D1535061

THE NEW TESTAMENT AS CANON:
AN INTRODUCTION

BREVARD S. CHILDS

THE NEW TESTAMENT
AS CANON:
AN INTRODUCTION

FORTRESS PRESS   PHILADELPHIA

Library of Congress Cataloging in Publication Data

Childs, Brevard S.
  The New Testament as canon.

  Includes index.
  1. Bible. N.T.—Introductions. 2. Bible. N.T.—
Canon. 3. Bible. N.T.—Theology. I. Title.
BS2330.2.C493 1985   225.1'2   84–21169
ISBN 0–8006–0739–2

1281184   Printed in the United Kingdom   1–739

To Cathy
much loved daughter
a new generation of faith

CONTENTS

PART THREE

THE ACTS

PART FOUR

THE PAULINE CORPUS

PART FIVE

THE CATHOLIC EPISTLES

PREFACE

An initial word of explanation is in order as to why an Old Testament specialist should undertake to write a New Testament Introduction. In 1978, when I finished the preparation of my *Introduction to the Old Testament as Scripture*, it became clear to me that my position regarding a canonical approach to the Bible remained incomplete and vulnerable without attention to the remaining part of the Christian Scriptures. The response of the reviewers confirmed my judgment that my work needed to be extended to the New Testament. It is my hope that as least some of the misunderstanding regarding the first volume will be removed by this second.

My academic interest in the New Testament is long standing. One of the great advantages of a European theological education was that, at least during my study in the early 1950s, the iron curtain which separates the two Testaments in American universities had not yet fallen. I am grateful to have been trained by some of the giants in the New Testament field: O. Piper, B. M. Metzger, O. Cullmann, K. L. Schmidt, and G. Bornkamm. In 1964 I spent several months in Tübingen and experienced the full impact of E. Käsemann, who was at the height of his influence. Then for almost a decade I tried intermittently to attend the New Testament lectures of my Yale colleague, Nils A. Dahl, and I am much in his debt for my own development. I have also greatly appreciated the conversations with other Yale colleagues in the field: Paul Schubert, Paul Minear, Abraham Malherbe, and Leander Keck.

Another sabbatical in Tübingen in the summer of 1981 allowed me to attend lectures and read widely in the writings of P. Stuhlmacher, M. Hengel, O. Hofius, and O. Betz. Finally, two summers at the Jewish Theological Seminary, four years of attending Judah Goldin's midrash seminars, and a year at the Hebrew University studying midrash gave me a rich background in Jewish studies.

Obviously I hold none of my esteemed teachers and colleagues responsible for my approach to the New Testament, but I remain grateful for their generous aid.

Some fifteen years ago, when I had just completed a book on biblical theology, I was shaken by a conversation with a New Testament colleague. He remarked that he did not so much disagree with my presentation, but felt that the perspective was dominated by Old Testament concerns. I had touched on few issues which were of real interest to a New Testament scholar. Upon reflection I realized the force of his argument.

In recent years it has been a practice of some Old Testament scholars often to include a section on New Testament themes, or the like, in their writings. Usually the approach entails simply an extension of Old Testament categories into the New Testament literature. Little wonder that New Testament scholarship has not taken these volumes very seriously. For this reason I have tried to hold in check Old Testament questions, and to saturate myself fully in strictly New Testament issues. For over five years my primary research energy has gone into New Testament studies and I have read as widely as possible in an effort to do justice to the integrity of this discipline.

I would like to emphasize that this volume is an Introduction to the New Testament. It is not a biblical theology, nor does it attempt to treat in detail a whole range of questions which involves the relation of the two Testaments. It is, of course, still my hope to have time and energy one day to address these issues.

Although this introduction is in some sense a companion volume to my earlier Old Testament work, it is more narrowly conceived. For example, it has not attempted to enter the pre-modern history of interpretation. Moreover, it has intentionally passed over many questions which properly belong to the field of New Testament introduction. Therefore, my treatment is not intended to replace the standard works of Zahn, Jülicher, Kümmel, Wikenhauser, Vielhauer, and Schenke.

My concern is to raise a whole set of important literary and theological issues which have not been adequately addressed by these standard works. Even though the questions associated with the canon are more central in the New Testament than in the Old, I have been surprised to see what little influence the present heated debates respecting the canon in the Old Testament have entered the contemporary field of New Testament, particularly within the English-speaking world. I shall consider this volume successful if it at least stimulates a fresh perspective and a different kind of debate. In the introductory chapters I have tried to describe some of the things which are involved in taking seriously the task of studying the New Testament as authoritative Scriptures of the church. In the end, I would rather speak of a new vision of the text rather than in terms of method.

As in the case of Old Testament studies, I find myself often critical of the classic positions regarding the approach to the New Testament both on the left and the right. Yet I freely admit that I have learned much from both Zahn and Wrede, from Jeremias and Käsemann, and from Lagrange and Loisy. Certain authors have appeared to me of particular insight and illumination. In spite of the diversity of perspective, I am indebted to J. Schniewind, K. Barth, G. Bornkamm, G. Eichholz, C. E. B. Cranfield, A. Vögtle and N. A. Dahl. A special note of gratitude is extended to H. Schürmann, a masterful exegete, whose understanding of the role of canon has offered invaluable support to my own work.

It should be obvious that much hard work has gone into this task. The need to carry a full teaching load in Old Testament during these last years in addition to my New Testament research has required early rising hours, long periods at night, and many summers of intensive study. My deepest gratitude extends to my incomparable wife, Ann, whose supportive role cannot be fully expressed in words.

New Haven
May 1984

ABBREVIATIONS

AB	The Anchor Bible, New York
AbTANT	Abhandlungen zur Theologie des Alten und Neuen Testaments, Zürich
AnBib	Analecta Biblica, Rome
AnThR	*Anglican Theological Review*, New York
ANTT	Arbeiten zur neutestamentlichen Textforschung, Berlin
ASNU	Acta seminarii neotestamentici upsaliensis, Upsala
ASTI	*Annual of the Swedish Theological Institute*, Leiden
Augs	Augsburg Commentaries, Minneapolis
AustrBR	*Australian Biblical Review*, Melbourne
AzKG	Arbeiten zur Kirchengeschichte, Berlin
BBB	Bonner biblische Beiträge, Bonn
BBET	Beiträge zur biblische Exegese und Theologie, Frankfurt
BETL	Bibliotheca Ephemeridum Theologicarum Loveniensium, Louvain, Gembloux
BEvTh	Beiträge zur *Evangelische Theologie*, Munich
BFChTh	Beiträge zur Forderung christlicher Theologie, Gütersloh
BGBE	Beiträge zur Geschichte der biblischen Exegese, Tübingen
B/HNTC	Black's/Harper's New Testament Commentaries, London and New York
BHT	Beiträge zur historischen Theologie, Tübingen
Bibl	*Biblica*, Rome
BibRes	*Biblical Research*, Chicago
BiLe	*Bibel und Leben*, Düsseldorf
BJRL	*Bulletin of the John Rylands Library*, Manchester
BSt	Biblische Studien, Neukirchen-Vluyn

BTB	*Biblical Theology Bulletin*, Rome
BTS	Biblisch-theologische Studien, Neukirchen-Vluyn
BU	Biblische Untersuchungen, Regensburg
BWANT	Beiträge zur Wissenschaft vom Alten und Neuen Testaments, Leipzig, Stuttgart
BZ	Biblische Zeitschrift, Freiburg, Paderborn
BZNW	Beihefte zur *Zeitschrift für die neutestamentliche Wissenschaft*, Giessen, Berlin
CB	Cambridge Bible for Schools and Colleges, Cambridge
CBQ	*Catholic Biblical Quarterly*, Washington
CBQMS	Catholic Biblical Quarterly Monograph Series, Washington
CGTC	Cambridge Greek Testament Commentaries
CGTSC	Cambridge Greek Testament for Schools and Colleges, Cambridge
CNEB	Cambridge Bible Commentary, New English Bible, Cambridge
CNT	Commentaire du Nouveau Testament, Neuchâtel
ConNT	Coniectanea neotestamentica, Lund
CTM	*Concordia Theological Monthly*, St Louis
DBHastings	*A Dictionary of the Bible*, ed. J. Hastings, Edinburgh and New York, 1900–1904
DBSuppl	*Dictionnaire de la Bible*, Supplément, Paris
DThC	*Dictionnaire de Théologie Catholique*, Paris
ÉB	Études bibliques, Paris
Einl.	*Einleitung in das Neue Testament* (see Bibliography to ch. 1)
EKK	Evangelisch-katholischer Kommentar zum Neuen Testament, Zürich, Neukirchen-Vluyn
ET	English Translation
ETL	Ephemerides Theologicae Lovanienses, Louvain
EvQu	*Evangelical Quarterly*, London, Exeter
EvTh	*Evangelische Theologie*, Munich
Exp	The Expositor, London
ExpB	Expositor's Bible, London
ExpGT	Expositor's Greek Testament, ed. W. R. Nicoll, London 1897–1910
ExpT	*Expository Times*, Edinburgh
FRLANT	Forschungen zur Religion und Literatur des Alten und Neuen Testaments, Göttingen

FS	Festschrift
FTS	Frankfurter theologische Studien, Frankfurt
FzB	Forschung zur Bibel, Stuttgart
GA	*Gesammelte Aufsätze*
Greg	*Gregorianum*, Rome
GS	*Gesammelte Schriften*
HAW	Handbuch der Altertumswissenschaft, Munich
HCNT	Kurzer Handcommentar zum Neuen Testament, Tübingen
Herm	Hermeneia, Philadelphia
HNT	Handbuch zum Neuen Testament, Tübingen
HTR	*Harvard Theological Review*, Cambridge, Mass.
HTKNT	Herders theologischer Kommentar zum Neuen Testament, Freiburg
HUT	Hermeneutische Untersuchungen zur Theologie, Tübingen
IB	*Interpreter's Bible*, 12 vols., Nashville 1951–57
ICC	International Critical Commentary, Edinburgh and New York
IDB	*The Interpreter's Dictionary of the Bible*, Nashville 1962
IDB Suppl	*The Interpreter's Dictionary of the Bible*, Supplementary Volume, Nashville 1976
Interp	*Interpretation*, Richmond
InterpC	Interpretation Commentaries, Atlanta
Intr.	*Introduction to the New Testament* (see Bibliography to ch. 1)
ITQ	*Irish Theological Quarterly*, Maynooth
JAAR	*Journal of the American Academy of Religion*, Boston
JAC	*Jahrbuch für Antike und Christentums*, Münster
JETS	*Journal of the Evangelical Theological Society*, Jackson, Miss.
JR	*Journal of Religion*, Chicago
JSNT	*Journal for the Study of the New Testament*, Sheffield
JTS	*Journal of Theological Studies*, Oxford
KEHNT	Kurzgefässtes exegetisches Handbuch zum Neuen Testament, Leipzig
KNT	Kommentar zum Neuen Testament, ed. T. Zahn, Leipzig
KS	*Kleine Schriften*
KuD	*Kerygma und Dogma*, Göttingen

MbThSt	Marburger Theologischer Studien, Marburg
MeyerK	H. A. W. Meyer, Kritisch-exegetischer Kommentar über das Neue Testament, Göttingen
MNTC	Moffatt New Testament Commentary, London
MüThSt	Münchner Theologische Studien, Munich
MüThZ	*Münchner Theologische Zeitschrift*, Munich
NCeB	The Century Bible, New Series, London
NClB	The New Clarendon Bible, Oxford
NF	Neue Folge
NICNT	New International Commentary on the New Testament, Grand Rapids
NKZ	*Neue Kirchliche Zeitschrift*, Erlangen
NovT	*Novum Testamentum*, Leiden
NovTSupp	*Novum Testamentum* Supplements
ns	New series
NTA	*New Testament Abstracts*, Weston, Mass.
NTAbh	Neutestamentliche Abhandlungen, Münster
NTApoc	*New Testament Apocrypha*, ed. E. Hennecke and W. Schneemelcher, ET ed. R. McL. Wilson, 2 vols., London and Philadelphia 1963–5, repr. 1973–4
NTD	Das Neue Testament Deutsch, Göttingen
NTF	Neutestamentliche Forschungen, Gütersloh
NTS	*New Testament Studies*, Cambridge
ÖTK	Ökomenischer Taschenbuchkommentar zum Neuen Testament, Gütersloh, Würzburg
OTS	*Oudtestamentische Studien*, Leiden
Pel	Pelican New Testament Commentaries, London, Baltimore
PNT	De prediking van het Nieuwe Testament, Nijkerk.
PTR	*Princeton Theological Review*, Princeton
Pw	A. Pauly and G. Wissowa, *Realencyklopädie der klassischen Altertumswissenschaften*, Stuttgart
QR	*Quarterly Review*, Nashville
RAC	*Reallexikon für Antike und Christentum*, Stuttgart 1950ff.
RB	*Revue Biblique*, Paris
RBén	*Revue Bénédictine*, Maredsous
RE[3]	*Realencyklopädie für protestantische Theologie und Kirche*, Leipzig [3]1896ff.
RechScR	*Recherches de Science Religieuse*, Paris
RelStR	*Religious Studies Review*, Hanover, Pa.

RestQ	*Restoration Quarterly*, Macon, Ga.
RevExp	*Revue and Expositor*, Louisville
RevQ	*Revue de Qumran*, Paris
RevSR	*Revue des Sciences Religieuses*, Strasbourg
RGG	*Die Religion in Geschichte und Gegenwart*, Tübingen [2]1927–31; [3]1957–65
RHE	*Revue d'Histoire Ecclésiastique*, Paris
RHPhR	*Revue d'Histoire et de Philosophie Religieuses*, Strasbourg
RHR	*Revue de l'Histoire des Religions*, Paris
RNT	Regensburger Neues Testament, Regensburg
RSR	*Recherches de Science Religieuse*, Paris
RSV	Revised Standard Version of the Bible, London, New York 1952
SAB	Sitzungsberichte der Preussischen Akademie, Berlin
SANT	Studien zum Alten und Neuen Testament, Munich
SB	La Sainte Bible, ed. L. Pirot, A. Clamer, Paris
SBB	Stuttgarter biblische Beiträge, Stuttgart
SBL	Society of Biblical Literature, Philadelphia, Missoula, Chico
SBLDS	Society of Biblical Literature Dissertation Series
SBLMS	Society of Biblical Literature Monograph Series
SBM	Stuttgarter biblische Monographien, Stuttgart
SBS	Stuttgarter Bibelstudien, Stuttgart
SBT	Studies in Biblical Theology, London and Naperville, Ill.
SEA	*Svensk Exegetisk Arsbok*, Lund
SJT	*Scottish Journal of Theology*, Edinburgh, Cambridge
SoBi	Sources Bibliques, Paris
SNT	*Die Schriften des Neuen Testaments*, Göttingen [3]1917–18
StNT	Studien zum Neuen Testament, Gütersloh
SNTSM	Studiorum Novi Testamenti Societas, Monograph Series, Cambridge
StEv	*Studia Evangelica* (published in TU), Berlin
StPatr	*Studia Patristica* (published in TU), Berlin
StTh	*Studia Theologica*, Lund, Aarhus
SUNT	Studien zur Umwelt des Neuen Testaments, Göttingen
SWJT	*Southwestern Journal of Theology*, Fort Worth, Tx.
TB	Torch Bible Commentary, London

TDNT	*Theological Dictionary of the New Testament*, ET of *TWNT*, Grand Rapids 1964–1976
ThB	Theologische Bücherei, Munich
ThBl	*Theologische Blätter*, Leipzig
ThExH	*Theologische Existenz Heute*, Munich
ThF	Theologische Forschung, Hamburg
THKNT	Theologische Handkommentar zum Neuen Testament, Berlin
ThJb	*Theologische Jahrbücher*, Tübingen
ThR	*Theologische Rundschau*, Tübingen
ThRev	*Theologische Revue*, Münster
ThStKr	*Theologische Studien und Kritiken*, Hamburg, Leipzig, Berlin
ThQ	*Theologische Quartalschrift*, Tübingen
ThSt	*Theological Studies*, Woodstock, Md.
ThStud	Theologische Studien, Zürich
ThViat	*Theologia Viatorum*, Petersburg
TLZ	*Theologischer Literaturzeitung*, Leipzig
TRE	*Theologische Realenzyklopädie*, Berlin and New York
TThS	Trierer Theologische Studien, Trier
TU	Texte und Untersuchungen zur Geschichte der altchristlichen Literatur, Leipzig, Berlin
TWNT	*Theologisches Wörterbuch zum Neuen Testament*, ed. G. Kittel, Stuttgart 1932ff.
Tyn	Tyndale New Testament Commentary, London
TynB	*Tyndale Bulletin*, London
TZ	*Theologische Zeitschrift*, Basel
VD	*Verbum Domini*, Rome
VF	*Verkündigung und Forschungen*, Munich
VigChr	*Vigiliae Christianae*, Leiden
WC	Westminster Commentaries, London
WdF	Wege der Forschung, Darmstadt
WMANT	Wissenschaftliche Monographien zum Alten und Neuen Testament, Neukirchen-Vluyn
Word	Word Biblical Commentary, Waco, Tx.
WTJ	*Westminster Theological Journal*, Philadelphia
WuD	*Wort und Dienst, Jahrbuch der Theologische Schule*, Bethel
WUNT	Wissenschaftliche Untersuchungen zum Neuen Testament, Tübingen
ZBK	Zürcher Bibelkommentare, Zürich

ZKT	*Zeitschrift für Katholische Theologie*, Innsbruck, Vienna
ZNW	*Zeitschrift für die neutestamentliche Wissenschaft*, Giessen, Berlin
ZSTh	*Zeitschrift für systematische Theologie*, Güterloh
ZTK	*Zeitschrift für Theologie und Kirche*, Tübingen
ZWTh	*Zeitschrift für wissenschaftliche Theologie*, Jena, Halle, Leipzig

PART ONE

THE NEW TESTAMENT: INTRODUCTION

1

THE ROLE OF THE CANON WITHIN
NEW TESTAMENT INTRODUCTION

Bibliography

B. W. **Bacon**, *An Introduction to the New Testament*, New York ²1907; W. **Bauer**, *Orthodoxy and Heresy in Earliest Christianity*(1934), ET London and Philadelphia 1971; F. C. **Baur**, 'Die Einleitung in das Neue Testament als theologische Wissenschaft', *ThJb* 9, 1850, 463–556; 10, 1851, 70–94, 222–53, 292–329; F. **Bleek**, *Introduction to the New Testament*, ET, 2 vols., Edinburgh 1869; R. **Bultmann**, 'Die Bedeutung der "dialektischen Theologie" für die neutestamentliche Wissenschaft', *ThBl* 7, 1928, 57–67; ET in *Faith and Understanding* I, London and New York 1969, 145–64; *Theology of the New Testament* II, ET London and New York 1955, 127–44; H. **von Campenhausen**, *The Formation of the Christian Bible*, ET Philadelphia and London 1972; (J. A. **Cassels**), *Supernatural Religion*, 3 vols., London 1874, Boston 1875; R. F. **Collins**, *Introduction to the New Testament*, Garden City, N. Y. and London 1983; C. A. **Credner**, *Einleitung in das Neue Testament*, Halle 1836; *Zur Geschichte des Kanons*, Halle 1847.

S. **Davidson**, *Facts, Statements and Explanations connected with the Publication of the 10th ed. of Horne's Introduction*, London 1857; *An Introduction to the Study of the New Testament, Critical, Exegetical and Theological*, 2 vols., London 1868, ³1884; M. **Dibelius**, *A Fresh Approach to the New Testament and Early Christian Literature*, ET London and New York 1936; E. **Dinkler**, 'Bibelkritik', *RGG³*, I, 1187–90; J. G. **Eichorn**, *Einleitung in das Neue Testament*, 5 vols., Leipzig 1804–27; V. P. **Furnish**, 'The Historical Criticism of the New Testament. A Survey of Origins', *BJRL* 56, 1973/4, 336–70; C. R. **Gregory**, *Canon and Text of the New Testament*, Edinburgh and New York 1907; H. E. F. **Guericke**, *Historisch-kritische Einleitung in das Neue Testament*, Leipzig 1843; D. **Guthrie**, *New Testament Introduction*, rev. ed. London 1981; 'Questions of Introduction', *New Testament Interpretation. Essays on Principles and Methods*, ed. I. H. Marshall, Exeter 1977, 105–25.

F. **Hahn**, 'Die neutestamentliche Wissenschaft', in *Wissenschaftliche Theologie im Überblick*, ed. W. Lohffs and F. Hahn, Göttingen 1974, 28–38; A. **von Harnack**, *The Origin of the New Testament*, ET London and New York 1925;

History of Dogma, ET, 7 vols., London 1894–99, Boston 1899–1903; H. **Heppe**, *Die Dogmatik der evangelisch-reformierten Kirche*, ed. E. Bizer, Neukirchen 1935; ET *Reformed Dogmatics*, London 1950, repr. Grand Rapids 1978; A. **Hilgenfeld**, *Der Kanon und die Kritik des Neuen Testaments*, Halle 1863; H. J. **Holtzmann**, *Lehrbuch der historisch-kritischen Einleitung in das Neue Testament*, Freiburg [3]1892; H. **Höpfl**, B. **Gut**, *Introductio Specialis in Novum Testamentum*, ed. A. Metzinger, Rome [5]1949; T. H. **Horne**, *An Introduction to the Critical Study and Knowledge of the Holy Scriptures*, London 1818, Philadelphia 1825, [9]1846; E. **Hoskyns**, N. **Davey**, *The Riddle of the New Testament*, London 1931, [3]1947; J. L. **Hug**, *Introduction to the New Testament*, ET London 1827, Andover Mass. 1836; H. **Hupfeld**, *Über Begriff und Methode der sogenannten biblischen Einleitung*, Marburg 1844.

E. **Jacquier**, *Histoire des livres du Nouveau Testament*, 4 vols., Paris [11]1928–35; A. **Jülicher**, E. **Fascher**, *Einleitung in das Neue Testament*(1894), Tübingen [7]1931, ET 1904; L. E. **Keck**, 'Is the New Testament a Field of Study? or, From Outler to Overbeck and Back', *The Second Century*, I, 1981, 19–35; H. **Koester**, 'New Testament Introduction: A Critique of a Discipline', *Christianity, Judaism and other Greco-Roman Cults, FS Morton Smith*, ed. J. Neusner, Part I, New Testament, Leiden 1975, 1–20; *Introduction to the New Testament*, 2 vols., ET Berlin, New York and Philadelphia 1982; G. **Krüger**, *Das Dogma vom Neuen Testament*, Giessen 1896; W. G. **Kümmel**, '"Einleitung in das Neue Testament" als theologische Aufgabe', *EvTh* 19, 1954, 4–15; *Introduction to the New Testament*, ET, rev. ed., Nashville and London 1975; *The New Testament: The History of the Investigation of its Problems*, ET Nashville and London 1972; 'Einleitungswissenschaft II', *TRE* 9, 469–82.

N. **Lardner**, *Credibility of the Gospel History*, 12 vols., London 1727–55; H. **Lietzmann**, *Wie wurden die Bücher des Neuen Testaments heilige Schrift?* Tübingen 1907; J. B. **Lightfoot**, *Essays on the Work entitled Supernatural Religion*, London and New York 1889; W. **Marxsen**, 'Die Bedeutung der Einleitungswissenschaft für die Predigtarbeit', *Der Exeget als Theologe*, Gütersloh 1968, 115–28; *Einleitung in das Neue Testament*, Gütersloh 1964, [4]1978; ET of 1st ed., *Introduction to the New Testament*, Oxford and Philadelphia 1968; *The New Testament as the Church's Book*, ET Philadelphia 1972; O. **Merk**, *Biblische Theologie des Neuen Testaments in ihrer Anfangszeit*, MbThS 9, 1972; J. D. **Michaelis**, *Introduction to the New Testament* (1750), ET of 4th ed., Cambridge 1793–1801; W. Michaelis, *Einleitung in das Neue Testament*, Bern [3]1961; J. **Moffatt**, *An Introduction to the Literature of the New Testament*, Edinburgh and New York 1911; C. F. D. **Moule**, *The Birth of the New Testament*, London and San Francisco [3]1981; S. **Neill**, *The Interpretation of the New Testament, 1861–1961*, London and New York 1964; F. **Overbeck**, 'Über die Anfänge der patristischen Literatur', *Historische Zeitschrift* 48, 1882, 417–72; reprinted Darmstadt 1954; E. **Pagels**, *The Gnostic Gospels*, New York and London 1979; N. **Perrin**, *The New Testament. An Introduction*, New York 1974; E. **Preuschen**, *Analecta II. Zur Kanongeschichte*, Tübingen 1910.

M. **Rese**, 'Zum gegenwärtigen Stand der neutestamentlichen Einleitungswissenschaft', *VF* 12, 1976, 29–38; E. **Reuss**, *Die Geschichte der Heiligen Schriften des Neuen Testaments*, Braunschweig ⁵1874; H. N. **Ridderbos**, *The Authority of the New Testament Scriptures*, Grand Rapids 1963; J. M. **Robinson**, H. **Koester**, *Trajectories through Early Christianity*, Philadelphia 1971; G. **Salmon**, *An Historical Introduction to the Study of the Books of the New Testament*, London 1885; W. **Sanday**, *The Gospels in the Second Century*, London 1876; H. M. **Schenke**, and K. M. **Fischer**, *Einleitung in die Schriften des Neuen Testaments*, 2 vols., Berlin 1978–9; F. **Schleiermacher**, *Einleitung ins Neue Testament, Sämmtliche Werke* VIII, Berlin 1845; H. **Schmid**, *Die Dogmatik der evangelisch-lutherischen Kirche*, Frankfurt ⁵1863; J. S. **Semler**, *Abhandlung von freier Untersuchung des Canon*, 4 vols., Halle 1771–75; Vol. 1 reprinted Gütersloh 1967; R. **Simon**, *Histoire Critique du Texte du Nouveau Testament*, Rotterdam 1689; reprinted Frankfurt 1968.

P. **Vielhauer**, *Geschichte der urchristlichen Literatur*, Berlin 1975; B. **Weiss**, *Lehrbuch der Einleitung in das Neue Testament*, Berlin ³1897; ET of 1st edition, London and New York 1889; C. **Weizsäcker**, *The Apostolic Age of the Christian Church*, 2 vols., ET London and New York 1894–95; P. **Wernle**, *The Beginnings of Christianity*, 2 vols., ET London and New York 1903–04; B. F. **Westcott**, *A General Survey of the History of the Canon of the New Testament*, London 1855, London and New York ⁷1896; W. M. L. **de Wette**, *Lehrbuch der historisch-kritischen Einleitung in die kanonischen Bücher des Neuen Testaments*, Berlin 1826; A. **Wikenhauser**, *New Testament Introduction*, ET of 2nd ed., New York 1958; revised by J. Schmid, *Einleitung in das Neue Testament*, Freiburg ⁶1973; W. **Wrede**, *Über Aufgabe und Methode der sogenannten neutestamentlichen Theologie*, Göttingen 1897; T. **Zahn**, *Geschichte des neutestamentlichen Kanons*, 2 vols., Erlangen 1888–90; 'Einleitung in das Neue Testament', *RE*³ V, 1898, 261–74; *Introduction to the New Testament*, 3 vols., ET Edinburgh and New York 1909.

I

The traditional Christian form of viewing the New Testament within the framework of dogmatic theology emerged in the post-Reformation period as the result of a variety of doctrinal controversies in the late sixteenth and seventeenth centuries. A theological understanding of canon was, of course, an integral part of the early church's reflection, but it received a different form when joined with the developing science of biblical introduction which appeared during the Renaissance.

On the one hand, the Reformers sought to establish the sole authority of scripture against the Roman Catholic claims of ecclesiastical authority. To some extent they continued to acknowledge the church's participation within a historical development, but they sought to restrict its theological significance. On the other hand, the resistance to seeing the Bible as an infallible rule of truth was raised by the increasingly strong voice of rationalists, Socinians, and Remonstrants. By the end of the seventeenth century, in spite of significant differences in emphasis between the Lutheran and Reformed theologians, a dogmatic formulation of the role of the New Testament canon was established which, ironically enough, shared at least many formal features with the Roman Church. The New Testament was seen as a collection of apostolic writings, universally acknowledged by the Church as authoritative in its entirety, written under the inspiration of the Holy Spirit, and guarding the truth of Christianity against all heresy in order to provide an eternal norm for church doctrine (cf. Heppe, Schmid, Hoepfl).

By the eighteenth century increasingly under the pressure from the Deists, the discussion of the canon was shifted by its orthodox Protestant defenders away from its primary debate with Rome in order to provide a first line of defence for the historical credibility of the gospel records. Typical of this move was the enormously learned apology of Nathaniel Lardner, *Credibility of the Gospel History*, who was surprisingly a Unitarian minister. He subsumed the issue of canonicity within the categories of historical trustworthiness and used the testimonies of the Church Fathers along with non-Christian writers as evidence for historicity and genuineness.

Vestiges of this dogmatic, apologetic understanding of the New Testament can still be seen in J. D. Michaelis' influential *Einleitung* of 1750 which is considered by many to be the first modern New Testament Introduction. He also treated the subject of New Testament canon under the rubric of its authenticity which was conceived of in largely historical terms. Michaelis distinguished sharply between authenticity and inspiration and used the latter as a support for its divine quality. Increasingly in the later editions the term inspiration was eroded until it was virtually abandoned in the fourth edition. Inspiration had lost its rationale because the evangelists could still function to provide historical evidence of genuine antiquity in the role of completely human authors.

It is generally acknowledged that the modern study of the subject of the biblical canon was inaugurated by the epoch-making investigation of J. S. Semler, *Abhandlung von freier Untersuchung des Canons* (1771–1775). Semler set out to destroy the dogmatic, apologetic concept of the canon into which the New Testament had traditionally been placed. Rather than the canon's being an authoritative form of the apostles' writings, virtually coterminous with the literature itself, historically uniform and structurally monolithic, Semler argued that these elements were wholly fictitious. He sought to substitute a purely historical description of the biblical canon which originally had nothing to do with a book's normative status, but simply indicated its inclusion within a catalogue of books to be used in a liturgical context.

Semler was remarkably successful in radically shifting the understanding of canon away from the traditional approach. In spite of the continuing controversy over the formation of the New Testament canon, both conservatives and liberals agreed in treating the problem largely as an historical issue. Conservative scholars such as Hug and Guericke sought to establish the process of canonization as closely as possible to the age of the apostles in order to defend the historical continuity and thus the authenticity of the writings. Conversely, liberals such as Eichhorn and de Wette tended to focus on the elements of discontinuity and to drive a wedge between the actual authorship of the New Testament and subsequent traditional dogma.

In F. Schleiermacher's *Einleitung ins Neue Testament*, which was published posthumously in 1845 from lecture notes, the author brilliantly develops some of the hermeneutical and exegetical issues involved in the critical understanding of the New Testament canon. He carefully distinguishes between the New Testament concept which the collecting process effected and the original setting of each of the books. The task of critical exegesis rested on recovering the position of the original hearer (7) and this was dependent on stripping away the subsequent accretions. Interpretation could not longer rest on the authority of the church, but had become a scientific enterprise (13) which must evaluate the various authors behind these historical writings. The clarity of Schleiermacher's vision stands in striking contrast to the confused and idiosyncratic theological observations of Semler, Eichhorn, and Credner, among others.

Another significant stage in the search for critical clarity was made by H. Hupfeld's brief monograph of 1844. He argued that a critical appraisal of the literature was the main contribution of an introduction rather than its being a loosely conceived compendium of archeological, historical, and geographical treatises which such volumes had traditionally comprised.

The next major advance in the study of canon in its relationship to the critical interpretation of the New Testament was first signalled by F. C. Baur in his early essay and later summarized in his famous article of 1850–51, 'Die Einleitung in das Neue Testament als theologische Wissenschaft'. Baur strove to set the discussion of canon into a far broader historical context in a reaction against the predominantly negative, formalistic treatment of de Wette and others. He argued that the New Testament grew within the development of Christian theology and that the history of dogma began, not after, but before the New Testament. The gospels must be viewed not solely in terms of their historicity, but as *Tendenzschriften* within the developmental sequence of early Christianity which progressed in its resolution of inner tension and sharp polarities. One of Baur's students, A. Hilgenfeld, summarized the effect of this newer approach in his book, *Der Kanon und die Kritik des Neuen Testaments*. He envisioned the chief task of an introduction to correct the false historical understanding which the tradition within the canon had fostered. The intensity of the controversy which Baur and his students unleashed dominated much of the third quarter of the nineteenth century, and in the end greatly contributed to the historical study of the New Testament by the radical nature of its challenge.

Even as late as 1850 the study of the New Testament in England had remained largely traditional and conservative, and was still represented by such textbooks as T. H. Horne's *Introduction*. However, the literary critical issues which the Germans had raised were slowly mediated through a variety of channels. Samuel Davidson's revision of Horne in 1856 had raised a storm of protest because of its mildly critical stance and was finally forced to appear as a separate volume. *Essays and Reviews* appeared in 1860 in which Jowett popularized some of the ideas current in Germany. Equally as controversial was the publication of the highly polemical, anonymous work entitled *Supernatural Religion* in 1874 (by J. A. Cassels). In the second part of the book the author sought to demonstrate the general unreliability of the New Testament by drawing on contemporary continental criticism of the history of the canon. The book itself was of less importance than the response which it evoked. A series of great Anglican scholars (Westcott, Lightfoot, Sanday) arose in defence of the traditional understanding of the New Testament which established the broad lines of English scholarship well into the twentieth century. J. B. Lightfoot, who was equipped with enormous patristic learning, was able to show numerous errors by the author of

Supernatural Religion. Through his review articles he largely convinced the English-speaking world that the traditional view of the New Testament rested on a solid historical foundation.

Particularly in B. F. Westcott's *A General Survey of the History of the Canon of the New Testament* the nineteenth-century response to both Semler and Baur received its classic Anglican formulation. On the one hand, Westcott's book offered a genuine break with the older dogmatic concept of canon in seeing the subject historically. On the other hand, he placed his historical description within the theological assumption that the unity of the one catholic church had been from the first. The canon had not arisen, as the newer critics had claimed, from a fusion of discordant elements at the end of the second century, but represented a gradual unfolding of a broad tradition directed by providential power which stood in direct historical and theological continuity with apostolic teaching.

It is significant to note that English scholars did not produce any serious, scholarly introductions to the New Testament during the last quarter of the nineteenth century. (Salmon is a peculiar type of exception.) Their contribution lay rather in Bible dictionaries, substantial commentaries, learned monographs especially on the Gospels, and, above all, text criticsm. However, this lack of indigenous introductions was compensated for in part by the translations of the best conservative examples from Germany, F. Bleek (1869), E. Reuss (1884), and B. Weiss (1886). Hilgenfeld and Holtzmann remained untranslated.

In contrast to the predominantly conservative trend of English New Testament scholarship in the last quarter of the nineteenth century, a different sort of consensus had begun to emerge in Germany during this same period. The heated controversy surrounding Baur's Tübingen school had subsided, and a more balanced reconstruction of the development of the New Testament and its canon had been finally established. In the classic literary critical introduction of H. J. Holtzmann the great strides, particularly in the analysis of the synoptic problem, were set forth. There was also a widespread agreement that the fixing of the first stage of the canon had occurred at the end of the second century. It resulted from a long history of debate in which finally a decision was made which marked off the boundaries of what were recognized as normative writings from a far larger group of books in use. However, this process was virtually irrelevant to the actual shaping of the New Testament literature

itself. Holtzmann saw the canonical form of the tradition as developing within the history of the Catholic church which modern
Protestants were obliged to hold in some suspicion, allegedly in the
critical spirit of the Reformation.

Toward the end of the nineteenth century T. Zahn offered the
last major attempt by conservative Protestantism to establish the
historical continuity of New Testament tradition by defending the
thesis that the major portion of the New Testament canon had
actually been fixed by the first part of the second century. However,
in spite of his impressive learning, his position continued to be judged
by the majority as unconvincing and even idiosyncratic in emphasis.
The new critical position represented by Harnack and Leipoldt
among others found a lucid summary in Jülicher's *Einleitung* (1894;
⁷1931). Although the placing of the discussion of the canon within
the critical introduction either at the beginning or at the end of the
book continued to fluctuate, there was no uncertainty that the study
of the New Testament's formation was independent of the later issues
of their collection within a canon.

Within the English- speaking world the shift in perspective from
a nineteenth-century conservative position to the reigning critical
position of the continent occurred quite rapidly. It was prepared by
the steady stream of English translations of Wernle, Weizsäcker,
Jülicher, and above all, of Harnack. The English translation of Zahn's
three-volume *Introduction* in 1909 made little impact in reversing the
new direction, but to many English scholars his position, which was
closest to the nineteenth-century Anglican consensus of Westcott
and Lightfoot, now seemed anachronistic. The appearance of J.
Moffatt's *Introduction* in 1911 as part of the famous International
Theological Library series which had been preceded by C. R.
Gregory's volume on *Canon and Text of the New Testament* (1907)
brought much of England fully in line with the critical German
consensus. In North America critical scholarship had long before
broken with the Anglican consensus as is clear in the introduction of
B. W. Bacon. Both Bacon and Moffatt were explicit in delineating
their task as a scientific investigation of the origins of the New
Testament writings apart from the traditional stance from which
they afterward came to be viewed.

Two major new developments emerged within the field at the
beginning of the twentieth century and have remained of major
significance up to the present, namely the history-of-religions

approach (*Religionsgeschichte*) and form criticism. In a certain sense they both served to reduce even further the significance of the canon for the interpretation of the New Testament. From the side of the history-of-religion school, A. Eichhorn, G. Krüger, and W. Wrede all regarded canonical categories as arising from an artificial dogmatic bias which obscured the scientific necessity of viewing the New Testament literature as differing in no way from the rest of Hellenistic writings. In the most recent times this approach has again been taken up and defended with great vigour by Helmut Koester. By exploiting Bauer's historical argument that the distinction between orthodoxy and heresy was anachronistic for the early church and a result of later political and dogmatic developments, Koester has again called for a radical suspension of all talk of New Testament canon in the traditional sense.

From the side of form criticism the formation of a New Testament canon has also been largely viewed in a negative light. The concern of this discipline was to trace the history of the development of primitive Christian literature in its oral stages by means of the interaction between literary forms and sociological setting. Although F. Overbeck used the emergence of the canon as an additional sign to confirm the sharp break in the forms of the early Christian *Urliteratur* from later church writing, he regarded the canon itself as a death certificate which functioned to seal off the real life of the New Testament.

R. Bultmann likewise shared with Overbeck a largely negative evaluation of the role of canon. It arose along with the office of bishop in an effort to secure right doctrine and succeeded in imposing a relative degree of ecclesiastical unity upon literature which was highly diversified. Again, M. Dibelius in his chapter on canonical and apocryphal literature first set out the broad lines of the history of the canon which agreed with the late nineteenth-century consensus. He was, by and large, more positive than Bultmann in regarding the canonical process as 'successful in high degree' in collecting the classical witnesses of primitive Christianity. However, since his interest lay in studying the forms and categories of the literature, he felt constrained to deal with canonical and extra-canonical literature in exactly the same manner. Indeed, in the context of Dibelius' literary endeavour it is difficult to deny that the force of his argument carries great weight.

To summarize up to this point: As a result of the historical critical study of the New Testament a broad consensus emerged by the end of the nineteenth century which continued into the twentieth century in which the New Testament canon was regarded solely as a post-apostolic development without any real significance for understanding the shaping of the New Testament itself.

II

In spite of the approach to canon which won hegemony in the nineteenth century and which continues to be widely represented in various modern introductions and manuals, I would like to argue the case that there has been a shift in perspective regarding certain important elements in the formation of the New Testament which offers the potential of throwing a different light on the relation of canon and New Testament Introduction.

First, from a historical point of view it has become increasingly clear that the canonical process was not simply a post-apostolic development undertaken by the early catholic church which could be sharply separated from the formation of the New Testament literature. Although F. C. Baur had already pointed out in the mid-nineteenth century that the New Testament grew within the broad context of a developing Christian theology, his insight was lost by the later Tübingen school. Only recently have some of the correct implications been drawn. Particularly von Campenhausen, in his brilliant book on *The Formation of the Christian Bible*, has located the beginnings of the process of canonization within the New Testament itself. Although entitling his chapter 'The Pre-History of the New Testament Canon', he has described those elements within the gospels and the Pauline corpus which resulted in the emergence of a full-fledged canon consciousness.

The genuine advance of von Campenhausen over his teacher Harnack is clear. Harnack described a number of motives within the early church which led to the creation of the New Testament. Several had their roots within the New Testament itself – reverence for Jesus' words, a prophecy and fulfilment pattern – but the major focus of Harnack's understanding of canon fell on the post-apostolic period's liturgical use of Christian writings to give them canonical status. In contrast, von Campenhausen is bold in asserting: 'But it is a sheer historical fact that the permanent basic assumption of the Christian

Bible is a Pauline conception . . . and to that extent the Christian Bible is inconceivable without him' (37). Far different in emphasis and much more representative of the older approach is the position of W. G. Kümmel. For him the necessity of a canon arose from the need to preserve in writing the truth of the oral tradition once the first generation of witnesses had died and to limit the scope of authentic writings from erosion by dubious authorities. Although one cannot dismiss these factors from the post-apostolic development of canon, Kümmel has continued to describe the canonical process in such a way as to remain irrelevant for the formation of the New Testament books themselves.

Secondly, the history-of-religion approach to the New Testament has made an important contribution in demonstrating the variety of different theological options which were available within the highly pluralistic milieu of early Christianity. To portray the formation of the New Testament canon as a natural growth of universally recognized authoritative writings into a normative apostolic collection fails to deal adequately with the enormous controversies and tensions which lay behind the individual books and their subsequent collection. Much of Käsemann's attack on Cullmann's position appears to me in this respect justified. The recovery of the Gnostic library of Nag Hammadi has made it abundantly clear that the struggle to define the nature of the gospel did not follow the fixing of the New Testament, but was an integral part of the process in which the decisions of the early church regarding canonicity were made.

Indeed, only recently have the full implications of the history-of-religion approach begun to emerge. The major thrust of E. Pagels' latest book, *The Gnostic Gospels*, is to suggest that there is now another avenue available apart from the allegedly tendentious shaping of the material by the Catholic party from which to reach back to an earlier, more authentic vision of Jesus' original message. Thus, also for Pagels the issue of the New Testament canon, even if judged negatively, has been pushed into the front of the debate.

Thirdly, from a literary perspective the development of the form-critical, traditio-historical approach as a means of interpreting the sociological forces at work in shaping the literature, particularly in the oral stages, has had profound implications on one's larger vision of the New Testament. No longer is the literature viewed in terms of a simple relationship between an original author and his composition. Rather, the complexity of the process has emerged in which the shape of the material has been greatly affected by the circle of tradents to which the literature was addressed and by whom the tradition was transmitted. The multi-layered quality of the Gospels and many of the epistles has further demonstrated the active participation of the community for whom the literature had a variety of religious functions. The tremendous contribution of Bultmann should not be confused with some of his specific literary theories, but lies in his consistent attention to the shifting perspectives through which the New Testament material has been filtered. Much of the conservative reaction of J. Jeremias or V. Taylor has simply missed the major point at issue.

The recognition of the multi-layered quality of the New Testament has also afforded a new perspective on an old question. How can one speak of a canonical influence, both intentional and unintentional, when the New Testament writers themselves did not write with the idea of creating holy scriptures? First, the multi-layered state of the literature indicates that the process of ordering and collecting left a profound and deep stamp on the material. Again, the process of canonical shaping stood in close theological continuity with the original kerygmatic intention of the New Testament writers to use their medium as a means of proclaiming the gospel and not to preserve an archive of historical records.

Fourthly, the nature of the New Testament as profoundly theological in essence which continues to resist simple historical or sociological solutions, has emerged with great clarity within recent years. Fifty years ago, Edwyn Hoskyns pointed out in *The Riddle of the New Testament* the extent to which the theological dimension of the New Testament formed the heart of the riddle of its interpretation, but he was unable to break out of the dialectic of faith and history. More recently, C. F. D. Moule (*The Birth of the New Testament*) has sought to complement the usual critical introduction by viewing the literature as the early church's attempt to explain itself theologically in various stages of self-awareness. Then again, Willi Marxsen (*Introduction to the New Testament*) has sought to write a different sort of critical introduction which would do justice to the theological questions often lost in the usual critical approach. Significantly, Marxsen found himself forced to confront head-on the problem of the canon with the provocative title of his monograph, *The New Testament as the Church's Book*. In spite of the host of unresolved questions in Marxsen's approach, he is unequivocal in describing the New Testament as the church's earliest extant volume of preaching.

Finally, in an article which outlined his approach, 'New Testament Introduction: A Critique of a Discipline', H. Koester returns to a discussion of the subject of canon. He rejects using the New Testament canon as a historical restriction in the scholarly study of the full range of Hellenistic literature. Nevertheless, he argues that 'the canon was created as a critical weapon in a religious and cultural revolution' (8). He then suggests that the task of a genuinely historical introduction would be to translate the theological intention of canon into a modern context by assessing the theological purpose of each ancient document as part of an ongoing process. Regardless of whether Koester's own *Introduction to the New Testament* has succeeded in fulfilling this function, at least he has correctly seen the theological dimension as lying at the centre of the critical enterprise of the New Testament Introduction.

To conclude: In the light of these shifts in perspective regarding the relation of introduction to canon, it comes as a challenge to develop the potential of a new approach to this discipline. Although the attempt to sketch the broad lines of a new vision of the text can never be a substitute for the detailed, painstaking research of the biblical scholar, such technical work can easily run into the sand if the larger concept of the enterprise has been lost.

2

THE CANON AS AN HISTORICAL AND THEOLOGICAL PROBLEM

Bibliography

K. **Aland**, 'Das Problem des neutestamentlichen Kanons' (1962), reprinted Käsemann, ed., *Das Neue Testament als Kanon*, 134–58; N. **Appel**, *Kanon und Kirche*, Paderborn 1964; J. **Barr**, *Holy Scripture: Canon, Authority, Criticism*, Oxford and Philadelphia 1983; K. **Barth**, *Church Dogmatics* I/2, ET Edinburgh and New York 1956, 473–537; E. **Best**, 'Scripture, Tradition and the Canon of the New Testament', *BJRL* 61, 1978/9, 258–89; H. **Braun**, 'Hebt die heutige neutestamentlich-exegetische Forschung den Kanon auf?' (1960), reprinted Käsemann, ed., *Das NT als Kanon*, 219–32; R. E. **Brown**, *The Critical Meaning of the Bible*, New York 1981; F. F. **Bruce**, *Tradition Old and New*, London 1970; 'New Light on the Origins of the New Testament Canon', in *New Dimensions in New Testament Study*, ed. R. N. Longenecker and M. C. Tenney, Grand Rapids 1974, 3–18; D. **de Bruyne**, 'Prologues bibliques d'origin marcionite', *RBén* 24, 1907, 1–14; 'Les plus anciens prologues latins des Évangiles', *RBén* 40, 1928, 193–314.

H. **von Campenhausen**, *The Formation of the Christian Bible*, ET London and Philadelphia 1972; O. **Cullmann**, 'The Tradition. The Exegetical, Historical and Theological Problem', ET *The Early Church*, London and Philadelphia 1956, 59–99; N. A. **Dahl**, 'Anamnesis. Memory and Commemoration in Early Christianity' (1948), ET *Jesus in the Memory of the Early Church*, Minneapolis 1976, 11–29; 'Form-Critical Observations on Early Christian Preaching', ibid., 30–36; 'The Origin of the Earliest Prologues to the Pauline Letters', *Semeia* 12, 1978, 233–77; H. **Diem**, 'Das Problem des Schriftkanons', (1952), reprinted Käsemann, ed., *Das NT als Kanon*, 159–74; D. L. **Dungan**, 'The New Testament Canon in Recent Study', *Interp* 29, 1975, 339–51; J. D. G. **Dunn**, *Unity and Diversity in the New Testament*, London and Philadelphia 1977; 'Levels of Canonical Authority', *Horizons in Biblical Theology* 4, 1982, 13–60.

C. F. **Evans**, *Is 'Holy Scripture' Christian?*, London 1971; W. R. **Farmer**, *Jesus and the Gospel, Tradition, Scripture, and Canon*, Philadelphia 1982; I. **Frank**, *Der Sinn der Kanonbildung*, Freiburg 1971; L. **Goppelt**, 'Die Pluralität der Theologien im Neuen Testament und die Einheit des Evangeliums als ökumenisches Problem', in *Evangelium und Einheit*, ed. V. Vajta, Göttingen 1971, 103–25.

B. **Hägglund**, 'Die Bedeutung der "regula fidei" als Grundlage theologischer Aussagen', *StTh* 11, 1957, 1–44; F. **Hahn**, 'Das Problem "Schrift und Tradition" im Urchristentum', *EvTh* 39, 1970, 449–68; 'Die Heilige Schrift als älteste christliche Tradition und als Kanon', *EvTh* 40, 1980, 456–66; A. **von Harnack**, *Die ältesten Evangelien-Prologe und die Bildung des Neuen Testaments*, *SAB*, Phil.-Hist. Klasse, 1928; R. G. **Heard**, 'The Old Gospel Prologues', *JTS* 6, 1955, 1–16; E. **Käsemann**, 'The Canon of the New Testament and the Unity of the Church', *Essays on New Testament Themes*, ET, SBT 41, 1964, 95–107; ed., *Das Neue Testament als Kanon*, Göttingen 1970; E. R. **Kalin**, 'The Inspired Community: A Glance at Canon History', *CTM* 42, 1971, 541–49; H. **Koester**, 'Häretiker im Urchristentum als theologisches Problem', *Zeit und Geschichte, Dankesgabe an R. Bultmann*, ed. E. Dinkler, Tübingen 1964, 61–76; ET in *The Future of our Religious Past*, ed. J. M. Robinson, London and New York 1971, 65–83; 'New Testament Introduction. A Critique of a Discipline', *Christianity, Judaism and other Greco-Roman Cults*, ed. J. Neusner, Part I, New Testament, Leiden 1975, 1–20; W. G. **Kümmel**, 'Notwendigkeit und Grenze des neutestamentlichen Kanons' (1950), reprinted in Käsemann, ed., *Das NT als Kanon*, 62–97; H. **Küng**, 'Der Frühkatholizismus im Neuen Testament als kontrovers-theologisches Problem', *ThQ* 142, 1962, 385–424; reprinted in Käsemann, ed., *Das NT als Kanon*, 175–204; J. **Kunze**, *Glaubensregel, Heilige Schrift und Taufbekenntis*, Leipzig 1899.

I. **Lönning**, '*Kanon im Kanon*', Oslo and Munich 1972; W. **Marxsen**, *The New Testament as the Church's Book*, ET Philadelphia 1972; F. **Mildenberger**, *Die halbe Wahrheit oder die ganze Schrift*, Munich 1967; 'The Unity, Truth, and Validity of the Bible', *Interp* 29, 1975, 391–405; C. F. D. **Moule**, 'Collecting and Sifting the Documents', *The Birth of the New Testament*, London and San Francisco ³1981, 235–69; R. **Murray**, 'How did the Church determine the Canon of Scripture?', *Heythrop Journal* 11, 1970, 115–26; S. M. **Ogden**, 'The Authority of Scripture for Theology', *Interp* 30, 1976, 242–61; K. H. **Ohlig**, *Woher nimmt die Bibel ihre Authorität?*, Düsseldorf 1970; *Die theologische Begründung des neutestamentlichen Kanons in der alten Kirche*, Düsseldorf 1972; A. C. **Outler**, 'The "Logic" of Canon-making and the Task of Canon-criticism', *Texts and Testaments*, ed. W. E. March, San Antonio 1980, 263–76; H. **Paulsen**, 'Die Bedeutung des Montanismus für die Herausbildung des Kanons', *VigChr* 32, 1978, 19–52; S. **Pedersen**, 'Die Kanonfrage als historisches und theologisches Problem', *StTh* 31, 1977, 83–136; J. **Regul**, *Die antimarcionitischen Evangelienprologe*, Freiburg 1969.

A. **Sand**, 'Die Diskrepanz zwischen historischen Zufälligkeit und normativen Charakter des neutestamentlichen Kanons als hermeneutisches Problem', *MüThZ* 24, 1973, 174ff.; *Kanon, Handbuch der Dogmengeschichte*, ed. M. Schmaus et al., 1–3a, Freiburg/Basel/Wien 1974; W. **Schrage**, 'Die

Frage nach der Mitte und dem Kanon im Kanon des Neuen Testaments in der neueren Diskussion', *Rechtfertigung, FS E. Käsemann*, ed. E. E. Ellis and E. Grässer, Tübingen 1976, 415–42; A. **Souter**, *The Text and Canon of the New Testament*, revised by C. S. C. Williams, London ²1954; H. **Strathmann**, 'Die Krisis des Kanons der Kirche' (1941), reprinted in Käsemann, ed., *Das NT als Kanon*, 41–61; P. **Stuhlmacher**, *Vom Verstehen des Neuen Testaments*, Göttingen 1979, 32–44; A. C. **Sundberg**, 'Towards a Revised History of the New Testament Canon', *StEv* IV, TU 102, 1968, 452–68; 'Canon Muratori: A Fourth Century List', *HTR* 66 1973, 1–41; 'The Biblical Canon and the Christian Doctrine of Inspiration', *Interp* 29, 1975, 354–71; G. H. **Tavard**, *Holy Writ or Holy Church*, London 1959, New York 1960; G. **Wainwright**, 'The New Testament as Canon', *SJT* 28, 1975, 551–71; B. B. **Warfield**, *The Inspiration and Authority of the Bible*, Philadelphia 1948, London 1951; T. **Zahn**, 'Kanon des Neuen Testaments', *RE*³, IX, 768–96; A. **Ziegenaus**, 'Die Bildung des Schriftkanons als Formprinzip der Theologie', *MüThZ* 29, 1978, 264–83.

Although the New Testament canon cannot be fully understood without attention both to its historical and theological dimensions, the nature of the problem can perhaps be more clearly presented if these two aspects are initially treated separately.

I

First, it should be noticed that a remarkable consensus among modern scholars has emerged regarding certain features of the history of the canonization of the New Testament. There is broad agreement that the canon of the New Testament gradually developed as a part of the larger growth of the Christian church during the second century. By AD 200 the four gospels were widely reckoned as Scripture on a par with the Old Testament along with a corpus of Pauline letters. However, the process of determining the outer limits of the apostolic writings developed, often in heated debate, until the end of the fourth century at which time both the Eastern and Western branches of the church reached a decision regarding the canon's scope which then generally became normative for the ancient church. Traditional distinctions within the canon, such as the *homologoumena* and the *antilegomena* of Eusebius, continued to play a subordinate role even after the various ecclesiastical decisions, which stabilized the canon's scope (cf. Kümmel, Campenhausen, Sand).

One of the important effects of this modern consensus has been the almost universal rejection of a traditionally earlier dating for the first stage of the New Testament's canonization during the first half of the second century which was defended with great learning by Zahn and which has continued to attract conservative scholars ever since.

However, in spite of this apparent consensus it would be a serious mistake to suppose that the major historical problems regarding the canonical process of the New Testament have been finally resolved. Far from it. Much controversy still surrounds the exact role of Marcion in relation to the process. Von Campenhausen's continued defence of Harnack's position, which assigned the first canonical collection to Marcion, appears less and less convincing (cf. Dahl, 'The Origin of the Earliest Prologues . . .'). Again, many historical factors are unclear regarding the early formulation of the fourfold Gospel collection and the process by which the Pauline corpus evolved. Or again, an important and highly debatable issue turns on determining the direction from which the New Testament canonical process proceeded. Did the canonization of the New Testament develop in analogy to an Old Testament process which had largely reached its goal of stabilization before the New Testament period, or rather did the major canonical force stem from the side of the Christian church (Gese, Stuhlmacher, Sundberg), which resulted in the definition of the Jewish Scriptures as an Old Testament within the larger Christian Bible? Specialists differ and more historical research is needed on this issue. Still it is possible that the polarity between these two positions has been overdrawn, and that both a historical continuity with the Old Testament process obtained as well as a sharply different christological judgment regarding the significance of a normative canon for the Christian church.

If there is a consensus regarding certain aspects of the historical problems associated with the development of the New Testament canon, the same cannot be said about the theological interpretation of canon. One of the major effects of the recovery of new interest in the subject of the New Testament canon has been the eruption of a fierce debate concerning numerous, highly controversial theological issues. Some of the more important German articles have been collected into a single volume by E. Käsemann (*Das Neue Testament als Kanon*). However, Käsemann's selection represented only a small choice from a much wider collection of German-speaking writers, and many fresh contributions have appeared during the last decade (e. g. Schrage, Ohlig, Sand). Moreover, equally important essays have appeared in Scandanavia (Lönning, S. Pedersen), in England (Best, Dunn, Barr), and in the United States (Sundberg, R. E. Brown, Koester).

The theological debate regarding canon has focused on a variety of crucial issues:

1. How is one to handle the great diversity of perspectives represented within the New Testament canon? Is Käsemann correct in his formulation that the canon, far from being the basis for the church's unity, offers instead major grounds for its disunity? The same emphasis on the New Testament as a complex of contradictions and tensions is given by Dunn, who then attempts to salvage one strand of continuity in the common concept of Jesus as the Exalted One. How is one to decide what is actually the authentic gospel among the many conflicting voices? Must each person opt for a 'canon within the canon'?

2. Is it useful and necessary to speak of levels of canonical authority (Brown, Dunn)? To what extent is the theological function of the New Testament canon dependent on the recovery of the particular historical moment in which authority was first attributed to a level of tradition? Is it correct to speak of canon as 'tradition frozen in time', and which serves simply to illustrate how Christians once understood authority (Best)?

3. Again, how much theological authority can be attributed to the canonical decisions of the early church? Increasingly the role of time-conditioned, cultural features has emerged which played a decisive role in the process. To what extent was the New Testament canon a defensive overreaction to the threat of the Montanists and Gnostics? Is the claim of orthodoxy against heresy simply the assertion by the victors in an internal church struggle without any historical or theological legitimacy (Bauer, Koester, Dunn)? If many of the criteria by which canonicity was decided, such as apostolicity, have been shown to be historically questionable, how can the results of such decisions have any lasting authoritative role for the modern church?

4. Then again, what should be the effect of the historical critical recovery of the decisive role of tradition in the formation of the New Testament on the older, classic debate respecting 'word and tradition'? Would it be wiser for modern Christians either to abandon

the Reformers' terminology of '*sola scriptura*', or seriously to modify it, or even to replace it, as has been suggested, with the allegedly more suitable '*sola traditio*'?

5. Finally, what effect should the fact of a New Testament canon whose formation is closely intertwined with the present structure of the literature be on the actual exegesis of a text? Is it the case that canonical categories are wholly inappropriate for the historian's interpretive task? Is there an unbridgeable chasm between a hard-nosed, modern critical exegesis, and the ecclesiastical form which tradition has attached to the sacred writings?

II

Although it would be unrealistic and even arrogant for any person to claim that a new understanding of canon could resolve all these genuinely perplexing questions, I would like to move in a direction which perhaps will throw some fresh light on the debate.

Certainly some of the difficulty from the outset arises from a widespread mistaken understanding of the nature of the New Testament canon. It is assumed by many that the formation of a canon is a late, ecclesiastical activity, external to the biblical literature itself, which was subsequently imposed on the writings. Many of the questions which pose a polarity between the New Testament's real historical development and its ecclesiastical function, or between its genuine meaning and the sense later ascribed to it by clerics, reflect this basic confusion. Rather, it is crucial to see that the issue of canon turns on the authoritative role played by particular traditions for a community of faith and practice. Canon consciousness thus arose at the inception of the Christian church and lies deep within the New Testament literature itself. There is an organic continuity in the historical process of the development of an established canon of sacred writings from the earliest stages of the New Testament to the final canonical stabilization of its scope. That the continuity was hammered out in continuous conflict is also true.

Because the issue of canon is not an extraneous force, but integral to the transmission and shaping of the literature throughout its development, the usual method of treating the subject of canon at the conclusion of an introduction (Jülicher, Kümmel, Vielhauer) badly distorts the investigation of the literature itself. Even when the subject of canon precedes the section of Special Introduction (Holtzmann, Wikenhauser), the lack of any integral connection between the two sections issues in the same effect. The basic error involved arises from the assumption that the literature was shaped by historical, literary, sociological, and history-of-religion forces, but that the theological struggle of its tradents with the literature's normative function was insignificant.

In an important article S. Pedersen has recently argued that the discussion of the New Testament canon has to be removed from treating it as a formal enterprise which lacks any theological content. Rather 'the establishing of the canon rests on a dialectual combination of historical and theological criteria' (89). He then describes certain aspects of the struggle to bring to bear content-oriented norms on the process of selecting and ordering the New Testament writings which are reflected in such passages as Luke 1.1–3, John 20.30, II Peter 3.15–16, and Rev. 1.3. Since I had arrived at these same passages without knowledge of Pedersen's essay, his article came as a welcome confirmation.

Equally important as the recognition of the deep historical roots of canon consciousness within the tradition, is an understanding of the nature of the process. Far from being objective conduits of received tradition, the tradents, authors, and redactors of the New Testament effected a massive construal of the material by the very process of selecting, shaping and transmitting it. At the heart of the process lay a dialectical move in which the tradents of the developing New Testament were themselves being shaped by the content of the material which they in turn were transmitting, selecting, and forming into a scriptural norm. Central to the canonical process was the concern to render the occasional form in which the gospel was first received into a medium which allowed it faithfully and truthfully to render its witness for successive generations of believers who had not directly experienced Christ's incarnation and resurrection. When J. Barr evaluates the subject of canon as a formal, even accidental occurrence, without any hermeneutical significance, he has badly misinterpreted its true significance (*Holy Scripture*, 67).

This understanding of canon provides a critical judgment on the more recent evaluation of the New Testament canon which agrees on its deep roots within the tradition, but describes it as the 'freezing of tradition in particular contexts' (Best, 265), which serves 'as an illustration of what that norm meant in certain particular contexts'

(285). Similarly, J. Dunn argues for different levels of canonical authority which were normative for the self-understanding of the communities which used them. Because each level reflects a diversity of authority, 'we cannot ask after the canonical authority of any text at any level without having regard to the historical context of that level' (36). He also speaks of the 'freezing of tradition' which is 'so contingent on the peculiarities of particular historical circumstances' as to call into question any lasting significance (37). Finally, R. E. Brown's distinction between a text's literal, canonical, and ecclesiastical meaning,which is a more sophisticated interpretation than either Best or Dunn, still understands the canonical level of the text as tied to a specific historical level of the initial collectors of the tradition (34ff.).

I am critical of this approach to the New Testament canon for a variety of reasons. First, it reflects essentially a historicist reading of the biblical text which assumes that the meaning of a text derives only from a specific historical referent. It seems unaware that the function of canonical shaping was often precisely to loosen the text from any one given historical setting, and to transcend the original addressee. The very fact that the canonical editors tended to hide their own footprints, largely concealing their own historical identity, offers a warrant against this model of historical reconstruction.

Again, the motivation for establishing a canon runs directly in the face of the above interpretation when it sought to render the reality of the gospel in such a way as not to tie it to the past, but to address every future believer. There was no one hermeneutical device used by which to achieve this actualization. Certainly the material was not merely abstracted or dehistoricized. To suggest that the collectors simply universalized the teachings of Jesus is badly to misconstrue the Gospels. Even a casual perusal of the Synoptics shows how frequently the sayings of Jesus were applied to different historical contexts, and therefore were reinterpreted to new situations with considerable freedom. At times a saying has been firmly attached to an original historical situation, but at other times *logia* are reordered in a topical fashion which have lost their original setting and been replaced with a purely literary one. The Pauline letters, in spite of the high level of historical particularity which has been retained, have generally been edited in a conscious effort to render these occasional writings into a normative collection for universal application within the community of faith. The point must be emphasized that there never developed within the New Testament any single device by which to make the transition, but the effect of the canonical process finally was to assign a dynamic for its interpretation which was often quite different from its original historical role.

In sum, the canonical process created a flexible framework, the dynamic of which is distorted by the historicist's rigid model. Even when the original setting has been carefully preserved, as is clearly the case at times, its continuing canonical function for future believers is largely destroyed if an iron curtain is dropped between the different levels of the tradition. The point is not to suggest that the historical process is unimportant for New Testament exegesis, but the crucial hermeneutical issue turns on establishing the proper relation between text and process. It is simply inadequate to speak of the New Testament as an 'illustration' of how the gospel was heard (Best) or as an example of early Christian preaching (Marxsen). The function of a normative canon is to encompass the significance of the process within the contours of a normative text, and this multi-layered text thus becomes the vehicle for the theological witness to the gospel. In my judgment, the objections of the Reformers to the traditional four senses of Scripture apply equally well to the modern appeal to levels of canonical authority. In the end, this serves to blunt the authority of the plain meaning of the text, which, in my terminology, is its canonical sense.

III

It should be clear by now that in the argument being mounted the term 'canon' has been greatly broadened, and a defence for this usage is called for. There is an initial agreement on the etymology of the term (Westcott, Beyer, Sand). The Greek work κανών with its Semitic cognate originally signified a reed, then a tool for measurement and linear rule. The term developed in two directions in subsequently acquiring a figurative sense. On the one hand, it signified a norm, standard, or rule within both a grammatical and religious context. Thus, one finds the term in church usage since the middle of the second century as the 'rule of faith' (κανὼν τῆς πίστεως). On the other hand, the term was used to describe a list, a register, or catalogue, and was used for mathematical and chronological tables. In this sense the term was used by Eusebius in his 'canons' of the Gospels which were tables for establishing the Gospel parallels.

As is well known, in the middle of the fourth century the term canon was applied to the collection of sacred scriptures for the first time. It has long been debated from which of the two senses this use respecting the Bible was derived. Beyer in Kittel's *Theological Dictionary* (III, 596–602) opted for the first meaning, namely norm. Zahn conversely argued for the second, namely list or catalogue (*RE*[3], IX, 769–73). Although this etymological discussion remains significant, its resolution is not crucial to my argument. As I have already suggested, the process of the formation of authoritative religious writings long preceded the particular designation of the collection as canon in the fourth century. For this reason I am using the term canon in a broader sense than is traditionally the practice in order to encompass the entire process by which the formation of the church's sacred writings took place.

I am including under the term not only the final stages of setting limits on the scope of the sacred writings – canonization proper – but also that process by which authoritative tradition was collected, ordered, and transmitted in such a way as to enable it to function as sacred scripture for a community of faith and practice. Essential to the process is a hermeneutical function which structured occasional writings of varied historical and geographical background into such a form as to allow them to perform a particular role in the life of every succeeding generation of the faithful. The canonical process which established a special relationship between scripture and people reflected both the influence of the historical communities on the shaping of the literature and conversely the influence of the sacred writings on the self-understanding of the community.

Recently this usage of the term canon has been sharply criticized by James Barr (*Holy Scripture*, 75ff.) who alleges that it is incoherent and ambiguous. He analyses my usage into three distinct meanings which include canon as a fixed collection, canon as the final form of a book or group of books, and canon as a principle of finality and authority. Barr has provided an important service in calling for clarity. My initial impression is that when Barr separates and analyses these various usages in isolation he misses the major phenomenon for which the term is used. I am suggesting that a religious reading of Israel's tradition arose early in its history and extended in different ways throughout the oral, literary, and redactional stages in the growth of the material until it reached a final form of relative stability. The process did not happen all at once; there was no one overarching hermeneutic to realize the goal; some attempts were more successful than others.

I use the term canon for this entire theological construal to avoid the error of traditional Protestant orthodoxy (cf. H. Heppe, *Reformed Dogmatics*, 22) when it spoke of the authority of scripture as lying in the mind of God without regard for its human reception (αὐτόπιστος). I have broadened the term canon to express both the process and effect of this transmitting of religious tradition by a community of faith toward a certain end in all its various aspects. That different things were involved in this construal on the oral, literary, and redactional layers is clear, but as I shall attempt to demonstrate, the elements of continuity in terms of agency and purpose are strong enough, in my opinion, to justify this usage.

I feel that it is important to retain the term canon to emphasize that the process of theological interpretation by a faith community left its mark on a literary text which did not continue to evolve and which became the normative interpretation of the events to which it bore witness for those identifying with that religious community. The term guards the factuality of a sacred text and does not allow it to be replaced by a mode of consciousness, a move still current in liberal Protestant circles.

Of course, a crucial methodological issue turns on whether or not one can rightly encompass such a variety of different forces at work in the formation of the various stages of the New Testament within the one term 'canonical', even if one allows the term to be broadened to include an entire process. Certainly it would be erroneous to suggest that the process was unilinear and uniform in nature. Rather, the opposite is closer to the truth. However, I would argue that there is a basic continuity between the early stages of the New Testament's formation and those theological forces which finally effected an authoritative canonical collection.

In the earliest stages of oral transmission the stories of Jesus' teaching and healing were not preserved in church archives, nor transmitted as detached historical reports, but rather were proclaimed in such a way as to evoke faith in their hearers. Clearly the kerygmatic nature of the earliest preaching lay at the centre of the disciples' activity and its discovery by the early form critics (Bultmann, Dibelius, K. L. Schmidt) did much to undercut the older liberal search for a Jesus apart from faith. N. Dahl has rightly modified the term kerygmatic to include also the process of recollection ('Anamnesis', 11 ff.), but the major theological point is not altered. Already in the oral tradition there was a move to retroject into the earthly life of Jesus the full mystery of his person and authority which had only emerged in view after his resurrection. Because Christ was proclaimed as a risen Lord who continues to confront each new generation with power, the various stages of his original self-disclosure during his earthly life were frequently collapsed together before the consciousness of his living presence.

Similarly, the forces within the canonical process were at work in shaping the Gospel material in its literary stages. The writer of Mark structured the basic form of his Gospel by joining the apostolic witness to Christ's redemptive work in his death and resurrection with the tradition of his teaching. Moreover, Mark wrote an account of Christ's words and deeds because he believed that the power of Jesus was still available. Jesus was not just a figure of past history, but one who continued to address his readers and whose coming in power was about to be realized. In Mark the challenge of an obedient response constantly shifts from the original disciples who usually appear as a foil, to every successive generation of followers.

Finally, on the redactional level, the final shaping imprint did not stem merely from an effort to update the material in order to suit the needs of a later historical period, but offered a fresh perspective on the text by which to guide the community of faith in its understanding of the gospel. In the fourth Gospel the reader is continually being instructed in the true significance of a statement or of an event, and thus put into a different position from the disciples from whom the mystery was still hidden (cf. 6.6; 7.39; 8.27; 11.51). In this way the final redactional hand confirmed the explicit purpose of the author who wrote: 'These are written that you may believe that Jesus is the Christ, the Son of God, and that believing you may have life in his name' (20.30).

IV

In a fundamental sense the New Testament canon established a context from which the evangelical tradition was to be interpreted. One sees this effect very clearly in the formation of the sacred literature. The period of the early church during the first and second centuries was a time of intense rivalry among competing traditions and interpretations. The various Christian churches spread across the Roman Empire sought to weigh and balance the claims of authoritative writings. At the heart of the Christian faith lay the conviction that ultimate authority rested with the gospel of Jesus Christ, but the issue at stake was in determining the nature of the gospel. Christians in Rome, Antioch, and North Africa along with Gnostics, Judaizers, and mystics sought to give shape to its content.

It soon became evident that much turned on the context from which one viewed the material. Irenaeus complained that the Gnostics took bits and pieces of the gospel which, when correctly ordered, depicted the king, but they made a picture of a fox or dog from the same pieces (*adv. haer.* I. 9.4). They operated from the wrong context. They had no true concept of the whole. He therefore appealed to the church's rule-of-faith, the *regula fidei*. This comprised a holistic reading of the gospel which included the sum of tradition constituting the true revelation on which the faith was grounded and to which Scripture testified (Kunze, Hägglund). The early church thus made a judgment as to what it understood to be the apostolic witness. The church's concern, however, was in preserving the gospel and not with explaining its own identity (*contra* Moule, *Birth*). By establishing a canon it set apart the apostolic witness and drew a distinction between it and later church tradition. However, it was a conscious evaluation of the early church regarding the apostolic witness which established the parameters of the canon. The *skandalon* of the canon is that the witness of Jesus Christ has been given its normative shape through an interpretive process of the post-apostolic age. Significantly, the theological polarity was not between 'word and tradition' – admittedly the word created the tradition – but between different forms of tradition, the canonical being the authoritative and later church tradition being derivative of the canonical.

The result of establishing a New Testament canon was that a fixed context was set for understanding the gospel. Often it consisted of establishing boundaries inside of which the true witness was to be found. Thus, there were four evangelists, not more. Each of the four Gospels had its own integrity and no one dared fuse them as Tatian had attempted. At times a line was drawn which distinguished two generally similar books. Hebrews was finally judged to be an apostolic witness, but Barnabas was excluded. Then again, sometimes a check was established to prevent a misreading of a witness, such as the function of James which guarded against a false reading of Paul. The canon therefore provided a context for the gospel, but did not attempt a final formulation of its message. It marked the arena in which each new generation of believers stood and sought to understand afresh the nature of the faith. It did not establish one doctrinal position, but often balanced several or fixed the limits within which Christians might rightly disagree.

This flexibility was possible because the New Testament in its canonical shape continued to be treasured by a community of faith and practice. It was read and sung in worship, and heard in anticipation of a fresh illumination from the Spirit. Certainly Kümmel is correct in stating that the New Testament literature has a 'special character' (*Intr.*, 29), but because he fails to clarify adequately the nature of its uniqueness in terms of its canonical function, he is vulnerable to the criticisms of Marxsen (*Einl.*, ⁴1978, 14). In sum, the canon of sacred scripture was a living vehicle through which the Lord of the church continued to address his people. It was not moored in the past, but was a word from the ever-present Saviour.

In his book *Unity and Diversity in the New Testament,* James Dunn continues to press hard the issue of the diversity within the New Testament. Unquestionably an important role of the canon was in preserving a wide range of diverse witnesses, however, in a way far different from that projected by Dunn. He shares an approach which is common to one school of German theology of describing the New Testament as a *complex oppositorum*. Dunn first isolates a doctrinal position through historical and literary reconstruction and then sets it in direct opposition to another New Testament strand. The assumptions involved in his procedure are enormous. Moreover, Dunn fails to examine the traditions within the canonical context in order to determine how the material was actually heard, but on the basis of a modern reconstruction poses tensions within the canon which historically were often never thus perceived. To draw an analogy from the Old Testament, II Isaiah may seem to a modern critical scholar to be irreconcilably in tension with I Isaiah, but neither the synagogue nor the church ever heard it in this way before the Enlightenment. Dunn's method juxtaposes these varying perspectives by abstracting them from their literary context and then finding a series of blatant contradictions.

The significance of the New Testament canon lies, not in denying the presence of great variety of perspective, but in its role as offering guidelines on how the variety was to be understood in the light of the unity in Christ. The early church never celebrated theological diversity as such in spite of the persistent counterclaims of liberal Protestantism. Dunn's error, following Käsemann among others, lies in greatly oversimplifying the variety of relational possibilities available to a religious community. Conflicting perspectives can function in different ways depending on the interpretive model used. They can serve as different poles within an ellipse, as two sides of the same coin, or as addressing different audiences in varying situations. In my judgment, it belongs to an essential part of the exegetical task to describe from the New Testament literature itself how different tensions were received and handled within a canonical context. Fortunately, some scholars, such as G. Eichholz, have always been aware of this responsibility. When seen in an historical or literary isolation an enormous chasm separates Galatians from the Pastoral epistles. However, from within the New Testament canon the Pastorals have been assigned a particular function which is certainly neither to be identified with the early Pauline letters nor characterized as hopelessly contradictory.

In a similar fashion the modern debate concerning the need for a 'canon within the canon' reflects much theological confusion. That communities or individuals have always had favourite texts is beside the point. Rather, the issue at stake is whether the traditional scope of the New Testament provides an established context which has been received by the Christian church as faithfully reflecting the full dimensions of the gospel. The canon provides this point of standing from which one's identity with the church universal is made. The recognition of the full canon serves to rule out an interpretive move which, on principle from the outset, has narrowed the tradition, regardless of whether it be by an appeal to the love commandment or to justification by faith.

However, recognition of the authority of the whole Christian canon does not mean for a moment that the canon functions within the community of faith as a monolithic block. Within the canon itself different parts have already been subordinated to one another. Indeed to what extent the Eusebian terminology of *homologoumena* and *antilegomena* is still theologically appropriate is far from settled. Moreover, the church stands in a living relation to its scriptures and awaits a different message for different situations. The canon provides for innumerable fresh combinations of its witness which flexibility in no way calls into question the authority of the entire corpus of writings as a vehicle of the Spirit.

A significant point to be emphasized in the search to understand the nature of the New Testament canon is that the early church was never at any period of its history without a canon of authoritative writings. The Christian church simply assumed the authority of Israel's scriptures. As von Campenhausen has forcefully stated, the problem of the early church was not what to do with the Old Testament in the light of the gospel, which was Luther's concern, but rather the reverse. In the light of the Old Testament which was acknowledged to be the true oracles of God, how was one to understand the Good News of Jesus Christ (*Formation*, 64f.).

Still the process of relating the witness to Jesus Christ by the canonical scriptures of the Old Testament was neither simple nor obvious. No one understanding of the relationship of the two testaments emerged as normative, nor were literary techniques by which the ancient texts were rendered by the church the same. Indeed the dynamics involved in an extension of the Jewish canon by the Christian church gave this history a very different movement from that by which Israel had originally formed its scriptures. Nevertheless, the presence of an Old Testament canon of normative writings, with its recognized conventions as to how its authority functioned for the Jewish community, ultimately established a pattern by which the varying qualities of writings within the church were measured. One can distinguish the formation of a New Testament canon of authoritative writings in contrast to the authority of oral tradition, or of authoritative spokesmen, by the attribution of the same divine status to the new writings as obtained for the sacred scriptures of the Old. Thus, both Irenaeus and Tertullian identified the two collections as having the same divine source in their manner of scriptural citation.

The process of stablizing a canon of authoritative New Testament writings was effected within the process of the church's continued use of them. The selection and shaping of the books of scripture took place in the context of the worship of the struggling church as it determined canonicity by the use and effect of the books themselves. There is an element of truth in H. Diem's one-sided characterization of the criterion of canonization as that which 'allows itself to be preached' (Käsemann, ed., *Das NT als Kanon*, 174). Of course, the ancient catholic church developed criteria by which to test the claims of canonicity. These included apostolicity and catholicity, among others (Ohlig, *Die theologische Begründung*, 24ff.). However, the process of theological reflection on the application of these criteria was a far more complex and subtle one than is often realized. A writing must be apostolic to be judged canonical, but conversely, if a writing was acknowledged to be canonical, such as Mark and Luke, it must be apostolic. It is hard to escape the impression that the later expositions of the criteria of canonicity were, in large part, after-the-fact explanations of an expression of the church's experience of faith in Jesus Christ which were evoked by the continued use of certain books. When the second- and third-century theologians spoke of a rule-of-faith in their battle with the Gnostics, they were giving expression to a holistic understanding of the gospel which they had received and which they acknowledged to be the grounds of their faith.

Finally, there is another highly important side to the issue of the New Testament canon which raises a different set of problems from those concerned with the historical origins of the collection. The issue has to do with the effect of the canonical collection in its final form on the shaping of the tradition for those who treasured these writings as scripture. In the first century and well into the early second, the authority of the preached gospel lay in the living voice of Christ, whose collected words carried unique power. Later, authority was accorded Christian prophets, and accrued to certain offices within the early church. Certainly during his lifetime Paul's claim to apostolic authority did not rest in his letters, but was attached to his person and spoken word. Both Papias and Justin bear testimony in the middle of the second century as to how highly the oral tradition, in distinction from the written word, was held.

With the growth of a written corpus of acknowledged authoritative writings which reached its first stage of stabilization by the end of the second century, a new literary dynamic was set in motion. The written word not only became the vehicle of the gospel tradition, but provided an interpretation of the tradition which often transcended the earlier stages of its growth. When we speak about the canonical shape of the New Testament books, we are including both these historical forces within the canon's development which formed the tradition toward the goal of the church's continued kerygmatic use, as well as the effect which the collection had in unleashing a new potential within the literature for each new generation of hearers. The written word thus assumed an autonomy which it had not first possessed, but one which continued to show continuity with its origins by firmly attaching its authority to Jesus Christ, the sole source of the Good News.

3

THE RATIONALE OF A CANONICAL APPROACH

Bibliography

R. E. **Brown**, '"And the Lord said"? Biblical Reflections on Scripture as the Word of God', *ThSt* 42, 1981, 3–19; 'What the Biblical Word Meant and What it Means', *The Critical Meaning of the Bible*, New York 1981, 23–44; R. **Bultmann**, *Faith and Understanding* I, ET London and New York 1969; R. F. **Collins**, 'Historical-Crictical Methodology', *Introduction to the New Testament*, Garden City, N. Y. and London 1983, 41–74; O. **Cullmann**, 'The Necessity and Function of Higher Criticism', ET *The Early Church*, London and Philadelphia 1956, 3–16; E. **Dinkler**, 'Bibelkritik', *RGG*³, I, 1188–90; G. **Ebeling**, 'The Significance of the Critical Method for Church and Theology in Protestantism', ET *Word and Faith*, London and Philadelphia 1963, 17–61; 'Hermeneutik', *RGG*³, III, 242–62.

F. **Hahn**, 'Problems of Christological Criticism', ET *Historical Investigation and New Testament Faith*, Philadelphia 1983, 13–33; P. D. **Hanson**, *The Diversity of Scripture*, Philadelphia 1982; E. **Käsemann**, 'Vom theologischen Recht historisch-kritische Exegese', *ZTK* 64, 1967, 259–81; E. **Krentz**, *The Historical Critical Method*, Philadelphia 1975; H. **Küng**, J. **Moltmann**, eds., *Conflicting Ways of Interpreting the Bible*, Concilium 138, Edinburgh and New York 1980; K. **Lehmann**, 'Der hermeneutische Horizont der historisch-kritischen Exegese', *Einführung in die Methode der biblischen Exegese*, ed. J. Schreiner, Würzburg 1971, 40–80; G. **Maier**, *The End of the Historical-Critical Method*, ET St Louis, 1977; I. H. **Marshall**, ed., *New Testament Interpretation. Essays in Principles and Methods*, Exeter 1977; W. A. **Meeks**, Review of H. Koester's *Einführung in das Neue Testament*, *JBL* 101, 1982, 445–8; P. -G. **Müller**, 'Destruktion des Kanons – Verlust der Mitte. Ein kritisches Gespräch mit Siegfried Schulz', *ThRev* 73, 1977, 177–86; D. E. **Nineham**, *New Testament Interpretation in an Historical Age*, London 1976; *The Use and Abuse of the Bible*, London 1976, New York 1977.

J. A. **Sanders**, 'The Gospels and the Canonical Process: A Response to Lou H. Silberman', *The Relationships among the Gospels*, ed. W. O. Walker, Jr., San Antonio 1978, 219–36; H. **Schlier**, 'Was heisst Auslegung der

Heiligen Schrift?', *Besinnung auf das Neue Testament* II, Freiburg 1964, 35–62; E. **Schweizer**, 'Scripture – Tradition – Modern Interpretation', *Neotestamentica*, Zürich and Stuttgart 1963, 203–35; R. **Smend**, 'Nachkritische Schriftauslegung', *Parrēsia, FS Karl Barth*, Zollikon-Zürich 1966, 215–37; P. **Stuhlmacher**, 'Neues Testament und Hermeneutik–Versuch einer Bestandaufname', *ZTK* 68, 1971,121–61; *Historical Criticism and Theological Interpretation of Scripture*, ET Philadelphia 1977; *Vom Verstehen des Neuen Testaments. Eine Hermeneutik*, Göttingen 1979; H. **Zimmermann**, *Neutestamentliche Methodenlehre*, Stuttgart 1978, 17–31.

I

To suggest that a new approach to the discipline of New Testament Introduction is needed is not to propose a return to a traditional, pre-Enlightenment understanding of the Bible. Such an endeavour is not only wrong in concept, but impossible in practice. Moreover, there is a wide consensus to which I belong that the last serious, profoundly learned attempt of T. Zahn to offer an historical defence of the traditional positions respecting authorship, dating, and compositional history of the New Testament books was largely unsuccessful. I would also include within this failure a host of relatively conservative manuals which continue to practise a kind of 'soft' historical criticism, which, while expressing openness to modern methodologies, actually represent a last-ditch defence of a pre-nineteenth- century interpretation. I think that the hermeneutical issues at stake are of a far more complex nature than recognized by any easy compromise and require a more radical and comprehensive resolution.

Only someone who is unacquainted with the contribution which two hundred years of critical research has achieved could lightly disparage its significance. Yet along with its massive accomplishments lie major problems respecting its adequacy in handling the biblical text. First, there is the assumption, which has been increasingly challenged from the side of both general literary criticism and philosophical analysis, that the historical critical approach is suitable, indeed, mandatory for every correct reading of the Bible. The point at issue is whether different usages of the text require different approaches, and whether the critical approach has a restricted role which cannot be simply universalized. The critical method generally assumes that there are a set of proper procedures through which the biblical text must be subjected before it can be correctly understood. It includes the establishment of a text's milieu, probable date, author, audience, and literary growth, among other things.

Secondly, the critical method reflected in most introductions rests on the assumption of a uniformly historical-referential reading of the biblical text. At least from a theological perspective the serious objection must be raised that the Bible bears witness to a multi-dimensional theological reality which cannot be measured solely on the basis of such a correspondence theory of truth. The relation between biblical testimony and critical assessment of its measurable effect within common human experience remains a subtle one and touches on basic epistemological judgments. To run the gambit between secular historicism and ecclesiastical dogmatism requires, at the very least, a subtle dialectical approach which has not been represented up to this point in a New Testament Introduction.

Thirdly, critical Introductions have been dominated by an approach which identifies the key to a text's meaning with a determination of its historical origin. Hence the enormous energy which is expended in tracing the history of the growth of a New Testament book from both liberal and conservative stances. At times such insights are indeed helpful, but they can also work adversely in severely hampering the hearing of other literary notes within a book which only sound from the synchronic level. The point is not to overemphasize the contrast between historical and literary approaches, but to recognize that these avenues can be both useful or detrimental for interpretation, depending on how the method is applied to a given biblical passage. Fortunately, there are some examples of modern Introductions successfully illuminating a New Testament writing even when the specific interpretation relates only very loosely to a previously announced methodology.

Finally, and above all, the historical critical Introduction – whether in a liberal or conservative form is irrelevant – has not done justice in interpreting the New Testament in its function as authoritative, canonical literature of both an historical and a contemporary Christian community of faith and practice. A special dynamic issues from its canonical function which is not exhausted by either literary or historical analysis, but calls for a theological description of its shape and function. Crucial to the point is that the descriptive and hermeneutical task of interpretation cannot be held apart, as if to determine what a text meant and what it means could be neatly isolated.

Another way of stating the issue is to propose that what is needed is a new vision of the biblical text which does justice not only to the demands of a thoroughly post-Enlightenment age, but also to the confessional stance of the Christian faith for which the sacred scriptures provide a true and faithful vehicle for understanding the will of God. To assert that the Christian stands in a special relation to these writings is not to disavow the legitimacy of numerous other approaches to the text, both within and without a stance of faith. Although the right to a pluralistic handling of the Bible was first raised in the Enlightenment, it had fully established itself by the nineteenth century, at least within modern Western culture. The theological issue turns on the Christian church's claim for the integrity of a special reading which interprets the Bible within an established theological context and toward a particular end, namely the discerning of the will of God, which is constitutive of the hermeneutical function of canon.

II

Lest the approach being suggested be immediately dismissed as a form of uncontrolled subjectivity – fideism is often the word used – the full implications of a canonical approach must be spelled out in further detail. At the outset it must be stressed that the term canon designates an established body of literature which the early church recognized as both authoritative and fixed in scope. It belongs to the descriptive task to analyse the particular shape and function of this literature in relation to the community of faith which treasured and fashioned it. The task is descriptive because what is primarily being described is the testimony of these first Christians and not the faith of the modern reader.

Moreover, the descriptive task shares some peculiar features because of the nature of the New Testament canon. It was constitutive of the manner according to which the early Christian testimony was received and transmitted that this witness was not simply frozen in time. Rather, the Gospel material and the apostolic epistles were received as authoritative and used by the congregations in preaching, teaching, and liturgy. The writings thus entered into a process which eventually led to canonization, but which also involved growth and reinterpretation as they continued to serve an ongoing theological function within the church which was often different from the original situation of composition. By the collecting and reordering of once independent writings into an authoritative corpus of scripture, a new dynamic was established which profoundly influenced the interpretation of the parts (cf. the analysis of the Pauline epistles as an example).

The descriptive task of the New Testament canonical literature involves far more than attempting to reconstruct the original historical intentionality of its author. Nor does the appeal to canon suggest that the task is somehow arbitrarily restricted to certain books. The descriptive task required by the canon is of a very different order. What is called for is an analysis which combines both historical and theological description. It seeks to pursue not only the motives for giving the literature its peculiar shape, but also the function which the literature now performs in its special form within the smaller and larger units of the collection. To describe the various layers reflected within the Fourth Gospel may often have significance for understanding the final form of the book, but this approach is not to be simply identified with the canonical meaning of the Gospel. The prehistory of the Fourth Gospel stands in an indirect, dialectical relation to its final form and aids to the extent in which it illuminates the canonical intentionality.

In one sense, this descriptive task can be performed by anyone regardless of religious commitment, who has insight and empathy with the canonical literature in all of its literary, historical and theological dimensions. In recent years students of comparative literature have often proven themselves unusually perceptive in seeing how religious literature functions. Although such a descriptive enterprise cannot be characterized as 'objective, scientific' in a narrow sense, such observations on the form and function of a canonical text can be confirmed or refuted by other interpreters especially in terms of the quality of the exegesis as illuminating or idiosyncratic. Thus, for example, the arguments involved in assessing the literary, historical, and theological relation of John 21 or Romans 16 to author intentionality and in interpreting the effect of these chapters on the books as a whole must share in the commonly accepted rules of rational discourse.

Nevertheless, the lines begin to blur and the complexity of the descriptive task of canonical literature emerges when one includes within the enterprise the pursuit of the inner theological logic of the canon's witness. It is still possible for someone who does not share the theological concerns of the canonical literature to describe the theological struggle of a biblical text in bearing witness to a theological reality of the Christian faith, the testimony to which transcends – some would say, distorts – the dimensions of historically verifiable accounts. Still it is rare to find penetrating theological exegesis of the New Testament by one who shares little or nothing of the faith reflected by the literature. A different scale of priorities within the exegetical task usually leads these scholars into different concerns with the text. The hermeneutical issue at stake is not the piety of the interpreter which provides a capacity for proper interpretation – this confusion is inherent in all forms of pietism – but rather the willingness to work within a received context of faith, which lies at the heart of the canon's normative function.

I am fully aware of the irony of the exegetical task being described, when scholars in the past who stood outside the arena designated by the church as authoritative have often been able to illuminate important dimensions of the canonical text in a way in which pious study has not been able to achieve. One thinks of the lasting contributions of de Wette, Baur, Wellhausen, etc. Nevertheless, the dialectical relation between an inner and outer context of the biblical text does not call into question the integrity of a search for the logic of the canon which gave witness to the faith of the early church. Rather, the presence of other contexts, not at all hermetically sealed off from the canonical, provides both an important check on ecclesiastical dogmatism and a caution against immodest claims of divine sanction.

There is one final aspect of the model being proposed for canonical interpretation which forms an integral part to the hermeneutical task. To suggest that it consists of a homiletical application of the text by the modern reader is badly to misunderstand the issues at stake. Up to this point we have stressed the coercion exercised by the text upon the reader, and the need of a descriptive analysis which does justice to the peculiar intertextuality of the canon, which combines theological, literary, and historical dimensions. The shape which the canon has given the New Testament offers a peculiar construal of the Christian tradition which the early church provided. This canonical construal took place within a particular context which developed through the church's reception of these writings as authoritative and was to be used to shape the Christian life. A chief motivation lying behind the canonical process was in rendering the tradition in such a way as for its message of the gospel to be accessible to every succeeding generation of Christians.

The modern reader thus finds in the biblical text signs which aid the reader in understanding how the canon sought to construe the material according to its understanding of the gospel. This observation is not to suggest that the New Testament contains a full-blown hermeneutic or one unified rule-of-faith. Certainly this is not the case. However, the canonical construal has left crucial indices within the text by means of which it sought to transmit its understanding of the gospel.

It belongs to the exegetical task that the modern reader takes his point of standing within the authoritative tradition by which to establish his identity with the Christian church. From the scriptures he confesses his faith in the same Lord, Jesus Christ, whose life, death, and resurrection was testified to him in the Spirit through whom his redemption was appropriated, and in the church through which the gospel was transmitted. Yet the canonical scriptures do not serve as a frozen deposit of tradition or doctrine, but a living vehicle through which the will of God is perceived. The hermeneutical task of interpreting scripture requires also an act of construal on the part of the reader. This interaction between text and reader comprises every true interpretation.

Decisive for this process of interpretation is the context in which it is carried on. The function of canon is to assure its involving a received tradition which has been shaped toward the end of engendering faith in the Risen Lord of the scriptures. However, a canonical context includes not only the scope of the sacred literature, but the means by which the reader engages the scriptures, namely an expectation of understanding through the promise of the Spirit to the believer. Within this context the modern Christian interpreter strives to discern how the time-conditioned, historical witness of the Bible becomes the medium of revelation of God's present and enduring will. There is no one method by which this translation is made; however, the task of extending the kerygmatic testimony of the New Testament into an encounter with the modern reader is constitutive of interpreting the Bible as a canonical, rather than an antiquarian enterprise.

III

It should be clear by now that we have used the term canon in a number of different ways. It comprises a fixed body of sacred literature which the early church once designated as normative. It also involves a particular theological construal of the tradition which it provided to the literature by means of the shape and intertextuality it formed within the collection of writings. Finally, the term includes the interpretive activity of the modern Christian reader who seeks not only to identify with the received tradition but also truthfully to appropriate the message and to be a faithful recipient of the gospel for the present age.

It is constitutive of the theological task of biblical exegesis that a dialectical relationship obtains between the past and the present, between descriptive and constructive, between the time-conditioned and the transcendent. Although there are exegetical steps which afford a more appropriate sequence than others, as we shall seek to demonstrate throughout the book, in principle there is no one correct point of entry. Nor can the different dimensions of interpretation involved in canon be neatly separated into exegetical stages or levels of meaning.

In seeking to explain the canonical approach in my *Introduction to the Old Testament as Scripture*, I emphasized the significance of the final form of the text in a polemical debate with the commonly accepted critical method which assumed that the biblical text must be first put through a critical sifting to determine dating, author, levels of composition and historical referent before it could be correctly understood. I stressed the integrity of the received text within the canonical model as the object of interpretation. However, my intention was to suggest that the final form functioned as the starting point for canonical exegesis. Only by beginning with the final form can the peculiar features of a passage's intertextuality be discerned which is blurred if one first feels contrained to force the text through a critical sieve. Yet the final form of the text is not to be regarded as a monolithic block. The interpreter still has the exegetical responsibility of seeking to discern the canonical, that is, kerygmatic shaping of the text for its witness within the whole by its selecting, reordering, and stressing of certain aspects of the tradition. In sum, to take the canon seriously does not mean that all texts are treated on the same level, or that inherited tradition is appropriated uncritically (cf. the chapter on the book of Revelation). It is precisely the function of the canonical shaping to render the received material in different critical ways.

For this reason much of the debate over a canon-within-the-canon has been misplaced. The issue at stake is not whether one needs material criteria by which to interpret the whole, but rather what is the nature of the criteria. In my judgment, the entire biblical canon in the sense of the whole New Testament collection must remain the authoritative starting point for all exegesis; however, the interpreter must constantly strive to discern afresh a theological construal which does justice to the variegated texture of biblical thought in its dialectical relation to the modern world of the interpreter. The appeal to the theological resources of the whole Christian canon serves as a major check against ideologies which often have some biblical rootage, but are made to function in such a way as to obviate large parts of the New Testament's message.

Often the criticism has been lodged against the canonical approach that it is static in nature and a contrast is projected with a dynamic traditio-historical process (cf. Hanson). In my judgment, this criticism derives from a misunderstanding of what is being proposed. The issue at stake is not the contrast between static text and dynamic process, but the nature of the process which is considered normative and its relation to the canonical text. Usually for the critical method, using the tools of tradition history, a process is reconstructed which seeks to traverse the period from the material's inception to its final, stabilized textual form. In some contexts of interpretation such a projection is useful in highlighting the growth and diversity of various traditions. However, the procedure is largely hypothetical. It usually falls in periods in which evidence is lacking and it functions as an abstraction of the tradition from actual historical communities. No one historical community ever heard the material according to the schemata being hypothesized.

In contrast, the canonical approach to the New Testament begins with those historical communities who received and heard the gospel in ways congruent with portions of the New Testament canon. They found their identity in these particular apostolic construals which served finally to overcome earlier historical diversities within early Christianity. In spite of the constant emphasis on the diversity within the New Testament by modern scholars, historically by the end of the second century, if not before, the gospels were being read holistically as a unity within the circumference proscribed by a rule-of-faith (cf. Papyrus Egerton 2, *NTApoc I*, 94–97).

Interest in the process by which this particular rendering of the New Testament message developed remains an integral part of canonical exegesis. The approach identifies with this particular perspective within the text's history, in the development of which whole areas containing other theological options were either subordinated or ruled out (e. g. the Gnostic). However, the process itself has no independent theological significance apart from the canonical text in which it left its interpretations. Conversely, the text cannot be isolated from the actual tradents of the tradition who participated in the canonical process. Ironically enough, the canonical approach being suggested offers the potential of actually being more historical, in a genuine sense of the term, than a critical method which is prone to abstraction and speculation regarding groups, traditions, and motivations.

Often the criticism has been levelled against the canonical approach that it is reductionistic because it lays primary interest on the text's theological dimension. In a brilliant review of Koester's *Introduction*, W. A. Meeks pinpoints the issue in his arguing that 'the category "theology" alone is not adequate to indicate what is significant about the life of Christian communities . . . it does not follow that it is only the theological statements or beliefs that the sources contain or imply that are important to us. What is important depends upon some larger conception of what theology's task is . . .' (*JBL* 101, 1982, 448).

I would agree with Meeks that it is one's larger conception of theology's task which defines 'what is important'. The formation of the New Testament canon performed exactly this function for the early church. These writings were preserved, not because of interesting historical, religious, or sociological data, but solely for their theological role in speaking of God's redemption in Jesus Christ. That the New Testament contains all sorts of other things is undisputed; however, the canonical approach identifies with the early church's evaluation of the Bible's function. As modern Christians we are more aware than our forebears of the role in which cultural features shaped this theological message, but the priority of the theological for the Christian church is aggressively reaffirmed by the focus on the canon. The inconsistency of Koester's position which would dispense with the New Testament canon, and yet seek a normative theological function for historical research, is demonstrated decisively by Meeks.

Finally, a word is in order concerning the stability of the lines which form the parameters around the New Testament canon. By canon we indicate those writings which were received as authoritative. The New Testament canon did not fall from heaven, nor is any view of its formation adequate which does not assign the historical early church the active and dominant role in its formation. Of course, it is theologically crucial to see that the church never claimed to have 'created' a canon, but it saw its task in discerning among competing claims what it recognized as apostolic. This process took hundreds of years to complete, and involved much controversy and uncertainty. Any claims for infallibility for these decisions are out of the question. The canon's authority, much like a creed, derives from its unique witness to Jesus Christ, the Lord of the church. The church lives from the promise that God continues to reveal his will through this vehicle, earth-bound and fragile in its very nature. Although I do not believe that the Eusebian categories for designating different qualities within the canon in the light of the diverse history of reception for different books can be directly appropriated without modification, in principle his distinctions remain theologically legitimate. Such distinctions correctly reflect the flexibility associated with the canonical norm. That certain Christian communities draw the outer limits of the canonical circle in a slightly different fashion is another warrant for retaining the maximum element of theological flexibility. However, in the end, the shape of the church's christological confession depends closely on the stability assigned to the unique apostolic witness. I judge it to be a major threat to Christian theology when the New Testament loses this function of unique witness to be regarded merely as a 'classic' or as an illustration of something else, whether a process, a mode of consciousness, or a religious ideology.

IV

Although an Introduction is hardly the place to enter into a lengthy debate with competing models of New Testament interpretation, a brief discussion may aid in sharpening the profile of the canonical proposal.

In recent years as the historical critical method has increasingly come under attack both from within and without the scholarly guild, numerous responses have sounded in its defence to assure their modern readers that the basic structure which emerged since the Enlightenment is both intact and indispensable. Several well-known scholars have launched passionate defences and sought to ground its theological legitimacy in the Reformation (e. g. Ebeling, Käsemann, Krentz).

I have no doubt that some of the claims made by these modern apologetes are true. Historical criticism is here to stay. Much of the conservative opposition is badly misplaced and even docetic in nature. Nevertheless, I remain largely unsatisfied with this defence and feel that the basic issues of the critical method in interpreting the Bible have been inadequately treated. Perhaps an analogy to the problem can be derived from Melanchthon's example. On the one hand, he sought to persuade his students of the indispensability of studying Aristotle's rhetoric. One could not learn to understand the use of language, concepts and logical categories of theological discourse without the masterful guidance of the great philosopher. On the other hand, he could also flatly state that to build one's theology on Aristotle was to effect a disaster beyond description. For him, as for Luther, Aristotle and the gospel were alien to each other and irreconcilable opponents.

To apply the analogy, I would agree that historical criticism is an indispensable teacher. From it the interpreter learns a multitude of things about the text, its meaning, history, and audience. Exegesis performed without its aid seems naive, often crude, and flat in its dimensions. Yet also in this case, this information stands in a dialectical relation to the biblical witness which has a unique story to tell about God and his redemption which enters the world of time and space, but shatters its laws and mores through endless surprises. It is the claim of the critical method for exclusively first priority which is the issue at stake. To allow the theology of the church to add a homiletical topping after the basic critical work has been done is small comfort. The theological battle has been surrendered at the outset. When Krentz confidently asserts: 'Historical criticism provides a way for the Scriptures to exercise their *proper critical function* for the church' (65), he has not grasped, in my judgment, the full dimensions of the claims which the critical method is demanding of the church.

Then again, P. Stuhlmacher has sought to delineate a new approach to exegesis in several recent articles and monographs. He criticizes the functionalism of historical criticism because of its method of historical distancing of the past from the present and in its use of a general principle of historical analogy. In fact, criticism is still dominated by Troeltsch's three principles. As a way out of the impasse he proposes a 'hermeneutics of consent' (*eine Hermeneutik des Einverständnisses*) which seeks to achieve an openness to the truth claims 'about man, his world, and transcendence' (*Historical Criticism*, 85). What is needed, according to Stuhlmacher, is a new perception which is 'the readiness to take up and work through the claims of the tradition' (*ZTK* 68, 148). Although the proposal is theologically serious and calls for a detailed response, it appears to me that the appeal to a 'dimension of transcendence' as a final exegetical move built onto a historical critical exegesis suffers from major problems. It assumes that the critical method is basically sound, but simply stands in need of an additional dimension which is, of course, a move different in kind from his historical exegesis. His suggestion remains vague and diffuse because it does not take into account the actual canonical shaping of the New Testament literature. Rather, he appeals for aid to a 'history of exegesis' (*Wirkungsgeschichte*) which, however, never achieves an integral relationship to the biblical text itself. As his commentary on Philemon illustrates, this history becomes an appendix to his critical historical and literary analysis. His actual exegesis fails to reflect the peculiar features of the letter's canonical intertextuality.

Finally, R. E. Brown addresses the issue of canon in an essay with the title 'What the Biblical Word Meant and What it Means' (*The Critical Meaning*, 23–44). Brown approaches the problem in terms of the various senses of the New Testament and distinguished several different levels of meaning. The literal sense is its meaning when it left the hand of its author or redactor, the canonical sense is its meaning when seen in the context of the larger canonical collection, and an ecclesiastical meaning which is an extension of the canonical is how the later church understood its sense. Brown argues for the basic priority of the literal sense as recovered by the historical critical method, but he does allow for the legitimacy of derived levels of meaning. He questions 'canonical critics' as to what preponderance one gives to the meaning derived from historical criticism and is suspicious of its centrality being eroded.

My major criticism of Brown's approach is that his hermeneutic separates the biblical text into different levels which destroys the fundamental dialectic between what a text meant and what it means which is the essence of canon. As a result of his levels of meaning the special texture of the biblical text which combines the past and the present is irreparably rent. By giving over the basic task of exegesis to the usual methods of historical criticism, Brown shatters the genuinely theological dimension of the text and effects a multiple reading which is reminiscent of the medieval church's appeal to the four senses of scripture with all its ensuing problems. In my judgment, the inability of Brown's method to deal adequately with the theological dimensions of the text emerges most clearly from his book on *The Birth of the Messiah* (New York 1977). In spite of impressive critical analysis the theological yield is small indeed and the separation between description and constructive theological exegesis is never overcome.

4

METHODOLOGY OF CANONICAL EXEGESIS

It is now in order to turn from the more theoretical discussion of the hermeneutical issues involved in exegesis, and to focus on the more specific task at hand. How does the canonical approach affect actual exegesis? What factors, perspectives, or rules govern the study of individual books? How does one proceed?

Interpretation begins with the canonical form of the text (cf. the excursus on text criticism). The move is obvious because to speak of the New Testament canon is to identify that corpus received as scripture. The canonical form marks not only the place from which exegesis begins, but also it marks the place at which exegesis ends. The text's pre-history and post-history are both subordinated to the form deemed canonical. The goal of the enterprise is to illuminate the writings which have been and continue to be received as authoritative by the community of faith. However, in between the point of beginning and ending lies a complex exegetical process. The interpreter enters into a dialogue with the text in an effort to discern how each writing within the New Testament canon construes its material in order to bear truthful witness to the gospel of Jesus Christ. The interpreter is reading the text toward a particular goal, namely, one which is congruent with the kerygmatic character of the scriptures in bearing testimony to God's redemption of the world in Christ. The focus on discerning a writing's canonical shape derives from the conviction that the text's kerygmatic purpose functions within the peculiar form of that witness. The canon as a designation of the collection marks the parameters of the scriptures, but the canonical shaping of the text leads the interpreter to discern how the material within the canon was fashioned through a particular intertextuality to render its special message.

The search for the canonical shape of the text begins with a reading which looks for traces either of how the author intended the material to be understood, or of the effect which a particular rendering has on the literature. The point is to take seriously a writer's expressed intentionality, but without pulling text and intention apart. At times the canonical text receives a meaning which is derivative of its function within the larger corpus, but which cannot be directly linked to the intention of an original author (cf. ch. 10 below, on Gospel Harmony).

One of the first places to look for indications of canonical shaping lies in the structure of the book. Obviously the formal means by which the material is ordered affects the content of the book in an integral way. However, within the books of the New Testament the structure of the whole is often unclear. Therefore, it is important from a canonical perspective to observe whether a book's structure is equivocal and lends itself to a variety of possible interpretations (cf. Matthew). A construal of the structure which in fact eliminates portions of the book should be viewed with suspicion (cf. Luke 1–2). Frequently patterns of interchange between dogmatic and paraenetic sections (cf. Hebrews) play a more significant canonical function than a book's overarching structure. Within the gospels, attention to the manner in which the narrative features render the material is of great importance.

The purpose of the author is often most clearly stated in the praescript or in the conclusion (Luke 1.1–4; Acts 1.1–5). Conversely the effect of a lack of a praescript on the reading of an epistle can give important leads on how the letter now functions (e. g. Hebrews). Similarly, conclusions often indicate a writer's intention (John 20.30), or provide an important canonical setting (Heb. 13.22; II Tim. 4.6ff.). Finally, the significance of the superscriptions should not be underestimated. They were added during the final stages of canonization, but frequently give a valuable clue on how the church first heard the message (cf. Hebrews, Revelation).

Another crucial feature in discerning how a writer construed his material is the search for the particular context in which it was placed. A major polemic of the canonical approach is directed against the manner in which historical critics often treat this problem by assuming the centrality of a hidden historical reference even when omitted by the writer, or by assigning a major force to be the effect of the delay of the parousia (Luke, Acts), or of a developing 'early

Catholicism' (Acts, Ephesians, II Peter). While a canonical approach is well aware of the variety of historical forces at work in the development of a composition, it seeks carefully to determine to what extent such forces have been consigned to a text's distant background or assigned a major role in the foreground. The historical critical method being criticized is one which reconstructs an allegedly original historical context and then refocuses the composition on the basis of such a theory (cf. Matthew). The search for the theological function of a writing can be only correctly achieved when the peculiar form of a passage's intertextuality is recognized which always stands in a subtle dialectical relationship with its original historical referent. Thus, although it is possible that John's Gospel arose in an environment which shared some significant features with a proto-Gnosticism, the present form of the Gospel has largely subordinated this inheritance and even rendered it inoperative in conscious opposition to its theology (cf. also Colossians).

It is erroneous to infer that the canonical approach which is being outlined is opposed to historical criticism in principle. The issue at stake turns on how it is used. Recovery of the pre-history of a composition, such as Q, can be useful in measuring both the continuity and discontinuity with the present canonical function. However, to insist on finding the key to the final form of the text in this early stage of development can easily become a hindrance in discovering its canonical role. Most modern commentators agree that the Fourth Gospel shows abundant evidence of being a multi-layered text. Yet to read the present Gospel according to a reconstructed theory of its levels easily results in badly misconstruing its canonical function (cf. ch. 8 below, on John). Similarly to assume that proper interpretation of a text depends on the critic's ability to provide the needed antecedents of understanding runs in the face of a canonical approach which seeks to correlate the function of the text with the information provided by the fourth evangelist. Nevertheless, a positive value of the historical critical method is the aid which it offers in sharpening the interpreter's ability to distinguish different voices within a text, and to guard against the conservative tendency of traditional exegesis to translate the New Testament canon into a single monolithic block by means of easy harmonization. The discovery of diversity is not the goal of exegesis, but its presence remains an important factor which has been worked into the texture of the canon.

A basic feature of the approach being outlined is the careful attention in discerning how the material is rendered into scripture in order to provide an access to its witness by successive generations of Christians who did not themselves experience at first hand Christ's ministry. The very phenomenon of a canon provides a basic warrant for inferring that the material of the New Testament was shaped toward engendering faith and did not lie inert as a deposit of uninterpreted data from a past age. A variety of different techniques were used in the collection and reshaping of the Pauline corpus which sought to expand the canonical function beyond the scope of the original addressee, and yet to retain a high level of particularity. The occasional nature of the Pauline corpus was largely retained, but significantly modified in many of the letters.

Then again, the four Gospels shaped the tradition in different ways in order to provide the reader access to the evangelical message. Mark retained the perspective of the pre-resurrection disciples for whom Jesus' real identity was hidden throughout most of his Gospel, whereas the Fourth Gospel was written consistently from the vantage point of Christ's mission as the Divine Son, who was sent from God. For Luke-Acts the category of proof-from-prophecy provided the means by which to span history from prophecy to fulfilment. At times the original context was blurred into an intentional ambiguity in order to bear witness to a new theological reality. Sometimes high levels of literary and theological tension were retained (II Corinthians), whereas at other times the speeches of individual apostles were fashioned into one uniform pattern (Acts).

At this juncture much of the controversy with the historical critical method emerges. The canonical approach regards it as a threat to exegesis when critics historicize the New Testament material by assuming that the sharper the historical focus, the better the interpretation (cf. the debate over Romans). Often the effect of postulating a specific, concrete referent is to destroy those very canonical features by which the message is rendered in its unique form. Therefore, in spite of a plethora of new information, the true theological witness of the text is rendered mute. The critic presumes to stand above the text, outside the circle of tradition, and from this detached vantage point adjudicate the truth and error of the New Testament's time-conditionality. In contrast, the canonical interpreter stands within the received tradition, and, fully conscious of his own time-conditionality as well as that of the scriptures, strives critically to discern from its kerygmatic witness a way to God which overcomes the historical moorings of both text and reader. The difference between the methods does not lie in an alleged polarity between tradition and criticism, but between the nature of an analytic approach and one which is consonant with the theological function of a normative religious canon.

A frequent indication of how the New Testament seeks to transcend its original historical context lies in carefully observing the function of the addressee of a composition. At times the original disciples are precisely portrayed in their historical context and only by subtle analogies are subsequent readers addressed. At other times the disciples become an obvious transparency for the one obedient response of the church (cf. John). A shift within a narrative or a letter from singular to plural, from 'I' to 'we', frequently signals a form by which to confront subsequent readers (cf. Acts). Finally, a variety of different techniques are employed by which to expand the original recipients of a letter in order to encompass the larger Christian church (cf. I Peter, Ephesians).

The canonical approach to the New Testament concerns itself with authorship, but in a fashion different from the debates generally engaged in between conservatives and liberals. It seeks to pay close attention to the theological function of eyewitness claims (Luke 1.3; John 21.24) without immediately translating the biblical testimony into a question of historical referentiality. Similarly it attempts to interpret the function of a claim to Pauline authorship of a letter which appears to have extended the witness beyond the historical period of Paul's ministry (cf. the Pastorals). Again, it seeks to explore the role of a canonical portrait of Paul or Peter which is only partially congruent with a critical reconstruction of the historical apostles. Thus the canonical approach accepts as helpful many of the interpretive options which stem from the model of pseudepigraphy, but remains critical of the appeals of these categories in doing full justice to the theological function of indirect authorship which has a special function within the canon (cf. the Pastorals, I Peter).

Of particular interest to the method being proposed is the concern to deal seriously with the effect which the shape of the canonical collection has on the individual parts. At times the larger corpus exerts a major influence by establishing a different context from that of a single composition. The effect of a holistic reading of the four gospels can be seen in the longer ending of Mark which functioned to bring Mark's gospel into harmony with the fourfold collection. A major canonical issue arises in seeking to explore the effect of including the Pastorals within the Pauline corpus, or of severing the original linkage of Luke's two-volume work into two parts, with separate and distinct functions within the canon assigned to Luke and to Acts. Likewise the relation in one canon between books so different as Galatians and James calls for careful reflection. Finally, a canonical approach seeks to determine whether a canonical 'harmony' of the four gospels is possible which avoids the pitfalls of both rationalism on the right and historicism on the left. How does attention to the canon's role aid the interpreter in dealing in a theologically responsible fashion with both the unity and diversity of the gospel witnesses? (cf. ch. 10 below on Harmony).

In conclusion, the principal concern of the canonical approach can be briefly summarized. Its aim is not to provide a short-cut to exegesis, nor is it to offer an interpretation of each passage within the New Testament. Rather, it seeks to sketch a different vision of the biblical text which profoundly affects one's concept of the enterprise, but which also makes room for the continuing activity of exegesis as a discipline of the church. It is likely that future scholars who work seriously with the implications of the canon will arrive at different interpretations of individual passages and indeed of the entire books. Such correction is all to the good. However, the nature of the debate will be vastly different among those who share a canonical vision of interpreting the New Testament as sacred scripture of the church. One test of continuity between generations of readers will be to determine the extent of a genuine family resemblance which reflects both diversity and individuality within the discipline.

PART TWO

THE GOSPELS

5

MATTHEW

Commentaries

A. Plummer, 1909
B. Weiss, [5]1910
W. C. Allen, ICC (1907), [3]1912
J. Wellhausen, [2]1914
A. H. McNeile, 1915
T. Zahn, KNT (1903), [4]1922
T. H. Robinson, MNTC, 1928
A. Schlatter, 1929
J. Wilkens, 1934–37
E. Klostermann, HNT, [3]1938
M.-J. Lagrange, ÉB, [4]1941
W. Michaelis, ZBK, 1948–9
J. Schniewind, NTD, [5]1950
S. E. Johnson, *IB*, 1951
E. Lohmeyer, MeyerK, 1956

F. V. Filson, B/HNTC, 1960
K. Stendahl, Peake, 1962
J. C. Fenton, Pel, 1963
P. Gaechter, 1963
J. Schmid, RNT, [5]1965
P. Bonnard, CNT, [2]1970
W. F. Albright, C. S. Mann, AB, 1971
W. Grundmann, THKNT, [3]1972
D. Hill, NCeB, 1972
E. Schweizer, NTD (1973), ET 1975
F. W. Beare, 1981
R. Gundry, 1982

Bibliography

E. L. **Abel**, 'Who Wrote Matthew?', *NTS* 17, 1970/71, 138–52; B. W. **Bacon**, 'The "Five Books" of Matthew against the Jews', *Exp*, VIIIth series, 15, 1918, 56–66; *Studies in Matthew*, New York and London 1930; H. **Baltensweiler**, 'Die Ehebruchsklauseln bei Matthäus', *TZ* 15, 1959, 340–56; G. **Barth**, 'Matthew's Understanding of the Law', Bornkamm, Barth and Held, *Tradition and Interpretation in Matthew*, q. v., 58–164; F. W. **Beare**, 'The Mission of the Disciples and the Mission Charge. Matthew 10 and Parallels', *JBL* 89, 1970, 1–13; K. **Berger**, *Die Amen-Worte Jesu*, BZNW 39, 1970; *Die Gesetzesauslegung Jesu*, I, WMANT 40, 1972; O. **Betz**, *Offenbarung und Schrifterforschung*, WUNT 6, 1960; E. P. **Blair**, *Jesus in the Gospel of Matthew*, New York 1960; P. **Bonnard**, 'Mattieu, éducateur du peuple chrétien', *Mélanges Bibliques*, FS B. Rigaux, ed. A. Descamps, Gembloux 1970, 1–7; K. **Bornhaüser**, *Die Bergpredigt*, BFChTh 2.7, 1923;

G. **Bornkamm**, 'Das Doppelgebot der Liebe', *Neutestamentliche Studien für R. Bultmann*, ed. W. Eltester, BZNW 21, 1954, 85–93; 'Bergpredigt', *RGG*³, I, 1957, 1047–50; 'Der Lohngedanke im Neuen Testament', *Studien zu Antike und Urchristentum*, *GA* II, Munich 1959, 69–92; 'End Expectation and Church', *Tradition and Interpretation in Matthew* (below), 15–51; 'The Stilling of the Storm in Matthew', ibid., 52–8; *Jesus of Nazareth*, ET London and New York 1960, 221–5; 'The Authority to "Bind" and "Loose" in the Church in Matthew's Gospel: The Problem of Sources in Matthew's Gospel', in *Jesus and Man's Hope*, ed. D. G. Miller, Pittsburg 1970, 37–50; reprinted G. Stanton, ed., *The Interpretation of Matthew*, q. v., 85–97; 'The Risen Lord and the Earthly Jesus: Matt. 28: 16–20', *The Future of our Religious Past*, ed. J.M. Robinson, London and New York 1971, 203–29; 'Der Aufbau der Bergpredigt', *NTS* 24, 1977/8, 419–32; G. **Bornkamm**, G. **Barth**, H. J. **Held**, *Tradition and Interpretation in Matthew*, ET London and Philadelphia 1963, ²1983; G. **Braumann**, 'Der sinkende Petrus. Matthäus 14, 28–31', *TZ* 22, 1966, 403–14; R. E. **Brown**, *The Birth of the Messiah*, New York and London 1977; S. **Brown**, 'The Matthean Community and the Gentile Mission', *NovT* 22, 1980, 193–221; B. C. **Butler**, *The Originality of St Matthew. A Critique of the Two-Document Hypothesis*, Cambridge 1951.

K. W. **Clark**, 'The Gentile Bias in Matthew', *JBL* 66, 1947, 165–72; O. L. **Cope**, *Matthew: A Scribe Trained for the Kingdom of Heaven*, CBQMS 5, 1976; N. A. **Dahl**, 'The Passion Narrative in Matthew', ET *Jesus in the Memory of the Early Church*, Minneapolis 1976, 37–51; W. D. **Davies**, *The Setting of the Sermon on the Mount*, Cambridge 1964; J. D. M. **Derrett**, *Law in the New Testament*, London 1970; M. **Dibelius**, 'Jungfrauensohn und Krippenkind', *Botschaft und Geschichte* I, Tübingen 1953, 1–78; *The Sermon on the Mount*, New York 1940 = 'Die Bergpredigt', *Botschaft und Geschichte* I, 79–174; M. **Didier**, ed., *L'Évangile selon Matthieu. Redaction et Théólogie*, BETL 29, Gembloux 1972; E. **von Dobschütz**, 'Matthäus als Rabbi und Katechet', *ZNW* 27, 1928, 338–48; ET in G. Stanton, ed., *The Interpretation of Matthew*, 19–29; C. H. **Dodd**, *Gospel and Law. The Relation of Faith and Ethics in Early Christianity*, Cambridge and New York 1951; 'Matthew and Paul', *New Testament Studies*, Manchester 1953, New York 1954, 53–66; 'The Beatitudes. A Form-critical Study', *More New Testament Studies*, Manchester and Grand Rapids 1968, 1–10; J. **Dupont**, 'Le point du vue de Matthieu dans le châpitre des paraboles', in Didier, op. cit., 221–59; G. **Eichholz**, 'Die Aufgabe einer Auslegung der Bergpredigt', *Tradition und Interpretation*, Munich 1965, 35–56; *Auslegung der Bergpredigt*, Neukirchen ³1975.

W. R. **Farmer**, *The Synoptic Problem*, New York and London 1964; F. V. **Filson**, 'Broken Patterns in the Gospel of Matthew', *JBL* 75, 1956, 227–31; A. **Finkel**, *The Pharisees and the Teacher of Nazareth*, Leiden and Köln 1964; A. T. **France**, 'The Formula-Quotations of Matthew and the Problem of Communication', *NTS* 27, 1980/1, 233–51; H. **Frankemölle**, *Jahwebund und Kirche Christi. Studien zur Form- und Traditionsgeschichte des 'Evangeliums' nach Matthäus*, NTAbh 10, 1974; 'Neue Literatur zur Berpredigt', *ThRev* 79, 1983,

177–98; V. P. **Furnish**, *The Love Command in the New Testament*, Nashville 1972, London 1973; P. **Gaechter**, *Die literarische Kunst im Matthäus-Evangelium*, Stuttgart 1965; B. **Gärtner**, 'The Habakkuk Commentary (DSH) and the Gospel of Matthew', *StTh* 8, 1954, 1–24; D. E. **Garland**, *The Intention of Matthew 23*, NovTSuppl 52, 1979; B. **Gerhardsson**, *The Testing of God's Son* (Mt 4:1–11 and Par.), Lund 1966; *The Mighty Acts of Jesus according to Matthew*, Lund 1979; J. **Gnilka**, *Die Verstockung Israels. Isaias 6, 9–10 in der Theologie der Symoptiker*, SANT 3, 1961; 'Die Kirche des Matthäus und die Gemeinde von Qumran', *BZ* 7, 1963, 43–63; M. D. **Goulder**, *Midrash and Lection in Matthew*, London 1974; H. B. **Green**, 'The Structure of St Matthew's Gospel', IV/1, TU 102, 1968, 47–59; H. **Greeven**, 'Die Heilung des Gelähmten nach Matthäus', *WuD* 4, 1955, 65–78; R. A. **Guelich**, *The Sermon on the Mount: A Foundation for Understanding*, Waco, Tx, 1982; R. H. **Gundry**, *The Use of the Old Testament in St. Matthew's Gospel*, NovTSuppl 18, 1967; E. **Haenchen**, 'Matthäus 23', *ZTK* 48, 1951, 38–63; reprinted *Gott und Mensch*, Tübingen 1965, 29–54; D. R. A. **Hare**, *The Theme of Jewish Persecution of Christians in the Gospel according to St Matthew*, SNTSM 6, 1967; H. J. **Held**, 'Matthew as Interpreter of the Miracle Stories', in G. Bornkamm et al., *Tradition and Interpretation In Matthew*, 165–299; M. **Hengel**, *Nachfolge und Charisma*, BZNW 34, 1968; ed. P. **Hoffmann**, 'Der Petrus-Primat im Matthäusevangelium', *Neues Testament und Kirche, FS R. Schnackenburg*, ET, *The Charismatic Leader and His Followers*, Edinburgh 1981; J. Gnilka, Freiburg 1974, 94–114; B. J. **Hubbard**, *The Matthean Redaction of a Primitive Apostolic Commissioning: An Exegesis of Matthew 28: 16–20*, Missoula 1974; H. **Hübner**, *Das Gesetz in der synoptischen Tradition*, Witten 1973; R. **Hummel**, *Die Auseinandersetzung zwischen Kirche und Judentum im Matthäusevangelium*, BEvTh 33, ²1966; M. D. **Johnson**, *The Purpose of the Biblical Genealogies*, SNTSM 8, 1969; 'Reflections on a Wisdom Approach to Matthew's Christology', *CBQ* 36, 1974, 44–64.

E. **Käsemann**, 'The Beginnings of Christian Theology', *New Testament Questions of Today*, ET London and Philadelphia 1969, 82–107; G. D. **Kilpatrick**, *The Origins of the Gospel according to St Matthew*, Oxford 1946, ²1950; J. D. **Kingsbury**, 'The "Jesus of History" and the "Christ of Faith" ', *CTM* 37, 1966, 500–10; *The Parables of Jesus in Matthew 13*, Richmond and London 1969; 'The Composition and Christology of Matt. 28: 16–20', *JBL* 93, 1974, 573–84; *Matthew: Structure, Christology, Kingdom*, Philadelphia and London 1975/6; *Matthew* (Proclamation Commentaries), Philadelphia 1977; 'The Figure of Peter in Matthew's Gospel as a Theological Problem', *JBL* 98, 1979, 67–83; W. S. **Kissinger**, *The Sermon on the Mount: A History of Interpretation and Bibliography*, Metuchen, N. J. 1975; G. **Kittel**, 'Die Bergpredigt und die Ethik des Judentums', *ZSTh* 2, 1924–5, 555–94; E. **Krentz**, 'The Extent of Matthew's Prologue. Toward the Structure of the First Gospel', *JBL* 83, 1964, 409–14; G. **Künzel**, *Studien zum Gemeindeverständnis des Matthäus-Evangeliums*, Stuttgart 1978.

J. **Lange**, ed., *Das Matthäus-Evangelium*, Darmstadt 1980; B. **Lindars**,

New Testament Apologetic, London 1961, Philadelphia 1962; H. **Ljungman**, Das Gesetz Erfüllen. Mt. 5, 17ff und 3, 15 untersucht, Lund 1954; E. **Lohmeyer**, 'Mir ist gegeben alle Gewalt', In Memoriam E. Lohmeyer, ed. W. Schmauch, Stuttgart 1951, 22–49; U. **Luz**, 'Die Jünger im Matthausevangelium', ZNW 62, 1971, 141–71; ET G. Stanton, ed., The Interpretation of Matthew, 98–128; T. W. **Manson**, The Teaching of Jesus, Cambridge 1931; The Sayings of Jesus, London 1949; J. P. **Meier**, Law and History in Matthew's Gospel, Rome 1976; The Vision of Matthew, New York 1978; 'John the Baptist in Matthew's Gospel', JBL 99, 1980, 383–405; B. M. **Metzger**, 'Formulas introducing Quotations of Scripture in the New Testament and Mishnah', JBL 70, 1951, 297–307; O. **Michel**, 'Der Abschluss des Matthäusevangeliums', EvTh 10, 1950/51, 16–26; ET G. Stanton, ed., The Interpretation of Matthew, 30–41; P. S. **Minear**, 'False Prophecy and Hypocrisy in the Gospel of Matthew', in Neues Testament und Kirche, FS R. Schnackenburg, J. Gnilka, ed. Freiburg 1974, 76–93; C. F. D. **Moule**, 'St Matthew's Gospel: Some Neglected Features', StEv II, TU 87, 1964, 91–99.

F. **Neirynck**, 'The Gospel of Matthew and Literary Criticism', in Didier, op. cit., 37–69; 'Les Femmes au Tombeau. Étude de la rédaction Matthéenne', NTS 15, 1968/69, 168–90; P. **Nepper-Christensen**, Das Matthäusevangelium. Ein judenchristliches Evangeliums?, Aarhus 1958; D. E. **Nineham**, 'The Genealogy in St Matthew's Gospel and its Significance for the Study of the Gospels', Explorations in Theology I, London 1977, 166–87; R. **Pesch**, 'Beobachtungen zu den Zitationsformeln der Reflexionszitate', Bibl 48, 1967, 393–420; W. **Pesch**, Matthäus der Seelsorger. Das neue Verständnis der Evangelien am Beispiel von Matt 18, Stuttgart 1966; W. **Rothfuchs**, Die Erfüllungszitate des Matthäus-Evangeliums, WMANT V, 8, 1969.

A. **Sand**, Das Gesetz und die Propheten. Untersuchungen zur Theologie des Evangeliums nach Matthäus, BU 11, 1974; G. **Schille**, 'Bemerkungen zur Formgeschichte des Evangeliums, II. Das Evangelium des Matthäus als Katechismus', NTS 4, 1957/8, 101–14; A. **Schlatter**, Die Theologie der Apostel, Stuttgart ²1922, 64–87; Die Kirche des Matthäus, Gütersloh 1930; O. **Schmitz**, 'Thurneysens christologische Deutung der Bergpredigt', Jahrbuch der theologischen Schule Bethel 9, 1938, 17–36; G. **Schneider**, Botschaft der Bergpredigt, Würzburg 1969; H. **Schürmann,** Traditionsgeschichtliche Untersuchungen zu den synoptischen Evangelien, Düsseldorf 1968; 126–56; S. **Schulz**, Die Stunde der Botschaft, Hamburg ²1970; E. **Schweizer**, 'Anmerkungen zum Gesetzesverständnis des Matthäus', Neotestamentica, Zürich und Stuttgart, 1963, 399–406; 'Gesetz und Enthusiasmus bei Matthäus' (1970), reprinted J. Lange, ed., op. cit., 350–76; Matthäus und seine Gemeinde, Stuttgart 1974; pp. 138–70 translated as 'Matthew's Church', in G. Stanton, ed., The Interpretation of Matthew, 129–55; D. P. **Senior**, The Passion Narrative according to Matthew, BETL 39, Gembloux 1975; P. L. **Schuler**, A Genre for the Gospels – the Biographical Character of Matthew, Philadelphia 1982; C. W. F. **Smith**, 'The Mixed State of the Church in Matthew's Gospel', JBL 82, 1963, 149–68; T. **Soiron**, Die Bergpredigt Jesus. Formgeschichte, exegetische und theologische

Erklärung, Freiburg 1941; G. **Stanton**, ed., *The Interpretation of Matthew*, London and Philadelphia 1983; K. **Stendahl**, *The School of Matthew and its Use of the Old Testament*, Philadelphia ²1968; 'Quis et Unde? An Analysis of Mt 1–2', *Judentum – Urchristentum – Kirche, FS J. Jeremias*, ed. W. Eltester, BZNW 26, 1960, 94–105; reprinted G. Stanton, ed., *The Interpretation of Matthew*, 56–66; G. **Strecker**, *Der Weg der Gerechtigkeit. Untersuchungen zur Theologie des Matthäus*, FRLANT 82, ³1971; 'Das Geschichtsverständnis des Matthäus', *EvTh* 26, 1966, 57–74; ET in G. Stanton, ed., *The Interpretation of Matthew*, 67–84; M. J. **Suggs**, *Wisdom, Christology and Law in Matthew's Gospel*, Cambridge, Mass. and London 1970.

K. **Tagawa**, 'People and Community in the Gospel of Matthew', *NTS* 16, 1969/70, 149–62; W. G. **Thompson**, *Matthew's Advice to a Divided Community: Matthew 17: 22–18:35*, AnBib 44, 1970; 'An Historical Perspective in the Gospel of Matthew', *JBL* 93, 1974, 243–62; E. **Thurneysen**, *The Sermon on the Mount*, ET of 5th ed., Richmond 1964; W. **Trilling**, *Das Wahre Israel*, SANT 10, ³1964; 'Amt und Amtverständnis bei Matthäus' in A. Descamps and A. de Halleux, eds., *Mélanges bibliques en hommage au Béda Rigaux*, Gembloux 1970, 29–44; 'Zum Petrusamt im Neuen Testament', *ThQ* 151, 1971, 110–33; A. **Vögtle**, 'Das christologische und ekklesiologische Anliegen von Mt 28, 18–20', in F. L. Cross, ed., StEv II, TU 87, 1964, 266–94; 'Die Genealogie Mt. 1, 2–16 und die matthäische Kindheitsgeschichte', *BZ* NF 8, 1964, 45–58, 239–62; 9, 1965, 32–49; reprinted *Das Evangelium und die Evangelien*, Düsseldorf 1971, 57–102; 'Das Schicksal des Messiaskindes', *BiLe* 6, 1965, 246–79; R. **Walker**, *Die Heilsgeschichte im ersten Evangelium*, FRLANT 91, 1967; H. **Windisch**, *The Meaning of the Sermon on the Mount* (1929), ET Philadelphia 1951; H. T. **Wrege**, *Die Überlieferungsgeschichte der Bergpredigt*, WUNT 9, 1968.

When we turn to the Gospel of Matthew, the methodological issues involved in a canonical approach can be immediately illustrated in detail.

First, the painstaking analysis of several generations of source critics has made out a very convincing case for seeing Matthew as dependent upon a collection of sources – to what extent oral or written remains debatable – which includes Mark, Q, and a special source (*contra* W. R. Farmer, et al.). The crucial hermeneutical issue at stake is the role to which this literary insight is assigned in interpreting the present Gospel. The canonical approach contests the literary model which makes the interpretation of Matthew dependent on the exegete's ability to reconstruct the diachronistic relationship between the Gospel and its sources. Of course, within the New Testament discipline itself an attack has been launched against the overemphasis on source analysis (cf. Dahl, 'Passion Narrative'). Nevertheless, from a canonical perspective the chief objection lies in giving such priority to the forces of literary development as to overlook the new dynamic introduced by the canonical function of the book as a whole within its new theological context. This reservation does not imply a rejection of the source-critical approach in principle – certainly not along the traditional, conservative lines – but it does relativize its importance and relegates it to the prehistory of the canonical text. Unquestionably source criticism of Matthew can greatly enrich and sharpen the interpreter's perspective, but it can never be a substitute for recovering the new canonical function which Matthew's Gospel has acquired.

Secondly, a canonical approach can make use of the modern redactional method without accepting it as the fundamental key to the proper interpretation of Matthew. The great contribution of recent redactional studies has been in the discovery of the specific and unique shaping of Matthew's Gospel by an editor who shared a particular theological perspective and who wrote from a definite historical context. However, the asumption that the many tensions within the Gospel are to be resolved by sharply distinguishing between tradition and redaction (cf. Strecker, Schulz) renders impossible a canonical reading of the Gospel as a whole. Thus the judgment that portions of ch. 5 are 'traditional ballast' which distort Matthew's real intention, is a highly tendentious approach. Nor can the recovery of the original setting of the Gospel – Bacon's 'new lawbook', Kilpatrick's 'liturgical manual', Stendahl's 'exegetical handbook' – provide the key to the role which the canon ultimately assigned Matthew's Gospel. However, it is also clear that the final canonical function stands in some continuity with its prehistory and employs features from its past by which to express its new function. Therefore, it is necessary that the insights of redactional criticism be fully exploited.

Finally, the canonical study of Matthew makes critical use of many studies regarding the historical age and milieu of the Gospel. It is not exegetically irrelevant to determine when the various levels of the text assumed a shape, and to understand the nature of Matthew's audience. Was the evangelist (or his redactor) fighting on several fronts? However, the basic hermeneutical issue turns on seeing to what extent such features have been assigned a canonical role. This statement is not to deny the validity of reading the biblical text obliquely from any number of non-canonical perspectives. However, our present concern is to demonstrate the integrity and indeed theological necessity for hearing Matthew's Gospel as scripture of the church.

I. The Structure of Matthew

We begin the search for the canonical shape of Matthew by examining the structure of the book. Certainly the observation is correct that one's concept of the book's structure affects one's understanding of the content. This close relationship is immediately apparent in the widely accepted structural analysis of Bacon ('The "Five Books"'). Bacon took his lead from the fivefold repetition of the phrase 'and when Jesus finished these sayings . . .' (7.28; 11.1; 13.53; 19.1; 26.1) to divide the Gospel into five books, each section consisting of narrative material which was then followed by a didactic discourse (e. g. Book 1: narrative, 3.1–4.25; discourse, 5.1–7.27). Chapters 1–2 form the book's prologue and 26.3–28.20 its epilogue. On the basis of this analysis Bacon drew the conclusion that Matthew had fashioned his material for apologetical reasons to supersede the fivefold Old Testament Pentateuch as a new law book for Christians. Criticism of Bacon's scheme has fallen on a number of points, but a crucial objection to his structural analysis turns on the improbability of conceiving of Jesus' death and resurrection as being an epilogue to the Gospel.

Again, a highly influential article of Krentz has argued that the key to the structural division of Matthew is found in the twice repeated phrase 'from that time Jesus began to . . .' (4.17; 16.21) which serves to introduce programmatic statements about the general content of Jesus' teching. Krentz then argues that 1.1–4.16 constitutes the first section of the book and sets out a perspective of Jesus which is necessary for the reader properly to evaluate Jesus' words and actions. More recently Kingsbury (*Matthew: Structure*) has further extended Krentz's insight to divide the Gospel into three sections (1.1–4.16; 4.17–16.20; 16.21–28.20) which he closely relates to his larger christological interpretation of the entire book. However, these larger divisions have not met with wide acceptance, and many still prefer to see a major introduction in 3.1.

In my opinion, the point to be drawn from this discussion is that there are significant signs of structural breaks and repetitions within the composition which reflect conscious accentuations, but that the attempt to establish objectively a comprehensive structural analysis has not been successful. This observation is not intended to undercut the importance of careful formal analysis. Certainly Stendahl's argument for joining the genealogy in 1.17 to the subsequent narrative 1.18–25 is illuminating. Nor should one deny the significance of the repetition of the various formulae. However, it does seem likely that the concern to determine a comprehensive structure reflects a modern mentality and attitude to literature which were not shared to the same extent in the ancient world. Moreover, from a theological point of view, the canonical shape of the Gospel – how it functioned religiously within the community of faith – does not appear to be integrally attached to an overarching formal structure.

Nevertheless, there are some particular characteristics of the Gospel of Matthew, comprising both formal and material aspects, which are highly significant to a canonical interpretation, and set it apart from the rest of the New Testament. First, the Gospel has arranged its material in an historical narrative which extends from the birth of Jesus, the beginnings and continuation of his ministry, the final journey to Jerusalem, and his death and resurrection. In terms of Mark's outline, Matthew has substantially extended his narrative both at the beginning and at the end. Secondly, Matthew has systematically ordered his material topically into larger speech units: Sermon on the Mount (5–7); mission charge (10); parables (13); communal instructions (18); Pharisees (23); the final expectations (24f.). Thirdly, Matthew makes use of citations from the Old Testament to establish a context into which his understanding of Jesus' ministry has been placed. These so-called formula citations (1.23; 2.6, 15, 18; 4.14, etc.) are to be distinguished from other uses of the Old Testament which Matthew shares in common with the other Gospels (cf. 3.2). It will be part of our task to determine what role these features play within a canonical reading of the Gospel.

II. The Church's Access to Christ

Perhaps the first crucial canonical issue to be investigated turns on determining how the Gospel of Matthew sought to interpret the church's access to Jesus Christ. What role did the earthly life of Jesus play in respect to the continuing faith of the church? Wherein lay the continuity? If the resurrected Christ was now alive and reigning as the exalted Lord of the church, in what sense was his earthly ministry of theological significance?

Within modern Matthaean scholarship one of the most consistent attempts to address this question has been the monograph of G. Strecker, *Das Weg der Gerechtigkeit*. In this book Strecker argues that Matthew has constructed the Gospel material into a history of salvation which was divided into consecutive periods along a linear time span: the time of the Fathers, the time of the prophets, the time of Jesus, and the time of the church. Matthew relegated the time of Jesus to the past by historicizing it into a 'life of Jesus'. Especially is this noticeable in the addition of the birth story and in the use of the formula citations. The only continuity between this past period and the present life of the church lay in the ethical challenge of Christ's teaching – the way of righteousness – in response to which the promised eschatological salvation was actualized.

Certainly Strecker has made a contribution by sharply posing the central canonical question, but his answer is basically unsatisfactory. In fact, his learned book remains a classic example of a seriously distorted thesis which continually runs against the grain of the Gospel. The responses by others (Kingsbury, *CTM*, 502ff.; G. Barth, 103) have made it abundantly clear that Matthew's unique construal of time moves in almost the exactly opposite direction. The decisive feature of Matthew's Gospel is that the author has fused the 'time of the earthly Jesus' with 'the time of the church'. Because Jesus is confessed as alive, Matthew's portrayal of the Christ encompasses, in its full dimension, both the pre-resurrection time of Jesus on earth and the post-resurrection time of the church. Thus the historical lines between the earthly Jesus and the later church's experience of his presence as Lord have been blurred. The issue as to whether this manner of handling his material derived always from an intentional move by the evangelist is difficult to decide. In certain cases, signs of a highly reflective intentionality are evident, as we shall attempt shortly to demonstrate. In other cases, a literary reflex may be present with far less conscious motivation. However it may be, the canonical effect of Matthew's Gospel is to provide the tradition of the Gospel with a quality of transparency by means of which the time of Jesus becomes an avenue to the future rather than a barrier from the past.

No passage more clearly illustrates Matthew's understanding of eschatological time that the 'great commission' passage (28.16–20) with which the book closes. Indeed, Michel has suggested that this section provides the major key to understanding the entire Gospel and that in a certain sense the book should be read from the end forward.

The disciples go to the mountain in Galilee to which they had been directed (28.7). The reaction on seeing the risen Christ is highly significant: 'they worshipped him, but some doubted'. Moreover, in the commission which follows no visible assurances are extended by which to overcome their doubt. The emphasis of the passage does not fall on seeing Jesus, but rather on understanding and obeying the words of the exalted one, which are his legacy to the church. The passage divides into three sections: (a) the full authority of the resurrected Christ (18b); (b) the commission to his disciples (19, 20a); (c) the promise (20b).

Christ addresses his disciples with the authority of the exalted Lord whose full power now extends throughout the universe. What follows is not a farewell address, but an act of enthronization in which the enthroned Christ lays claim upon all earthly powers and peoples. The similarity in language to Daniel 7 has long been noticed, but, as Vögtle has correctly observed (*StEv*), the function of the paralleled imagery is not to point to the fulfilment of the parousia, but rather to the present status as exalted and already enthroned *Kyrios*.

Secondly, one sees in the commission to the disciples which follows that the purpose of the passage is not to distinguish the exalted Christ from the earthly Jesus, but rather to bind the two indissolubly together. The new feature lies in the extension of his power over heaven and earth. The disciples are sent forth to make disciples of all nations. The prior restriction to the house of Israel (10.5) has now been removed and a universal mission flows from the unlimited authority of the resurrected one. Moreover, the content of the disciples' evangelization by which the church is constituted remains the commandments of the earthly Jesus. The past tense of the Greek verb ('have taught') makes it clear that it is the words of the earthly Jesus which remain normative also for the post-resurrection church. His revelation of the will of God points to the 'way of righteousness' for all time (cf. Bornkamm, 'The Risen Lord'). Therefore, the passage establishes not only the identity of the earthly Jesus and the exalted

Christ, but the continuity of the one message. The historical dimension of Jesus' life on earth has been neither destroyed nor devalued, but rather given a new canonical function in the light of the exaltation of Christ.

Finally, the commission of Christ closes with the promise: 'I am with you always to the close of the age.' The theme of Christ's continuing presence, of his being with his people, which was found in his name as Emmanuel, now brackets the entire Gospel. It promises the living presence of Christ in their midst, not only for the future, but as a reality which has always been the case (18.20). Indeed, it is the theological understanding reflected in this passage which allows the author to project features of the exalted Lord back into his description of the earthly ministry of Jesus.

A second set of passages in which Matthew's special understanding of the relation of the past to the present focuses on the role assigned to the disciples. In contrast to Luke's portrayal which retains a distinction between the reaction of the disciples before and after the resurrection, Matthew depicts the disciples from a very different perspective. Because the distinction between the time of the earthly and the risen Jesus has coalesced, Matthew assigns the disciples a special role. They have been made representatives of the future church, that is to say, vehicles from which continuing paraenetic examples can be drawn. Rather than historicizing the twelve and assigning them a role within the past (so Strecker), they have been depicted by Matthew as transparencies of the Christian church. By their very failures a note of warning is sounded against all false certainty which obscures the faithfulness of Christ on which the church is grounded. For this reason many situations of the post-resurrection church, by means of which the true nature of discipleship was defined, have been projected back into the portrayal of the Twelve.

Kilpatrick and others have long recognized that the historical background reflected in Matthew's Gospel is often of a later period than the lifetime of Jesus, but they have usually failed to grasp the theological and canonical significance of this phenomenon. Because the time of Jesus and the time of the church have been fused, the disciples function in a way which transcends their historical role and allows them to represent future generations of disciples as well.

For example, the original historical setting of the initial sending out of the Twelve is at first retained, even with the distinctive

Matthaean tradition not to approach the Gentiles (10.5–6). But shortly, the mission to the Gentiles (10.18) is joined to the mission to the Jews. One hears of Christian persecutions and the sharp separation between church and synagogue reminiscent of John's Gospel (17ff.). Moreover, the disciples are equipped with the authority of the exalted Lord (v. 8), and fulfil the same signs of the kingdom which Jesus himself had done in the previous two chapters.

To speak of Matthew's 'idealization' of the disciples is also seriously to miss the nature of his portrayal. In spite of their sharply differing role from that of Mark's which is largely negative, Matthew does not turn them into saints. Rather, as G. Barth has clearly shown (106), Matthew employs a different concept of faith from that of Mark. For Matthew a distinction is made between faith and understanding. The noetic element is largely removed from πίστις. Thus the disciples can understand Jesus' teaching, but they lack trust in the person of Jesus. They are frequently accused of being men 'of little faith'. Bornkamm's essay on the storm at sea (8.23ff.) is unusually helpful in first relating Matthew's shaping of this story into a paradigm by which to instruct every generation of future disciples regarding the nature of faith in the power of the exalted Christ, who is with them always (28.20).

Another confirmation of the effect of Matthew's coalescing of time in his depiction of the disciples is the manner in which the disciples consistently address Jesus as Lord (*Kyrios*). Over against the inherited tradition which is still reflected in Mark, Matthew reserves the designation of 'Lord' to the disciples, thus indicating their response to the exalted Christ. Similarly in Matthew's passion account, his emphasis falls on Jesus as the Son of God endowed with power who voluntarily suffers (26.63ff.). Moreover, Dahl has observed (46) how frequently Matthew's passion account has been illuminated and interpreted by the faith of the church. The hearers of Matthew's passion account knew all the time that he who was crucified was also the resurrected one. Again, the enemies of Jesus repudiate him by mocking him in the very words of the later Christian confession: 'tell us if you are the Christ, the Son of God' (26.63).

However, it would be a serious misunderstanding of Matthew's Gospel to suppose that his projecting the knowledge of the resurrected Christ back into the pre-Easter period has had the effect of rendering the entire Gospel into timeless homilies. Nothing could be further from the truth. Rather, the time of Jesus and the time of the church could be blurred because all of history stood under the threat of the coming eschatological judgment. The full implication of this radical future orientation for Matthew's Gospel will become shortly apparent.

III. Matthew's Use of the Old Testament

Up to this point in the discussion of the canonical shape of Matthew the emphasis has fallen upon the theological significance of Christ as the enthroned Lord. However, Matthew's christological interests extend far beyond the use of the one title. A major concern of Matthew's Gospel is to bear witness to Jesus as the promised Messiah of Israel. Indeed, the full range of Old Testament messianic representations is applied to him: he is the Messiah (16.16; 26.63), son of David (1.18ff.; 22.41–46), Emmanuel (1.23), Son of God (3.17; 4.1ff.; 14.33; 16.16), the new Moses (5.1ff.), Son of man (9.6; 12.1–8), servant of God (12.18–21), the wisdom of God (13.35), king of Israel (21.5), eschatological ruler (16.28; 19.28; 24.30), chief corner stone (21.42), and bridegroom (22.1–10).

Moreover, the most characteristic feature by which Matthew develops his christology is his use of the Old Testament, more specifically, his application of the 'formula citations' (*Reflexionszitate*). The term has been coined to designate a series of citations which are unique to Matthew and differ from the application of inherited Old Testament material common to the other gospels. These citations are characterized by set formulaic introductions, and by an Old Testament text which differs from the normal dependence on a Septuagintal text tradition. The following are usually included: 1.23f.; 2.5f., 15, 17f., 23; 4.14ff.; 8.17; 12.17ff.; 13.35; 21.4f.; 26.56; 27.9f.

There remains much controversy within modern Matthaean studies regarding the origin and function of these citations (cf. Kilpatrick, Stendahl, Strecker, Gärtner, Gundry, and Rothfuchs). It is debated to what extent the citations derive from an oral or written source, and the nature of Matthew's own redactional contribution in respect to his *Vorlage*. Without rehearsing the full debate, several points relate specifically to our canonical concerns. First, the citations of Matthew differ from the typical Jewish midrashic usage in that the Matthaean citations do not attempt to

interpret a specific Old Testament text, but rather use the Old
Testament text to illuminate a historical phenomenon in the life of
Christ. Nor are the Matthaean citations related to Jewish *pesher*
exegesis, common to Qumran (*contra* Stendahl), because they do
not take their lead from the Old Testament text, but serve as a
commentary on the meaning of what has happened in events which
constitute the gospel (cf. Betz, 79). Secondly, the citations are
misunderstood when they are described as completely artificial,
wooden applications of the text, dictated by catchword connections,
which attempt to historicize external events in the life of Jesus, largely
for polemical reasons (Strecker). Such an approach fails to reckon
with the prophetic context from which the entire Old Testament was
read. Thirdly, the attempt to distinguish sharply between tradition
and redaction, and limit the exegetical significance only to the latter
stage is not only difficult and often arbitrary, but undercuts the basic
canonical function within the Gospel.

The significance of the formula citations for Matthew's Gospel lies
in several functions which they perform. First, the Old Testament
citations provide a theological context within the divine economy of
God with Israel by which to understand and interpret the significance
of Jesus' life and ministry. The entire Old Testament is viewed as a
prophetic revelation of God's purpose pointing to the future which
has now been fulfilled in Jesus Christ, God's promised Messiah. The
term 'reflexion citation' is helpful in emphasising the role of the
citation in evoking an activity of reflection, meditation, and interpretation on the part of the reader in striving to grasp the relationship
between Old Testament prophecy and New Testament fulfilment.
The New Testament technique of citing a specific passage is badly
misunderstood if one concludes that Matthew's interests are
narrowly construed or largely apologetic. Rather, the specific text
functions as a transparency into the larger prophetic dimension
represented by the entire Old Testament.

Secondly, the formula citations are a form of Christian proclamation. The Gospel writer bears witness from the context of Israel's
prior experience of God to the realization of the divine will, now
through the Messiah. On the one hand, Matthew reads the Old
Testament from the perspective of the gospel, and testifies to the
unity of the one plan of God within the scheme of prophecy and
fulfilment. On the other hand, the very meaning of the gospel to
which he bears witness receives its definition from the Old Testament.

Thirdly, the citations serve as a means of actualizing the presence of the promised Messiah who is now experienced as the resurrected and exalted *Kyrios*. Thus, when Matthew calls to mind the servant figure of Isaiah 42 by a citation in Matt. 12.17ff. in order to interpret the significance of Jesus' healing ministry, he bears witness to the post-resurrection church of the present reality of Christ's salvation within the community of faith (cf. Rothfuchs 183). The hope for which the Jews wait is already being experienced by Christ's church.

IV. The Problem of the Law

No problem is more central to Matthew's Gospel than his presentation of Christ's relation to the law. Not only is a large amount of space relegated to this issue in the Sermon on the Mount (chs. 5–7), and in many controversy scenes with the Pharisees, but the basic question of how Jesus, the promised Messiah and fulfiller of the Old Testament, relates to the divine Torah of the old covenant dominates the entire Gospel.

Once again, the methodological issue of how to evaluate the evidence is of central importance, especially in the light of the frequent tensions within the text relating to matters of the law (cf. Matt. 5.17ff.). The contribution of modern critical study has been highly significant in resisting attempts of easy harmonization and in striving to hear the differing notes sounded with great precision. However, there has frequently been a danger of resorting to a literary, historical, or redactional device by which to resolve the tension. For example, various strata have been distinguished – Jewish vs. Hellenistic, traditional vs. redactional, Judaizers vs. antinomian – and played against each other. From a canonical perspective an insistence that the tension within the final form of the received text be maintained and addressed is basic to the theological task of interpretation.

Jesus' disagreement with the representatives of Judaism regarding the law emerges sharply both in his actions and in his words as is made clear in the series of controversies with the Pharisees (9.1–8, 9.13; 12.1–8; 15.1–20; 19.1–9: cf. Hummel and G. Barth). The depth of the disagreement is underestimated when scholars suggest that Jesus was only opposing the Pharisaic tradition of the law, but leaving the Mosaic law itself intact. Nor is the controversy adequately described by claiming that Jesus sought only to dispense with the Old Testament ceremonial law while retaining the ethical imperatives. Rather, the issue turned on Jesus' claim to be the true interpreter of the will of God as revealed in the law. 'The Son of man is lord of the sabbath' (12.8).

According to Matthew's presentation, the major function of Jesus as Israel's Messiah lies, above all, in the interpretation of the law. Bornkamm expresses it succinctly: 'as the Scriptures legitimated Jesus in his messianic role and status, so the law legitimated him in his teaching' ('Expectation', 32). The emphasis of Matthew falls on the authoritative new teaching of Jesus. 'You have heard it said of old . . ., but I say to you . . .' However, the teachings of Christ are integrally related to his messianic role as one who perfectly fulfilled the law of God. The term 'fulfil' (5.17) bears the sense of 'accomplish' or 'effect' and is contrasted with 'abolishing' or 'dispensing with' the law.

Matthew's understanding of the law as a fundamental element in his witness to Christ as Messiah can be described under several headings:

(a) The law of Moses is not a temporary measure which has now been superseded in the kingdom of heaven, but rather represents the eternally valid will of God. 'Until heaven and earth pass away, not an iota, not a dot, will pass from the law until all is accomplished' (5.18). Entrance into the kingdom of God which is the way of righteousness is still measured by the law. Lawlessness (ἀνομία) is the epitome of evil. Jesus has come to establish the law in its true meaning, and not to abolish it. He seeks no new law (lex nova), but brings the old into full reality as realizing the will of God.

(b) Jesus does not restrict the scope of the Mosaic law by a process of selection. He neither liberalizes nor internalizes its function. Rather, he radicalizes its imperatives by stripping away the various human ploys to avoid its full force. Thus, he confronts his hearers with the radical dimension of God's will for righteousness. In the six antitheses of the Sermon on the Mount the form of Jesus' reinterpretation of the tradition varies from outright repudiation to sharpest reformulation, but the effect is the same (cf. Barth and Bornkamm). The law is established as the supreme will of the God of righteousness, who demands from his people a response commensurate to his being.

(c) The law is not a list of stipulations, nor a catalogue of virtues, but, because it expresses the living will of God, it can be both summarized and clarified as to its essentials. The Pharisees are criticized for clinging to externals and for neglecting the 'weightier matters of the law' (23.23). They have misunderstood the nature of God's will by failing to understand what Hosea meant by works of justice and mercy (Matt. 9.13; 12.7). Moses made concessions to Israel's sinfulness, but originally the will of God was clear in its intent (19.3ff.). Above all, the heart of the law can be summarized in the love of God and the love of neighbour (22.34–40). 'On these two commandments hang all the law and the prophets' (v. 40). Indeed, Bornkamm has mounted a serious case for understanding this 'double law of love' as Matthew's exegetical principle for his entire Gospel ('Das Doppelgebot').

(d) Again, the law is actualized by the radical claim of discipleship as a following in the way of righteousness demanded by the law. The challenge to follow the commandments of the earthly Jesus formed the heart of the commission given by the resurrected Christ (28.20). Matthew has consistently shaped the miracle stories in such a way as to emphasize the continuing call to discipleship (cf. Held). Moreover, the final challenge to the 'rich young ruler' (19.16ff.) to sell all and to follow Jesus, served to bring home the radical nature of the will of God and laid bare the man's attempt to domesticate the imperatives of discipleship. In the doing of the will of God, in following the path of suffering and humility, the presence of the exalted Christ is continually actualized.

(e) Finally, it remains a fundamental tenet of Matthew's Gospel to place his discussion of the law always within the eschatological framework of the impending final judgment. Only in Matthew does the portrayal of the day of judgment occupy such an important position (7.21ff.; 13.36ff.; 25.31ff.). The followers of Christ are offered no institutional privileges nor special status over against the Jews, but all persons alike face the final reckoning at which time their actions will be measured in the light of the divine demand for righteousness (cf. Bornkamm, 'End Expectation').

V. The Sermon on the Mount

Within the context of Matthew's discussion of the law, the chapters traditionally known as the 'Sermon on the Mount' (chs. 5–7) play a particularly significant role. The need to address the difficult problem of interpreting this corpus is acute. Can one speak of a canonical shaping of this material?

The great variety of exegetical models represented in the history of exegesis reflect the difficulty of the problem (cf. Barth, *TRE* II, 618ff.; W. S. Kissinger; Guelich). The early church sought to assign the 'higher morality' demanded by the Sermon to the clergy. The Reformers interpreted the Sermon along Pauline lines, and saw its function to illustrate the sinfulness of man before God's law. Later liberal Protestant theology either internalized the demands of the Sermon (Ritschl), or relegated it to an 'interim ethic' before the expected end of the world (Schweitzer), or understood it as a time-conditioned response to Judaism (Windisch, Bornhäuser, Davies). Finally, a consistently christological interpretation which made Christ the sole fulfiller of the law has been suggested (Thurneysen). Within the more recent discussion (cf. Bornkamm, Eichholz, Barth, Strecker) certain elements of consensus have emerged. It is agreed that Matthew's Sermon has its own particular theological integrity which resists being interpreted through the eyes of Paul. Again, the emphasis of the Sermon is on Jesus' teaching, not his person. Thirdly, there are indicative and imperative elements within the Sermon which posit a special interrelatedness.

Bornkamm's critique of those offering a christological interpretation is highly significant in focusing the problem. He argues that the Sermon on the Mount represents the teachings of Christ, and nowhere are the demands of the Sermon related to the person of Jesus as fulfiller, except in the redactional addition of 5.17, which cannot be made an exegetical key to the whole sermon. Therefore, to interpret the Sermon christologically is to confuse the genuine exegetical task of interpreting the words of the Sermon with the situation caused by the reader for whom the words evoke the larger questions regarding the law (Bornkamm, *Jesus*, ET 108f.; *RGG* [3]I, 1049). But is this not to raise the canonical question? The Sermon of Jesus was not preserved by the evangelist apart from his concern that the words of Jesus function kerygmatically for succeeding generations of readers. The very distinction which Bornkamm insists must be maintained by the modern interpreter has been consistently blurred by the evangelist. Indeed, he has fashioned the Sermon on the Mount in light of the context of the community of faith who live with the larger questions concerning the will of God in his law.

The task of discerning the canonical shape of the Sermon on the Mount lies precisely in recognizing those features within the text by which the larger context, in this case different from the context of the original sermon, was introduced as a hermeneutical guide. Several features have long been recognized. The Sermon is set within the framework of the two sets of verses (4.23 and 9.35) which summarize Jesus' ministry. Furthermore, the 'Christ of the word' (5–7) is paralleled to the 'Christ of the deed' (8–9) (so Schniewind). The present form of the Sermon is characterized further by a tension created by the introduction of the beatitudes (blessings) which function as indicatives, and the succeeding series of imperatives which dominate the remaining sermon. This tension is further exacerbated by the concluding section of the Sermon which focuses on the demand for responding to the will of God in concrete deeds.

The effect of this ordering of the material within its final form is to re-emphasize and buttress the significance of Christ's own role within the Sermon which functions in no way as an isolated verse: 'I have not come to abolish the law and the prophets, but to fulfil them' (5.17). The result of the shaping is clear. Matthew has presented a form of Jesus' preaching of the law in which the stress falls on his teaching the way of righteousness with its overwhelming ethical demands. However, Matthew's awareness that he is presenting the teachings of Jesus to a Christian community which both remembers the life, death, and resurrection of God's Messiah, and also continues to experience the presence of the resurrected Lord is evident precisely in this arrangement of the material. Matthew has shaped his material in a way different from Paul (cf. Eichholz, *Auslegung*, 162ff.). Christ is not presented in the Sermon on the Mount as the end of the law (Rom. 10.4) Nevertheless, a canonical shaping of the material which guides the reader to see the imperatives of the kingdom in the light of the king should not be denied. If it is a mistake to resolve Matthew's tension by means of Pauline theology, it appears equally unsatisfactory to maintain that in the end the Sermon reflects only a 'hopeless tension' between the will of God and those who hunger after righteousness (Bornkamm, *Jesus*, ET 109). Rather, the tension evoked by the Sermon continues to lay claim on its hearer because the possibility of its resolution has already been demonstrated by the earthly life of Jesus through whose vindication the community of faith continues to experience an eschatological fulfilment.

VI. The Way of Righteousness

A problem closely associated with Matthew's interpretation of the law turns on the issue of what is meant in the Gospel by the frequently used term 'righteousness'. Beside the repeated occurrence of the noun (3.15; 5.6; 5.20; 6.33), one meets the phrases 'the way of righteousness' (21.32), 'God's righteousness' (6.33), and a 'greater righteousness' (5.20). Often mention is made of the 'righteous' (13.17; 23.29). What is one to understand from this cluster of expressions?

The modern debate over the significance of this terminology has been greatly intensified by the aggressive position which has been developed by Strecker in his book on the theme of 'The Way of Righteousness'. The author argues that righteousness is an ethical imperative demanded by God for the entrance into the kingdom of heaven. For Matthew righteousness is in no sense a gift of God, but an ethical requirement represented by the teachings of Christ (155). In the doing of deeds of righteousness commensurate with the ethical teachings of Jesus, who is both *Kyrios* and coming world judge, eschatological salvation is actualized in the present. S. Schulz (190) further elaborates on the implications of Strecker's interpretation. Matthew stands firmly within the growing tradition of 'early Catholicism' with his emphasis on good works. Matthew's criticism of Judaism lies only in the latter's failure to achieve a high enough level of ethical behaviour.

Our response to Strecker's interpretation has already been adumbrated in the previous discussion of the Sermon on the Mount. First, it is fully clear that Matthew works with a concept of both the imperative and the indicative. Righteousness is both a demand by God, and also a gift from God (5.6; 6.33). The evangelist does not develop these two sides of righteousness in a dialectical fashion after the manner of Paul; however, the two aspects are firmly held together. Indeed, it is the tendency of the two to fall apart in Judaism that has evoked Matthew's criticism (cf. Barth, 130; Luz, 164ff.). Secondly, the concept of righteousness is closely related to Matthew's whole christology. Jesus fulfils 'all righteousness'. This righteousness is not understood in a legalistic fashion, but rather, by his identification with the poor and sinful, the earthly Jesus addressed the will of God in its entirety and united in his action both the divine justice and mercy (Barth, 136). Thirdly, Matthew conceives of the demands for righteousness not as a bigger and better Pharisaism, but in a new and radical quality of behaviour which in its obedience to the will of God partakes of an eschatological reality. The coming kingdom is a quality of action made possible by Christ's having demonstrated the way of righteousness.

VII. Israel and the Church

The final issue to be discussed is Matthew's portrayal of Israel and the church. The canonical interest of Matthew in this subject is evident, more than in any of the other Gospels, to delineate a portrait of the community of faith as the Christian church.

With the resurrection of Christ the exclusive mission of the earthly Messiah to Israel was ended (10.6; 15.24) and the way was opened for the mission to the nations (28.16ff.). Matthew does not conceive of this mission in terms of a *heilgeschichtliche* process, as if first to the Jews and then to the nations. Rather, the theme of Israel's guilt in the rejection of God's Messiah dominates his portrayal. This note is sounded clearly in the trial scene before Pilate. The Jews choose Barabbas instead of Jesus even though he is 'that righteous man' (27.19) and is acknowledged as such by Pilate (27.24). They take upon themselves the sole responsibility of his death, significantly extending the guilt even unto their children (27.25). The kingdom of God is therefore taken away from Israel and 'given to a nation producing fruits' (21.43). The kingdom which had once been given to Israel has been transferred to a people who understand the way of righteousness. There has been long debate over exactly what stage in the historical relations betwen synagogue and church is here reflected. From a theological perspective the separation depicted between the old and the new appears quite decisive, even if histor- ically less developed than in John's Gospel.

Of all the Gospels Matthew is the only one employing the term ἐκκλησία to describe the church (16.18; 18.17). Moreover, the reference to an entity with an external, historical shape within the world is not an isolated phenomenon. It fits in with his general portrayal of a concrete, established order of community (ch. 18), with bearers of offices (23.8ff.) which possess ecclesiastical authority to 'bind and loosen' (16.16ff.) and to forgive sins (9.2ff.). The role of Peter in the Gospel does not function as a type of the individual

Christian (*contra* Schulz, 217) but Peter serves a unique function to establish theological continuity between the earthly Jesus and a community which confesses his lordship (Hoffmann, 106). Not only does he receive Christ's special blessing (16.16ff.), and the guardianship of the 'keys' (v. 19), but it is Peter who is addressed with the continuing questions which occupy the post-resurrection church (17.24, etc.).

However, it is equally important to observe that nowhere does Matthew transfer the name of Israel upon the church. Nor are any of the ancient titles of honour designating the people of God in the old covenant applied to the Christian community. They are not the 'elect', 'the true Israel', or the 'remnant'. Here the contrast with the Qumran community is striking. Rather, in Matthew the imagery of the family and a household are used to describe the new community of faith (ch. 18). Thus Matthew emphasizes that the church receives its identity, not through institutional marks, but in relation to the exalted Lord of the church.

Finally, it is basic to observe that Matthew assigns no place of special privilege to the church in regard to the coming day of judgment. There is never a simple identification between the church and the kingdom of heaven, but the church stands under the constant warning, along with all persons, before the great divine reckoning. Then those who performed the works of righteousness, who visited the sick, fed the hungry, clothed the naked, will be invited to inherit the kingdom (25.31). It is particularly characteristic of Matthew's handling of his material that the paraenetic element assumes a highly existential quality in an intensive and direct appeal to the Christian audience (25.31ff.). Significantly, it is a voice that can address Jesus as 'Lord' to whom it is said in rejection, 'as you did it not to one of the least of these, you did it not to me . . .' (25.45).

To summarize, Matthew actualizes the gospel in terms of the presence of an exalted Lord of the church who fulfilled the promise of Israel's Messiah in his words and deeds. By his teaching of the will of God he opened the way to the kingdom of heaven whose eschatological reality is already manifest among those doing the will of God.

6

MARK

Commentaries

E. P. Gould, ICC, 1896
H. J. Holtzmann, HCNT, [3]1901
B. Weiss, MeyerK, [9]1901
A. Menzies, 1901
H. B. Swete, [3]1909
J. Wellhausen, [2]1909
J. Weiss, SNT, [3]1917
A. E. J. Rawlinson, WC, 1925
M.-J. Lagrange, ÉB, [5]1929
G. Wohlenberg, KNT, [3]1930
F. Hauck, THKNT, 1931
E. Klostermann, HNT, [4]1950
H. Branscomb, MNTC, [6]1952
J. Schniewind, NTD, [6]1952

J. Schmid, RNT, [4]1958
S. E. Johnson, B/HNTC, 1960
E. Lohmeyer, MeyerK, [16]1963
D. E. Nineham, Pel, 1963
C. E. B. Cranfield, CGTC, [2]1963
E. Haenchen (Der Weg Jesu), 1966
V. Taylor, [2]1966
E. Schweizer, (NTD), ET 1970
W. Grundmann, THKNT, [5]1971
W. L. Lane, NICNT, 1974
J. Gnilka, EKK, 1978
R. Pesch, HTKNT, [3]1980
L. Williamson, InterpC, 1983

Bibliography

Cf. G. **Wagner**, *An Exegetical Bibliography of the New Testament. Matthew and Mark*, Macon, Ga. 1983.

P. J. **Achtemeier**, 'Toward the Isolation of Pre-Markan Miracle Catenae', *JBL* 89, 1970, 265–91; 'The Origin and Function of the Pre-Markan Miracle Catenae', *JBL* 91, 1972, 198–221; *Mark* (Proclamation Commentaries), Philadelphia 1975; 'Mark as Interpreter of the Jesus Tradition', *Interp* 32, 1978, 339–52; '"And He Followed Him": Miracles and Discipleship in Mark 10:46–52', *Semeia* 11, 1978, 115–45; A. M. **Ambrozic**, *The Hidden Kingdom*, CBQMS 2, 1972; D. E. **Aune**, 'The Problem of the Messianic Secret', *NovT* 11, 1969, 1–31; B. W. **Bacon**, 'The Prologue of Mark: A Study of Sources and Structure', *JBL* 26, 1907, 84–106; *The Gospel of Mark: Its Composition and Date*, New Haven 1925; H. W. **Bartsch**, 'Der Schluss des Markus-Evangeliums', *TZ* 27, 1971, 214–54; E. **Best**, *The Temptation and the Passion: The Marcan Soteriology*, SNTSM 2, 1968; 'Mark's

Preservation of the Tradition', in *L'Évangile selon Marc*, ed. M. Sabbe, 21–34; 'The Role of the Disciples in Mark', *NTS* 23, 1976/77, 377–401; *Following Jesus: Discipleship in Mark's Gospel*, *JSNT* Suppl. 4, 1981; *Questions about Mark's Gospel*, Leiden 1983; J. L. **Blevins**, *The Messianic Secret in Markan Research, 1901–1977*, Washington 1981; T. E. **Boomershine**, 'Mark 16:8 and the Apostolic Commission', *JBL* 100, 1981, 225–39; and G. L. **Bartholomew**, 'The Narrative Technique of Mark 16:8', *JBL* 100, 1981, 213–23; R. **Bultmann**, *The History of the Synoptic Tradition*, ET Oxford and New York 1963; T. A. **Burkill**, 'The Cryptology of Parables in St Mark's Gospel', *NovT* 1, 1956, 246–62; *Mysterious Revelation*, Ithaca, N. Y. 1963; *New Light on the Earliest Gospel*, Ithaca 1972; 'Blasphemy: St Mark's Gospel as Damnation History', in *Christianity, Judaism, and other Greco-Roman Cults, FS Morton Smith*, ed. J. Neusner, I, Leiden 1975, 51–74.

    C. E. B. **Cranfield**, 'St Mark 4.1–34', *SJT* 4, 1951, 398–414; N. A. **Dahl**, 'The Parables of Growth' (1951), reprinted, *Jesus in the Memory of the Early Church*, Minneapolis 1976, 141–66; 'The Purpose of Mark's Gospel' (1958), ET, ibid., 52–65; J. **Dewey**, *Markan Public Debate*, SBLDS 48, Chico 1980; C. H. **Dodd**, 'The Framework of the Gospel Narrative' (1932), reprinted *New Testament Studies*, Manchester 1953, New York 1954, 1–11; J. R. **Donahue**, *Are You the Christ?*, SBLDS 10, Missoula 1973; J. **Drury**, 'The Sower, the Vineyard, and the Place of Allegory in the Interpretation of Mark's Parables', *JBL* 24, 1973, 367–79; J. D. G. **Dunn**, 'The Messianic Secret in Mark', *TynB* 21, 1970, 92–117; reprinted C. Tuckett, ed., *The Messianic Secret*, 116–31; H. J. **Ebeling**, *Das Messiasgeheimnis und die Botschaft des Marcus Evangelisten*, BZNW 19, 1939; W. R. **Farmer**, *The Last 12 Verses of Mark*, SNTSM 25, 1974; W. **Feneberg**, *Der Markusprolog*, SANT 36, 1974; M. E. **Glasswell**, 'The Use of Miracles in the Markan Gospel', in C. F. D. Moule, ed., *Miracles*, London 1965, 151–62; J. **Gnilka**, *Die Verstockung Israels*, SANT 3, 1961.

    G. **Hartmann**, *Der Aufbau des Markusevangeliums*, Münster 1936; D. J. **Hawkin**, 'The Incomprehension of the Disciples in the Markan Redaction', *JBL* 91, 1972, 491–500; M. D. **Hooker**, *The Son of Man in Mark*, London and Montreal 1967; D. **Juel**, *Messiah and Temple*, SBLDS 31, Missoula 1977; S. P. **Kealy**, *Mark's Gospel: A History of its Interpretation*, New York 1982; L. E. **Keck**, 'Mark 3:7–12 and Mark's Christology', *JBL* 84, 1965, 341–58; 'The Introduction to Mark's Gospel', *NTS* 12, 1965/66, 352–70; H. C. **Kee**, 'Mark as Redactor and Theologian', *JBL* 80, 1971, 333–63; *Community of the New Age. Studies in Mark's Gospel*, Philadelphia and London 1977; 'Mark's Gospel in Recent Research', *Interp* 32, 1978, 353–68; W. H. **Kelber**, *The Kingdom in Mark*, Philadelphia 1974; *Mark's Story of Jesus*, Philadelphia 1979; F. **Kermode**, *The Sense of an Ending*, New York 1967; *The Genesis of Secrecy*, Cambridge, Mass. 1979; K. **Kertelge**, *Die Wunder Jesu im Markusevangelium*, SANT 23, 1970; J. D. **Kingsbury**, 'The Gospel of Mark in Current Research', *RelStR* 5, 1979, 101–7; *The Christology of Mark's Gospel*, Philadelphia 1983; H. D. **Knigge**, 'The Meaning of Mark', *Interp* 22, 1968, 53–70;

H. W. **Kuhn**, *Ältere Sammlungen im Markusevangelium*, SUNT 8, 1971; R. H.
Lightfoot, *History and Interpretation in the Gospels*, London and New York
1935; *The Gospel Message of St Mark*, Oxford 1950; U. **Luz**, 'Das Geheimnis-
motiv und die markinische Christologie', *ZNW* 56, 1965, 9–30; ET C.
Tuckett, ed., *The Messianic Secret*, 75–96; R. P. **Martin**, *Mark. Evangelist
and Theologian*, London 1972; W. **Marxsen**, 'Redaktionsgeschichtliche
Erklärung der sogenannten Parabel-theorie des Markus', *ZTK* 52, 255–71;
Mark the Evangelist, ET Nashville 1969; R. P. **Meye**, *Jesus and the Twelve.
Discipleship and Revelation in Mark's Gospel*, Grand Rapids 1968; C. F. D.
Moule, 'The Intention of the Evangelists', *New Testament Essays in Memory
of T. W. Manson*, ed. A. J. B. Higgins, Manchester 1959, 165–79; F.
Neirynck, *Duality in Mark. Contributions to the Study of the Markan Redaction*,
BETL 31, 1972; G. W. E. **Nickelsbury**, 'The Genre and Function of the
Markan Passion Narrative', *HTR* 73, 1980, 153–84; D. E. **Nineham**, 'The
Order of Events in St Mark's Gospel – An Examination of Dr Dodd's
Hypothesis', *Studies in the Gospels. Essays in Memory of R. H. Lightfoot*, ed. D.
E. Nineham, Oxford 1955, 223–39.

P. **von der Osten-Sacken**, 'Streitgespräch und Parabel als Formen
markinischer Christologie', in *Jesus Christus in Historie und Theologie, FS H.
Conzelmann*, ed. G. Strecker, Tübingen 1975, 373–94; E. **Percy**, *Die Botschaft
Jesu*, Lund 1953, 271–99; N. **Perrin**, *A Modern Pilgrimage in New Testament
Christology*, Philadelphia 1974; 'The Interpretation of the Gospel of Mark',
Interp 30, 1976, 115–24; Q. **Quesnell**, *The Mind of Mark*, AnBib 38, 1969;
H. **Räisänen**, *Das 'Messiasgeheimnis' im Markusevangelium*, Helsinki 1976; K.-
G. **Reploh**, *Markus – Lehrer der Gemeinde*, Stuttgart 1969; H. **Riesenfeld**,
'Tradition und Redaktion im Markusevangelium', *Neutestamentliche Studien
für R. Bultmann*, ed. W. Eltester, BZNW 21, 1954; 157–64; J. M. **Rist**, *On
the Independence of Matthew and Mark*, SNTSM 32, 1978; J. M. **Robinson**,
The Problem of History in Mark, SBT 21, 1957; 'On the *Gattung* of Mark (and
John)', in *Jesus and Man's Hope*, ed. D. G. Miller, Pittsburgh 1970; 99–129;
J. H. **Ropes**, *The Synoptic Gospels*, Cambridge, Mass. 1934.

M. **Sabbe**, ed., *L'Évangile selon Marc*, Louvain 1974; W. **Schenk**, *Der
Passionsbericht nach Markus*, Gütersloh 1974; G. **Schille**, 'Bemerkungen zur
Formgeschichte des Evangeliums I: Rahmen und Aufbau des Markus-
Evangeliums', *NTS* 4, 1957/8.1–24; K. L. **Schmidt**, *Der Rahmen der Geschichte
Jesu*, Berlin 1919; J. **Schniewind**, 'Messiasgeheimnis und Eschatologie', in
E. Kähler, ed., *Nachgelassene Reden und Aufsätze*, Berlin 1952, 1–13; E.
Schweizer, 'Anmerkungen zur Theologie des Markus', *Neotestamentica et
Patristica: FS O. Cullmann*, ed. W. C. van Unnik, NovTSupp 6, 1962, 35–46;
'Die theologische Leistung des Markus', *EvTh* 24, 1964, 337–55; 'The
Portrayal of the Life of Faith in the Gospel of Mark', *Interp* 32, 1978, 387–404;
'The Question of the Messianic Secret in Mark', ET C. Tuckett, ed., *The
Messianic Secret*, 65–77; E. **Sjöberg**, *Der verborgene Menschensohn*, Lund 1955,
100–32; E. **Stegemann**, 'Von Kritik zur Feindschaft. Eine Auslegung von
Markus 2,1–3,6', in *Der Gott der Kleinen Leute*, ed. W. Schottroff and W.

Stegemann, II, Munich 1979, 39–57; H.-H. **Stoldt**, *History and Criticism of the Marcan Hypothesis*, ET Macon, Ga. and Edinburgh 1980; N. B. **Stonehouse**, *The Witness of Matthew and Mark to Christ*, Philadelphia 1944; G. **Strecker**, 'The Theory of the Messianic Secret in Mark's Gospel', ET C. Tuckett, ed., *The Messianic Secret*, 49–64; G. M. **Styler**, 'The Priority of Mark', in C. F. D. Moule, *The Birth of the New Testament*, London and San Francisco ³1981, 285–316; R. C. **Tannehill**, 'The Disciples in Mark: the Function of a Narrative Role', *JR* 57, 1977, 386–405; E. **Trocmé**, *The Formation of the Gospel according to Mark*, ET London 1975, Philadelphia 1976; G. W. **Trompf**, 'The First Resurrection Appearance and the Ending of Mark's Gospel', *NTS* 18, 1971/2, 308–30; C. **Tuckett**, ed., *The Messianic Secret*, London and Philadelphia 1983; 'Introduction: The Problem of the Messianic Secret', ibid., 1–28; P. **Vielhauer**, 'Erwägungen zur Christologie des Markusevangeliums' *Aufsätze zum Neuen Testament*, Munich 1965, 199–214; H. **Waetjen**, 'The Ending of Mark and the Gospel's Shift in Eschatology', *ASTI* 6, 1965, 114–31; T. J. **Weeden**, 'The Heresy that Necessitated Mark's Gospel', *ZNW* 59, 1968, 145–58; *Mark, Traditions in Conflict*, Philadelphia 1971; W. **Wrede**, *Das Messiasgeheimnis in den Evangelien*, Göttingen 1901; ET *The Messianic Secret*, London and Cambridge 1971.

I. The Purpose of Mark

Recent research on the Gospel of Mark has generally agreed in seeing certain characteristic features of the book. First, in striking contrast to the traditional estimate of Mark as an abbreviation of Matthew's Gospel, a broad consensus has emerged which would not only continue to defend Mark's priority among other Gospels, but which would stress the creative, literary skill of the author in composing his book. Indeed, ever since the early form-critical work of K. L. Schmidt the chronological sequence of the stories has been viewed largely as a literary rather than historical relationship. Secondly, Mark's Gospel is a highly theological composition – it is a Gospel – which does not lend itself to being read as biography since it has omitted all interest in Jesus' character development, his inner motivations, and physical appearance. Thirdly, much of the difficulty of interpreting this Gospel turns on the problem of understanding the role of the so-called 'messianic secret' which is a theme closely tied to most of the other complexities within the book: his theory of the parables, the largely negative description of the disciples, the dominant role of the passion, and its abrupt ending.

However, in contrast to this widespread consensus respecting certain important features within the Gospel, no agreement whatever has emerged regarding the purpose for which the book was written (cf. Kümmel, *Intr.*, 92). A wide range of hypotheses have been offered in an attempt to break out of the impasse. Bultmann proposed that Mark sought to unite the Hellenistic kerygma about Christ with the Palestinian tradition of the story of Jesus (*History of the Synoptic Tradition*, 347f.). J. M. Robinson's formulation differs slightly – Mark combined an aretalogy cycle with the passion narrative (*Trajectories*, 189) – but in general his position was akin. Then again, a considerable number of scholars described Mark's major purpose as an effort to counteract a false christology which sought to fit Jesus into the mould of the popular Hellenistic religious hero, usually described as a *theios-anēr* theology (Perrin, *Pilgrimage*, 110; Weeden, *Mark*, 164f.; Achtemeier, 'Origin and Function', 209ff.). Others such as Kelber (*Kingdom in Mark*, 129ff.) argued that Mark wrote in Galilee after the destruction of the temple, and, using the disciples to personify his enemies, wrote to show Christians that Galilee was the place where the kingdom was to be realized.

At the other extreme from these historicizing interpretations Marxsen envisioned Mark as a writer with an eye on the church of his own age, who was not interested in preserving a memory of Jesus' ministry, but rather intended his book to serve as a proclamation which 're-presents Jesus', that is, makes the risen Lord manifest (*Intr.*, 138). Finally, Dahl argues that Mark's purpose in writing his Gospel was not to persuade readers to believe in the message, but rather to remind those within the church of the content of discipleship which was inseparable from a hidden and misunderstood Messiah ('Purpose', 58f.).

My aim in rehearsing these various theories regarding Mark's intention in writing his book is not to dismiss them all as inadequate. To the contrary, it is difficult to deny elements of truth in almost all of these proposals, although obviously some of the theories are far stronger than others. Rather, my major criticism of this history of research is that the peculiar canonical shape of this Gospel has not emerged with sufficient clarity. That is to say, the focus on how the book functioned as scripture for the Christian community which treasured it as such has often been lost when the attention has fallen chiefly on probing the author's original intention, or in exploring the historical milieu, or in reconstructing a profile of the community being addressed. I would argue that such features can certainly play a significant role in the book's canonical function, but an essential part of the exegetical task is to determine to what extent this is the case rather than assuming the crucial role of historical reconstruction for every interpretation. Consequently, many of the excellent critical observations which led to the above-mentioned theories will be fully exploited, but the focus of my investigation will be redirected toward the canonical question.

II. The Hidden and Revealed Messiah

In many ways, the credit for posing the crucial interpretive question for Mark's Gospel goes to W. Wrede. He was the first to see clearly that the problem of the 'messianic secret' lies at the heart of the Gospel of Mark. Wrede argued that the Gospel contained two traditions: an older, that Jesus first became Messiah at his resurrection, and a later one, that he was the Messiah during his lifetime. In order to harmonize this tension Mark introduced his theory of the hidden Messiah which was a theological construct. Criticism of Wrede's interpretation has come from many quarters (Ebeling, Schniewind, Percy, Sjöberg), but it has become increasingly clear that the theme of the hidden Messiah was firmly anchored in the tradition which Mark had received. Moreover, it seems highly unlikely that a tradition of a non-messianic Jesus had ever been preserved in the church. Still Wrede correctly saw that a tension existed in the Gospel between two traditions, namely, between a pre-resurrection tradition which viewed Jesus' earthly life as a hidden messiahship and a post-resurrection tradition which confessed that he was the Messiah, the Son of God. Unquestionably the evangelist shared fully this latter confession.

The crucial exegetical question turns on the issue of why the author should have continued to recount the pre-resurrection tradition in which Christ's true identity was hidden at a time in which the secret had been revealed. Not only was the evangelist fully aware of Christ's messiahship but it seems highly likely that his readers also shared the mystery of his identity. Moreover, the theme of Christ's hidden messiahship does not function in the book as an apologetic or as a purely literary device, but was deeply embedded in the theological content of the Gospel. Clearly Mark's concern to preserve the pre-resurrection tradition of Christ's hidden identity did not arise out of mere historical interest, but was theological in nature. Why then did the evangelist feel constrained to recount the pre-resurrection history of Jesus' hidden identity as Messiah when his true messianic identity was now manifested in the post-resurrection form of the risen Lord?

To address this question is to raise the basic canonical question of Mark's Gospel. The issue turns on the way in which the author rendered his traditions in order to bear witness to Jesus Christ for succeeding generations of hearers. The case has recently been made that Mark only appeared to be describing the historical period of Jesus' ministry while all the time actually addressing his own generation. Indeed Marxsen has argued that Mark had no interest in preserving the memory of Jesus' past deeds, but rather intended solely to make the risen Lord manifest (*Intr.*, 138). In a similar vein Perrin claimed that in the Gospel of Mark past, present, and future all flow together because he is addressing an apocalyptic community which he envisions as standing between the resurrection and the imminent parousia (*Intr.*, 144f.). Although it is theoretically possible for the evangelist to have fashioned his material into such a shape because of his theological concerns, it remains an exegetical question to determine if, in fact, he chose this mode of rendition.

I would argue that Mark's understanding of the relationship between Jesus the Messiah who was truly manifested as the risen Lord by his resurrection and the hidden Jesus of the pre-resurrection period was of a very different order. Moreover, his use of the messianic secret was only one means among others by which to give his Gospel its canonical shape. Although the evangelist was fully aware of Christ's true identity, the form of his presentation of the tradition makes it clear that there was no avenue open to the resurrected Christ which had not first gone the way of his hidden ministry as the suffering, and crucified Jesus. According to Mark, the relation between the hidden and revealed saviour is not simply chronological, but ontological. The two forms of revelation are inextricably bound together.

The shape of Mark's Gospel thus establishes an analogy between the first generation of disciples who experienced Christ in his hidden revelation and every successive generation of hearers which confronts a similar challenge. It belonged to the essence of Christ's identity that it was made known through his suffering and death. Similarly, it is constitutive of Christian faith that Christ's true identity is revealed only by the way of the cross. Thus, Mark does not recount the hidden ministry of Jesus for purely historical reasons, nor to serve as merely a backdrop against which to unfold the present Lord of the church. Rather, the forms of the pre-resurrected and post-resurrected Jesus belong together, and there is no way to divorce the two, either in the past or the future.

III. The Canonical Shape of the Gospel

We turn to the Mark's Gospel and attempt to demonstrate exegetically those features which have given the book its special canonical shape.

There has been much discussion in recent years regarding the structure of Mark's Gospel. Several very detailed outlines have been suggested (e. g. V. Taylor, 107ff.; Schweizer, 'Anmerkungen', 42; R. Pesch, *Das Markusevangelium*, I, 32ff.). It is difficult to deny that several possible outlines are illuminating in highlighting important features within the book. However, it is equally difficult to establish conclusively the superiority of any one scheme (cf. Gnilka's caution, *Markus*, I, 25ff.). At least one can agree that the first eight chapters treat in general Jesus' ministry in Galilee and that a major break occurs at 8.26 with Peter's confession at Caesarea Philippi. The last part of the book focuses on Jerusalem which leads up to the passion and death of Jesus.

The Gospel of Mark begins with a programmatic introduction (1.1–15) which sets forth the intention of the evangelist (cf. Keck, 'Introduction'). 1.1, which is probably to be read as a title to the entire book, characterizes the content of his message as the 'gospel of Jesus Christ'. This gospel is the proclamation of the saving work of Jesus Christ which had been promised by the prophets of Israel. Mark is not offering a report of Jesus' own preaching, but rather a theological construal of the meaning of his entire ministry. The gospel of Jesus Christ is the proclamation about Jesus Christ who thus is identified as the content of the message.

Mark's reference to the 'beginning of the gospel' is not a chronological designation of when his public career began, the first phase of an historical movement, but the beginning of God's saving acts which continue to exert power in Jesus Christ. The Marcan introduction thus establishes the canonical perspective for the entire book. The evangelist will be recounting the words and deeds of Jesus, but he has indicated to his readers from the outset that he will be understanding them in the light of their true significance because Mark knows that Jesus himself is the mystery of the kingdom of God (1.15). What follows is to be heard as proclamation about Jesus. From this canonical perspective the Jesus of the synoptics and the Christ of Paul do not stand in opposition, but both bear witness to the true theological significance of his life and death as God's saving acts for the redemption of humanity. Mark's Gospel has already fused the proclaimer with the proclaimed.

The first eight chapters of Mark focus attention on the mighty acts of Jesus, the Christ. Various themes have been closely intertwined. First, Jesus teaches and acts with divine authority (1.22). His deeds evoke amazement and awe: 'We never saw anything like this' (2.12). His messiahship is indeed a fact. John bears witness to his divine mission; the heavenly voice announces him as the 'beloved son' (1.11) for whom Israel waited. He cleanses the leper (1.40), heals the afflicted (2.12), forgives (2.5), and casts out demons (3.11), thus opposing the kingdom of Satan (3.26). He feeds the hungry crowd which wanders in the desert (6.30ff.; 8.1ff.). He announces his mission as one of calling sinners to repentance (2.17) because the kingdom of God has arrived in power (1.15). He exerts sovereign power over the unruly wind and sea (4.35ff.; 6.48). He is lord even of the Sabbath who is possessed with authority from God to free from sin (2.10) and to cut the cords of human tradition which enslaves (7.14ff.). He can actually raise the dead (5.35). Nevertheless, he does not permit the demons to make him known. His true identity as 'Son of God' cannot be revealed in this manner (3.11f.). This avenue to his hidden messiahship is closed off. Even those whom he has healed are silenced (5.43; 7.36). Thus Jesus refers to himself only as the 'Son of man', and forces his hearer to identify his person through his saving acts.

Secondly, Jesus' mission calls forth bitter opposition from the religious and civil authorities. The first eight chapters are filled with conflict stories. The scribes challenge his authority and designate his actions as blasphemy (2.7). The plot of the Pharisees and the Herodians to destroy him climaxes immediately in the narrative (3.6), and the first indication of his death is foreshadowed already in the second chapter (2.19). Then Jesus is thought to be mad by his friends (3.21), and rejected by his home town (6.1–6). John's death is reported as a foreshadowing of the Messiah's fate (6.14ff.). Yet the evangelist makes it abundantly clear that Jesus did not come to cause a political disturbance or to excite the mob. He came to do good (3.4ff.), to destroy evil (3.26; 7.20ff.). Jesus is perceived as a threat to the old order who sees clearly that no compromise with the new is possible.

Thirdly, Jesus calls disciples 'to be with him' (3.14). They are challenged 'to follow him' (2.14). He establishes a new beginning and sends them forth with his authority to preach and heal (6.7ff.). Often he takes them apart from the crowd to explain to them privately his message (3.7; 4.33). The call to discipleship transcends the natural ties of family and is redefined as obedience to the will of God (3.31ff.). However, the overwhelming emphasis of the Gospel of Mark is on the inability of the disciples to comprehend either Christ's true identity or his mission. They react in awe and fear during the storm at sea and are chided for lack of faith by Jesus (4.35ff.). When the woman with a flow of blood touches his garment and finds her faith rewarded, the disciples miss the significance of the event completely. They do not understand about the loaves and are twice described as 'hardened of heart' (6.52; 8.14ff.). In the subsequent chapters this theme will grow in intensity.

Within the first half of the Gospel, ch. 4 on the parables of the kingdom performs a programmatic role and serves to link the various themes which have already been introduced (cf. Excursus II). Clearly Mark does not record Jesus' parables in order to provide some typical examples of his teaching. Nor does he recount them to educate the dull-witted disciples. Rather, Mark intends the parable of the sower to offer a key by which to interpret all the parables (4.13). It explains the nature of Christ's hidden ministry; the parable guards the mystery of his identity. There is an organic unity between Jesus' present ministry and the future kingdom of God (cf. Dahl). In spite of the apparent insignificance of Jesus' earthly ministry, the hidden rule of God has begun. Much of the seed sown will be lost, but still the crop will be enormous (4.8). The smallest seed of all will grow into the largest of trees, thus fulfilling Daniel's vision of God's future kingdom which encompasses the world (4.19ff.).

According to 4.11f. Jesus deliberately chose the form of the parable – the *mashal* – both to reveal and to conceal his true meaning. To those inside they reveal the secret of the kingdom; to those outside they function as riddles preventing an understanding of the mystery. Yet what at first appears to be an absolute distinction between Jesus' disciples who are 'inside', and the uninitiated public who are

'outside', proves to be misleading. The typology is not to be understood historically, but theologically. That perennial people of heavy
ears and closed eyes described by Isaiah 6, who is incapable of
perceiving God's redemptive activity in the world, is contrasted with
those disciples to whom God has unlocked the mystery of his eternal
purpose in Jesus Christ. Actually Jesus' own disciples, those of the
Gospel narrative, have not yet entered into the mystery. They do not
understand his true identity nor comprehend his parables. They
continue to stumble in ignorance before the mystery of the hidden,
rejected, and crucified Messiah.

Chapter 4 is programmatic for the canonical shape of the Gospel
because it bears witness to the nature of Christ's revelation to
every successive generation of Christian. The hiddenness of Christ's
identity remains a mystery to those outside for whom the crucified
Messiah is an offence. Yet for those who are inside – those disciples
who understand the secret – the parables testify to the ultimate
triumph of God's rule whose vindication has already begun.

The issue continues to be debated to what extent the confession of
Peter at Caesarea Philippi (8.27ff.) marks a turning point in the
ministry of Jesus (Lightfoot, *Mark* 33f.; Achtemeier, *Mark*, 36ff.). A
consensus has developed that the incident plays no role for the
evangelist in setting forth a mental or spiritual development within
Jesus. He did not change tactics, nor did his disciples reach a new
stage of understanding. Yet within the narrative the incident does
seem to mark the second major portion of the book which begins to
fall more and more under the shadow of the climactic events of
Jerusalem. The first prediction of his death occurs in 8.31, followed
in succession by two more (9.31; 10.33f.). The call to discipleship as
participating in the death of Christ (9.34f.; 10.43) becomes more
explicit, and its implications are spelled out in a whole chapter just
before the entrance into Jerusalem (ch. 10).

In the Marcan version of Peter's confession, the title of the Christ
is neither accepted nor refused, but is explicitly encompassed within
the messianic secret (8.30). Peter speaks the truth, as had the demons
before him, but is silenced. His confession does not offer the true
path to the secret as is immediately demonstrated in the scene
which follows. Jesus predicts his suffering and death and is flatly
misunderstood by Peter who will know nothing of a suffering Christ.
The call to follow Christ to the cross is then addressed to the multitude
and no longer just to the Twelve. The call clearly transcends the

historical context of the narrative and confronts every successive would-be-disciple.

The transfiguration scene (9.2ff.) presents a momentary unveiling of Christ's true identity for the sake of the disciples. At no time before, except at his baptism, is the secret made more clearly known. Jesus is the promised Messiah, testified to by the law and the prophets, and identified as the beloved Son (Ps. 2) by the heavenly voice. This scene, coming as it does just before the events of Jerusalem, removes any possible doubt as to the true identity of the suffering Son of man. However, the metamorphosis is temporary. The disciples did not understand and were afraid to ask (9.32). Still for the readers of Mark who know the messianic secret his transfiguration serves as a foretaste of Christ's glorious triumph at his parousia.

With the triumphal entry (ch. 11) Jesus rides into Jerusalem as the prince of peace (Gen. 49.11; Zech. 9.9), and by his action evokes the proper response to his messiahship (Ps. 118.26). Lightfoot (*Mark*, ad loc.) speaks of his action as straining the Marcan doctrine of the secret messiahship to the breaking point, but the ovation of the festival crowd is ambivalent. The entrance neither produced any results nor reflected a true grasp of his real identity, as the subsequent chapters emphasize with considerable irony (15.8ff.). For Mark the true figure of the humble Messiah did not arise unambiguously from the Old Testament. Rather, what Jesus now did was to fill the prophet's concealed word with its true meaning.

In the preceding chapters the healing of the epileptic boy (9.14–29) and the blind Bartimaeus (10.46–52) had been already construed with symbolic meaning and testified that faith can see even when the covenant people has been rendered blind. Now the symbolic judgment of the old order is given its most powerful representation with the cursing of the fig tree (11.12ff.) and the cleansing of the temple (11.15ff.). Lightfoot is surely right in seeing the apocalyptic discourse in ch. 13 as designed to introduce the passion (*Mark*, ad loc.). The portrayal of the revealed eschatological 'Son of man coming in the clouds with great glory' for all to see (v. 26) stands in its most violent contrast with the reviled and rejected servant.

IV. Mark's Passion Account

There is still a widespread consensus (*contra* Kelber) that Mark found the passion story in a largely completed form with the major components already established. Nevertheless, Mark left his redactional stamp on the material in chs. 14ff. which brings to completion his original purpose. Clearly the passion of Jesus is the climax of his Gospel, which had been foreshadowed from the beginning. The events of Christ's rejection, suffering, and death realized the fundamental mystery of his Messiahship and rendered Mark's whole Gospel intelligible.

For Mark the passion story reflects a profound, dialectical relationship betwen human and divine causation (14.21). On the one hand, Christ suffered and died because of the plottings of evil men. There is a tight historical nexus of events established which began with the resolution in 3.6 to destroy Jesus, and which culminates in his betrayal, arrest, trial and crucifixion. On the other hand, Christ's passion falls under the divine necessity ($\delta\epsilon\tilde{\iota}\,\tau\grave{o}\nu\,\upsilon\grave{\iota}\grave{o}\nu\ldots\pi\alpha\theta\epsilon\tilde{\iota}\nu$, 8.31). Christ fulfils the divine will in accordance with scripture (14.49). He prays to have 'the cup removed' (14.36), but accepts the will of God to die.

Mark portrays the cost of the Messiah's final victory through obedience as being his complete abandonment. In Gethsemane his disciples cannot share his vigil, but sleep and do not know what to answer (14.40). When he is arrested, 'all forsook him and fled' (14.50). He is denied by Peter (14.66ff.) and delivered over to the crowd by Pilate (15.15). At his crucifixion he is identified with the suffering innocent one of the Psalter who is abandoned by God (15.34) and who cries out in the darkness. He dies as the 'king of the Jews' (15.18, 26), whose identity is indeed announced, but totally misunderstood.

Yet there is another theme which runs through the passion account. Christ's eschatological kingdom is anticipated and already experienced before his final victory. He is anointed by a woman whose deed of faith is recognized in every succeeding generation (14.3ff.). At the Last Supper the disciples participate in the 'blood of the covenant' which is a foretaste of the eschatological meal within God's rule (14.22ff.). The centurion who witnesses his death bears testimony to his true identity (15.39). Thus the passion story further develops a theme of the whole Gospel that even in his lifetime

Jesus was indeed God's chosen one whose true identity, although concealed, was life-giving.

The canonical significance of this particular shaping of the tradition is to render the Gospel material in such a way that the entire account of Jesus' earthly life can be read by subsequent generations of believers with a different level of meaning from those who originally participated in the events. The positive element in the pre-resurrection tradition which offers a momentary recognition of his true identity functions to reinforce the hermeneutical point made by the emphasis on the hidden secret of Christ's messiahship. For a post-resurrection disciple the challenge presented in the pre-resurrection experience of his lordship collapses the time differential into one single moment of discipleship.

V. The Resurrection according to Mark

We turn finally to ch. 16.1–8, Mark's resurrection account, and seek to analyse its canonical function within the book. Several unique features in these verses have long been noticed and require interpretation. First, the textual evidence is conclusive in establishing the two additional, traditional endings (vv. 9–20, the longer ending; the one additional verse after v. 8, the shorter ending) as secondary. Therefore, regardless of the reasons by which to explain the present state of the text, Mark's original ending is now confined to vv. 1–8. Secondly, although the announcement of Jesus' resurrection is central to the passage (v. 6), there are no resurrection appearances recorded. Thirdly, further events beyond the resurrection between Jesus and his disciples are envisioned which explicitly repeat an earlier theme (v. 7). Fourthly, the women who visited the tomb react in trembling, astonishment, and fear and are silent in communicating the message of Christ's resurrection.

How is one to understand these features of the narrative? It is clear at the outset that one's interpretation depends on an initial assessment of whether the present ending (1–8) represents the intended ending of the evangelist or whether the concluding portion of the chapter has been lost. The issue can hardly be resolved definitively, given our present state of knowledge. However, I think it fair to say that increasingly a majority has emerged which reckons with vv. 1–8 as Mark's intended conclusion, although there also remains an important dissenting minority opinion. If one then works with the majority hypothesis, the question immediately arises why no resurrection appearances are recorded by the evangelist. Clearly Mark is not trying to conceal the resurrection. He has been aware of it from the outset, and he has shaped his whole Gospel from this perspective. Indeed it is decisive even for the final chapter.

Yet Mark does not present the resurrection as a message directed toward unbelievers in an effort to evoke belief. The message is written for believers which suggests that its purpose lies elsewhere. The resurrected Christ has a message for his disciples of which he had previously spoken (16.7; cf. 9.9). Their relationship with him continues and is oriented toward the future when they shall again meet. It seems, therefore, likely that Mark simply assumes the knowledge of the appearances. At least he needs only the fact of the resurrection, and not the fuller tradition, to make his main point.

Equally significant is the reaction of the women to the announcement of the resurrection. They respond in fear and trembling. As a result, they do not communicate the angel's message. This reaction would imply that their reaction of fear is not viewed by the evangelist as a positive response. Dahl's interpretation ('Purpose of Mark', 55) is intriguing when he suggests that the goal of the evangelist 'was not to awaken faith but to recall the character of the resurrection as a mystery and wonder which could elicit fear and awe'. The evangelist continues his theme of the hidden and revealed secret of Christ's messiahship. Although both Mark and his audience know Christ's true identity, his account of the women's response makes clear that even the resurrection did not remove the mystery of Christ's identity. It was still possible not to understand and to react in unbelieving fear and astonishment.

Dahl's interpretation appears to me correct that Mark's intention is not to evoke faith in unbelievers, but is addressed to the church. Moreover, his purpose appears to be to remind his audience that the need for a believing response to the crucified Lord – a theme which had dominated his whole gospel – had not been changed by the resurrection. The mystery of Christ's revelation as both concealing and revealing his identity continues past the resurrection. It is still possible to misunderstand. The mystery of Christ's pre-resurrection identity still obtains for the post-resurrection community because, even following Christ's vindication by God, his followers can continue in fear and astonished unbelief. For Mark, the resurrection does not, therefore, render obsolete the pre-resurrection tradition, but rather confirms the same message. Mark addresses his book to the church in order to call to mind the true nature of discipleship for every generation subsequent to the resurrection. The call to participate in Christ's death has not changed, but has been confirmed by the resurrection.

VI. The Canonical Significance of the Longer Ending

There is one concluding problem of canonical shaping to address. The original ending of the Gospel of Mark – whether originally by intent or accident is now irrelevant – has been expanded. At least by the middle of the second century two additional endings were attached to the end of 16.8. First, a shorter ending which in the major textual traditions always preceded the longer ending. Secondly, a longer ending which displaced the shorter ending to become the accepted ending for the Byzantine (koine) text.

The significance of the expanded ending has usually been disregarded by modern critical scholarship, but it is wide-ranging in effect. Mark's Gospel received its canonical shape by the addition of an ending which clearly does not stem from the original author. Yet the addition is not simply a pious gloss attached to one late textual tradition, but rather an early expansion which helped to form the dominant canonical tradition. Moreover, the longer ending consists of a catena of passages taken from the other three canonical Gospels in addition to other sources (cf. Nestle's edition). This evidence supports the conclusion that the expanded ending to Mark entered the text during the process of forming a fourfold Gospel collection. If from an historical perspective Mark's Gospel provided the primary source for Matthew and Luke, there is at least one highly important example within the canonical process of the reverse influence at work.

What is the canonical effect of the longer ending on the reading of Mark's Gospel? First, the addressee of the Gospel has not been altered. The message is still directed primarily to those within the Christian church. However, for this next generation of post-resurrection Christians, knowledge of the resurrection appearances by means of oral tradition can no longer be assumed. The grounds for Christian belief must now be set forth in written form. Moreover, the vehicle for the resurrection tradition has now become the other written Gospels. For Mark to function within the fourfold collection his Gospel has been brought into conformity with the other three. That is to say, the oral tradition which undergirded Mark's final chapter has now been spelled out and shaped in accordance with the tradition provided by the larger collection. The canonical Mark has thus been fashioned in such a way as to harmonize with the other three (cf. ch. 10 below). The hermeneutical implications of this canonical shape would provide a strong warrant for resisting theories of interpretation which would read Mark as an idiosyncratic witness in open conflict with the other three (e. g. Weeden, Kelber).

Secondly, the same theological point made by the original ending of Mark (16.18) has been retained, but extended. The emphasis of the longer ending falls fully on the disciples' unbelief even in the face of the resurrection (vv. 11, 12, 14, 16). The longer ending, in addition, functions as a commentary on the first eight verses and plainly rules out interpreting the astonishment and awe of the women in a positive fashion. Their unbelief is upbraided by the resurrected Christ, who equates belief and unbelief with salvation and judgment (v. 16).

Finally, the function of the Gospel of Mark in its larger canonical shape has now been expanded beyond the role of calling the disciples to remember the nature of their discipleship to the crucified and rejected Messiah. The disciples are now commissioned to evangelize the world, much in the style of Matthew's commission. Mark's original 'anamnetic' focus (Dahl) has been made to serve a new role, in conformity with the other Gospels, which addresses those both inside and outside the fellowship of believers.

7

LUKE

Commentaries

B. Weiss, MeyerK, ⁷1883
F. Godet, ET 1887–89
H. J. Holtzmann, HCNT, ²1892
J. Wellhausen, 1904
A. Plummer, ICC, ⁵1922
A. Loisy, 1924
B. S. Easton, 1926
E. Klostermann, HNT, ²1929
J. M. Creed, 1930
T. Zahn, KNT, ⁴1930
H. K. Luce, CGTSC, 1933
F. Hauck, THKNT, 1934
M.-J. Lagrange, ÉB, ³1948
N. Geldenhuys, NICNT, 1954

A. Schlatter, ²1960
J. Schmid, RNT, ⁴1960
G. B. Caird, Pel, 1963
H. Schürmann, HTKNT, 1969
K. Rengstorf, NTD, ¹⁴1969
F. W. Danker, 1972
E. E. Ellis, NCeB, ²1974
G. Schneider, ÖTK, 1977
J. Ernst, RNT, 1977
W. Grundmann, THKNT, ⁸1978
I. H. Marshall, NICNT, 1978
W. Schmithals, ZBK, 1979
J. A. Fitzmyer, AB, 1981–5
E. Schweizer, (NTD), ET 1983

Bibliography

Cf. the exhaustive bibliography in J. A. **Fitzmyer**, AB.

P. J. **Achtemeier**, 'TheLucan Perspective on the Miracles of Jesus', *JBL* 94, 1975, 547–62; H. **von Baer**, *Der Heilige Geist in den Lukasschriften*, WMANT 39, 1926; C. K. **Barrett**, *Luke the Historian in Recent Study*, London 1961; H. W. **Bartsch**, 'Zum Problem der Parusieverzögerung bei den Synoptikern', *EvTh* 19, 1959, 116–31; *Wachtet aber zu jeder Zeit*, Hamburg 1963; O. **Bauernfeind**, 'Vom historischen zum lukanischen Paulus', *EvTh* 13, 1953, 347–53; 'Zur Frage nach der Entscheidung zwischen Paulus und Lukas', *ZSTh* 23, 1954, 59–88; O. **Betz**, 'The Kerygma of Luke', *Interp* 22, 1968, 131–46; J. **Blinzler**, 'Die literarische Eigenart des sogenannten Reiseberichts im Lukas-Evangelium', *Synoptische Studium, FS A. Wikenhauser*, ed. J. Schmid and A. Vögtle, Munich 1953, 20–52; P. **Borgen**, 'From Paul to Luke: Observations toward Clarification of the Theology of Luke-Acts', *CBQ* 31, 1969, 168–82; K. **Bornhäuser**, *Studien zum Sondergut Lukas*,

Gütersloh 1934; G. **Bornkamm**, 'Die Verzögerung der Parusia', (1951), reprinted *Geschichte und Glaube* I (*GA* III), Munich 1968, 46–55; F. **Bovon**, *Luc le Théologien. Vingt-cinq ans de recherches* (1950–1975), Neuchâtel and Paris 1978; G. **Braumann**, 'Das Mittel der Zeit – Erwägungen zur Theologie des Lukasevangeliums', *ZNW* 54, 1963, 117–45; *Das Lukas-Evangelium. Die redaktions- und kompositionsgeschichtliche Forschung*, Darmstadt 1974; R. E. **Brown**, *The Birth of the Messiah*, New York and London 1977; S. **Brown**, 'The Role of the Prologues in Determining the Purpose of Luke-Acts', in Talbert, *Perspectives*, 99–111; A. **Büchele**, *Der Tod Jesu im Lukasevangelium: Eine redaktionsgeschichtliche Untersuchung zu Lk 23*, FTS 26, 1978; U. **Busse**, *Die Wunder des Propheten Jesus: Die Rezeption, Komposition und Interpretation der Wundertradition im Evangelium des Lukas*, FzB 24, 1977.

H. J. **Cadbury**, *The Making of Luke-Acts*, New York and London 1927; 'Commentary on the Preface of Luke', *The Beginnings of Christianity*, ed. F. J. Foakes Jackson, II, 489–510; ' "We" and "I" in Luke-Acts', *NTS* 3, 1956/7, 128–32; R. J. **Cassidy**, *Jesus, Politics, and Society: A Study of Luke's Gospel*, New York 1978; H. **Conzelmann**, *Die Mitte der Zeit. Studien zur Theologie des Lukas*, BHT 17, 1954, ⁵1964, ET *The Theology of St Luke*, London and New York 1960; O. **Cullmann**, *Christ and Time*, ET London and Philadelphia 1950; 'Parusieverzögerung und Urchristentum', *TLZ* 83, 1958, 1–11; *Salvation in History*, ET London and New York 1967; N. A. **Dahl**, 'The Story of Abraham in Luke-Acts', *Studies in Luke-Acts*, ed. Keck and Martyn, 139–58; 'The Purpose of Luke-Acts', *Jesus in the Memory of the Early Church*, Minneapolis 1976, 87–98; F. W. **Danker**, *Luke* (Proclamation Commentaries), Philadelphia 1976; H. J. **Degenhardt**, *Lukas – Evangelist der Armen. Besitz und Besitzversicht in den lukanischen Schriften*, Stuttgart 1965; G. **Delling**, ' ". . . als er uns die Schrift aufschlosst". Zur Lukanischen Terminologie der Auslegung des Alten Testaments', *Das Wort und die Wörter, FS G. Friedrich*, ed. H. Balz and S. Schulz, Stuttgart 1973, 75–84; M. **Dibelius**, *Jungfrauensohn und Krippenkind* (1932), in *Botschaft und Geschichte*, I, Tübingen 1953, 1–78; R. J. **Dillon**, *From Eye-Witness to Ministers of the Word. Tradition and Composition in Luke 24*, AnBib 82, 1978; C. H. **Dodd**, 'The Fall of Jerusalem and the "Abomination of Desolation"', in *More New Testament Essays*, London and Grand Rapids 1968, 69–83; J. **Drury**, *Tradition and Design in Luke's Gospel: A Study in Early Christian Historiography*, London 1976; I. I. **Du Plessis**, 'Once More: The Purpose of Luke's Prologue (Lk i 1–4)', *NovT* 16, 1974, 259–71.

E. E. **Ellis**, 'Present and Future Eschatology in Luke', *NTS* 12, 1965/6, 27–41; J. **Ernst**, 'Schriftauslegung und Auferstehungsglaube bei Lukas', *Schriftauslegung*, ed., J. Ernst, Munich 1972, 177–92; *Herr der Geschichte. Perspektiven der lukanischen Eschatologie*, SBS 88, 1978; C. F. **Evans**, 'The Central Section of St Luke's Gospel', *Studies in the Gospels, Essays in Memory of R. H. Lightfoot*, ed. D. E. Nineham, Oxford 1955, 37–53; A. **Feuillet**, 'Le récit lucanien de la tentation (Lc 4.1–13)', *Bibl* 40, 1959, 613–31; H. **Flender**, *St Luke: Theologian of Redemptive History*, ET London and Philadelphia 1967; F. J. **Foakes-Jackson**, K. **Lake**, *The Beginnings of Christianity*, 5 vols., London and New York 1922–1939; E. **Franklin**, *Christ the Lord: A Study in the Purpose and Theology of Luke-Acts*, London and Philadelphia 1975.

A. **George**, *Études sur l'oeuvre de Luc*, Paris 1978; J. **van Goudoever**, 'The Place of Israel in Luke's Gospel', *NovT* 8, 1966, 111–23; M. D. **Goulder**, *Eschatology in Luke*, Philadelphia 1972; E. **Grässer**, *Das Problem der Parusiever-zögerung in den synoptischen Evangelien und in der Apostelgeschichte*, BZNW 22, ³1979; W. **Grundmann**, 'Fragen der Komposition des lukanischen "Reise-Berichts"', *ZNW* 50, 1959, 252–70; E. **Haenchen**, 'Historie und Verkündi-gung bei Markus and Lukas', *Die Bibel und Wir*, Tübingen 1968, 156–81; G. **Harbsmeier**, 'Unsere Predigt im Spiegel der Apostelgeschichte', *EvTh* 10, 1950/51, 353–68; A. **von Harnack**, *New Testament Studies*, I: *Luke the Physician. The Author of the Third Gospel and the Acts of the Apostles*, ET London and New York 1908; A. J. B. **Higgins**, 'The Preface to Luke and the Kerygma in Acts', *Apostolic History and the Gospel, Biblical and Historical Essays Presented to F. F. Bruce*, ed. W. W. Gasque and R. P. Martin, Exeter and Grand Rapids 1970, 78–91; T. **Holtz**, *Untersuchungen über die alttestamentlichen Zitate bei Lukas*, TU 104, 1968; A. J. **Hultgren**, 'Interpreting the Gospel of Luke', *Interp* 30, 1976, 353–65.

J. **Jeremias**, *Die Sprache des Lukasevangeliums*, Göttingen 1980; J. **Jervell**, *Luke and the People of God: a New Look at Luke-Acts*, Minneapolis 1972; L. T. **Johnson**, *The Literary Function of Possessions in Luke-Acts*, SBLDS 39, Missoula 1977; E. **Käsemann**, 'The Problem of the Historical Jesus', ET *Essays on New Testament Themes*, SBT 41, 1964, 15–47; L. E. **Keck**, J. L. **Martyn**, eds., *Studies in Luke-Acts, Essays in Honor of Paul Schubert*, Nashville 1966; G. **Klein**, 'Lukas 1, 1–4 als theologisches Programm', in *Zeit und Geschichte, FS R. Bultmann*, ed. E. Dinkler, Tübingen 1964, 193–216; reprinted in *Das Lukas-Evangelium*, ed. G. Braumann, Darmstadt 1974, 170–203; W. S. **Kümmel**, '"Das Gesetz und die Propheten gehen bis Johannes" – Lukas 16, 16 im Zusammenhang der heilsgeschichtlichen Theologie der Lukasschriften', *Verborum Veritas, FS G. Stählin*, ed. O. Böcher and K. Haacker, Wuppertal 1970, 89–102; reprinted *Heilsgeschehen und Geschichte* II, Marburg 1978, 78–86; 'Lukas in der Anklage der heutigen Theologie', *Heilsgeschehen und Geschichte* II, 87–100; J. **Kürzinger**, 'Lk 1, 3 . . . ἀκριβῶς καθεξῆς σοι γράψαι', *BZ* 18, 1974, 249–55.

G. W. H. **Lampe**, 'The Holy Spirit in the Writings of St Luke', *Studies in the Gospels: Essays in Memory of R. H. Lightfoot*, ed. D. E. Nineham, Oxford 1957, 159–200; R. **Laurentin**, *Structure et Théologie de Luc I-II*, Paris 1957; K. **Löning**, 'Lukas-Theologe der von Gott Geführten Heilsgeschichte', in *Gestalt und Anspruch des Neuen Testaments*, ed. J. Schreiner and G. Dautzenberg, Würzburg 1969, 200–28; G. **Lohfink**, *Die Himmelfahrt Jesu*, SANT 26, 1971; *Die Sammlung Israels*, SANT 39, 1975; E. **Lohse**, *Die Auferstehung Jesu Christi im Zeugnis des Lukasevangeliums*, BSt 31, 1961; 'Lukas als Theologe der Heilsgeschichte', *EvTh* 14, 1954, 256–75; reprinted *Die Einheit des NT*, Göttingen 1973, 145–64; 'Missionarisches Handeln Jesu nach dem Evange-lium des Lukas', *Die Einheit des Neuen Testament*, 165–77; U. **Luck**, 'Kerygma,

Tradition und Geschichte bei Lukas', *ZTK* 57, 1960, 51–66; reprinted in Braumann, ed., *Das Lukas-Evangelium*, 95–114; I. H. **Marshall**,*Luke: Historian and Theologian*, Exeter and Grand Rapids 1970; A. J. **Mathill**, Jr., 'Naherwartung, Fernerwartung and the Purpose of Luke-Acts', *CBQ* 34, 1972, 276–93; *Luke and the Last Things: A Perspective for the Understanding of Lukan Thought*, Dillsboro, N. C. 1979; P. S. **Minear**, 'Luke's Use of the Birth Stories', *Studies in Luke-Acts*, ed. Keck and Martyn, Nashville 1966, 111–30; *To Heal and to Reveal: The Prophetic Vocation according to Luke*, New York 1976; D. P. **Moessner**, 'Luke 9:1–50: Luke's Preview of the Journey of the Prophet Like Moses of Deuteronomy', *JBL* 102, 1983, 575–605; R. **Morgenthaler**, *Die lukanische Geschichtsschreibung als Zeugnis: Gestalt und Gehalt des Kunst des Lukas*, AbTANT 14, 15, 2 vols., 1949; F. **Mussner**, 'καθεξῆς im Lukas-prolog', *Jesus und Paulus, FS W. G. Kümmel*, ed. E. E. Ellis et al., Göttingen 1975, 253–55.

F. **Neirynck**, ed., *L'Evangile de Luc: Problèmes littéraires et théologiques, Mémorial Lucien Cerfaux*, Gembloux 1973; B. **Noack**, *Das Gottesreich bei Lukas*, Uppsala 1948; G. **Ogg**, 'The Central Section of the Gospel according to St Luke', *NTS* 18, 1971/2, 39–53; H. H. **Oliver**, 'The Lucan Birth Stories and the Purpose of Luke-Acts', *NTS* 10, 1963/4, 202–26; P. **von der Osten-Sacken**, 'Zur Christologie des lukanischen Reiseberichts', *EvTh* 33, 1973, 476–96; O. A. **Piper**, 'The Virgin Birth. The Meaning of the Gospel Accounts', *Interp* 18, 1964, 131–48; F. **Rehkopf**, *Die lukanische Sonderquelle*, WUNT 5, 1959; M. **Rese**, *Alttestamentliche Motive in der Christologie des Lukas*, SNT 1, 1969; 'Neuere Lukas-Arbeiten', *TLZ* 106, 1981, 225–37; W. C. **Robinson**, Jr., *Der Weg des Herrn – Studien zur Geschichte und Eschatologie im Lukas-Evangelium*, ThF 36, 1964.

H. **Sahlin**, *Der Messias und das Gottesvolk: Studien zur protolukanischen Theologie*, Uppsala 1945; É. **Samain**, 'La notion de APXH dans l'oeuvre lucanienne', in *L'Evangile de Luc*, ed. F. Neirynck, 299–328; R. **Schnacken-burg**, 'Der Sinn der Versuchung Jesu bei den Synoptikern', *TQ* 132, 1952, 297–326; 'Der eschatologische Abschnitt Lukas 17, 20–37', in *Schriften zum Neuen Testament*, Munich 1971, 220–43; G. **Schneider**, 'Zur Analyse des lukanischen Reiseberichtes', in *Synoptische Studien, FS A. Wikenhauser*, Munich 1953, 207–229; *Verleugnung, Verspottung und Verhör Jesu nach Lukas 22, 54–71, Studien zur lukanischen Darstellung der Passion*, SANT 22, 1969; *Parusiegleichnisse im Lukas-Evangelium*, SBS 74, 1975; 'Zur Bedeutung von καθεξῆς im lukani-schen Doppelwerk', *ZNW* 68, 1977, 128–31; J. **Schniewind**, *Die Parallelperi-kopen bei Lukas und Johannes*, Leipzig 1914; *Das Gleichnis vom verlorenen Sohn*, Göttingen 1940; T. **Schramm**, *Der Markus-Stoff bei Lukas – Eine literarkritische und redaktionsgeschichtliche Untersuchung*, SNTSM 14, 1971; P. **Schubert**, 'The Structure and Significance of Luke 24', *Neutestamentliche Studien für R. Bultmann*, BZNW 21, 1954, 165–86; H. **Schürmann**, 'Evangelienschrift und kirchliche Unterweisung. Die repräsentative Function der Schrift nach Lk 1, 1–4'; reprinted *Traditionsgeschichtliche Untersuchungen zu den synoptischen Evangelien*, Düsseldorf 1968, 251–340; *Der Paschamahlbericht (Lk 22, (7–14)*

15–18, Münster ²1968; *Der Einsetzungsbericht, Lk 22, 19–20*, Münster ²1970; *Jesu Abschiedsrede, Lk 22, 21–38*, Münster ²1977; 'Zur Traditionsgeschichte der Nazareth-Perikope Lk 4, 16–30', in *Mélanges Biblique en hommage au B. Rigaux*, ed. A. Descamps et A. de Halleux, Gembloux 1970, 187–205; S. **Schulz**, 'Gottes Vorsehung bei Lukas', *ZNW* 54, 1963, 104–16; 'Lukas', *Die Stunde der Botschaft*, Hamburg, 1967, 235–96; E. **Schweizer**, *Luke. A Challenge to Present Theology*, ET Atlanta 1983; G. **Sellin**, 'Komposition, Quellen und Funktion des lukanischen Reiseberichtes (Lk. ix 51–xix 28)', *NovT* 20, 1978, 100–35; N. **Stonehouse**, *The Witness of Luke to Christ*, London and Grand Rapids 1951; *Origins of the Synoptic Gospels*, Grand Rapids ²1983, 118–28.

C. H. **Talbert**, *Luke and the Gnostics: An Examination of the Lucan Purpose*, Nashville 1966; 'The Lukan Presentation of Jesus' Ministry in Galilee: Luke 4:31–9:50', *RevExp* 64, 1967, 485–97; 'The Redaction Critical Quest for Luke the Theologian', in *Jesus and Man's Hope*, ed. D. G. Miller, Pittsburgh 1970, 171–222; *Literary Patterns, Theological Themes, and the Genre of Luke-Acts*, SBLMS 20, Missoula 1974; ed., *Perspectives on Luke-Acts*, Danville and Edinburgh 1978; R. C. **Tannehill**, 'The Mission of Jesus according to Luke IV 16–30' in *Jesus in Nazareth*, BZNW 40, ed. E. Grässer et al, 1972, 51–75; W. B. **Tatum**, 'The Epoch of Israel: Luke i-ii and the Theological Plan of Luke-Acts', *NTS* 3, 1966/7, 184–95; V. **Taylor**, *Behind the Third Gospel*, Oxford 1926; *The Passion Narrative of St Luke*, Cambridge 1972.

W. C. **van Unnik**, 'Remarks on the Purpose of Luke's Historical Writings (Lk 1, 1–4)', reprinted *Sparsa Collecta* I, Leiden 1973, 6–15; P. **Vielhauer**, 'Das Benedictus des Zacharjas', *Aufsätze zum Neuen Testament*, Munich 1965, 28–46; 'On the "Paulinisms" of Acts', Keck and Martyn, eds., *Studies in Luke-Acts*, 33–50; A. **Voegtle**, 'Was hatte die Widmung des lukanischen Doppelwerks an Theophilos zu bedeuten?', *Das Evangelium und die Evangelien*, Düsseldorf 1971, 31–42; 'Offene Fragen zur lukanischen Geburts- und Kindheitsgeschichte', ibid., 43–56; M. **Völkel**, 'Der Anfang Jesu in Galiläa. Bemerkungen zum Gebrauch und zur Funktion Galiläas in den lukanischen Schriften', *ZNW* 64, 1973, 222–32; 'Exegetische Erwägungen zum Verständnis des Begriffs καθεξῆς im lukanischen Prolog', *NTS* 20, 1973/4, 289–99; P. **Wanke**, *Die Emmauserzählung: Eine redaktionsgeschichtliche Untersuchung zu Lk 24, 13–35*, Leipzig 1973; U. **Wilckens**, *Die Missionsreden der Apostelgeschichte*, WMANT 5, ³1974, 100–86; W. **Wilkens**, 'Die theologische Struktur der Komposition des Lukasevangeliums', *TZ* 34, 1978, 1–13; L. E. **Wilshire**, 'Was Canonical Luke Written in the Second Century? – A Continuing Discussion', *NTS* 20, 1973/4, 28–51.

The problem of how to interpret the biblical text in accordance with its canonical shape is nowhere more sharply posed than with the Gospel of Luke. The crucial theological issue at stake turns on the way in which the writer understood the redemptive events, accomplished by Jesus Christ, to apply to the ongoing life of the Christian church (cf. Conzelmann's correct formulation, 11f.). How did Luke construe the gospel toward its salvific applications? Even a superficial reading of Luke's Gospel indicates striking differences in the manner by which the evangelical message was actualized when compared with the other Gospels.

I. The Critical Debate

The canonical issue regarding the understanding of Luke has been greatly intensified during the last thirty years by the emergence of a highly learned, impressive school of interpretation, which has sought specifically to address the basic hermeneutical problems involved. Beginning in the early 50s with the publications of Käsemann, Vielhauer and Conzelmann, and then picked up and expanded by others within the larger Bultmann school (Grässer, Haenchen, Klein, Schultz, etc.), a very sharply profiled portrait of Luke emerged which was worked out on the basis of the two-volume work of the one author of Luke-Acts.

The main lines of the approach to these two books can be briefly outlined:

(a) Largely because of the delay in the expected return of Christ in the parousia, Luke abandoned the eschatological hope of the early Christians and replaced it with a new theory of history in order to accommodate the changing historical situation which he had experienced. Luke was able to 'de-eschatologize' the Christian message by anchoring the life of Jesus in the past as an historical event, which he sharply set apart from the continuing history of the church. Luke thus modified the Marcan terminology respecting the gospel, dropped references to the imminent return of Christ (contrast 9.27 with Mark 9.1), and historicized eschatological references by referring them to the past (Luke 21) (cf. Conzelmann, 36ff.; Schulz, 235ff.; Haenchen, *Acts*, 141).

(b) Luke divided his history into three sharply differentiated periods in order to achieve his goal of distinguishing those elements in the message which were relegated only to the past and those which continued to have authoritative relevance. Accordingly, there was first the period of Israel which ended with John the Baptist (cf. Luke 16.16). This period was followed by the life of Jesus which he designated 'the centre of history', and concluded with the period of the church which began with Christ's ascension (Conzelmann, 14f.).

(c) Because of his view of history and tradition, Luke provides the warrant for 'early Catholicism'. This is to say, the apostolic tradition becomes a fixed entity whose tradents, by means of an historical succession, become the sole guarantees for its purity and proper transmission (Käsemann, 29).

(d) Luke's ability to translate the Christian message into the post-apostolic period which adjusted to a non-Jewish, Roman milieu was achieved at a great cost. Luke's apology for natural theology and *Heilsgeschichte* resulted in a loss of all sense of Paul's doctrine of justification by faith, of the atoning death of Christ, and the eschatological entrance of God's kingdom (Vielhauer, 'Paulinisms').

One of the more powerful features of this modern school of Luke-Acts interpretation lies in the combination of literary penetration and theological reflection. In a certain sense, Conzelmann formulated the issue 'canonically' when he raised the issue at the outset as to the material's use for successive generations of Christians. Similarly, the intensity of Käsemann's attack on Luke's alleged misconstrual of the gospel derives from its wider canonical implications, especially respecting the Pauline corpus.

As one would expect in the light of the seriousness of this critical proposal, the new position has called forth a variety of rejoinders which have tended to focus on specific issues of the interpretation. Cullmann, whose *heilsgeschichtliche* interpretation of the entire New Testament appeared to be most seriously affected by Conzelmann, sought to contest the redactional originality of Luke as well as the negative assessment of his accomplishment (*Salvation in History*, 29ff.). He reiterated his position from the earlier debate with A. Schweitzer and M. Werner that the delay of the parousia had played only a minor role in reshaping the Gospels because of the early church's understanding of eschatology. However, in spite of some good insights most scholars questioned whether Cullmann had been successful in checking the momentum generated by Conzelmann.

Flender's monograph also attempted to attack Conzelmann along a broad front. His emphasis on the multi-dimensional understanding of history by Luke, particularly the role of a horizontal and vertical eschatology in relation to the Spirit, was more successful in demonstrating the one-sidedness of Conzelmann's position. However, Flender's categories were criticized as stemming more from systematic theology than from biblical exegesis, and the impact of the book was lessened.

Far more successful were those books and articles which focused on specific points of weakness within the new exegetical construal. W. C. Robinson's dissertation did much to call into question Conzelmann's interpretation of Luke's use of geography and eschatology. Then again, Kümmel's articles focused on the complexity of building such a superstructure on the foundation of the one verse, Luke 16.16. Likewise, Minear was highly convincing in showing the significance of the Lucan birth stories which served to modify Conzelmann's theory of periodization. Finally, the important essays of Luck, Braumann and above all of Schürmann (HTKNT), raised serious questions, especially from the perspective of the prologue, as to whether Luke's fundamental purpose had been adequately handled.

To summarize: the intense debate over the interpretation of Luke's Gospel has successfully eroded some of the more extreme features of the profile which members of the Bultmann school had sketched. However, many of the important redactional observations initially made by Conzelmann, such as an historical periodization, appear to have been widely accepted and defended by recent commentators well outside the Bultmann circle (e.g. Schneider, Ernst). Moreover, because no overarching interpretation of the Gospel has emerged which offered as comprehensive a treatment as Conzelmann's, his position continues to represent the dominant interpretation among most modern handbooks and introductions. Perhaps one of the major contributions of a canonical approach to this Gospel will be to bring together a variety of important observations which have already been made in various contexts, but without the benefit of a consistently sharp focus on the question of canonical function.

II. The Lucan Prologue, 1.1–4

The Gospel of Luke begins with a carefully worded, highly stylized statement of the author's purpose in writing his book. Luke's use of the literary conventions common to the antique writings of the Hellenistic world have long been noticed and exhaustively described (E. Norden, *Agnostos Theos*, Darmstadt 1956, 311ff.; Cadbury, Preface of Luke; Fitzmyer, 278ff.). The conventional style of the proemium differs markedly from the rest of the book, but demonstrates from the outset the author's concern to address his book to a wider audience rather than direct it only to a group of believers. (Voegtle, 'Was hatte die Widmung', 31ff.).

The prologue to Luke's Gospel offers a classic example of a literary form which has been shaped in order to serve primarily a canonical function. Among modern New Testament scholars, H. Schürmann has recognized this fact most clearly and even speaks of a 'kanonische Gesamtdarstellung' ('Evangelienschrift', 270). The biblical author is concerned to establish from the outset how the events transmitted by the tradition relate to the present and future generation of believers. Indeed, the issue turns on the change effected when the oral proclamation of the gospel is set down in narrative, written form by a chain of tradents different from the original eyewitnesses.

Luke begins by noting the fact that 'many' ($\pi o\lambda\lambda o\acute{\iota}$) have already attempted to put into writing a 'report' ($\delta\iota\acute{\eta}\gamma\eta\sigma\iota\nu$) of the nature of the events associated with Jesus Christ. The content of these events is left unspecified in Luke's Gospel prologue, but is clearly assumed to include 'all that Jesus began to do and teach until the day when he was taken up' (Acts 1.1). The problem addressed by Luke is strikingly different from that of Mark who bears witness to the preaching of the good news. Luke does not offer further examples of proclamation. His concern is with offering a legitimization of the new proclamation and therefore he addresses the problem raised by the presence of a new medium of witness, namely the report ($\delta\iota\acute{\eta}\gamma\eta\sigma\iota\varsigma$). Luke's characterization of the prior attempts is only implicit and somewhat neutral. He does not dismiss them as false; however, the need for his new attempt does imply an inadequacy. It is going beyond the evidence to assume that Luke is contesting Mark's Gospel in particular.

The subject matter of the report is the 'events which have been fulfilled among us' (v. 1). Luke speaks of events, and not just prophecies, which have been fulfilled. The verb is not to be understood simply as a neutral term indicating occurrence, but rather it serves to characterize the events as 'fulfilled time' (*Erfüllungszeit*). The eschatological dimension of the events is expressed in several ways. Although the events lie in the past and share the quality of an accomplished sequence, the events have not been bound temporally to the past as ordinary historical events (*contra* Klein), but continue to impinge upon the present. The events have been fulfilled 'among us' (v. 1). Particularly, Klein has pointed out the difficulty involved in this expression. Clearly the same first person plural pronoun in v. 2 is distinguished in time from the original eyewitnesses. How then can the 'we' in v. 1 be contemporaneous with 'the events fulfilled among us'? The problem is not to be resolved by an appeal to a traditional critical development (Klein), but rather along the theological lines carefully developed by Schürmann (op. cit). The eschatological nature of these events encompasses both the past, present and future and encompasses the 'we' of Luke's generation along with the original eyewitnesses.

Nevertheless, Luke's eschatological understanding of the redemptive events has not removed the important effect of his periodization of history. He is describing the events which have a beginning and ending, and which do not encompass the subsequent acts of the apostles (cf. Schürmann's decisive arguments against Cadbury et al.). Moreover, Luke is concerned to retain the difference between those historical eyewitnesses, and those who came later. Luke makes no claim to have an independent access to the events which would rival that of the eyewitnesses. Rather, he has received the tradition through the 'ministers of the word', which he now attempts to set down in writing.

Luke next describes both his procedure and the goal of his literary production. He has followed 'all things from the beginning' ($\check{\alpha}\nu\omega\theta\varepsilon\nu$, cf. Acts 26.4), and 'accurately' ($\dot{\alpha}\varkappa\varrho\iota\beta\tilde{\omega}\varsigma$, cf. Acts 18.26). He expresses his intention to set out 'an orderly' account ($\varkappa\alpha\theta\varepsilon\xi\tilde{\eta}\varsigma$). The exact meaning of this latter expression continues to be much disputed (cf. Kürzinger, Mussner, Schneider, Fitzmyer). However the element of chronological ordering certainly belongs within its semantic field. He is concerned to follow the 'way of Jesus' which unfolded as a sequence. Luke's activity comprises both careful collecting and critical sorting of the material. He stands within the chain of tradition, yet he is clearly more than just a collector. The traditional and critical are joined in his theological and critical enterprise. In my opinion, Schürmann's description of Luke as a 'blessed churchman' is not well chosen and leaves him open to severe criticism that he is making Luke an apologist for early Catholicism (cf. Busse, 7). However, Schürmann's main emphasis is surely squarely on the target.

A final and crucial canonical factor forms the climax of the prologue. The decisive goal of Luke's book, which is dedicated to Theophilus, is 'that you may know the dependable certainty

(ἀσφάλεια) about those things of which you have been informed'
(v. 4). His purpose is directed to securing the faith of Christian
believers, both for the present time and beyond, by demonstrating
the solid grounds of the tradition on which it is grounded. Luke does
not conceive of his work primarily as an apologetic task which seeks
to defend the faith by producing external proofs to support the
internal claims of faith. Yet it is also clear that there is no sharp
demarcation drawn between an inner and outer circle. His critical
defence of the tradition, both as theologian and historian, is addressed
to the faithful, but within the context of a public forum. Thus the
'historical' and the 'redemptive historical' elements within the
composition have retained their coherence.

The canonical implications of the prologue for the book as a whole
are many and difficult to overestimate. Luke is addressing precisely
the problem of how the past events of Christ's life are appropriated
for salvation by successive generations of believers. The threats of
distortion and misunderstanding form the background of the task
(Luke 10.3; Acts 20.29).

Luke is concerned to set down accurately the redemptive events
because it is through these events that the eschatological reality of
Christ's salvation impinges on every successive generation. The
'record' continually bears witness – even in this new literary form –
to the *paradosis* through which the apostolic word is actualized. The
great events transpired in history, indeed in a series of acts which
now lie in the historical past. Yet these events are not moored in past
history but continue to be fulfilled time 'for us'. Right at this crucial
juncture the direction of Conzelmann and his colleagues badly misses
the exegetical point, and has introduced a totally uncanonical reading
of Luke's Gospel which in fact turns the basic theological concern of
the author on its head. Rather, as Schürmann correctly states: 'in
the apostolic parodosis the redemptive events retain their imperative
contemporaneity' (HTKNT, 269). Luke thus confirms the authoritative quality of the apostolic tradition which he attempts to render
in its most accurate form for the sake of the church, and which he
sharply sets apart from all later teachings.

III. Luke's Understanding of Time

The importance of Luke's concept of time has continued to play a major role in the interpretation of the gospel ever since Conzelmann's thesis appeared. The steady stream of articles and monographs over several decades has confirmed the significance of the issue. From a canonical perspective already in the prologue one senses the importance of the issue. Because both Conzelmann and Käsemann have consistently addressed the issue in terms of its canonical implications, they have intensified the challenge as to whether Luke has been correctly understood.

At the outset, it is important to recognize that Luke has introduced a definite periodization of history which sets his work apart from the other synoptics (so also Fitzmyer). The time of Jesus has a beginning (ἤρξατο; Acts 1.1; 10.37) and an end (ἀνελήμφθη; Acts 1.2, 11). The time of the church follows the time of Jesus. It is built upon the prior witness but not fused with it (Luke 24.44ff.; Acts 1.1). The time of Jesus unfolds in a series of chronological events which move from Galilee to Judaea to Jerusalem. Jesus' life is described as a journey which reflects a consistent purpose from the start (Luke 9.51). Similarly, the time of the apostles begins at Jerusalem, extends to Judaea and then to the end of the earth (Luke 24.47; Acts 1.8). It is not by chance that Luke's understanding requires a two-volume work in order to cover the two distinct periods of history. Moreover, the time of Jesus is set apart from the period of Israel (Luke 16.16) as promise is distinguished from fulfilment.

Yet the crucial issue lies in determining the exact scope of this schematization and in understanding its theological significance. Conzelmann's division of three sharply distinguished periods has suffered considerable erosion. W. C. Robinson has successfully shown the lack of any rigid consistency in separating John's ministry from the period of Jesus (Der Weg, 9ff.). Kümmel has rightly criticized the overemphasis on Luke 16.16 as providing the warrant for Luke's basic intentionality ('Das Gesetz'). Similarly, Minear has demonstrated Luke's much wider and more flexible historical horizon by including the birth stories in the literary analysis (Studies in Luke-Acts, 111ff.).

Perhaps the most controversial issue at stake lies in the assumption that Luke's theory of history derived ultimately from the failure of the hope of Christ's return to materialize. His theory of history was then an accommodation to actual experience and was effected by de-eschatologizing those elements of the tradition which were the tradents of this disrupted hope. Accordingly, John the Baptist was isolated from the preaching of the kingdom, the parables were reinterpreted to remove any trace of imminent expectation, and the parousia was extended into the distant future which followed the unfolding history of the church. It is to an examination of these issues that I now turn.

A. *The Role of the Spirit*

The programmatic function of Jesus' first appearance in the synagogue of Nazareth (Luke 4.16–30) has long been recognized. Luke's intentional ordering of this sequence is supported by the change from the Marcan position (6.1–6) and from an element of friction within the chapter derived from the older scheme (4.23). Jesus is portrayed as being led by the Holy Spirit into Galilee (4.14) following the temptation. His first public appearance begins in the synagogue and the role of the new emerges immediately in conflict with the old.

Jesus defines his mission in terms of Israel's prophetic writings. He reads from the book of Isaiah and preaches on the biblical text. (Luke offers a mixed LXX text of Isa. 61.1f. and 58.6.) His is not a rabbinic exegesis, nor does he recapitulate the ancient prophetic promise. Rather, the claim is made in the clearest language possible that everything of which the prophets spoke was at that moment fulfilled in his word. Isaiah had spoken of the anointing of the prophet by the Spirit in order to proclaim the jubilee year of God's salvation which brought good news to the poor, liberty to the imprisoned, and healing to the sick. This salvation has arrived at the moment of his preaching. 'Today' in the presence of his person, salvation has arrived. The time of fulfilment has come. All the 'new' of the messianic hope has taken a concrete form in Jesus of Nazareth as the promised eschatological time becomes a reality.

Through the Holy Spirit Jesus announced the realization of prophetic time in history. Those who heard his word had access to God's salvation, not through a *heilsgeschichtliche* scheme, but by means of the Spirit. Jesus' preaching unleashed an eschatological dimension of God's salvation through the Spirit which guaranteed its continued force within the present time. The outpouring of the Spirit began with Jesus' proclamation of 'today', but the Spirit continues throughout

Luke's history to manifest the sign of God's salvation in the midst of every new generation of believers (Acts 1.1ff., 38; 4.8; 9.17). The 'today' announced by Jesus continues to contemporize the present without preventing God's plan from unfolding in the history of Israel and the church. The word of salvation does not remain merely a 'gracious word' (Luke 4.23). It belongs to God's 'visitation' that the old resists the new, and Jesus leaves the place of his youth to preach the good news of the kingdom to those outside according to the plan of God (4.43f.).

It is certainly possible to speak with Conzelmann of Jesus' life as the middle of time in the sense that Jesus' life was preceded by Israel and followed by the church in an historical sequence. However, the witness of Luke is badly distorted if one does not bear in mind that Jesus' life is also fulfilled time. In his word the salvation of God's kingdom was brought into the present once and for all, and made accessible to all believers through his Spirit. This eschatological dimension of time in Luke's Gospel resists the effort to confine Jesus to past history or to restrict his power to ecclesiastical mediation.

B. *The Delay of the Parousia*

One of the most frequently discussed problems relating to Luke's understanding of time concerns the issue of the delay of the parousia. For the Bultmann school the effect of the delay was thought to be a crucial factor in shaping Luke's understanding of history. Two groups of passages within Luke reflect most clearly the problem at issue: the so-called parables of the parousia (12.35–38, 39–40, 41–46; 19.12–27), and the eschatological passages (17.22–37; 21.5ff.).

Luke 12.35–46 contains a series of smaller units and isolated logia of Jesus which have been linked and which address the problem of the parousia. The issue as to the text's prehistory is complex, and commentators differ on the details of what can be safely attributed to a Q source, and what to a Lucan redaction (cf. Schneider, *Parusiegleichnisse*, ad loc.). However, in general it would seem clear that considerable continuity obtained between Luke and his *Vorlage*. Nevertheless, the marks of Luke's particular redactional stamp are evident and widely recognized in the crucial verses, especially when compared with Matthew.

References to the delay in the parousia appear explicitly in several of the parables (12.38, 45). Luke 18.7, when properly translated, also relates to the delay in the final judgment. However, perhaps the most obvious reference to the delay is Luke's introduction to the parables of the talents (19.11ff.): 'He proceeded to tell a parable . . . because they supposed that the kingdom of God was to appear immediately.' Grässer (115ff.) concludes that the major function of the parable in Luke was an attempt to come to terms with the perplexing postponement of the imminent return.

Although I would fully agree that the effect of the delay is present in these texts, and a development beyond the Gospel of Matthew is probable, the crucial issue turns on how the delay is theologically understood within the witness of Luke's Gospel. It is inadequate simply to assume that this experience provided the major force for Luke' theology without a close hearing of the text. First, there is no sign that the eschatological hope was either abandoned or replaced by a theory of history in these texts. The polemical edge of the parable is indeed directed against those who would fix a date, but the recognition of an extended period of time preceding the return has not in itself undercut the eschatological expectation. Again, the major thrust of Luke's interpretation is to highlight the suddenness and unexpected quality of the return (12.35ff.; 46ff.). Finally, Luke's application of the parables is basically misconstrued if it is assumed that his reinterpretation stems from an effort to make the best out of an embarrassing predicament. Far from it. Rather, the recognition of the period of the church preceding the return of Christ fits consistently within Luke's theological understanding of the gospel. The certainty of the future derives from the plan of God who visits his people with his presence in judgment and redemption, and thus calls forth a continuing response to the imperatives of discipleship. The eschatological hope in Luke's Gospel is not a partially digested vestige, but derives from careful theological reflection.

c. The Approaching End, Luke 21

Luke 21 is generally assumed by the members of the Bultmann school to offer the clearest example of a passage which shows the strongest effect of the delay of the parousia. The chapter lends itself especially to redaction criticism because of the parallel passages in Mark 13 and Matthew 24.

There is general agreement that in Mark the tribulation which precedes the end (v. 7b) begins with wars and rumours of wars (vv.

7f.). The beginning of suffering for the saints commences with the start of intense persecution. Those enduring to the end will be saved (v. 13). The acceleration leading up to the consummation of the world is pictured in apocalyptic imagery drawn from Daniel ('the desolating sacrilege', Dan. 9.27; 11.27). The persecution reaches such an intensity that had not God shortened the days, none of the elect would survive. Then in direct sequence with this chain of apocalyptic events the Son of man appears along with cosmological judgment and brings the age to an end (vv. 24ff.). This pattern is generally similar in Matt. 24.

However, an examination of the parallel passages in Luke reveals some striking differences. Luke has grouped the eschatological material into two different sections (17.22–37 and 21.3–28), and provided a slightly different introductory context for the latter. Once again the future is described in a sequence which begins with wars and tumults (v. 9), but the reader is immediately instructed that 'the end will not be at once' (v. 9). There follows the fearful persecution. The emphasis now falls on a faithful witness even unto death by which eternal life is secured (vv. 13ff.), rather than just holding on until the end. However, at this point the most striking difference in Luke appears. In place of the Marcan reference to the desolating sacrilege (13.14) Luke offers a description of the destruction of Jerusalem by surrounding armies (21.20ff.). Moreover, the picture of destruction of Jerusalem results in an extended period of submission (v. 24) and is sharply set apart from the eschatological, cosmological events of vv. 25ff. which introduce the end of the world.

It is chiefly on the basis of this latter change that Conzelmann and others describe Luke's approach as an historicizing of the tradition in order to remove its eschatological elements. It is alleged that Luke has replaced the language of Daniel with a sober, this-worldly description of Jerusalem's destruction which the author had already experienced in AD70 and now viewed as past history. Klostermann speaks of his bringing the prophecy up to date in the light of his experience. Accordingly, the destruction of Jerusalem has been sharply marked off from the coming of the Son of man which event has been projected into the distant future to make place for the time of the church.

This widespread interpretation of Luke 21 by Conzelmann and Grässer, among others, has met some serious criticism (cf. Bartsch, Flender, Braumann). Certainly Braumann has raised a significant point when he questions whether the delay of parousia was only one factor which was taken up into Luke's reinterpretation along with other elements, such as persecution ('Das Mittel', 140f.). Nevertheless, in my judgment, the basic exegetical shape of Luke has not yet been adequately described.

First, the point needs to be stressed that within the present narrative structure of the chapter the destruction of Jerusalem continues to be depicted as a future event (vv. 20ff.). To suggest that for Luke, who wrote after AD70, the destruction was an event in the past is to introduce a basic confusion. Rather, within the narrative of ch. 21 the destruction of Jerusalem is viewed as part of a future sequence leading up to the end. Indeed Luke writes from a post-AD70 historical position, and his description of the city's destruction can be classified as *post eventum*. However, the decisive point to make is that this literary device now performs a special canonical function, as frequently occurred in the Old Testament (I Kings 13; Dan. 11). Luke has confirmed the truth of the eschatological hope by filling out the details of the prophecy with concrete details gained from his historical experience. The purpose of this historicization, however, is neither to call into question the promise, nor to transpose the events into the past. The future orientation of the prophecy remains untouched. Rather, by providing the original prophecy with a concrete description from the actual historical destruction of Jerusalem the reader is given a further confirmation of the truth of the proclamation. The first reader of Luke's Gospel, and every successive generation for whom the events of AD70 are past history, recognize in the fulfilment of the prophecy a foretaste of the entire prophecy. However, to speak of Luke's purpose as de-eschatologizing in intent is badly to misconstrue the canonical function of the chapter.

Secondly, the claim that Luke has broken the eschatological pattern of Mark 13 in order to compensate for the delay in the parousia has oversimplified the text and missed the central effect of Luke's witness. That Luke has made a point different from Mark is clear, and that the delay of the parousia may also have played a role is fully possible. However, the crucial issue is the nature of the change. Luke has not withdrawn the eschatological hope, but rather given it a different shape. He has made it conform to a common Old Testament apocalyptic pattern which now provides the commentary on the church's future hope. The key is provided in Luke 21.24. The distress of Jerusalem in which the church, as true Israel, finds itself

will extend until 'the times of the Gentiles are fulfilled'. As once
Israel had to endure the period of her 'indignation' from the first
destruction of Jerusalem by the nations until the coming of God's
kingdom (Dan. 7.27f.), so Luke now envisions the church living in
between the times. The church still awaits the coming of the kingdom,
but according to God's plan, the 'times of the Gentiles must be
fulfilled'. The destruction of Jerusalem is simply further confirmation
of the certain execution of the divine dispensation. In sum, Luke has
not de-eschatologized the promise, but reshaped it and made it
conform more closely to the traditional Old Testament pattern. That
the delay of the parousia provided an impetus is probable, but many
other factors also played a role in forming Luke's witness, not least
of which was the sense of continuity between the old and the new
Israel as the people of God among the nations.

IV. Proof-from-Prophecy

The above interpretation of Luke 21 reflects only one instance from
a much wider perspective, namely Luke's understanding of Christ's
mission in terms of the Old Testament. A major danger in seeking
to react to the contemporary debate over Luke's purpose is to neglect
important features of the Gospel in the heat of controversy. A decisive
corrective to the widespread lack of interest in the Old Testament
by the Bultmann school has come from scholars such as P. Schubert,
N. A. Dahl, and J. Jervell, among others. A confirmation of the
central importance of Luke's use of a prophecy-fulfilment pattern
will be seen in its continuation and even expansion in his second
volume, Acts.

In his Gospel Luke portrays a continuous series of promises and
fulfilments which closely link the history of ancient Israel with the
life of Jesus. The counsel of God (βουλή) receives its concrete
interpretation from this perspective (contra Schulz, ZNW 54) as the
proof-from-prophecy marks the unbroken movement in history from
expectation to realization. Beginning with the infancy narratives
(1.32–35, 68–75), the story of Jesus is set within the context of God's
chosen one, who was foretold by the prophets and anointed by the
Spirit. Then Jesus, filled with the Spirit, confirms the fulfilment of
the messianic hope (4.16ff.). Luke's emphasis falls especially on the
fulfilment of the prophecies of Christ's suffering and death (9.20ff.)

and the divine necessity of his journey to Jerusalem in order to die
(9.51ff.). The 'beloved son' who is cast out of the vineyard confirms
the prophecy of Ps. 118 (20.17f.).

The climax of Luke's Gospel comes in ch. 24. Through the risen
Christ the disciples are made to see that the whole life of Jesus,
in his suffering, death, and resurrection is unfolded in the Old
Testament. After the resurrection it suddenly became clear to them
that it was not only God's plan for the Christ that had been
prophesied, but also their mission to preach repentance and forgiveness to the nations (24.47ff.).

N. A. Dahl has made another important point which has brought
Luke's particular use of the Old Testament into sharpest focus. Luke
often has developed his proof-from-prophecy in a two-stage pattern
('The Purpose of Luke-Acts', 89ff.). This is to say, Luke is not simply
concerned, as was Matthew, to establish a prophecy-fulfilment
pattern from the Old Testament to the New. Rather, Luke is
interested first in establishing the nature of the messianic hope, as it
were, from the side of the Old Testament. Thus, he begins his
argument by determining the peculiar features of the Old Testament's description of the Messiah, specifically his suffering and
resurrection (Acts 2.25ff.). Acts 17.3 expresses it '. . . explaining and
proving that it was necessary for the Christ to suffer and to rise from
the dead . . .'. Then the second step in the pattern is to establish that
it is Jesus and no other who is the Christ (Acts 2.25ff.; 13.33ff.; 17.3).
In Luke's Gospel the clearest formulation of the approach is found
in 24.44ff., but a key passage for Luke is Ps. 118.22, 'the rejected
stone' (Luke 20.17; cf. Acts 4.11).

Luke's use of the Old Testament proof-from-prophecy is badly
misunderstood if it is taken to be a rigid *heilsgeschichtliche* schema.
Rather, Luke's interpretation is integrally connected to his theology
of the Spirit. Luck ('Kerygma', 104ff.) is certainly correct in stressing
that for Luke the Old Testament is the living witness of the Spirit.
The ancient prophets' authority lies in their speaking through the
voice of the same Holy Spirit. A classic expression of Luke's theology
is found in Acts 28.25: 'The Holy Spirit was right in saying to your
fathers through Isaiah the prophet. . .'.

However, it is equally erroneous to play scripture and Spirit
against each other, as Luck tends to do (109ff.). The two together
form a unity in Luke's thought. Scripture through the Spirit bears
witness to the Christ who is Jesus. It speaks of his resurrection from

the dead, and of his bringing salvation to the Gentiles (2.32; 2.68, etc.). Scripture thus bears living witness both to God's 'mighty works, wonders and signs' (Acts 2.22), but also to 'the definite plan and foreknowledge of God' (Acts 2.23). For Luke the Old Testament bears testimony to this divine plan, which is both real and truthful, whether recognized or not (Acts 28.25ff.).

Because of this unity of scripture and tradition, Luke can portray two different strategies for mission. When addressing Jews, the apostles are pictured as arguing from scripture 'explaining and proving that it was necessary for the Christ to suffer and rise' (Acts 17.2; cf. also the speeches of Peter and Paul, Acts 2.14ff.; 4.5ff., etc.). Proof-from-prophecy is the means by which the witness to the Jews is made. A major point of Luke's prologue – 'to show the truthfulness of the great events fulfilled among us' – fits in with this same approach. However, when addressing non-Jews the appeal can be made directly to the witness of the Spirit. Thus, Peter makes his defence in Jerusalem that God has given to the non-Jews the gift of the same Spirit (Acts 11.17). Peter does not make his witness to the Gentile, Cornelius, by means of a proof-from-prophecy, yet he still testifies that the gospel he preaches is supported by all the prophets (10.43). Scripture through the Spirit speaks of a divine reality which has been fixed by the counsel of God. Although the strategy employed in different contexts within the pluralism of the Roman world can vary greatly, this diversity in approach in no way represents a tension within Luke's theology.

Several larger theological implications can be drawn from Luke's use of the Old Testament. The scriptures of the Jews provide the context from which Jesus' life is read and understood. Above all, Luke does not attempt to christianize the Old Testament, but to let it speak in its own voice of the coming salvation. This characterization is not to deny that Luke's own perspective and Hellenistic environ-ment provided a filter through which the Jewish scriptures were read. After all it was the Septuagint which he consistently used. Nevertheless, the major point to be made is that Luke's explicit intention was to relate the story of Jesus to the story of Israel. Therefore, to address the subject of the canonical shape of Luke's Gospel is also to come to grips with Luke's understanding of the continuity between Israel and the church.

Again, a confirmation of the centrality of the Old Testament prophecy for Luke's Gospel is found in his ecclesiology (cf. especially

Lohfink, *Die Sammlung Israels*). Luke does not speak of the 'founding' of the church or even of the formation of a 'new Israel'. Rather, Jesus' call to faith serves both to gather and to divide Israel. From his disciples, who form the core of the true Israel, the proclamation extends to all the nations and Israel's mission is brought to completion. To characterize Luke's theology as the 'beginning of Christendom' (*initium Christianismi*) which is Käsemann's formulation ('The Problem of the Historical Jesus', 29), finds no warrant in this depiction of the church's role.

V. The Canonical Shape of Luke as a Separate Book

A final question regarding the canonical shape of Luke's Gospel turns on the issue of the effect of the canonization process which separated Luke's two volumes and assigned each a different canonical function within the larger corpus of the New Testament. This issue will be discussed at greater length in the chapter on the book of Acts. However, two initial observations concerning Luke are in order:

(*a*) First, on the basis of the prologue to Luke's Gospel the case has been made for the original integrity of the gospel as a separate entity. The second volume of the Acts was added later. Accordingly, the form of Luke's first volume as a gospel did not derive from the later canonical decision to divide the work into two. At most the separation of the two books left its literary mark on the final section of the Gospel but did not determine the genre of the first volume. The Gospel of Luke often reflects the life of the post-resurrection church, but does not show a literary knowledge of the book of Acts.

(*b*) Secondly, the placing of Luke's Gospel within the larger context of a fourfold Gospel collection affected the reading of Luke, as it did each of the individual Gospels, by enlarging the original context. However, specifically the new position of Luke within the larger corpus served to relativize Luke's prologue. That is to say, regardless of how one understood Luke's references to the 'many earlier attempts' (1.1), Luke's claim to give a superior account was not honoured in regard to the canonical Gospels. The integrity of his witness was fully accepted, but neither as superior nor inferior to the other three.

8

JOHN

Commentaries

H. A. W. Meyer, MeyerK, 1834
(^{5}1896)
F. A. G. Tholuck, ET 1859
F. Godet, ET 1876–77
B. F. Westcott, 1880
B. Weiss, MeyerK, ET ^{8}1893
J. Wellhausen, 1908
W. Heitmüller, *SNT*, ^{3}1918
A. Loisy, ^{2}1921
T. Zahn, KNT, $^{5/6}$1921
J. H. Bernard, ICC, 1928
G. H. C. MacGregor, MNTC, 1929
H. Odeberg, 1929
W. Bauer, HNT, ^{3}1933
F. Büchsel, NTD, ^{2}1935
M.-J. Lagrange, ÉB, ^{5}1936
E. Hoskyns, F. N. Davey, ^{2}1947
R. H. Lightfoot, 1956
A. Schlatter, ^{3}1960

A. Wikenhauser, RNT, ^{3}1961
H. Strathmann, NTD, ^{10}1963
J. Marsh, Pel, 1963
J. N. Sanders, B. A. Mastin,
B/HNTC, 1968
R. E. Brown, AB, 1966–70
R. Bultmann, MeyerK, ^{16}1959; ET
1971
L. Morris, NICNT, 1972
B. Lindars, NCeB, 1972
J. Schneider, THKNT
(Sonderband) 1976
S. Schulz, NTD, ^{14}1978
C. K. Barrett, (1955), ^{2}1978
E. Haenchen, 1980
J. Becker, ÖTK, 1979–81
R. Schnackenburg HTKNT
1965–75, ET 1968–82

Bibliography

B. W. **Bacon**, *The Gospel of the Hellenists*, New York 1933; J. A. **Bailey**, *The Traditions common to the Gospels of Luke and John*, SNTSM 7, 1963; W. **Baldensperger**,*Der Prolog des Vierten Evangeliums. Sein polemisch-apologetischer Zweck*, Freiberg 1898; C. K. **Barrett**, 'The Old Testament in the Fourth Gospel', *JTS* 48, 1947, 155–69; *The Gospel of John and Judaism*, London and Philadelphia 1975; *Essays on John*, London and Philadelphia 1982; F. C. **Baur**, 'Zur johanneischen Frage', *ThJb* 16, 1857, 209–57; H. **Becker**, *Die Reden des Johannesevangeliums und der Stil der gnostischen Offenbarungsrede*, FRLANT 68, 1956; J. **Becker**, 'Aufbau, Schichtung und theologiegeschichtliche Stellung des Gebets in Johannes 17', *ZNW* 60, 1969, 56–83; 'Wunder und Christologie: zum literarkritischen und christologischen Problem der Wunder im Johannes-Evangelium', *NTS* 16, 1969/70, 130–48; 'Die Abschiedsreden Jesu im Johannesevangelium', *ZNW* 61, 1970, 215–46; J. **Blank**, *Krisis. Untersuchungen zur johanneischen Christologie und Eschatologie*, Freiburg 1964; J. **Blinzler**, *Johannes und die Synoptiker*, SBS 5, 1965; M.-É. **Boismard**, 'Le Chapître XXI de Saint Jean', *RB* 54, 1947, 473–501; *Le Prologue de Saint Jean*, Paris 1953; 'Saint Luc et la rédaction du quatrième évangile', *RB* 69, 1962, 185–211; P. **Borgen**, *Bread from Heaven*, Leiden 1965; G. **Bornkamm**, 'Zur Interpretation des Johannes-Evangeliums', *EvTh* 28, 1968, 8–25; reprinted *Geschichte und Glaube* I (*GA* III), Munich 1968, 104–21; J. W. **Bowker**, 'The Origin and Purpose of St John's Gospel', *NTS* 11, 1964/5, 398–408; F. M. **Braun**, *Jean le Theologien*, 3 vols., Paris 1959–68; H. **Braun**, *Qumran und das Neue Testament*, 2 vols., Tübingen 1966; R. E. **Brown**, 'The Paraclete in the Fourth Gospel', *NTS* 13, 1966/7, 113–32; 'The Kerygma of the Gospel according to John', *Interp* 21, 1967, 387–400; *The Community of the Beloved Disciple*, New York 1979; R. **Bultmann**, 'Der religionsgeschichtliche Hintergrund des Prologs zum Johannesevangelium', *Eucharisterion*, *FS H. Gunkel*, ed. H. Schmidt, FRLANT 36, 1923, II, 3–26; reprinted *Exegetica*, Tübingen 1967, 10–35; 'Die Bedeutung der neu erschlossenen mandäischen und manichäischen Quellen für das Verständnis des Johannesevangelium', *ZNW* 24, 1925, 100–46; reprinted *Exegetica*, 55–104; 'Untersuchungen zum Johannesevangelium', *ZNW* 27, 1928, 113–63; ibid. 29, 1930, 169–92; reprinted *Exegetica*, 124–97.

K. L. **Carroll**, 'The Fourth Gospel and the Exclusion of Christians from the Synagogue', *BJRL* 40, 1957/8, 19–32; D. A. **Carson**, 'Understanding Misunderstandings in the Fourth Gospel', *TynBul* 33, 1982, 59–91; J. H. **Charlesworth**, ed., *John and Qumran*, London 1972; O. **Cullmann**, 'Der johanneische Gebrauch doppeldeutiger Ausdrücke als Schlüssel zum Verständnis des vierten Evangeliums', *TZ* 4, 1948, 360–72; *Early Christian Worship*, ET, SBT 10, 1953; *Peter: Disciple, Apostle, Martyr*, ET London and Philadelphia ²1962; *The Johannine Circle*, ET London and Philadelphia 1976; R. A. **Culpepper**, *The Johannine School*, SBLDS 26, Missoula 1975; *Anatomy of the Fourth Gospel*, Philadelphia 1983; N. A. **Dahl**, 'The Johannine Church and History' (1962), reprinted, *Jesus in the Memory of the Early Church*, Minneapolis 1976, 99–119; C. **Dekker**, 'Grundschrift und Redaktion im Johannesevangelium', *NTS* 13, 1966/7, 66–80; J. D. M. **Derrett**, 'Water into Wine', *BZ* 7, 1963, 80–97; C. H. **Dodd**, *The Interpretation of the Fourth Gospel*, Cambridge 1953; *Historical Tradition in the Fourth Gospel*, Cambridge 1963; J. D. G. **Dunn**, 'John VI – a Eucharistic Discourse', *NTS* 17, 1970/1, 328–38; R. T, **Fortna**, *The Gospel of Signs*, SNTSMS 11, 1970; 'From Christology to Soteriology – A Redaction-Critical Study of Salvation in the Fourth Gospel', *Interp* 27, 1973, 31–47; 'Christology in the Fourth Gospel', *NTS* 21, 1974/5, 489–504.

P. **Gardner-Smith**, *Saint John and the Synoptic Gospels*, Cambridge 1938;

E. R. **Goodenough**, 'John a Primitive Gospel', *JBL* 64, 1945, 145–82; E. **Grässer**, 'Die antijüdische Polemik im Johannesevangelium', *NTS* 11, 1964/5, 74–90; A. **Guilding**, *The Fourth Gospel and Jewish Worship*, Oxford 1960; R. **Gyllenberg**, 'Die Anfänge der johanneischen Tradition', *Neutestamentliche Studien für R. Bultmann*, ed. W. Eltester, BZNW 21, 1954, 144–7. K. **Haacker**, *Die Stiftung des Heils*, Stuttgart 1972; E. **Haenchen**, 'Aus der Literatur zum Johannesevangelium 1929–56', *ThR* 23, 1955, 295–335; 'Johanneische Probleme', *ZTK* 56, 1959, 19–54; 'Der Vater, der mich gesandt hat', *NTS* 9, 1962/3, 208–16; 'Probleme des johanneischen Prologs', *ZTK* 60, 1963, 305–34; 'Das Johannesevangelium und sein Kommentar', *TLZ* 89, 1964, 881–98; F. **Hahn**, 'Der Prozeß Jesu nach dem Johannesevangelium', *EKK* 2, 1970, 23–96; A. **von Harnack**, 'Über das Verhältnis des Prologs des vierten Evangeliums zum ganzen Werk', *ZTK* 2, 1892, 189–231; 'Das "Wir" in den johanneischen Schriften', *SAB* (Phil.-hist. Klasse), 1923, 96–113; J. R. **Harris**, *The Origin of the Prologue to St John's Gospel*, Cambridge 1917; E. **Hirsch**, *Studien zum vierten Evangelium*, Tübingen 1936; W. F. **Howard**, *The Fourth Gospel in Recent Criticism and Interpretation*, revised by C. K. Barrett, London and Naperville [4]1955.

J. **Jeremias**, 'A Comparison of the Marcan Passion Narrative with the Johannine', *The Eucharistic Words of Jesus*, ET, rev. ed., London and New York 1966, 89–96; G. **Johnston**, *The Spirit-Paraclete in the Gospel of John*, SNTSM 12, 1970; M. **de Jonge**, *Jesus: Stranger from Heaven and Son of God*, Missoula 1977; ed., *L'Évangile de Jean: Sources, rédaction, theologie*, BETL 44, 1977; E. **Käsemann**, *The Testament of Jesus*, ET London and Philadelphia 1968; 'The Structure and Purpose of the Prologue to John's Gospel', ET, *New Testament Questions of Today*, London and Philadelphia 1969, 138–67; A. **Kragerud**, *Der Lieblingsjünger im Johannesevangelium*, Oslo 1959; R. **Kysar**, *The Fourth Evangelist and His Gospel*, Minneapolis 1975; H. **Leroy**, *Rätsel und Missverständnis*, BBB 30, 1968; B. **Lindars**, 'The Fourth Gospel: An Act of Contemplation', in *Studies in the Fourth Gospel*, ed. F. L. Cross, London 1957, 23–35; *Behind the Fourth Gospel*, London 1971; E. **Lohse**, 'Wort und Sakrament im Johannesevangelium', *NTS* 7, 1960/61, 110–25.

J. L. **Martyn**, *History and Theology in the Fourth Gospel* (1968), Nashville [2]1979; *The Gospel of John in Christian History*, New York 1978; W. A. **Meeks**, *The Prophet-King. Moses Traditions and the Johannine Christology*, NovTSuppl 14, 1967; 'The Man from Heaven in Johannine Sectarianism', *JBL* 91, 1972, 44–72; '"Am I a Jew?" Johannine Christianity and Judaism', *Christianity, Judaism and other Greco-Roman Cults, FS Morton Smith*, ed. J. Neusner, I, New Testament, Leiden 1975, 163–86; P. S. **Minear**, 'The Audience of the Fourth Gospel', *Interp* 31, 1977, 339–54; 'Logos Ecclesiology in John's Gospel', *Christological Perspectives, Essays in Honor of H. K. McArthur*, ed. R. F. Berkey and S. A. Edwards, New York 1982, 95–111; 'The Original Function of John 21', *JBL* 102, 1983, 85–98; J. P. **Miranda**, *Der Vater, der mich gesandt hat*, Bern/Frankfurt 1972; F. **Mussner**, *Zoe. Die Anschauung von 'Leben' im vierten Evangelium*, Munich 1952; 'Die johanneischen Parakletsprüche und die apostolische Tradition', *BZ* 5, 1961, 56–70; W. **Nicol**, *The Sēmeia in the Fourth Gospel. Tradition and Redaction*, NovTSuppl 32, 1972; B. **Noack**, *Zur johanneischen Tradition*, Copenhagen 1954.

B. **Olsson**, *Structure and Meaning in the Fourth Gospel*, Lund 1974; E. **Pagels**, *The Johannine Gospel in Gnostic Exegesis*, Missoula 1973; S. **Pancaro**, 'The Relationship of the Church to Israel in the Gospel of John', *NTS* 21, 1974/75, 396–405; P. **Parker**, 'Two Editions of John', *JBL* 75, 1956, 303–14; 'John the Son of Zebedee and the Fourth Gospel', *JBL* 81, 1962, 35–43; R. **Pesch**, *Der reiche Fischfang (Lk 5, 1–11/ Jo 21, 1–15). Wundergeschichte – Berufungsgeschichte – Erscheinungsbericht*, Düsseldorf 1969; T. E. **Pollard**, *Johannine Christology and the Early Church*, SNTSM 13, 1970; F. **Porsch**, *Pneuma und Wort. Ein exegetischer Beitrag zur Pneumatologie des Johannesevangeliums*, Frankfurt 1974; G. **Reim**, *Studien zum alttestamentlichen Hintergrund des Johannesevangelium*, Cambridge 1974; K. H. **Rengstorf**, ed., *Johannes und sein Evangelium*, WdF 82, 1973; G. **Richter**, *Studien zum Johannesevangelium*, BU 13, 1977; J. M. **Robinson**, 'The Johannine Trajectory', *Trajectories through Early Christianity*, Philadelphia 1971, 232–68; J. A. T. **Robinson**, 'The Destination and Purpose of St John's Gospel', *NTS* 6, 1959/69, 117–31, reprinted *Twelve New Testament Studies*, SBT 34, 1962, 107–25: 'The Relation of the Prologue to the Gospel of St John', *NTS* 9, 1962/3, 120–9, reprinted *Twelve More New Testament Studies*, London and Philadelphia 1984, 65–76; E. **Ruckstuhl**, *Die literarische Einheit des Johannesevangeliums*, Freiburg 1951; 'Zur Aussage und Botschaft von Johannes 21', in *Die Kirche des Anfangs*, FS H. *Schürmann*, ed. R. Schnackenburg, Leipzig 1977, 339–62.

J. N. **Sanders**, *The Fourth Gospel in the Early Church*, Cambridge 1943; A. **Schlatter**, *Sprache und Heimat des vierten Evangelisten*, Gütersloh 1902; H. **Schlier**, '"Im Anfang war das Wort". Zum Prolog des Johannesevangeliums', in *Die Zeit der Kirche*, Freiburg, ³1962, 274–87; R. **Schnackenburg**, 'Joh 12, 39–41. Zur christologischen Schriftauslegung des vierten Evangelisten', *Neues Testament und Geschichte*, FS O. *Cullmann*, ed. H. Baltensweiler and B. Reicke, Zürich and Tübingen 1972, 167–77; 'Das Anliegen der Abschiedsrede in Joh 14', *Wort Gottes in der Zeit*, FS K. H. *Schelkle*, ed. H. Feld and J. Nolte, Düsseldorf 1973, 89–104; J. **Schniewind**, *Die Parallelperikopen bei Lukas und Johannes*, Leipzig 1914; reprinted Darmstadt ³1970; L. **Schottroff**, *Der Glaubende und die feindliche Welt*, WMANT 37, 1970; H. **Schürmann**, 'Jesu letzte Weisung Jo 19, 26–27a', *Ursprung und Gestalt*, Düsseldorf 1970, 13–28; S. **Schulz**, *Untersuchungen zur Menschensohnchristologie im Johannesevangelium*, Göttingen 1957; *Komposition und Herkunft der johanneischen Reden*, BWANT 5. 1, 1960; E. **Schwartz**, 'Aporien im vierten Evangelium', *Nachrichten von der königlichen Gesellschaft der Wissenschaft zu Göttingen*, Phil. -hist. Klasse, Berlin 1907, 342–72; 1908, 115–88, 497–560; E. **Schweizer**, *Ego Eimi*, FRLANT 56, 1939, ²1965; 'The concept of the Church in the Gospel and Epistles of St John', *New Testament Essays, Studies in Memory of T. W. Manson*, ed. A. J. B. Higgins, Manchester 1959, 230–45; G. T. **Sheppard**, *Wisdom as a Hermeneutical Construct*, BZAW 151, 1980; J. S.

Siker-Gieseler, 'Disciples and Discipleship in the Fourth Gospel: A Canonical Approach', *Studia Biblica et Theologica* 10, 1980, 199–225; A. J. **Simonis**, *Die Hirtenrede im Johannes-Evangelium*, AnBib 29, 1967; S. S. **Smalley**, 'Diversity and Development in John', *NTS* 17, 1970/71, 276–92; 'The Signs in John XXI', *NTS* 20, 1973/4, 275–88; *John, Evangelist and Interpreter*, Exeter 1978; D. M. **Smith**, 'The Sources of the Gospel of John. An Assessment of the Present State of the Problem', *NTS* 10, 1963/4, 336–51; *The Composition and Order of the Fourth Gospel*, New Haven 1965; 'Johannine Christianity: Some Reflections on its Character and Delineation', *NTS* 21, 1974/5, 222–48; *John* (Proclamation Commentaries), Philadelphia 1976.

H. M. **Teeple**, *The Literary Origin of the Gospel of John*, Evanston 1974; W. **Thüsing**, *Die Erhöhung und Verherrlichung Jesu im Johannesevangelium*, Münster 1970; H. **Thyen**, 'Aus der Literatur zum Johannesevangelium', *ThR* 39, 1974/5, 1–69, 222–52, 289–330; 'Entwicklungen innerhalb der johanneischen Theologie und Kirche im Spiegel von Joh 21 und der Lieblingsjüngertexte des Evangeliums', in M. de Jonge, ed., *L'Évangile*, 259–99; W. C. **van Unnik**, 'The Purpose of St John's Gospel', (I), TU 73, 1959, 382–411; M. F. **Wiles**, *The Spiritual Gospel. The Interpretation of the Fourth Gospel in the Early Church*, Cambridge and New York 1960; W. **Wilkens**, *Die Entstehungsgeschichte des vierten Evangeliums*, Zürich-Zollikon 1958; 'Die Erweckung des Lazarus', *TZ* 15, 1959, 22–39; *Zeichen und Werke*, Zürich 1969; H. **Windisch**, 'Der Johanneische Erzählungsstil', *Eucharisterion* II, *FS H.* Gunkel, FRLANT 36, 1923, 174–213; *Johannes und die Synoptiker*, Leipzig 1926; *The Spirit-Paraclete in the Fourth Gospel*, ET Philadelphia 1968; W. **Wrede**, *Charakter und Tendenz des Johannesevangeliums*, Tübingen ²1933.

The literature of modern scholarship on the Gospel of John is quite overwhelming and far exceeds any one person's ability to master it. Fortunately, there has also been a steady stream of books and articles over the years which have tried to summarize and evaluate the state of the field (e. g. Barrett's rev. ed. of Howard, Haenchen, Kysar, Brown, Smith).

In my opinion, this important history of research stands in a dialectical relationship to a canonical reading. Because of the nature of the questions raised and the answers given, historical critical scholarship can never be disregarded; however, seldom does it offer an adequate solution to the hermeneutical issues at stake. The issue is not that criticism is radical or skeptical in its assumptions. (I do not share this conservative apologetic.) Rather, a different relationship to the text is held from that usually assumed by the historical critical approach. I am fully aware that in suggesting that an understanding of John's Gospel does not stand in a relationship of direct dependency upon theories of the book's origin, historical setting, and authorship one runs in the face of a wide consensus. Thus, I disagree heartily with the common critical view recently expressed by B. Lindars. He writes: 'The effort to get behind the Fourth Gospel is not simply a literary-critical game, but an inescapable task in the process of discovering the real meaning. . . .' (*Behind the Fourth Gospel*, 22). However, rather than pursuing the issue further in a theoretical fashion, I shall try to demonstrate with the material itself the nature of the canonical approach's indirect relationship to the historical critical enterprise.

I. Historical-critical Questions in Canonical Perspective

A. *Structure and Style*

There is general agreement regarding the larger structure of the book that it falls into two main sections (1.19–12.50 and 13.1–20.29). The book is introduced by a prologue (1.1–18) and concluded with an epilogue (21.1–25). However, there are major literary problems which have continued to resist a fully satisfactory solution. On the one hand, there is a strong stylistic unity and thematic coherence to the book. On the other hand, the transitions by which the various episodes are linked are frequently very rough and chronologically confusing. Moreover, the movement of the narrative is of such redundancy and complexity as to cause Hoskyns to speak of its spiral quality (66f.).

The peculiarities of John's literary style have long been noticed (cf. Wrede's classic description). Putative events are first described which toward the end of a unit begin to dissolve into speeches with little indication of when the narrative concludes (e.g. ch. 3). The people who are portrayed in various situations also tend to lose their sharp profiles and become representative figures. However, the fundamental problem of style with which critical scholarship has wrestled has to do with the peculiarities of the Fourth Gospel which stand in striking discontinuity with the synoptic gospels. In the place of the succinct, aphoristic sayings which dominate the other gospels, the Jesus of John's Gospel engages in lengthy monologues. The familiar parables of the synoptics are also missing, and the frequent reports of miracles have been replaced by allegorical-like signs. The effect of this peculiar form of narrative on the portrait of Jesus has, of course, emerged as a major issue for generations of interpreters.

B. *Purpose of the Gospel*

The debate as to the author's intention in writing this gospel has tended to focus on the so-called 'first conclusion' of the book in 20.30f. Upon an initial reading it would appear that the author has set down his purpose in a completely straightforward fashion: 'these are written that you may believe that Jesus is the Christ . . .'; however, upon closer examination a variety of problems of interpretation has emerged.

First, the textual problem of the verb in 20.31 raises the question as to whether the verse should be translated in the present subjunctive – 'that you may continue to believe' – which would imply the writer's purpose was to strengthen those already in the faith. Or is the aorist subjunctive to be preferred – 'that you might come to believe' – which would suggest the book was directed to non-Christians? Secondly, it has been argued (cf. Bultmann) that this ending originally marked the conclusion of the 'book of signs' and does not adequately formulate the purpose of the entire book. In fact, several commentators suggest that each individual hand at work on the book's composition may have had a different purpose. Finally, the ending is thought to be far too general and vague to explain the complexity of the book and the specific function within a concrete, historical milieu (so Cullmann).

For these reasons scholars have sought for clues elsewhere in the book and indeed outside the book by which to explain the original intention lying behind the writing of the gospel. The various theories are well known and rehearsed in every manual. For example, J. A. T. Robinson and van Unnik have argued that the Gospel served as a missionary handbook to convert the Diaspora Jews. Baldensperger saw an apologetic purpose to counter the sectarianism of a group around John the Baptist. Wilkens finds the Gospel's intention to be primarily one of opposing gnostic heresy and docetic teachings. R. E. Brown, Martyn, and Meeks agree in focusing on the book's role in establishing a community's social identity in the context of conflicting group struggle. Finally, Barrett, as a reaction to the stress on external factors, argues for the primacy of the author's internal reasons which were independent of whether the book was ever read by others.

In my judgment, each of these various theories regarding the author's intention has found some biblical evidence from which at least to begin. Nor are all the hypotheses mutually exclusive. However, I would argue that these interpretations do not do justice to the canonical function of this first conclusion. The various theories seek to give to the passage an historical concreteness which it simply does not have. More importantly, the search for the author's intentionality has tended to flatten the theological dimension of the conclusion by failing to follow the direction which the ending has acquired in its larger canonical role.

It is not by chance that the conclusion follows closely the conversation of the risen Christ with Thomas. Thomas' belief based on his encounter with the risen Christ is contrasted with those who are commended for their belief without having actually seen the Christ. The conclusion continues this same line of thought as it addresses an unspecified audience which is designated 'you'. The question as to whether these persons are Christian or non-Christian plays no significant role. Rather, the weight of the ending falls elsewhere. A selection of Jesus' signs has been made from many which he had given. This is to say, only a portion of the tradition has been presented as a summary statement of the whole book. The signs are related no longer either to an alleged sign source, or just to the resurrection, but encompass the whole ministry of Christ. The evangelist bears witness to Christ's earthly life, lived in the presence of his disciples, yet the witness is directed to another audience different from those original disciples. This audience is not explicitly identified with the future generation of readers. However, by distinguishing the addressee from the original audience, and identifying it with the readership of the present book, the ending functions in effect as a canonical device for addressing every succeeding generation.

This ending has shaped the Gospel material in a canonical fashion by designating the book as the medium through which future generations who did not encounter the earthly Jesus are challenged to believe. Moreover, the ending makes explicit that the selection of material is not designed to provide a biography of Jesus, but serves rather to evoke faith in Jesus as the Christ. The two christological formulations, 'Jesus is the Christ', 'the Son of God', are used in a fully Christian sense and are not indications of a specific first-century constituency. The evangelist thus renders the material into a Gospel, that is, its construal points toward the goal of salvation. It is not enough to report the resurrection appearances, but essential is a faithful response which is appropriate to this divine offer of life through his name.

c. The Addressee of the Gospel

Closely linked to the purpose of the Gospel is the question regarding the addressee of the book. In addition to the peculiarities of the literary form of the Fourth Gospel, the unusual content has intensified the search for the specific historical milieu of the book as one important avenue for illuminating its many perplexing features.

Toward the end of the nineteenth century and well into the twentieth century, the debate regarding the book's background and historical addressee was polarized about the issue of whether Hellenistic or Jewish (rabbinic) influences were primary (Harnack, Bacon vs. Schlatter, Billerbeck). However, increasingly it has become evident that this way of posing the historical questions rested on a construct which did not reflect the complexity of first century Syro-Palestine. A much more subtle description was called for which also resisted the geographical polarization between Palestine and the diaspora. In recent years much effort has been expended in sketching features of an alleged Gnostic milieu, although debate continues regarding the evangelist's direct relation to Gnosticism itself. Increasingly, however, a critical consensus has emerged which characterizes the immediate milieu of the gospel as a syncretistic form of heterodox Judaism and which has sought support from both Qumran and Nag Hammadi. Still a considerable diversity exists in the detailed profiling of the environment (cf. Odeberg, Cullmann, R. E. Brown). Research in comparative religion has also thrown considerable light on peculiar features of the Johannine idiom such as Braun's study of wisdom, Schweizer's '*ego eimi*' formula, and Borgen's targum-like exegesis.

There is another aspect to the problem of determining the addressee of the book. Because of the complexity of the history of the book's composition, many scholars have begun to question whether the issue of establishing one addressee has all but lost its meaning. Some would argue that a variety of different historical addressees are involved which shift according to the individual layer of tradition or stage of redaction. Finally, some would argue that even in its final form the semantic level on which the Fourth Gospel is to be read has not been established and therefore the addressee can fluctuate from level to level, depending on the function assigned to symbolic language within the Gospel.

One of the basic hermeneutical issues at stake in this debate turns on the problem of the antecedents of understanding. An axiom of the critical method is that a proper interpretation of John's Gospel is dependent upon a correct historical assessment of the decisions affecting the material prior to John's appropriation of it. The hermeneutical issue turns on whether the canonical shape provides its own key to the antecedents of understanding. It is significant that the evangelist (or redactor) has supplied the reader with a running commentary on a variety of subjects which do require additional information. The commentary is of different sorts. Often a Hebrew term is translated for the benefit of a reader whose comprehension of the situation requires specific knowledge (1.38, 41; 4.25; 5.2; 9.7; 19.17; 20.16). At other times, material is supplied which provides the needed historical context. Thus, 4.9 explains the historical relation between Jews and Samaritans as a needed commentary on Christ's conversation. Again, Jewish religious practices are explained, important geographical places are indicated (6.1), or distinctions between persons clarified to avoid misunderstanding (14.22). Finally, the writer makes explicit reference to the Old Testament scriptures as establishing the context from which an event was to be understood (19.28). Specifically in terms of the issue of the book's addressee the crucial canonical issue focuses on determining to what extent the canon has provided its own information commensurate with the kind of understanding it seeks to evoke.

My concern in offering a different approach to the problem is not to denigrate the prior efforts, nor to contest the complexity of the literary and historical evidence. Rather, it is to raise the question as to whether sufficient attention has been paid to the effect of the book's canonical shaping on the issue of the addressee. In other words, can one speak of a canonical addressee in the Fourth Gospel who is not simply identified with an historical audience? Does the depicted addressee function differently in the Fourth Gospel, say, from that of the Johannine epistles?

P. Minear once observed that the Gospel of John makes a significant distinction between 'disciples at first hand', and 'disciples at second hand'. Particularly in John 17 Jesus prays not only for his disciples to whom he has given his words (v. 8), but also for those who come to faith through the word of that first generation: 'who believe in me through their word'. Minear argues that this latter group is to be identified with a second generation of disciples and that the evangelist goes to considerable effort in overcoming a generation gap. It is certainly possible that Minear is right in sensing a problem which did emerge historically between the first two generations of disciples. However, R. E. Brown is closer to describing the canonical function of this distinction when he understands the addressee of the second group as being 'Christians of all times'. Certainly the weight of the distinction falls on those who were with him during his earthly ministry and those who know him only through his word. Whether the gap is of one generation or a hundred does not affect how belief in the exalted Christ is evoked.

Nevertheless, to suggest that the disciples are portrayed as models for future believers, both in their acceptance and misunderstanding of Jesus' word (de Jonge, *Jesus*, 15), does not fully reflect the canonical function to which the disciples have been assigned by the Fourth Gospel. In the canonical shaping of the Fourth Gospel the theme of discipleship has been developed along two lines, disciples and discipleship. (I am indebted to J. S. Siker-Gieseler's essay for this insight.) The disciples, as the historic Twelve, function primarily on the surface level in John. They are chosen by Jesus and accompany him. They are portrayed as doing many things in John's Gospel, some negative and some positive. They follow, believe, confess, misunderstand, object, and are confused. What is striking in the treatment of the disciples is that the evangelist frequently provides a commentary which sets the reader apart from the historical disciples. The disciples' objections and misunderstandings (4.31; 7.34; 8.21) derive from a surface meaning which misses the real depth of Jesus' sayings, but the reader is informed as to its true signficance. In one sense the disciples are the foils of true discipleship which will encounter similar issues, but needs to respond in a way different from the original Twelve.

The positive side of discipleship in John's Gospel is portrayed in separate scenes within a narrative context (cf. Siker-Gieseler). In the conversation with the Samaritan woman the nature of true faith is explicated as the woman is progressively led from the surface discussion to a depth knowledge of Christ's offer of eternal life.

However, the climax of the chapter comes when the Samaritans from the city are led to believe in Jesus as the Messiah because of his words (4.42). Again, the Capernaum official (4.46ff.) is challenged to believe on the basis of Jesus' word without first seeing signs and wonders. Likewise, the man born blind (9.1–41) is slowly led to believe in Christ through a lengthy debate with his detractors and finally confesses his faith before Jesus which, however, had already emerged from his healing power at a time when Jesus was not present. In all these narratives the emphasis falls on what it means to be a disciple after the departure of Jesus. These disciples are never pictured as accompanying him, but rather they believe because of his word. Conversely those who oppose faith in Christ, and are designated as the 'Jews', represent a theological construct, and not a specific historical entity. They are characterized as belonging to the hostile world of unbelief.

D. *The Authorship of the Fourth Gospel*

The authorship of the Fourth Gospel has been hotly debated for over 150 years. The traditional view has sought to defend the church's identification of the author with John, the son of Zebedee, on both internal and external grounds. Conversely, the critical view has questioned the identification on the same grounds, and sought to reconstruct more plausible historical theories of composition. In my opinion, the most striking feature of this debate has been that neither the traditional nor the critical perspectives have been sufficiently concerned to deal seriously with the theological function of the problem of authorship within the Gospel. The one obvious exception is the sensitive theological treatment of Hoskyns, which comes the closest in offering a canonical reading of this element of the Gospel.

The initial point to make is that the anonymity of the author has been preserved throughout the Gospel. Never once is John, the son of Zebedee, mentioned as the author, rather the writer's identity is intentionally veiled. A major criticism of the traditional position which has been defended most ably by such giants in the field as Westcott, Lightfoot, Zahn and Lagrange, is that they seem unaware of running in the face of the canonical shaping. This statement is not to suggest that the historical question of the authorship of the Gospel is illegitimate, but that the traditional defence of the Johannine authorship derived from another concern which has greatly confused the theological issue. The traditional defence sought to establish the theological authority of the gospel by proving that its author was an eyewitness. Thus, the truth of the gospel and its historicity were equated. As a result, not only was the true canonical function of the Gospel's authorship overlooked, but a set of modern philosophical assumptions were introduced which seriously affected the exegetical task. Ironically, the critical position which largely succeeded in casting doubt on the traditional position took over and extended the same philosphical perspective as it sought to reconstruct the book's real authorship in order to evaluate its truth.

Nevertheless, it cannot be denied that the question of authorship is a genuine issue which is raised by the Gospel itself. 21.24 clearly poses the problem: 'This is the disciple who is bearing witness to these things, and who has written these things.' The reference is to the 'beloved disciple' who appeared in the previous paragraph. In this passage a misunderstanding of a saying of Jesus regarding this disciple has been corrected. Jesus did not say that the beloved disciple would not die before Christ's return. The implication of this passage is rather clear that he has indeed died. In v. 24 a voice, clearly different from that of the beloved disciple, now identifies the beloved disciple with the author of 'these things'.

The beloved disciple is first introduced in 13.23ff. during the last supper, but the remaining references all relate to Christ's death and resurrection (19.25–27; 20.2–11; 21.7; 21.20–23; 21.24). His role as the one who bears witness is explicitly made in 19.20 which offers the closest parallel to 21.24. The issue at stake in both these passages is the authority and truthfulness of his witness of which the book is testimony. Although the veil of his anonymity is never lifted, this disciple is placed at the cross as a witness. He also experiences the empty tomb and bears witness to Christ's resurrection.

Moreover, the authority of this disciple is confirmed by another voice: 'we know that his testimony is true' (21.24). The testimony of the apostolic community which had first borne witness to Christ's glory (1.14) confirms the truth of this Gospel. Harnack has argued that the 'we' in the Fourth Gospel was a fluctuating *persona* capable of expanding from singular to plural. However, I think that this interpretation confuses the historical dimension of the sequence of witnesses. The beloved disciple has died, but his witness lives on in a book and the living generation bears testimony to the truthfulness and authority of his words through whom they have believed. The

witness of the beloved disciple is not attested to by an historical
identification, but taken up into the living voice of the community
of the apostolic faith whose testimony now encompasses the entire
book.

The crucial methodological issue at stake is doing justice to the
theological function of the book's witness to authorship without
converting the question immediately into one of historicity. The
function of the book's authorship is not to establish an objective
historical source whose eyewitness can be confirmed by a neutral
public scrutiny. Rather, the author bears witness to a belief which
has arisen as a consequence of his seeing. He is given a vision of
reality which is inextricably grounded in his first-hand experience
with the earthly Jesus, but his witness cannot be construed as a
source whose authority derived from historical correspondence with
putative events and which are brought into conformity with the
canons of modern historical science. In sum, the issue of authorship
is a theological issue which functions in relation to the authority of
the witness within a community of faith. H. Schürmann expresses it
as follows: 'Jesus himself from the cross declares this gospel in a
certain sense to be "canonical" and normative for the church'
('Jesu Letzte Weisung', 25). Yet this theological witness leans over
backwards in insisting that the apostolic testimony is grounded in
an encounter with the Jesus who lived among them. Indeed, 'that
which . . . we have seen with our eyes, which we have looked upon
and touched with our hands, concerning the word of life. . . .'.

Finally, a word is in order concerning the important theological
function which the modern historical study of the book's composition
performs. By showing the multi-layered quality of the Fourth Gospel
whose composition extended over several generations within the first
century, an important corrective is provided against flattening the
theological issue of authorship into a simplistic relationship between
author and composition which has remained the nemesis of the
traditional reading of the gospel. Conversely, the inability of historical studies to identify historical authors does not require that the
historical lacunae be filled with speculative theories of authorship
before the exegetical task can be accomplished.

E. Tradents of the Tradition

No issue within the modern study of the Fourth Gospel illustrates better the shift of interest from the earlier focus on the peculiarities of an individual author to the new interest in the history of tradition. In spite of the impressive stylistic unity of the book, there is a widespread consensus that the text of the gospel is multi-layered and reflects a complex history of the growth of tradition.

One of the most notable features of the modern study of the Fourth Gospel concerns the relationship between it and the Synoptics. Much debate was carried on well into the 1930's regarding the extent of John's knowledge of the Synoptics. Opinion varied from those holding some knowledge on the part of the Fourth Gospel of all the other three, to knowledge only of a single Gospel. A corollary to this discussion focused then on the motivation for John's Gospel in the light of his remarkable discontinuity with the Synoptics. The most radical thesis suggested that the author had consciously sought to suppress the three earlier Gospels (Windisch, *Synoptiker*).

Usually the contemporary shift in perspective is attributed to the little monograph of Gardner-Smith in 1938. Clearly the law of diminishing returns had already begun in respect to the older theories of partial dependency and the discipline was predisposed to a fresh formulation of the relationship. Dodd's support of Gardner-Smith's theory that John's Gospel rested on independent oral tradition did much to enhance its credibility. In addition, the new insights which it brought respecting a more serious study of tradition was its greatest confirmation.

Much of the recent scholarly debate has turned on the nature of the sources – both oral and literary – used by John. Bultmann's elaborate source analysis has been a major catalyst. It is unnecessary once again to rehearse his theories (cf. D. M. Smith, *Composition*). Generally speaking, his hypothesis regarding a 'sign source' has received considerable support and has been vigorously pursued by Fortna, Nicol, and Teeple, among others. One of the great attractions of a source theory is that it enables one to distinguish more sharply between tradition and redaction which is a concern lying at the heart of much of the interest in Johannine source analysis (cf. also J. M. Robinson's 'Johannine Trajectory' depiction, *Trajectories*). However, it should also be noted that a strong minority voice continues to question the possibility of sharply distinguishing between tradition and redaction. Thus, Dahl has no doubt regarding the complicated history of traditions preceding the present literary form of the Gospel, but opposes Bultmann's analysis by identifying the evangelist with the so-called ecclesiastical editor of the tradition ('The Johannine Church', 119).

In my opinion, the crucial hermeneutical question respecting the issue of sources has been correctly posed already by Hoskyns:

> The important question is not whether the Fourth Gospel depends upon oral tradition, or upon written documents, or upon both, but whether it is, or is not, a work existing in its own right, and whether it is or is not to be interpreted independently and by itself (68).

To the extent in which source analysis can aid in understanding the final form of the Gospel, it is to be welcomed. That this function has not been usually supported (e.g. Bultmann, Robinson, etc.) should not call into question its genuine potential for interpretation.

F. Levels of Tradition

There is another issue regarding the role of the tradents of Johannine tradition which has emerged in recent years as a problem of major proportion. The scholar whose work lies at the centre of the debate is clearly J. L. Martyn. In addition, many others have entered into the discussion and the arguments continue to be developed (G. Richter, O. Cullmann, Boismard, etc.). R. E. Brown has recently formulated the basic issue with his customary clarity: 'The Gospel must be read on several levels, so that it tells us the story both of Jesus and of the community that believed on him' (*Community*, 17). The credit for first developing a comprehensive theory for reading the Gospel on different levels goes to Martyn. Starting with his monograph, *History and Theology in the Fourth Gospel* (1968) and refined and summarized a decade later ('Glimpses', *The Gospel of John in Christian History*), Martyn has developed the thesis that the Fourth Gospel is to be interpreted as a multi-layered text which reflects the various struggles within the history of the Johannine community. In his latest essay, he traces three periods of conflict: early, middle, late. The most important was the middle period during the late 80s in which the synagogue leaders introduced into the liturgical service a reworked form of the *birkat ha-minim* (the ban on deviators) in order to identify and to expel those Jews who confessed Jesus as the Messiah.

the hermeneutical effect of this reconstruction of the history of the Johannine church is then developed by Martyn in a detailed exegesis of John 9. According to his reading, the text must be read on two different levels. It is a witness to a discrete event in Jesus' earthly life, but it is also a witness to the experience of the Johannine church. The evangelist used this literary device of dual textual levels to show how the risen Lord continues his earthly ministry in the ongoing proclamation of the church. Martyn therefore reads the story as a drama reflecting the community's struggle with Judaism leading up to and following the synagogue ban.

There is a wide consensus that Martyn has greatly illuminated the text by seeing it in relation to the expulsion from the synagogue. A comparison of commentaries on the Fourth Gospel which precede Martyn's work demonstrates the new dimension of historical particularity which Martyn has been able to achieve. Yet the crucial hermeneutical issue remains whether Martyn has correctly assessed the canonical function of this material within the final shape of the text. To offer a historical reconstruction of the Johannine community of ch. 9 is not to be equated with an exegesis of the biblical text, even though the text does indeed reflect historical material from a period long after the ministry of Jesus. I would argue that to take the canonical shape of the Gospel seriously is to recognize that the text's authoritative, kerygmatic witness is not identical with its historical development, but must be discerned from the literary form of the text itself.

Thus, at the outset, the text of ch. 9 offers no hint that the passage is to be read on two separate levels. The manner by which the ministry of the earthly Jesus relates to the continuing ministry of the church does not follow a pattern determined by the text's historical growth. Rather, the text of John is completely tied to the ministry of Jesus; however, the story which has been shaped by subsequent historical events is expanded in such a way as to bear testimony to how Jesus addressed issues which became crucial in the life of the church. The historical experience of the early church has been structured into the canonical text itself and made subservient to the canon's intentionality.

This criticism is not to suggest that Martyn has completely misinterpreted the canonical shape of ch. 9. He has certainly seen several of its central features: (a) the ministry of Jesus is paralleled to the continuing function of the Christian preacher, (b) the debate over Christ's identity is carried on in the narrative in such a way that Jesus is absent from the scene. However, in Martyn's concern to do justice to the various levels of this multi-layered text, he has separated elements whose coherent unity belongs to an essential witness of the text. Thus, the story is actualized for subsequent readers in a way different from that envisioned by Martyn. For example, it is clear that in the present form of the text a major movement within ch. 9 is the role reversal from the blind man to the blindness of the Pharisees (vv. 1 and 40f.). Moreover, the process by which Christian faith is engendered, in contrast to the growth of disbelief through wilful denial of the works of God, plays a dominant role in the witness of the chapter. In sum, Martyn's thesis is useful to the extent in which it illuminates features of the canonical text. However, it is to be resisted when it interprets the chapter to conform to an historical reconstruction which actually runs in the face of the final form of the canonical story itself. Martyn is correct in seeing a dimension of the church's actualization built into the biblical text, but his theory can be contested in not doing justice to the subtlety of the gospel's intertextuality.

G. The Historical Jesus and the Christ of Faith

One of the persistent questions arising from the Fourth Gospel for the modern reader is the relationship between the earthly Jesus and the Christ of faith. At the beginning of the nineteenth century critics such as Schleiermacher could still assign their major attention to John's portrayal of Jesus. However, beginning with D. F. Strauss the opinion became increasingly axiomatic that the Fourth Gospel must be excluded as an historical source of the life of Jesus, according to the modern sense of the term. Of course, the twentieth century has experienced somewhat of a reaction to this historical scepticism, and particularly among English scholars, the historical reliability, even superiority, of certain Johannine traditions has been defended (cf. Dodd). However, the issue of the Gospel's historicity is of a different order from the theological question and only secondarily related. The primary issue turns on the function of the witness to the earthly life of Jesus within the Fourth Gospel. This problem lies at the heart of a canonical reading of the book.

It is essential for John's presentation to reckon with the identity of the earthly Jesus with the exalted Christ. There is no distance, either of time or space, which needed to be overcome. A sharp line of demarcation between the earthly ministry of Jesus and the activity of the Spirit in the church, such as Luke draws, is never made by John. During his entire earthly ministry Jesus was the saviour of the world. Even imperfect faith, such as possessed by the disciples, could see his glory. The difference in perspective from, say, Mark's Gospel is striking in this regard. The Fourth Gospel insists that the eternal Word who became flesh (1.14) also became tired and thirsty and ate and drank with his disciples. Nevertheless, the evangelist portrays Jesus' possession of a unique knowledge and he derives the motivation of his actions solely from a divine commission rather than being conditioned by external affairs of the world.

Yet it is also evident that the Fourth Gospel preserved a distinction between the time of the earthly ministry of Jesus and that of the post-resurrection church. The glorified Christ of the present has not simply absorbed the earthly Jesus. For that reason, Jesus is portrayed in the Gospel as not having as yet been glorified. The Spirit has not been sent, the faith of the disciples is still imperfect, and Jesus' ministry is limited in space to the Jews (cf. Dahl, 101ff.).

The evangelist of the Fourth Gospel bears witness to the life of Jesus in various ways. He has chosen to use the genre of a Gospel, following the movements of his earthly life, rather than to write a theological tractate. Indeed, by virtue of this medium he seeks to illuminate the relation of Jesus' earthly life to the post-resurrection community of faith. The glorified Christ, who is present in the life of every believer after the ascension, was also anticipated in the earthly life of Jesus. As Dahl expresses it: 'the witness borne to his historical ministry is, therefore, at the same time a testimony to his presence here and now' (104). The church of the present cannot understand the exalted Christ apart from his earthly incarnation. The role of the Spirit is not to add anything new, but to shed light on the acts and words of those who had been with Jesus from the beginning (de Jonge, *Jesus*, 12). The Spirit forms the link between the church and the risen Christ, but through the medium of the gospel.

In an analogous fashion the scriptures of the Old Testament bear witness to the exalted Christ in the period before his earthly witness. These witnesses do not function to establish a *heilsgeschichtliche* preparation for Jesus' earthly life, but rather bear testimony to his true identity as the glorified Messiah, which witness stands in contrast to the unbelief of the Jews who do not therefore understand their own scriptures. The witness of the Old Testament demonstrates the continuity between believers before and after his earthly life in the one exalted Lord.

There is still missing an essential element in the Gospel's portrayal of the earthly Jesus as identical with the exalted Christ. The centrality of his earthly life lies in the evangelist's conviction that Jesus' glorification was achieved through his death and resurrection. The very grounds for the church's existence and for the gospel itself derives from the hour of exaltation through the events leading to his final vindication. It is in the vision of Christ that his glory is revealed. This essential relation resists every Gnostic move to see Christ as a heavenly figure who merely passed through the earth on a journey coming from the Father and returning to him. From a canonical perspective the imagery of the Man from heaven can neither be demythologized (Bultmann), historicized (Käsemann), nor rendered into a mute sociological force (Meeks). Rather, its continuing christological function serves to profile the witness to the dual nature of Christ's identity as truly God and man.

II. On Reading the Fourth Gospel Canonically

In the following section I shall attempt to sketch a few broad lines towards what I construe to be a reading of the Fourth Gospel which is consonant with its canonical role.

A. The Prologue, 1.1–18

The exegetical problems associated with the prologue are numerous, but need not be rehearsed in detailed (cf. Harnack, Harris, Bultmann, Käsemann, Haenchen for the modern debate). The problems focus on the structure of the prologue, the nature of the antecedents in the traditions used, the relation of the prologue to the rest of the book, and the theological intention involved in the use of such unusual vocabulary.

It has long been recognized that two Old Testament passages are reflected at the outset, namely, Genesis 1 and Proverbs 8. However, the exact relationship between these two biblical allusions and the theological significance of the combination has not been satisfactorily explained. I would argue that the canonical shaping of the prologue has not been adequately assessed up to now. First of all, the prologue does not begin simply with a juxtaposition of two Old Testament passages. The relationship is of a different order completely. The creation of the world as obviously reflected in Genesis 1 has been construed by means of a wisdom construct (cf. Sheppard). This is to say, a sapentializing process which had already begun toward the end of the Old Testament period and developed by Sirach and Baruch, reinterpreted the narrative, legal, and prophetic traditions from the perspective of wisdom. By reading one portion of the canon, such as the Torah, through the prism of another section of the canon, a theological construct emerged which sought to discern the unity among the variety of Israel's witnesses. The word which brought the world into being (Gen. 1.1) was the selfsame manifestation of wisdom which was with God from the first (Prov. 8). The word of wisdom was 'in the beginning with God; all things were made through him, and without him was not anything made . . . .'. What the evangelist has done in the Prologue is to adopt a typical wisdom construal, which was a common exegetical technique of contemporary Judaism, but he then fashioned an even wider construal which encompassed both creation and wisdom within christology. The Word of God which was with God in creation 'became flesh and dwelt among us'. In a conscious polemic against the synagogue the claim is being made by the evangelist that the hermeneutical key to the divine will is not to be found merely in an identity of wisdom and torah, but in the incarnation of Jesus Christ in whom both the wisdom and law of God is united.

The canonical function of the prologue thus establishes a perspective for reading the Gospel tradition of John. The material is not simply being interpreted from a post-resurrection retrojection, but rather on the basis of the resurrection faith, the evangelist has construed his tradition from a perspective which encompasses the Gospel within the eternal will of God for the redemption of the world. That the evangelist felt free throughout his Gospel to make use of the Gnostic-like language akin to Hellenistic philosophy should not obscure the central theological issue at stake which the prologue makes clear.

B. *The Book of Signs, 1.19–12.50*

From a canonical perspective several features are especially significant in the Johannine portrayal of the ministry of the earthly Jesus.
First, in the signs of Jesus the glorification of Jesus is anticipated,
but in such a way as not to destroy the distinction between the
pre-resurrection and post-resurrection church (Dahl). Thus, the
cleansing of the temple which is placed at the beginning of his
ministry provides the witness that Jesus has replaced the temple as
the sign of God's presence within a new order. Again, the historic
contrast between Jew and Samaritan has been overcome, and the
'living water' replaces that of Jacob's sacred well. The Samaritans
themselves testify to the truth which anticipates the coming of the
Spirit at Christ's ascension.

Secondly, the true nature of Jesus which supports the evidence
from his signs is provided by the witness of the Old Testament.
Without simply allegorizing the Old Testament, the evangelist uses
it as a prior witness which reveals his sonship (5.39). Moses thus
becomes the great accuser of the Jews, who are refuted from their
own scriptures (5.45). Similarly, Abraham rejoiced over Jesus'
coming (8.56) and Isaiah saw his glory (12.41). Following the
resurrection the disciples' belief is grounded both in the scriptures
and the words of Christ (2.22).

Thirdly, the evangelist continually supplies editorial commentary
to the narrative which explains either the reason for an action of
Jesus (6.6; 7.79), or the reaction of others to him (2.21; 7.39). The
effect is to clarify the force behind the sequence of events which
constitute his earthly life. His acts are all linked to a divine motivation
which enters into human time and space, but is never a result of
ordinary human history.

c. *The Farewell Addresses. Chs. 13–17.*

The major canonical significance of the farewell addresses is that
they provide a context within the life of Jesus for the community of
faith which lives without the benefits of the earthly Jesus. Christ, in
anticipation of his imminent departure, describes the continuing role
of the Paraclete in providing instruction for every future generation
of believer. The Spirit fashions the link between the glorified Christ
and the community of faith.

Again, a key to these chapters is given in Christ's prayer for those 'who believe in me through their word' (17.20). Faith in the resurrected Christ is now mediated through the witness of that first generation of believers. Although earthly fellowship with the disciples was ending, there would shortly be a new beginning which would have no end. Only through his death could this glorification occur and allow for the coming of the Paraclete.

D. The Passion of Christ, chs. 18–19

My concern at this point is not to pursue the issue of the earliest form of the tradition lying behind the Johannine account, or even to offer a detailed comparison with the Synoptics, although such analyses often aid in bringing into sharper focus the peculiar shape of John's passion account (cf. R. E. Brown, II, 787ff.). Rather, my summary is again limited to those features in which a canonical concern is most evident.

The Johannine passion account brings to a climax a major theme of the Gospel that the crucifixion ushers in the hour of Christ's glorification. No one takes his life from him, but he lays it down voluntarily (10.18). In his being lifted up, he will now draw all men to himself (12.32f.). Jesus is depicted throughout as knowing everything which will befall him and of being completely the master of his fate. The Johannine account omits all the details which add to the horror of the crucifixion – Gethsemane, darkness, taunts, cry – but allows Jesus' glory to shine through his humiliation.

The context for understanding the meaning of the events is provided by the Old Testament which supplies the real causal force behind the sequence of the passion (18.32; 19.24, 28ff., 36f.) as a fulfilment of a divine purpose to which the Old Testament spoke. In addition, there is a running commentary by the evangelist which is at times explicitly addressed to the reader (19.35). It both provides necessary information, and also interprets the significance of the events (18.4, 14, 40; 19.28, etc.) with the purpose of evoking belief in the hearer (19.35). The effect is that the crucifixion is portrayed in terms of its salvific relevance for Christ's followers.

A high sense of irony provides a major vehicle for the Johannine witness. The kingship of Christ is revealed in its true character by the trial. Although Jesus is addressed as king by Pilate and is crucified as King of the Jews, the Jews confess to having no king but Caesar

(19.15). Jesus is judged by the world's power although the trial is actually a judgment of the world (12.31) and Pilate's power is a derivative of God's (19.11).

Both Pilate and the Jews are presented as representatives of the world who oppose God's will, yet both become unconscious witnesses to the Christian truth. Jesus challenges Pilate to recognize the truth which is being revealed, but Pilate seeks to escape the decision. Jesus bears a good testimony (18.19) and is actually declared innocent of any crime. Yet he is still delivered over to the powers of darkness.

A particular feature of the Johannine passion is its transparency to symbolic meaning. Schnackenburg's reluctance to see symbolism in these chapters is dictated by his inability to prove a conscious author intentionality. However, if one deals seriously with the Christian reader response in the light of the whole canon, it is hard to avoid seeing the peculiar symbolic function of the Johannine passion. Jesus carries his own cross as an example of Christian martyrdom. He is the good shepherd who does not lose a single sheep (18.9). He dies as the passover lamb and in his death flows the water of baptism and the blood of the eucharist (19.34). In sum, the evangelist does not allegorize the passion account, but he shapes it with such a density as to allow the events to be actualized by means of its symbolic function in innumerable ways for future generations of readers.

E. *The Resurrection, ch. 20*

Ch. 20 is closely connected to the preceding account of the passion, but the evangelist of the Fourth Gospel, to an even greater degree, focuses his attention on the nature of faith by which the life of the resurrected Christ could be appropriated by the believer. To emphasize this Johannine feature of the canonical shaping is not to imply that the text's meaning has been separated from its ostensive referentiality, but rather to characterize this particular construal as one which points forward rather than backward.

In a carefully balanced sequence of episodes the coming of faith, both of individuals and of groups of Christians, is portrayed. Each individual (Mary, the beloved disciple, Thomas) reflects a different aspect in experiencing Christ, and each conveys the message to the larger group. An important climax occurs with the appearance to Thomas who is pictured in a position comparable to every successive generation of believers who has not seen the risen Christ. The blessing to those who believe without having seen is then universalized by the didactic form of the beatitude (v. 29).

The continuing presence of Christ in personal relationship with his disciples is picked up as a theme from the earlier chapters (14ff.). The stress first falls on the continuity between the earthly and the resurrected Christ who shows his hands and his side. However, the relationship of the risen Christ to the believer is not simply a return to the earlier period. Mary appears to think so in seeking to touch him, and is instructed that something lies beyond in the future which must be accomplished by his ascension before communion is fully established (v. 17). The disciples are then commissioned to their task of ministry and given the Holy Spirit as a continuing gift toward its accomplishment.

The conclusion of the chapter overlaps with the conclusion of the book, and reflects an important canonical function. The collection of a portion of Jesus' signs in written form to which the disciples were witnesses has as its function to evoke faith in Jesus the Christ. The conclusion therefore ties the editorial process in the formation of an authoritative scripture to its kerygmatic function as proving a continuing testimony to Christ as the source of life.

f. *After the Resurrection, ch. 21*

The final chapter is often regarded as an appendix or epilogue. Yet Schnackenburg is correct (III, ET 344) that ch. 21 does not offer just more of the same, but presents a special stance which affects how the entire Gospel is rendered. In short, the chapter offers an excellent example of canonical shaping which reflects on issues addressing the mission of the church in future generations, indeed from the resurrection to the return of Christ.

The real hermeneutical issue is lost, however, when the central problem of the chapter is translated into one of authorship. Those who defend the evangelist's authorship of the chapter tend to subordinate the chapter's peculiar features in order to defend a unified intentionality of the one writer (Lagrange). Those who characterize the chapter as a later appendix usually isolate the chapter from the rest of the gospel and find no integral connection between the two (Dodd). I would rather argue that a different layer of tradition is highly probable, but that the chapter has been shaped with the entire Gospel already in mind and with a conscious theological purpose.

The Fourth Gospel ends, not with another attempt to create faith in the resurrected Christ, but rather with the issue of how Christ's disciples were to minister to the world in the light of the resurrection. In a real sense, the chapter functions as an application of the farewell addressed in ch. 14–17. The issue is not simply to include ecclesiastical concerns, but how the next generation of believers responds to the new life which they have experienced.

The two disciples, Peter and the beloved disciple, are closely linked in the concluding chapter, but their functions in the church's continuing ministry are carefully distinguished. Peter is rehabilitated and commissioned to a pastoral office of sustaining the flock. Conversely, the beloved disciple is sustained in his role as the authentic witness to Christ, whose witness extends beyond his own lifetime and is now transmitted in written form. A new canonical stage is clearly reflected in these verses which are concerned to preserve an authentic testimony with the passing of the apostolic generation, symbolized in the beloved disciple. The community of faith ('we') serves to guarantee the authority of his work and to testify to the truth of his witness.

A major emphasis of ch. 21 is to stress the continued presence of Jesus with his disciples. The stories of the fishing and the meal function as transparencies to assure succeeding generations of Christ's ability to meet their needs. This presence is actualized by different forms of symbolism which encompass the entire chapter. Christ feeds his disciples as in the eucharist. He is not recognized except by his gracious gifts. The unity of the church is adumbrated in the miraculous catch.

Finally, it is of signficance to note that the canonical book which now contains the evangelist's authentic witness to Christ is linked to his second coming (v. 23). In spite of this theme being different from the major eschatological emphasis of the book itself, a canonical context has been established by which the Fourth Gospel is to be read and which links the Gospel to the larger Johannine corpus (cf. Revelation).

9

THE CANONICAL PROBLEM OF THE
FOUR GOSPELS

Bibliography on the Harmony and Disharmony of the Gospels

K. L. **Carroll**, 'The Creation of the Fourfold Gospel', *BJRL* 37, 1954/5, 68–77; J. H. **Crehan**, 'The Fourfold Character of the Gospel', *StEv* (I), TU 73, 1954, 3–13; O. **Cullmann**, 'The Plurality of the Gospels as a Theological Problem in Antiquity', ET *The Early Church*, London and Philadelphia 1956, 40–56; H. **Cunliffe-Jones**, 'The Fourfold Gospel as a Theological and Pastoral Problem for Today', *StEv* (I), TU 73, 1959, 14–24; C. H. **Dodd**, *The Apostolic Preaching and its Developments*, London 1936, New York 1937; G. **Ebeling**, *Evangelische Evangelienauslegung. Eine Untersuchung zu Luthers Hermeneutik*, Munich 1942; J. H. A. **Ebrard**, *Wissenschaftliche Kritik der evangelischen Geschichte*, Frankfurt ³1868; M. **Else**, *Tatian und seine Theologie*, Göttingen 1960.

B. **Hägglund**, *Die heilige Schrift und ihre Deutung in der Theologie Johann Gerhards. Eine Untersuchung über das altlutherische Schriftverständnis*, Lund 1951; E. **Hirsch**, *Die Theologie des Andreas Osiander und ihre geschichtlichen Voraussetzungen*, Göttingen 1919; E. **Hoskyns**, *The Riddle of the New Testament*, London 1931, ³1947; E. **Käsemann**, 'The Canon of the New Testament and the Unity of the Church', ET *Essays on New Testament Themes*, SBT 41, 1964, 95–107; H. **Koester**, 'One Jesus and Four Primitive Gospels', *Trajectories Through Early Christianity*, Philadelphia 1971, 158–204; 'New Testament Introduction: A Critique of a Discipline', *Christianity, Judaism and other Greco-Roman Cults, FS Morton Smith*, ed. J. Neusner, I, New Testament, Leiden 1975, 1–20; W. **von Loewenich**, *Luther als Ausleger der Synoptiker*, Munich 1954; H. K. **McArthur**, *The Quest Through the Centuries*, Philadelphia 1966; H. **Merkel**, *Die Widersprüche zwischen den Evangelien. Ihre polemische und apologetische Behandlung in der Alten Kirche bis zu Augustin*, WUNT 13, 1971; R. **Morgan**, 'The Hermeneutical Significance of Four Gospels', *Interp* 33, 1979, 376–88.

C. **Pesch**, 'Über Evangelienharmonien', *ZKT* 10, 1886, 225–44, 454–80; R. **Pesch**, R. **Kratz**, *So Liest Man Synoptisch*, 7 vols., Frankfurt 1975–80; D. **Schellong**, *Calvins Auslegung der synoptischen Evangelien*, Forschungen zur

Geschichte und Lehre des Protestantismus 10, 38, Munich 1969; G. **Strauss**, *Schriftgebrauch, Schriftauslegung und Schriftbeweis bei Augustin*, BGBE 1, 1959; B. H. **Streeter**, *The Four Gospels*, London 1924, New York 1925, 3–23; C. H. **Talbert**, 'The Gospel and the Gospels', *Interp* 33, 1979, 351–362; H. J. **Vogels**, *St. Augustins Schrift 'De consensu evangelistarum'. Unter vornehmlicher Berücksichtigung ihrer harmonistischen Anschauungen*, Frankfurt 1908; *Beiträge zur Geschichte des Diatessaron im Abendland*, Münster 1919; W. O. **Walker** jr., ed., *The Relationship among the Gospels*, San Antonio 1978; B. F. **Westcott**, *An Introduction to the Study of the Gospels*, London 1851, New York 1857, [5]1875, [7]1892; D. **Wünsch**, *Evangelienharmonien im Reformationsjahrhundert*, AzKG 52, Berlin 1982; T. **Zahn**, 'Das vierfaltige Evangelium', I, *Geschichte des Neutestamentlichen Kanons*, Erlangen 1888, 150–192.

A Selection of Gospel Harmonies and Synopses

St **Augustine**, *The Works of Aurelius Augustine*, vol. VIII, *The Sermon on the Mount and the Harmony of the Evangelists*, ET Edinburgh 1873; J. A. **Bengel**, *Richtige Harmonie der vier Evangelisten*, Tübingen 1736, [3]1766; J. **Calvin**, *Commentary on a Harmony of the Evangelists, Matthew, Mark, and Luke* (1555), ET Edinburgh 1845, reprinted Grand Rapids n. d,; M. **Chemnitz**, *Harmonia Quatuor Evangeliorum, quam ab eodem feliciter inchoatam Polycarpus Lyserus et Johannes Gerhardus, is quidem continuavit, hic perfecit* (1593ff.), Hamburg 1704; J. **Clericus (LeClerc)**, *Harmonia Evangelica, cui subjecta est historia Christi ex quatuor evangeliis concinnata*, Amsterdam 1699; J. J. **Griesbach**, *Synopsis evangeliorum*, Halle 1774; C. **Jansenius**, (Gandavensis), *Commentarii in suam concordiam ac totam historiam evangelicam*, Louvain 1549, Antwerp 1558.

B. **Lamy**, *Commentarius in harmoniam sive concordiam quatuor evangelistarum*, Paris 1699; N. **Lardner**, *The Credibility of the Gospel History*, Part I, London 1727; J. **Lightfoot**, *The Harmony, Chronicle, and Order of the New Testament. The Text of the Four Evangelists methodised*, London 1654; vol. 1 of *Works*, London 1682; J. **MacKnight**, *A Harmony of the Four Gospels, in which the Natural Order of each is preserved*, 2 vols., London 1756, [2]1763; W. **Newcome**, *An Harmony of the Gospels*, Dublin 1778; A. **Osiander**, *Harmoniae Evangelicae Libri Quatuor, Graece et Latine*, Basel 1537; E. **Robinson**, *A Harmony of the Gospels in Greek*, Andover, Mass. 1834; W. **Stroud**, *A New Greek Harmony of the Four Gospels*, London 1853; K. **Wieseler**, *A Chronological Synopsis of the Four Gospels*, ET London 1864.

I. The History of the Formation of the Fourfold Collection

In spite of the very fragmentary knowledge regarding the exact history of the formation of the Gospels into a collection of four, there is a rather wide consensus among modern scholars about certain aspects of this complex process:

(*a*)At least by the end of the second century, the four canonical Gospels had acquired an authoritative status in the ancient church, replacing an earlier practice of local churches being dependent on individual Gospels.

(*b*)The collection of the four into a corpus implied both a limiting of the authority of other books claiming to be genuine Gospels as well as a rejection of the option of reducing the plurality of witnesses to one condensed or combined account. Tatian's continued use in the Syrian church is an exception which confirms the rule.

(*c*)The criteria for the selection turned on a number of factors of which apostolicity was the major one. The concept involved a combination of historical and theological judgments which allowed for the apostolicity of Mark and Luke whose authors were never considered apostles in a strictly historical sense. Theories of authorship soon attached themselves to the tradition, such as the Petrine origin of Mark's Gospel.

(*d*)The order of the fourfold collection varied considerably at first, but in time became increasingly fixed, but without a single normative sequence.

II. Classic Attempts at Harmonization

The difficulties resulting from the plurality of the Gospels within the canonical collection are continually testified to in the writings of the church fathers (cf. Merkel). In the early church, apologetic defences were soon mounted against attacks on the inconsistencies of the Gospels from outside critics, and several very different solutions were proposed for handling the alleged contradictions. Two classic approaches emerged shortly which were represented by Augustine and Origen.

Augustine developed the most elaborate case ever made within the ancient church for rationally harmonizing the tensions within the Gospels. In his famous treatise *On the Unity of the Gospels (de consensu evangelistarum)* he set forth a sophisticated series of rules by which to bring conflicting testimonies into a unity, which became the dominant model within the church until the rise of the historical critical approach. Thus, his rule of inclusion and omission defended the integrity of the combined account which he constructed by conflating the accounts. Again, the rule of the unity of sense rather than letter accommodated the variety in reporting the identical event. His rule of dissimilation posited two different events which removed the need for harmonization of differing accounts. Finally, his rule of anticipation and recollection introduced a psychological dimension into the interpretation by which to accommodate disloc- ation in sequential order among the Gospels. One need only compare Augustine's approach with the elaborate rules for harmonization offered by the illustrious Jean Le Clerc in 1699 (*Harmonica Evangelica*) to see confirmed the continuity in harmonizing method which extended over a thousand years.

Although at times in his exegesis of the Gospels Origen could make use of similar traditional rules for harmonization, his basic approach differed markedly from Augustine. For example, in his *Commentary on John* (Book X.2ff.), Origen went to great lengths in comparing the Gospels to demonstrate the impossibility of harmonizing the accounts in their literal sense. With a precision worthy of Bultmann, Origen demonstrated the difficulties of fitting the period of the forty-day temptation given in the Synoptics into the narrative framework of John's Gospel. Of course, Origen then argued that the contradictions were intentional and functioned merely as signals to force the reader to seek the true spiritual and mystical sense of the passage. In this context appears his often quoted sentence: 'The spiritual truth was often preserved, as one might say, in the material falsehood' (*John* X.4). Unfortunately, the exegetical and theological potential offered by Origen of seeing in the Gospels a literary genre different from that of historical reporting was not pursued. Rather, Origen's legacy, transmitted through Clement, Jerome, and others, resulted frequently in a simplistic use of allegory which moved, as if by reflex, away from concern with the literal sense of the text to various forms of applied meanings. The effect was to resolve the problem of the gospel's plurality, but at a frightful cost.

The problems evoked in attempting to harmonize the four Gospels continued to persist in the church and received a new impetus toward resolution through the forces which were unleashed by the Renaissance and Reformation. Of the many impressive harmonies which appeared in the sixteenth and seventeenth centuries (cf. the discussion in Schellong and Wünsch especially), one stands out by the extremes to which it was willing to go. In 1537 A. Osiander attempted once and for all to resolve the problem of harmonizing the inner contradictions of the Gospels by developing the theory that each Gospel recorded a completely consistent chronology of the life of Jesus. Tensions between conflicting reports were removed by positing a separate event for every variation in the accounts. Thus, Jesus healed a blind man by Jericho four times, Peter warmed himself by the fire four times, and twice a crown of thorns was placed on Jesus' head. Interestingly enough, both Luther and Calvin polemicized against Osiander's harmonizations. Nevertheless, Osiander's attempt remains significant in the working out in a highly consistent and rigorously rational manner the most extreme option which was logically possible. In spite of the influence which Osiander's approach continued to exert among conservative groups well into the nineteenth and even into the twentieth century (e. g. MacKnight's harmony), its patent artificiality spelt in actuality the bankruptcy of the whole enterprise of harmonization of the gospels as traditionally conceived (cf. Wünsch).

One final example of Gospel harmonization in the nineteenth century deserves to be mentioned. B. F. Westcott's famous book, *An Introduction to the Study of the Gospels*, provided a last major effort by one of England's leading New Testament scholars to seek to address the old issue of harmony by means of a reformulation of the problem. Westcott proposed that the unity of the four Gospels should be set in the context of a broad, dynamic view of divine inspiration. The Bible was envisioned as the revelation of divine truth for the church and the world which had been slowly prepared by stages during the history of the Jewish nation and in classical Graeco-Roman philosophy. Accordingly, the Gospels reflect a moral harmony which transcends the diversity of their human expression. He wrote: 'Behind the differences of the letter lies a perfect unity of the Spirit' (5th ed., 44), whose symmetry can only be grasped by those approaching the writings in search of their spiritual purpose. The closest analogy to the diversity of the Gospels is found in the world of nature in which the particularity of human vision perceives only limited aspects of the mysterious unity of the whole.

Several elements in Westcott's theory of harmonization are noteworthy. First, Westcott separated himself at the outset from the traditional, often rationalistic attempt, to harmonize the discrepancies, particularly after the manner of Osiander. Secondly, Westcott was fully aware of the striking differences among the Gospels, especially in terms of style, structure, and purpose. Finally, Westcott was much concerned to do full justice to the theological nature of the

Gospels in such a way as not to impair the human side of the revelation.

However, Westcott's effort at harmony suffered from some serious flaws which largely accounted for its ultimate demise. First, he regarded the chief problem of harmonization to be the divergence among the Gospels in temporal sequence which he sought to meet by insisting on a moral unity rather than a chronological one. However, the real problems of harmony proved to be deeper than Westcott ever envisioned. Secondly, his positing of a common oral tradition underestimated the nature of the struggle within the early church and did not adequately address the literary interdependence of the Gospels. Finally, and a crucial point, Westcott's solution was constructed completely along the lines of nineteenth-century idealistic philosophy. His contrasts were always between the literal and the spiritual, the outward and the inner, the temporal and the absolute. His major move in harmonization was to abstract the differing accounts according to higher conceptual principles. Thus, even though Westcott appeared to hold back the tide of radical German criticism for a time, the rise of the Oxford school of Synoptic studies had relegated Westcott's theory to oblivion by 1900.

III. The Collapse of the Canonical Categories

Although the historical critical study of the Gospels at first worked within the framework of the traditional harmony, very shortly it succeeded in breaking out and with a vengeance. One of the first disruptions came when the English Deists separated sharply the Gospel of John from the Synoptics and rejected the former as not being a genuine historical source. By and large, the discussion of the eighteenth century was dominated by the conflict between dogmatic and historical questions which called forth both the rationalistic attacks of Anthony Collins as well as the learned, traditional response of Nathaniel Lardner. However, it was no longer taken as an assumption by either side that the four Gospels functioned as a unified, truthful witness of apostolic tradition.

Nineteenth-century scholarship was dominated by the literary study of the Gospels. Even the epoch-making *Life of Jesus* by D. F. Strauss (1837) which in many ways brought to an end the critical questions of the Deists, acquired much of its impact through its particular literary perception which was combined with a radical construal of myth. However, the discovery of the literary (source) relationship among the Synoptic Gospels did more than anything else to undercut the grounds for harmonization. No longer could the Gospels be treated as independent witnesses which were arranged according to logical rules of narrative consistency. Rather, their relationship was now linked in a close historical sequence by the use of literary sources. The increasing acceptance of the two-source theory of composition in the latter part of the nineteenth century which argued for the priority of Mark and the role of a source 'Q' did much to damage the traditional views of authorship. Particularly in England, where the intensive study of the literary interdependence of the Gospels was carried on largely by Anglican clergy (Hawkins, Sanday, Streeter), the break with the church's tradition did not stem from a shift in confessional stance, as frequently occurred in Germany. Nevertheless, the abandonment of the traditional approach to the harmony of the four canonical Gospels was just as complete as in Europe.

The development and application of the form-critical method to the Gospels which occurred in Germany in the 1920s momentarily shifted attention away from the dominant questions of source criticism, but it only served to distance itself even more from concern with the canonical form of the Gospels. Interest focused on tracing the complex oral history of the material in its preliterary stages, of analysing the variety of different literary forms, and of establishing the historical, sociological settings of the material according to the evidence derived from the new approach. Equally significant was the application of a history-of-religions approach to the New Testament texts by the first generation of form critics (Bultmann, Dibelius, Schmidt) which they had appropriated from their illustrious teachers (Bousset, Reitzenstein, Jülicher, Heitmüller), and further developed in conjunction with the new directions afforded by form criticism. One of the effects was to broaden the angle of vision far beyond the scope of the canonical gospels and to derive many of the decisive historical forces from outside the areas of biblical religion. One of the more impressive modern legacies from Bultmann's work is the formation of a school around H. Koester of Harvard, who with J. M. Robinson, has called for a radical dismantling of the New Testament categories which would eradicate the last vestiges of canonical bias.

Then again, the growing influence of redactional criticism starting from the period following World War II up to the present has contributed substantially in further reducing the significance of treating the Gospels as a canonical unit. The redactional critics have been able to demonstrate conclusively the peculiar features and independent stamp which each editor left on his material. Moreover, there has been considerable success in relating the unique features of each Gospel to the needs of the particular first-century communities which influenced the traditioning process. Within this approach the issue of the relationship among the four Gospels in traditional terminology has largely lost its significance. When the older questions of harmony are raised, they are usually set within a polemical context to serve only as a foil by which to demonstrate the extent of the discontinuity.

The theological effect of the various forms of the historical critical study of the Gospels can best be seen by comparing some modern representatives. In the period of the 1930s a rather strong reaction set in against the growing atomization of the Gospels through critical scholarship and a call was sounded for a theological synthesis. Edwyn Hoskyn's influential book, *The Riddle of the New Testament* (1931) sought to argue the case that critical scholarship had successfully revealed the complex nature of the historical development of the New Testament, but that the genuine riddle of the book could only be resolved theologically. At the heart of the New Testament's diversity lay a series of historical events which ultimately determined the shape of the witness. Accordingly, the New Testament writers did not impose extrinsic categories upon the synoptic material, but reflected the paradoxes of a history which was derived from the conscious intention of Jesus, the Messiah, to fulfil the Jewish scriptures. Hoskyns thus grounded his theological perception of the New Testament, not on a traditional view of canon, but on an historical intentionality in the mind of Jesus.

Of even more importance in this period – at least for the Anglo-Saxon world – was the work of C. H. Dodd. In 1936 Dodd called for a synthesis of the New Testament material which would serve to balance the analytical emphasis of the prior generation. He found the unity of the Gospels to lie in the kerygma, which he distinguished from the teachings (*didache*). In his own way, Dodd supported the new theological interest which had arisen in Germany on recovering a kerygmatic unity underlying the Gospels. However, significantly, all these attempts sought to ground the unity in phenomena lying behind, and clearly distinguished from, the canonical form of the Gospels. Similarly, G. Kittel's widely acclaimed *Theologisches Wörterbuch* illustrated the concern of that era to penetrate beyond the gains of critical, analytical, and historical study of the New Testament to some grounds for theological unity. However, none of these representative approaches sought to recover a central role for the canonical categories, but assumed that the unity was to be sought elsewhere. Ironically enough, some of the most theologically conservative efforts from this period, such as those of J. Jeremias or T. W. Manson, were most radical in rejecting canonical categories.

However, the present generation of New Testament scholars has seen a strong reaction against even this formulation of the unity of the New Testament. Käsemann's provocative formulation of the theological problem of the canon is well known and need not be rehearsed in detail (*Essays on NT Themes*, 95ff.). Käsemann's insistence that the various parts of the New Testament are often in sharpest conflict with one another resulted in his call for a 'discerning of the spirits' to discover what is true among the conflicting voices within the canon. For Käsemann the fact of a canon works precisely to exclude the possibility of finding unity within the New Testament.

Finally, the work of H. Koester has moved in exactly the opposite direction from that of Hoskyns. Hoskyns had argued that the kerygma of the early Christian community stemmed from a direct response to events in the earthly life of Jesus and therefore provided a basic unity among the four Gospels. However, for Koester the claims for historical continuity by the apocryphal and Gnostic writings stand in equal, if not closer, proximity with the earthly Jesus and are similarly creations of rival groups within the ancient Hellenistic world. The theological effect of Koester's work thus drains the canonical status of the New Testament literature of its last vestiges of significance. The formation of the canonical Gospels simply served to establish the superiority of those writings which were prized by the party which had won political hegemony.

IV. The Theological Function of the Four Gospels within the Canon

It is my basic thesis that modern New Testament scholarship has moved in a wrong direction when it has allowed its genuine insights into the history of the formation of the New Testament literature, won through painstaking research, to destroy the significance of the canonical collection of the four Gospels. Although it is fully agreed that there can be no return to the older traditional form of the harmony of the Augustine model, the crucial theological issue turns on assessing the lasting theological significance of the particular canonical shape in which the Gospels were collected in order to serve as authoritative for the Christian church.

There is a widespread consensus that by the end of the second century the four Gospels had been joined into a fixed corpus. Several factors in the history of this development bear witness that this process had not taken place unthinkingly nor without controversy. Tatian's attempt to fuse the four Gospels into one continuous account certainly presented another clear option, which, however, was finally rejected by the ancient church. Similarly, Marcion's move critically to sift the material according to one dogmatic perspective and to retain only portions of the Gospel tradition was seen as a fundamental threat to the catholicity of the faith and also rejected. Finally, the numerous Gnostic Gospels which purported to contain esoteric, hidden teachings of Jesus did not succeed in supplementing or supplanting the four.

A closer analysis of the form of the four canonical Gospels is now in order. Each of the four now bears the title 'the Gospel according to ($\varkappa\alpha\tau\acute{\alpha}$) so-and-so'. These titles do not form part of the original Gospels, but stem from the collectors of the gospels who used the titles to provide the material with a unified shape. The Greek preposition, $\varkappa\alpha\tau\acute{\alpha}$, does not designate simply a genitive of authorship, although authorship is not excluded, but rather it implies a conformity to a subject which has been treated by others. Accordingly, there is only one Gospel, but it has been rendered by four different evangelists. The collectors therefore provided this material with a new context which allowed for its diversity, yet laid claim also on its unity.

Moreover, the effect of the new context provided by the fourfold corpus in several instances ran in the face of the original context supplied by a single evangelist to his material. For example, the original literary entity which encompassed Luke-Acts has been broken, and the two parts of the original work have been assigned different functions within the New Testament canon. Luke's Gospel now belongs to the Gospel collection and is to be interpreted in the context of the other Gospels, whereas the book of Acts has been assigned a separate role as a bridge to the apostolic witness of the Pauline and Catholic epistles. The implied superiority of presentation, especially in its ordering, which is expressed in the prologue of Luke's Gospel, has been considerably relativized both by its simple juxtaposition with the other Gospels and by its position as one among several in a larger series.

From a canonical perspective it is fuly legitimate, and indeed mandatory, that the integrity of each single Gospel be maintained. The canonical ordering neither fused the Gospels nor subordinated one to another. Therefore, when modern redaction criticism seeks to pursue the peculiar stamp which each author has left upon his composition, the method cannot be faulted for its pursuit of diversity. However, it is equally important in doing justice to the canonical shape of the Gospels that the nature of the Gospel's unity be pursued with equal vigour. To suggest that the search is of minor importance and is simply a vestige from a precritical era, is to disregard not only the literary shape given the collection, but it is also to run in the face of its ancient and fully justifiable usage within the community of faith as a single corpus. Although the assembled congregation hears different pericopes from single Gospels read each Sunday, members of the community possess Bibles with four different witnesses, and at least a memory of the other testimonies is retained which demands that the larger canonical question of the unity in the variety of testimony be addressed.

The approach of redaction critics can only be welcomed when they focus their full attention on clarifying the unique imprint of each evangelist by scrutinizing the literary features of the individual Gospels. However, to leave the theological questions at this stage is to miss the basic function of the canonical writings which was not to instruct the reader on the ideology of an author, but to bear witness to its subject matter, the Gospel. The individuality of the human author is subordinated to the theological significance of the life, death, and resurrection of Jesus Christ. From a canonical perspective, the primary function of the Gospels is theocentric, not anthropocentric.

How then is the unity of the four Gospels to be envisioned? Both the older harmonies and the nineteenth-century 'life-of-Jesus' research worked with the assumption that the Gospel accounts were to be read in terms of an historical referent. The Gospel accounts received their meaning when made to correlate with a biography of

Jesus which lay behind the witness. One of the great contributions of the early form critics was in showing the fundamental error at stake in this approach, which was shared by both conservatives and liberals. It has now become a truism in recognizing that the Gospels do not have as their purpose to describe a life of Jesus. All the characteristics of a biography are missing in the Gospels. Rather, the Gospels are kerygmatic in nature. I use the term in its broadest sense. They bear witness to the proclamation of divine salvation through the life and death of the Saviour. Now what is true for each individual Gospel pertains also to the canonical collection. Therefore, it is a basic misconstrual of the New Testament material when one seeks to reconstruct from the Gospels a life of Jesus, either by the addition of the parts into a complete harmony, or the subtraction and critical sifting of the evidence in order to discover the real Jesus behind the levels of accretion. However, if the unity does not consist in merely combining the four Gospels into a harmonious whole, nor in a biographical substratum behind the text, wherein does it lie?

V. Gospel Harmony and Canon

I would like to argue the case that the question of the unity of the Gospels is closely related to the formation of the New Testament canon. The failure to regard the peculiar form in which the canon has structured the material lies at the heart of many of the misconstruals of the unity.

The canon has preserved four distinct literary entities, which are similarly entitled, as bearing witness to the one Gospel. Of course, the presence of different sources within a collection was not unusual for the Old Testament canon. There is much paralleled material found in different Hebrew books which have maintained their separate canonical integrity, such as Kings and Chronicles. Similarly, the Pentateuch, which forms a discrete canonical collection, consist of at least four separate literary sources which have been combined to form a single composition.

Nevertheless, the crucial point to make is that none of the forms of canonical literature which appear in the Old Testament offers an exact parallel to the New Testament Gospels. In spite of the great variety with which the Hebrew canon shaped its material (cf. my *Introduction to the Old Testament as Scripture*), there is nothing which can be considered as a direct analogy. Indeed, the differences are far more striking that the similarities. Within the Pentateuch the sources have been intertwined to form a fixed composition. The effect is that the relationship between the sources has been once-and-for-all established within the history of the literature's formation and subsequent collection. For example, in Genesis the Priestly source not only introduces the book, but provides the overarching framework into which the earlier Yahwistic source has been placed. The combination of sources has thus determined the semantic level on which the combined text is to be read which often differs from its original narrative function.

The striking characteristic of the collection of the four Gospels is that this combining of sources, that is to say, the separate Gospels, has not happened. In terms of the canonical collection each Gospel retains its discrete integrity. None is subordinated to another, either literarily or historically. Even though modern scholarship has painstakingly tried to establish the degree of overlap among the Gospels, and even determined with a high probability the literary priority of Mark's Gospel, these critical judgments are not reflected in the present form of the canonical shape. No one Gospel is made the hermeneutical key, as would have happened had John's Gospel been constructed into an overarching framework and the three Synoptics inserted into its story. Interestingly enough, the well-known tradition preserved in the Muratorian Canon interpreted the formation of the fourfold collection as if the history had happened just in this manner. According to this, all the disciples gave their material to John who wrote, as it were, the official Gospel for them all. However, the tradition is apocryphal and not sustained by the present canonical form of the Gospels. The individual Gospels have not been reworked through the canonical process in such a way as to establish for the reader signs which indicate the interrelationship of the various gospels. As a result, in spite of the large amount of common material, both in form and content shared by the evangelists, the major formal sign of canonical shaping of the collection is the juxtaposition of the four books with titles which introduce the books as witnesses to the one gospel.

Wherein then does the unity of the fourfold Gospel collection lie according to its canonical shaping? The unique feature of the Gospel's shape is that the unity is asserted, but never established in a fixed literary form. According to the canonical shape the unity must be determined from reading the four, but no one definitive entrance – neither literary, nor historical, nor theological – has been established by the shape of the canonical text. Fluidity, therefore, is constitutive of the canonical shape of this corpus. The basic error of the traditional harmony was the assumption that the canonical process had been deficient in leaving the Gospels in their plural form rather than completing the process by fusing them into a fixed, authoritative interpretation. Because this development did not take place within the canonical process, but in fact was flatly rejected, the plural form remains constitutive of the canonical shape. Conversely, the basic error of the historical critical position was the assumption that the canonical shape was of no exegetical significance and that valid interpretation depended on a critical reconstruction which re-aligned the Gospels in their original historical sequence. Consequently both from the right and left the canonical shaping of the fourfold Gospel collection has been disregarded which is one of the major reasons for the present impasse in New Testament scholarship.

The theological implications of the canonical shaping are highly significant. The unity of the one Gospel lies within its fourfold witness, but each new generation of readers is challenged to discern that unity. Nowhere is it presupposed that the one correct interpretation lies hidden, waiting the day to be finally uncovered. Rather, the richness of the witness to the gospel is such that each new reading challenges its hearers to reflect theologically on its testimony to the one Lord.

However, rather than continue to discuss in general terms the effect of the canonical shape on the nature of the Gospel's unity, it is more useful to turn to specific texts within the canon and seek to illustrate exegetically a canonical approach to the Gospels.

10

A CANONICAL HARMONY OF THE
GOSPELS

I. The Infancy Narratives

Bibliography

Cf. the exhaustive bibliographies in R. E. **Brown**, *The Birth of the Messiah*, and in J. A. **Fitzmyer**, *The Gospel according to Luke I–IX*, 330ff. K. **Bornhäuser**, *Die Geburts- und Kindheitsgeschichte Jesu*, BFChTh 2. 23, 1930; R. E. **Brown**, *The Birth of the Messiah: A Commentary on the Infancy Narratives in Matthew and Luke*, New York and London 1977; R. **Bultmann**, *The History of the Synoptic Tradition*, ET Oxford and New York 1963, 320–28; O. **Cullmann**, 'Infancy Gospels', *NTApoc* I, 363–417; M. **Dibelius**, *Jungfrauensohn und Krippenkind: Untersuchungen zur Geburtsgeschichte Jesu im Lukas-Evangelium* (1932), reprinted in *Botschaft und Geschichte* I, Tübingen 1953, 1–78.

R. **Lauretin**, *Structure et théologie de Luc I–II*, Paris 1957; A. R. C. **Leaney**, 'The Birth Narratives in St Luke and St Matthew', *NTS* 8, 1961/2, 158–66; P. S. **Minear**, 'Luke's Use of the Birth Stories', in *Studies in Luke-Acts*, ed. L. E. Keck and L. Martyn, Nashville 1966, 111–30; E. **Nellessen**, *Das Kind und seine Mutter*, Stuttgart 1970; E. **Norden**, *Die Geburt des Kindes: Geschichte einer religiösen Idee*, Stuttgart 1924; K. H. **Schelkle**, 'Die Kindheitsgeschichte Jesu', in *Wort und Schrift: Beiträge zur Auslegung und Auslegungsgeschichte des Neuen Testaments*, Düsseldorf 1966, 59–75; H. **Schürmann**, 'Aufbau, Eigenart und Geschichtswert der Vorgeschichte, Lk 1–2', *Bibel und Kirche* 21, 1966, 106–11; reprinted in *Traditionsgeschichtliche Untersuchungen zu den synoptischen Evangelien*, Düsseldorf 1968, 198–208; K. **Stendahl**, 'Quis et Unde? An Analysis of Mt 1–2', *Judentum–Urchristentum–Kirche, FS J. Jeremias*, ed. W. Eltester, BZNW 26, 1964, 94–105; H. **Usener**, 'Geburt und Kindheit Christi', *ZNW* 4, 1903, 1–21.

P. **Vielhauer**, 'Kindheitsevangelien', *Geschichte der urchristlichen Literatur*, Berlin 1975, 665–79; A. **Vögtle**, 'Offene Fragen zur lukanischen Geburts- und Kindheitsgeschichte', *Bibel und Leben* 11, 1970, 51–67; reprinted *Das Evangelium und die Evangelien: Beiträge zur Evangelienforschung*, Düsseldorf 1971, 43–56.

A. *Attempts at Harmonization*

The relation between the two accounts of Jesus' infancy (Matt. 2 and Luke 2) has always appeared as a major problem for harmonists. The difficulty lies in relating two stories which are told independently of each other, and which cannot be easily synchronized. Luke's account moves in an unbroken sequence from the birth of Jesus, to the appearance of the shepherds, to his circumcision on the eighth day, to the purification rites in Jerusalem on the fortieth day, to the public acknowledgement from Simeon and Anna, to his settlement in Nazareth. In contrast, Matthew depicts a sequence from the coming of the Magi to Jerusalem, the finding of the child, a dream warning of danger, the flight to Egypt, the slaughter of the children, the death of Herod, and the settlement in Nazareth.

The historical solution of the harmonists falls roughly into two major options with several minor variations possible. Either one argues that the wise men came before the purification at Jerusalem, or that their visit followed the purification. The first option has been the more traditional choice which, in its most familiar form, designated the visit of the Magi on the thirteenth day after Christ's birth. Several reasons were brought forth to defend this interpretation. Jesus was still living in Bethlehem which would be more difficult to assume once he had been taken to the temple at Jerusalem. Again, Luke ties closely together the end of the purification with the return to Nazareth (2.39). However, the difficulty arises of synchronizing the threat which followed closely after the Magi's visit with the visit to Jerusalem for purification. Would his parents have taken him to the very place which would appear to expose him to the greatest danger possible? Calvin seeks to minimize the difficulty by having the purification take place quickly when passing through Jerusalem on the way to Egypt! Augustine tries to avoid the problem by suggesting that Herod had forgotten about the wise men and the child until he was reminded of the incident by rumours of Jesus' visit to the temple (also Chemnitz). A few harmonists (Clericus) even felt constrained to have Joseph's warning in a dream occur while in Jerusalem during the purification, or in Nazareth, rather than in Bethlehem, but the difficulty of relating these ploys to the two stories is obvious.

The second option, of having the wise men appear after the purification, has also had its defenders (Bengel, Wieseler, Robinson).

One of the reasons supporting this preference is that it seems to cause less strain on the individual sequence of the stories when they are joined with as little temporal overlap as possible. As an additional warrant for this reconstruction it was often argued that, had the Magi's visit occurred before the purification, their gifts of gold would have made it impossible for the family to have offered a pair of birds (Luke 2.24) which was restricted to the very poor (cf. Osiander, Newcome and Calvin's rejoinder). Finally, it was reckoned that the Magi needed sufficient time for the journey to Jerusalem unless it be assumed that the star appeared before Christ's birth. However, one of the major difficulties in this theory was in suggesting a reason why the parents of Jesus would ever have returned to Bethlehem after the purification to be found by the Magi, especially in the light of the inhospitable reception. In addition, how is one to reconcile the public recognition of Jesus as the Messiah by Simeon and Anna with the ignorance of his birth when the Magi appeared subsequently?

B. *The Approach of Historical Criticism*

With the rise of the historical critical method the difficulties between the two accounts which had occupied the traditional harmonists paled into virtual insignificance. A whole host of fresh issues emerged which stressed the degree of radical divergence in the two infancy narratives. Accordingly, it was argued that Matthew's account assumed that Bethlehem was the home of Mary and Joseph. They leave not because their home is elsewhere, but, because of a warning of the threat from Herod, they flee to Egypt. They would have returned to Bethlehem had not the fear of Herod's son, mediated through a dream, driven them to Nazareth. Whereas in Luke, Nazareth is the home of Joseph and Mary. They proceed to Bethlehem to register for the Roman census because it was the home of Joseph's ancestors. After the completion of Mary's purification, they return home to Nazareth without any flight to Egypt or regard for the rule of Archelaus.

The tension between the stories is further exacerbated when one approaches the material form-critically. M. Dibelius' famous essay offers a classic study from this perspective. He analyses two totally different cycles of legend arising from different settings, and treasured by different tradents for wholly different purposes. In the light of the history of traditions lying behind the formation of these two cycles, the attempt to harmonize the accounts into a coherent whole loses its rationale completely.

Finally, the effect of recent redactional studies has greatly contributed to sharpening the perspective for viewing the two stories as separate entities. Stendahl, for example, feels that the vestiges from the earlier harmonistic approach have been a major deterrent from seeing each story in its individual integrity. For him, the structure of Matthew's Gospel rules out even speaking of a birth narrative. Rather, the point of this evangelist is to present an argument about how Jesus was engrafted into the Davidic pedigree, which apology was buttressed in ch. 2 with a geographical focus on the two cities, Bethlehem and Nazareth. In contrast, the redactional studies of the structure of Luke's infancy narrative focus completely on this one presentation, and it is felt that the older question of harmony is basically irrelevant for close analysis of the theological stamp of Luke-Acts.

c. A Critique of the Two Approaches

In my judgment, both of the two major approaches reflect strengths and weaknesses. The great strength of the older harmony was, at least, in raising the canonical question of the relationship between these two strikingly different accounts, but the solutions offered suffer from major problems. First of all, from a literary perspective, regardless of how one decides on synchronizing the two accounts, the combination of passages which the harmonists suggest effects a major distortion within each of the discrete cycles. A new context is established which severely blurs the witness of the separate Gospels. For example, the dynamics of the story of the family of Jesus fleeing for its life to Egypt and escaping just in the nick of time from the terrifying slaughter of the innocent children is completely lost if the family is allowed the leisure of breaking its flight to perform all the religious rites in the temple. Again, it is a poor historical method which treats its sources uncritically on the flat so as logically to deduce new historical information by simple conflation without first exploring the form and function of the individual sources. Certainly the argument that the purification offering of the poor would no longer be suitable after the visit of the Magi reflects a simplistic historical methodology.

Finally, the theological argument against this method of harmonizing the birth stories must be considered. The approach fails to do justice to the kerygmatic nature of the evangelists. Rather, it handles the biblical texts as sources for reconstructing a biography of Jesus on which its theological reflection depends. It treats the explicit witness of an evangelist on the same level with conclusions which are rationally deduced according to general patterns of human behaviour. The theological issue at stake is the underlying assumption that there are many different avenues to the reality testified to in the Gospels and that the canonical texts perform no special function as vehicles of divine revelation.

The historical critical approach to the infancy narratives also exhibits strengths and weaknesses. Its great contribution lies in its concern to hear each individual Gospel in a precise manner which will do justice to all its particularity. Thus, Stendahl has made a contribution in stressing the unique structural shape of the revelation to Joseph (1.18ff.) and its integral relation to the preceding genealogy with Matthew's Gospel. Likewise, by tracing the prehistory of both cycles of stories, Dibelius has been able to hear the final form of each story with a new sensitivity both respecting detail as well as general tone and movement.

However, what is the effect of the refusal to deal seriously with the relation of the two stories within the canonical collection? From a literary perspective the question has not been addressed whether or not a new entity has been formed by the canonical process which may affect the reading of the single Gospels. More importantly, the critical method, as usually practised, fails to address the central canonical question respecting the relation of these two witnesses to the one gospel. Therefore, it tends to limit the role of exegesis to an analysis of the differing concepts of the two evangelists without being able to go beyond these witnesses to address the subject matter itself, namely, Christ's infancy as a revelation of his divine mission.

D. A Canonical Approach to the Infancy Narratives

Within the collection of the fourfold Gospel the two accounts of Christ's infancy are simply juxtaposed. That is to say, there is no structural or redactional linkage between the stories. This situation, therefore, poses a different hermeneutical problem from, say, the two parallel creation stories of Genesis which have been literarily linked.

Nevertheless, the similarity of content within the two different stories pointing to a common historical referent makes the question of establishing their relationship within the one literary corpus necessary. The nature of the overlap between the stories is highly significant. The stories are joined at the beginning by the birth of Jesus at Bethlehem (Matt 2.1; Luke 2.1–7), and again at the conclusion with his settlement at Nazareth (Matt. 2.23; Luke 2.39). However, the rest of the stories are independent of each other, and go their separate ways without internal crossing. (It is not necessary to repeat that both stories form part of a larger literary structure, reflecting different literary functions and that each has developed through a separate prehistory).

The hermeneutical issue, in this instance, is also clear. The linkage is not derived from any individual author's intentionality, nor from a subsequent redactional editing of the collection. Rather, it stems from the result of the canonical collection which has effected a new and larger context for originally independent material. Thus, from a canonical perspective the internal relationship between the story of the Magi and the shepherds is not to be logically deduced. The attempt to intertwine the two stories runs in the face of the present shaping. Moreover, there is nothing to suggest that the effect of the juxtaposition of the two raises the semantic level of the stories within their new context by shifting the mode of discourse to that of metaphor or symbol which is once removed from its original sense. Neither can one say that the new context subordinates one of the stories to the other. Finally, one cannot rightly speak about the two stories functioning as two sides of one coin, since the elements in common hold only for the two extreme ends.

In the light of this canonical situation, I would rather argue that the two stories are related to each other holistically, that is to say, the stories are to be compared to each other in their entirety, and not according to their independent parts. First, the two stories bear witness to the hidden and revealed elements of Jesus' birth. Matthew's story contrasts the lack of knowledge of his birth in Jerusalem with the wonderful revelation of the event to the wise men from a distant land, while Luke pictures the hidden quality of the child in the manger with the glorious revelation to the world in the angels' song. Again, Luke depicts the humility of his birth with no place in the inn, whereas Matthew pictures the recognition of his majesty with the royal gifts from the Magi. Finally, Luke focuses on the joy at the birth by both angels and shepherds with only a hint of the coming sorrow (2.34f.), whereas Matthew's presentation of the joy of the Magi (2.10) is overshadowed almost completely by the themes of threat, intrigue, flight, and fear at his coming. Obviously, each of these contrasting features could be pursued theologically in depth.

At this juncture, it is important to make the point that this comparison is not simply homiletical, but entails in this instance both literary and theological reflection which is commensurate with the new canonical function within the fourfold Gospel. However, because there are features of the canonical approach shared in common with homiletics, a determination of the exact relationship between the disciplines of exegesis and proclamation is important. Within the framework of these two infancy stories within the canon no one fixed set of comparisons has been established. The relationship between the stories is a variable one within a wide range of possibilities which are altered according to the particular reader competence of the interpreter. However, this flexibility does not imply that the enterprise is wholly subjective. The two texts exert a coercion upon the reader which stems both from the literary elements of the stories and their theological content. The major difference between canonical exegesis and homiletics in respect to the interaction between literary analysis and creative imagination is that the homilist is required to extend the significance of the biblical stories into the contemporary world and to apply the text to the specific situation of his modern audience.

Then again, a canonical analysis shares with the homilist the theological responsibility of approaching the text kerygmatically, which is to say, both readings are predisposed to hearing the biblical text as a witness to the good news of God's redemption in Christ. The text is not a neutral source to be simply scrutinized. Finally, it should be pointed out that in the history of exegesis a close relationship has always existed between the harmony of the gospel – even when poorly executed – and the homiletical application of its message. The harmonies of Calvin and Chemnitz are classic examples of this union of descriptive exegesis and homiletical application.

What is the relationship of such a canonical interpretation to the historical enterprise? What really happened historically during the early years of Jesus' infancy? The answer cannot be generalized to form a single hermeneutical principle valid for all of scripture. In regard only to these two infancy narratives, the common historical reference is restricted to the beginning and end of the two stories. No additional historical information is needed in order for the two stories to function together within the canonical context. The inner nexus of the two sequences remains unsettled. The joint witness functions without having resolved the historical problem.

If this situation appears strange, even intolerable, reflect for a moment as to how the biblical stories of Christ's infancy actually function for a modern congregation. Most Christians would know that Jesus was born in Bethlehem, and some that he grew up in Nazareth. Almost all would know of the visit of the Magi and the story of the shepherds on Christmas morning. This information stems from various exposures to the Gospels through Sunday school instruction, in sermons, and in the church's liturgy. Yet if the average Christian were to be asked about the exact sequential relationship of the shepherds to the Magi, the answer would reflect widespread uncertainty and confusion. The reason is clear. This information does not, and never did, form an integral part of the New Testament's witness to the incarnation. In this case, the Christian church continues to live and celebrate the Good News without having this historical problem ever resolved, nor feeling in any way that the gospel is impaired.

One final comparison may aid in clarifying the method which is being proposed. A comparison between the two infancy stories and the two announcement stories (Matt. 1.18–25; Luke 1.26–38) is highly revealing. In the announcement stories the impending birth of Christ is announced to two different persons, Joseph and Mary, but in different ways for different purposes. However, in at least six different places the individual narratives are closely linked by both stylistic and content similarity. Both Joseph and Mary are counselled not to fear (Matt. 1.20; Luke 1.30). Both accounts make explicit mention of there being no prior marital relation between the couple (Matt. 1.18; Luke 1.34). Both speak of the birth from the Holy Spirit (Matt. 1.20; Luke 1.35). In both the command to call the child's name Jesus is given (Matt. 1.21; Luke 1.31), and in both his mission is outlined in terms of Old Testament prophecy, with varying emphases (Matt. 1.21–23; Luke 1.32f.). Finally, in both the reaction to the message is of acceptance and obedience.

Although the two annunciation stories are equally diverse as the infancy stories, and reflect different literary functions and a separate history of tradition, they are linked by similarities in style and content which unleash a very different dynamic from that of the infancy stories. The annunciation stories recount the different ways in which Joseph and Mary learned of the wondrous child, but the variations interplay as counterpoint on the basic themes which the two stories share. Although the creative imagination of the reader clearly affects the way in which the stories are heard together, the parallel structure and overlap in content provide a more closely defined area into which the interpretation must fit in order to do full justice to their intertextuality.

II. John the Baptist

Bibliography

K. **Aland**, ed., *Synopsis quattuor evangeliorum*, Stuttgart 1964, 20–27; E. **Bammel**, 'The Baptist in Early Christian Tradition', *NTS* 18, 1971/2, 95–128; J. **Becker**, *Johannes der Täufer und Jesus von Nazareth*, BSt 63, 1972; M. É. **Boismard**, 'Les traditions johanniques concernant le Baptiste', *RB* 70, 1963, 5–42; R. **Bultmann**, *History of the Synoptic Tradition*, ET London and New York 1963, 245–7; H. **Conzelmann**, *The Theology of St Luke*, ET London and New York 1960, 18–27; M. **Dibelius**, *Die urchristliche Überlieferung von Johannes dem Täufer*, Göttingen 1911; C. H. **Dodd**, *Historical Tradition in the Fourth Gospel*, Cambridge 1963, 251ff.; M. S. **Enslin**, 'John and Jesus', *ZNW* 66, 1975, 1–18; A. **Huck**, *Synopse der drei ersten Evangelien*, Tübingen ⁹1950; ET ed. H. Lietzmann and F. L. Cross, Berlin 1936.

   C. **Kraeling**, *John the Baptist*, New York 1951; E. **Lohmeyer**, *Das Urchristentum, I: Johannes der Täufer*, Göttingen 1932; W. **Marxsen**, 'John the Baptist', *Mark the Evangelist*, ET Nashville 1969, 30–53; C. C. **McCown**, 'The Scene of John's Ministry', *JBL* 59, 1940, 113–31; W. **Michaelis**, *Täufer, Jesus, Urgemeinde*, Gütersloh 1928; R. **Pesch**, R. **Kratz**, *So Liest Man Synoptisch*, I, Frankfurt 1975, 17–41; J. A. T. **Robinson**, 'The Baptism of John and the Qumran Community', *HTR* 50, 1957, 175–91; reprinted *Twelve New Testament Studies*, SBT 34, 1962, 11–27; 'Elijah, John and Jesus: An Essay in Detection', *NTS* 4, 1957/8, 263–81, reprinted ibid., 28–52; H. **Schürmann**, *Das Lukasevangelium* I, Freiburg 1969, 148–83; B. H. **Streeter**, 'St Mark's Knowledge and Use of Q', *Studies in the Synoptic Problem*, ed. W. Sanday, Oxford 1911, 166–83; J. **Weiss**, *SNT*³, 1917, I, 75f.; W. **Wink**, *John the Baptist in the Gospel Tradition*, SNTSM 7, 1968.

The initial sections related to John the Baptist are found in Matt. 3.1–17, Mark 1.1–11, Luke 3.1–22, and John 1.6–34. This material can be grouped into various subsections which include his appearance, preaching, and baptism of Jesus (cf. Huck, Aland).

A. *Attempts at Harmonization*

The material in these sections offers a number of classic problems for the traditional harmony of the gospels. First, there is an apparent contradiction between John's reluctance to baptize Jesus, which presupposes some prior knowledge from a previous acquaintance (Matt. 3.13f.), and the statement of John recorded twice in the Fourth Gospel: 'I myself did not know him' (1.31, 33) (cf. Augustine, Jansen, ad loc.). A similar problem relates to the role of Elijah in which the Fourth Gospel appears to conflict with the other three. Secondly, the exact sequence of the events of the baptism was much discussed among the harmonists, especially the conflicting function of the adverb 'immediately' (εὐθύς) in the parallel passages of Matt. 3.16 and Mark. 1.10 (cf. Chemnitz). Finally, the variety in the reporting of the words from the heavenly voice as well as the scope of the audience who perceived the sight evoked controversy.

The manner in which these problems were reconciled within a harmony is also significant. Augustine states at the outset that the reader is not at liberty to suppose any one of the evangelists is false (II. 12.28) – a sentiment universally shared by the ancient catholic church. Nevertheless, he is also acutely aware of the differences among the Gospels in respect to John the Baptist. First, he argues, one must recognize that different modes of speech have been employed which allow each evangelist some freedom in shifting the idiom from the third person to the first without any distortion of meaning (II. 14.31). This literary argument is then extended to defend the principle that identity of sense is the criterion for truth and not verbal coincidence. Calvin prefers the term 'substance'. Matthew differs from Mark and Luke because he offers the *summam doctrinae*, whereas they record in their own words. Augustine pursues the same approach in a somewhat different direction by suggesting that the evangelist has considerable freedom respecting the words he registers as long as he ascertains 'what is in the mind of the person who speaks' (*quid velit ille qui loquitur*, II. 12.29). The full implications of his theory of intentionality remained undeveloped in this pericope, but appeared later in fuller form.

Finally, the explanation occurs in every harmony that the dissonance among the Gospels stems from the evangelists either reporting sentences which were given on two different occasions (dissimilation), or by providing only a portion from a saying which was complemented by another writer. Thus, Augustine simply adds together the differing accounts of two Gospels as forming the whole: 'whose shoe lachet I am not worthy to unloose, and whose shoes I am not worthy to bear'. Newcome opts for the explanation of different occasions. Interestingly enough, one of the earliest extant examples which applies these same techniques of harmonization of Jesus' baptism is found in the Gospel of the Ebionites, which has been dated in the first half of the second century (cf. *NTApoc* I, 157f.).

B. *The Approach of Historical Criticism*

Few pericopes illustrate better the shift of perspective which modern historical criticism has introduced. Even when the starting point appeared to be the same – to what extent was John acquainted with Jesus – the ensuing discussion moved in a strikingly different direction.

The presence of different literary sources constituting the material about John the Baptist emerged clearly from early Synoptic studies. Whereas in the introduction of John the Baptist, Mark's basic outline is followed by Matthew and Luke, John's preaching of repentance occurs only in Matthew 3.7–10/Luke 3.7–9 and was assigned early on to Q. However, the complexity of the classic literary critical solution of the source problem is also illustrated in this material. The Q material recording John's preaching continues in Matthew 3.11f./Luke 3.16f., but has also a parallel in Mark's Gospel (1.7f). Since it seems clear that Matthew and Luke did not derive these verses from Mark, but from the same Q source from which they obtained the preceding and following verses, one must assume an overlap between Mark and Q (cf. Streeter, 166ff.).

Without pursuing the details of this literary problem which has not yet come to rest, some of the hermeneutical impact of the crucial literary approach is immediately apparent. The four accounts of John's ministry, instead of being treated as independent witnesses to a common reality, as in the traditional manner of the harmony, were now viewed as standing in an historical relationship or interdependence which introduced into the discussion a crucial new depth dimension. The classic harmonistic device of reconciling differences by means of dissimilation or conflation was dealt a hard blow.

The historical critical study of the Gospels also brought an important shift of perspective in its approach to the historical background of the Gospel tradition about John the Baptist. It raised the question of the historical relation between the followers of John and Jesus, and sought to supply historical motivation for a continuing rivalry, explaining Matthew's conversation (3.13–15) as an early Christian apologetic. Then again, it pursued the nature of the tradents of the various traditions surrounding John (cf. Bultmann's discussion), and sought to evaluate more precisely the colouring which the changing sociological milieu introduced. By classifying the material form-critically a different dynamic was produced which eclipsed the older harmonistic questions. Some scholars, particularly in the nineteenth century, sought to probe behind the text to uncover the growth of Jesus' messianic consciousness at the time of his baptism, applying to the event the general psychological principles which govern all human development (e. g. J. Weiss).

The effect of recent redactional study on the Baptist traditions has also been noteworthy. Rather than seeing the variations among the Synoptics as merely stylistic, redaction critics sought to uncover marks of a larger and consistent theological perspective regarding the significance of the baptism. A typical analysis of this approach is found in R. Pesch's synoptic reading. He argues that Mark has organized the Baptist tradition christologically in contrast to Matthew's ecclesiastical orientation. Luke, for his part, has assigned John's role completely to the Old Testament age and sharply separated even the baptism of Jesus from the activity of John who had already been imprisoned prior to the event (3.19ff.). As a result, earlier attempts to reconcile the Fourth Gospel's denial of John as an Elijah figure with the Synoptics' affirmation lost its significance and soon dropped out of sight.

My reason for reviewing the conflicting methodologies of the traditional harmonist with the modern historical critical approach is not to affirm one wholeheartedly nor to reject the other out of hand. The hermeneutical issue is a complex one and requires many subtle distinctions. On the one hand, the older harmonist's approach, in spite of its serious methodological weaknesses, has retained some elements of theological truth which have not been rendered obsolete by the critical method. When setting out a canonical approach, I shall try not to support this statement with specific detail.

On the other hand, the approach of historical criticism has brought a wealth of new material to bear on the text along with a depth of fresh insights which can only be welcomed by an interpreter. Nevertheless, the newer methodologies are also not without some serious problems and cannot be simply accepted without critical scrutiny. Clearly one must henceforth reckon with literary sources and a literary interrelationship. Moreover, that the John the Baptist tradition has a richer and more varied history than appears in the canonical Gospels is even evident from the book of Acts (19.1ff.). Finally, the study of the redactional stamp has sharpened the interpreter's focus on the text, as a comparison of the recent commentators such as Schweizer or Conzelmann with those of the previous generation such as V. Taylor or Schniewind demonstrates. Again in our canonical analysis we shall attempt to offer specific criticisms of the application of historical method to this cycle of stories.

c. A Canonical Harmony of the John the Baptist Accounts

The crucial hermeneutical question is whether one can develop a canonical approach which will not only make use of the strengths of both methods, while avoiding their weaknesses, but which will do justice to the peculiar integrity of the fourfold Gospel corpus in recovering an important dimension of this biblical literature. We begin by seeking to discern the effect of the canonical shape of the collection on the presentation of John the Baptist by the individual Gospels.

At the outset, the Fourth Gospel provides the key to the new hermeneutical function of the fourfold collection. In order to make this point clear it is necessary to distinguish between the shape of the Fourth Gospel as a literary composition with a discrete integrity, and its function within the canonical collection. The unique features of the fourth evangelist's account of the John the Baptist traditions have long been recognized. The fourth evangelist assumes a knowledge of the tradition on the part of his readers. Whether it derives from all of the Synoptic Gospels, from only certain of them, or from independent tradition (Gardner-Smith) remains debatable. The Fourth Gospel does not describe the origin or appearance of John. He was simply sent from God (1.6). Nor does he even depict the baptism of Jesus. Rather, John's role is restricted to that of a witness. His baptizing with water is contrasted with Jesus' baptism with the Holy Spirit which John confirms with his testimony to the descent of the dove (1.32).

With the formation of the Gospels into a fourfold collection some significant alterations in the function of the Fourth Gospel transpire respecting this particular material. If from an historical critical perspective the issue is unresolved whether or not the Fourth Gospel used the Synoptics or independent oral tradition, when joined in a canonical collection, a new relationship is formed. The effect of the parallelism in content with its verbal overlap between the Synoptics and John establishes a new literary context in which the Fourth Gospel functions as a commentary on the Synoptic accounts. In other words, the Fourth Gospel assumes a tradition of which only a few lines are sketched. However, when viewed canonically in the context of the fourfold collection, the Synoptic Gospels, which share a common outline with John, function as providing the full content of that tradition which John assumed. We are not suggesting that the new context which the canon has provided has resolved the historical problem of the relationship of the Gospels. Such a move issues in a confusion of categories. Rather, we are suggesting that a new literary entity emerged through the process of canonical shaping which offered a theological interpretation of the material in its fourfold testimony, and which has its own peculiar dynamic.

It can be debated to what extent Bultmann is historically correct in assuming that the presence of close parallels in John's Gospel with the Synoptics (e.g. 1.15, 30, etc.) stems from the hand of an ecclesiastical redactor who has introduced synoptic material secondarily into John's Gospel. However, the effect of the parallelism within the context of the collection is to bind the Gospels into a peculiar form. Accordingly, the Fourth Gospel is not merely summarizing tradition in general, but that very tradition of which the other three Gospels speak. Moreover, John's Gospel now functions as a type of commentary on the true significance of the events testified to by the Synoptics. Thus, according to this canonical shaping of the Baptist material, the four Gospels are not to be read on the same level, as four independent witnesses, but John's Gospel provides a theological framework by which to interpret the three.

There is a second alteration in the function of the Fourth Gospel which the canonical process has effected. Clearly John's Gospel made use of a peculiar mode of discourse. The description of John in terms of a witness, who understands the true nature of Jesus as Son of God on whom the Spirit rests forms a coherent part of the larger structure of this Gospel. However, it is only when the Fourth Gospel, with its peculiar mode of discourse is integrally related to the Synoptics by means of the canonical process that the nature of John's commentary becomes clear. John offers neither a targum nor a midrash of the Synoptics. He does not smooth out the tensions or fill in the gaps of the narrative. Rather, the effect of his mode of discourse with the larger collection is to alter the semantic level of the Synoptic material.

The Synoptics had spoken of one coming 'after' John who is 'mightier' than he (Matt. 3.11/ Mark 1.7/ Luke 3.16). John's interpretation parallels the Synoptics (1.30): 'after me comes a man who ranks before me, for he was before me.' However, John has altered the temporal language in order to talk about Christ's pre-existence (cf. Brown, *John*, I, ad loc.). Then again, the Synoptics portray John in various ways as fulfilling the role of Elijah, the eschatological prophet of the endtime (Matt. 3.4; Mark 1.3; Luke 3.4). But the Fourth Evangelist denies flatly that John can be identified with Elijah (1.21). The reason does not derive solely from his use of another tradition, but by shifting the level of discourse from regarding Elijah as a messenger to that of a voice, John finds the historical concretization no longer suitable to the new role. Finally, the whole discussion of John's not 'knowing' Jesus before the heavenly revelation no longer moves on the simple historical plane and thus conflicts with the historical portrayal, especially of Matthew. For the Fourth Gospel the polarity lies between human knowledge and revelation from heaven, with the creator of the world yet unrecognized by his own, and between being born of the Spirit and not of the flesh. Therefore, the Fourth Gospel's statement cannot be made to fit into the Synoptic sequence according to the older harmonist's strategy as if the tension could be removed by simple addition or dissimilation. Conversely for the historical critics to insist on finding an irreconcilable contradiction with the Synoptics is to misunderstand its new canonical function.

There is a third alteration in the function of the Fourth Gospel caused by the canonical process which demands our attention. The new role of the Fourth Gospel as a theological commentary to the Synoptics in this pericope has the effect of relativizing the differences among the Synoptics and drawing their witnesses together in a loose unity. In contrast to the *logos* christology of the Fourth Gospel which has reinterpreted the role of John the Baptist to serve as a witness to the revelation of the eternal Word who became flesh, the three Synoptics have in common a christology which presents the role of John the Baptist in relation to Jesus as one of anticipation to fulfilment. All the Synoptics have in common the seeing of John the Baptist in the role of an Old Testament preparation for the coming of the beloved Son (servant) of Isaiah 40. The variations in their presentation now function canonically as sounds of different notes within the one melody. In the light of this canonical effect, both Augustine and Calvin were right in emphasizing the similarity of substance among the Synoptics.

At this juncture an important difference between redaction criticism and the canonical approach emerges. Both methods agree in the need to hear each Gospel in its own integrity. The disagreement turns on how one evaluates the individual stamp of the different redactors. The concern of redaction criticism is to reconstruct a context in terms of the historical and sociological forces at work on the author and from this vantage point to understand the editorial changes. The danger inherent in the method is to exaggerate the extent of the differences and to force the material into theological systems which are highly speculative. Thus, Conzelmann's interpretation of the Lucan account of Jesus' baptism separates it sharply from the activity of John who, according to the previous verse (3.20) was already in prison and who in Lucan theology could have no role in the ministry of Jesus. Space is too limited for a full debate, but, in my judgment, Conzelmann has turned a structural device of the author into a full-blown theological system. In the light of the common tradition who could doubt John's participation in Jesus' baptism? Conzelmann has read far too much into a feature of literary stylization of Luke's Gospel. Similarly, the sharp distinction made by R. Pesch between a christological and ecclesiastical editing of the material concerning John the Baptist seems overly refined and more dictated by a theory of a redactor's intentionality than from the text itself.

In contrast to the redactional approach, the canonical method is concerned to interpret the Gospels, not only according to the intentionality of the individual evangelists, but also according to the function with the parts accrued in the light of the larger canonical collection. Of course, the modern interpreter does not know the mind of the canonical shapers any better than that of the redactors, but we do have an indication in the effect on the text which the canonical collection gave the literature. The material has been joined in such a way as to highlight some features and to subordinate others. It is my contention that, at least in terms of the John the Baptist material, the canonical ordering of the role of the Fourth Gospel and its effect on the Synoptic parallels has produced a centripetal force which has contracted the original variations rather than exacerbating the differences after the model of the redactional critics.

There is one final, important point to be made. The tensions between the witness of the Fourth Gospel and that of the Synoptics respecting the Baptist tradition have not been fully removed. Indeed the fourth evangelist offers a christological reading of the Synoptic tradition which has shifted the semantic level of the text and has viewed the material in terms of a consistent *logos* theology. However, the canonical shape has not fused the various accounts into one homogeneous whole. The Synoptics have been pulled closer together, but their combined witness remains in considerable tension with the Fourth Gospel. Accordingly, the relationship between John the Baptist and Jesus continues to be incomplete. John does not become a follower of Jesus, and his followers remain separate. Moreover, John's message of the coming judgment does not easily accord with the preaching of Jesus. The later account of John's doubt (Matt. 11.2–6/Luke 7.18–23) only confirms the continuing discrepancy. The Synoptics continue to bear witness to the difference between the expectation and its fulfilment. Therein lies a great theological significance which has not been destroyed by the very different stance offered by the fourth evangelist.

The canonical shaping of the Baptist tradition has given literary and theological clues as to how the material was to be ordered and interpreted. The two major christological construals are not to be fused by a unifying dogmatic system nor raised to a new level of abstraction. In this respect, a canonical reading offers a major correction to the traditional harmony. Nevertheless, there are theological connections between the two christological interpretations being offered. Both stress the unique status of the Son, the breaking in of the new, and the work of the Spirit through Christ's ministry. It remains the ongoing task of theological reflection, which is fully commensurate with the canonical approach, to reflect on the relationship which offers a rich variety of combinations, especially when viewed from the changing perspective of each generation of readers.

III. Peter's Confession at Caesarea Philippi

Bibliography

F. W. **Beare**, *The Earliest Records of Jesus*, London and Nashville 1962, 139; R. **Bultmann**, 'Die Frage nach dem messianischen Bewusstsein Jesu and das Petrusbekenntnis', *ZNW* 19, 1919/20, 165–75 = *Exegetica*, Tübingen 1967, 1–10; *The History of the Synoptic Tradition*, ET London and New York 1963, 257–9; T. A. **Burkill**, 'The Injunction to Silence in St Mark's Gospel', *TZ* 12, 1956, 585–604; O. **Cullmann**, *Peter: Disciple, Apostle, Martyr*, ET London and Philadelphia ²1962; E. **Dinkler**, 'Petrusbekenntnis und Satanswort. Das Problem der Messianität Jesu', *Zeit und Geschichte*, FS R. *Bultmann*, ed. E. Dinkler, Tübingen 1964, 127–53; ET, 'Peter's Confession and the "Satan" Sayings: The Problem of Jesus' Messiahship', *The Future of our Religious Past*, London and New York 1969, 169–202.

R. N. **Flew**, *Jesus and His Church*, London 1938, 123–36; E. **Haenchen**, 'Die Komposition von Mk 8, 27–9, 1 und Parr', *NovT* 6, 1963, 81–109; M. **Hooker**, *The Son of Man in Mark*, London and Montreal 1967, 174–88; R. H. **Lightfoot**, *The Gospel Message of St Mark*, Oxford 1950, 31ff.; W. **Mundle**, 'Die Geschichtlichkeit des messianischen Bewusstseins Jesu', *ZNW* 21, 1922, 299–311; R. **Pesch**, 'Das Messiasbekenntnis des Petrus (Mk 8, 27–30). Neuverhandlung einer alten Frage', *BZ* NF 17, 1973, 178–95; K. L. **Schmidt**, 'Die Kirche im Urchristentum', *Festgabe für A. Deissmann*, Tübingen 1927, 258–319; A. **Vögtle**, 'Messiasbekenntnis und Petrus-verheissung. Zur Komposition Mt 16, 13–23', in *Das Evangelium und die Evangelien*, Düsseldorf 1971, 137–70.

A. *Introduction to the Problems*

The parallel passages occur in Matt. 16.13–23, Mark 8.27–33, and Luke 9.18–22. Traditional harmonies of the Gospels did not recognize any great problems in combining the accounts (cf. Origen, Augustine, Calvin). The presence of significant additions and omissions was easily overcome by conflating the varying presentations into a single, unified scene.

One of the useful contributions of the modern critical method was in discovering some important new dimensions in the exegesis of these passages which had long been overlooked. First, the nature and extent of the differences among the Gospels showed up very sharply. It was argued that the Matthaean additions completely altered the context from that offered by Mark, and that such contradictory perspectives regarding the role of Peter could not be easily joined. Secondly, the different function of this pericope in the larger structure of each Gospel was clearly perceived. Although this insight was often misapplied in a psychologizing move by the life-of-Jesus movement, nevertheless the prime importance of the passage, especially for Matthew and Mark, was correctly discerned. Thirdly, the tension between the historical narrative concerning the ministry of Jesus and its post-Easter form which reflected the concerns of the later Christian church, was observed early in the nineteenth century. At first this issue was treated within a narrow literary approach in terms of 'genuine' and 'non-genuine' passages, but more recently the focus has been broadened into a history-of-traditions problem to include a study of the historical shape of the peculiar tradents of the material.

B. *The Canonical Shaping of the Tradition*

Considerable debate continues regarding the historical development of this passage. The controversy has focused particularly on the relation between the pre-Easter and post-Easter elements within the material. In my judgment, there are several signs, such as the geographical location, to indicate that the tradition was hardly created out of whole cloth (*contra* Bultmann). However, the material in all the Gospels is now thoroughly impregnated with a post-Easter perspective. Precisely this reforming of the tradition – both in the oral and literary stages – in order to preserve and address the ongoing community of faith is a process which we have entitled 'canonical shaping'. Although at times it is exegetically significant to be able to distinguish carefully between the different layers of this process, it is by no means axiomatic that the historical dimension functions always as a decisive factor for interpreting a biblical pericope. As we have tried to demonstrate, the material within each individual Gospel has been incorporated within an entity with its own discrete dynamic and the exegesis of a pericope is not directly dependent upon one's ability to trace the tradition's growth within every stage.

(i) Mark

Mark has set the scene at Caesarea Philippi which probably reflects a genuinely historical element. Jesus' question appears at first strange because confessions as to his identity have been unwanted up to that point in this Gospel. His question functions as a literary device which forms the backdrop for Peter's affirmation. The answers which are first offered are all positive – there would have been those who thought him mad – but they fall short of his true identity. Then Peter articulates the belief which the church continues to confess: 'You are the Christ' (Mark 1.1; John 20.31; Acts 17.3; 18.28). However, Jesus enjoins his disciples to silence.

There is nothing in the text to suggest that Jesus repudiated the title, but the narrative makes it immediately clear that the mystery of Christ's identity as the suffering Messiah required a different mode of revelation. Who Jesus was would only become clear through the experience of suffering and death which history would effect and which the disciples would witness. Jesus had made himself known in his acts of healing (1.29ff.), in forgiveness (2.9ff.), in signs of divine power (4.36ff.), and in teaching with authority (1.27). Now Mark introduces a new intensity into his narrative with the first of the prophecies of Christ's impending death (8.31; 9.31; 10.32ff.). Moreover, for the first time the implications for discipleship of the mystery of Christ's sufferings are made explicit.

Peter's rebuke and Jesus' response follow a larger pattern within Mark's Gospel. Each of the announcements of Jesus' role as the suffering Messiah called forth an example of misunderstanding (9.33ff.; 10.35ff.). In this passage Peter functions as an illustration of Christian misunderstanding, whereas Jesus spells out the true implications of discipleship. His call to the multitude for discipleship is set within an eschatological context of life and death. The parallel with Mark 13.30 identifies this 'adulterous and sinful generation' as the last before the entrance of God's kingdom in power. Before the convulsion of the old age, each Christian is enjoined to gain his life by losing it. Although Jesus' words in their Marcan form are addressed specifically to that second generation of Christians who are facing the threat of martyrdom (cf. Haenchen), in their canonical role they transcend this original historical particularity to confront each new generation of Christians with the cost of true discipleship.

(ii) Matthew

Initially Matthew follows Mark's outline quite closely with some slight variation. His rephrasing of the question in terms of the Son of man (16.13) does not seriously alter the sense (cf. the *koine* text). Similarly, Peter's confession is represented in a fuller form of Christian faith: 'You are Christ, the Son of the living God'.

The major addition of Matthew occurs in vv. 17–19. Whereas Peter's confession according to Mark is met with an admonition to silence, Matthew interposes a blessing on Peter which has the effect of shifting the structure of the passage significantly. The close Marcan connection with Jesus' call to discipleship is loosened and his teachings now form a separate section.

Peter is commended for his confession. He is designated as the foundation for Christ's church. Of course, Peter is assigned this role, not simply as a human being, but as an apostle. The church which shares Peter's confession is pictured as the temple of the new age. Peter is blessed for his confession and the emphasis falls on the divine origin of the truth concerning Christ which has been revealed to him.

Obviously the prehistory of this ecclesiastical tradition has been much debated. However, the exact relationship between its pre-Easter content and its post-Easter stamp is not crucial for determining its function within Matthew's Gospel. A very different dynamic from that of Mark has been established. The confession has been momentarily detached from the discourse on suffering, and the confessional context has been expanded in terms of an ecclesiastical actualization. The uniqueness of Christ is matched by the uniqueness of his church. The church which is grounded on this apostolic confession is promised an eternal existence against all the forces of opposition.

Matthew then picks up the Marcan sequence. Verse 21 introduces the altercation with Peter and the subsequent implication for discipleship as a separate scene 'from that time onward'. However, the linkage between the two scenes has not been completely severed. The image of Peter as the rock (v. 18) is juxtaposed with Peter as the stumbling-block (v. 23). Thus, Peter the apostle, the tradent of the church's faithful confession, stands in sharpest contrast with Peter, the representative Christian, who basically misunderstands the mission of his Lord.

Finally, one notices that the razor-sharp eschatological message of Mark's call to discipleship has been somewhat dulled. Matthew no longer addresses 'this sinful and adulterous generation' before whom the Christian disciple is tempted to be ashamed, nor does he speak of the kingdom's coming 'in power'. Rather, the challenge of discipleship is now formulated more in terms of rewards for obedience and of public confession (Matt. 10.33ff.).

(iii) Luke

In Luke the pericope concerning Peter's confession has not been assigned the prominent place that it has in the other Synoptic Gospels. The incident stands in close proximity to the feeding miracle which resulted from the omission of the Marcan material of 6.45–8.26, but which may find a parallel in a Johannine tradition (6.66ff.). Luke has a different setting with no mention of Caesarea Philippi. Peter's confession is also distinct from the other Synoptics. Jesus is 'the Christ of God'. But most uniquely, Luke has omitted all reference to a controversy with Peter. He moves directly from Peter's initial confession to an announcement of Jesus' own death and the call to discipleship.

The particular concern of Luke's Gospel emerges with his formulation of this latter theme. The phrase 'to take up one's cross' had already been used metaphorically by the other Synoptics. Now the call to discipleship is even further actualized in a universalized direction. The call is 'to all' ($\pi \acute{a} \nu \tau a \varsigma$). Moreover, Luke now adds the adverb 'daily'. The effect is to alter the radical eschatological perspective of Mark and to apply the call as a continual witness which extends over an indefinite period of time. The same theological intention is expressed in Luke 14.27: 'Whoever does not bear his own cross and come after me, cannot be my disciple'.

A summary is now in order. Each of the three Gospels has in common a tradition of Peter's confession with its close linkage to Christ's imminent death. Each of the Gospels has actualized the tradition in different ways in terms of its implication for Christian discipleship. For Mark, the secret of Christ's identity as the servant Messiah is set in stark opposition to Peter's confession and the call to discipleship is actualized in an eschatological context of the end of the age. For Matthew, the implication of Peter's confession is extended to the new community of faith, whose existence is grounded on an apostle who confesses Jesus as the Christ. For Luke, the call to discipleship is universalized as a repeated challenge to bear one's own cross in suffering for Christ's sake.

c. Hermeneutical Implications of the Larger Canonical Context

Up to this point we have been attempting to argue the case that the usual approaches to the diversity of the Gospels have been inadequate. On the one hand, the three Synoptic accounts of Peter's confession cannot be merely fused into a unity. Such a move fails to do justice to the different roles of the individual Gospels and the unique texture of each witness. On the other hand, the critical advice not to attempt to establish any larger canonical relationship beyond that of historical development (Beare, ad loc.), or to historicize the account in terms of a Palestinian or Hellenistic milieu does not begin to come to grips with the theological problem of scripture's role for a community of faith. How then is the diverse forms of Peter's confession to be interpreted within the larger canonical context of the fourfold Gospel corpus?

Peter's confession of Christ's identity and the implications for Christian discipleship have been actualized in different ways in the Synoptics. Each gospel applies the challenge to discipleship in a particular historical situation. The hermeneutic effect is that of refracting a beam of light through a prism with its multiform results. The initial canonical implication is to reinforce the position that there is not one fixed response which is always commensurate with the call to discipleship. Post-Easter Christians live in a different historical moment from pre-Easter disciples, and the implications of being a faithful follower of Christ continued to grow and develop for the church. The three Gospels have in common a similar witness to Christ's identity from Peter's confession, but implications for Christian discipleship are drawn in different ways and function as examples of a variety of genuine responses.

Secondly, the larger canonical collection offers a theological guide for the later Christian community by which to interpret and correct the historical particularity of each Gospel. It is clear that Mark's Gospel viewed its generation as the last before the consummation of Christ's kingdom. However, within the context of the fourfold corpus, Mark's interpretation has been balanced by two other forms of actualization which reckon with the continuation of discipleship in the church. Matthew has retained an eschatological understanding of the entrance of Christ's kingdom without tying its consummation specifically to that first generation. Luke has translated the call to discipleship into a metaphorical mode.

Then again, Matthew's famous addition of vv. 17–19 could lead to a distorted theology of the church triumphant unless it is constantly kept in relation to Mark's account of Peter's confession which has closely linked in the one oracle Peter's true confession with the immediate threat of its misunderstanding.

Finally, this pericope has some important theological implications for the larger theological problem posed by the canon. How can the witness of such fragile tradents who were so prone to the misunderstanding of Christ's message ever become the normative witness for successive generations of Christians? Was not much of Christ's teaching misunderstood and in need of reconstruction in order to recover its purer form? Particularly Matthew's form of this pericope addresses this larger hermeneutical issue. A sharp distinction is made between Christ's church which is grounded upon an apostolic testimony revealed by God himself, and those fully human disciples who were inclined to error and misunderstanding. The church's acceptance of the authoritative role of the canonical witness rests on the belief that God has chosen to use the testimony of the apostles in such a way as to guide his church in spite of the frailty of the vehicle of revelation.

IV. The Rich Young Ruler

Bibliography

B. W. **Bacon**, *The Beginnings of the Gospel Story*, New Haven and London 1909, 140–42; D. **Bonhoeffer**, *The Cost of Discipleship*, ET London and New York 1948, 50–69; G. **Bornkamm**, *Jesus of Nazareth*, ET London and New York, 1960, 146–52; R. **Bultmann**, *History of the Synoptic Tradition*, ET Oxford ²1968, 21f.; K. M. **Fischer**, 'Asketische Radikalisierung der Nachfolge Jesu', *Theologische Versuche* 4, Berlin 1972, 11–26; W. **Harnisch**, 'Die Berufung des Reichen Mk 10, 17–27', *FS E. Fuchs*, ed. G. Ebeling, Tübingen 1973, 161–76; J. **Jeremias**, *Unknown Sayings of Jesus*, ET London ²1964, 33–6; R. P. **Martin**, *New Testament Foundations: A Guide for Christian Students*, vol. 1, *The Gospels*, Exeter 1975; C. G. **Montefiore**, *The Synoptic Gospels I*, London ²1927; N. B. **Stonehouse**, *Origins of the Synoptic Gospels*, Grand Rapids 1963, London 1964, 93–112; N. **Walter**, 'Zur Analyse von Mc 10, 17–31', *ZNW* 53, 1962, 206–18; B. B. **Warfield**, 'Jesus' Alleged Confession of Sin', *PTR* 12, 1914, 177–228; reprinted *Christology and Criticism*, New York 1929, 97–145; J. **Weiss**, ' "Zum reichen Jüngling" Mk 10, 13–27', *ZNW* 11, 1910, 79–83.

A. Introduction to the Problems

The parallel passages for this pericope are as follows: Matt. 19.16–23; Mark 10.17–22; Luke 18.18–23. Our study will focus only on the first part of the larger narrative.

The pericope of the so-called 'rich young ruler' – a traditional nomenclature which derives from a conflation of the accounts – did not emerge as a serious problem for the older harmonists. The reason for this reaction is also immediately clear. The *koine* (Byzantine) text had already harmonized the parallels by conforming Matthew's text to that of Mark and Luke. Only when the more original text of Matthew was recovered in the ancient uncials did the sharp differences appear. Instead of Mark's reading (closely followed by Luke): 'Good teacher, what must I do to inherit eternal life?', and Jesus' response: 'Why do you call me good?', Matthew reads 'Teacher, what good thing must I do to have eternal life? And he said to him, "Why do you ask me about what is good? One there is who is good" '.

Once the more original text had been recovered, various other reasons contributed to the great interest which critical scholarship brought to bear on this passage. First of all, the Matthaean text appears to illustrate especially well the peculiar literary techniques of this evangelist. Not only did he show considerable freedom in altering the syntax of the adjective 'good', which he found in Mark, but he characteristically eliminated the expressions of emotion for the young man which had been attributed to Jesus (10.21). Secondly, and far more important, it was argued that Matthew had been offended by Mark on 'doctrinal grounds' (V. Taylor, *Mark*, 424f.) because he attributed to Jesus an acknowledgment of sin (Montefiore, I, 239f.), and thus Matthew 'softens' Jesus' response in order to alter the christology. Thirdly, commentators argued that Matthew had substituted a moralistic understanding of faith in the place of Mark's 'evangelical' one. Whereas for Mark the keeping of the law fails by omitting the crucial element of the cross, in Matthew eternal life can be gained by moral perfection (Bacon, *Gospel Story*, 132). More recently, Haenchen (*Der Weg Jesu*, 355ff.) has defended the view that Matthew represents a form of ascetic Judaism which provided the warrant for the later Roman Catholic doctrine of 'supererogatory works' which made possible a double standard within Christian morality.

In response to these allegations, conservative scholars sought to defend the 'orthodoxy' of Mark. Warfield argued that the passage at stake was not christological in focus but offered Christ's affirmation of the Old Testament commandments as the continuing expression of the one will of God. Stonehouse came to similar conclusions, but along a different route. He felt that the evidence was lacking by which to infer that Matthew found Mark's text to be a stumbling block and he sought to minimize the differences between the Gospels as doctrinally inconsequential.

B. *A Canonical Approach*

Because I am not fully satisfied with either of the approaches which have been briefly outlined, I would like to examine another alternative which explores the effect of the canonization process on the issue. Our study will deal only with Matthew and Mark. Luke's account appears to be an abbreviation of Mark and does not affect the exegetical issues at stake.

Mark's Gospel begins with a colourful description of the man who accosted Jesus as he was leaving for a journey. Running up to him, he knelt down and posed his question: 'Good teacher, what must I do to inherit eternal life?' Several things are noteworthy in the question. There is general agreement among New Testament scholars (cf. Lohmeyer) that the title of address used was an unusual one by which to address a rabbi. However, there is nothing in the text to determine why he used it, as if he considered Jesus more than an ordinary human being or was using the title as a means of flattery. The content of the question was not particularly surprising, but expressed a common pious aspiration of Judaism which stemmed from the Old Testament. How does one gain entrance into the kingdom of God? How does one obtain the blessings of future life in God's presence? Jesus' response clearly indicates that he rejected the question, although there is nothing to suggest that it was because of the man's insincerity or flattery. Rather, he repelled the question because it impinged upon the goodness of God. In the context of this question, God alone was the source from which goodness derived, and to whom all obedience was due. Then on the basis of this corrected formulation, Jesus answers the man's question. God has revealed his will in his commandments, the doing of which insures eternal life. Even in his role as 'good teacher', Jesus had nothing to offer which would countermand the law. Mark's account makes it particularly clear that Jesus was not purporting to say anything new, but reiterating the obvious which every Jew should know.

However, the questioner is not satisfied with the answer. He pushes the issue one step further. 'Teacher' – at least he has accepted Jesus' rebuke – 'all these commandments I have observed from my youth.' Implied in the statement is the question: 'What do I still lack?' The main point of the story now emerges with clarity. The questioner also agrees that the commandments reveal God's will. There is no question of lack of sincerity or failure in religious devotion. Mark explicitly confirms this point by depicting Jesus' reaction to the man: '. . . Looking upon him he loved him' (v. 21). Then Jesus responds: 'You lack one thing. Go, sell what you have, give it to the poor, and come, follow me.'

The major exegetical crux, of course, lies in determining the significance of Jesus' respose. Protestants have generally tended to argue, often in Pauline terms, that Jesus' reply sought to expose the moralism and 'works-righteousness' which formed the grounds for the whole discussion (so Zahn). Jesus had assumed the role of a legalist only as a device by which to destroy its entire structure. However, there is nothing in the text to suggest that Jesus' citing of the Old Testament Decalogue was only a device, or that a polarity between faith and works is at stake. Then again, traditional Roman Catholic exegesis has seen Jesus' answer as demanding something in addition to the usual commandments in order to offer him the special challenge of discipleship, but such an interpretation also lacks support from what precedes and what follows. Finally, there are innumerable psychological interpretations which see Jesus' response as a pedagogical attempt to correct a superficial view of the law, or to deepen the man's understanding of commitment.

The basic point to be made is that the challenge to sell all and to follow Jesus was not an eleventh commandment. It was not given as an additional requirement by which to achieve a special status of morality. Rather, Jesus' challenge must be seen in closest relationship to the Old Testament commandments. The call to sell all never functioned as a general imperative, but rather as an *ad hoc* challenge to this man, by which all the commandments assumed their correct perspective. Jesus thus radicalized the entire law by his demand for complete commitment. What the questioner lacked was therefore *everything* because he had not loved the Lord his God with complete abandonment. The issue turned on a qualitative omission, not quantitative.

If one now turns to Matthew's account, one notices immediately the sharply abbreviated form of the narrative which has dispensed with the background material of Mark. The crucial shift in formulation comes in the initial exchange between Jesus and the young man. The question becomes: 'What good thing must I do to have eternal life?' To this Jesus replies: 'Why do you ask me about the good?' It is highly possible that Matthew was disturbed by the Marcan form of the question. Certainly the change seems to be an intentional one and not simply derived from stylistic alterations of oral transmission. To ask about 'doing the good' in Jewish circles was not just to pose a philosophical question. It had long been established by the Old Testament that 'the good' was what God demanded of his people (Amos 5.14f.). In the context of the covenant, doing good was equivalent to establishing justice and fulfilling one's obligations toward one's neighbour. The questioner thus inquires what God requires for a person in order to enter the kingdom.

When Jesus replies: 'keep the commandments', Matthew sharpens the dialogue by having the young man then interject: 'Which commandments?' According to Matthew, Jesus then cites from the Decalogue and concludes with the summarizing imperative from Lev. 19.18: 'You shall love your neighbour as yourself.' The effect is that Matthew excludes any misunderstanding of the Old Testament commandments as simply legalistic stipulations by drawing out the full implications of what the Old Testament law really intended from the start. The addition helps eliminate the misinterpretation of Jesus' intention as if he were contrasting an older moralism with a new and higher commandment. Finally, the Matthaean addition in v. 21, 'If you would be perfect, go, sell what you possess', is basically misunderstood if viewed moralistically as a higher state of ethical perfection. Rather, the term is in accord with the earlier expansion from Leviticus and encapsulates the heart of the Old Testament law: 'Be ye perfect (holy) as I am perfect' (19.2, etc.). The goal of the law is to fashion God's people after his own likeness which is holiness. As in Mark, the parallel passage in Matthew turns on a qualitative omission in fulfilling the law, not one of quantity.

If we now expand the context of our study to examine the relationship between these two parallel accounts, it has become apparent that the two accounts of the story are making the same point in slightly different form. The parallels present, as it were, two sides of the same coin. In both, the witness concerns the relationship between the eternal will of God expressed in the Old Testament commandments and the messianic claim of Christ. In the context of the fourfold Gospel collection the two parallel passages function as mutually interpretive commentaries which are neither to be fused, nor torn apart, but heard in concert in terms of their christological witness.

c. Some Larger Implications of the Canonical Harmony

This passage offers a good opportunity for exploring some important hermeneutical issues in somewhat more detail.

(*a*) Modern literary and redactional criticism has enabled the interpreter to understand better the process by which a given composition took shape. By casting light on the peculiar propensities of an author, regarding both style and content, one brings the text into sharper focus. Thus, it is significant to see how Matthew has abbreviated and how he had expanded his text, and, if possible, to discern his characteristic moves and peculiar motivations. The effort of conservatives to minimize the differences between the accounts and to blur elements of redactional individuality in an effort to buttress traditional authorship is not constructive.

However, the attempt to ground interpretation in the intentionality of an author fails to reckon with the crucial problem of canon. The Gospel texts have not only been written by different authors, but were received and transmitted by different audiences over an extended period of time. Moreover, how the message was heard has now been incorporated within these multi-layered texts. The concern to ground interpretation in the final form of the text rests on the conviction that it is the received, canonical text which is authoritative. Thus, for example, Matthew may well have been offended by the Marcan form of the initial question: 'Good teacher . . .'. But ultimately an interpretation of the canonical text does not depend upon Matthew's motivation, but the shape which his text received by its hearers. Within the final form of Matthew's account, his alleged taking offence at Mark does not play any significant role. The effect of the redacted text has not built this factor into its message. It may be a valid literary observation to say that Matthew tends to eliminate from his Marcan *Vorlage* expressions which

attribute emotions to Jesus. However, the crucial issue for interpretation is whether or not the picture of Jesus given by Matthew was
heard and transmitted as depicting a different Christ from Mark.

(b) What significance does the larger canonical context of a fourfold
collection have for the charge that Mark reflects the vestiges from an
older, unorthodox christology? Assuming for a moment that Mark's
christology was in fact very different from Matthew's – a charge
which has not been established for this passage – what role would
the larger canonical context play in the issue? I have argued the case
that the formation of the canon effected a theological ordering of the
diverse material, and thus reflected how the various Gospels were
received and heard. In regard to this passage, Matthew and Mark
(Luke) were arranged as mutually interpretive witnesses to the one
event. One was not subordinated to another, nor was the semantic
range altered, nor the historical referent changed. Rather, the effect
of the canonical collection was to present one basic testimony with
complimentary features. In sum, Mark's account was not heard
as offering a radically different christology in competition with
Matthew, but as multiple testimonies to the one gospel.

The same case can be made to the charge that Matthew has
seriously altered the ethical imperative of Jesus as presented by
Mark, and transformed it into a form of early Catholic asceticism.
Although such an exegesis would be difficult to sustain even on the
basis of Matthew's Gospel alone, it is thoroughly eliminated when
viewed from the perspective of the larger canon.

(c) As we have seen, the text-critical issue assumes major exegetical
significance in Matthew's account of the 'rich young ruler'. My
concern is to explore the hermeneutical issues involved which have
often been overlooked in the allegedly scientific recovery of the best
and most original text (cf. Excursus I).

Certainly no one would contest the significance of recovering an
earlier form of Matthew's text which differs markedly from that of
Mark and Luke. Rather, the critical issue turns on evaluating the
significant fact that Matthew's text in its transmission has been
harmonized to the other Gospels. If the goal of New Testament
exegesis is to recover the earliest text, then the significance of its
transmission history can be largely dismissed as illustrating only a
process of subsequent corruption. However, if the canonical process
includes the reception of the text as part of the 'data' of the

authoritative tradition, then the form of its textual history is also significant.

It would be a serious error simply to identify the *koine* text with the canonical text. The *koine* or Byzantine text is a post-canonical development which sought to preserve, usually by conflation, what it regarded to be the apostolic witness. However, the history of the transmission also of this text type involved continuous accretion and innumerable errors which blurred its form. Thus the task of New Testament criticism must involve a critical sorting of the evidence in search for the best form of the received apostolic tradition.

The broad scope of early testimony to the unharmonized text of Matt. 19.16 offers convincing evidence that this reconstructed text is closer to the canonical text than the *Textus Receptus*. However, the harmonized reading also offers a significant testimony to confirm that these Gospel accounts were not heard as being significantly different. Although one cannot identify the apostolic testimony of the New Testament which constitutes canonical scripture with the subsequent traditional readings of later generations, there is often a significant continuity between the generations of Christian readers which cannot be discounted. For this reason attention to the traditional (*koine*) text remains theologically significant for exegesis when it is done within the context of the canon.

V. The Cursing of the Fig Tree

Bibliography

Cf. the extensive bibliographies in R. **Pesch**, *Das Markusevangelium* II, Freiburg 1977, 201f., and W. R. **Telford**, *The Barren Temple*, 272–86. P. J. **Achtemeier**, *Mark* (Proclamation Commentaries), Philadelphia 1975, 23–6; H. W. **Bartsch**, 'Die "Verfluchung" des Feigenbaums', *ZNW* 53, 1962, 256–60; J. **Buse**, 'The Cleansing of the Temple in the Synoptics and in John', *ExpT* 70, 1958/9, 22–4; H. **Cousin**, 'Le figuier desséché. Un exemple de l'actualisation de la geste évangélique', in *Foi et Vie, FS Suzanne de Dietrich*, ed. J. Ellul, Paris 1971, 82–93; J. W. **Doeve**, 'Purification du Temple et desséchement du figuier', *NTS* 1, 1954/5, 297–308; H. **Giesen**, 'Der verdorrte Feigenbaum – Eine symbolische Aussage', *BZ* 20, 1976, 95–111; W. L. **Knox**, *Some Hellenistic Elements in Primitive Christianity*, London 1944; R. H. **Lightfoot**, *The Gospel Message of St Mark*, Oxford 1950, 60–69; G. **Münderlein**, 'Die Verfluchung des Feigenbaumes (Mk. XI. 12–14)', *NTS* 10, 1963/4, 89–104; R. **Pesch**, R. **Kratz**, 'Jesu Fluch über den

Feigenbaum', *So Liest Man Synoptisch*, VI, Frankfurt 1979, 75–7; A. de Q. **Robin**, 'The Cursing of the Fig Tree in Mark', *NTS* 8, 1962/3, 276–81; C. W. F. **Smith**, 'No Time for Figs', *JBL* 79, 1960, 315–27; W. R. **Telford**, *The Barren Temple and the Withered Tree, JSNT*, Suppl. 1, Sheffield 1980.

A. *Introduction to the Problems*

The parallel passages are found in Mark 11.12–14, 20–25 and Matt. 21.18–22. For the traditional harmonist two major sorts of problem have emerged. One has to do with the apparently different chronology in which the event was set. The second problem turns on harmonizing the conflicting presentations of the event.

According to Mark, Jesus entered Jerusalem (11.11), looked around the temple, but as it was late, departed to Bethany to spend the night. On the next day, leaving Bethany he cursed the fig tree and subsequently cleansed the temple. In the evening of this second day he again left the city. On the morning of the third day, his disciples observed the withered fig tree and received Jesus' instruction as to its meaning.

According to Matthew, Jesus rode into Jerusalem, entered the temple and cleansed it. He then left the city and lodged in Bethany. On the morning of the second day, when he was returning to the city, he cursed the fig tree, and, when the disciples saw that it withered at once, he instructed them concerning its meaning. Thus, Mark portrays the cursing of the fig tree before the cleansing of the temple, whereas Matthew places it after. Mark depicts an interval of time between the cursing and the recognition of its withering while Matthew portrays the cursing and the withering at the same moment of time.

Several characteristic ways to reconcile the accounts are represented by the traditional harmony. Apart from the moral difficulties which have been a problem from the outset, the most frequent issue demanding a resolution is the chronology. Augustine and Calvin are representative in reconstructing a historical sequence by combining the two accounts on the assumption that both evangelists have used considerable freedom in their portrayals. Clericus' reconstruction is more radical and he is forced to transfer the entry in Mark 11.11 after 11.15 in order to harmonize the passage with Matthew's sequence. Another approach is to suggest that Jesus began to cleanse the temple on one day, and completed it on the next, and that the tree began immediately to wither (so Matthew), but was not observed until the next day by the disciples (so Mark). Finally, the more consistent harmonists fell back on the theory of dissimilation and had several cleansings (Lightfoot) and several cursings (Osiander). Of course, the major criticism of all these attempts is that the biblical text is badly bent in an effort to achieve harmony. The peculiar features of the individual Gospels are treated as obstacles to be overcome and so consistently blurred.

With the rise of critical scholarship a variety of new interpretations were offered, some of which have persisted. At times it was argued that the story derived from a parabolic saying of Jesus (cf. Luke 16), which was externalized into the form of a miracle in the course of its growth (Knox 82), or that it was an etiology which subsequently intruded into the passion narrative (Haenchen, *Der Weg Jesu*, 381). Montefiore is frank: 'The story has, in any case, no moral or religious value for us today' (*Synoptic Gospels* I, 266). Several commentators agree that the story now functions symbolically even though its original role is unclear (Lohmeyer, Schniewind, Schweizer).

In recent years the work of redaction critics has successfully begun to illuminate this passage in a fresh way. For example, Achtemeier offers an excellent summary in regard to Mark's use of the episode (23ff.). He points out that the evangelist has offered an interpretation of the story by using it as a bracket for the cleansing of the temple. He thus indicates that he intends the two stories to be understood in relation to each other. The effect is that the temple is now interpreted as cursed like the tree, and the story functions as a symbolic act of bringing the worship of the temple to an end. In my judgment, this close literary reading of the text has made an important contribution in correctly interpreting the Gospel of Mark and also in pointing the way to its larger canonical role.

When we next turn to Matthew, the difficulty in discerning the evangelist's intention increases. Telford (72) underscores the problem of trying to make any redactional sense of the story in the context of ch. 21. In the end, he argues that Matthew's redaction has been prompted by his disapproval of the symbolic tones in Mark and that he transforms the tradition to make a didactic point (80). In spite of many excellent observations, I remain unconvinced that Telford has correctly heard the peculiar emphasis of the Matthaean text.

Clearly Matthew has shaped his material in a way quite differently from Mark. Following his entry into Jerusalem which was accompanied by messianic shouts of Hosanna (Ps. 118.26), Jesus enters the temple and cleanses it. Then Matthew includes another event which also occurred in the temple, namely, the healing of the blind and the lame. Moreover, he identifies those healed with those who had earlier greeted Jesus with shouts of Hosanna (v. 15). The effect is that the cleansing of the temple is now bracketted by a response of true faith. His rejection by the old is accompanied with his reception by the new. Along with the purging of the old order the concrete signs of new and wonderful things have already emerged.

At this point in the narrative Matthew has inserted the cursing of the fig tree, but this negative illustration is provided immediately with a positive interpretation by Jesus. He teaches the disciples the power of faith (vv. 21ff.). This theme of faith and belief is then continued in the controversy and parable which are both linked to the ministry of John the Baptist. One son said yes and refused; the other said no, but agreed. An interpretation is offered in v. 32. The chief priests and Pharisees did not believe, but the tax collectors and harlots have faith. A similar point is made in the following parable. The kingdom of God has been taken away from them and given to a nation producing fruits. Matthew's explicit reference three times to the 'season of fruit' (or the like, 34, 41, 43) is thus linked to the withered fig tree which failed to produce fruit.

The effect of Matthew's formation of the material is that the cursing of the fig tree now functions as a parable, along with 28ff. and 33ff. All three first make a negative point respecting the old religious order, but all three add to this a positive interpretation which supports the original bracketing of the temple cleansing with a response of faith. The vineyard is given to a nation producing fruit (v. 43). The old order of the temple worship has already died (cf. παραχρῆμα = 'immediately'), and has been replaced by those recipients of faith who are already signs of the messianic age. Matthew has shifted the focus of the withering of the fig tree to become a marvellous sign (vv. 20, 42) to those who live by faith and prayer.

B. The Search for a Canonical Harmony

Once each of the passages has been heard in its own distinctiveness and purpose, we are in a position to return to the larger canonical question. How are the two passages to be harmonized within the context of the fourfold Gospel collection? What is now obvious is that the crucial hermeneutical interpretation of the fig tree episode has already occurred on the redactional level. It is very unlikely that the cursing of the fig tree functioned originally on a symbolic level. Lohmeyer makes the excellent point that the grounding of the story in the genuine hunger of Jesus does not support an original didactic role (*Markus*, 235). However, regardless of the prehistory of the tradition, both evangelists have interpreted the event symbolically. Their theological points vary slightly in each Gospel. Matthew complements the completely negative purpose of the cursing of Mark with a positive understanding of the new nation of faith which, in its response to the kingship of Christ, has replaced the old order. Because both parallels have been assigned a symbolic interpretation, the two stories easily complement each other. However, the nature of this harmony also reveals the crucial differences between the canonical and the traditional approaches.

The two accounts are to be harmonized kerygmatically, that is to say, in respect to their witness to the one gospel of Jesus Christ. The traditional harmony has attempted its interpretation always on the grounds of reconstructed history without taking seriously the peculiar canonical shape by which the material has been assigned a function for the continuing community of faith. Secondly, a canonical harmony does not fuse the stories into one fixed literary composition, but establishes a flexible context in which further theological reflection on the christological context of the varying witnesses can be pursued. Both Mark and Matthew interpret the fig tree incident symbolically, but how their two witnesses to the messianic action of Christ relate demands a disciplined reflection within the context of the entire New Testament which is hardly exhausted in one formulation.

VI. The Anointing of Jesus

Bibliography

R. E. **Brown**, *The Gospel according to John, I-XII*, New York 1966, London 1971, 447–54; D. **Daube**, 'The Anointing at Bethany and Jesus' Burial', *AnThR* 32, 1950, 186–99; J. **Delobel**, 'L'onction par la pécheresse', *ETL* 42, 1966, 415–75; J. D. M. **Derrett**, 'The Anointing at Bethany', *StEv* II, TU 87, 1964, 174–82; C. H. **Dodd**, 'The Anointing at Bethany (xii 1–8)',

Historical Tradition in the Fourth Gospel, Cambridge² 1965, 162–73; H. **Drexler**, 'Die grosse Sünderin Lc 7, 36–50', *ZNW* 59, 1968, 159–73; J. K. **Elliott**, 'The Anointing of Jesus', *ExpT* 85.1974, 105–07; P. **Gardner-Smith**, *St John and the Synoptic Gospels*, Cambridge 1938, 42–50; W. **Henss**, *Das Verhältnis zwischen Diatessaron, christlicher Gnosis und 'Western-Text'*, BZNW 33, 1967; J. **Jeremias**, 'Die Salbungsgeschichte Mc 14, 3–9', *ZNW* 35, 1936, 75–82; A. **Legault**, 'An Application of the Form-Critique Method to the Anointings in Galilee and Bethany', *CBQ* 16, 1954, 131–41; R. **Pesch**, 'Die Salbung Jesu in Bethanien (Mk 14, 3–9). Eine Studie zur Passionsgeschichte', *Orientierung an Jesus. FS J. Schmid*, ed. P. Hoffmann, N. Brox and W. Pesch, Freiburg 1973, 267–85; R. **Pesch**, R. **Kratz**, 'Jesus wird in Bethanien gesalbt', *So Liest Man Synoptisch* VII, Frankfurt 1980, 22–28; H. **Sahlin**, 'Zwei Fälle von harmonisierendem Einfluss des Matthäus-Evangeliums auf des Markus-Evangelium', *StTh* 13, 1959, 166–79; L. **von Sybel**, 'Die Salbungen. Mt 26, 6–13, Mc 14, 3–9, Lc 7, 36–50, Joh 12, 1–8', *ZNW* 23, 1924, 184–93.

A. *Introduction to the Problems*

The passages which concern the anointing of Jesus are as follows: Matt. 26.6–13; Mark 14.3–9; Luke 7.36–50; John 12.1–8. The problems encountered by the traditional harmony are set forth clearly and in full by Newcome (*Harmony*, 120), although many of them had already been discussed by earlier harmonists. The problem had been greatly intensified for the traditionalists when H. Grotius brilliantly attempted to derive the various Gospel accounts from one event (cf. especially the response of Clericus).

Briefly stated, the problems which the harmonies faced were numerous. First, the anointing of Jesus is recorded by Matthew and Mark as occurring two days before passover, but in John it appears to have occurred six days before passover. Moreover, in John the anointing precedes the triumphal entry, but in Matthew and Mark it follows the event. Secondly, the scene is laid in different places, namely, in the house of Mary and Martha (Lazarus), or in that of Simon the leper, or Simon the Pharisee. Thirdly, Matthew and Mark speak of anointing Jesus' head, John of his feet. Fourthly, the woman doing the anointing is unnamed in Matthew and Mark. She is identified as Mary in John and called a sinner in Luke. Fifthly, the disciples object in Matthew and Mark, whereas according to John it is Judas who objects. Finally, the response of Jesus varies among the Gospels.

The traditional ways of harmonizing such problems are familiar by now and need not be pursued in detail. The chronology is adjusted by assuming a period of time between vv. 1 and 2 of John 12, or by recourse to a theory of subsequent recollection which is different from the historical sequence. The differences in details between John and Matthew/Mark are thought to be complementary. Most significant, however, the account in Luke is almost universally attributed to a different event and removed from the need of harmonization.

In striking contrast to the harmonists' view, the modern critical approach introduced an historical depth which appeared to resolve the problems at one stroke. Indeed, the force of the argument is hard to deny. Especially C. H. Dodd set forth the growth of the material in a clear, and largely convincing, manner. The variations arose in the course of oral transmission. Two different patterns emerged, the one of Mark-Matthew, the other the form used by Luke. In the first, an unknown woman anoints Jesus' head in the house of Simon the leper. In the second, in the house of Simon the Pharisee a harlot anoints his feet, and weeping, dries them with her hair. Subsequently, John combined elements of these two patterns into his story with some additions. The woman is identified with Mary, but she also dries with her hair his feet which she has anointed.

R. E. Brown (*John*, ad loc.) agrees in general with the depiction of such an historical growth, but prefers the theory that two basic events lay at the beginning of the development rather than just one. Luke's account derives from a penitent sinner who weeps in Jesus' presence. There is no anointing with perfume, but she scandalizes the Pharisees by loosening her hair in public. Mark's account refers to a scene at Bethany in which a woman – probably Mary – anointed Jesus' head with an expensive perfume to express her devotion to him. The two stories then grew and mutually influenced each other. Brown prefers to think that John's account depends on a form of oral tradition in which the admixture of detail had already occurred, rather than to assume a direct knowledge of different Synoptic Gospels.

B. *The Witness of the Individual Gospels*

The basic hermeneutical issue at stake turns on the question as to whether the function which the canonical collection of the fourfold Gospels assigns these passages has been correctly understood. My argument is that their role has not been adequately assessed either

by the traditional harmony, which depends upon a strained reconstruction of an allegedly original historical sequence, or by recovering
a traditio-historical development of the material's prehistory. What
then is the special canonical dynamic of this passage?

We turn first to examine the role which the anointing passage
plays within Luke's Gospel. Clearly there is a historical relationship
between this account and the other Gospels. However, regardless of
whether Dodd or Brown is correct in deriving Luke's account from
a separate event or from one in common with the rest of the Gospels,
Luke's Gospel has clearly assigned this passage a different function
from that of its parallels. Within Luke, the passage has been
completely disconnected from the passion narrative and located in
Galilee within a different chronological framework. Moreover, the
anointing scene is unrelated to the death of Jesus, but serves as the
occasion for a parable which addresses the question of forgiveness.
Whether the sayings produced the situation or the reverse
(Bultmann, *Synoptic Tradition*, 20f.) is not directly relevant to determining its role within the final form of Luke's Gospel. Thus, although
the historical critics are undoubtedly right that the oral form of
Lucan tradition has influenced the shape of the other Gospels, the
harmonists are also correct in arguing for a discrete, non-parallel
function within the final form of the canon.

The Gospel of Matthew follows that of Mark closely, using the
same larger narrative framework and retaining a verbal parallelism
with only minor abbreviations. For our purposes, the role which it
assigns the passage is similar to that of Mark's. Therefore, the crucial
issue turns on the relationship between Mark and John. We begin
by studying the role of the anointing passage in each of these Gospels
before raising the question of the effect of the canonical collection.

In Mark, the passage of the anointing (14.3–9) has been inserted
between the announcement of the Jewish leaders' determination to
destroy Jesus by stealth (vv. 1f.), and Judas' offer to betray Jesus to
them (vv. 10–11). This introduction affords a guide to the meaning
of the passion narrative for Mark. The passion week of 14.1 begins
two days before the feast and ends in 16.1 two days after passover.
Lohmeyer notes how carefully Jesus' last twenty-four hours are
divided into three-hour sections (14.26, 72; 15.1, 25, 34, 42).

The scene is set in Bethany at the house of Simon the leper. No
one else is mentioned by name. We hear merely of 'a woman' and of
'some' present who complained. She broke a jar of costly ointment

over Jesus' head while he sat at table. Those present then objected to this waste, suggesting it would have been better used for serving the poor. Jesus defended her action at considerable length. 'She has done a beautiful thing to me . . . you will not always have me with you . . . she has anointed my body for burial . . . wherever the gospel is preached, her deed will be remembered to her credit.'

Jesus' defence of the woman offers the key to the interpretation of the event according to Mark. The woman's action does not focus on her love for Jesus. None of her emotions are depicted, nor is she given a name (contrast Luke and John). Rather, the stark objective character of her deed is emphasized. There is no indication of how she got the ointment or how the others immediately knew the cost. The woman's significance lies in her witness to the uniqueness of Christ in his passion. She testifies to his office as the royal Messiah, anointing him on his head. Jesus confirms that she has done a good work which is indeed commensurate with his status. Moreover, what the woman has done in his honour takes priority over the care of the poor which is a perennial duty. This eschatological moment in history comes only once because in this hour Jesus' true identity is revealed. The woman has responded in a way suitable to that special hour by her extravagant gift. She has anointed the Messiah in anticipation for the grave. She has not only foreseen his death prophetically, but actually performed an historical act whose full significance lay in the future. According to Mark, the woman thus becomes the first witness to the revelation of the suffering Messiah. Her testimony has actually entered into the preaching of the gospel of Christ's redeeming death which would continue in the proclamation of the church (14.9).

John's presentation of the anointing scene differs not only in detail, but in its structure and significance as well. The raising of Lazarus from the dead, which story preceded the anointing of Jesus, had evoked the harshest opposition of the Jews. The formation of their conspiracy to kill him constitutes the introduction of the anointing scene. The close connection between the resurrection of Lazarus and the Jews' plot is again seen at the conclusion of the anointing passage (12.10). Moreover, Lazarus 'whom Jesus had raised from the dead' (v. 2) plays a prominent role in the anointing story as the host to Jesus along with Mary and Martha.

The sharp contrast which the signs of Jesus called forth is built into the structure of the anointing story. Instead of being in the house of Simon the leper, or the hostile Simon the Pharisee of Luke's Gospel, Jesus is entertained by his closest friends whose deepest devotion has already been expressed in the previous chapter. Conversely, the opposition to this expression of love by Mary is provided, not by a group of insensitive disciples, but by Judas, the evil betrayer (v. 4) whose apparent concern for the poor was motivated by his personal greed. This sharp antithesis between faith and unbelief continues a central Johannine theme that divine judgment is meted out in accordance to one's response to Jesus who is the Christ (3.17ff.).

John's understanding of the approaching passion also has a different focus from that of Mark's. Jesus came into the world to do the will of God. When he is lifted up he will draw all men to himself (12.32). When his hour comes, then the Son of man will be glorified (12.23). Previously, because his hour had not yet come, no one could lay their hands on him (7.30; 8.20). But now the hour has come and Jesus goes to the feast of the passover in Jerusalem to fulfill the will of God and to be delivered unto death. He does not pray to be spared from the hour of his death because through it God will be glorified (12.27).

According to John's Gospel, Jesus is anointed by Mary before his triumphal entry into Jerusalem (12.12ff.). She shows her devotion to him by expending her costly gift. She anoints his feet and wipes them with her hair. Jesus commends the act: she has anointed him for his burial. Mary honours him as king, but not as the crowd who did not understand (12.12ff.). Rather, she anoints him as the Christ who is about to die. Jesus explains why Mary did not give the money to the poor (v. 7). She had reserved her gift for his burial. Mary had recognized the need for Jesus to die, and in an expression of genuine devotion had consciously anticipated his burial. Thus, Jesus enters Jerusalem as a king anointed for burial and unfolds the truth of his life through his death for all mankind.

It has often been suggested that the end of v. 3 is to be interpreted symbolically: 'the house was filled with the fragrance of the ointment' (cf. Westcott, Hoskyns, Bultmann). In my judgment, this is not the case when one's attention is confined to John's presentation. Only when one sets the verse in parallelism to Mark's saying about the gospel's being preached in the whole world (14.9) does a non-literal meaning to John's statement appear. However, it should be recognized that this interpretation rests on a larger canonical context and does not derive solely from a reading of John.

c. The Search for a Canonical Harmony

Once we have attempted to interpret each Gospel on its own terms, it is now appropriate to search for its canonical significance within the fourfold collection.

We have seen that the Gospels of Mark and John bear witness to the same event, the account of which is set at the beginning of the passion week. In both Gospels the anointing story offers a theological guide to what follows. Yet it is also clear from a study of each individual Gospel that their differing chronology is not to be harmonized, either as to what day the events occurred or as to its relationship to the triumphal entry. The stories in their canonical form do not function on the same plane. A different theological understanding of time is at stake. For Mark, the anointing of Jesus begins a chain of events in which the secret identity of Christ is manifested in his death as Israel's suffering Messiah. The moment of eschatological disclosure enters into a given period of history and forms part of the Gospel from that point on. However, for John the unfolding of the eternal plan of God reaches its final hour when Christ, the obedient Son, fulfils the divine will by his voluntary death on the cross, and in his glorifying of the Father reveals his salvation to all the world.

Similarly, the personnel in the two accounts of the event play different theological roles. Mark portrays the objective testimony of an unknown woman whose honouring of Jesus by anointing his head bore witness to the uniqueness of his person as the suffering, royal Messiah, and who unknowingly anticipated his impending death, whereas John sets the event in the house of Jesus' closest friends, and portrays the love and sacrificial devotion of Mary who, sensing the threatening evil contrived by the leaders and personified by Judas, anoints his feet for burial. Thus, it follows that the event of the anointing has a different significance in the interpretation of the passion for the two Gospels, which is severely damaged if the details of the story are formed into an allegedly single, consistent story.

In what manner then are the Gospel accounts to be related which will do justice to the new function which the formation of the fourfold collection has effected? The canonical shape bears testimony to the one gospel in its multiple form, but it is the task of each generation

of interpreters to strive to discern its unity. We thus approach the
collection with the question: What does this pericope within the
fourfold Gospel tell us of Jesus Christ?

In all the accounts of Jesus' anointing there is a preparation for
his death in some fashion. The basic theological problem turns on
understanding the relationship between Christ's death which was
the culmination of a chain of human actions, devised and carried out
by evil men, and the eternal plan of God which encompassed the
evil of human contrivance, and which had been derived from the
foreordained will of God for the salvation of the entire world. The
two anointing stories of Mark and John reflect different approaches
to both history and eschatology, but both are wrestling with aspects
which together constitute the heart of christology.

Again, different aspects of faith in Christ are portrayed in the
stories. To characterize the relationship as one of objective and
subjective is not fully on target, but this contrast at least begins to
catch some of the theological polarity. Both Mark and John agree
on a response of faith which is represented by the extravagant
and reckless expenditure of perfume, a gift which dramatizes the
honouring of Christ with all one's costliest possessions. Moreover,
both accounts see the anointing as an act of Christian devotion
which is incorporated within the message of redemption itself, and
overcomes the opposition of earthly power to fill the world.

However, does not such an approach drain the Gospels of their
historical character and substitute theological meaning for the
element of positivity? I would argue that the canonical shaping of
each Gospel has preserved its own relationship to the historical
events. An overarching relationship cannot be generalized. Specifically in terms of these anointing stories, the act of Christ's anointing
before his death constitutes a non-reducible element in the witness
of Matthew/Mark and John. Indeed, because this essential relationship to this event is missing in Luke's Gospel, whatever its theological
significance, it has been set apart by the canonical process from the
other three Gospels.

It should be stated immediately that these christological reflections
on the canonical shape of the anointing stories by no means exhaust
the possibilities, but are only illustrative of the continuing theological
task involved in reading the fourfold Gospels. Precisely because
no one literary interrelationship among the Gospels has become
normative, a flexible variety of moves is called for. Thus, although

the Lucan account of the anointing of Jesus has been detached from the passion narrative, it would still be fully in order to compare, say, Jesus' response to human affection as found in Luke with that of Matthew or John. Similarly, there is a certain parallel in the story of Jesus blessing the children (Mark 10.13ff.) with the anointing story, particularly as given by Mark. In both there is a rational objection from the disciples who have another scale of highest priority. In both stories Jesus blesses the response of transparent love and spontaneous affection.

To summarize: the anointing stories reflect a theological ordering of the tradition which has its own distinct integrity and canonical dynamic which is different from the historical process by which the compositions developed. At this point a canonical approach to the Gospels finds itself at odds with a critical methodology which identifies correct interpretation with its correlation to historical development. The canonical shape first limited the range of diversity within the tradition by assigning a separate function to Luke's account. Although some of Luke's unique tradition was retained in the Johannine account, these features performed a special function within the Fourth Gospel. The effect of the canonical ordering of this material was therefore to provide complementary dimensions of christology by means of diverse narrative accounts, whose tensions were carefully modified in places, but largely retained.

VII. The Resurrection Narratives

Bibliography

P. **Althaus**, 'Die Auferstehung der Toten', reprinted *Theologische Aufsätze*, Gütersloh 1929, 119–39; K. **Barth**, *The Resurrection of the Dead* (1924), ET London and New York 1933; P. **Benoit**, 'Marie-Madeleine et les disciples au tombeau selon Jn 20, 1–18', *Judentum – Urchristentum – Kirche, FS J. Jeremias*, ed. W. Eltester, BZNW 27, 1960, 141–52; H. D. **Betz**, 'The Origin and Nature of Christian Faith according to the Emmaus Legend', *Interp* 23, 1969, 32–46; E. L. **Bode**, *The First Easter Morning*, AnBib 45, 1970; L. **Brun**, *Die Auferstehung Christi in der urchristlichen Ueberlieferung*, Oslo 1925; R. **Bultmann**, 'Karl Barth, "Die Auferstehung der Toten"', *ThBl* 5, 1926, 1–14; ET, 'Karl Barth, *The Resurrection of the Dead*', *Faith and Understanding* I, London and New York 1969, 66–94; *Theology of the New Testament* I, ET London and New York 1951, 42ff., 292ff.; H. **von Campenhausen**, 'The Events of Easter and the Empty Tomb', *Tradition and Life in the Church*, ET

London and Philadelphia 1968, 42–89; C. H. **Dodd**, 'The Appearances of the Risen Christ: an Essay in Form-Criticism of the Gospels', *Studies in the Gospels, Essays in Memory of R. H. Lightfoot*, ed. D. E. Nineham, Oxford 1957, 9–35; J. H. A. **Ebrard**, *Wissenschaftliche Kritik der evangelischen Geschichte*, Frankfurt [3]1868; C. F. **Evans**, *Resurrection and the New Testament*, SBT II. 12, 1970; G. **Friedrich**, 'Die Auferweckung Jesu, eine Tat Gottes oder ein Interpretament der Jünger?', reprinted *Auf das Wort kommt es an, GA G. Friedrich*, Göttingen 1978, 319–53; R. H. **Fuller**, *The Formation of the Resurrection Narratives*, London and New York 1972.

P. **Gardner-Smith**, *The Narratives of the Resurrection: A Critical Study*, London 1926; H. **Grass**, *Ostergeschehen und Osterberichte*, Göttingen [4]1970; G. **Hartmann**, 'Die Vorlage der Osterberichte in Joh 20', *ZNW* 55, 1964, 197–220; E. **Hirsch**, *Die Auferstehungsgeschichten und der christliche Glaube*, Tübingen 1940; P. **Hoffmann**, 'Auferstehung Jesu Christi; II.1 Neues Testament', *TRE* 4, 1979, 478–513; J. **Kremer**, *Die Osterbotschaft der vier Evangelien*, Stuttgart 1968; W. **Künneth**, *The Theology of the Resurrection* ([2]1934), ET London and New York 1965; K. **Lake**, *The Historical Evidence for the Resurrection*, London and New York 1907; J. **Lange**, *Das Erscheinen des Auferstandenen im Evangelium nach Matthäus*, Würzburg 1973; A. R. C. **Leaney**, 'The Resurrection Narratives in Luke (xxiv. 12–53)', *NTS* 2, 1955/6, 110–14; B. **Lindars**, 'The Composition of John xx', *NTS* 7, 1960/61, 142–7; E. **Lohse**, *Die Auferstehung Jesu Christi im Zeugnis des Lukasevangeliums*, Neukirchen 1961; J. **MacKnight**, *A Harmony of the Four Gospels*, 2 vols., London [2]1763; R. **Mahoney**, *Two Disciples at the Tomb. The Background and Message of Jn 20, 1–10*, Berne-Frankfurt 1974; W. **Marxsen**, *The Resurrection of Jesus of Nazareth*, ET London and Philadelphia 1970; F.**Morison**, *Who Moved the Stone?*, London and New York 1930; C. F. D. **Moule**, ed., *The Significance of the Message of the Resurrection for Faith in Jesus Christ*, SBT II. 8, 1968.

F. **Neirynck**, 'Les femmes au tombeau: Étude de la rédaction Matthéenne (Mt 28.1–10)', *NTS* 15, 1968/9, 168–90; R. R. **Niebuhr**, *Resurrection and Historical Reason*, New York 1957; W. **Pannenberg**, 'Die historische Problematik der Auferweckung Jesu', in *Grundzüge der Christologie*, Gütersloh 1964, 85ff.; N. **Perrin**, *The Resurrection according to Matthew, Mark and Luke*, Philadelphia 1977; R. **Pesch**, R. **Kratz**, 'Die Auferstehungbotschaft am leeren Grab', *So Liest Man Synoptisch* VII, Frankfurt 1980, 150–65; A. M. **Ramsey**, *The Resurrection of Christ: an Essay in Biblical Theology*, London 1945, Philadelphia 1946; K. H. **Rengstorf**, *Die Auferstehung Jesu*, Witten 1952; J. A. T. **Robinson**, 'The Resurrection in the New Testament', *IDB* IV, 43–53; P. **Schubert**, 'The Structure and Significance of Lk 24', *Neutestamentliche Studien für R. Bultmann*, BZNW 21, ed. W. Eltester, 1954, 165–86; P. **Stuhlmacher**, 'Das Bekenntnis zur Auferweckung Jesu von den Toten und die Biblische Theologie', *ZTK* 70, 1973, 365–403; C. H. **Talbert**, ed., *Reimarus: Fragments*, ET London and Philadelphia 1971, 153–210; J. **Wanke**, *Die Emmauserzählung*, Leipzig 1973; B. F. **Westcott**, *The Gospel of the*

Resurrection, London [2]1869, New York [7]1891; 'The Resurrection', *An Introduction to the Study of the Gospels*, London [5]1875, 29–36; U. **Wilckens**, *Auferstehung. Das biblische Auferstehungszeugnis historisch untersucht und erklärt*, Stuttgart [2]1977.

Both the importance and difficulty of understanding the resurrection accounts of the four Gospels are obvious to anyone who has studied the New Testament. The continuing interest of systematic theology in the detailed exegesis of these Gospel pericopes further testifies to the centrality of the subject matter for Christian theology. Indeed, some have suggested that the interpretation of the resurrection accounts offers a model for developing a modern theology which is in direct dialogue with the historical critical enterprise (Grass). As a result of these overlapping interests from many disciplines within the field of theology, the secondary literature is overwhelming and can only be selectively represented. Our present interest is in relating this larger debate to the issue of the canonical interpretation of biblical texts.

A. *Harmonistic Attempts*

The parallel passages in the Gospels are the following: Matt. 28.1–20, Mark 16.1–8 (9–20), Luke 24.1–53, John 20.1–31; 21.1–25. In the traditional harmonies (e.g. Augustine, Calvin, Clericus) attention focused on reconciling apparent contradictions of chronology, such as when the women brought the spices, and at what time of day they set forth to visit the tomb. The problem of harmonizing the various descriptions of the angels and the exact sequence of Jesus' appearances also evoked explanation.

However, with the rise of Deism in England and Lessing's publication of the fragments of Reimarus in Germany, the task of harmonizing the resurrection accounts entered a new phase of intense struggle. In Edward Robinson's *Harmony* (1834) the author not only set out his own elaborate scheme for harmonizing the time, persons, and appearances of the four Gospels, but in addition appended the synthetic reconstructions of G. Benson (1764) and N. Lardner (1764). One is struck immediately by the new and tortuous complexity of the schemata which posit numerous visits to the tomb and an artificial multiplication of scenes. Perhaps the nadir in this harmonization attempt is reached by James MacKnight's *Harmony* (1756). In order to explain why the disciples and the women never met, although both were constantly shuttling back and forth between the sepulchre and Jerusalem, MacKnight suggests that they used different streets in Jerusalem and so continually missed each other (656f.). In the end, the trivalization of the Gospel accounts into something resembling a bad home movie is the greatest indictment of this method of interpretation.

The later attempts of harmonists such as Ebrard to recognize the very diverse perspectives from which the Gospel accounts were narrated (cf. also Westcott), moved in a more promising direction. However, their perceptive literary observations were invariably tied to elaborate psychological ploys which blocked the avenue toward a fresh concept of Gospel harmony.

B. *The Application of the Historical-critical Method*

In spite of the continual refinement of exegetical tools over the last hundred and fifty years, the historical critical method shares the common assumption that the various biblical accounts must be critically examined in terms of origin, development, and social function before the material can be understood in any synthetic way by the modern reader. It was soon recognized, both from form and content, that the resurrection accounts of the Gospels were not simply eyewitness accounts which could be spliced together to produce a historical report. Rather, the various accounts reflected different traditions, each with its own life, which had undergone a complex history of change and growth. As a result, the whole enterprise of Gospel harmony lost its rationale and was rejected out of hand as hopelessly naive.

Very early it was argued by many that a comparison of the resurrection tradition in I Corinthians 15 suggested that Paul's earliest kerygmatic formulation was unaware of the empty tomb tradition, which accretion was thought to have emerged secondarily in order to address a variety of new issues in the early church (cf. Grass, 138ff.). However, a significant minority continued to reject this hypothesis (Moule, Brown). The tension between appearances in Galilee and in Jerusalem was attributed to different circles of tradents and often related to Pentecost. Only at a much later time was the inner friction partially harmonized by the Fourth Gospel.

Similarly, the Matthaean tradition of guarding the tomb has generally been considered a late development which arose as an apologetic weapon in the continuing controversy between church and synagogue. In terms of the form-critical debate, scholars differ somewhat in the description of the growth of the material. Dodd's influential article ('Appearances') outlined two basic types of resurrection narratives from which the later expansions developed, whereas R. E. Brown (*John*, 966ff.) prefers seeing one basic form at the source and later accretions. Significantly the various attempts to determine the historicity of the kernel of the 'mythopoetic' tradition ('subjective' visionary; 'objective' visionary, etc.) relate only loosely to a literary analysis, but rather derive more from independent hermeneutical and theological commitments of the scholar (cf. the representative collection of essays edited by C. F. D. Moule).

c. The Interpretation of Karl Barth

In distinction from the two classic options of conservative and liberal theology, Karl Barth offered an interpretation which cut against both positions, although obviously the brunt of his attack focused on the liberal position. Barth first developed his interpretation in his 1924 exegesis of I Corinthians, but later expanded it in his *Church Dogmatics* (III/2, ET 1960, 530ff.; IV/1, ET 1956, 311ff., 826ff.). Barth's initial monograph called forth an immediate reply from Bultmann and Althaus in which the former was far more positive than the latter.

Barth observed that, whereas the death of Jesus is portrayed by the Gospels in detail, the resurrection of Jesus is never described. What is left of a historical context is at best the 'residue': empty tomb and grave clothes. They serve as testimony to the resurrected one whose presence evoked the gospel's response. They function only as the sign of the reality. Barth then developed the thesis that the resurrection of Christ is an eschatological act of God which is different in kind from common events of history. It marks the end of the old order and the beginning of the new. Because this history is unique, it offers no continuity with the events of the old age. The resurrection cannot be understood from the residue! To use his analogy: at best one can catch a momentarily fixed image of a bird in flight which only points to the reality without being able to encompass it.

In response to the criticism that Barth has de-historicized the resurrection, Barth insisted that it occurred in real time and space. However, for him the issue at stake turns on what one means by 'history'. He rejects the critical assumption that, because the resurrection does not fit the categories of scientific history (*Historie*) which can be measured with critical tools, the event did not occur. He also argues that the Gospels function truthfully as witness irrespective of their literary forms and thus cannot be successfully demythologized. Barth's basic attack on Bultmann – and on the historical-critical method in general – is that he has turned the text on its head by construing it in anthropological rather than theological terms.

D. *The Hermeneutical Issues at Stake*

In the interpretation of the resurrection accounts which now follows we shall attempt to indicate the way in which a canonical harmony both agrees and disagrees with various features of these three different approaches which we have briefly sketched. However, it might first be useful to outline the nature of the hermeneutical problem of the resurrection accounts which has emerged and which must be adequately addressed by any new proposal.

First, there are elements of both historical continuity and disconti-nuity between the earlier portrayals of Jesus found in the Gospels and the resurrection accounts. On the one hand, Paul can enumerate as a series of events Christ's death, burial, resurrection and appear-ances (I Cor. 15.3ff.). The resurrected Christ bears the nail prints; he can be touched and he eats with his disciples as before (John 21). On the other hand, he is not recognized by his disciples (Luke 24), or by Mary (John 20.11ff.). The resurrected Jesus appears to reflect a new and different existence. He passes through closed doors (John 20.19) and cautions Mary not to lay hands on him since he has not yet ascended. Above all, Paul talks of a new and different resurrected body which the believer through faith shares with Christ.

Secondly, there is a tension between the presentations of the resurrection as the cause of faith and the resurrection as the result of faith. Clearly the major witness of all four Gospels is in testifying to the power of the resurrected Lord in evoking faith from unbelief. Barth has correctly stressed this central aspect of the biblical witness. Yet, it is also the case that the form of the gospel witness bears the stamp of its reception and transmission by a community of faith which shaped the accounts. Indeed, one can often locate a concrete setting within the communal life which gives evidence of the crucial factor of Christian faith in construing the witness, a point repeatedly stressed by Bultmann and the proponents of historical exegesis.

Thirdly, it remains a persistent hermeneutical problem how to deal adequately with both the unity and diversity of the fourfold Gospel witness. There is a single-minded attention to the one event of Christ's resurrection. Conversely the variety of emphases within the Gospels reflects a diversity of description concerning what occurred which is seldom encountered with such intensity within the New Testament.

E. The Search for a Canonical Harmony

At the outset it is basic in any attempt to sketch the lines of a suggested canonical harmony to be conscious that the combined reading of the Gospels cannot be different in kind from the individual witnesses. It is, therefore, important to review certain characteristic features by means of which the resurrection has been rendered in the separate accounts.

The resurrection is not described in any of the canonical Gospels, but – with the exception of Mark – the accounts focus on the appearances of the resurrected Christ. Again, all the Gospels emphasize the elements of surprise, enigma, wonder and fear concerning events which are difficult to grasp. Then again, the accounts of the appearances are construed in highly theological language which often obscures the elements of exact historical sequence. Matthew speaks in terms of enthronement (28.16ff.), Luke of prophecy and fulfilment (24.44ff.), and John of his glorification and the role of the Spirit (20.22). A massive theological interpretation of the event was an essential part of the evangelical witness to the resurrection from the outset. Finally, in spite of the lack of historical continuity in the presentation of the resurrection, the accounts do comprise literary narratives with common elements of time and space clearly represented. To describe the resurrection accounts as a collage of incoherent impulses akin to a modern expressionistic painting is certainly badly to misconstrue the narratives.

Since our main concern now lies in seeking to interpret the Gospel accounts in a harmony consonant with the shape of the fourfold canonical corpus, it seems reasonable to begin with an investigation of the so-called longer ending of Mark which is the oldest attempt at harmonization available. The dependence of the longer ending on the canonical Gospels (with the exception of vv. 17f.) is readily apparent: vv. 9–11 = John 20.11–18; vv. 12f. = Luke 24.13–35; vv. 14–16 = Matt. 28.16–20; v. 19 = Luke 24.50–53.

What are the characteristic features in the harmonistic attempt of the longer ending? First, all the three other gospels are used without any discernible order because all speak of the one resurrection. Moreover, the individual accounts are construed kerygmatically in terms of their function as witnesses. Mary went and 'announced' to them the good news (v. 10). Similarly, the two disciples 'announced' to the rest what they had experienced (v. 13). The disciples are commissioned to 'preach the gospel' (v. 15). Then again, the harmony of the longer ending has rendered the combined accounts into a consistent theological construal. The writer has reordered the material under the theme of the disciples' unbelief in spite of the evidence (vv. 11, 13, 14). Obviously such a move finds its warrant in portions of the other Gospels, but the writer of the ending has gone beyond his sources in emphasizing this one feature (cf. especially v. 13). However, an even more important indication of the writer's theological interest is found in v. 19. Much in accord with the ancient tradition of I Corinthians – 'died and . . . raised according to the scriptures' – the writer describes Christ's ascension and enthrone-ment at the 'right hand of God' (cf. Acts 7.55f.; Rom. 8.34; Eph. 1.20, etc.). Thus, the writer has used a primitive Christian formula, which had been adopted from the Old Testament, in order to describe the continuing role of the resurrected one in relation to the ministry of his disciples. The historical sequence of the narrative has been broken off because the reality of the present, reigning Lord of the church now transcends the patterns which obtain in ordinary human life.

Finally, in spite of the effect of a new eschatological understanding of time and space which the resurrection entailed, the writer of the longer ending has not abandoned completely the elements of historical sequence in his harmony. He begins with a reference to the time of the day when Christ first appeared (v. 9), and he links the various appearances in a loosely temporal order by means of a series of adverbial phrases ('after this', 'next', etc.). It is also clear that these elements of narrative are passive in quality. They remain in the background of the story and show no effort at closely joining the separate incidents. In sum, they function as a formal device to aid the reader in linking the parts, but without playing an important interpretive role in establishing a definite historical order.

We next turn to the four Gospel accounts of the resurrection in an effort to discern some lines of canonical harmony. It is significant that from a purely literary perspective the effect of reading the four Gospels together does not focus the major attention upon discerning the exact historical sequence of the events described. The impression of having only a fragment of a narrative is not overcome by the joining together of the four accounts. The appearance of the resurrected Christ forms the centre, but the different reactions radiate from the centre in a disorganized, largely unexpected fashion with no close inner coherence. Thus, at the outset, the attempt to harmonize the accounts by reconstructing a fully consistent, unified narrative is to do an injustice to the literary shape of the material. The fragmentary, episodic reactions to an unexpected wonder do not cohere without a high degree of tension. Thus, the search for a canonical harmony does not depend on historically correlating the number of angels at the scene, or the relation between appearances in Galilee and Jerusalem.

Moreover, theological reflection growing out of the peculiar nature of the eschatological witness to the resurrection confirms the literary evidence. Barth has correctly emphasized the shattering of the elements of historical continuity by characterizing them as the 'residue'. One cannot move directly from the empty tomb to the resurrected Christ, nor derive one from the other. This aspect of the witness, which is an essential feature of each Gospel, is not altered by the shape of the canonical corpus. One is left with gaps, with confusion, and with fragments of the whole which cannot be pieced into a unity on the historical plane. Rather, the unity of the Gospels lies in the resurrected one of whom all the voices speak.

It is not even satisfactory theologically to explain the relationship between pre-Easter and post-Easter experience by using the analogy of sign and reality. At least in biblical terminology, the sign partakes of the selfsame reality as its object and anticipates it in time as a foretaste. The empty tomb does not function in this sense as a sign of the resurrection. It is different in kind and reflects rather the relation of negative to positive.

Nevertheless, while insisting on the priority of the elements of discontinuity when speaking of the resurrection of Christ, it is important to recognize that there are features of continuity within the narrative which are even highlighted by the larger canonical collection. It is not by chance that the harmony offered in the longer ending of Mark links the various accounts in a loose, temporal sequence. That the accounts were received as a form of a story in spite of discontinuous and fragmentary qualities belongs to the activity of receiving a tradition which purports to have transpired in time and space. The resurrection accounts speak of earlier and later incidents, of locations in Galilee and Jerusalem. To attempt to hear the four accounts together in some sense entails introducing elements of logical and temporal ordering. The empty tomb is linked in a narrative form with the appearance of the resurrected Christ in spite of their different functions within the Gospel witness. The main point to be made is that the elements of continuity, especially in retaining the narrative form within the harmony, remain a necessary, formal element which is essential as a vehicle of human discourse, but not having an independent, kerygmatic function within the collection.

One of the continuing controversies regarding the meaning of the resurrection turns on the debate between the so-called 'subjective-objective' interpretations (cf. Moule, 2ff.). Did the resurrection evoke the Christian faith, or did the faith shape the resurrection stories? Karl Barth would be a good representative of the 'objective' interpretation, Bultmann of the 'subjective'. Our present concern is to suggest that attention to a canonical harmony may offer some direction for overcoming this stalemate.

Certainly historical critical study has made a significant contribution in demonstrating the degree to which the four Gospel accounts have been shaped by different forms of Christian faith, often within very concrete historical settings during the second half of the first century. One criticism of Barth's interpretation is that insufficient attention has been paid to this process of the text's being received, shaped, and transmitted over a lengthy period of time. Yet it is crucial to recognize that in this process of development, which we designate as the canonical process, the biblical accounts of the resurrection have been rendered by those transmitting the text in a particular fashion. All the Gospels point in a distinctively theocentric direction. That is to say, they consistently bear witness to the resurrection as an act of God, and not to their own faith. The evangelists who shaped the Gospel texts in faith testify to the force of the resurrection in evoking that very faith.

The hermeneutical problem of the resurrection is misconstrued when viewed in a polarity between a subjective and an objective approach. Rather, both dimensions are involved but the crucial issue turns on how the relationship is conceived. The problem with the usual application of the historical critical method – the so-called subjective option – is not in its recognizing the sociological setting of the tradents of the tradition. Rather, it rests in allowing these factors to determine the text's meaning even when such an interpretation runs against the explicit testimony of those who shaped the text. As a result of claiming to know better than the text itself, they only succeed in rendering its theological witness mute.

The Gospel accounts of the resurrection testify to a variety of different experiences of the risen Christ by means of a variety of literary forms. Their testimony is not restricted to one moment in historical time. By recognizing the eschatological dimension of the resurrection, they bear testimony to its continuing reality which extended far beyond Easter morning and was experienced by the Christian community. Thus, Luke's witness to the risen Christ speaks of Jesus who was (and is) known in the eucharist, in the 'breaking of bread' (24.35). Mark's longer ending testifies to the enthroned Lord who continues to work with his disciples through signs. Matthew bears witness to the exalted Christ who commissions his disciples for ministry and whose presence is with them to the close of the age. John focuses on the faith of those who have not themselves seen the earthly Jesus, but who partake of his eternal life through the testimony of others. In all the Gospels the Christ, whose resurrection brings into being a new eschatological age, can never be grasped simply by a noetic process, but is experienced by the church in the faithful exercise of Christian discipleship.

Obviously an exegetical method which derives meaning from the New Testament only when it conforms to the ordinary conventions of human behaviour has difficulty fitting the Gospel accounts into such categories. However, in spite of the remarkable variety of ways by which the risen Christ is actualized by the Christian church, one can still discern a canonical harmony within the corpus of the four Gospels.

PART THREE

THE ACTS

11

THE ACTS OF THE APOSTLES

Commentaries

F. Overbeck, KEHNT, [4]1870
H. J. Holtzmann, HCNT, [3]1901
E. Preuschen, HNT, 1912
H. H. Wendt, MeyerK, [5]1913
R. Knopf, *SNT*, [3]1917
A. Loisy, 1920
T. Zahn, KNT, [2/3]1921–22
E. Jacquier, ÉB, 1926
F. J. Foakes-Jackson, MNTC, 1931
K. Lake, H. J. Cadbury, 1933
A. C. Clark, 1933
O. Bauernfeind, THKNT, 1939
R. B. Rackham, WC, [14]1951

R. R. Williams, TB, 1953
F. F. Bruce, NICNT, 1954
H. W. Beyer, NTD, [9]1959
A. Wikenhauser, RNT, [4]1961
C. S. C. Williams, B/HNTC, [2]1964
R. P. C. Hanson, NClB, 1967
J. Munck, AB, 1967
G. Stählin, NTD, [13]1970
E. Haenchen, MeyerK, ET 1971
A. Weiser, ÖTK, 1980
J. Roloff, NTD, [17]1981
G. Schneider, HTKNT, 1980–82

Bibliography

Cf. the bibliography of A. J. **Mattill, jr.**, M. B. **Mattill**, *A Classified Bibliography of Literature on the Acts of the Apostles*, Leiden 1966.

B. W. **Bacon**, 'The Chronological Scheme of Acts', *HTR* 14, 1921, 137–66; H. **von Baer**, *Der Heilige Geist in den Lukasschriften*, WMANT 39, 1926; L. W. **Barnard**, 'Saint Stephen and Early Alexandrian Christianity', *NTS* 7, 1960/61, 31–45; C. K. **Barrett**, *New Testament Essays*, London 1972; 'Acts and the Pauline Corpus', *ExpT* 88, 1976/77, 2–5; 'Paul's Address to the Ephesian Elders', in *God's Christ and His People, FS Nils A. Dahl*, ed. W. A. Meeks and J. Jervell, Oslo 1977, 107–21; O. **Bauernfeind**, 'Vom historischen zum lukanischen Paulus', *EvTh* 13, 1953, 347–53; 'Zur Frage nach der Entscheidung zwischen Paulus und Lukas', *ZSTh* 23, 1954, 59–88; H. D. **Betz**, 'The Conference at Jerusalem', *Galatians* (Herm), 1979, 81–3; 'The Conflict at Antioch', ibid., 103–5; O. **Betz**, 'Die Vision des Paulus im Tempel von Jerusalem. Apg 22, 17–21 als Beitrag zur Deutung des Damaskuserlebnisses', *Verborum Veritas, FS G. Stählin*, ed. O. Böcker and K.

Haacker, Wuppertal 1970, 113–23; W. **Bieder**, *Die Apostelgeschichte in der Historie. Ein Beitrag zur Auslegungsgeschichte des Missionsbuches der Kirche*, ThStud 61, 1960; P. **Borgen**, 'From Paul to Luke', *CBQ* 31, 1969, 168–82; G. **Bornkamm**, 'The Missionary Stance of Paul in I Corinthians and in Acts', in L. E. Keck, J. L. Martyn, eds., *Studies in Luke-Acts*, (below) 194–207; U. **Borse**, 'Paulus in Jerusalem', in *Kontinuität und Einheit, FS F. Mussner*, ed. P.-G. Müller and W. Stringer, Freiburg 1981, 43–64; F. **Bovon**, *Luc le théologien: vingt-cinq ans de recherches (1950–1975)*, Neuchâtel and Paris 1978; J. W. **Bowker**, 'Speeches in Acts: A Study in Proem and Yalemmedenu Form', *NTS* 14, 1967/68, 96–111; S. **Brown**, 'The Role of the Prologues in Determining the Purpose of Luke-Acts', in Talbert, ed., *Perspectives* (below), 99–111; F. F. **Bruce**, *The Speeches in the Acts of the Apostles*, London 1945; 'The Holy Spirit in the Acts of the Apostles', *Interp* 27, 1973, 166–83; 'Is the Paul of Acts the Real Paul?' *BJRL* 58, 1975/76, 282–305; R. **Bultmann**, 'Zur Frage nach den Quellen der Apostelgeschichte', *Exegetica*, Tübingen 1967, 412–23; C. **Burchard**, *Der dreizehnte Zeuge. Traditions- und kompositionsgeschichtliche Untersuchung zu Lukas' Darstellung der Frühzeit des Paulus*, FRLANT 103, 1970; 'Paulus in der Apostelgeschichte', *TLZ* 100, 1975, 881–95.

H. J. **Cadbury**, *The Style and Literary Method of Luke*, London and Cambridge, Mass. 1920; *The Making of Luke-Acts*, New York and London 1927; 'The Hellenists', *Beginnings*, ed. Foakes-Jackson and Lake, V, 59–74; 'The Titles of Jesus in Acts', ibid., 354–75; 'The Summaries in Acts', ibid., 392–402; *The Book of Acts in History*, London 1955; 'Acts and Eschatology', *The Background of the New Testament and Its Eschatology, Essays in honour of C. H. Dodd*, Cambridge 1954, 300–21; '"We" and "I" Passages in Luke-Acts', *NTS* 3, 1956/7, 128–32; 'Four Features of Lucan Style', in Keck and Martyn, eds., *Studies in Luke-Acts*, 87–102; H. **von Campenhausen**, 'The Apostles', ET *Ecclesiastical Authority and Spiritual Power in the Church of the First Three Centuries*, London and Stamford 1969, 12–29; D. R. **Catchpole**, 'Paul, James and the Apostolic Decree', *NTS* 23, 1976/77, 428–44; H. **Conzelmann**, *The Theology of St Luke*, ET London and New York 1960; 'The Address of Paul on the Areopagus', in Keck and Martyn, eds., *Studies*, 217–30; 'Luke's Place in the Development of Early Christianity', ibid., 298–316; J. H. **Crehan**, 'The Purpose of Luke in Acts', *StEv* II, TU 87, 1964, 354–68.

N. H. **Dahl**, 'A People for his Name', *NTS* 4, 1957/8, 318–27; 'The Story of Abraham in Luke-Acts', in Keck and Martyn, eds., *Studies*, 139–58; 'The Purpose of Luke-Acts', *Jesus in the Memory of the Early Church*, Minneapolis 1976, 87–98; F. W. **Danker**, *Luke* (Proclamation Commentaries) Philadelphia 1976; G. **Delling**, 'Israels Geschichte und Jesusgeschehen nach Acta', in *Neues Testament und Geschichte, FS O. Cullmann*, ed. H. Baltensweiler and B. Reicke, Zürich 1972, 187–97; 'Das letzte Wort der Apostelgeschichte', *NovT* 15, 1973, 193–204; M. **Dibelius**, *Studies in the Acts of the Apostles*, ET London 1956; W. **Dietrich**, *Das Petrusbild der lukanischen Schriften*, BWANT 94, 1972; C. H. **Dodd**, *The Apostolic Preaching and its Developments*, London

1936, reprinted 1951; J. **Dupont**, *The Sources of Acts*, ET London and New York 1964; 'La conclusion des Actes et son rapport à l'ensemble de l'ouvrage de Luc', in Kremer, ed., *Actes des Apôtres*, 359–404; *The Salvation of the Gentiles. Essays on the Acts of the Apostles*, ET New York 1979; B. S. **Easton**, *The Purpose of Acts*, London 1936; A. **Ehrhardt**, 'The Construction and Purpose of the Acts of the Apostles', *StTh* 12, 1958, 45–79; E. E. **Ellis**, 'The Role of the Christian Prophet in Acts', in *Apostolic History and the Gospel, Essays presented to F.F. Bruce*, eds. W. W. Gasque and R. P. Martin, Exeter and Grand Rapids 1970, 55–67; W. **Eltester**, 'Lukas und Paulus', in *Eranion, FS H. Hommel*, ed. J. Kroymann, Tübingen 1961, 1–17; M. S. **Enslin**, 'Once Again: Luke and Paul', *ZNW* 61, 1970, 253–71; C. F. **Evans**, ' "Speeches" in Acts', *Mélanges Bibliques, FS B. Rigaux*, ed. A. Deschamps and A. de Halleux, Gembloux 1970, 287–302.

E. **Ferguson**, 'The Hellenists in the Book of Acts', *RestQ* 12, 1969, 159–80; J. A. **Fitzmyer**, 'Jewish Christianity in Acts in Light of the Qumran Scrolls', in L. E. Keck and J. L. Martyn, eds., *Studies*, 233–57; H. **Flender**, *St Luke: Theologian of Redemptive History*, ET London and Philadelphia 1967; F. J. **Foakes-Jackson**, K. **Lake**, eds. *The Beginnings of Christianity*; Part I: *The Acts of the Apostles*, 5 vols., London and New York, 1920–1933; E. **Franklin**, *Christ the Lord. A Study in the Purpose and Theology of Luke-Acts*, London and Philadelphia 1975; B. **Gärtner**, *The Areopagus Speech and Natural Revelation*, Uppsala 1955; W. W. **Gasque**, 'The Speeches of Acts. Dibelius Reconsidered', in *New Dimensions in New Testament Study*, ed. R. N. Longenecker and M. C. Tenney, Grand Rapids, 1974, 232–50; *A History of the Criticism of the Acts of the Apostles*, BGBE 17, 1975; M. D. **Goulder**, *Type and History in Acts*, London 1964; E. **Grässer**, 'Die Apostelgeschichte in der Forschung der Gegenwart', *ThR* NF 26, 1960, 93–167; 'Acta-Forschung seit 1960', *ThR* NF 41, 1976, 141–94; 42, 1977, 1–68; 'Die Parusieerwartung in der Apostelgeschichte', in J. Kremer, ed., *Les Actes* (below), 99–127; H. **Grass**, *Ostergeschehen und Osterberichte*, Göttingen ⁴1970, 30–51.

E. **Haenchen**, 'Tradition und Komposition in der Apostelgeschichte' (1955), in *Gott und Mensch*, Tübingen 1965, 206–26; 'Das "Wir" in der Apostelgeschichte und das Itinerar', (1961), ibid., 227–64; 'Judentum und Christentum in der Apostelgeschichte', (1963), in *Die Bibel und Wir*, Tübingen 1968, 338–74; 'Die Apostelgeschichte als Quelle für die christliche Frühgeschichte', (1966), ibid., 312–57; 'Die Einzelgeschichte und der Zyklus. Eine methodologische Glosse zur Acta', *Neues Testament und Geschichte, FS. O. Cullmann*, Zurich 1972, 199–205; G. **Harbsmeier**, 'Unsere Predigt im Spiegel der Apostelgeschichte', *EvTh* 10, 1950/51, 352–68; A. **Harnack**, *The Acts of the Apostles*, ET London 1909; H. J. **Hauser**, *Strukturen der Abschlusserzählung der Apostelgeschichte (Apg 28, 16–31)*, AnBib 86, 1979; C. W. **Hedrick**, 'Paul's Conversion/Call: A Comparative Analysis of the Three Reports in Acts', *JBL* 100, 1981, 415–32; M. **Hengel**, 'Zwischen Jesus und Paulus, die "Hellenisten", die "Sieben" und Stephanus', *ZTK* 72, 1975, 151–206; *Acts and the History of Earliest Christianity*, ET London and

Philadelphia 1979; E. **Hirsch**, 'Die drei Berichte der Apostelgeschichte über die Bekehrung des Paulus', *ZNW* 28, 1929, 305–12; T. **Holtz**, 'Die Bedeutung des Apostelkonzils für Paulus', *NovT* 16, 1974, 110–48; B. J. **Hubbard**, 'The Role of Commissioning Accounts in Acts' in Talbert, ed., *Perspectives*, 187–98; A. J. **Hultgren**, 'Paul's Pre-Christian Persecutions of the Church: Their Purpose, Locale and Nature', *JBL* 95, 1976, 97–111; J. **Jeremias**, 'Untersuchungen zum Quellenproblem der Apostelgeschichte', *ZNW* 36, 1937, 205–21; J. **Jervell**, *Luke and the People of God. A New Look at Luke-Acts*, Minneapolis, 1972; L. T. **Johnson**, *The Literary Function of Possessions in Luke-Acts*, SBLDS 39, Missoula 1977.

E. **Käsemann**, 'Ephesians and Acts', in L. E. Keck and J. L. Martyn, eds., *Studies*, 288–97; R. J. **Karris**, 'Missionary Communities. A New Paradigm for the Study of Luke-Acts', *CBQ* 41, 1979, 80–97; L. E. **Keck, J. L. Martyn**, eds., *Studies in Luke-Acts, Essays presented in honour of Paul Schubert*, Nashville 1966; J. J. **Kilgallen**, *The Stephen Speech: A Literary and Redactional Study of Acts 7, 2–53*, AnBib 67, 1976; G. **Klein**, *Die zwölf Apostel. Ursprung und Gehalt einer Idee*, FRLANT 77, 1961; O. **Knoch**, *Die 'Testamente' des Petrus und Paulus*, SBS 62, 1973, 32–43; J. **Knox**, 'Acts and the Pauline Letter Corpus', in L. E. Keck, J. L. Martyn, eds., *Studies*, 279–87; J. **Kremer**, ed., *Les Actes des Apôtres. Traditions, rédaction, théologie*, Gembloux 1979; G. **Krodel**, *Acts* (Proclamation Commentaries), Philadelphia 1981; D. W. **Kuck**, *The Use and Canonization of Acts in the Early Church*, STM Thesis, Yale University 1975; K. **Lake**, 'The Holy Spirit', in *Beginnings*, V, 1933, 96–111; 'Paul's Controversies', ibid., 212–23; 'The Chronology of Acts', ibid., 445–74; J. **Lambrecht**, 'Paul's Farewell Address at Miletus (Acts 20, 17–38)', in Kremer, ed., *Les Actes*, 307–37; G. W. H. **Lampe**, 'The Holy Spirit in the Writings of St Luke', in *Studies in the Gospels. Essays in memory of R. H. Lightfoot*, Oxford 1955, 159–200; 'Miracles in the Acts of the Apostles', in *Miracles*, ed. C. F. D. Moule, London ²1966, 163–78; A. R. C. **Leaney**, 'Why there were Forty Days between the Resurrection and the Ascension in Acts 1, 3', *StEv* IV, TU 102, 1968, 411–19; B. **Lindars**, *New Testament Apologetic*, London and Philadelphia 1961; O. **Linton**, 'The Third Aspect. A Neglected Point of View. A Study in Gal. 1–2 and Acts 9 and 15', *StTh* 3, 1949, 79–95; G. **Lohfink**, *Paulus vor Damaskus*, SBS 4, 1965; *Die Himmelfahrt Jesu*, SANT 26, 1971; *Die Sammlung Israels. Eine Untersuchung zur lukanischen Ekklesiologie*, SANT 39, 1975; E. **Lohse**, 'Die Bedeutung des Pfingstberichtes im Rahmen des lukanischen Geschichtswerkes', *EvTh* 13, 1953, 422–36; reprinted *Die Einheit des Neuen Testaments*, Göttingen 1973, 178ff.; 'Lukas als Theologe der Heilsgeschichte', *EvTh* 14, 1954, 256–76; K. **Löning**, *Die Saulustradition in der Apostelgeschichte*, NTAbh, NF 9, 1973.

I. H. **Marshall**, *Luke: Historian and Theologian*, Exeter and Grand Rapids 1970; A. J. **Mattill**, jr., 'A Spectrum of Opinion on the Value of Acts as a Source for the Reconstruction of the Life and Thought of Paul', in Talbert, ed. *Perspectives*, 63–83; P.-H. **Menoud**, 'Remarques sur le textes de l'ascension dans Luc-Actes', *Neutestamentliche Studien für R. Bultmann*, ed. W.

Eltester, BZNW 21, 1954, 148–56; 'Le plan des Actes des Apôtres', *NTS* 1, 1954/5, 44–51; 'Le salut par la foi selon le livre des Actes', *Foi et Salut selon S. Paul*, Rome 1979, 255–72; H. J. **Michel**, *Die Abschiedsrede des Paulus an die Kirche Apg 20 17–38*, SANT 35, 1973; P. S. **Minear**, 'Dear Theo. The Kerygmatic Intention and Claim of the Book of Acts', *Interp* 27, 1973, 131–50; *To Heal and to Reveal. The Prophetic Vocation according to Luke*, New York 1976; R. **Morgenthaler**, *Die lukanische Geschichtsschreibung als Zeugnis*, AbTANT 14, 15, 2 Bände, Zurich 1949; C. F. D. **Moule**, 'The Christology of Acts', in L. E. Keck, J. L. Martyn, eds., *Studies*, 159–85; P. G. **Müller**, 'Die jüdische Entscheidung gegen Jesus nach der Apostelgeschichte', in J. Kremer, ed. *Les Actes*, 525–31; J. **Munck**, 'Discours d'adieu dans le Nouveau Testament', *Aux Sources de la Tradition Chrétienne, Mélanges à M. Goguel*, Neuchâtel 1950, 155–70; *Paul and the Salvation of Mankind*, ET London and Richmond 1959.

F. **Neirynck**, 'The Miracle Stories in the Acts of the Apostles: An Introduction', in Kremer, ed., *Les Actes*, 169–213; J. C. **O'Neill**, *The Theology of Acts in its Historical Setting*, London ²1970; R. F. **O'Toole**, 'Why Did Luke Write Acts (Lk-Acts)?', *BTB* 7, 1977, 66–76; *Acts 26. The Christological Climax of Paul's Defense (Ac 22:1–26:32)*, AnBib 78, 1978; 'Activity of the Risen Jesus in Luke-Acts', *Bibl* 62, 1981, 471–98; E. **Plümacher**, *Lukas als hellenistischer Schriftsteller. Studien zur Apostelgeschichte*, SUNT 9 1972; 'Wirklichkeitserfahrung und Geschichtsschreibung bei Lukas. Erwägungen zu den Wir-Stücken der Apostelgeschichte', *ZNW* 68, 1977, 2–22; 'Apostelgeschichte', *TRE* III, 1978, 483–528; 'Die Apostelgeschichte als historische Monographie', in Kremer, ed., *Les Actes*, 457–66; F. **Prast**, *Presbyter und Evangelium. Die Abschiedsrede des Paulus in Milet (Apg 20.17–38) im Rahmen der lukanischen Konzepten der Evangeliumsverkündigung*, Stuttgart 1979; W. **Radl**, *Paulus und Jesus im lukanischen Doppelwerk. Untersuchungen zu Parallelmotiven im Lukasevangelium und in der Apostelgeschichte*, Bern and Frankfurt 1975; W. M. **Ramsay**, *St Paul the Traveller and the Roman Citizen*, London and New York 1895; K. H. **Rengstorf**, 'Die Zuwahl des Matthias (Apg 1, 15ff.)', *StTh* 15, 1961, 35–67; M. **Rese**, 'Die Funktion der alttestamentlichen Zitate und Anspielungen in den Reden der Apostelgeschichte', in Kremer, ed., *Les Actes*, 61–79; V. K. **Robbins**, 'The We-Passages in Acts and Ancient Sea Voyages', *BibRes* 20, 1975, 5–18; H. G. **Russell**, 'Which was Written First, Luke or Acts?', *HTR* 48, 1955, 165–74.

G. **Schille**, 'Die Fragwürdigkeit eines Itinerars der Paulusreisen', *TLZ* 84, 1959, 165–74; 'Die Leistung des Lukas in der Apostelgeschichte', *Theol. Versuche* 7, 1976, 91–106; W. **Schneemelcher**, 'Die Apostelgeschichte des Lukas und die Acta Pauli', in *Apophoreta, FS E. Haenchen*, ed. W. Eltester, BZNW 30, 1969, 236–50; G. **Schneider**, 'Der Zweck des lukanischen Doppelwerks', *BZ* 21, 1977, 45–66; 'Stephanus, die Hellenisten und Samaria', in Kremer, ed., *Les Actes*, 215–40; P. **Schubert**, 'The Final Cycle of Speeches in the Book of Acts', *JBL* 87, 1968, 1–16; 'The Place of the Areopagus Speech in the Composition of Acts', *Transitions in Biblical*

Scholarship, ed. J. C. Rylaarsdam, Chicago and London 1968, 235–61; H. **Schürmann**, 'Das Testament des Paulus für die Kirche' (1962), reprinted *Traditionsgeschichtliche Untersuchungen zu den synoptischen Evangelien*, Düsseldorf 1968, 310–40; E. **Schweizer**, 'Concerning the Speeches in Acts', in L. E. Keck and J. L. Martyn, eds., *Studies*, 208–16; M. **Simon**, *St Stephen and the Hellenists in the Primitive Church*, London and New York 1958; V. **Stolle**, *Der Zeuge als Angeklagter. Untersuchungen zum Paulusbild des Lukas*, BWANT 102, 1973; G. **Strecker**, 'Die sogenannte zweite Jerusalemreise des Paulus (Act 11, 27–30)', *ZNW* 53, 1962, 67–77; A. C. **Sundberg**, 'Toward a Revised History of the New Testament Canon', *StEv* IV, TU 102, 1968, 452–61; C. H. **Talbert**, *Literary Patterns, Theological Themes, and the Genre of Luke-Acts*, Missoula 1974; ed. *Perspectives on Luke-Acts*, Danville and Edinburgh 1978; D. L. **Tiede**, *Prophecy and History in Luke-Acts*, Philadelphia 1980; E. **Trocmé**, *Le 'Livre des Actes' et l'histoire*, Paris 1957.

W. C. **van Unnik**, 'The "Book of Acts" – Confirmation of the Gospel' (1960), in *Sparsa Collecta* I, Leiden 1973, 340–73; 'Die Apostelgeschichte und die Häresien', ibid., 402–9; 'Luke's Second Book and the Rules of Hellenistic Historiography', in Kremer, ed., *Les Actes*, 37–60; F. **Veltmann**, 'The Defense Speeches of Paul in Acts', in Talbert, ed. *Perspectives*, 325–39; P. **Vielhauer**, 'Zum "Paulinismus" der Apostelgeschichte', *EvTh* 10, 1950, 1–15; ET 'On the "Paulinism" of Acts', in L. E. Keck and J. L. Martyn, eds., *Studies*, 33–50; U. **Wilckens**, 'Die Bekehrung des Paulus als religionsgeschichtliches Problem', *ZTK* 56, 1959, 273–93; *Die Missionsreden der Apostelgeschichte. Form- und traditionsgeschichtliche Untersuchungen*, WMANT 5, ³1974; A. N. **Wilder**, 'Variant Traditions of the Resurrection in Acts', *JBL* 62, 1943, 307–38; S. G. **Wilson**, *The Gentiles and Gentile Mission in Luke-Acts*, SNTSM 23, 1973; H. **Windisch**, 'The Identity of the Editor of Luke and Acts, III. The Case Against the Tradition', *Beginnings* II, 1922, 298–348; R. F. **Zehnle**, *Peter's Pentecost Discourse. Tradition and Lukan Reinterpretation in Peter's Speeches of Acts 2 and 3*, SBLMS 15, Nashville 1971.

I. The Contemporary Debate over Acts

The basic questions of interpretation have seldom been so directly related to the issues of canon as with the book of Acts. In recent years the form of the discussion has often taken a negative turn, but the force of the argument and the widespread implications of the debate present an unusual challenge to the biblical exegete and theologian. It has been argued that the book of Acts reflects a tendentious ideology of its author which has idealized the early history of the church, badly skewed the ministry of Paul, and seriously misunderstood many of the central tenets of the Gospels. Far from being a canonical bridge between the fourfold Gospel collection and the apostolic letters, the book of Acts offers a theological option which did justice neither to the Gospels nor to Paul, but rather provided a biblical warrant for the establishment of Christendom (Vielhauer, Conzelmann, Haenchen).

Fortunately, this extreme formulation of the problems of Acts has met with much resistance from within the New Testament discipline itself. Often the defence of a more positive interpretation of the literary, theological, and historical functions of Acts has resulted in modifications and cautious reformulations of the issue. Thus, for example, the book of Acts appears to have more historical integrity than once thought (Hengel, Gasque). Certain lines of theological continuity between Luke and Paul have been underestimated (Bauernfeind, O. Betz), and the presence of both traditional eschatological expectations and *heilsgeschichtliche* schemata can be discerned (Kümmel, *Intr.*, Flender).

However, these efforts at rehabilitating the book of Acts have seldom resulted in a thoroughly new and convincing analysis which does full justice to the canonical function of the book. The critical debate has settled down to a somewhat weary give-and-take situation within set scholarly parameters (cf. Plümacher, *TRE*). The task remains to inquire afresh after the canonical shape, to discern how the material addresses successive generations of Christian readers, and to explore the history of the book's composition to see how its growth aids in interpreting the received form of the book.

II. The Actualization of the Gospel in Acts

At the outset the question regarding the purpose of the book of Acts must be raised. A whole host of answers have been given, many of which demand serious reflection (cf. Foakes-Jackson and K. Lake). The old Tübingen school of F. C. Baur saw the book as a compromise document which sought to mediate the tensions from an internal Christian debate between Judaizers and Hellenists. Others construed the major force behind the book's composition to be political in describing how Christianity spread throughout the Roman empire. Still others have explained the book's main intention to be in offering a description of the transition from Judaism to Gentile Christianity. Then again, an apologetic motivation has been suggested which

mounted a defence for Christianity's being a recognized religion
within the state (*religio licita*). Finally, a theological purpose arising
out of the loss of the hope of the imminent return of Christ has been
defended, which restructured the faith in terms of a theology of
history and legitimated the role of the church as the official tradent
of the sacred traditions and sole vehicle of divine salvation (Grässer).

It would be hard to deny that each of these proposals has found
some significant evidence upon which to build its case. Yet it is also
true that each of the theories finds the decisive factor to be some force
behind the biblical text, or one which is only partially congruent with
the book's own articulation of intentionality. One of the great
contributions of van Unnik's illuminating article ('The "Book of
Acts"') was in raising the question whether the book's own formulation of purpose has been adequately considered. To read the book
for its kerygmatic witness is not to deny the influences of other forces
upon the book's composition, but it is to insist that its canonical
function for a community of faith and practice is integrally connected
to its theological intentionality.

The book of Acts sees itself in direct continuity with the Gospel of
Luke. Another prologue is offered in a similar style which is addressed
to the same recipient, Theophilus, and explicit reference is made to
the prior volume. Beyond this, the two books are related in a
conscious pattern of promise and fulfilment which is emphasized by
the overlapping material at the end of Luke and the beginning of
Acts. Luke closes with the 'promises of the Father' to be realized in
Jerusalem (24.49) and with the ascension. Acts begins with an
extended description of the ascension and the coming of the Spirit
at Pentecost.

The prologue of Acts also serves to confirm the initial prologue of
Luke. The period of Jesus' earthly ministry comprises a fixed period
which has ended. Jesus ascends into heaven and leaves his disciples.
Something new has begun with the age of the church. The crucial
theological issue, which is explicitly addressed by the author, is the
major canonical question. What is the relationship between the
ministry of Jesus Christ and that of his church? Canonically
expressed, what is the theological link between the book of Acts and
the Gospel of Luke?

In traditional Christian exegesis the relationship between the two
books was thought to be a very simple one. Luke presented the
earthly ministry of Jesus, whereas Acts portrayed the ascended

Christ at work in the Spirit. However, the canonical shaping of the Lucan material offers a far more complex and subtle relationship which requires closer attention to a variety of other factors. In other words, Luke did not develop a theology of the continued presence of Christ along the lines of the Pauline doctrine of being 'in Christ', but rather he sought to actualize his tradition in another manner.

In his second prologue the author once again lays emphasis upon the continuity between the past and the present. He is well aware that the earthly ministry of Christ has passed to become part of history. What now occurs with Christ's disciples is not a prolongation of the gospel, nor are they to strive for an existential recovery of Christ's presence. Rather the theme of the apostles as chosen of God for a specific task is picked up (1.2) and the 'certainty' (Luke 1.4) of the truth of the resurrection confirmed 'with many proofs' (1.3). The continuity theme is also emphasized by Jesus himself, as the resurrected-but-not-yet-ascended Christ, who instructs his disciples regarding the kingdom of God for forty days (v. 3). The tension caused by this extended period in Acts with its omission in Luke's account (24.44ff.) has long been noticed. However one explains the prehistory of the tradition of the forty days in Acts (cf. Menoud, Wilson, etc.), its canonical role within the introduction is clear. Luke summarizes Jesus' ministry in terms of the kingdom of God which ministry is then passed on to the apostles. As the chosen vehicles for the witness of the resurrection, they have been instructed by Christ himself. The continuity between the two eras of God's redemptive history has been assured by Jesus and confirmed by the unique office of apostle (1.21ff.).

However, the relation between the two eras is not a simple one of historical continuity. The decisive new factor is the presence of the Spirit for whom the apostles are to wait. The fulfilment of the promise comes on the day of Pentecost. The ministry of witnessing to the 'end of the earth' is supported by the gift of language. The testimony to Christ is not confined to the Jews alone, but all the nations begin to hear the message in their own tongue.

The decisive role of the Spirit of God in the book of Acts is a clear signal that the author is not merely writing a history of the rise of Christianity. This false conclusion has often been drawn because of Luke's awareness of historical time. However, Luke's intention is clearly different from ordinary historical writing, as immediately becomes evident in what follows.

Luke sets out to describe the effect of God's plan in equipping the apostles with his Spirit. The witness is made through the 'word of God', which results from being filled with the Holy Spirit (4.31). The importance of the word of God as the vehicle for the witness is confirmed by the constant reference to the word (4.4, 29, 31; 6.4; 8.14; 10.44; 11.1, etc.), the effect of which is then summarized as comprising the actual substance of the book. 'The word of God increased and the number of disciples multiplied greatly' (6.7). The focus of the writer is on the history of the word as it unfolds within the plan of God (12.24). To characterize Acts merely as a history of the church is to miss its most important dimension.

In addition, the function of the word of God is crucial for understanding how the author conceived of the relation between his first and second compositions. The book of Acts does not serve as a commentary on the Gospel. It is in no sense a midrash. Rather, the relationship is of a different order. The word which is preached is 'in the name of Jesus Christ', or 'by his name' (4.30). Forgiveness of sins is proclaimed through his name (10.43), demons driven out by the name (16.18), and Paul is ready to die for the name. In one sense, this idiom represents the Lucan form of the presence of Christ. Through his name Christ is present in his full reality, but the name is not the avenue for actualizing his benefits. Rather, the preached word becomes the channel for unleashing the power of the resurrected Christ. The Spirit forms the bridge between the earthly Jesus and the ascended Lord.

A closer look at the sermons in the book demonstrates how the preached word functions as the means of actualizing the present significance of the gospel (cf. Dibelius, Wilckens). A consistent pattern emerges throughout the book. First, the sermon recounts the life of Jesus culminating in his death. These events did not occur by accident, but according to the plan of God. Then God raised his servant Jesus from the dead and vindicated him. The sermon closes with the apostolic witness to the certain fact that Christ is alive and reigning with God. Finally, on the basis of these 'mighty works of God', an appeal for repentance is made.

The remarkable and consistent feature of this preaching which occurs throughout the book of Acts is the portrayal of Christ as belonging both to the past and to the present. Fully in accordance with the Gospel of Luke, Jesus' life is portrayed in a sequence of historical events. He was a man attested to by his mighty works, who was crucified and killed (2.22f.). He went about doing good and healed all those who were oppressed (10.38). Yet at the same time, this same Jesus has been vindicated through his resurrection and been appointed by God both Lord and Christ (2.36). Although put to death, the apostle bears witness that 'he *is* the one ordained by God to be the judge of the living and the dead' (10.42; cf. 7.55ff.).

At this point it is crucial to understand how the author of Acts makes theological use of his recounting the mighty acts of God. On the basis of what God has done, a direct appeal is made to the listeners for repentance (2.38). What is being offered is characterized in different ways. It consists of forgiveness of sins, of blessing, of the gift of the spirit, of the good news of peace. At times it is designated as salvation (4.12; 13.26). Obviously the content of that being offered is well known and can be simply referred to. The point of the sermon and the content of the good news is that the ancient promises offered to the fathers have been fulfilled. References to repentance, forgiveness of sins, and the gift of the Spirit serve as catchwords or convenient summaries of the entire Old Testament message of salvation. Paul confesses to Agrippa that he says nothing 'but what the prophets and Moses said would come to pass' (26.22).

Because the content of the Christian message is largely defined in terms of the Old Testament by Luke, it becomes crucial for him to defend his interpretation of the significance of Jesus on the basis of the Old Testament. The proof-from-prophecy method which first appeared in the Gospel of Luke becomes even more prominent in the book of Acts. Chapters 3, 7, and 13 offer classic illustrations of the approach. Luke is not attempting a christological reading of the Old Testament. Rather, the Old Testament is cited as providing the content of the message which was then fulfilled by Jesus. Thus, Ps. 16 is frequently quoted as evidence that God's Holy One was not allowed to experience corruption, a situation which was then realized by Jesus' resurrection from the dead (Acts 2.25ff.; 13.35). Similarly, the Old Testament expectation that the Messiah would be exalted to God's right hand was testified to by Ps. 110 (Acts 2.34) and now confirmed to the apostles by Jesus' ascension.

The author of Acts does not relate his contemporary hearers to Jesus by actualizing the figure of the resurrected Christ. He does not describe the age of the church as a history of the direct encounter with the ascended Lord. Although it is true that the ascended Christ appeared to Paul, and Stephen addressed Jesus directly in prayer

(7.59), these incidents are not typical of Luke's approach in relating the mighty deeds of the past with the present community of faith. Rather, Christ's achievement as vindicated Lord resulted in his realizing Israel's salvation which is now made accessible in faith and which is testified to by the preached word of his appointed apostles. There is now a teaching, that is to say, a message with a content which is transmitted and confirmed by personal testimony (2.42).

Luke goes to great lengths to spell out the means by which this salvation, accomplished by Christ, is to be appropriated by the new generation who had not participated in the earthly ministry of Jesus. Indeed, the consistent and detailed outlining of the steps on the way to salvation appears almost as an *ordo salutis*. In reaction to the preached word the question is asked by those hearing: 'What then shall we do?' (3.37). The apostles' response had already been prepared by the Old Testament proof text (2.21; cf. Joel 2.32). 'Repent, be baptized in the name of Jesus Christ for the forgiveness of sins; receive the gift of the Holy Spirit' (2.38). The formulation in 3.19 varies, but the substance is the same: 'Repent . . . turn again, that your sins may be blotted out, that times of refreshing may come from the presence of the Lord' (cf. 10.43). 13.39 speaks of the believer being freed from sins, but then further defines it as being 'freed from everything from which you could not be freed by the law of Moses'. The act of appropriation is described as 'receiving the word' (17.11), 'believing' (10.43), and 'obeying' (5.32).

The role of the Holy Spirit plays a decisive role within the description of the conversion. The key event for understanding the Spirit's function in Acts is, of course, the day of Pentecost (Acts 2) in which Peter interprets the meaning of the coming of the Spirit from Old Testament texts as the confirmation of the fulfilment of the eschatological hope of the day of the Lord. The long promised kingdom of God has arrived, the last days have begun, and the signs of the new age are everywhere evident. What first took place only for the apostles repeats itself for every believer throughout the book of Acts. Following repentance and baptism, the gift of the Spirit is promised (2.38). The Spirit is said to 'fall' upon those who hear (10.44). It is always given as a gift (5.32). Although it appears often as the final element within a sequence of acts, Luke lays great emphasis upon the freedom of the Spirit. It comes as a surprise and is always seem as stemming directly from God (11.17). It cannot be controlled or purchased (8.14ff.), although the apostles become vehicles for its transmission by the laying on of hands (8.18). Significantly, the coming of the Spirit within Acts is not bound within a fixed scheme of an *ordo salutis*. In Paul's case, the Spirit came before his baptism (9.17ff.), and at Corinth baptism in the name of Jesus was required of John's disciples before the gift of the Spirit (19.1ff.).

The gift of the Spirit serves as a visible sign of one's entrance into the salvation of God through the name of Christ. Both in the case of Cornelius (11.15ff.), and in that of the apostolic assembly (15.6ff.), the fact that God has given to the Gentiles the same gift of the Spirit proves to be the decisive sign of their divine acceptance. The experience of the Spirit confirmed the entrance of Gentiles into the promised salvation.

The universal scope of the appeal to receive God's salvation was sounded from the very start, at the day of Pentecost. All the nations heard 'in their own tongue the mighty works of God' (2.11). Similarly, Peter finds in the Old Testament a further warrant for this universal offer: 'Whoever calls on the name of the Lord will be saved' (2.21). That the inclusion of the Gentiles in the salvation of God was an essential part of the Old Testament's promise, proves to be a major theme of the book of Acts (13.47). However, it is fundamental to Luke's understanding of the salvation which is being offered to the Gentiles, that it is the hope of Israel which is being realized. This important insight has been especially developed in the essays of Dahl and Jervell. Luke does not describe the rejection of the Jewish people and God's raising up a new people of God. Rather, faithful Israel does respond. In spite of the obduracy of a disobedient portion, the promise of Israel's restoration has been accepted and the Gentiles enter into this legacy of Israel as part of the one people of God. The initial offer of God's salvation to the Jews, prior to the mission to the Gentiles, was not merely strategically motivated by the author of Acts, but was grounded theologically in the unity of the one people of God.

III. The Church of the Future

Up to this point in our search for the canonical shape of the book of Acts, attention has been directed to describing the process of the actualization of the great acts of God in Jesus Christ for the succeeding apostolic period. However, there is another crucial passage which focuses its emphasis on the subsequent transition from the apostolic age to the post-apostolic church. Paul's farewell address to the elders at Miletus (Acts 20.17–35) has largely been studied in the past for its potential aid in tracing the development of the early church's understanding of ecclesiastical offices. However, because this historical issue is tangential to the literary function of the passage, we shall not pursue the debate (cf. von Campenhausen; G. Bornkamm, *TDNT*, VI, 651–83). It is to the great credit of H. Schürmann to have seen the crucial canonical implications of this passage. Schürmann even speaks of 'the great theological achievement of Luke in seeking to be "canonical" for the church of every age' (322).

The farewell address of Paul marks the end of the apostolic period within Luke's understanding of *Heilsgeschichte*. Paul is portrayed as the last of the apostles, both as representative of the Twelve and also dependent upon them (Bornkamm). The passage reflects Luke's theological concern sharply to distinguish between the beginning of the gospel (Luke 1.2), the period of the apostles, and finally the period after the apostolic age ('after my departure', v. 29). Paul's farewell is directed to the elders of Ephesus, but it is clear that his last will and testament has been shaped to address the post-apostolic church as well. Far from being simply a 'bishop's manual', the speech is a word 'to all the flock' (v. 28). Moreover, Paul's focus begins with the past, moves to the present, and then centres its major attention on the future. In the sense that the passage serves to interpret the tradition for successive generations, both in its continuity and discontinuity, it is a classic example of canonical shaping.

The speech turns on two major points: the continuity of the apostolic tradition and the office of guardian of the flock. Paul is portrayed as the model of the apostolic ministry. He has been faithful to his ministry which he received from the Lord Jesus (v. 20) in testifying to the gospel. The issue is of the continuity of the tradition. Paul has declared to the church 'the whole counsel of God'. The issue is of completeness. He has served the Lord in humility by ministering unstintingly to the flock. The issue is of giving of the church's welfare priority over personal gain.

In the light of this model, he addresses the present and future leaders of the church. They are to build on the tradition which they have received ('remember'). The apostles have laid the foundation, have determined its parameters ('the whole counsel of God'), and have demonstrated the praxis of the faith in the care for the church's needs (vv. 34f.). The goal of the ministry is not the preservation of pure doctrine for its own sake, nor is it the administration of social services. Rather, being grounded in the good news of the kingdom (v. 25), as received from the testimony of the apostles, the church lives out its confession in the service of the weak (v. 35) under the grace of God's word (v. 32). Nowhere in this passage do the bearers of the tradition acquire their authority through an official status, nor is the office defined in terms of an established channel of succession. Nevertheless, the responsibility of maintaining the continuity of the gospel and providing for the welfare of the church is not assigned to chance or charismatic leaders. Because of the threat against the church, from both within and without (29f.), the hope of the future lies in maintaining the faithful ministry through the grace of God (v. 32) which has been established upon the testimony of the apostles.

Among modern commentaries, it has long been regarded as a major problem of this chapter that Paul establishes himself as a model for Christian ministry. A variety of psychological ploys have been offered by which to circumvent the problem of alleged immodesty. In more recent studies a literary solution has been proposed. Because the farewell speech does not stem from Paul, but from Luke, the offence of self-esteem can be mitigated. However, neither of these modern approaches has come to grips with the theological issue at stake, nor adequately interpreted the canonical function for which this portrait of Paul has been drawn. The witness of this passage is not to Paul's personality, but to his representative role as bearer of the apostolic tradition. Luke offers a 'canonical' portrayal of Paul which is to serve as a model for future generations. In this portrayal one sees both the continuity and discontinuity between the so-called historical Paul and the Paul of the church.

First, in respect to the elements of continuity, no passage in the Acts shows such a conscious effort to reflect the actual vocabulary of Paul himself (cf. Schürmann, 312). Whether this presentation rests on received tradition (F. F. Bruce), or is largely Luke's construction (Haenchen), does not effect the intentionality of the composition. Secondly, in respect to the element of discontinuity, the portrait of Paul does not conform closely to the reconstructed, historical Paul of the letters, but is the Paul who has been heard as teacher of the church. That is to say, the picture of the canonical Paul has already been abstracted from the historical situation of his original letters to function in a representative, apostolic role for a later age.

IV. Critical Issues in Luke's Theology

At this point in the discussion of the Pauline portrayal in Acts 20, we have touched upon the first of a series of highly controversial issues involved in the canonical shaping of the book of Acts. It seems wise to attempt to address some of these issues in a more systematic, topical fashion, while at the same time, seeking further to explore the canonical shape of central passages within the book of Acts.

A. Luke's Historical Portrayal

The charge has often been made that the description of the history of the early church in the author of Acts represents a highly idealized picture which distorts the actual course of events. Neither the complexity of the history, nor the inner tensions have been correctly presented. Rather, according to this view, the book of Acts has construed his account in an idealizing manner in order to create an edifying story of how the church began ('*Erbauungsgeschichte*', Haenchen). Over against this view a sizeable number of more conservatively oriented New Testament scholars have tried to defend the historicity of Acts as reflecting a reasonably accurate portrayal, if admittedly selective in nature (cf. Gasque, Marshall).

In my opinion, neither of these approaches has adequately addressed the hermeneutical issue at stake, nor has been able to resolve the real exegetical problems. The error lies in assuming that the author is attempting to write history in the modern sense of the word, and that the truth of the book can be measured in terms of correspondence to common historical referentiality. Because the book frequently does not comply with the modern standards of historical verisimilitude, it is then characterized as an edifying story. Such an interpretation has assumed a hermeneutic of historical referentiality, but finding little support, derived the sources of its referentiality from the creative imagination of its author. The conservative rejoinder which is inclined to turn to rationalistic apologetics, also effects a flattening of the biblical text even when combined with learned archaeological research (cf. W. M. Ramsay).

However, the book of Acts is not a history of the early church according to the usual connotation of the term. Rather, as we have attempted to show, the author is describing the effect of the preaching of the word of God and the resulting salvation realized by the gift of the Spirit. The referentiality is of a theological order which involves the entrance of the eschatological kingdom of God and the formation of a 'people for his name'. The nature of this reality is badly skewed when it is made to conform either to modern historical or to philosophical categories. This hermeneutical stance does not deny that historical elements – indeed, in the modern sense of the term – are frequently reflected in the biblical account. Moreover, the scientific analysis of the biblical account from the perspective of critical historical research is fully legitimate and often aids in sharpening the profile of the theological witness. However, the theological task of relating biblical exegesis to historical research cannot be one of simple identification, but requires a delicate balance of theological sophistication. In sum, the form of the question of historical idealization has already biased the answer and needs to be reformulated for a theologically responsible reply.

Perhaps this hermeneutical issue can be best illustrated by focusing on the Lucan account of the apostolic decree (Acts 15) which seems to be in marked conflict with Paul's description in Galatians 2. The discrepancy appears to involve a variety of different problems, including conflicting chronology, sequence of events, role of the protagonists, and nature of the decrees. Because the critical issues have been discussed at length in the commentaries, it is unnecessary to rehearse them in detail (cf. K. Lake, *Beginnings* V, 195ff.). The initial problem turns on the chronological relation between Acts 15 and Galatians 2. The classic solutions are familiar. Lightfoot identifies the event portrayed in Acts 15 with that of Galatians 2 and seeks to explain away Paul's explicit word that his visit in Galatians 2 was his second (1.18ff.) and not his third visit. Ramsay resolves the chronological difficulty by choosing to identify the visit of Galatians 2 with Acts 11, but then he must explain why the later conference had to resolve the same issue once again. Zahn identifies Galatians 2 with Acts 15 but then assumes that Galatians 2 has dispensed with chronology which allows the author the freedom to reconstruct his own sequence. Linton tries to recover an earlier tradition differing from both Galatians and Acts. Finally, there is the widespread theory represented by Weizsäcker (*Apostolic Age*) who distributes the accounts of Acts between a reconstructed Antiochene and a Jerusalem source, and regards the conflation as clumsy. The effect is that the sequence of Galatians has usually been assumed to be correct and that of Acts reordered and reinterpreted to bring it into historical conformity.

The purpose of reviewing this history of exegesis is not to dismiss it as irrelevant. The historical problems are real, and cannot be obscured. However, it is equally important to recognize that no solution to this problem has been attempted in relation to the canonical shaping of the two books. An exegesis of ch. 15 in the context of the book of Acts does not necessarily depend upon the resolution of this historical crux. To raise the question as to the canonical function of these two accounts is to approach the text from a particular perspective.

The problem described by Acts 15 which resulted in the apostolic conference turns initially on the issue of circumcision. It is of importance to note that two very different formulations of the problem are offered. According to v. 1, some from Judaea argued that salvation depended upon being circumcised after the law. According to v. 5, the issue concerned the necessity for observing the law of circumcision by those Gentiles who had already been saved, that is, become Christians. In Peter's response once again the two issues are intertwined. He begins by testifying that God had confirmed the salvation of the Gentiles through faith by the gift of the Spirit. He then raises the question of requiring of them anything of the law as a prerequisite of salvation (v. 10), and concludes that both Jew and Gentile are saved without distinction by the grace of Jesus Christ (v. 11).

What is significant to observe is that the book of Acts does not sharply distinguish between the issue of receiving salvation apart from the law, and the issue of a subsequent way of life freed from the law. Rather, it addresses them both in terms of the grace of Jesus Christ. However, the theological point made is clear enough: both the entrance into God's salvation and the manner of life within his salvation depend solely on the grace of God apart from obedience to the law. The function of the Old Testament citation is to prooftext this agreement with a biblical warrant.

When subsequently the issue of the apostolic decree is brought up (vv. 19ff.), the narrative in Acts assumes as settled the theological issue of the right of the Gentiles to be saved apart from the law. The issue now turns to the strategy for maintaining the unity of the church between Jew and Gentile. It does not offer a retreat from the theological point already made. For the sake of unity, Gentile

Christians are 'advised' – the language is consistently conciliatory – to follow a manner of life which will be less offensive for Jews and which has its warrant in the freedom allowed Gentiles within the law.

Turning now to the controversy in Galatians 2, both the similarities and differences are significant. The theological issue which Paul addresses also focuses on the controversial problem of circumcision. However, the context of Galatians is very different. The two basic theological questions respecting the law and Gentile Christians have become separated. Even by Paul's opponents, it has been accepted that uncircumcised Gentiles can hear the gospel and receive the Spirit of God. The issue at stake is whether once they have entered into the salvation of God, they are also required to fulfil the law of Moses. Paul argues that these two questions are not to be separated, but are theologically indivisible. If the Galatians had correctly understood the nature of their salvation through God's grace, they would also have understood that the obedient life is lived according to the guidance of the Spirit and not in fulfilment of the works of the law.

For Paul, the demand of the Judaizers for continued obedience of the law not only fundamentally misconstrues the truth of salvation by God's grace through faith, but also threatens the basic freedom of the Christian which Christ has won (2.4). Paul, therefore, opposes vigorously any compromise with Jewish tradition in order to preserve the truth of the gospel which frees the believer to walk as a new creation in the Spirit.

To summarize, the basic theological point respecting the gospel and the Jewish law is similar in both Acts and Galatians. In both the entrance into God's salvation and the ordering of life within his salvation depend solely on the grace of God apart from obedience to the law. Within Acts the chapter marks the decisive transition to the Gentile mission. However, the differences are equally important. Luke draws the theological implications regarding the unity of the church and thus advises Gentile Christians to observe certain Jewish practices. Paul, in contrast, focuses on the freedom of the Gentile believer which refuses to be subject to human tradition. Unquestionably, the level of theological precision is greater in Galatians, and the intensity of the struggle differs enormously. However, Paul's theological unfolding of the internal dimensions of the gospel in respect to the law serves to complement rather than subvert Luke's more formal understanding of law.

The canonical shaping of these two New Testament books has not attempted to resolve a variety of historical and literary problems. Rather, its function has been to preserve the integrity of each witness and to establish the semantic level on which these two witnesses are to be related. It has resisted all attempts to neutralize the tension on historical, literary, or theological grounds. Acts 15 cannot be dismissed as an idealization, which has been dictated by an ideology, nor can this chapter be forced to reflect the identical historical perspective of Galatians. The canonical shape thus serves to establish theological parameters for interpreting these texts, but the development of the theological potential of relating Christian freedom to church unity within these two chapters depends on the further reflection of the biblical theologian.

B. *Luke's Portrayal of Paul*

Much of the credit for first having posed the question of a peculiar Lucan portrait of Paul goes to P. Vielhauer. In his incisive article of 1950 Vielhauer argued that the picture of Paul given in Acts differs greatly from the Paul of the genuine letters. He focused on four main areas of disagreement under the headings: natural theology, law, christology, and eschatology. Vielhauer's interpretation was pursued further by Conzelmann, Grässer, and Haenchen among others. What emerged in Acts was a figure of Paul whose theology of missionary strategy differed in no way from Peter or James, who was a pious observer of the Jewish law, sustaining circumcision and fasting, and who had replaced the radical Pauline eschatology of the letters with a church-oriented *Heilsgeschichte*. In addition, lest the profound theological implications of this analysis be somehow missed, Käsemann spelt them out in his characteristically polemical fashion. Luke had seriously distorted the basic Pauline theology. As a representative of early catholicism he offered a false theological alternative which had to be rejected in the name of the gospel.

Several significant reactions to this highly controversial analysis of Acts should be immediately noted. Conservative critical scholars, such as Bauernfeind and Schürmann, offered carefully worked out rebuttals of this position which they characterized as extreme. Bauernfeind in particular made the significant point that Vielhauer had erected an artificially sharp contrast by reconstructing an allegedly 'historical' Paul from his so-called genuine letters, and that such a critical reconstructed portrait had never functioned in the literature or community of the early church. Again, Scandinavian New Testament scholars such as Dahl, Jervell, Munck and Borgen sought to erode the sharp contrast by indicating elements of continuity betwen the Pauline letters and Acts. Borgen was successful in showing the *heilsgeschichlichte* dimensions of Romans 9–11, the use of signs and wonders as proof of the apostolic office (II Cor. 12.11ff.), and a common resurrection tradition between Luke and I Corinthians 15. Similarly, Dahl's brilliant study of the phrase 'a people for his name' in Acts 15.14 did much to call into question the analysis which attributed the entire chapter to Luke's literary creativity without any recourse to tradition.

Although I am certainly in agreement with these important critical modifications of Vielhauer's position, I would argue that the hermeneutical issues at stake have not been adequately handled so far within the debate. Moreover, the crucial importance of the canonical shaping of Acts has not been raised, which means that the conservative response has only succeeded in chipping away at the edges without striking to the heart of the theological issue.

First of all, the figure of the apostle Paul has been assigned a variety of roles within the book of Acts. This observation is not to suggest that his portrait derived solely from a literary projection on the part of its author. Without denying Luke's literary creativity, the evidence is also clear that Luke stood within a tradition (cf. Schürmann, Dahl, Jervell), and was not simply creating out of whole cloth. Luke makes very little, if any, use of the letters of Paul. Paul is portrayed as he was received and heard within the early Christian community. This is to suggest that in his role as teacher of Israel, Paul has been removed from the historical particularity which is present in his individual letters. Paul is not sketched from a historical reconstruction, but his role has been generalized, universalized, and made representative. He is the last of the Pharisees, the first of the Gentile missionaries, and the apostolic representative for the Twelve. The canonical Paul is, thus, a theological composite, at least one stage removed from the Paul of the letters, who now addresses the future needs of the Christian church (Acts 20). The canonical shapers of the Lucan portrait have already rendered the historical figure in such a way as to serve the ongoing community of faith.

c. Literary Techniques and Canonical Shape

Several generations of New Testament scholars have expended great energy in tracing the variety of literary techniques used by the author of Acts. Unfortunately, much of this excellent work has never been related to its theological, that is, canonical, function. Thus, the research of Dibelius and Wilckens has been highly successful in showing the stereotyped speech patterns used by both Peter and Paul which have obliterated the historical particularities of these speeches. Both speakers have been assigned the role of bearing witness to the one common Christian faith. The truth of the accounts was not measured in terms of its accuracy in representing an original historical incident, but in its correspondence to the one apostolic witness of the faith in Jesus Christ on which the Christian church was grounded.

Or again, it has long been recognized that the real audience to whom the speeches in Acts were directed tends to transcend the narrative framework. For example, the alleged inconsistencies in Paul's speech before Agrippa and Festus arise from the fact that the real addressees emerge as the readers of Luke's story (cf. O'Toole, 19ff.). The point is not that the narrative framework is purely fictional, but that the peculiar canonical function to which Acts was directed increasingly affected the shaping of the material. Similarly, Paul's farewell address begins with a genuinely historical situation with Ephesian elders meeting at Miletus, but the shape of Paul's last will leaves that historical moment to address the future leaders of the church faced with typical threats.

Finally, irrespective of the issue of prior sources, the effect of the introduction of the 'we' passages in Acts is to bring a broader confirmation of the apostolic witness and ground the material in a communal experience. The effect of the first person plural usage is to render the testimony in a peculiar fashion which serves to bridge the gap between the original author and the subsequent reader.

d. The Defence of Paul

There is another set of texts in which the peculiar canonical function of Paul emerges with some clarity, namely, those passages which relate to Paul's early life and conversion (chs. 9, 22, 26). It is not the place to rehearse the history of research on this controversial problem, but the search for an adequate explanation of why the conversion incident is repeated three times in Acts continues to engage interpreters.

Lohfink (*Paulus*) offers a helpful review of why the traditional conservative attempts at harmonization into one unified account have failed. His criticism of the critical resolution through an appeal to different literary sources is also incisive. Lohfink's own form-critical analysis has illuminated individual forms within the growth of the tradition, but has hardly resolved the major problems within the book of Acts. For this reason, Burchard's redactional study is more representative of the newer approach. Indeed, Burchard has often been successful in his careful distinguishing between Luke's use of inherited tradition and his own literary contribution. His major conclusion is certainly correct that Luke was concerned to present Paul as a fully legitimate apostolic witness, different from the Twelve, but equal in rank with them. However, Burchard has not adequately worked out the canonical function of the three accounts within the book of Acts. His chief interest remains in distinguishing the various elements within the literary composition. His synthetic category of the 'outer' and 'inner' function of the passages (129ff.), in my judgment, does not do justice to the canonical shape.

The problem at issue, therefore, is how the conversion accounts function within the book of Acts in relation to a Christian community which sought to hear therein a continuing witness for the faith. That Luke has made use of a variety of literary techniques in order to heighten the effect of the story is clear (cf. Lohfink), but such literary observations do not in themselves penetrate to the heart of the issue. Neither is it adequate to see in the three accounts a representative move to present typical audiences for whom Paul adjusted his experience, e.g. ch. 22 to Jews, ch. 26 to Gentiles. Nor is Paul's conversion ever pictured as something to be actualized by later generations of Christians.

Rather, the repetition of Paul's conversion points to its great importance within the framework of the theological history which Luke is setting forth in his second composition. Paul's conversion is first recorded in Acts 9 as another example of the power of the gospel to spread through the working of the Spirit. Indeed, Luke depicts Paul's conversion with some unique features, but akin to the eunuch of ch. 8 and Cornelius of ch. 10. There is a certain objective quality about the first account. The scene is recorded in the third person, and Paul's commission as a chosen instrument is communicated in a dialogue with Ananias. The effect of the conversion is of amazement (v. 21) and the immediate confrontation of Paul with the Jews (v. 22).

The many variations on the two later accounts (chs. 22 and 26) have long been noticed. However, even so critical a scholar as Haenchen has observed that many of the differences in the details, such as what was seen and heard, and by whom, do not distract, but rather contribute to the particular effect of each presentation of the story. One of the crucial canonical issues is that both chs. 22 and 26 present the story within the explicit framework of Paul's defence. In ch. 22 he defends himself before the Jews of Jerusalem, in ch. 26 before King Agrippa. However, it is also obvious that the audience being addressed, and the theological issues being discussed, transcend the original narrative setting of the defence. In ch. 22 the specific account of the conversion experience on the Damascus road closely follows that of ch. 9, but this central section has been both preceded and followed by a different formulation of the tradition. In vv. 3ff. Paul uses his background and early history as a proof of his zeal for the Jewish faith and the law. Again, in ch. 22 Ananias, who is characterized as a devout and faithful Jew, makes the point it is the 'God of our fathers' who appointed Paul 'to know his will, to see the Just One and to hear a voice from his mouth'. Therefore, Paul's commission to witness to what he has seen stems from the will of the God of the Old Testament.

However, lest it be thought that ch. 22 is an attempt to justify Paul's witness before a Jewish audience, the succeeding paragraph (vv. 17–21) moves in a totally different direction. Paul, who is portrayed as the still faithful Jew praying in the temple at Jerusalem, is now informed by Jesus in a vision that his testimony will not be accepted by the Jews of Jerusalem. When Paul objects and again makes reference to his record as a zealot for the law, he is nevertheless sent far away to the Gentiles. It is clear that Paul is not seeking to convince the Jews of Jerusalem, but is offering a defence of why his mission to the Gentiles is not a defection from true Judaism, but stems from the will of the God of the fathers. Paul has not severed his connection with the Old Testament faith, but his true witness has been rejected in Jerusalem against all reason.

In ch. 26 the defence before Agrippa again makes use of the same form of the conversion experience (vv. 12–15), but greatly alters the subsequent form of the tradition by eliminating completely the intermediatory role of Ananias. Moreover, the speech summarizes at the outset the major issue at stake in ch. 26: the hope in the promise of the God of the fathers. Paul emerges as a defender of the genuine Jewish faith. He can still represent himself as a Pharisee, faithful to the strictest interpretation of the law. He stands in direct continuity with the faith of Judaism. What was prophesied through the Hebrew prophets has now been realized through Jesus. The appearance of the risen Lord to Paul confirms the Old Testament promise and is therefore crucial to his case. Thus, Paul can argue that he is preaching nothing which is not found in Moses and the prophets.

Again in ch. 26, the defence is not addressed to a contemporary Jewish audience. The Jews have already become a distant party. Rather, Agrippa and Festus serve as representatives of the wider world of the Gentiles (vv. 20–23) who are challenged to share in the promise of the Father, now offered to all in Christ. Moreover, Agrippa confirms the complete innocence of Paul in respect to the charges of the Jews.

To summarize, the function of Paul's often repeated conversion accounts is closely connected with the larger problem of his defence which occupied the last chapters in the book of Acts (21–28). In my judgment, Jerwell's interpretation has been largely confirmed. The real problem is not a justification before Rome, but the theological issue of the status of Paul. Because the church shares in Israel's salvation any justification of the charge that Paul had become apostate by rejecting the law would be a major threat to the unity of the church. The defence of Paul as the unique bridge between the old covenant and the Gentile mission has crucial theological significance for Acts.

V. The Canonical Effect of Acts within the New Testament

A concluding, and extremely important aspect of the canonical shape of the book of Acts, remains to be discussed concerning the final effect of the canonical ordering of the book within the New Testament collection. The issue has recently played a significant role in the larger debate over the history of New Testament canonization. In the view of some (Harnack and von Campenhausen) the canonization

of the book of Acts was crucial in providing a historical link between
the Gospels and epistles, and thus served to assure the catholicity of
Paul within the church. This once generally accepted view has
recently been challenged by Sundberg and Kuck who contest the
theory of a conscious formation of the core of the canon in the second
century, arguing rather for a much later date for the decisive
formation of the New Testament. Especially Kuck has proposed that
Acts did not play a significant role in structuring the New Testament,
but that well before the book of Acts came into view, the two
authorities of Christ and his apostles were already established. He
concludes: 'The placement of Acts in the canon lists shows that it
was not important for the structure of the New Testament, for it
never found any consistent placement in the order of these lists' (92).

In my judgment, two different, if related issues, are at stake in this
debate. The first one concerns a larger revisionist view of the New
Testament canon which contests the consensus that a core had been
established as canonical by AD 200. The second issue concerns the
canonical role of the book of Acts within the New Testament
collection. In regard to the first issue, I disagree with Sundberg's
revisionist theory and I think that his redating of the Muratorian
canon to the fourth century as a crucial support for his hypothesis is
tendentious and unproven. Moreover, I do not accept his sharp
distinction between the concept of 'scripture' and 'canon' ('Toward
a Revised History', 454), which, in my opinion, distorts the basic
theological dynamic of the canonical process by regarding it as a late
ecclesiastical valorization. However, in regard to the second issue,
Sundberg and especially Kuck have made a strong case against
Harnack's position in showing that the historical evidence does not
support the central role of Acts in the formation of the New Testament
corpus. What then was the role of the book of Acts in the canonical
process?

The literary evidence is unequivocal that the books of Luke and
Acts once formed a two-volume work by the same author. A theory
has been developed by Menoud among others, largely to explain the
tension between the conclusion of Luke and the beginning of Acts,
that the books were divided at the moment of canonization. However,
the theory is highly unlikely and rests on the assumption of the
simultaneous canonization of both books. It seems far more probable
that Luke was first assigned a canonical sanctity and only subsequently did Acts acquire a similar status.

However, the crucial point to be made is that the original two-volume work was divided and the individual books assigned different canonical functions. Luke became part of the fourfold Gospel collection and received its interpretation within the context of this corpus. Acts was assigned another position as bearer of the apostolic witness which was clearly distinguished from that of the evangelists.

It is important to emphasize that the canonical function of Acts was not determined by the order of its placement within the New Testament collection. Already Zahn had described the great variety within the ordering of the New Testament books which the early lists and church fathers reflect (*Geschichte des Neutestamentlichen Kanons*, II, 280–383). Usually the Gospels came first in order, but the book of Acts could both precede and follow the Pauline epistles, or could precede and follow the catholic epistles as well. Zahn concluded that the order of the books of the New Testament was not a subject of great significance for the ancient church, but was rather an issue of later editors and publishers (383).

The canonical significance of Acts lies elsewhere, regardless of its order within the New Testament collection. First, the canonical collectors sought to preserve both the Pauline letters and the book of Acts. By so doing they established a context for the reading of Acts which was different from that of the original author of Acts who composed his book without recourse to the Pauline letters. Secondly, the literary effect of this new context is clear, regardless of whether or not the church fathers gave explicit formulation to its role. Because Acts offers a narrative of Paul's ministry with fixed chronological and geographical sequence, it provided the framework into which Paul's letters which lacked a sequence were fitted. This traditional use of Acts as the interpretive guide to the Pauline letters has been assumed by the church because of the canonical collection and not challenged until the rise of the critical method discovered tension between the materials.

Thirdly, the canonical ordering of Acts and the Pauline letters was part of a larger process which both preceded and followed the decision respecting Acts' inclusion within the New Testament. The process involved the editing of the individual apostolic letters within a larger, universalizing canonical corpus and the addition of books (deutero-Pauline, Pastorals), which appeared to have arisen after the period of the historical Paul. This redactional process reflects a portrait of Paul akin to that of Acts. The effect of this canonical process was also to interpret the historical Paul of the letters in the light of a larger theological construct of the Paul of the church. Thus, the canonical function of Acts had the canonical effect of rendering the material in a way commensurate with a larger, more general canonical pattern and of strengthening the unity of the whole. To this extent Harnack's theory that Acts assured the catholicity of Paul within the church retains its validity.

Finally, what are the the implications for the modern interpreter of the canonical role of Acts within the New Testament? The issue has become acute in the light of the tension discovered by critical research between Luke and Paul. Even to suggest with some conservative scholars that these two bodies of material be held in a dialectical relationship of constant tension is to offer a modern theological option which has no warrant from within the shape of the canon itself. Rather, the canon has retained the Pauline letters, but within the framework of Acts which provides hermeneutical guidelines for their interpretation. The content of the letters of Paul and the portrayal of Acts are certainly not to be simply identified, nor can one be allowed to destroy the witness of the other. However, Acts instructs the community of faith in one direction in which to move by translating the significance of Paul's original life and message for a different generation of readers who did not share in Paul's historical ministry.

PART FOUR

THE PAULINE CORPUS

12

ROMANS

Commentaries

M. Luther, 1515–16, ET 1961
P. Melanchthon, 1532
J. Calvin, 1539
F. A. G. Tholuck, ⁵1856
C. Hodge, ²1864
F. Godet, ²1883
E. H. Gifford, 1886
H. C. G. Moule, ExpB, 1894
W. Sanday, A. C. Headlam, ICC, 1895
R. Cornely, 1896
B. Weiss, MeyerK, ⁹1899
J. Denney, ExpGT, 1900
A. Jülicher, *SNT*, ³1917
T. Zahn, KNT, ³1923
C. H. Dodd, MNTC, 1932
K. Barth, ⁶1929, ET 1933
H. Lietzmann, HNT, ⁴1933

A. Schlatter, 1935
E. Gaugler, ZBK, 1945, 1952
P. Althaus, NTD, ⁶1949
M.-J. Lagrange, ÉB, ⁶1950
A. Nygren, ET 1952
K. Barth, Shorter Com., ET 1959
C. K. Barrett, B/HNTC, 1957
O. Kuss, 1957, 1959
J. Murray, NICNT, 1960, 1965
O. Michel, MeyerK, ⁴1966
J. C. O'Neill, 1975
C. E. B. Cranfield, ICC, 1975, 1979
H. Schlier, HTKNT, ²1979
U. Wilckens, EKK, 1978–82
E. Käsemann, HNT, ⁴1980, ET 1980
R. A. Harrisville, Augs, 1980

Bibliography

K. **Barth**, *Christ and Adam: Man and Humanity in Romans 5*, ET Edinburgh 1956, New York 1957; G. **Bauer**, 'Zur Auslegung und Anwendung von Röm 13, 1–7 bei Karl Barth', *Antwort, FS K. Barth*, Zollikon-Zürich 1956, 114–23; F. C. **Baur**, 'Ueber Zweck und Veranlassung des Römerbriefs und die damit zusammenhängenden Verhältnisse der römischen Gemeinde. Eine historisch-kritische Untersuchung', *Tübinger Zeitschrift für Theologie*, 1836, Heft 3, 59–178; reprinted *Ausgewählte Werke in Einzelausgaben*, ed. K. Scholder, I, Stuttgart 1963, 147–266; J. C. **Beker**, *Paul the Apostle*, ET Philadelphia and Edinburgh 1980; C. J. **Bjerkelund**, *PARAKALŌ. Form, Funktion und Sinn der parakaló-Sätze in den paulinischen Briefen*, Lund 1967; G.

Bornkamm, 'Die Offenbarung des Zornes Gottes (Röm 1–3)', *Das Ende des Gesetzes*, Munich 1966, 9–33; 'Taufe und neues Leben (Röm 6)', ibid., 34–50; 'Sünde, Gesetz und Tod (Röm 7)', ibid., 51–69; 'Paulinische Anakoluthe im Römerbrief', ibid, 76–92;'The Letter to the Romans as Paul's Last Will and Testament', ET in K. P. Donfried, ed., *The Romans Debate*, 17–31; U. **Borse**, 'Die geschichtliche und theologische Einordnung des Römerbriefes', *BZ* NF 16, 1972, 70–83;E. **Brandenberger**, *Adam und Christus*, WMANT 7, 1962; R. **Bultmann**, 'Das Problem der Ethik bei Paulus', *ZNW* 23, 1924, 123–40, reprinted *Exegetica*, Tübingen 1967, 36–54; 'Römer 7 und die Anthropologie des Paulus', ibid., 198–209; ET in *Existence and Faith*, ed. S. Ogden, New York 1960, 147–57; 'Glossen im Römerbrief', ibid., 278–84; 'Adam und Christus nach Römer 5', ibid., 424–44.

W. S. **Campbell**, 'Why did Paul write Romans?', *ExpT* 85, 1973/4, 264–9; C. E. B. **Cranfield**, 'Paul's Purpose or Purposes in Writing Romans', *The Epistle to the Romans* II, ICC, 1979, 814–26; H. **Cremer**, *Die paulinische Rechtfertigungslehre im Zusammenhang ihrer geschichtlichen Voraussetzungen*, Leipzig 1909; N. A. **Dahl**, 'Two Notes on Romans 5', *StTh* 5, 1951, 37–48; 'The Particularity of the Pauline Epistles as a Problem in the Ancient Church', *Neotestamentica et Patristica, FS O. Cullmann*, ed. W. C. van Unnik, NovTSupp 6, 1962, 261–71; 'Missionary Theology in Romans', *Studies in Paul*, Minneapolis, 1977, 70–94;W. D. **Davies**, 'Paul and the People of Israel', *NTS* 24, 1977/78, 4–39; H. **Dietzfelbinger**, *Paulus und das Alte Testament*, Munich 1961; E. **Dinkler**, 'The Historical and Eschatological Israel in Romans 9–11', *JR* 36, 1956, 109–27; K. P. **Donfried**, ed., *The Romans Debate*, Minneapolis 1977; 'False Presuppositions in the Study of Romans', ibid., 120–48; W. **Doty**, *Letters in Primitive Christianity*, Philadelphia 1973; G. **Eichholz**, *Die Theologie des Paulus im Umriss*, Neukirchen-Vluyn 1972; E. E. **Ellis**, *Paul's Use of the Old Testament*, Edinburgh and Grand Rapids 1957; V. **Furnish**, *Theology and Ethics in Paul*, Nashville 1968; H. **Gamble**, *The Textual History of the Letter to the Romans*, Grand Rapids 1977; D. **Georgi**, *Die Geschichte der Kollekte des Paulus für Jerusalem*, ThF 38, Hamburg 1965; E. **Grafe**, *Über Veranlassung und Zweck des Römerbriefs*, Freiburg and Tübingen 1881; *Die Paulinische Lehre vom Gesetz nach den vier Hauptbriefen*, Freiburg ²1893; E. **Güttgemanns**, 'Heilsgeschichte bei Paulus oder Dynamik des Evangeliums? Zur strukturellen Relevanz von Röm 9–11 für die Theologie des Römerbriefes', *Studia linguistica neotestamentica*, Munich 1971, 34–58.

F. **Hahn**, 'Das Gesetzesverständnis im Römer- und Galaterbrief', *ZNW* 67, 1967, 29–63; D. **Hall**, 'St Paul and Famine Relief', *ExpT* 82, 1971, 394–41; G. **Harder**, 'Der konkrete Anlass des Römerbriefes', *ThViat* 6, 1959, 13–24; A. **von Harnack**, 'Das Alte Testament in den Paulinischen Briefen und in den Paulinischen Gemeinden', *SAB*, Berlin 1928, 124–41; F. J. A. **Hort**, *Prolegomena to St Paul's Epistles to the Romans and the Ephesians*, London and New York 1895, 1–61; H. **Hübner**, *Das Gesetz bei Paulus*, FRLANT 119, 1978; L. W. **Hurtado**, 'The Doxology at the End of Romans',

New Testament Textual Criticism. Essays in Honour of Bruce M. Metzger, ed. E. J. Epp and G. D. Fee, Oxford 1981, 185–99; J. **Jervell**, 'The Letter to Jerusalem', in Donfried, ed., *The Romans Debate*, 61–74; E. **Jüngel**, 'Das Gesetz zwischen Adam und Christus', *ZTK* 60, 1963, 42–74;*Paulus und Jesus*, HUT 2, ³1967.

E. **Käsemann**, 'The Righteousness of God in Paul', ET *New Testament Questions of Today*, London and Philadelphia 1969, 168–82; 'Worship in Everyday Life: a Note on Romans 12', ibid., 188–95;'Principles of the Interpretation of Romans 13', ibid., 196–216;'The Faith of Abraham in Romans 4', ET *Perspectives on Paul*, London and Philadelphia 1971, 79–101;'Zum Verständnis von Röm 3, 24–26', *Exegetische Versuche und Besinnungen*, Tübingen 1960, I, 96–100; E. **Kamlah**, *Traditionsgeschichtliche Untersuchungen zur Schlussdoxologie des Römerbriefes*, Diss. Tübingen 1955; R. J. **Karris**, 'Romans 14:1–15:13 and the Occasion of Romans', in Donfried, ed., *The Romans Debate*, 75–99; L. E. **Keck**, 'The Poor among the Saints in the New Testament', *ZNW* 56, 1965, 100–29; *Paul and His Letters* (Proclamation Commentaries), Philadelphia 1979; K. **Kertelge**, *'Rechtfertigung' bei Paulus*, Münster 1966; 'Paulinische Anthroplogie nach Römer 7', *ZNW* 62, 1971, 105–14; G. **Klein**, 'Röm 4 und die Idee der Heilsgeschichte', *EvTh* 23, 1963, 424–47; 'Romans, Letter to the', *IDB Suppl*, 752–54; 'Paul's Purpose in Writing the Epistle to the Romans', ET in Donfried, ed., *The Romans Debate*, 32–49; J. **Knox**, 'Romans 15:14–23 and Paul's Conception of his Apostolic Mission', *JBL* 83, 1964, 1–11; W. G. **Kümmel**, *Römer 7 und die Bekehrung des Paulus*, Leipzig 1929, reprinted Munich 1974; 'Die Probleme von Röm 9–11 in der gegenwärtigen Forschungslage', *Heilsgeschehen und Geschichte II*, Marburg 1978, 245–60; O. **Kuss**, *Paulus. Die Rolle des Apostels in der theologischen Entwicklung der Urkirche*, Regensburg 1971, 161–204.

F. **Lang**, 'Gesetz und Bund bei Paulus', *Rechtfertigung, FS E. Käsemann*, ed. J. Friedrich, Tübingen 1976, 305–20; J. B. **Lightfoot**, 'The Structure and Destination of the Epistle to the Romans', *Biblical Essays*, London and New York 1893, 287–374; W. **Lütgert**, *Der Römerbrief als historisches Problem*, Gütersloh 1913; U. **Luz**, *Das Geschichtsverständnis des Paulus*, Munich 1968; 'Zum Aufbau von Röm 1–8', *TZ* 25, 1969, 161–81; S. **Lyonnet**, 'Justification, jugement, redemption, principalement dans l'Epître aux Romains', *RB* 5, 1960, 168–84; 'L'histoire du salut selon les chapître vii de l'épître aux Romains', *Bibl* 43, 1962, 117–51; T. W. **Manson**, 'St Paul's Letter to the Romans – and Others', *Studies in the Gospels and Epistles*, Manchester and Philadelphia 1962, 225–41; reprinted in Donfried, ed., *The Romans Debate*, 1–16; O. **Merk**, *Handeln aus Glauben: die Motivierung der paulinischen Ethik*, MbThSt 5, 1968; O. **Michel**, *Paulus und seine Bibel*, BFChTh 2.18, 1929; P. S. **Minear**, *The Obedience of Faith. The Purposes of Paul in the Epistle to the Romans*, SBT II.19, 1971; C. D. **Morrison**, *The Powers that Be: Earthly Rulers and Demonic Powers in Romans 13.1-7*, SBT 29, 1959; C. **Müller**, *Gottes Gerechtigkeit und Gottes Volk. Eine Untersuchung zu Röm 9–11*, FRLANT 86, 1964; J. **Munck**, *Paul and the Salvation of Mankind* (1954), ET London and Richmond 1959;*Christ and Israel: an Interpretation of Romans 9–11*, ET Philadelphia 1967;

K. F. **Nickle**, *The Collection: A Study in Paul's Strategy*, SBT 48, 1966; A. **Oepke**, *Die Missionspredigt Paulus*, Leipzig 1920; P. **von der Osten-Sacken**, *Römer 8 als Beispiel paulinischer Soteriologie*, FRLANT 112, 1975; E. **Pagels**, *The Gnostic Paul*, Philadelphia 1975; H. **Paulsen**, *Überlieferung und Auslegung in Römer 8*, WMANT 43, 1974; K. H. **Rengstorf**, 'Paulus und die älteste Christenheit', *StEv* II, TU87, 1964, 447–64; H. N. **Ridderbos**, *Paul*, ET Grand Rapids 1975.

E. P. **Sanders**, *Paul and Palestinian Judaism*, London and Philadelphia 1977; J. A. **Sanders**, 'Torah and Christ', *Interp* 29, 1975, 372–90; H. M. **Schenke**, 'Aporien im Römerbrief', *TLZ* 92, 1967, 881–8; H. **Schlier**, 'Von den Heiden. Röm 1, 18–32', *Zeit der Kirche*, Freiburg ²1958, 29–37; 'Von der Juden. Röm 2, 1–29', ibid., 38–47; 'Die Taufe nach dem 6. Kapitel des Römerbriefs', ibid., 47–56; 'Das Mysterium Israels', ibid., 232–44; W. **Schmithals**, 'The False Teachers of Romans 16:17–20', ET *Paul and the Gnostics*, London and Nashville 1972, 219–38; *Der Römerbrief als historisches Problem*, StNT 9, 1975; R. **Schnackenburg**, 'Römer 7 im Zusammenhang des Römerbriefs', in *Jesus und Paulus, FS W. G. Kümmel*, ed. E. E. Ellis and E. Grässer, Göttingen 1975, 283–300; J. **Schniewind**, 'Das Seufzen des Geistes, Röm 8, 26–27', *Nachgelassene Reden und Aufsätze*, Berlin 1952, 81–103; R. **Scroggs**, *The Last Adam*, Philadelphia and Oxford 1966; Oxford 1967; K. **Stendahl**, *Paul among Jews and Gentiles*, Philadelphia 1976; 'The Apostle Paul and the Introspective Conscience of the West' (1963), ibid., 78–96; M. L. **Stirewalt**, Jr., 'The Form and Function of the Greek Letter-Essay', in Donfried, ed., *The Romans Debate*, 175–206; S. **Stowers**, *The Diatribe and Paul's Letter to the Romans*, SBLDS 57, Chico 1981; A. **Strobel**, 'Zum Verständnis von Röm 13', *ZNW* 47, 1956, 67–93; P. **Stuhlmacher**, *Gerechtigkeit Gottes bei Paulus*, FRLANT 87, ²1966; 'Das Ende des Gesetzes. Über Ursprung und Ansatz der paulinschen Theologie', *ZTK* 67, 1970, 14–39; M. J. **Suggs**, ' "The Word is Near You": Romans 10:6–10 within the Purpose of the Letter', *Christian History and Interpretation. Studies Presented to John Knox*, ed. W. R. Farmer, C. F. D. Moule and R. R. Niebuhr, Cambridge 1967, 289–312.

R. C. **Tannehill**, *Dying and Rising with Christ*, BZNW 32, 1967; H. E. **Weber**, *Das Problem der Heilsgeschichte nach Römer 9–11*, Leipzig 1911; W. **Wiefel**, 'The Jewish Community in Ancient Rome and the Origins of Roman Christianity', in Donfried, ed., *The Romans Debate*, 100–19; U. **Wilckens**, 'Die Rechtfertigung Abraham nach Röm 4', reprinted *in Rechtfertigung als Freiheit. Paulusstudien*, Neukirchen-Vluyn 1974, 33–49; 'Was heisst bei Paulus: "Aus Werken des Gesetzes wird kein Mensch gerecht?" ', ibid., 77–109; 'Über Abfassungszweck und Aufbau des Römerbriefs', ibid., 110–70; 'Römer 13, 1–7', ibid., 203–45; W. **Wuellner**, 'Paul's Rhetoric of Argumentation in Romans', *CBQ* 38, 1976, 330–51; reprinted in Donfried, ed., *The Romans Debate*, 152–74; D. **Zeller**, *Juden und Heiden in der Mission des Paulus. Studien zum Römerbrief*, FzB 1, 1973.

I. The Critical Debate

It has long been recognized that the interpretation of the letter to the Romans involves some of the most difficult problems within the New Testament. The extreme length of the letter, its frequently broken style, its range of topics, and, above all, its highly complex chain of argument have confronted generations of readers with the sheer enormity of the exegetical task. Textual problems have also added to the interpreter's difficulty.

Within the modern era the debate over understanding the book has repeatedly focused on the search for the original setting of the letter and on Paul's motivation for writing to Rome. There has developed a widespread consensus that the book represents a genuine, occasional letter, arising from a given historical moment, and that this time-conditioned origin prevents the letter from being properly understood as a timeless theological tractate. Two major alternative interpretations of the cause which motivated Paul's writing of Romans have emerged. One group of scholars have derived the letter from Paul's concern to address specific problems within the church at Rome. Another group sees the motivation for the letter to lie rather in Paul's own existential situation.

The first approach emerged with F. C. Baur's initial challenge to the traditional theological interpretation of Romans (1836). Baur argued that the heart of the entire letter was to be found in chs. 9–11 for which the previous section, 1–8, was only a preparation. Paul confronted the Jewish Christians of Rome who saw in the inclusion of Gentile Christians into the church a threat to the promise of God for his people. Baur's contribution was in describing a concrete historical setting, a hypothesis which offered a unified interpretation for the entire letter. Of course, the one-sidedness of Baur's thesis was not convincing for many and shortly others (Weizsäcker, *Apostolic Age*, Lütgert) returned to the older view that Paul's main addressees were Gentile Christians (cf. Holtzmann, *Lehrbuch*, ²1886, 256f. for the nineteenth-century debate). However, the effect of Baur's insistence on a historical setting has left a permanent mark on the way in which the question of motivation was now posed.

Within the modern debate a large group of scholars continues to represent Baur's initial insight in seeking a concrete historical cause within the church at Rome (cf. Donfried). One of the more attractive theories (Wiefel, Gamble) sees in the disturbance caused by Claudius' expelling the Jews from Rome the background for the tension within the Roman church. Then again, one of the bolder attempts at a detailed reconstruction has been offered by Minear who seeks to identify specific parties from chs. 14–15 to which Paul was writing.

In opposition to this approach of recovering the original setting of Romans, a second group of scholars have located the decisive motivation for Paul's writing of the letter from within the ministry of Paul himself. They argue that because the Roman church was unknown to Paul, the letter marks an exception within the Pauline corpus. T. W. Manson's influential essay did much to support this direction by arguing on the basis of the textual variants that the letter was originally a 'round letter', which was later sent to Ephesus with the specific greetings of ch. 16. The letter was, therefore, never addressed to the historical needs of one community.

Then again, a different attempt to locate the specific concerns of the book within Paul's ministry was presented by Jervell, who argued that the letter was actually concerned with Paul's impending trip to Jerusalem. Paul was seeking the support of the Roman church to present a unified position for the Gentile churches. The relation between Jewish and Gentile Christians lay at the heart of the book. A similar position has been defended by Stendahl with slight modifications. A variation of the theory was that Paul sought to introduce himself to the Roman community by means of the letter before asking for financial and spiritual help. Finally, one of the more impressive hypotheses within the second category is that of Bornkamm ('Paul's Last Will'). He argues that the book is a summary of Paul's teaching, indeed a last will and testament of the apostle, which he has abstracted from the concrete situations of past letters in the light of his imminent departure for Jerusalem. Finally, Wilckens lays more emphasis on the effect of Paul's own history since the Galatian controversy, but basically agrees with the major lines of Bornkamm's thesis.

One of the difficulties within this debate up to now has been the inability of either side to score a decisive victory. Some elements of truth appear to lie on both sides, but both work with numerous elements of unproven reconstructions. Some recent commentators have attempted a compromise and have spoken of a variety of different causes (Cranfield). However, in very recent times a new front has opened up which has sought to bridge the critical impasse by focusing its attention on the peculiar literary and rhetorical features of the letter. At first building on the literary analyses of Deissmann, Bultmann, Schubert, and Roller, the effort was made to bring new precision to the study of the epistolary form of Paul's letter on the assumption that the major time-conditioned force on the writer was in its giving shape to fixed literary genres. In spite of some advances, in the end, the approach produced diminishing returns. For this reason Wuellner among others has recently sounded a call to shift the focus from genre studies to recovering the rhetorical setting of Paul's letter. Wuellner has opened up a new vista by tracing the peculiar function of Pauline argumentation, in which he made use of the tools of modern rhetorical science. However, in the end Wuellner's approach seems to raise as many problems as it has resolved. One is amazed by the formalistic quality of the argument which has virtually removed the interpretation from its historical and theological content. According to Wuellner the rhetorical form of Romans can be classed as 'epideictic' which serves 'to strengthen the disposition toward action by increasing the adherence to values it lauds'. However, by arbitrarily defining the rhetorical genre within which Paul's argument allegedly functions, the modern interpreter has also largely determined its hermeneutical role.

II. The Hermeneutical Problem of Romans

The purpose of rehearsing the various critical attempts to determine more precisely the original setting of Paul's letter to the Romans is not to belittle the critical enterprise because of its inability to resolve the problem. Unquestionably many fresh and useful insights have emerged from the debate. Moreover, the criticism levelled against the traditional reading of the letter as a timeless compendium of dogmatic theology (Melanchthon) has been of lasting exegetical significance.

Nevertheless, I would argue that the basic hermeneutical issue of interpreting Romans, which is closely tied to its canonical function, has not been adequately faced. Of course, it might seem strange that during all this lengthy debate the issue of interpreting Romans as canonical literature has not been raised as a serious option. Yet the reason is clear. Another hermeneutical model has been simply assumed which provided the rationale for the critical approaches which have been undertaken. Donfried's formulation makes clear the working assumption: 'The reason is simple: The implication and challenge of the New Testament for the twentieth century can only be made clear when one knows the setting of each New Testament book in its original context. In other words, if one does not know the original intention of a document, one can hardly interpret its contemporary meaning with accuracy and precision.'

This proposal assumes that the interpreter first establishes the original setting, and then, if inclined, attempts to show its contemporary theological relevance. I would have thought that a proper theological understanding of the hermeneutical function of canon would have reversed the process. That is to say, one begins by attempting to discern the canonical shape of the present text, and in the process seeks to determine the role that both the original and the subsequent elements play in the final form of this religious text. My canonical proposal does not deny that one can read Romans from a variety of perspectives and for different purposes. It can be studied for its philological, historical, and literary contributions. The position which is being attacked is the widespread hermeneutical assumption, expressed clearly by Donfried, that a correct *theological* interpretation is dependent upon first reconstructing an original setting.

A variation of Donfried's assumption is offered by Stendahl, but with more theological sensitivity, when he raises the question: 'How can letters which Paul directed to specific churches in specific situations be the word of God for the church at large and in all times?' (*Paul among Jews*, 6). Stendahl then argues for a critical recovery of Paul's original intention and for keeping the Pauline letters separate without homogenization ' . . . for the purpose of making sure what questions the apostle intended to answer. Even the divinely right answer is not heard aright if it is applied to the wrong question' (ibid.).

I would agree that Stendahl has made a significant point. His own essay which traced the effect of reading Romans from the perspective of the 'introspective conscience of the West' is often convincing. Indeed, historical criticism has an important negative and positive role to play, both in demolishing false exegetical constructs and in sharpening the critical perception of a biblical text. It can thus aid in hearing Paul's right questions. However, a major point to make in response is that historical-critical exegesis has been and can be just as vulnerable as traditional exegesis in failing to discern the actual questions of the book. Stendahl's suggestion of hearing each letter for itself is surely not wrong up to a point, but it does not greatly aid in breaking out of the exegetical impasse. Above all, it does not address the basic hermeneutical issue of the function of the church's canonical literature in providing its own normative interpretive context which is not necessarily to be identified with the original author's intention.

III. The Shape and Reception of Romans

When we turn to analyse specifically the canonical shaping of Romans, two important factors need to be carefully studied. The first has to do with the effect of the collecting process on the letter itself. The second concerns the effect of the context on the reception of the book.

We turn first to the effect of the collecting process. Several modern studies have suggested that the present form of Romans has undergone a process of extended expansions (O'Neill), or minor glossing (Bultmann). Along the same line, Schmithals has proposed that two independent books were joined to constitute the final form of the book. As far as I can determine, none of these literary theories has received serious support from the field, and therefore can be passed over quickly.

The real problem of determining the nature of the book's growth and reinterpretation lies elsewhere. It can best be seen from the book's textual history. The major problem concerns the place of the doxology (16.25–27), and the final chapter of the epistle. The variant textual traditions confirm that the book was circulated in more than one recension. There is a similar tradition of textual variants in 1.7,15 in which the omission of the geographical designation of the letter ('in Rome') occurs. Without repeating the debate, which has been treated fully by Gamble, the major implications for interpreting Romans should be stated. N. A. Dahl, and his student H. Gamble, have made a convincing case that the chief canonical problem of the Pauline epistles lay in their high level of particularity which resisted wider application in the post-Pauline churches. During the early period of its transmission various attempts were made to generalize the message of Romans by omission of the specific references to people and places which were contained in the praescript and final chapter. The addition of the doxology would be another example of this generalizing effort on the part of the later editors. However, Dahl's main conclusion is that in the end the particularity of the letter to the Romans was retained with some minor expansions within the canonical corpus. The book was allowed to function in its canonical role with the final chapter of personal greetings. Therefore, at least for Romans there is no indication that the process of editing the letter for the canonical collection altered substantially the original form of the letter.

We turn next to the second factor of canonical significance, namely, the effect of the reception of the book. How was the book heard? Obviously much depends on the context in which the letter functioned and the interaction between text and interpreter. Meaning is not something chipped out of an inert text. An interpretation which regards the book as a timeless theological tractate fails to reckon either with the historical elements of particularity constituting Paul's mission theology which have been given a canonical role within Romans, or the eschatological context within God's economy to which the reader is pointed. Conversely an interpretation which seeks to reconstruct an original context usually assumes a hermeneutic of historical referentiality which establishes a different context from that of the canonical text itself. In contrast to these two common options, a canonical approach to Romans recognizes the peculiar blend of material from the concrete, historical context of Paul's ministry to a first-century, Jewish-Christian congregation at Rome with a theological message, grounded in christology, which provides its own special dynamic of eschatological and universal transcendence. In the following sections the concern will be to sketch some of the broad lines of such a canonical interpretation.

IV. The Beginning and Ending of the Letter

Paul begins the praescript of the letter (1.1–7) by defining himself and his ministry in terms of a christological statement: 'Apostle . . . set apart for the gospel of God . . . concerning his Son'. He has been commissioned to his office as an apostle by the risen Christ to bear testimony to the gospel. In Pauline usage 'gospel' and 'apostle' are correlative terms within his theology of mission. He does not proclaim himself nor reflect on his peculiar conversion experience, but identifies himself in terms of his call to the proclamation of the gospel in the world. The content of his preaching is 'the gospel of God . . . concerning his Son'. The gospel is about God's history and his activity in Jesus Christ. Indeed, the entire Old Testament bears witness to this gospel through its promises. Christ entered into human history in a line of human descendents, and through his resurrection disclosed God's redemptive purpose for the world. Paul does not transmit stories about the earthly Jesus of a past age, but bears witness to the eschatological meaning and explosive power of the resurrected one for past, present, and future time. The gospel intersects history, but it transcends its sequence in both time and space. It can never be solely about events of the past because it unleashes a divine power for present and future. Thus, the history of God's action in Christ is not addressed simply to individuals, or to the Christian church, but it lays claim on the entire cosmos, on the world and all it encompasses.

The gospel is proclaimed to bring about 'the obedience of faith . . . among all the nations . . . including yourselves'. Paul does not stand outside the history of salvation and reflect on a theological structure. As an apostle he testifies to his special role as an ambassador of the gospel between the resurrection and the parousia, and he argues theologically to make this missionary congregation understand its place within the divine plan (Dahl, 'Missionary Theology', 71). Paul does not address this congregation according to its own self-understanding, but completely from the perspective of the crucified one. He seeks to engender a faithful response commensurate with his subject, Jesus Christ, among all the nations, but including those at Rome.

The broader implications from the praescript for understanding Paul's entire letter are far reaching. Indeed, Paul shatters the traditional epistolary form in order to anticipate the themes of the whole book. The content of his letter is radically christological. It sets the context for his own role, the content of his message, and the purpose of his ministry to them. It is God's history which impinges on him, on them, and on the nations. Whatever Paul will have to say to this congregation, its particularity finds its significance in the light of what God has done and is doing in his Son.

Significantly Romans closes with a doxology which has been patterned after the praescript and which serves to encompass the entire book within the same consistently christological context. Again one hears of the 'gospel and the preaching of Jesus Christ', which 'was made known through the prophets', 'for all the nations', and 'for the obedience of faith'. The doxology, however, does go beyond the praescript in speaking of the 'revelation of the mystery which has been now revealed and through scripture is made known'. Our present concern is not to pursue the canonical function of the doxology in forming a link with the expanded witness of Colossians and Ephesians, but rather to limit our study to its canonical role within Romans.

The doxology functions, first of all, to render the final word of Paul to the Roman church. The doxology is not a liturgical response of the letter's recipients to Paul's words, but a liturgical response of Paul to the subject of his book. The doxology is primarily addressed, of course, to God, but the church is included as if a secondary addressee and incorporated within the hymn. Paul is not speaking to God about them, but rather, continuing to address the Romans as 'you', he commends them into God's keeping. The whole point of the gospel about which he has been speaking in his letter has been to realize in them an 'obedience of faith' commensurate with the preaching of Jesus Christ. Theology and mission are inextricably bound, as they are throughout the letter.

Then again, the consistently christological perspective emerges with force. Paul does not end with a final exhortation to obey, but rather points them to the source of the new life in a confession of praise. His final use of the doxology confirms the theological context from which he has been working all through his book (cf. 7.25; 11.36; 15.33). Paul cannot speak long about what God has done in Christ, without shifting his mode of discourse and addressing God directly in praise. God is not an object about which he calmly discourses, but the all-encompassing power of life to whom one must respond.

Finally, Paul concludes with a last summary of his message. The gospel of God which he has been preaching to them had long been hidden, but now in Jesus Christ has been revealed. When Paul speaks of the gospel, it is always from an eschatological perspective which subsumes the past, present, and future within the eternal will of God for the world.

To summarize, the praescript and concluding doxology serve to establish a christological context from which to interpret Paul's missionary activity to the Romans. The reader is made immediately aware that the logic of what follows unfolds from its christological subject matter. Any interpretation which abstracts the content from this kerygmatic centre into timeless truths misses the eschatological thrust of the message by which the Romans are confronted. Similarly, any interpretation which seeks to locate the key to Paul's letter within a nexus of literary, historical, and religious sequences fails to grasp either the content or the logic of the letter.

V. The Righteousness of God as Theme

There is a widespread agreement that the theme of Romans is sounded in 1.16: 'The gospel is the power of God for salvation to everyone who has faith, to the Jew first and also to the Greek.' Two sub-themes then follow in v. 17 and vv. 18ff. which are integrally related by a series of conjunctions. In the gospel the righteousness of God and the wrath of God are revealed. It is not our concern at this juncture to review the long and continuing debate over the significance of the theme of the righteousness of God for Romans, but rather to focus on its relation to the canonical shaping of the book. The crucial theological and hermeneutical issue turns on the context from which the term is understood.

In traditional Protestant commentaries, especially in orthodox Lutheran circles, justification by faith was treated as a separate theological doctrine which was central to the entire Christian faith. Modern critical scholarship, which has wrestled hard with this issue since the late nineteenth century, questioned the isolating of this one theme from the literary and historical context of the letter. W. Wrede (1904) characterized the doctrine as a 'polemical doctrine' (*Kampfeslehre*) of limited scope. Similarly, A. Schweitzer attacked the centrality of the theme for Paul and described it as subsidiary (*Nebenkrater*). A. Schlatter and E. P. Sanders have continued in this direction and emphasized Paul's 'participatory' theology as being most basic. Righteousness by faith is considered a restricted meta-phor of limited polemical significance within Paul's larger theological scheme. A somewhat different line of approach has been pursued by Stendahl. He argues against the centrality of the theme that the doctrine of justification by faith originated in Paul's mind from his grappling with the problem of defending the place of the Gentiles among the Jews (*Paul among Jews*, 26f.). It thus arose as a legitimation and apologetic for his Gentile mission.

Over against these various interpretations, Eichholz and Cranfield have argued—correctly in my judgment—that the confusion in understanding the theme of justification in Paul has arisen from the failure to establish its proper context. The doctrine of justification by faith is a derivative of Paul's christology. It was developed in an attempt to interpret the theological consequences of Christ's death and resurrection within his missionary theology. When justification is divorced from God's action in Jesus Christ, either by grounding it in the general human condition, or by interpreting it as a time-conditioned metaphor of limited function, its centrality within the letter to the Romans, and indeed within the entire theology of Paul, is seriously impaired.

The terminology of the righteousness of God stems originally from the Old Testament. H. Cremer made the decisive point in rediscovering that the Hebrew *şedaka* does not denote revenging or distributive justice, but God's saving righteousness which he establishes in relation to his people. The use of the term in this sense was widespread both in Qumran and in pre-Pauline tradition, and did not originally derive from a polemical context, as its role within a baptismal setting proves (cf. Dahl). However, Paul did greatly sharpen the term and developed it polemically in the debate with Judaism in order to exclude completely the works of the law from God's righteousness in Christ.

In the light of the lengthy modern debate regarding the syntax of the phrase 'righteousness of God' (Bultmann, Käsemann, Stuhlmacher, Conzelmann, Sanders, etc.), Eichholz has made a crucial theological point in insisting that the heart of Paul's doctrine cannot be reached simply through a study of the terminology. The crucial issue at stake is its function within the context of Paul's argument. As 3.21–26 makes fully clear, Paul does not work with a general concept of righteousness which he applies to Christ, but *vice versa*. In the light of what God has done in Jesus Christ, Paul seeks to interpret the consequences of this eschatological event in the terms of God's righteousness. Starting from the confrontation which occurred in the death and resurrection of Christ, Paul draws the consequence that God's righteousness has been revealed apart from the law, as a gracious gift, for all who believe without distinction.

God's righteousness includes both the righteousness by which God himself is righteous and the righteousness by which God makes the believer righteous (Dahl). Although Paul's theology of justification addressed first a Jewish audience who stood within the Old Testament tradition, the effect of the Christ event, which broke down the barrier between Jew and Gentile, resulted in extending the theology of justification beyond the Jew. 'Is God the God of Jews only? Is he not the God of Gentiles also?' (3.29). Not by chance Paul then addresses man in his universal dimension: 'We hold that a man is justified by faith apart from the works of the law' (3.28). In the chapters which follow in the letter to the Romans (chs. 4, 5, 9–11) Paul continues to draw the theological consequences of Christ's salvific intervention into human history in terms of a theology of justification.

The hermeneutical significance of Paul's understanding of justification for a canonical reading of the letter lies in recognizing the christological context of Paul's argument which both establishes the content of his message and the implications for its reception. Within his missionary theology to the Roman church, Paul's presentation of the gospel not only addresses that historic community with the significance for them of God's act, but confronts every subsequent generation of reader, both Jew and Gentile, with the consequences of what Christ accomplished.

The christological content of Paul's doctrine of justification prevents limiting its significance to the 'introspective conscience' of Western man, as well as to an historical problem within the early church respecting Jews and Gentiles. The righteousness of God must retain its full eschatological, cosmic dimension. Nevertheless, the consequences of Christ's redemption confront anew each generation of mankind in its concrete historicality, which means in a time-conditioned situation. That the doctrine of justification was heard in different ways by Christians throughout the history of the church belongs to its proper canonical function. The crucial point is that its actualization in the life of the church be grounded in a christology which means its faithful application in the light of God's action in Jesus Christ.

VI. The Role of the Old Testament

Up to this point we have played down an important feature of the canonical shape of Romans which already occurs in both the praescript (1.2) and concluding doxology (16.26). The issue at stake is the role of the Hebrew scriptures, that is, of the Old Testament, in Paul's letter. Even a quick perusal makes the frequency and extent of its use immediately clear, not just in terms of actual citations which also abound, but in a variety of allusions, paraphrases, and general references. Chapter 3 cites a catena of passages from the Psalms and Prophets to confirm Paul's charge that all men, both Jew and Greek, are under the power of sin. Chapter 4 offers an interpretation of Abraham's faith (Gen. 15.6) which verse is combined with Ps.32.1f. to make the case that Abraham was justified through faith apart from circumcision to become the father of the nations. Chapter 5 sets Adam's representative role as a vehicle of sin and death in contrast to Christ's universal role as medium of life. Then again, the role of the Mosaic law which had been introduced in ch.2, is picked up in ch.5 and continued through ch.8. In chs. 9–11 the relation between Israel and the church is treated with one of the most extensive uses of the Old Testament within the entire Pauline corpus. Finally, even in the so-called paraenetic or ethical sections of the letter (chs.12ff.), Paul works out the moral implications of the Christian faith by an appeal to the Old Testament (12.19f.; 13.8ff.; 14.10ff.; 15.7ff.).

Our concern with this issue is not to pursue the complex issues related to text criticism and exegetical techniques involved in the New Testament's use of the Old, but rather to address the hermeneutical significance in terms of its canonical function within the letter to the Romans.

Two representative positions come to mind which set the scope of the modern debate. On the one hand, a *heilsgeschichtliche* approach is represented by scholars such as Cullmann and Munck, among others, who stress the continuity between the Old Testament history and its New Testament analogy. Using the traditional rubric of 'prophecy and fulfilment', they argue that Paul sees Christ as the 'goal' (*telos*, Rom.10.4) of Old Testament promise and brings to completion what had begun in the old covenant. This view is to be commended in respect to the seriousness with which it takes the Old Testament and in its search for the unity of the two Testaments.

However, several objections can also be directed against this position. First, it can be questioned whether the category 'prophecy and fulfilment' is really a Pauline formulation (cf. Dahl, *Studies in Paul*, 121ff.). More significant is the criticism that the radical discontinuity effected by Christ's death and resurrection has not been adequately interpreted. Is not Christ rather the 'end' of the law (10.4)?

On the other hand, scholars such as Harnack, Grafe, Dietzfelbinger and Klein argue that the issue of the Old Testament is in no way essential to the gospel. At best it provides metaphors which can be replaced in other contexts with more suitable language. The objection to this approach turns on whether Paul's use of the Old Testament has been reduced to such an extent as to lose its substantial theological function by identifying it merely as a literary device.

In reacting to these two exegetical options, I would argue that both have failed to deal adequately with Paul's christological starting point. For Paul Christ is not simply a continuation of Israel's history. The eschatological character of the gospel marks the radical end of the old, and a completely new entrance of divine power, different in kind from the old. However, when Paul begins to reflect on God's cosmic act in Jesus Christ, he is able to discern that the reality of the gospel has already been testified to in the old covenant. Dahl makes the significant distinction between prophecy and promise (*Studies in Paul*, 120ff.). With the former term the emphasis falls on establishing the truth of the fulfilment by means of a theory of correspondence, whereas in the latter term the stress falls on a word of God being a self-involving commitment, which calls for an exercise of power in confirming the divine will. It is this second use which lies at the heart of Paul's understanding of the Old Testament.

Within this christological perspective Paul uses a variety of different ways of employing the Old Testament. He can argue analogically in terms of a universal pattern relating Christ and Adam. Then again, Abraham can be pictured as the model for all believers who exercised a faith in God which continues to define the nature of Christian belief. Again, the entire Old Testament can be seen as prophetic oracles of God announcing beforehand the coming application of God's power for salvation (1.2; Gal. 3.8), or making known the mystery of Israel's rejection and restoration. Paul's christological perspective comes to the Old Testament to provide a commentary on what God has done in Jesus Christ. Yet it is a serious oversimplification to imply that he is merely imposing christological categories on his material with a heavy hand. Rather, once Christ has provided the key to his understanding of the Hebrew scriptures as promise, the inner dynamic of the Old Testament itself assumes the lead in his thought. Faith interprets faith, and the Old Testament fills in the content and reveals the full dimension of the gospel (16.26).

In sum, the canonical significance of Paul's massive use of the Old Testament lies in once again establishing the proper context from which Christ's redemption is to be understood. The nature of God's decisive intervention in human history is understood from the Old Testament as an eschatological reality which was announced in the old covenant as promise and confirmed both to Israel and the nations. The gospel ratified God's commitment which was guaranteed to Abraham's descendants (4.16). Yet the Old Testament witness continues to function for each new generation. The scriptures were written for 'our' sakes (4.24; 15.4). They function within Paul's theology of mission to the Romans to make known to them the will of God in order to bring about 'the obedience of faith'. The use of the Old Testament is, therefore, not merely a strategic concession to a Jewish milieu, but the unique vehicle by which the reality of Christ's deed is understood and actualized in every successive age (cf. Wilckens, *Romans* I, 64).

VII. The Problem of the Addressee

One of the recurring features of the canonical shape of Romans has been the role of the material by virtue of its special content and its unique function to influence the manner in which the letter was received by its reader. It is now necessary to pursue this topic in more detail.

It lies in the peculiar nature of Paul's presentation of the gospel that, although his letter is addressed to a historically circumscribed, concrete church at Rome, in the course of his discourse this original addressee is altered in a variety of different ways. In the first place, the literary character of the letter with its loose connection to the form of a diatribe, often appears to confront actual debating partners. Yet when Paul turns to lay his charge against his Jewish protagonist, the addressee suddenly assumes a representative form. 'Therefore you have no excuse, O man, whoever you are . . .'. Eichholz speaks of Paul's opening up a horizon of his theology of justification which suddenly extends to all of humanity (*Die Theologie des Paulus*, 225). Perhaps the clearest use of representative language appears in Paul's use of the Adam figure (ch.5). 'For as by one man's disobedience many were made sinners, so by one man's obedience many will be made righteous' (5.19). The effect of moving from the one to the many is to involve the reader who is suddenly drawn into a direct confrontation.

A somewhat akin, but more complex profiling of a representative addressee occurs in Rom. 7.7ff. The problem has long been debated as to whether the first-person subject—some claimed it to be directly autobiographical—should be set in a chronological sequence before or after the Christian conversion. Both attempts ran into insurmountable contradictions. It was to Kümmel's great credit (*Römer 7*) to have recognized the true nature of the addressee in this chapter. Paul was not writing an autobiography, but from the theological stance gained from the gospel, he was describing man under the law whose true condition was hidden from him and only disclosed in Christ. By profiling his description in a first-person idiom Paul sought to actualize in each hearer the existential nature of human life apart from Christ. However beyond the classic example of Romans 7, it belongs to a characteristic feature of Paul's letter that he continues to move from third-person language to the self-involving language of 'I', 'we', and 'you'. Already at the end of ch.4, which closely joins ch.5, Paul moves from the third person to the inclusive 'we'. Or again, in ch.6 Paul refutes the charge that he is advocating a licentious life by appealing to the common experience of all Christians: 'Do you not know that all of us who have been baptized into Christ Jesus were baptized into his death?'

The main thrust of Paul's argument in chs. 9–11 is that God has faithfully maintained his word of promise to Israel. 'But it is not as though the word of God had failed' (9.6). Yet in the course of defending his position exegetically Paul demonstrates that the issue is not addressed to some theoretical Jewish audience. Rather, he makes it immediately clear that the issue involves God's universal salvation and that the existence of the church is dependent upon Israel's future. 'If you boast, remember it is not you that support the root, but the root that supports you' (11.18). The young church in Rome which is being addressed wants nothing more to do with Israel. 'So do not be proud, but stand in awe. For if God did not spare the natural branches, neither will he spare you' (11.20f.). Paul's argument transcends completely the issue of regional prejudice, and grounds the church's salvation in the selfsame mercy of God which has been promised Israel. Just as Paul's concern for the Jerusalem collection began at the local, concrete level, but gave witness to the fundamental unity of the church, so the argument in chs. 9–11 touches on such basic theological realities as to confront existentially each new generation of believers.

Finally, a word is in order regarding the nature of the addressee in chs. 14–15, the so-called 'strong' and 'weak'. These chapters provide the major warrant for all the various attempts which have been made to identify concrete parties within the Roman church to whom Paul has focused his letter (cf. Minear). Against the search for a concrete addressee Bornkamm ('The Last Will', 22) has argued that a comparison with the parallel in I Cor. 8–11 confirms how much a concrete background is really lacking in the letter to the Romans. Of course, Bornkamm is concerned to show that Paul, also in these chapters, is summarizing previous debates and therefore purposely is increasing the level of abstraction and distance from the original situation. In my judgment, Bornkamm's argument for an intentional abstracting in these chapters is suggestive, but falls short of being conclusively demonstrated.

I would prefer to argue that regardless of the concrete character of Paul's original addressee, in their present literary form, the chapters serve to denote a genuine ambiguity. The occasional addressee recedes within the larger context and a universal referent emerges which far transcends local Roman party rivalries in order to speak a word for all. It is not by chance that the point of the chapters focuses on a universal appeal for radical Christian living which relativizes all such petty human factions. 'If we live, we live to the Lord, and if we die we die to the Lord; so then, whether we live or die, we are the Lord's. For to this end Christ died and lived again . . .' (14.8f.).

To summarize, the canonical shaping of the letter to the Romans does not lie in a heavy reworking by later redactional expansions. The present form of the book is virtually the same as when it came from the hand of Paul. Rather, the canonical shape of Romans lies in the book's potential to transcend the original concrete historical setting. When treasured and read as scripture by a community of faith the nature of Paul's witness to God's eschatological intervention in Jesus Christ for the redemption of the world establishes a new context and unleashes a continuing power by which to address each new generation of Christians with the implications of the gospel.

13

I CORINTHIANS

Commentaries

J. C. K. von Hofmann, ²1874
H. A. W. Meyer, MeyerK, ET 1881
A. P. Stanley, ⁵1882
F. Godet, ET 1886–7
T. C. Edwards, 1897
C. F. G. Heinrici, MeyerK, ⁸1896
J. Weiss, MeyerK, ⁹1910
A. Robertson, A. Plummer, ICC,
  ²1914
R. St John Parry, CB, 1916
W. Bousset, SNT, ³1917
A. Schlatter, 1934
P. Bachmann, KNT, ⁴1936
J. Moffatt, MNTC, 1936
O. Kuss, RNT, 1940

F. W. Grosheide, NICNT, 1953
E.-B. Allo, ÉB, ²1956
J. Héring, CNT, ²1959, ET 1962
M. E. Thrall, CNEB, 1965
C. K. Barrett, B/HNTC, 1968
H. D. Wendland, NTD, ¹²1968
H. Lietzmann, W. G. Kümmel,
  HNT, ⁵1969
F. F. Bruce, NCeB, 1971
H. Conzelmann, Herm, ET 1975
W. F. Orr, J. R. Walther, AB, 1976
R. S. Reif, Pel,1977
E. Fascher, C. Wolff, THKNT,
  ²1980–82

Bibliography

S. **Arai**, 'Die Gegner des Paulus im 1. Korintherbrief und das Problem der Gnosis', *NTS* 19, 1972/3, 430–37; E. **Bammel**, 'Herkunft und Funktion der Traditionselemente in 1 Kor. 15,1–11', *TZ* 11, 1955,401–19; C. K. **Barrett**, *From First Adam to Last*, London and New York 1962; 'Cephas and Corinth', *Abraham unser Vater, FS O. Michel*, ed. O. Betz, M. Hengel and P. Schmidt, Leiden 1963, 1–12; 'Christianity at Corinth', *BJRL* 46, 1963/4, 269–97; S. S. **Bartchy**, μᾶλλον χρῆσαι. *First Century Slavery and the Interpretation of 1 Cor 7,21*, SBLDS 11, Missoula 1973; K. **Barth**, *The Resurrection of the Dead*, ET London and New York 1933; R. **Baumann**, *Mitte und Norm des Christlichen. Eine Auslegung von 1 Kor 1, 1–3, 4*, NTAbh, NF 5, 1968; F. C. **Baur**, 'Die Christuspartei in der korinthischen Gemeinde, der Gegensatz des petrinischen und paulinischen Christentums in der alten Kirche, der Apostel Petrus in Rom', *Tübinger Zeitschrift für Theologie*, 1831, Heft 4,

61–206; reprinted *Ausgewählte Werke*, ed. K. Scholder, I, Stuttgart 1963, 1–146; W. **Bieder**, 'Paulus und seine Gegner in Korinth', *TZ* 17, 1961, 319–33; G. **Bornkamm**, 'Der köstlichere Weg (1.Kor 13)', *Das Ende des Gesetzes*, *GA* I, Munich 1958, 93–112; 'Herrenmahl und Kirche bei Paulus', *ZTK* 53, 1956, 312ff.; reprinted *Studien zu Antike und Urchristentum*, *GA* II, Munich ²1963, 138–76; 'The Missionary Stance of Paul in I Corinthians 9 and in Acts', ET *Studies in Luke-Acts*, ed. L. E. Keck and J. L. Martyn, Nashville 1966, 194–207; H. **Braun**, 'Exegetische Randglossen zum 1. Korintherbrief', *Gesammelte Studien zum Neuen Testament und sein Umwelt*, Tübingen ² 1967, 178–204; R. **Bultmann**, 'Karl Barth, "Die Auferstehung des Toten" ', *ThBl* 5, 1926, 1–14; ET, *Faith and Understanding* I, London and New York 1969, 66–94.

H. **von Campenhausen**, 'The Christian and Social Life according to the New Testament', ET *Tradition and Life in the Church*, London and Philadelphia 1968, 141–59; H. C. C. **Cavallin**, *Life after Death: Paul's Argument for the Resurrection of the Dead, 1 Corinthians 15*, Gleerup 1974; H. **Chadwick**, ' "All Things to All Men" (I Cor.ix.22)', *NTS* 1, 1954/5, 261–75; H. **Conzelmann**, 'Zur Analyse der Bekenntnisformel I Kor. 15, 3–5', *EvTh* 25, 1965, 1–11; N. A. **Dahl**, 'Paul and the Church at Corinth according to I Cor. 1:10–4:21', *Christian History and Interpretation, FS John Knox*, ed. W. R. Farmer et al., Cambridge 1967, 313ff.; reprinted *Studies in Paul*, Minneapolis 1977, 40–61; G. **Delling**, *Paulus' Stellung zu Frau und Ehe*, Stuttgart 1931; E. **Dinkler**, 'Zum Problem der Ethik bei Paulus', *ZTK* 49, 1952, 167–200; reprinted *Signum Crucis*, Tübingen 1967, 204–40; 'Korintherbriefe', *RGG*³ IV, 1960, 17–23; D. J. **Doughty**, 'The Presence and Future of Salvation in Corinth', *ZNW* 66, 1975, 61–90; G. **Eichholz**, *Was heisst charismatische Gemeinde? 1. Korinther 12*, Munich 1960; *Die Theologie des Paulus im Umriss*, Neukirchen-Vluyn ²1977; E. E. **Ellis**, 'Paul and His Opponents', *Prophecy and Hermeneutic in Early Christianity*, Grand Rapids 1978, 80–115; G. G. **Findlay**, 'The Letter of the Corinthian Church to St Paul', *Exp* VI.1, 1900, 401–7; B. **Fjärstedt**, *Synoptic Tradition in I Corinthians*, Uppsala 1974; R. W. **Funk**, 'Word and Word in I Corinthians 2:6–16', *Language, Hermeneutic, and the Word of God*, New York 1966, London 1967, 275–305.

A. S. **Geyser**, 'Paul, the Apostolic Decree and the Liberals in Corinth', in *Studia Paulina in Honorem Johannis de Zwaan Septuagenarii*, ed. J. N. Sevenster and W. C. van Unnik, Haarlem 1953, 124–38; R. M. **Grant**, 'Hellenistic Elements in I Corinthians', in *Early Christian Origins: Studies in Honor of H. R. Willoughby*, ed. A. Wikgren, Chicago 1961, 60–66; M.-L. **Gubler**, *Die frühesten Deutungen des Todes Jesu*, Fribourg and Göttingen 1977; J. **Hainz**, *Ekklesia. Strukturen paulinischer Gemeinde-Theologie und Gemeinde-Ordnung*, Regensburg 1972; M. D. **Hooker**, 'Beyond the Things which are Written', *NTS* 10, 1963/4, 127–32; R. A. **Horsley**, ' "How can some of you say, that there is no resurrection of the dead?" Spiritual Elitism in Corinth', *NovT* 20, 1978, 203–31; J. C. **Hurd**, jr., *The Origin of I Corinthians*, New York and London 1965; new ed. Macon, Ga. 1983; E. **Kähler**, *Die Frau in den* *paulinischen Briefen*, Zürich and Frankfurt 1960; E. **Käsemann**, 'Ministry and Community in the New Testament', ET *Essays on New Testament Themes*, SBT 41, 1964, 63–94; 'A Pauline Version of the "Amor Fati" ', ET *New Testament Questions of Today*, London and Philadelphia 1969, 217–35; J. J. **Kijne**, 'We, Us and Our in I and II Corinthians', *NovT* 8, 1966, 171–9; John **Knox**, *Chapters in a Life of Paul*, New York and London 1950; W. G. **Kümmel**, 'Verlobung und Heirat bei Paulus (I Cor 7,36–38)', in *Neutestamentliche Studien für R. Bultmann*, ed. W. Eltester, BZNW 21, 1954, 275–295; K. **Lake**, *The Earlier Epistles of St Paul: Their Motive and Origin*, London ²1914; J. B. **Lightfoot**, 'St Paul and the Three', *St Paul's Epistle to the Galatians*, London ¹⁰1890, 292–374; 'The Mission of Titus to the Corinthians', *Biblical Essays*, London and New York 1893, 271–84; W. **Lütgert**, *Freiheitspredigt und Schwarmgeister in Korinth*, BFChTh 12,3, 1908.

A. **Malherbe**, 'The Beasts at Ephesus', *JBL* 87, 1968, 71–80; K. **Maly**, *Mündige Gemeinde. Untersuchungen zur pastoralen Führung des Apostels im I. Korintherbrief*, SBM 2, 1967; T. W. **Manson**, 'St Paul in Ephesus: (3) The Corinthian Correspondence', *BJRL* 26, 1941/2, 101ff,; reprinted in *Studies in the Gospels and Epistles*, Manchester and Philadelphia 1962, 190–243; C. **Maurer**, 'Grund und Grenze apostolischer Freiheit', *Antwort, FS Karl Barth*, Zollikon-Zürich 1956, 630–41; W. **Meeks**, *The First Urban Christians*, New Haven 1983, 111–39, 157ff.; P. S. **Minear**, 'Christ and the Congregation: I Corinthians 5–6', *RevExp* 80, 1983, 341–50; J. **Munck**, 'The Church without Factions', *Paul and the Salvation of Mankind*, ET London and Richmond 1959, 135–67; J. **Murphy-O'Connor**, 'Freedom or the Ghetto (I Cor VIII, 1–13; X,23-XI,1)', *RB* 85, 1978, 543–74; P. **von der Osten-Sacken**, 'Die Apologie des paulinschen Apostolats in I. Kor. 15, 1–11', *ZNW* 64, 1973, 245–62; E. **Pagels**, ' "The Mystery of the Resurrection": A Gnostic Reading of 1 Corinthians 15', *JBL* 93, 1974, 276–88; B. A. **Pearson**, *The Pneumatikos-Psychikos Terminology*, SBLDS 12, Missoula 1973; G. **von Rad**, 'The Early History of the Form-Category of I Corinthians XIII.4–7', ET *The Problem of the Hexateuch and Other Essays*, Edinburgh and New York 1966, 301–17; M. **Rissi**, *Die Taufe für die Toten*, Zürich 1962.

W. **Schenk**, 'Der I. Korintherbrief als Briefsammlung', *ZNW* 60, 1969, 219–43; A. **Schlatter**, *Die korinthische Theologie*, Gütersloh 1914; H. **Schlier**, 'Über das Hauptanliegen des 1. Briefes an die Korinther', *Die Zeit der Kirche*, Freiburg 1956, 147–59; W. **Schmithals**, 'Die Korintherbrief als Briefsammlung', *ZNW* 64, 1973, 263–88; ET 'On the Composition and Earliest Collection of the Major Epistles of Paul', *Paul and the Gnostics*, London and Nashville 1972, 239–74; J. **Schniewind**, 'Die Leugner der Auferstehung in Korinth', *Nachgelassene Reden und Aufsätze*, Berlin 1952, 110–39; W. **Schrage**, 'Die Frontstellung der paulinschen Ehewertung in 1. Cor 7.1–7', *ZNW* 67, 214–34; A. **Schreiber**, *Die Gemeinde in Korinth*, NTAbh NF 12, 1977; H. **Schürmann**, 'Haben die paulinschen Wertungen und Weisungen Modellcharakter?', *Greg* 56, 1975, 237–71; J. H. **Schütz**, *Paul and the Anatomy of Apostolic Authority*, SNTSM 26, 1975, 187–213; E.

Schweizer, 'The Service of Worship. An Exposition of I Corinthians 14', *Neotestamentica*, Zürich and Stuttgart 1963, 333–43; 'I Korinther 15, 20–28 als Zeugnis paulinischer Eschatologie', *Jesus und Paulus, FS W. G. Kümmel*, ed. E. E. Ellis and E. Grässer, Göttingen 1975, 301–14; R. J. **Sider**, 'The Pauline Conception of the Resurrection of the Body of Corinthians', *NTS* 21, 1974/5, 428–39; H. **von Soden**, 'Sakrament und Ethik bei Paulus. Zur Frage der literarischen und theologischen Einheitlichkeit von I. Kor. 8–10' (1931) = *Urchristentum und Geschichte*, Tübingen 1951, 239–75; selections in ET, 'Sacrament and Ethics in Paul', *The Writings of St Paul*, ed. W. A. Meeks, New York, 1972, 257–68; D. M. **Stanley**, ' "Become Imitators of Me" ', Apostolic Tradition in Paul', *Bibl* 40, 1958, 859–77.

G. **Theissen**, *Sociology of Early Palestinian Christianity*, ET London and Philadelphia 1978; *The Social Setting of Pauline Christianity: Essays on Corinth*, ET London and Philadelphia 1982; A. C. **Thiselton**, 'Realized Eschatology at Corinth', *NTS* 24, 1977/8, 510–26; P. **Vielhauer**, 'Paulus und die Kephaspartei in Korinth', *NTS* 21, 1974/5, 341–52; L. **Vischer**, *Die Auslegungsgeschichte von I. Kor. 6,1–11: Rechtsverzicht und Schlichtung*, BGBE 1, 1955; U. **Wickert**, 'Einheit und Eintracht der Kirche im Präskript des ersten Korintherbriefes', *ZNW* 50, 1959, 73–82; U. **Wilckens**, *Weisheit und Torheit. Eine exegetisch-religionsgeschichtliche Untersuchung zu I. Kor. 1 und 2*, BHT 26, 1959; J. H. **Wilson**, 'The Corinthians Who Say There is No Resurrection of the Dead', *ZNW* 59, 1968, 90–107; W. **Wuellner**, 'Haggadic Homily Genre in I Corinthians 1–3', *JBL* 89, 1970, 199–204; J. **Zmijewski**, *Der Stil der paulinischen 'Narrenrede': Analyse der Sprachgestaltung in I Kor. 11,1–12,10 als Beitrag zur Methodik von Stiluntersuchungen neutestamentliche Texte*, BBB 52, 1978.

The nature of the first letter to the Corinthians is such that the crucial canonical questions are often raised even by non-professional readers. How can a book be considered normative for the Christian faith which seems to be so disjointed and haphazard in structure? How can one understand when only one voice in a dialogue is recorded? How authoritative is advice which appears to be utterly time-conditioned in perspective, even to suggesting that women be silent in church and wear veils?

By and large, the response of the historical-critical method has been to shift the focus of attention away from first addressing these larger theological problems. Critics prefer to work with a different scale of priorities, arguing that the major task of exegesis is first to understand Paul's letter in its original context, and only after this has been accomplished can one begin to address the theological issues of the letter's continuing normative role. Moreover, it is often thought that once the historical and literary problems have been addressed, then a variety of different theological options usually become available for resolving the questions of authority. The difficulty is that these two sets of legitimate issues do not always engage each other. Our approach will be to review briefly the critical discussion of I Corinthians before turning to a theological response to the canonical issues.

I. Critical Issues of I Corinthians

A. Literary Problems

Few would deny that the literary problems of the letter are considerable. Paul is concerned to address a wide range of issues, some of which have arisen from oral communications (1.11; 5.1), and some from a letter seeking the apostle's advice. The use of the formula περὶ δὲ ('concerning the . . .', 7.1,25; 8.1; 12.1; 16.1) seems to reflect his explicit response to the letter. These differing sources, which provide the motivation for Paul's writing, account in part for the lack of a close thematic unity. Following the praescript he begins by addressing the problem of the church's divisions (1.10–4.21). Next he turns to rebuke certain scandals about which he has heard (5.1–6.20). Then he addresses questions from the letter regarding sexual conduct, meat offered to idols, spiritual gifts, and worship (7.1ff.). In ch. 15 he discusses the nature of the resurrection which concern appears to be motivated from an oral report rather than from the letter. Finally, ch. 16 closes with a response to questions regarding the collection.

However, the real literary problems do not lie simply in the wide range of topics handled, but in the manner of their presentation. Scholars have long noted features of literary inconsistency. 6.1–11 appears to break the train of thought which moves from ch. 5 to 6.12ff. Chapter 9 departs from the main lines developed in 8–10. Chapter 13 interrupts the sequence of 12–14.

However, an even more serious charge of inconsistency of thought has been raised. It has been argued that two very different perspectives are reflected in chs. 8–10, which have conflated Paul's discussion of εἰδωλόθυτος ('sacrificed to idols', 8.1,4,7,10; 10.19), and εἰδωλολατρία ('idolatry', 10.7,14). According to J. Weiss (ad loc.), 10.1–22 represents a strict opinion forbidding outright any contact with meat which has been sacrificed, whereas 8; 10.23–11.1 reflects a much more lenient position which was defended by a liberal faction within the Corinthian church.

On the basis of these literary problems, coupled with the evidence that Paul had written a prior letter (I Cor.5.9), a variety of different theories have been formulated which contest the literary integrity of I Corinthians. It has often beèn held that I Corinthians comprises at least two letters, one of which is the reconstructed prior letter. The difference in perspective within the present composite letter has arisen either from this literary conflation (Weiss, Schmithals, Schenk), or from a development in Paul's attitude (Hurd). The original and most influential source theory remains that of J. Weiss, whose division lies at the centre of the several more recent modifications by Dinkler, Schmithals and Schenk. (Cf. Schenke and Fischer, *Einl.*, I, 99, and Hurd, *Origin*, 1965, 45, for convenient graphs of recent attempts at source division.)

Conversely, a very strong case for the literary integrity of I Corinthians has been made by another group of critical scholars. Perhaps their most incisive argument derives from a monograph of H. von Soden (1931) who defended the unity of chs. 8–10 by pursuing carefully the theological coherence of the chapters. Many scholars, such as Kümmel and Conzelmann, felt that von Soden had successfully removed the major obstacles to maintaining the book's unity. Similarly, Hurd (131ff.) suggested that the parallel to I Corinthians 8–10 in Romans 14–15 carried much weight in favour of the literary integrity of the central section of the letter. Finally, Dahl's discussion of chs. 1–4 has been useful in drawing these chapters more closely to the themes elsewhere found in I and II Corinthians.

To summarize, although a good number of literary problems remain, and the disjointed character of the letter is still acutely felt, the evidence for the radical solution offered by positing several conflated letters has not been convincing to a majority of critical scholars. The manner in which this position relates to the canonical function of the book will be discussed below.

B. Paul's Opponents

Hurd poses immediately a basic problem of I Corinthians when he writes: 'I Corinthians is to be understood as but one part of a conversation which took place between Paul and the church in Corinth' (xv). Because it has become a truism for New Testament scholarship that Paul's letters are to be interpreted against the background of their specific occasion, the quest for the other participants in the conversation has dominated the history of historical critical research.

It is unnecessary to repeat the debate in great detail because this research has been rehearsed many times (cf. Ellis; Conzelmann, 309f.; Schmithals, *Gnosticism*, 117ff.; Dahl, *Studies*, 40ff.). F. C. Baur's great contribution in his epoch-making essay of 1831 was in making the dissensions of I Cor.1.12 the point of entrance from which the whole history of early Christianity could be unlocked. He collapsed the four slogans into two opposing parties, the Pauline-Apollonine and the Petrine-Christine, and characterized Paul's opponents as Judaizers who claimed allegience to Paul as the means to direct contact with Christ. Baur also set the major lines for subsequent debate in focusing his attention upon critically reconstructing the concrete profile of the 'other voice' in Paul's debate as a desideratum for the letter's interpretation.

In the discussion which ensued Baur's scheme came under severe attack, but his questions continued to dominate scholarly interest. In England, although vigorously opposing Baur's historical construal of early Christianity, J. B. Lightfoot also identified Paul's opponents with Judaizers, but then went on to distinguish between Pharisaic and Gnostic types (*Galatians*, 372f.). A decisive break with Baur's theory of Judaizers came in Germany with Lütgert who characterized the 'Christ party' as spiritualistic enthusiasts who were an early type of libertinistic Gnostics. Many variations of his theory that the major opponents were Gnostics have been defended in recent times by Schmithals, Wilckens, Marxsen and others, and it would appear that at least a negative consensus has emerged in denying the presence of Judaizers at Corinth which Baur had proposed.

Three other significant opinions need to be discussed in this brief survey. J. Munck represents the far extreme from Baur. He even disputes the theory that parties were involved and argues that the dissension arose when Corinthians under Greek influence misunderstood Christianity as a form of wisdom, and envisioned their leaders as teachers of wisdom. Dahl's position offers significant modifications of Munck's, but he is agreed in seeing the various slogans, not as separate parties, but as declarations of independence from Paul.

Finally, Hurd, in spite of his singular theories of Pauline development, is characteristic of other scholars (Bultmann, Marxsen, *Intr.*)
in suggesting that Paul misunderstood the nature of his opposition
and that the modern interpreter must use critical means of recovering
a true historical profile.

My motivation in rehearsing this history of scholarship is not to
erect a straw man, nor to disparage the debate because of its tentative
nature. Rather, the critical discussion provides the necessary background for a canonical approach which, working with different
hermeneutical assumptions, attempts to set some exegetical controls
to the enterprise of historically reconstructing Paul's opponents.

C. The Time-conditionality of Paul's Responses

For well over a hundred and fifty years strenuous efforts have been
made to cast light on the background and social context of first-
century Christianity in order to understand the Pauline response to
the Corinthian church. It has long been thought that the imperatives
and advice which constitute Paul's ethics reflect a combination of
Jewish and Greek features. The great contribution of historical
research has been to discover the extent of Paul's continuity with
his cultural environment which has done much to undercut the
assumption that the apostle was only concerned with timeless
Christian doctrine. On the one hand, Paul's opposition to divorce
(7.10ff.), association with prostitutes (6.12ff.), and opinion on veils
(11.2ff.) was thought to be fully in line with strict Jewish tradition.
On the other hand, his advice regarding celibacy (7.1ff.) and
glossolalia (14.1ff.) appeared to have its roots in Greek circles
which were affected by Gnostic or proto-Gnostic traits. Increasingly,
however, the difficulty of separating divergent features into discrete
Jewish and Greek components has become painfully apparent.

Schmithals' learned and repeated attempts to correlate elements
found in Corinth with his reconstructed Gnostic system demonstrates
the possibilities inherent in such a construal even when the hypothetical nature of much of the reconstruction is admitted. At the
very least a new sensitivity to Gnostic-oriented language has been
developed among modern scholars.

Finally, the complexity of the problem emerges when one raises
the question of the shape of the tradition on which Paul is explicitly
dependent. Much of the controversy respecting the interpretation of

ch. 15 turns on the relationship of Paul to traditional formulations of the faith which he had received. Even when the tradition is rooted in the Old Testament scriptures, its subsequent filtering through Jewish-Hellenistic midrashic categories can hardly be denied (8.4ff.; 10.1ff.).

D. Paul's Authority

In the light of these various new critical endeavours to set Paul solidly within his historical environment, it should come as no surprise that the grounds of Paul's authority should also have emerged as a perennial problem closely associated with both I and II Corinthians. Once the classic 'catholic' solution of Clement, bishop of Rome (I Clem.42), was rejected as anachronistic for the first century, various attempts have been offered in an effort to address the question historically. J. Schütz's book is useful in reviewing the history of the debate.

Although the subject is complex and extends far beyond the scope of an introduction, it is closely connected with our concern to describe the canonical function of Paul's letters. It is helpful at least to sketch the two extreme positions in the present discussion as background to the canonical question. On the one side is the position of Käsemann ('Ministry and Community', 83ff.), who argues that Paul's authority was completely free from any office or ecclesiastical structure, but was fully dependent upon his exercise of the gifts of the Spirit, the charismata, which Käsemann describes as a projection of the doctrine of justification by faith into ecclesiology. On the other side is the position of Schlier who understands Paul's authority to be grounded in normative apostolic tradition which stood in direct continuity with the revelation of Christ himself. The word which Paul preached was thus indistinguishable from church dogma and was self-authenticating in its function. Between these two extremes lies a great variety of other interpretations which continue to be discussed. It will be our concern shortly to investigate how this problem relates to the canonical function of I Corinthians within the Pauline corpus.

II. A Canonical Approach to the Book

A. The Literary Problem

Critical scholarship has made a lasting contribution in its close reading of the book which has highlighted the disjointed literary quality of its composition. It is fully clear that I Corinthians does not offer an artistically constructed theological tractate, but is a composition which in its structure has been largely controlled by the historical situation, and which reacts even in its sequence to the issues raised by the Corinthian church. However, the point must be stressed that the canonical role of a biblical book does not depend upon the degree of literary unity, but on the function to which the material has been assigned in communicating the gospel to a community of faith and practice.

Although theoretically it is certainly possible that the present form of a Pauline letter within the canonical collection was comprised of a combination of once independent letters (cf. the discussion of II Corinthians), such literary theories do raise important hermeneutical issues which call for careful distinctions. The source division of I Corinthians, as proposed for example by Weiss, suggests that the present literary context of the book as received is misleading and largely unintelligible. Correct interpretation depends on reconstructing a new context which is thought to be the original historical one. Even if such a prehistory were available, a canonical approach would at least insist that the present shape of the book in its conflated form be carefully studied.

However, in respect to I Corinthians, the evidence for seeing in the book two independent letters which were subsequently joined fails to convince. The essay of von Soden on the integrity of chs. 8–10 has played a decisive role in critical circles because it has demonstrated to most scholars' satisfaction that the source-critical solution of these chapters has misunderstood the nature of Paul's dialectical handling of sacrament and ethics. By interpreting ch.8 and 10.23ff. as ethically permissive, and 10.1–22 as reflecting a more primitive, mythological concept, Weiss has not only introduced totally foreign categories, but has missed the heart of Paul's argument. On the basis of this classic example the point should be reiterated that the canonical approach which is being suggested sees as its chief goal, not to provide, as it were, the correct interpretation of a passage, but rather to establish a context from which the real exegetical task of interpretation can begin. In the case of I Corinthians, the literary source theory of Weiss, Dinkler and Schmithals has rendered virtually impossible a canonical hearing of the book.

B. The Voices of Paul's Opponents

As we have already noticed, it is a particular feature of I Corinthians that the book is largely a rejoinder to concrete questions of a historical community. This quality of containing only one voice from among many raises some important hermeneutical problems. Especially for a canonical approach which resists assigning a normative interpretive role to the recovery of a letter's original function, the issue is highly significant.

First of all, the canonical approach is unequivocal in assigning the normative theological role to Paul's voice. It is not the historical situation which provides the canonical authority, nor the dialogue within the church which bears the weight. Rather, Paul's response in its received canonical form comprises the witness which functions authoritatively for each subsequent generation of believers. Nevertheless, it is crucial for a canonical reading to recognize that Paul is not writing a timeless tractate. His witness is addressed to a specific historical situation and participates in the contingency of that moment. It seems obvious that the Corinthians once knew of the situation to which Paul referred in chs. 1–4, but which has become enigmatic to subsequent readers. To the extent to which historical critical research can aid in illuminating Paul's witness, it provides an invaluable interpretive tool.

However, an equally crucial hermeneutical issue at stake turns on the relationship between Paul's original context and the canonical context available to subsequent readers. Perhaps it would be wise to address the issue as it affects the exegesis of I Corinthians 15. Paul begins the chapter by setting forth the tradition which he has received regarding Christ's death and resurrection. He then turns in v. 12 to address a particular heresy respecting the resurrection which had surfaced in the Corinthian church. 'How can some of you say that there is no resurrection of the dead?' In the continuing debate over the interpretation of this chapter, it has become increasingly apparent that much turns on getting a sharp focus on the Corinthian opinion which Paul contests. If one derives the rejection of the resurrection of the dead from a position akin to the Saducees, or if one suggests that the motivation arises from general Hellenistic aversion to a bodily resurrection, then it is difficult to make sense of Paul's logic. It would appear that the Corinthians are not denying the resurrection of Christ, but only the general resurrection of the dead. Paul argues that if there is no resurrection of the dead, then Jesus Christ cannot have been raised, and the Christian faith is in vain.

The logic of Paul's case falls into place if one follows the lead of Schniewind and others who argue that the Corinthians are spiritual enthusiasts. They deny the future resurrection of the dead because of their conviction that they have already experienced the resurrection (cf. II Tim. 2.18). They have already entered fully into the new age, and being no part of the old, expect nothing more in the future. The thrust of Paul's argument is to show that their principle of no future resurrection in fact undercuts Christ's resurrection as well, who is the first fruit of the Christian hope, and the benefits which Christians derive from his divine vindication are destroyed.

How does this historical-critical reading relate to its canonical function? In ch.15 Paul uses the peculiar Corinthian misunderstanding as a backdrop against which to present his own positive witness to Christ's resurrection. The main function of the chapter turns on explaining the significance of his confession: '. . . but in fact Christ has been raised from the dead' (v. 20). The tools of critical research have been helpful in bringing into sharper focus the Corinthian misunderstanding and thus clarifying the logic of Paul's argument. In this instance the historical critic was not attempting to know better than the biblical text itself, but rather to illuminate a situation which had once been shared by the contestants, but which had become blurred for the modern reader However, it is also true that the major function of the chapter is to draw out the implications for the Christian faith of a denial of the resurrection, and to explain the eschatological significance of Christ's victory. In other words, the major canonical function of the chapter is blurred, but not seriously impaired, if the peculiar motivation lying behind the Corinthian denial appears enigmatic to a modern reader.

The point at issue comes out clearly in the history of the exegesis of this chapter. Ever since the Enlightenment and the development of modern scientific thought, the denial of the resurrection has been motivated by a very different philosophy from that reflected by the

Corinthian enthusiasts. A modern rationalist denies in principle that the dead are ever raised, and therefore his generalization includes the particular instance which Christian tradition has claimed for Jesus. The logic of this move is exactly the reverse of that developed in Corinth. However, ever since the modern period, Christians have generally read the chapter in the light of the modern context in which the denial was made.

The hermeneutical point to make is that even though the original historical context was somewhat out of focus in the traditional Christian interpretation, the chapter was able to function canonically because its witness did not depend upon the reader's exact knowledge of the motivation behind the Corinthian error. The fact of the denial was grounds enough to evoke Paul's positive teaching. From a theological perspective the chapter functions canonically as witness to the truth regardless of how the error respecting the resurrection arises. In other words, from a canonical perspective the function of the chapter is not tied only to the peculiar historical stance of the Corinthians, but also bears witness within the changing modern context of the reader who experiences the denial of the resurrection from a totally different perspective.

To summarize, the recovery of the original historical context of I Corinthians 15 proved in this case to aid the modern interpreter in discerning the apostle's message in all its sharpness. However, the content of the chapter was such that the message of the chapter could function truthfully even when the modern context of the reader provided a continuity only by a rough analogy to the original. For a modern preacher to develop his homily on I Corinthians 15 in the light of his own historical context and that of his modern congregation can, in this instance, be defended as a proper extension of the gospel tradition. An additional support for this argument would be that elsewhere in the New Testament the witness to the truth of the resurrection is threatened by denials which reflect other grounds from that represented by the Corinthian heresy (Mark 16.8; Luke 24.10ff.; John 20.24ff.; Acts 17.32ff., etc.).

C. The Time-conditionality of Paul

Implied in our initial query after the canonical authority of I Corinthians was the apparent incompatibility between the thorough time-conditionality of Paul's response and its continuing normative role. In this regard modern historical criticism has made a major contribution in having broken the widespread idealistic perspective of the nineteenth century which viewed biblical authority solely in terms of universal principles. Yet the historical-critical approach has seldom been able to go beyond its negative contribution in addressing the question at issue. It has frequently been content to comment on Paul's inconsistency in reflecting both 'liberal' and 'conservative' ethical biases, and in the end to find in his response to the Christian church very limited ethical authority for the modern church. However, the crucial theological task is neither to contest Paul's time-conditionality, nor to allow Paul's message unlimited autonomy, but rather to discover how it functions within its canonical context as scripture.

Karl Barth was the first commentator in modern times to suggest that I Corinthians 15 provides the key for interpreting the entire epistle. Indeed, in spite of the letter's literary disjointedness there is a consistently eschatological perspective which culminates in ch.15, and which extends throughout the whole book. At stake in ch.15 is the Corinthian misunderstanding of the eschatological nature of Christ's redemption. It is the relationship between the old and the new age in Paul's eschatology which has a consistent effect on his ethical instructions to the Corinthian church.

At the outset Paul expresses gratitude to the Corinthians 'who are not lacking in any spiritual gift as you wait for the revealing of the Lord Jesus Christ, who will sustain you to the end . . . ' (1.7f.). The saints have experienced the radical new—the victory has been won (15.57)—but they await the unveiling of what God has prepared for them in the future (2.9). They are admonished to continue to build on the foundation of the gospel (3.10), since every man's work will be tested by the coming judgment (4.5). Yet the judgment has in fact already fallen on the old age as the rulers of this world crucified the Lord of glory (2.6ff.).

Christians are those 'upon whom the end of the ages has come' (10.11). They have been freed in Christ (7.22) and all things are lawful (10.23). Because they have been bought with a price (7.23), they are no longer their own. They have been joined together in the body of Christ, in the unity of the one Lord (10.16). Although they continue to live in the world (5.10), the new life in Christ has fully relativized the things which the world holds dear. Therefore, those with wives are to live 'as though they had none', 'those who buy as though they had no goods, and those who deal with the world as though they had no dealings with it' (7.29ff.). They have thus become a spectacle to the world (4.9), like men sentenced to death (4.9).

In the light of this new eschatological life in Christ, Paul draws concrete ethical implications for Christian behaviour. How can Christians dare go to a civil court before unbelievers to settle their affairs? Do they not realize that 'the saints will judge the world'? (6.1ff). Again, it is unthinkable for 'members of Christ' to consort with prostitutes. Has not God made the body the temple of the Holy Spirit (6.12ff.), which God will raise from the dead as he did Christ (v. 14)? Similarly, Christians are to shun the worship of idols and not be partners with demons (10.20).

The dialectical quality of Paul's ethics emerges as a direct consequence of his eschatological perspective. The Corinthians have been made free in Christ. All things are lawful for them, and yet they have been made a 'slave to all' (9.19). In respect to eating food offered to idols, Paul makes absolutely clear that an idol has no real existence—'there is no God but one' (8.4)—and yet he calls upon the Christians in Corinth to restrict their freedom in love lest the conscience of the weak be injured.

The ethic of the new, eschatological age is one of freedom. The Christian is controlled by the gifts of the Spirit, not by the law, yet the believer lives 'in between the times'. Christ has become the first fruits of the new order (15.23), but the Christian still awaits the end (v. 24). Paul vigorously contests the Corinthian error, which feels that the Christian already lives a spirit-filled life which is completely of the new age, and which thus dissolves the eschatological tension which is constitutive of the life in Christ before the parousia. When Paul insists that the Corinthian women continue to wear veils during worship, it is to misconstrue his theological motivation to suggest that he is simply socially conservative in some matters. Rather, the issue at stake is the nature of Christian behaviour living in an eschatological tension between the old and the new ages. Apparently there were those women in Corinth who felt that the traditional distinctions in mores between male and female no longer applied, and in a symbolic gesture of their new freedom rejected the head covering. Paul disputes the move and argues for the maintenance of the symbolic veil.

Paul's response to the concrete ethical dilemmas of the Corinthian congregation is dominated by a consistently eschatological perspective. The heart of his argument is exposed in ch.15 in which the christological grounds for life in Christ are developed in detail. Yet Paul applies his ethics in different ways. He does not deviate from his basic position that Christians have been freed in Christ, that they have entered a new age, and that they are led by the Spirit. Nevertheless, Paul offers some rules as pastoral guides for Christian living 'in between the times'. These are not laws; they have no ontological or legal status, but function as guidelines for faithful Christian response. In 7.17 the apostle sets out one of these rules: 'let every one lead the life which the Lord has assigned to him', that is to say, 'every one should remain in the state in which he was called'. In the rest of the chapter Paul unfolds the reasoning behind this rule-of-thumb, and applies it in some detail. In a similar way he addresses the problem of spiritual gifts in chs. 12–14. His fundamental eschatological perspective is clear: 'for our knowledge is imperfect and our prophecy is imperfect, but when the perfect comes, the imperfect will pass away' (13.9f.). However, then Paul goes on to set forth some rules as an aid by which to decide concrete issues: 'all things should be done decently and in order' (14.40; cf.16.14).

In sum, to suggest that because Paul is thoroughly time-conditioned in his ethical advice, his epistle is of limited value to modern Christians is to miss the point of his theological contribution. The boldness of his ethical direction derives from an eschatology which is christologically grounded, and yet penetrates into the concrete struggles of Christian life in the world.

D. The Canonical Authority of Paul

The final problem to be discussed is Paul's authority. We have noticed the difficulty of understanding the nature of his authority and the complexity of the topic which relates to apostleship, office, charisma, and tradition. Our intention is not to suggest one resolution of this controversial problem, but rather to focus on one aspect of the issue. How does the authority which Paul exercised toward the historical church of Corinth relate to the authoritative function which was assigned to him by virtue of the canonization of I Corinthians? Does the process of canonization change one kind of authority into something different in kind?

One of the striking features of I Corinthians is the sharp distinctions which Paul employs in his exercise of authority toward his church.

At times he appeals to the authority of Christ as providing the grounds for his imperatives (7.10; 11.23). He can be apodictic, unequivocal, and uncompromising (5.3ff.). At other times he finds his authoritative warrant in the tradition which he has received (15.3). Then again, he often makes a clear distinction between Christ's authority and his own (7.12). Moreover, there is a tentative quality about many of Paul's expressions of advice. He thinks that he has the Spirit of God on a certain matter (7.40). Or he offers advice by way of concession, not of command (7.6), and characterizes his response as an 'opinion' which he trusts is dependable (7.25). Finally, he frequently appeals to knowledge which the congregation already possesses (8.1; 12.2ff.), and requests them to exercise their reason (10.15).

What effect did the process of canonization have on Paul's exercise of authority? Is his role changed now that his letter has been received as part of sacred scripture? Is the result of canonization that the different levels of Paul's historical exercise of power have been flattened into one form of scriptural legitimation? The issue is obviously important for anyone taking the canonical function of the New Testament seriously.

There is no indication that the process of canonization has left any deep marks on the structure of the original letter. The book has not undergone a heavy redactional reworking in order to enable it to function canonically. The only possible exception is the unusual form of the book's addressee in 1.2. Besides being directed to the church of God at Corinth, there is the supplement 'together with all those who in every place call on the name of our Lord Jesus Christ'. It remains debatable among scholars whether or not the latter is part of the original letter or a secondary expansion. Regardless of its literary history it now serves to extend the addressee of the letter far beyond its original recipients.

Apart from this one possible literary shaping, the issue of the influence of canonization on the book's authority is one of changing function. In what way has it been influenced by its place within the New Testament canon? First of all, the effect of the canonization of Paul's letter to the Corinthians was to assign a lasting religious authority to Paul within the Christian faith which extended far beyond the Corinthian church. Especially in the case of I Corinthians, the historical source provided by the Apostolic Fathers (Clement, Polycarp) shows dramatic evidence of the authoritative role which

Paul's letter had received within early Christianity. Yet it is also true that Paul did not write to the Corinthians a chatty, personal letter of solely casual advice which was then later elevated into an authoritative statement far removed from its initial intention. Rather, Paul wrote to his church as an apostle, in the name of Christ, and he consciously sought to exercise his apostolic authority upon them. In other words, the act of canonization was a broad acknowledgement of Paul's authority on the part of the larger church which simply extended the apostle's authority beyond its original recipients, but in continuity with its original intent.

Then again, there is nothing to suggest that the effect of canonization seriously altered the dynamic of Paul's original exercise of his apostolic authority. As we have already attempted to show, Paul grounded his message in an eschatological understanding of the Christian life which he derived from Christ's resurrection, but which he supported with some rules of behaviour in order to aid in concrete decisions. The effect of canonization did not transform his letter into a timeless tractate, nor reduce the flexibility within Christian freedom which Paul developed. The modern Christian continues to live between the times in the tension of eschatological expectation. Therefore, it is a misunderstanding of canonical function when Paul's letter is translated into a manual of right doctrine which renders it different in kind from its original function. Conversely, to dismiss Paul's ethics as merely time-conditioned opinion fails utterly to grasp the continuing authoritative role of the Bible as scripture of the church in all its time-conditionality.

14

II CORINTHIANS

Commentaries

J. C. K. von Hofmann, ²1877
A. P. Stanley, ⁵1882
H. A. W. Meyer, MeyerK, ET 1883
C. Hodge, ⁶1883
C. J. Ellicott, 1887
J. Denney, ExpB, 1894
G. Heinrici, Meyer, ⁸1900
J. H. Bernard, ExpGT, 1903
A. Menzies, 1912
A. Plummer, ICC, 1915
W. Bousset, *SNT*, ³1917
P. Bachmann, KNT, ²1922
H. Windisch, MeyerK, ⁹1924
A. Schlatter, 1934

R. H. Strachan, MNTC, 1935
O. Kuss, RNT, 1940
F. V. Filson, IB, 1953
E. -B. Allo, ÉB, ²1956
P. E. Hughes, NICNT, 1962
J. Héring, CNT, ET ²1967
H. D. Wendland, NTD, ¹²1968
H. Lietzmann, W. G. Kümmel,
HNT, ⁵1969
F. F. Bruce, NCeB, 1971
C. K. Barrett, B/HNTC, 1973
H. Bultmann, E. Dinkler, MeyerK
Sonderband, 1976

Bibliography

W. **Baird**, 'Letters of Recommendation', *JBL* 80, 1961, 166–72; M. **Barré**, 'Paul as "Eschatologic Person": a New Look at 2 Cor 11:29', *CBQ* 37, 1975, 500–26; C. K. **Barrett**, ψευδαπόστολοι (2 Cor 11.13)', *Mélanges bibliques en hommage au R. P. Bêda Rigaux*, ed. A. Descamps et al., Gembloux 1970, 377–96; 'Paul's Opponents in II Corinthians', *NTS* 17, 1970/71, 233–54; W. H. **Bates**, 'The Integrity of II Corinthians', *NTS* 12, 1965/6, 56–69; R. **Batey**, 'Paul's Interaction with the Corinthians', *JBL* 84, 1965, 139–46; H. D. **Betz**, 'Eine Christus-Aretalogie bei Paulus (2 Kor 12,7–10)', *ZTK* 66, 1969, 288–305; '2 Cor. 6,14–7,1: An Anti-Pauline Fragment?', *JBL* 92, 1972, 88–108; *Der Apostel Paulus und die sokratische Tradition. Eine exegetische Untersuchung zu seiner 'Apologie' 2 Korinther 10–13*, BHT 45, 1972; G. **Bornkamm**, 'Die Vorgeschichte des sogenannten Zweiten Korintherbriefes' (1961), reprinted *Geschichte und Glaube, GA* IV, Munich 1971, 162–94; F. F. **Bruce**, 'Paul on Immortality', *SJT* 24, 1971, 457–72; L. **Brun**, 'Zur

Auslegung von 2. Kor 5, 1–10', *ZNW* 28, 1929, 207–29; C. H. **Buck**, 'The Collection for the Saints', *HTR* 43, 1950, 1–29; R. **Bultmann**, 'Exegetische Problem des Zweiten Korintherbriefes' (1947), reprinted *Exegetica*, Tübingen 1967, 298–322; J. -F. **Collange**, *Énigmes de la deuxième épître de Paul aux Corinthiens—Étude exegetique de 2 Cor.2:14–7:4*, SNTSM 18, 1972; N. A. **Dahl**, 'On the Literary Integrity of 2 Cor. 1–9', *Studies in Paul*, Minneapolis 1977; 'A Fragment and its Content: 2 Corinthians 6:14–7:1', ibid., 62–9; J. T. **Dean**, 'The Great Digression. 2 Cor ii 14–vii 4', *ExpT* 50, 1938, 86–98; E. **Dinkler**, 'Die Taufterminologie in 2 Cor 1,21f.', *Neotestamentica et Patristica, Freundesgabe für O. Cullmann*, ed. W. C. van Unnik, NovTSupp 6, 1962, 173–91.

G. **Ebeling**, 'Geist und Buchstabe', *RGG*³ II, 1958, 1290–96; E. E. **Ellis**, '2 Cor 5,1–10 in Pauline Eschatology', *NTS* 6, 1959/60, 211–24; J. A. **Eschlimann**, 'La rédaction des épîtres pauliniennes d'après une comparaison avec les lettres profanes de son temps', *RB* 53, 1946, 185–96; A. **Feuillet**, 'Paul, Corinthiens (Les épîtres aux)', *DBSuppl* VII, 170–95; J. A. **Fitzmyer**, 'Qumran and the Interpolated Paragraph in 2 Corinthians 6:14–7:1', *CBQ* 23, 1961, 273–80; J. W. **Fraser**, 'Paul's Knowledge of Jesus: II Corinthians V.16 Once More', *NTS* 17, 1970/71, 293–313; G. **Friedrich**, *Amt und Lebensführung. Eine Auslegung von 2 Kor 6,1–10*, BSt 39, 1963; '*DIE* Gegner des Paulus im 2 Korintherbrief', *Abraham Unser Vater, FS O. Michel*, ed. O. Betz, M. Hengel and P. Schmidt, Leiden 1963, 181–215; D. **Georgi**, *Die Gegner des Paulus im 2 Korintherbrief*, WMANT 11, 1964; *Die Geschichte der Kollekte des Paulus für Jerusalem*, ThF 38, 1965; J. **Gnilka**, '2 Cor. 6:14–7:1 in the Light of the Qumran Texts and the Testaments of the Twelve Patriarchs', ET *Paul and Qumran*, ed. J. Murphy-O'Connor, Chicago and London 1968, 46–68; E. **Güttgemanns**, *Der leidende Apostel*, FRLANT 90 1966; A. **Hausrath**, *Der Vier-Capitel. Brief des Paulus an die Korinther*, Heidelberg 1870; C. J. A. **Hickling**, 'The Sequence of Thought in II Corinthians, chapter three', *NTS* 21, 1974/5, 380–95; N. **Hydahl**, 'Die Frage nach der literarischen Einheit des zweiten Korintherbriefes', *ZNW* 64, 1973, 289–306.

E. **Käsemann**, 'Die Legitimät des Apostels. Eine Untersuchung zu II. Kor 10–13', *ZNW* 41, 1942, 33–71; L. E. **Keck**, 'The Poor among the Saints in the New Testament', *ZNW* 56, 1965, 100–29; 'The Poor among the Saints in Jewish Christianity and Qumran', *ZNW* 57, 1966, 54–78; J. H. **Kennedy**, *The Second and Third Epistles of St Paul to the Corinthians*, London 1900; K. **Kertelge**, 'Das Apostelamt des Paulus, sein Ursprung und seine Bedeutung', *BZ* 14, 1970, 161–81; J. **Lambrecht**, 'The Fragment 2 Cor 6,14–7, 1. A Plea for its Authenticity', *Miscellanea neotestamentica* 2, ed. T. Baarda, NovTSupp 47, 1978, 143–61; J. B. **Lightfoot** , 'The Mission of Titus to the Corinthians', *Biblical Essays*, London and New York 1893, 273–84; T. W. **Manson**, 'St Paul in Ephesus, 3: The Corinthian Correspondence', *BJRL* 26, 1941/2, 101–20; 327–41; reprinted in *Studies in the Gospels and Epistles*, Manchester and Philadelphia 1962, 190ff.; J. L. **Martyn**, 'Epistemology at the Turn of the Ages: 2 Corinthians 5:16', *Christian History* *and Interpretation. FS John Knox*, ed. W. R. Farmer et al., Cambridge 1967, 269–87; A. Q. **Morton**, 'Dislocations in I and 2 Corinthians', *ExpT* 78, 1966/7, 119; C. F. D. **Moule**, 'St Paul and Dualism: The Pauline Conception of Resurrection', *NTS* 12, 1965/6, 106–23; J. **Munck**, *Paul and the Salvation of Mankind*, ET London and Richmond 1959, 168–95; K. F. **Nickle**, *The Collection: A Study in Paul's Strategy*, SBT 48 1966, 166.

J. L. **Price**, 'Aspects of Paul's Theology and their Bearing on Literary Problems of Second Corinthians', *Studies in the History and Text of the New Testament in Honor of K. W. Clark*, ed. B. D. Daniels and M. J. Suggs, Salt Lake City 1967, 95ff.; K. **Prümm**, *Diakonia Pneumatos—Der zweite Korintherbrief als Zugang zur apostolischen Botschaft*, 3 vols., Rome 1960–67; M. **Rissi**, *Studien zum Zweiten Korintherbrief*, AbTANT 56, 1969; W. **Schmithals**, *Gnosticism in Corinth*, ET Nashville ²1971; J. H. **Schütz**, *Paul and the Anatomy of Apostolic Authority*, SNTSM 26, 1975; S. **Schulz**, 'Die Decke des Moses', *ZNW* 49, 1958, 1–30; E. **Schweizer**, 'Die Mystik des Sterbens und Auferstehens mit Christus bei Paulus', *EvTh* 26, 1966, 239–57; J. B. **Souček**, 'Wir kennen Christus nicht nach dem Fleisch', *EvTh* 19, 1959, 300–14; P. **Stuhlmacher**, 'Erwägungen zum ontologischen Charakter der καινὴ κτίσις bei Paulus', *EvTh* 27, 1967, 1–35; C. H. **Talbert**, 'Again: Paul's Visits to Jerusalem', *NovT* 9, 1967, 26–40; S. H. **Travis**, 'Paul's Boasting in 2 Corinthians 10–12', *St Ev* VI, TU 112, 1973, 527–32; W. C. **van Unnik**, ''Η καινὴ διαθήκη – A Problem in the Early History of the Canon', *St Patr* IV, TU 79, 1961, 212–27; ' "With Unveiled Face". An Exegesis of 2 Corinthians iii, 12–18', *NovT* 6, 1963, 153–69; C. R. **Williams**, 'A Word-Study of Hebrews XIII', *JBL* 30, 1911, 129–36.

As one would expect, there are some important elements of continuity between the first and the second letters of Paul to the Corinthians. Once again there is much attention paid to Paul's opponents, to the defence of the apostolic office, and to eschatological hope. Yet the surprising thing is the recognition of how great are the discontinuities between the letters which often seem to outweigh those of continuity. Two main issues have dominated the modern critical discussion of II Corinthians: (*a*) the nature of the historical relationship of Paul and the church at Corinth between the writing of I and II Corinthians (included in this issue is the nature of Paul's opponents); (*b*) the apparent disunity within the second epistle. Both of these issues are closely related to each other and have important canonical implications as well. As it will shortly become apparent, the crucial canonical issue of II Corinthians turns on determining the nature of its canonical referentiality. Our procedure will be first to spell out the exact nature of the historical critical issues, and then to show their effect on the interpretation of the canonical shape of the book.

I. New Historical Reconstructions

The modern critical study of II Corinthians was made possible by breaking sharply with certain assumptions on which traditional interpretations had been largely based. (Tertullian's views were an exception, *de pud.* 13.) Until the early nineteenth century and even later, it had been assumed that the first Corinthian letter provided the immediate context from which II Corinthians was to be interpreted (cf. Stanley, Zahn). Following the account of Acts, interpreters thought that nothing very significant had happened between the writing of the two letters. Paul's opponents were considered to be the same, the 'wrong doer' of II Cor. 7.12 was identified with the immoral person of I Cor. 5.1ff., and the 'painful letter' (II Cor. 2.4; 7.8,12) was thought to be the apostle's characterization of I Corinthians. In sum, the canonical relationship between the two letters to the church at Corinth was translated by traditional exegesis into historical categories which greatly affected the meaning of the text.

The important critical change came about when it was discovered that much more history had occurred between Paul and the Corinthians than could be inferred from the book of Acts. Increasingly it became apparent that the context of I Corinthians did not match the situation envisioned in II Corinthians, but from the bits and pieces of the second canonical letter a very different picture of the relationship could be reconstructed. In 1830 Bleek first suggested that the 'painful letter' (*Tränenbrief*) of chs. 2 and 7 could not be identified with the letter of I Corinthians, but must have been written in the period between the two canonical epistles. Suddenly a host of unanswered questions emerged, which were then debated throughout the rest of the nineteenth century. How long was the interval between the letters? Did Paul pay a visit before or after I Corinthians? Who was the offender of II Corinthians 7, and what had happened to evoke the painful letter? (cf. Plummer, ICC, xivff.).

Although a wide variety of different theories continues to be entertained by critical scholars (cf. Georgi, *Die Gegner*, 25ff.), some agreement has emerged regarding the broad lines of the historical sequence. Accordingly, Paul made a second visit to Corinth which is not recorded in the book of Acts. In II Cor. 12.14 and 13.1 Paul spoke of his impending third visit. The second visit cannot have occurred before the writing of I Corinthians because there is nothing which anticipates the peculiar tensions which were to erupt in the first letter. The exact reason for the visit is obscure, but appears related to troubles instigated by new arrivals from Jerusalem. Also the relationship of this visit to the two announced travel plans in I Cor. 16.5ff. and II Cor. 1.15f. is unclear (cf. Windisch, MeyerK, 60ff.). However, there is no doubt but that Paul's visit was unsuccessful in dissolving the opposition, and that Paul was personally wronged by someone in the ensuing exchange. The apostle then withdrew and wrote a bitter letter demanding compliance (2.4; 7.8,12) which he sent by Titus. After waiting for a time in great agitation, he set out for Macedonia to meet Titus (2.13;7.5). Finally, Titus brought good news of the church's repentance and regret (7.5). Paul then composed yet another letter which constitutes portions of the canonical book of II Corinthians, in which he expressed his joy over the reconciliation.

II. New Literary Possibilities

Closely connected with the discovery of new historical dimensions has been the excitement produced by the new exegetical possibilities for resolving the many literary problems which have long baffled commentators. To many scholars it suddenly seemed possible to correlate disjointed literary fragments of II Corinthians with their true historical referent in a reconstructed original sequence. This endeavour has largely occupied the modern critical study of the book.

Even traditional commentators recognized that the book clearly divides into three sections following the introduction: 1–7, reconciliation with the Corinthian church; 8–9, ordering of the collection; 10–13, settling with the rebellious congregation. However, the extent of the discontinuities, both within and among the sections, only emerged through the careful scrutiny of modern critical research. First, the letter of reconciliation (1.3–2.13) is suddenly broken off and the narrative then continued in 7.5–16. Between this bracket is a section offering a justification of the apostolic office which appears to have the literary integrity of a once independent composition (2.14–6.13; 7.2–4). In addition, to make matters even more complicated, there is a widespread consensus (cf. Fitzmyer, Gnilka, Dahl) that the unit 6.14–7.1 is a later redactional unit which has its origin in a Jewish circle akin to Qumran.

Turning next to chs. 8 and 9, these two chapters on the collection are widely regarded as doublets. 9.1 uses an introductory formula which functions to introduce a new unit (cf. Windisch), and is not simply a further elaboration of what preceded. Moreover, the main points of the argument in ch.8 are rehearsed in a paralleled manner which does not add anything of substance. As a result, it is generally thought that the two chapters functioned independently of each other, and were part of separate epistles of Paul, probably written at different periods.

Finally, and the most difficult problem of all, is the relation of chs. 10–13 to the preceding chapters. The *Einleitung* of Schenke-Fischer is typical in finding 'the transition from 7.16 to 10.1ff. simply incomprehensible' (109). If the whole point of chs. 1–7 was to establish the complete reconciliation of Paul with his church, how then is one to explain the abrupt shift in tone to the harshest possible words of recrimination? Of course, there have been several traditional ploys used to harmonize the difficulties. Often psychological reasons are employed, such as Lietzmann's well-known suggestion of 'Paul's sleepless night' (HNT, 139) as providing sufficient cause for the sharp change in tone. More plausible is the proposal that Paul's habit of dictating his letters with periods of interruption accounts for the shift in perspective (Kümmel, *Intr.*) or that chs. 10–13 were directed to a restricted minority group of continuing opponents (Guthrie). However, these attempts at harmonization are not fully convincing to the majority of scholars and frequently appear strained even to those defending them.

A more radical solution for explaining the discontinuity of chs. 10–13 had already been offered by J. S. Semler (1776) in suggestng that these chapters should be seen as an independent letter. However, it was the theory of A. Hausrath (1870) which launched the modern critical study of the book. Hausrath conjectured that chs. 10–13 were not simply a fragment of an independent letter, but were actually the 'painful letter' of II Corinthians 2 which had been written before the rest of II Corinthians and was now preserved in a non-historical sequence.

Hausrath's theory did not evoke at first much positive response in Germany, but the theory received a strong reaction in England from J. H. Kennedy who developed a similar theory, independently of Hausrath. Kennedy added some additional evidence for considering chs. 10–13 as the 'painful letter', which had traditionally been regarded as lost. He linked three passages in chs. 1–9 which were all written in the past tense with three passages in 10–13 which were in the future tense, and sought thus to demonstrate that the latter must have preceded the writing of the former in 1–9 (1.23//13.2; 2.3//13.10; 2.9//10.6).

In the history of the research which followed, the literary theory was further expanded in an attempt to resolve the literary dislocations within the entire book. Bultmann's version, which was then defended by Dinkler (RGG^3, IV, 17ff.) became a commonly accepted hypothesis. II Corinthians consists of two letters. The earlier, the so-called 'painful letter', comprises 2.14–7.4; 9; 10–13; the later 1.1–2.13; 7.5–16; 8. However, more recently this source theory has come under increasing attack as unlikely since it has been contested that the painful letter could not have included such diverse elements as Bultmann's theory requires. The most recent refinement of the hypothesis is represented by Bornkamm, Georgi, and Schenke-Fischer. It posits four or five different stages which reflect Paul's complicated relationship with the Corinthians, and the sections are no longer viewed as strands of a larger unity. Georgi's theory (*IDB Suppl*, 183ff.) posits five fragments: A(2.14–7.4); B(10–13); C(1.1–2.13; 5.5–16); D(8); E(9). Of course, the danger of a complete literary atomization of the letter remains acute, particularly when one sees the even further divisions proposed by Schmithals.

Within this modern critical development, one of the more significant new perspectives has been that of Bornkamm. After first pursuing his interpretation of Paul's opponents as a type of wandering 'miracle worker' and showing their relation to the literary problems, Bornkamm raises the basic redactional question of how to explain the present shape of II Corinthians which he assumes has been secondarily assembled from disparate letter fragments. He argues that a redactional motivation can be determined at two significant junctures. The section 10–13 received its present position in analogy to a well established New Testament pattern because its function was then understood as a type of eschatological warning against expected heresy pointing to the endtime. Similarly, Paul's letter of reconciliation in 2.14ff. was introduced by a form of doxology in order to construe the apostle's journey as a triumphal march.

The chief significance of Bornkamm's redactional criticism was his recognition of an important theological referentiality which was not to be simply identified with a letter's original historical function. Shortly we shall return to Bornkamm's suggestion and discuss its relation to our canonical interpretation.

It would be misleading to imply that the modified form of Hausrath's theory of the reconstructed lost letter of Paul in chs. 10–13 has been universally accepted by critical scholars. An impressive minority voice continues to resist its acceptance (Kümmel, Hydahl, etc.). It remains a serious problem for the critical theory that the specific incident which called forth the painful letter in chs. 2 and 7 is not mentioned in chs. 10–13 (cf. Bornkamm's response, *GA* IV,174ff.). Similarly, the argument that chs.10–13 followed rather than preceded the reconciliation (Windisch) shows a significant divergence within the critical theory. However, in my judgment, the evidence for the modified Hausrath hypothesis is still more plausible than the theories of composition which seek to defend the book as an original unity (Schlatter, Bachmann, Kümmel, Guthrie). Nevertheless, the critical theory, in spite of its valuable insights, operates with a hermeneutical model which is seriously deficient and needs to be placed within a different interpretive context.

III. The Hermeneutical Problem at Stake

The exegesis of II Corinthians affords a classic example from which to illustrate once again hermeneutical issues which have occupied us throughout this volume. Because many of the issues have been treated before, the discussion can be brief.

(*a*) It has been almost universally assumed in the history of the modern study of II Corinthians, both by liberals and conservatives, that a correct exegesis of the book depends upon reconstructing the historical referent at the time of Paul's original writing. For this reason the ability to correlate the various sections of the letter with specific historical events in Paul's relationship to his church was considered an essential element. As a result, the multiple shadings of historical referentiality within the book were obliterated, and tentative reconstructions lifted to the same level as explicit historical argumentation. For example, Paul's mention of the 'one who did the wrong' refers to an explicit historical incident and functions as an essential part of his argument in chs. 2 and 7 for repentance and forgiveness. However, the lack of any reference to this incident in 10–13 is often supplied by commentators who need the specific historical reference in order to interpret these chapters in the same context as chs. 2 and 7.

(*b*) Traditionally conservative exegesis of II Corinthians has been equally committed to a theory of historical referentiality. It was a fatal move when the canonical status of the two letters to Corinth was translated historically to provide a concrete reference to passages which were indeterminate in II Corinthians. One of the great contributions of the historical-critical method was in destroying this erroneous historical move and in opening up the text to a fresh reading.

(*c*) Although the use of crass psychological ploys are generally suspect among critics as adequate grounds for literary dislocation, more subtle uses of psychological categories are widespread. Thus, the argument which undergirds Hausrath's hypothesis assumes that it is psychologically impossible for Paul to address the same congregation with such harsh words after he had just been reconciled. My point is not to dispute the force of all such arguments, nor to rule them automatically out of court. However, it is to question whether such psychological motivations can be disregarded or even overruled by a new canonical use of scripture which bears a witness to theological truth which is not identifiable with common human behaviour. Bornkamm's redactional explanation of the present position of chs. 10–13 at least recognized the possibility of another theological concern transcending the original historical situation.

(*d*) The exegesis of II Corinthians illustrates the need for a subtle discerning of a canonical shape which makes differing usages of the original historical relation of Paul to his church. On the one hand, it is impossible to ignore the possibility of recovering a sharper profile of events which were once known and understood by Paul's hearers and which constitute a crucial dimension of his theological witness. On the other hand, it is equally important to realize that the canonical role of the final form of this book has its own integrity which functions in a way distinct and often different from the original letters.

IV. The Canonical Shape of II Corinthians

Within the Pauline corpus it becomes apparent that several of the apostle's letters have been canonized in a form which is virtually identical with the original historical letter (e.g. Romans, Galatians). In such cases our concern has focused on determining to what extent the book has received a change in function because of its new canonical context within the larger corpus. However, II Corinthians reflects a different situation in which it seems reasonably clear that the present form of the book derives from a lengthy redactional activity. The hermeneutical and exegetical issue at stake is to clarify how the canonical approach which is being proposed for II Corinthians relates to, and yet differs from, redactional criticism.

We have already made mention of the contribution of Bornkamm in his perceptive analysis of the book. He argues that the editor of chs. 10–13 provided these chapters with a new literary function differing from its original role. The letter which originally did not share either the form or function of apocalyptic writings, was assigned by its positioning an eschatological role of providing a warning against future heresy and false prophecy (180–82). Bornkamm contends that the writer was employing a common pattern of early Christianity, found in the Gospels and epistles, which reflected a common theological perspective of the post-apostolic period. The opponents of Paul were thereby characterized as the false prophets of the endtime, and the apostle exalted as the true means of protection for the faithful church. He concludes that there were some questionable aspects to this development, particularly a tendency to identify Pauline teaching with pure doctrine.

Two issues are at stake in exploring the relationship of redactional criticism to a canonical interpretation. One turns on a methodological difference, the other on exegetical details respecting Bornkamm's interpretation of II Corinthians. The redactional critical method offers an historical interpretation of a biblical text which has extended the concept of authorship to include the intentional stamping of an earlier composition by a subsequent editor. The analysis seeks to determine the historical forces at work on the redactor as well as the effect of his editorial activity on the text.

The canonical approach which is being proposed focuses its attention on the effect of redactional activity on the biblical text as it is interpreted by a community of faith, including the past, present, and future, which reads it as normative scripture within the context of faith. The critical study of the historical intentionality of an author or redactor serves a canonical purpose in aiding the reader to determine the literary profile of the text. However, the text's meaning is not identified with its historically reconstructed intentionality, but emerges in an interraction between the historically formed text and the community of faith which reads it as a religious norm. Specifically in terms of II Corinthians, Bornkamm's redactional method restricts the interpretation of 10–13 to determining the historical and theological forces at work on the post-apostolic redactor and to relating the effect of his intentionality on the biblical text. The canonical approach seeks also to determine historical and theological forces at work, but it shifts the focus of interpretation from being an historical enterprise of the Hellenistic age, to a present interpretive activity which construes the shaped historical text in a particular manner.

Perhaps the issue will become clearer by turning to some exegetical details which distinguish Bornkamm's exegesis from a canonical. Bornkamm sees the redactional function of 10–13 to be an eschatological one which he sets apart from chs. 1–7. Yet a case can be made that the redactional insertion of 6.14–7.1 provides an important link with 10–13 and probably stems from the same redactional hand (Dahl, 68). The effect of the insertion of 6.14ff. is to establish a parallel between the situation envisioned in chs. 1–7 and in 10–13. Both 6.14ff. and 10–13 portray the church as the people of God in a battle against Satan (6.15//11.14). The specific function of 6.14ff. is to warn the church that a rejection of Paul's authority is tantamount to aligning itself with the enemy of God. Thus 6.14ff. provides an important dimension to the Pauline interpretation of his office which is the main subject at issue in chs. 1–7.

What this means is that the function of 10–13 within II Corinthians is not simply an eschatological one, directed to the future. It remains a real problem with Bornkamm's interpretation that the eschatological language of Paul occurs in chs. 1–7 and not in 10–13 (cf. 1.9f., 22; 2.15; 4.14, 16ff; 5.1ff. etc.). Rather, chs. 10–13 like 1–7 deal with a correct understanding of Paul's apostolic office which is constitutive both for the church's life and for the proclamation of the gospel. In both sections of the book the office of Paul is explained as sharing in the weakness and power of Christ, rather than in the wondrous signs of the superlative apostles (12.11). The threat to the gospel which is described in 10–13 and 6.14–7.1 was not only an eschatological danger, but one which is constitutive to the Christian faith and is integrally related to the office of the apostle. Indeed, the threat extends into the future, but the rejection of Christ's true apostle will recur in every generation. In a word, Bornkamm interprets chs. 10–13 as a redactor's intention to profile the future for the post-Pauline church. The effect of his redactional move is ultimately to historicize the text and to tie it to the editor's theological intention. In contrast, a canonical approach points the editorial shaping away from the author's motivation, and focuses on the effect which the move had on the biblical text for future generations who read the interpreted text as authoritative scripture. Chapters 10–13 offer a theological witness respecting the relation of the apostolic office to the Christian life which functions to overrule the psychological obstacle of using such harsh words to a church which has been reconciled to Paul in chs. 1–7.

According to Bornkamm there is another significant sign of redactional shaping in II Corinthians. The account of Paul's journey to Macedonia to meet Titus which begins in ch.2 has been abruptly broken off at v. 13 and is only resumed in 7.5. In between has been inserted a lengthy apology for the apostolic office in 2.14–6.13, 7.2–4. This apology, moreover, is introduced in 2.14 with a doxology which has the effect of idealizing the apostle and transforming his trip into Macedonia into a triumphal march. Once again the exegetical issue is whether Bornkamm's redactional analysis does justice to the present shape of the passage.

Paul's defence of his apostolic office, which was written before his reconciliation with the Corinthian church, has now been preserved in a form which lies bracketted between 1.3–2.13 and 7.5–16. What is the canonical effect of this position on the canonical reading of chs. 1–7? What theological witness has resulted from this apparently non-chronological arrangement of different portions of Paul's correspondence? I would argue that the point being made is that a correct understanding of Paul's apostolic office is constitutive for reconciliation with him and with the gospel he proclaims.

The doxology in 2.14 performs a significant function in establishing a canonical context for his apology. Paul gives praise to God who has given him the ministry of reconciliation (5.18). His reconciliation with the Corinthian church is only a reponse to the prior divine reconciliation. The ministry about which the apostle is talking is not just a defence of his action before the Corinthians, but relates to the gospel in the eternal purpose of God (4.5). Paul's function as Christ's ambassador is one which dispenses both life and death (2.15f.). What transpired between Paul and the Corinthians, including his trip to Troas, which was filled with suffering and misunderstanding, was a transparency of what his apostolic office was all about. The literary insertion of this apology (2.14ff.) now serves as an elaborate commentary on the true meaning of his relationship to his church. Reconciliation and apostolic office belong together constitutively. Paul's apology gives the grounds for the eschatological existence of which the trip was an illustration. Far from being an idealization of the apostle, it explains why his suffering was not simply an unfortunate accident, but offered the true evidence of his divinely commissioned apostolic office. The coupling of 1.3–2.13 with 2.14ff. transformed a record of an historical event into a description of an essential relationship which characterized the eschatological nature of both the apostolic office and the Christian life.

The bracketing of the two letter fragments makes clear not only the constitutive quality of Paul's office, but functions to incorporate the community of faith into a similar life of suffering. His apology constantly moves to a plural addressee 'we' (3.1ff.; 4.1ff.; 5.1ff.). In contrast to the old covenant which was symbolized by Moses' fading glory (3.7ff.), those who live by the Spirit of God have experienced the new creation (5.17). Their momentary affliction is only a preparation for the new order of which the Spirit of Christ is already its guarantee (5.5). The faithful community lives by the eschatological certainty of a resurrection future.

Finally, a word is in order regarding the canonical function of chs. 8–9. In my judgment, the literary evidence tips the scales in favour of a theory of two once independent portions of letters. However, the evidence is far from conclusive. Whatever the prehistory of these chapters, they now function within II Corinthians as a literary unit with minimal signs of internal friction. The repetition in 9.1 serves as a rhetorical device which increases the urgency of the request. The structure of the two chapters is virtually the same: theological warrant, derived argument, practical directives, but it is varied in part by a chiastic arrangement. The most important point to be made is that the theology which undergirds the chapters relating to the collection for Jerusalem flows directly from chs. 1–7 and derives from a Pauline view of office and community. Especially noticeable is the theocentric orientation which views the collection as a sign of

God's grace to the church (8.1) and parallels Christ's giving of himself to his people with the challenge of responding to the needs of the poor in like manner (8.8). It is only when the collection is viewed in terms of psychological strategy that the tension with chs. 10–13 is thought to be intolerable.

V. The Canonization of the Corinthian Correspondence

Our analysis has defended a different compositional development for the two canonical letters to the church at Corinth. We have argued for the virtual identity of I Corinthians with the original letter of Paul, but for a complex redactional process of II Corinthians in which the present canonical letter was formed from a collection of once independent writings. Moreover, the patristic evidence seems to confirm that the process by which the two letters were accorded canonical status also differed (cf. the primary and secondary evidence collected by Bornkamm, 187ff.). In brief, I Corinthians was known and widely cited by the Apostolic Fathers, particularly by Clement, whereas II Corinthians appears unknown until the clear reference in Marcion, even when the arguments of the Fathers would have been greatly strengthened by an appeal to the letter.

In my judgment, the difference in the history of the formation and ecclesiastical reception of the two letters reflects the growth of a consciousness of canon within the early Christian church. The objection has often been raised against redactional theories of the Pauline letters that such an editorial activity is without parallel among the other collections of Hellenistic letters. Although the truth of this axiom has been challenged, the major point to be made is that the early church's development of a canonical collection of authoritative scripture is without a close analogy among the Hellenistic letter collections (cf. Bornkamm, 198). The growth of this canon consciousness accounts for the difference in the handling of the two letters of Paul. It also explains why the Corinthian correspondence was canonized in the form of two separate letters and not just one. By the turn of the second century, Paul's occasional letters had increasingly been assigned a continuing authoritative status, and were being assembled into an expanding corpus. Within this context, independent letters and fragments were joined into a new composition largely from the conviction that their authority transcended the original situation to which they were first delivered.

Finally, the question needs to be raised to what extent the two Corinthian letters now constitute one unified canonical context. We have already discussed the injurious effect on exegesis when the canonical categories were interpreted in strictly historical terms. What then is the genuine relationship between the two letters within the Pauline corpus?

In spite of the important discontinuities on the historical plane—different opponents, new issues, contrasting tones—the continuity of theological witness, which was hammered out in reaction to the concrete problem of the one historic church, unites the letter within the larger, often disparate corpus. The defence of Paul's apostolic office, the christological grounding of his future hope, and the characterization of the Christian life as lived between the old and the new ages, join the two very different epistles into a profound canonical unity, which context serves mutually to enrich the parts.

15

GALATIANS

Commentaries

C. J. Ellicott, 1854
J. B. Lightfoot, 1865, ¹⁰1890
W. M. Ramsay, ²1900
A. Williams, CB, 1910
E. D. Burton, ICC, 1920
T. Zahn, KNT, ³1922
M.-J. Lagrange, ÉB, ³1926
G. S. Duncan, MNTC, 1934
O. Kuss, RNT, 1940
J. A. Allan, TB, 1951
H. N. Ridderbos, NICNT, 1953
R. Bring, ET 1961
H. W. Beyer, NTD, ⁸1962

J. Bligh, 1969
D. Guthrie, NCeB, 1969
H. Schlier, MeyerK, ¹⁴1971
H. Lietzmann, HNT, ⁴1971
P. Bonnard, CNT, ²1972
A. Oepke, J. Rohde, THKNT, ³1973
D. Lührmann, ZBK, 1978
H. D. Betz, Herm, 1979
J. Becker, NTD, ⁴1981
F. Mussner, HTKNT, ⁴1981
C. Cousar, InterpC, 1982
F. F. Bruce, NICNT, 1982

Bibliography

C. K. **Barrett**, 'The Allegory of Abraham, Sarah, and Hagar in the Argument of Galatians', *Rechtfertigung, FS E. Käsemann*, ed. J. Friedrich, Tübingen 1976, 1–16; W. **Bauer**, *Orthodoxy and Heresy*, ET London and Philadelphia 1971; J. C. **Beker**, *Paul the Apostle*, ET Philadelphia and 1980, 23–131; H. D. **Betz**, 'Spirit, Freedom, and Law: Paul's Message to the Galatian Churches', *SEA* 39, 1974, 145–60; 'The Literary Composition and Function of Paul's Letter to the Galatians', *NTS* 21, 1974/5, 353–74; 'In Defense of the Spirit: Paul's Letter to the Galatians as a Document of Early Christian Apologetics', *Aspects of Religious Propaganda in Judaism and Early Christianity*, ed. E. Schüssler Fiorenza, Notre Dame 1976, 99–114; U. **Borse**, *Der Standort des Galaterbriefes*, BBB 41, 1972; R. **Bring**, 'Der Mittler und das Gesetz. Eine Studie zu Gal.3,20', *KuD* 12, 1966, 292–309; F. F. **Bruce**, 'Galatian Problems: 1. Autobiographical Data', *BJRL* 51, 1968/9, 292–309; 'Galatian Problems: 2. North or South Galatians?', ibid.52, 1969/70, 243–66; 'Galatian Problems: 3. The "Other Gospel" ', ibid. 53, 1970/1, 253–71;

'Galatian Problems: 4. The Date of the Epistle', ibid. 54, 1971/72, 292–309; R. **Bultmann**, 'Zur Auslegung von Galater 2, 15–18' (1952), reprinted *Exegetica*, Tübingen 1967, 394–99; T. **Callan** , 'Pauline Midrash: The Exegetical Background of Galatians 3:19b', *JBL* 99, 1980, 549–67; N. A. **Dahl**, *Das Volk Gottes* (1941), reprinted Darmstadt 1963, 212–17; 'The Atonement – An Adequate Reward for the Akedah? (Ro 8:32)', *Neotestamentica et Semitica, Studies in Honour of M. Black*, ed. E. E. Ellis and M. Wilcox, Edinburgh 1969, 15–29; reprinted *The Crucified Messiah*, Minneapolis 1974, 15–29; 'Widersprüche in der Bibel, ein altes hermeneutisches Problem', *StTh* 25, 1971, 1–19; ET 'Contradictions in Scripture', *Studies in Paul*, 159–77.

G. **Ebeling**, *Die Wahrheit des Evangeliums. Eine Lesehilfe zum Galaterbrief*, Tübingen 1981; J. **Eckert**, *Die urchristliche Verkündigung im Streit zwischen Paulus und seinen Gegnern nach dem Galaterbrief*, BU 6, 1971; C. E. **Faw**, 'The Anomaly of Galatians', *BR* 4, 1960, 25–38; W. **Foerster**, 'Abfassungzeit und Ziel des Galaterbriefes', *Apophoreta, FS E. Haenchen*, ed. W. Eltester, BZNW 30, Berlin 1964, 135–41; E. **Grässer**, 'Das eine Evangelium. Hermeneutische Erwägungen zu Gal 1,6–10', *ZTK* 66, 1969, 306–44; W. **Grundmann**, 'Die Häretiker in Galatien', *ZNW* 47, 1956, 25–66; E. **Güttgemanns**, *Der leidende Apostel und sein Herr*, FRLANT 90, 1966; F. **Hahn**, 'Das Gesetzesverständnis im Römer- und Galaterbrief', *ZNW* 67, 1976, 29–63; A. E. **Harvey**, 'The Opposition to Paul', *StEv* IV, TU 102, 1968, 319–332; J. G. **Hawkins**, *The Opponents of Paul in Galatia*, Diss. Yale 1971; R. B. **Hays**, *The Faith of Jesus Christ: An Investigation of the Narrative Substructure of Galatians 3:1–4:11*, SBLDS 56, Chico 1983; A. **Hilgenfeld**, 'Zur Vorgeschichte des Galaterbriefes', *ZWTh* 27, 1884, 303–43; K. **Holl**, 'Der Streit zwischen Petrus und Paulus in Antiochien und seine Bedeutung für Luthers innere Entwicklung', *GA* III, Tübingen 1928, 134–46; R. **Jewett**, 'The Agitators and the Galatian Congregation', *NTS* 17, 1970/71, 198–211; P. **Jung**, 'Das paulinische Vokabular in Gal 3,6–14', *ZTK* 74, 1952, 439–49.

M. **Kähler**, *Der Brief des Paulus an die Galater*, Halle ²1884; K. **Kertelge**, 'Zur Deutung des Rechtfertigungsbegriffs im Galaterbrief', *BZ* 12, 1968, 211–22; G. **Klein**, 'Galater 2,6–9 und die Geschichte der Jerusalemer Urgemeinde', *Rekonstruktion und Interpretation*, Munich 1969, 99–128; H. **Koester**, 'Gnomai Diaphoroi: The Origin and Nature of Diversification in the History of Early Christianity', *Trajectories through Early Christianity*, Philadelphia 1971, 114–57; J. **Knox**, 'Galatians, Letter to the', *IDB*, II, 1962, 338–43; K. **Lake**, *The Earlier Epistles of St Paul*, London ²1914; J. **Lambrecht**, 'The Line of Thought in Gal. 2, 14b–21', *NTS* 24, 1977/78, 484–95; O. **Linton**, 'The Third Aspect: A Neglected Point of View, a Study in Gal. I–II and Acts IX and XV', *StTh* 3, 1949/50, 79–95; I. **Lönning**, 'Paulus and Petrus: Gal 2, 11ff. als kontroverstheologisches Fundamentalproblem', *StTh* 24, 1970, 1–69; D. **Lührmann**, *Das Offenbarungsverständnis bei Paulus und in den paulinischen Gemeinden*, WMANT 16, 1965; 'Tage, Monate, Jahreszeiten, Jahre (Gal 4,10)', in *Werden und Wirken des Alten Testaments, FS*

C Westermann, ed. R. Albertz, Göttingen und Neukirchen-Vluyn 1980, 428–55; W. **Lütgert**, *Gesetz und Geist: Eine Untersuchung zur Vorgeschichte des Galaterbriefs*, BFChTh 22.6, 1919; D. J. **Lull**, *The Spirit in Galatia: Paul's Interpretation of Pneuma as Divine Power*, SBLDS 49, Chico 1980; A. J. **Malherbe**, 'Ancient Epistolary Theorists', *Ohio Journal of Religious Studies* 5, 1977, 3–77; T. W. **Manson**, 'St Paul in Ephesus: (2) The Problem of the Epistle to the Galatians', *BJRL* 24, 1940, 59–80; reprinted *Studies in the Gospels and Epistles*, Manchester and Philadelphia 1962, 168–89; O. **Merk**, 'Der Beginn der Paränese im Galaterbrief', *ZNW* 60, 1969, 83–104; P. S. **Minear**, 'The Crucified World. The Enigma of Galatians 6,14', *Theologia Crucis—Signum Crucis, FS E. Dinkler*, ed. C. Andresen and G. Klein, Tübingen 1979, 395–407; J. **Munck**, *Paul and the Salvation of Mankind*, ET London and Richmond 1959, 87–134; F. **Mussner**, *Theologie der Freiheit nach Paulus*, Freiburg 1976.

J. C. **O'Neill**, *The Recovery of Paul's Letter to the Galatians*, London 1972; F. **Overbeck**, *Über die Auffassung des Streits mit Petrus in Antiochen (Gal 2,11ff.) bei den Kirchenvätern*, Basel 1877; reprinted Darmstadt 1968; J. **Roloff**, *Apostolat – Verkündigung – Kirche*, Gütersloh 1965; J. H. **Ropes**, *The Singular Problem of the Epistle to the Galatians*, London and Cambridge, Mass. 1929; J. T. **Sanders**, 'Paul's Autobiographical Statements in Galatians 1–2', *JBL* 85, 1966, 335–43; W. **Schmithals**, 'The Heretics in Galatia', ET *Paul and the Gnostics*, London and Nashville 1972, 13–64; *Gnosticism in Corinth*, Nashville and New York ²1971; G. **Stählin**, 'Galaterbrief', *RGG* ³II, 1958, 1187–9; A. **Strobel**, 'Das Aposteldekret in Galatien. Zur Situation von Gal I und II', *NTS* 20, 1973/4, 177–90; P. **Stuhlmacher**, *Das paulinische Evangelium, I: Vorgeschichte*, FRLANT 95, 1968; J. B. **Tyson**, 'Paul's Opponents in Galatia', *NovT* 10, 1968, 241–54; ' "Works of Law" in Galatians', *JBL* 92, 1973, 423–31; P. **Vielhauer**, 'Gesetzesdienst und Stoicheiadienst im Galaterbrief', *Rechtfertigung, FS E. Käsemann*, ed. J. Friedrich, Tübingen 1976, 543–56; K. **Wegenast**, *Das Verständnis der Tradition bei Paulus und in den Deuteropaulinen*, WMANT 8, 1962, 32ff.; U. **Wilckens**, J. Blank, 'Was heisst bei Paulus: "Aus Werken des Gesetzes wird kein Mensch gerecht" ', *Ev.-Kath. Kommentar zum Neuen Testament* (Vorarbeiten 1), Neukirchen-Vluyn 1969, 31ff.; R. M. **Wilson**, 'Gnostics in Galatia?', *StEv* IV, TU 102, 1968, 358–67; W. **Wuellner**, 'Paul's Rhetoric of Argumentation in Romans', *CBQ* 38, 1976, 330–51; reprinted K. Donfried, ed. *The Romans Debate*, 152–74.

It seems wise to begin the analysis of Galatians with a review of some of the critical problems of the book, and to place a suggested canonical approach in the context of the contemporary discussion in order to bring the issues at stake into sharpest focus. At times features of the modern debate will appear as mere foils of the canonical reading, but more often the insights of critical scholarship will be accepted and exploited, usually within a different hermeneutical framework.

I. Form and Function of the Letter

There is the widest possible consensus that the letter to the Galatians is a genuine letter of Paul, even written in his own hand to address a specific historical situation. Again, it appears likely that the present form of the letter within the canonical collection—a possible exception could be 2.7f.—is virtually identical with Paul's original composition. Moreover, it has been long recognized that Paul follows some of the conventions of Hellenistic letter writing, especially in his use of a praescript and conclusion, although it has been traditionally thought that these typical features were less pronounced in Galatians than in some of his other epistles. The debate over the structure of the letter continues, but a modification of Lightfoot's broad threefold division has been widely accepted (Williams, Oepke, Kümmel, etc.): 1.11(12)–2.21 = narrative, apologetic; 3.1–5.12 = argumentative, doctrinal; 5.13–6.10 = hortatory.

Within very recent times the form-critical question regarding the form and function of the letter—Paul Schubert's language—has entered a new phase, particularly in the emphasis on the rhetorical nature of Paul's argumentation by W. Wuellner and H. D. Betz, among others. The new concern is to go beyond an analysis of the epistolary conventions of genre criticism. The methods of Wuellner and Betz are not identical. The former attempts to bring the insights of modern rhetorical analysis which is akin to structuralism to bear on interpretation. The latter seeks, largely through historical analysis, to determine how Paul's argumentation was influenced by ancient Graeco-Roman rhetorical tradition, which he reconstructs from Quintilian, Cicero, and others. Since Betz has written a programmatic essay (*NTS* 21) and a major new commentary on Galatians, his position will form the basis for a critical evaluation.

Betz characterizes Galatians as an example of the 'apologetic letter' genre. In his essay and commentary he attempts to show in detail the similarity of Galatians to forms of traditional rhetoric and to demonstrate the similar rhetorical functions of the parts of the letter. The letter has a praescript (1.1–5) and a postscript (6.11–18) which contains the three conventional parts of the *peroratio*. The body of the letter begins with an *exordium* (1.6–11) which supplies the 'facts' that occasioned the letter, but are formulated with a partisan bias. The *exordium* is followed by the narrative (1.12–2.14) which is an exposition of the events supposed to have occurred. The decisive section is the *probatio* (3.1–4.31) which then presents the 'proof' of the argument. Throughout his exposition Betz stresses that the form and rhetorical function belong together and are to be interpreted in the light of ancient epistolography.

One cannot fault Betz in principle for his use of literary parallels to interpret the form and function of Paul's letter. The issue turns on how well the analogies are drawn and whether his thesis illuminates or obfuscates the biblical text. At the outset, it is difficult to determine the exact relationship between a text and a rhetorical tradition in Betz's application. Is it on a conscious or unconscious level? Is it a polemical or irenic relationship? Is the dependency a loose or tight one? It is one thing to suggest that recognition of Paul's cultural background aids in interpreting his letter, but quite another to argue that he has been deeply influenced by traditional Greek rhetoric. However, the truism of recognizing Paul's milieu is not what Betz is proposing. Rather, he is arguing that Paul is using a conscious rhetorical strategy as a schooled art of persuasion, and failure of the modern interpreter to recognize this device leads to misunderstanding his letter to the Galatians.

There are several different issues involved in evaluating Betz's thesis. The first problem concerns his assumption that Hellenistic letters function according to set rules of rhetoric which can be analysed within an established epistolographic system. However, the exact relationship between the standard manuals of Greek rhetoric and the actual practice of letter writing is a subtle one, as A. Malherbe has conclusively demonstrated. Certainly letters were influenced by rhetorical conventions, but two different kinds of material are involved in the theoretical discussions of the manuals and in the collections of sample letters. By identifying the two and imposing the whole theoretical system on the letters of Paul, Betz is building a construct which far exceeds the evidence. A further judgment on this issue lies beyond the competence of this writer and must be debated by the experts. However, the problem is of such importance as to threaten Betz's entire enterprise.

The second problem is more obvious and Betz faces it head-on. He writes: 'Rhetoric, as antiquity understood it, has little in common with the truth, but it is the exercise of those skills which make people believe something to be true' (*Galatians*, 24). The problem, of course, is to reconcile the use of such a psychological strategy with the motivation of the apostle. In response, Betz resorts to a very curious argument. Because Paul pronounces a conditional blessing upon those who remain loyal to the Pauline gospel, his letter assumes the literary function of being the carrier of blessing and curse. Betz designates it a 'magical letter', and claims it as another genre among ancient letters. Consequently, Paul does not simply rely on the rhetorical art of persuasion and its system of argumentation, but he has introduced the dimension of magic, which confronts the community automatically with judgment.

I think it is apparent that Betz's argument is here very weak. Not only is the category of 'magical letter' in itself highly suspect, but its application to Galatians is tenuous in the extreme. Betz's rhetorical construal runs in the face of Paul's ministry and the expressed purpose of the letter. Moreover, by posing his theory of rhetorical function Betz has skewed the real exegetical questions regarding rhetorical function and Paul's intentionality. In sum, in spite of much learning and some excellent detailed insights, his theory is a massive *tour de force* which largely obfuscates the reading of the canonical text.

There is a second major exegetical issue also relating to the form and function of Galatians, which has recently been raised by Nils Dahl ('Contradictions', *Studies in Paul*). He argues that the key to Galatians 3, and in some respects to the entire letter, lies in recognizing that Paul is making use of traditional rabbinic hermeneutics. Dahl argues that there is a traditional rabbinic rule going back to Hillel for treating two contradictory passages of scripture, according to which each must be maintained as equally valid in its respective context. 'The whole train of thought in Gal.3:10–12 rests on the presupposition that Hab. 2:4 and Lev. 18:5 contradict each other' (170). Accordingly, Paul's major problem lies in his solution of upholding the two contradictory passages, which he does by construing the entire law of Moses as a provisional, interim arrangement, which was valid for the pre-messianic period.

In my judgment, Dahl's interpretation of Galatians 3 is not fully convincing. First, in terms of the larger context of ch.3, vv. 10–12 serve as a negative argument against justification by the law and buttress the positive thesis of v. 7 that Abraham was justified by faith

(Oepke, Schlier, Betz). Secondly, Paul is contrasting faith and law as being opposed to each other in principle. He is not reading Hab.2.4 and Lev. 18.5 as being contradictory passages. Although logically the two passages do contradict, Paul is not reading Leviticus in this manner, but rather only to illustrate his thesis of opposing principles. Both passages provide a warrant for his one point: justification by faith. In sum, the contradiction is on a different level in Paul's argument from that envisioned by Dahl. For Paul two different principles of salvation are involved, and the issue is not analogous to the textual situation which rabbinic hermeneutics sought to address in midrash.

However, our real concern for reviewing Dahl's argument lies in pursuing certain basic hermeneutical problems which his essay has raised. What is the relation between original exegetical techniques employed by the biblical writer and the later hearing of the epistle by readers who no longer understand them? If one argues that the original context is normative, then a later canonical reading is completely dependent upon recovering this context by means of historical critical reconstruction along with all the ensuing problems. Conversely, if one argues that recovering the original intentionality carries no exegetical significance for a canonical exegesis because the later community of faith provides its own context, this decision not only robs critical research of its meaning, but appears to destroy the normative role of the historically conditioned, ancient canonical text.

Using Dahl's argument as an illustration, I would like to contend that there is a direction out of this hermeneutical impasse. The initial goal of exegesis of scripture is to discern its canonical shape, that is to say, to understand how the biblical text functions in bearing witness to its kerygmatic content. Critical scholarship can play a positive role in discerning the canonical shape, but its role is not to substitute an original reading in place of a canonical.

Specifically in terms of Galatians 3, Dahl has sharpened the exegete's perception by focusing on the issue of contradiction in the light of ancient rabbinic tradition. Theoretically it would have been possible that Paul was employing an historically conditioned ancient exegetical technique which had been either forgotten or misunderstood by later readers. Historical critical research would then have greatly aided in recovering the canonical shape of the passage which had incorporated rabbinic hermeneutics into its witness. The critical exegetical test would turn on the abililty of a critical reading to illuminate the actual canonical text, rather than some earlier historical level lying behind the biblical text itself. Moreover, an additional criterion would lie in determining the level of continuity between a fresh critical reading and the larger canonical function of the book for a community of faith. This is to say, it is constitutive of the function of canon that it renders its material by various means in order to address an ongoing community of faith. It is without analogy to find the essential key to a whole book to have been lost in some time-conditioned aspect of the literature which had been misunderstood from the beginning.

Again, in terms of Galatians, an understanding of the argument of Paul in Galatians 3 does not depend on recovering a lost rabbinical key. The canonical text does not function as Dahl reconstructs it. However, he has illuminated the background of the text. His research into the phenomenon of biblical contradiction does aid in seeing how Paul was at pains to reconcile the law and the promise of God. One's perception is sharpened in reading the canonical text which is not dependent on a lost key, but which stands in continuity with a larger canonical function of the letter in addressing a continuing community of faith in its own historical context.

II. The Letter's Occasion, Protagonists, and Recipients

It is not our present concern to review the lengthy debate on the exact occasion of Paul's letter and its historical recipients. As is well known, two different theories seek to interpret more precisely the meaning of the term Galatia. The South Galatian theory (or province), which is defended by W. Ramsay and T. Zahn, refers the term to the churches founded in Pisidia and Lycaonia on the so-called first missionary journey (Acts 13.14). The North Galatian theory (or territory), which is held by Lightfoot and Kümmel, among others, locates the recipients in the district of Galatia (Acts 16.6). A decision on the issue directly affects the dating of the latter. The South Galatian theory would tend to date the letter early, whereas the North Galatian theory would put it toward the end of the third missionary journey. Within recent years the majority appears increasingly to favour the North Galatian theory. From a hermeneutical perspective this debate would be an example of information which was assumed in the original historical situation, but subsequently was no longer precisely understood.

A far more important, and yet equally difficult problem concerns the question of the opponents of Paul against which he has directed his letter. Who are those who 'trouble' the Galatians (1.7), and 'want to pervert the gospel' (1.7), who seek to induce the churches to adopt circumcision (5.2; 6.12f.), obedience to the law (3.2; 5.4) and observance of festivals (4.10; 6.13, 16)? Traditionally the opponents have most often been described as the 'Judaizers', Christians usually but not always thought to be Jewish, who sought to impose the legal requirements of Judaism, especially circumcision as an essential element for salvation. However, a significant break with traditional exegesis was first proposed by Lütgert who argued that the libertine features of the opponents (5.13,16) suggest that Paul was actually fighting on two different fronts. His thesis was then radicalized by Schmithals who argued for seeing the opposition as Gnostic, Jewish Christians whose motivation was misunderstood by Paul. More recently a variety of compromise solutions have emerged which envision various forms of syncretism shared by both Jewish and Gentile Christians.

Because a similar problem has already occupied our attention in the discussion of I and II Corinthians, I can be brief. The hermeneutical issue at stake in this problem is how one uses the ability of modern critical research to bring the historical features of Paul's opponents into sharp focus, indeed, at times even sharper than it may have been for the apostle himself. One approach rests on the assumption that the clearer the historical focus becomes the better the interpretation of the biblical text. A new perspective provides the means of evaluating and even correcting the canonical text. Thus, Schmithals suggests that his rediscovery of Paul's opponents as Jewish Gnostics allows him correctly to assess the situation which Paul had misunderstood.

The canonical approach which I am proposing would rather suggest that the critical role of describing Paul's historical opponents could have genuine significance in interpreting certain features within the canonical text. However, the approach would avoid assuming that the witness of the apostle can be simply equated with historical reconstructions, even if more accurate historically. Paul's theological construal of the gospel to the churches of Galatia was written in response to a certain concrete historical situation and

incorporates historical features into his message. However, the
authoritative quality of this message lies in his bringing the content
of the gospel to bear on that situation affecting his churches. The
truth of his theological witness does not depend on the objective
accuracy of his historical knowledge. Rather, the significance of
Paul's relation to his opponents lies in his assessment of the theological dimensions of the disagreement. In Gal. 4.8f. Paul identifies
the Galatians' adoption of Jewish legalism with a return to serving
the elemental spirits of paganism. From the perspective of the history
of religions the analogy is misplaced. From the Pauline perspective
on the gospel, his identification formulates sharply the theological
implications involved. In sum, the canonical approach being suggested views the subject matter consistently from the perspective of the
canonical text, but uses extra-biblical evidence to aid in interpreting
the canonical intentionality. It recognizes that the subject matter of
the biblical text is not identical with common historical reality, but
it strives in principle neither to identify nor to isolate these two
spheres of reality.

Up to this point, the emphasis has fallen on trying to preserve the
integrity of the Pauline controversy with his opponents by resisting
any simplistic identification of his construal with objective historical
reality. However, the reverse attempt to sever Paul's description
from historical reality also poses a threat. It would have significant
theological implications for the study of Galatians if it could be shown
historically that Paul had basically misunderstood his opposition. If
his opponents had in fact not advocated the practice of circumcision
and were only speaking metaphorically, such a discovery would
certainly call into question Paul's witness. Of course, the example
chosen is extreme, but it would relate to the suggestion of Schmithals
and Marxsen (*Intr.*) who argue that Paul was fundamentally uninformed about the controversy. Actually there remains a large area
of historical agreement respecting Paul's opposition, and few would
contest that his antagonists were Christians who were attempting to
impose adherence to Jewish law as a requirement for salvation in
addition to faith.

III. The Canonical Function of the Letter

The basic canonical question at stake is to discern how a fully time-
conditioned letter which was written under severe stress in order to

address a specific historical situation in first-century Galatia could function as normative scripture for subsequent generations of Christians, namely for us. . . .

At the outset, there is agreement that the canonical function was not achieved for the epistle to the Galatians by literary redaction. The canonical form of the letter appears to be virtually identical with Paul's original composition. However, the context from which the letter was originally read and that of subsequent readers has changed. The canonical function is now tied to the peculiar shape of the literature through which the historical situation of the Galatians is now mediated. This statement is not to suggest that a literary context has replaced a historical, but that Paul's construal of the historical situation has become normative. The canonical text has incorporated history within its witness, and thus a crucial part of the exegetical task is to discern the particular function of the historical dimension, which is far from uniform throughout the Bible.

Paul's construal of the historical situation which provides the historical context is, first of all, highly selective and much narrower in scope than that in which the Galatian churches read his original letter. Although the canonical reader is made aware of certain tensions within the church, he is no longer privy to the full extent of the rivalry, nor of the relation among the various parties. For example, the reader is left uninformed on the relation between those once representing the strict Jewish wing before the apostolic conference (Acts 15), and those who became Paul's opponents in Galatia. Again, Paul's former relationship to his churches is sketched, but very briefly so as to focus on only certain aspects of his ministry.

Secondly, the canonical context provided by Paul is written from a highly subjective, personal perspective. His defence of his apostolic authority is made autobiographically (1.11ff.). His account of the conference in Jerusalem with the church leaders, which stands in considerable tension with Acts 15, is rehearsed in terms of its effect on his own ministry rather than as an agreement between the churches of Jerusalem and Antioch.

Finally, Paul's construal of the situation is continually set in analogy to Old Testament history (3.6ff.; 3.23ff.; 4.21ff.). A theological understanding of history has largely replaced viewing it in terms of a causal nexus of events. Paul confesses his astonishment at the quick desertion of his authority (1.6), but without pursuing the steps involved at great length, moves immediately to its theological implications. He argues his case by setting their historical situation in analogy to God's history with Abraham, and drawing the consequences.

To summarize the point: Although the original text of the letter to the Galatians has remained the same, the context in which the letter is read by later generations has changed from that of the original audience. Of course, there are large elements of continuity between the readings of the different communities of faith, but the importance of recognizing the distinctiveness of the canonical context over against the original should not be overlooked when seeking to discern the book's continuing theological function.

IV. Paul's Original Addressees and Subsequent Readers

On the basis of a change in commitment by the Galatian churches, Paul explains the threat of their action to the gospel. In the course of his argument he elaborates the positive nature of the Christian faith, especially in relation to justification, faith, and works of the law. The search for the canonical function of the letter requires a careful discerning of those elements which have been assigned by the letter to a unique and once-and-for-all role, and those which function as representative and typical for the Christian faith.

First, Paul argues that the errors of the Galatian churches pose an ontological threat to the gospel. The Galatians are historical representatives of an erroneous alternative offered by the law. They have embraced a way of salvation through works of the law which is opposite in principle from the faith in God who justifies the ungodly. Indeed, the law performed a pedagogical function in the plan of God before the coming of the Son, but to impose it on believers after Christ has won the world's redemption is to render his action meaningless (3.23ff.). The intensity and vehemence of the apostle's outbreak derive from the seriousness of the issue at stake. It also accounts for his absolute refusal to compromise. Faith and works stand juxtaposed in a massive 'either/or'. By grounding his argument in the faith of Abraham, Paul removes the debate from the sphere of merely contingent history. The Galatians have not just made a human misjudgment, but committed themselves to an alternative which severed their continuity with the father of the faith.

Although Paul is addressing a specific historical situation, he does it in terms of its being representative of an erroneous dimension of reality which a misuse of the law poses. The effect of Paul's argument is to involve the later reader of the canonical text with the same force as it did the original addressee. The alternative between faith and works reflects the same ontological issue for subsequent generations as it did for the Galatians. The canonical context allows for an easy translation of the representative role played by the Galatians into new historical situations by which to bear witness to recurring instances of the same essential threat to the truth.

Secondly, Paul's letter sets forth positively the truth of the Gospel which is constitutive of the Christian faith. He draws the implications of justification by faith in terms of freedom (5.1), walking in the Spirit (5.16), and love of neighbour (5.14). With little difficulty the biblical text effects an identification of the later reader with the apostle's appeal to the original recipients: 'For freedom Christ has set us free. Stand fast therefore . . .' (5.1). In addition, Paul's letter is characterized by formulations in terms of theological principles of the gospel: 'it is those of faith who are the sons of Abraham' (3.7). 'There is neither Jew nor Greek, slave nor free, male nor female, for you are all one in Jesus Christ' (3.28). 'In Jesus Christ neither circumcision nor uncircumcision is of any avail, but faith working through love' (5.6). By grounding his argument in the example of Abraham, the life of faith is freed from the contingencies of any one historical period. The promises which flow from faith are anchored in God's history which encompasses equally every successive generation of believers.

However, it is equally important to observe how Paul's letter bears witness to some events constituting the gospel which are not representative in nature, but unique and once-and-for-all in their effect on the Christian faith. 'When the time had fully come, God sent forth his son, born of woman, born under the law, to redeem those who were under the law . . . ' (4.4). Christ entered human history at a given moment and his redemptive work altered for ever and irreversibly God's relationship to humanity. Paul speaks of the new age which Christ ushered in through the unique death and resurrection of the Son (1.4). Although the apostle continues throughout all his epistles to wrestle with the theological problem associated with the Christian's appropriation of the death of Christ, never does the event itself become representative of human action, but it remains *sui generis* within the purpose of God.

There is yet another event which is unique and non-representative in Paul's epistles, namely his appointment as an apostle. The reason for the emotional defence of his apostleship against both internal and external attacks emerges with the greatest clarity in the first two chapters of Galatians.Paul grounds his authority upon direct revelation by God. His message is not derived from human tradition, but stems from divine disclosure. His office is not an exercise in personal power, but a special gift by which to bear testimony to the resurrection of Jesus Christ. The function of the Christian canon of Pauline letters is not to extend the office of the apostle, but rather to preserve for future generations the unique apostolic witness on which the Christian faith is established.

Much confusion has been engendered by the failure of critical biblical scholarship to understand the true nature of the canon's authority. J. C. Beker has recently written a serious book on Paul which seeks to illustrate on the basis of Romans and Galatians a dialectic in his theology between elements of contingency and coherence. However, Beker falls into a typical modern error by setting up contingency as the only viable theological alternative to viewing the New Testament as 'timeless doctrine'. The major point to be made is that the function of the Christian canon is to provide another alternative which avoids the impasse which Beker projects. Paul's letters have been preserved in a collection in which the original elements of contingency have been largely retained. However, the collection has been treasured by a community of faith, read in the context of the whole gospel, and shaped in various ways to guide their use for later generations of believers. Thus the canon has established its own dynamic, which when faithfully exercised, guides each future community through its own historicity into a living relation with the God and Father of Jesus Christ.

16

EPHESIANS

Commentaries

A. G. C. von Harless, ²1858
H. A W. Meyer, 1859
J. Eadie, ²1861
C. J. Ellicott, ³1864
H. von Soden, HCNT, 1891
H. Oltramare, 1891/2
T. K. Abbott, ICC, 1897
E. Haupt, MeyerK, ⁷1902
B. F. Westcott, 1906
J. A. Robinson, ²1907
G. G. Findlay, ExpB, ²1908
P. Ewald, KNT, ²1910
E. F. Scott, MNTC, 1930
F. C. Synge, 1941
M. Dibelius, HNT, ³1953
F. W. Beare, IB, 1953

C. Masson, CNT, 1953
H. Rendtorff, NTD, ⁷1955
J. A. Allan, TB, 1959
F. F. Bruce, 1961
E. Gaugler, ZBK, 1966
G. H. P. Thompson, CNEB, 1967
J. L. Houlden, Pel, 1970
H. Schlier, ⁷1971
C. L. Mitton, NCeB, 1973
J. Ernst, RNT, 1974
M. Barth, AB,I–II, 1974
J. Gnilka, HTKNT, ²1977
H. Conzelmann, NTD, ¹⁵1981
R. Schnackenburg, EKK, 1982
F. Mussner, ÖTK, 1982

Bibliography

J. A. **Allan**, 'The "In Christ" Formula in Ephesians', *NTS* 5, 1958/9, 54–62; C. P. **Anderson**, 'Who Wrote "The Epistle from Laodicea"?', *JBL* 85, 1966, 436–40; M. **Barth**, *The Broken Wall*, Chicago 1959; 'Die Parusie im Epheserbrief, Eph 4, 13', *Neues Testament und Geschichte, FS O. Cullmann*, ed. H. Baltensweiler and B. Reicke, Zürich and Tübingen 1972, 239–50; P. **Benoit**, 'L'unité de l'Église selon l'Épître aux Éphésiens', in *Studiorum Paulinorum Congressus*, I, Rome 1963, 57–77; 'Rapports littéraires entre les épîtres aux Colossiens et aux Éphésiens', *Neutestamentliche Aufsätze, FS J. Schmid*, ed. J. Blinsler, O. Kuss and F. Mussner, Regensburg 1963, 11–22; E. **Best**, 'Ephesians 1,1', *Text and Interpretation*, ed. E. Best and R. McL. Wilson, Cambridge 1979, 29–41; W. **Bieder**, 'Das Geheimnis des Christus nach dem Epheserbrief', *TZ* 11, 1955, 329–43; C. R. **Bowen**, 'The Place of

Ephesians among the Letters of Paul', *AnThR* 15, 1933, 279–99; R. E. **Brown**, *The Semitic Background of the Term 'Mystery' in the New Testament*, Philadelphia 1968; F. F. **Bruce**, 'St. Paul in Rome, IV. The Epistle to the Ephesians', *BJRL* 49, 1966/7, 303–22; H. J. **Cadbury**, 'The Dilemma of Ephesians', *NTS* 5, 1968/9, 91–102; G. B. **Caird**, 'The Descent of Christ in Ephesians 4,7–11', *St Ev* II, TU 87, 1964, 535–545; J. **Cambier**, 'La bénédiction d'Éphésiens 1,3–14', *ZNW* 54, 1963, 58–104; C. C. **Caragounis**, *The Ephesian Mysterion: Meaning and Content*, Lund 1977; H. **Chadwick**, 'Die Absicht des Epheserbriefes', *ZNW* 51, 1960, 145–53; C. **Colpe**, 'Zur Leib-Christi-Vorstellung im Epheserbrief', *Judentum – Urchristentum – Kirche, FS J. Jeremias*, ed. W. Eltester, BZNW 26, ²1964, 172–87; J. **Coutts**, 'Ephesians 1:3–14 and I Peter 1:3–12', *NTS* 3, 1956/7, 115–27; 'The Relationship of Ephesians and Colossians', *NTS* 4, 1957/8, 201–207; F. L. **Cross**, ed. *Studies in Ephesians*, London 1956.

N. A. **Dahl**, 'Adresse und Proömium des Epheserbriefes', *TZ* 7, 1951, 241–64; 'Christ, Creation and the Church', *The Background of the New Testament and its Eschatology, in honour of C. H. Dodd*, ed. W. D. Davies and D. Daube, Cambridge 1956, 422–43; 'Der Epheserbrief und der verlorene erste Brief des Paulus an die Korinther', *Abraham unser Vater, FS O. Michel*, ed. O. Betz, M. Hengel and P. Schmidt, Tübingen 1963, 65–77; 'Bibelstudie über den Epheserbrief', *Kurze Auslegung des Epheserbriefes*, Göttingen 1965, 7–83; 'Cosmic Dimensions and Religious Knowledge (Eph.3:18)', *Jesus und Paulus, FS W. G. Kümmel*, ed. E. E. Ellis and E. Grässer, Göttingen 1975, 57–75; 'Ephesians, Letter to the', *IDBSuppl*, 268f; R. **Deichgräber**, *Gotteshymnus und Christushymnus in der frühen Christenheit*, SUNT 5, 1967; G. S. **Duncan**, *St. Paul's Ephesian Ministry: A Reconstruction with Special Reference to the Ephesian Origin of the Imprisonment Epistles*, London 1929, New York 1930; J. **Ernst**, *Pleroma und Pleroma Christi*, BU 5, 1970; A. **Feuillet**, 'L'église plérôme du Christ d'après Éphésiens 1,23', *Nouvelle Revue Théologique*, Louvain 78, 1956, 449–72, 593–610; K. M. **Fischer**, *Tendenz und Absicht des Epheserbriefes*, FRLANT 111, 1973; D. **Flusser**, 'The Dead Sea Sect and Pre-Pauline Christianity', *Scripta Hierosolymitana* 4, 1958, 215–66.

M. **Goguel**, 'Esquisse d'une solution nouvelle du problème de l'épître aux Éphésiens', *RHPhR* 111, 1935, 254–85; 112, 1936, 73–99; J. **Gnilka**, 'Paränetische Traditionen im Epheserbrief', *Mélanges bibliques en hommage au B. Rigaux*, ed. A. Descamps et A. de Halleux, Gembloux 1970, 397–410; 'Das Kirchenmodell des Epheserbriefes', *BZ* 15, 1971, 161–84; 'Das Paulus-bild im Kolosser- und Epheserbrief', *Kontinuität und Einheit, FS F. Mussner*, ed. P.-G. Müller and W. Stringer, Freiburg 1981, 179–93; E. J. **Goodspeed**, *The Meaning of Ephesians*, Chicago 1933; 'Ephesians and the First Edition of Paul', *JBL* 70, 1951, 285–91; *The Key to Ephesians*, Chicago and Cambridge 1956; A. **Harnack**, 'Die Adresse des Epheserbriefes', *SAB* 1910, 696–709; P. N. **Harrison**, 'The Author of Ephesians', *St Ev* II, TU 87, 1964, 595–604; O. **Hofius**, ' "Erwählt vor Grundlegung der Welt" (Eph 1,4)', *ZNW* 62, 1971, 123–28; H. J. **Holtzmann**, *Kritik der Epheser- und Kolosserbriefe*, Leipzig 1872;

F. J. A. **Hort**, *Prolegomena to St Paul's Epistles to the Romans and the Ephesians*, London and New York 1895, 65–184; D. **Jayne**, ' "We" and "You" in Ephesians 1.3–14', *ExpT* 85, 1973, 151f.; E. **Kähler**, *Die Frau in den Paulinschen Briefen*, Zürich and Frankfurt 1960; E. **Käsemann**, *Leib und Leib Christi*, BHT 9, 1933; 'Epheserbrief', *RGG³*, II, 1958, 517–20; 'Ephesians and Acts', *Studies in Luke-Acts*, ed. L. E. Keck and J. L. Martyn, Nashville 1966, 288–97; 'The Theological Problem Presented by the Motif of the Body of Christ', ET *Perspectives in Paul*, London and Philadelphia 1971, 102–21; E. **Kamlah**, *Die Form der katalogischen Paränese im Neuen Testament*, Tübingen 1964; A. C. **King**, 'Ephesians in the Light of Form Criticism', *ExpT* 63, 1951/2, 273–76; J. C. **Kirby**, *Ephesians, Baptism and Pentecost. An Inquiry into the Structure and Purpose of the Epistle to the Ephesians*, London and Montreal 1968.

K. G. **Kuhn**, 'Der Epheserbrief im Lichte der Qumrantexte', *NTS* 7, 1960/61, 334–46; J. B. **Lightfoot**, 'The Destination of the Epistle to the Ephesians', *Biblical Essays*, London and New York 1893, 377–96; A. **Lindemann**, *Die Aufhebung der Zeit. Geschichtsverständnis und Eschatologie im Epheserbrief*, StNT 12, 1975; 'Bemerkungen zu den Adressaten und zum Anlass des Epheserbriefes', *ZNW* 69, 1976, 235–51; E. **Lohmeyer**, 'Das Proömium des Epheserbriefes', *ThBl* 5, 1926, 120–25; R. P. **Martin**, 'An Epistle in Search of a Life-setting', *ExpT* 79, 1967/8, 296–302; C. **Maurer**, 'Der Hymnus von Epheser als Schlüssel zum ganzen Brief', *EvTh* 11, 1951/2, 151–72; H. **Merklein**, *Das kirchliche Amt nach dem Epheserbrief*, SANT 33, 1973; *Christus und die Kirche. Die theologische Grundstruktur des Epheserbriefes nach Eph 2,11–18*, SBS 66, Stuttgart 1973; 'Zur Tradition und Komposition von Eph 2,14–18', *BZ* 17, 1973, 79–102; C. L. **Mitton**, 'Goodspeed's Theory Regarding the Origin of Ephesians', *ExpT* 59, 1947/8, 323–27; *The Epistle to the Ephesians: Its Authorship, Origin, and Purpose*, Oxford 1951; G. **Münderlein**, 'Die Erwählung durch das Pleroma-Bemerkungen zu Kol.1,19', *NTS* 8, 1962, 264–76; F. **Mussner**, 'Beiträge aus Qumran zum Verständnis des Epheserbriefes', *Neutestamentliche Aufsätze, FS J. Schmid*, ed J. Blinzler et al., Regensburg 1963, 185–98; *Christus, das All und die Kirche*, TThS 5, ²1968; W. **Nauck**, 'Eph.2,19–22 ein Tauflied?', *EvTh* 13, 1953/4, 362–71; D. E. **Nineham**, 'The Case against Pauline Authorship', *Studies in Ephesians*, ed. F. L. Cross, London 1956, 21–35; B. **Noack**, 'Das Zitat in Ephes.5,14', *StTh* 5, 1951, 52–64.

W. **Ochel**, *Die Annahme einer Bearbeitung des Kolosser-Briefes im Epheser-brief*, Würzburg 1934; E. **Percy**, *Die Probleme der Kolosser und Epheserbriefe*, Lund 1946; 'Zu den Problemen des Kolosser- und Epheserbriefes', *ZNW* 43, 1950/51, 178–94; P. **Pokorný**, *Der Epheserbrief und die Gnosis*, Berlin 1965; W. **Rader**, *The Church and Racial Hostility: A History of Interpretation of Ephesians 2, 11–22*, Tübingen 1978; A. E. J. **Rawlinson**, 'Corpus Christi', *Mysterium Christi*, ed. G. K. A. Bell and A. Deissmann, London and New York 1930, 225–44; J. M. **Robinson**, 'Die Hodojoth-Forme in Gebet und Hymnus des Frühchristentums', *Apophoreta, FS E. Haenchen*, ed. W. Eltester, BZNW 30, 1964, 194–235; A. **van Roon**, *Is Ephesians Authentic? An Investigation into the*

Authenticity of the Epistle of the Ephesians, NovTSuppl 39, 1974; H. **Sahlin**, 'Die Beschneidung Christi. Eine Interpretation von Eph 2,11–22', *Symbolae Biblicae Upsalienses* 12, Lund 1950, 5–22; J. P. **Sampley**, *'And The Two Shall Become One Flesh'. A Study of Tradition in Ephesians 5:21–33*, SNTSM 16, 1971; J. N. **Sanders**, 'The Case for Pauline Authorship', *Studies in Ephesians*, ed. F. L. Cross, London 1956, 9–20; M. **Santer**, 'The Text of Ephesians 1.1', *NTS* 15, 1968/9, 247f.; W. **Schenk**, 'Zur Entstehung und zum Verständnis der Adresse des Epheserbriefes', *Theologische Versuche* 6, 1975, 73–8; G. **Schille**, 'Der Autor des Epheserbriefes', *TLZ* 82, 1957, 325–334; H. **Schlier**, *Christus und die Kirche in Epheserbrief*, BHT 6, Tübingen 1930; J. **Schmid**, *Der Epheserbrief des Apostel Paulus. Seine Adresse, Sprache und literarischen Beziehungen*, BS 22.3–4, 1928; R. **Schnackenburg**, 'Gestalt und Wesen nach dem Epheserbrief', *Schriften zum Neuen Testament*, Munich 1971, 268–87; 'Christus, Geist und Gemeinde (Eph 4,1–16)', *Christ and Spirit in the New Testament: In honour of C. F. D. Moule*, ed B. Lindars and S. S. Smalley, London 1973, 279–96; S. S. **Smalley**, 'The Eschatology of Ephesians', *EvQu* 28, 1956, 152–7; F.-J. **Steinmetz**, 'Parusie-Erwartung im Epheserbrief?', *Bibl* 50, 1969, 328–36; K. **Wegenast**, *Das Verständnis der Tradition bei Paulus und in den Deuteropaulinen*, WMANT 8, 1962; K. **Weidinger**, *Das Problem der urchristlichen Haustafeln*, Leipzig 1928; *Die Haustafeln: ein Stück urchristlicher Paränese*, Leipzig 1928.

The book entitled Ephesians has emerged as a serious puzzlement to modern interpreters on several accounts. It has no specific addressee like the rest of the Pauline epistles, and has few features of a genuinely occasional letter. Again, it differs from the undisputed letters in style and content to such an extent as to cause many critical scholars to question its Pauline authorship. Finally, there is much unclarity regarding the letter's historical background and the actual purpose for which it was written. Because these are the questions on which recent critical scholarship has focused its attention, and to which a canonical approach must respond if it is to be taken seriously by the discipline, we shall begin with a more detailed examination of the current debate.

I. The Letter's Addressee

The first major problem turns on the issue of the book's addressee. Traditional exegesis, following the book's superscription and designation in 1.1, has understood the letter to be written for the church at Ephesus (cf. one of the last defences by Eadie). Yet this assumption runs immediately into major difficulties from the content of the letter itself. Although the book of Acts (18–20) records the long and intimate relationship between Paul and the Ephesian church (cf.20.17ff.), this epistle is characterized by its impersonal tone. Surprisingly no personal greetings whatever are offered. Clearly the writer has no direct acquaintance with his audience, but knows of their faith only by hearsay (1.15). Conversely, he is known by them also indirectly (3.2ff.). The conclusion appears unavoidable that the recipients of the letter were unknown to Paul. It was this evidence which forced Theodore of Mopsuestia to propose the unlikely thesis that Paul wrote to the Ephesians before he had first visited the church.

The textual evidence in the praescript (1.1) confirms the evidence derived from the letter's content (cf. Lightfoot, Abbott, Percy, 449ff.; Roon 72ff.). The words 'in Ephesus' are missing in the oldest Greek manuscripts of Vaticanus and Sinaiticus, and in the important minuscule 1789. They are also omitted from the texts used by Marcion, Tertullian, and Origen. On the basis of this evidence, there is a widespread agreement that the words in 1.1 are secondary.

In the light of this evidence a variety of different solutions have been proposed by which to resolve the problem of the original addressee of the letter. Several attempts to read the present Greek text without a local designation have been made ever since Origen, but they remain greatly strained. The stereotypical form of the praescript speaks against seeing any conscious attempt to distinguish between classes of saints. Nor have suggestions at textual emendation commended themselves. Because of Marcion's testimony and the note in Col.4.16, the theory has been proposed in various forms that the letter was originally destined for the church at Laodicea (Harnack), but the reasons given why this addressee, if original, would ever have been lost have not increased confidence in the theory (cf. Kümmel, *Intr.*, 353).

Perhaps the most popular modern theory, particularly among conservative scholars (e.g. Lightfoot, Hort, Zahn, Percy, Schlier), has been to view the letter as originally a circular letter intended for several communities. Using the background of Tychicus' impending visit (Col. 4.7; Eph. 6.21), it was conjectured that the original epistle had a space for the addressee which the messenger inserted at each occasion of reading the letter. To meet the objection that such a procedure was without any parallel in antiquity, Dahl offered an important modification of the encyclical theory ('Adresse', 244ff.). He argued that several copies of the original letter were made, each with a specific localization of the addressee. During the subsequent process of collecting the Pauline letters into a canonical corpus, a copy of the letter without an addressee had been used which had been preserved at Ephesus. He conjectures that this letter 'from Ephesus' was then misconstrued as being 'to Ephesus'.

Regardless of how one explains the present addressee, there has emerged a growing consensus that the present text derived from a complex historical process and that the earliest extant text reflects a stage within the canonical process rather than the original autograph.

II. The Problem of Authorship

The problem of the real authorship of the letter has remained a classic crux of critical scholarship since the early nineteenth century. In spite of the explicit self-claims for Pauline authorship (1.1; 3.1; 6.21f.), serious questions have continued to be raised which have not yet reached a final resolution. Indeed, it would seem that in recent years, in spite of the strong minority voices of Percy, Schlier, Roon, etc., the majority of critical scholars no longer support a direct Pauline authorship (Dahl, *IDB Suppl.*, Kümmel, Gnilka, Schelkle). What are the issues at stake?

First, it is generally agreed that the number of similarities of this letter with the undisputed letters of Paul are very great. Several themes of Ephesians have the closest parallels in the other Pauline writings: the description of unredeemed man ruled by the flesh, the role of the law, the privileged state of the Jews, the divine plan of salvation, and the nature of reconciliation. However, it is the close similarity with so many of Paul's letters which cuts both ways (cf. the exhaustive list by Goodspeed, *The Meaning of Ephesians*, 82ff.). Those who dispute the Pauline authorship contend that the parallels derive from an imitation of the apostle who would not have reproduced his earlier thought in such a way as to be more Pauline than Paul himself. Clearly the force afforded such arguments depends largely on the reader's prior stance.

Secondly, a more objective debate turns on evaluating the linguistic and stylistic evidence. (Abbott's commentary is still basic when supplemented by Percy.) Many of the same features which set

Colossians apart recur in Ephesians. One is struck by the extraordinary length of the sentences which exceed even those in Colossians (1.3–14, 15–23). There is a piling up of relative clauses (1.6–8, 2.2f.) and participial constructions (1.3,5,9,13). The frequent use of ἵνα clauses, infinitive constructions and prepositional expressions are singled out by both Abbott and Percy as unusual. Neither commentator would contend that these linguistic and stylistic features are unique to Ephesians and Colossians. Percy goes to great lengths to find parallels with passages of the homologoumena (202ff.). Rather, the issue focuses on the frequency and peculiarity of a usage which sets Ephesians apart from the characteristic style of the undisputed Pauline letters. How are these differences to be explained?

Thirdly, another issue which is closely related focuses on the literary problem of the relationship between Ephesians and the letter of Colossians. The similarity between the two letters has long been noticed, but it has been the contribution of modern critical scholarship to have investigated the problem in depth. Holtzmann's monograph (1872) offered an exhaustive description of the extent of the parallelism, and argued that the priority of relationship shifted back and forth between Colossians and Ephesians. He attempted to solve the problem on the literary level by means of a complex theory of interpolations and redactions. According to his theory, the author of Ephesians not only first imitated an original Colossians, but subsequently interpolated Colossians with material from Ephesians. Few have found the theory fully convincing.

More recent research has moved in two different directions. First, careful distinctions are made between the different types of contact. Parallelism of formal features within the praescript and conclusion is of a different order from overlapping terminology or concepts, and each area requires separate handling (cf. Gnilka, *Epheser*, 7ff.). Secondly, and more important, the solution to the problem is no longer restricted to the literary level, but the recognition of the role of tradition has shifted the nature of the debate. Much of Percy's research focuses on the traditional elements which underlie both books. Dahl ('Der Epheserbrief', 75f.) agrees with Flusser's important observation that the remarkable parallels between Ephesians and the literature of Qumran point to a common fund of tradition shared by Hellenistic communities of Jews and Christians ('The Dead Sea Sect'). As a result, most modern scholars are inclined to see a large element of common tradition in the two letters. However, this insight does not rule out the literary dimension which seems to point at times to seeing Ephesians as a secondary expansion of an earlier formulation in Colossians. Scholars remain divided on the extent to which this issue affects the decision regarding the authorship of Ephesians.

Of course, the problem of the traditional material underlying the Ephesian letter is not restricted to the relationship with Colossians. Much of the most exciting research in recent years has been in investigating the sources of the tradition upon which its author was dependent. Moreover, it is a fair characterization of the current debate to say that the divergence in modern interpretation lies in large measure upon one's understanding of the use of tradition.

The credit for raising the issue of the role of Gnostic material in Ephesians goes, above all, to Bultmann, and then to his students, Schlier and Käsemann. These scholars presented the challenge of reading Ephesians from the perspective of a mythological Gnostic system which presupposed a primordial redeemer figure whose descent from on high broke through the dividing wall, and who in his ascent through successive emanations gathered the members of his body to himself in a cosmic unity. That a consistent and coherent context emerged from which to interpret many of the basic terms of the letter can hardly be denied (e.g. head, body, dividing wall, knowledge, mystery, manifold, etc.). Of course, the fierce debate which continues to be waged turns on whether or not this Gnostic context did, in fact, exert the influence on the New Testament author which has been proposed. The early defenders of Gnostic influence have modified somewhat their initial hypothesis over the years, particularly in the light of a clearer view of Gnosticism which has moved the debate away from the broad and speculative reconstruction of Reitzenstein. In addition, a steady stream of books and articles have appeared which attacked the hypothesis from a variety of perspectives (cf. Percy, Mussner, M. Barth), or offered corrections on specific exegetical issues (Dahl). The issue has not been fully resolved and the debate continues. However, there has emerged a growing consensus shared even by its defenders that the interpretation of the traditions underlying Ephesians cannot be restricted to Gnostic influence.

Considerable attention has been given to pursuing the role of hymnic, liturgical material, at times derived from baptismal rites, which have been discovered to play a major role (cf. Schille,

Deichgräber, Nauck, Barth). Again, the significant role of Old Testament traditions which have been filtered through rabbinic and sectarian Jewish circles has been increasingly recognized (e.g. Sampley). Finally, the discovery of the Qumran literature proved to be an invaluable aid in providing an access into the syncretic background shared by first-century Hellenistic religions which has only begun to be exploited (Kuhn, Flusser, Dahl).

Once again the broadening of the field of investigation into the problems of tradition has not directly affected the decision respecting the book's authorship. For example, Schlier can still defend Pauline authorship in spite of his Gnostic hypothesis. Still one gains the impression that the focus on the new areas of research has shifted scholarly interest away from the original critical issues and in fact rendered them far less significant for the exegetical task. Moreover, the basic hermeneutical issues raised by Schlier's interpretation are hardly affected by his defence of the Pauline authorship of the letter.

Finally, and perhaps the crucial issue in determining the authorship of the letter, has to do with the evaluation of the theological perspective of Ephesians in relation to Pauline theology. As always, Käsemann has been the most aggressive in hurling down the gauntlet. 'Here the gospel is domesticated. . . . Christology is integrated with the doctrine of the church. . . .' (*Jesus Means Freedom*, 89). For Käsemann the main concern of the author of Ephesians, in striking difference from Paul, lies in ecclesiology rather than christology, which is the characteristic feature of the transition to 'early catholicism'. However, even a generally conservative scholar such as Kümmel can assert categorically: 'the theology of Ephesians makes the Pauline composition of the letter completely impossible. . . .' (*Intr.*, 360).

A variety of other theological differences between Ephesians and Paul are highlighted by those who contest the Pauline authorship. It is suggested that the expectancy of the imminent parousia has been replaced by the mission of the church to the world (Chadwick, 148). Again, the Pauline understanding of the church as a local manifestation has been expanded into a universal category with Christ envisioned as the head of the body. Finally, the role of the apostles as the foundation of the church is regarded as foreign to Paul's thinking.

However, once again the issue of the theological differences between the letter of Ephesians and the Pauline homologoumena extends far beyond the problem of authorship. Clearly there are theological differences reflected in Ephesians which must be addressed even by those scholars who defend the Pauline authorship. For example, it is significant that conservative scholars, such as Hort and M. Barth, are equally interested in recovering a sharp profile of the theology of Ephesians and not attempting to blur the lines of discontinuity (cf. Barth, *Ephesians* I, 220ff.).

To summarize the discussion regarding authorship, the critical issue at stake is how to explain the important elements of both continuity and discontinuity between the letter to the Ephesians and the uncontested Pauline corpus. On the one hand, a group of scholars continue to defend Pauline authorship as the most likely explanation of the book's innumerable problems. They argue that the letter's peculiar linguistic quality stems either from the book's unusual content, or from Paul's use of inherited liturgical material. They contest that the theological differences stand in crass contradiction to Paul and see them as a natural growth of ideas compatible with the undisputed letters. Finally, they argue that no projected pseudepigraphical situation is as plausible as the historical ministry of Paul in the years of his final imprisonment.

On the other hand, a group which has probably become the majority reject the direct authorship of Pauline authorship. At times this indirect relationship is explained in terms of a 'Pauline school' (Deutero-Pauline) with the emphasis falling on its pseudepigraphical function. Usually, it is argued that a post-Pauline period is reflected in the letter. These scholars find support for their evaluation in a consistent historical picture of the development of first-century Christianity into which Ephesians fits as a link in a trajectory (Bultmann, Koester).

III. The Purpose of the Letter

There is one last issue of importance in the current critical discussion of the book, namely, the purpose for which the book was written. Significantly, there is a considerable overlap in positions when describing the book's purpose among those who disagree on the question of authorship.

The issue of the author's purpose in writing the Ephesian letter is closely tied to the discussion of its form. There seems to be a rather firm agreement that it is not an occasional letter like the majority of Paul's correspondence. Several scholars question whether it should even be classed as a letter at all (Marxsen, *Intr.* 192). Käsemann describes it as a treatise merely clothed in the form of a letter (*RGG*[3], 517), and Schenk characterizes it as 'an edifying tractate' only using the pretence of being a letter (174). Schlier interprets the letter as belonging to a wisdom genre which offers a meditation on the mystery of Christ (*Epheser*, 21f.). Finally, and more illuminating, in my opinion, is Dahl's description which addresses both its form and rhetorical function. 'It belongs to a type of Greek letters – genuine and spurious – which substitute for a public speech rather than for private conversation. The epistolary purpose is to overcome separation and establish contact between sender and recipients . . . .' (*IDB Suppl*, 268).

Finally, the attempts critically to reconstruct the original purpose of the letter are very divergent, and demonstrate the complexity of the problem. Moreover, they are not all mutually exclusive theories. A number of scholars attempt to penetrate through the general language of the apostle and pinpoint a concrete historical problem in the life of the early church. Often the proposal focuses on the threat of a growing tension between Jewish and Gentile Christians which the author sought to meet in his appeal for church unity (Chadwick, Käsemann). Dahl suggested that the epistle was directed specifically to the recently baptized Gentile converts ('Adresse'). Others opt for a more general purpose such as that suggested by Lightfoot in which Paul sought 'to set forth the grand truths (of Colossians) in a broader form and in their more general relations' (394). Still others wonder whether there were several purposes and a broad front of issues which concerned the author (Gnilka, 47f.). For those scholars who defend the pseudepigraphical nature of the letter, an important purpose of the letter turns on the author's exercising the authority of the apostle in order to legitimate a theological point. However, since there is little interest in ecclesiastical structure in contrast, say, with the Pastorals, the attempt to find the object of the attempted legitimation, is more difficult and less convincing in effect.

One of the most ingenious theories which sought to resolve the purpose of the letter with great specificity was that of E. Goodspeed's so-called 'canonical' explanation (*The Meaning of Ephesians*). He argued that the author had been stimulated by the writing of Acts to try to recover the importance of Paul for the early church which had largely forgotten him. He therefore wrote the letter of Ephesians to serve as an introduction to the Pauline corpus. Goodspeed's theory explained brilliantly the writer's knowledge of the earlier Pauline letters, its peculiar style, and its generalizing, comprehensive content. However, in spite of its brilliance, the theory suffers from major problems so that even in the modified form given it by Mitton, it has very few defenders (cf. Schlier, 26ff.). There is no hint from within Ephesians itself that the letter served as an introduction to the corpus, nor did the book ever attain the first position in the ordering of the corpus. Equally serious is the assumption that Paul had passed into virtual oblivion and needed resuscitation (cf. the discussion in ch. 24 below).

To summarize up to this point: our intention in reviewing the critical debate on Ephesians is to sketch the broad range of issues which any responsible interpretation must address. The lines of continuity between the modern critical debate and our suggested canonical interpretation will be obvious, but it should also become clear that a different hermeneutical stance can alter the interpretation radically.

IV. The Canonical Shape of Ephesians

In his 'Bibelstudie' of Ephesians, N. Dahl first discusses briefly the usual historical critical problems associated with the letter. However, before he turns to his actual exegesis, he directs a sentence to his modern audience: 'We ought to read this letter today as addressed to us' (9). How is this possible? In what sense can an ancient epistle, written in Greek, to someone else, in a different age and situation, be said to address us? Is this simply a rhetorical gesture to elicit the reader's empathy which would apply equally well to the reading of Chaucer or Shakespeare? The answer is not obvious, and regardless of how one finally decides, the question lies at the heart of the problem of understanding the letter to the Ephesians as canon.

Basic hermeneutical issues are at stake as to how one approaches the biblical text. I disagree with those who feel that the appeal to the modern reader is simply a pious convention, left over from a past uncritical era, and more suitable for homilists than exegetes. Nor do I feel that the theological issue involved is to be restricted to a final stage of reflection, as if the question of the modern addressee could only properly be raised after the solid, objective task of historical interpretation had been completed. Rather, it seems to me an essential part of the descriptive task to seek to understand how this ancient letter was transmitted, shaped, and interpreted in order to render its message accessible to successive generations of believers by whom and for whom it was treasured as authoritative. The hermeneutical issue is therefore an integral part of the exegetical task and not merely a luxury for theologians.

For this reason it is our concern to address the basic issue in determining wherein the canonical function of Ephesians lies. The approach is not an anti-critical one, as if the review of historical scholarship were simply a foil, but a different way of posing the critical questions. A change in stance emerges clearly in the interpretation of Ephesians. Most critical scholars seem to assume that first one constructs a profile of the 'historical Paul', and then one determines to what extent one can or cannot include Ephesians within Pauline theology. Even among so-called conservative scholars the same historical assumptions are axiomatic. For example, A. van Roon writes: ' . . . the verdict of scholarship will decide the allotted place of the epistle within the framework of the New Testament as a whole. If the final verdict is that the work is not authentic . . . it will nevertheless have to be relegated to the periphery of the New Testament . . . if the contrary emerges . . . the results will be . . . to recognize it as a critical source of information' (1f.).

In my opinion, such an approach has turned the purpose of the New Testament canon on its head and badly misconstrued its theological function. The primary issue is not whether or not Ephesians is Pauline. The canonical process has already incorporated it within the Pauline corpus. Rather, the exegetical issue is to determine the effect which the inclusion of the letter has on its shape and on the understanding of the corpus. The canonical decision has rendered a theological judgment as to what constitutes the 'canonical Paul'. Although it remains a valid and important question to consider the relation between the 'canonical' and the 'historical' Paul, the two entities cannot be identified, nor can the latter determination establish the parameters of the former. The function of canon is to establish the shape of the vehicle through which the true Pauline witness to the gospel is made.

The critical study of Ephesians has pointed out correctly the many unusual features of this letter in terms of language, style, and content. Regardless of how one understands this indirect relation of Ephesians to the historical Paul, a point to be emphasized is that the apostle never becomes the object of the epistle's witness, but its subject. This stance towards the material emerges clearly from the praescript (1.1), in the body of the letter (3.1), and in its conclusion (6.21ff.). When Paul speaks of himself in 3.1ff., his witness functions to bind his office of apostle to the Gentiles with the divine plan of uniting Jews and Gentiles together in the same body. It is certainly possible, as many scholars feel, that the letter to the Ephesians reflects elements of a post-Pauline perspective (cf. 2.20, 3.2–11; 4.11–14). However, the use of the term pseudepigraphy runs in the face of the canonical function of the letter, not because of implying an indirect authorship, but by altering the function of the apostle from subject to object, from first person to third (cf. ch. 21 below). For the canonical approach being suggested, the issue remains open as how best to explain the historical factors which led to the peculiar shape of the letter. The use of an associate in prison or the intermediary role of a later 'Pauline school' are both possible options. Regardless of this decision, the canonical role of the letter is closely tied to the first person witness of the Apostle Paul, whose office legitimates his message.

As we saw earlier, there has been much discussion concerning the form of the letter to the Ephesians. The problem emerged because the occasional features which are so characteristic of Paul's other letters are missing. Yet the alternative of viewing the letter as a theological tractate is unattractive because it appears to describe an abstract discourse, which is foreign to the epistle and threatens to lose the specific hymnic and liturgical elements which constitute its real message.

Our study of the canonical process of shaping the Pauline corpus has sought to demonstrate that the form-critical distinction between an occasional letter and a theological tractate has been increasingly blurred. The effect has been to subordinate the different original forms of literature into vehicles for suitable theological witness. Whether one regards Ephesians as a letter or theological tractate is unimportant as long as these terms are given their content by the literature's actual function. In a real sense, Ephesians establishes a true canonical model for defining the nature of genuine theological reflection. Far from its being a detached, abstract exercise, the letter establishes the liturgical context for divine praise in theological reflection which moves from the indicatives of the gospel to concrete implications for Christian living in the world and which is grounded in God's present activity on behalf of his creation. It is basically to misunderstand the function of the letter when commentators characterize it as abstract because it lacks features of an occasional letter. Rather, in the context of the Christian faith the letter meditates on the concrete quality of God's historical salvation in Jesus Christ and develops a specific reponse commensurate with this revelation of divine grace (cf. Schlier, *Epheser*, 20).

One of the basic keys to the letter's canonical function lies in understanding the hermeneutical function of the epistle's peculiar addressee. Paul directs his letter, not to Gentile Christians in general, but to a particular group of believers (cf. Dahl, 'Adresse'). 1.13 makes clear that there are those new Christians who have been sealed in the Holy Spirit, and with whom the Apostle is unacquainted. The contrast between 'you' and 'us' is not one between Gentile and Jewish Christians, but between different generations of Christians.

The purpose of the letter is set forth in 1.15ff. Having heard of their faith and being deeply concerned for their welfare, the apostle sets out to explain what is the greatness of God's power in the community of believers 'according to the working of his great might which he accomplished in Christ' (vv. 19,20). Paul is desirous that the new generation of Christians understand the nature of God's present exercise of power in their lives according to the divine purpose which he accomplished in Christ and which encompasses the entire universe.

We have already reviewed the textual problem in 1.1 and seen that the oldest textual witness was without a local addressee. The present reference to the Ephesian church reflected a later canonical stage when the letter had been collected within the Pauline corpus. Whether or not the original letter once designated a specific congregation, the canonical form served to generalize the addressee in a manner commensurate with the content of the epistle, which is directed to the newly baptized in Christ. The subsequent addition of the designation 'to the Ephesians' should be regarded as a type of commentary by the collectors, which may well have confused the source of an exemplar of the letter with its original addressee. Be that as it may – and no theory of the origin of the reading is without some difficulty – the commentary can serve to confirm the canonical function and need not run in the opposite direction to engender confusion. If Paul directs his letter to the Ephesian church which he once knew so well, the reader of the epistle would be led to infer that the purpose of his letter must be to address that new generation of Ephesians about whose faith he had only heard secondhand. However, it is also important to recognize that this later interpretive concretizing of the tradition could engender confusion if the addressee is not related to the content of the letter. An obvious example of the danger is Theodore's attempt to construe the entire letter in the light of chronological consistency required by the Ephesian addressee and as a result to ride roughshod over the more evident intentions of the letter.

There are some important implications to be drawn from this description of the letter's canonical function. What distinguishes the Ephesian letter from the great majority of Pauline letters is that the canonical intention to shape the original letter in such a way as to render it accessible to later generations of believers did not take place on the redactional level. The textual expansion in 1.1 only confirms this basic point. Rather, it is reflected in the primary level of the composition, which is to say, that it derives from the author's own intention. The concern to address a new generation of Christians, unknown to Paul, is a small step removed from a growing consciousness of the role of the canon which performed a similar function. The point to be made is that the grounds for the subsequent canonical process extend back into the actual compositional level of the New Testament literature itself.

The writer of this epistle begins with an outpouring of blessing to God for the overwhelming riches of his grace which the church ('we') has experienced and which is rooted in the eternal decision of favour in Jesus Christ. God has revealed the secret of his decision which is even now being accomplished in a plan to unite all things under the one head in Christ, both in heaven and on earth. Moreover, this working out of God's purpose incorporates also those who have been newly baptized and have been sealed with the promised gift of the Holy Spirit (1.13f.).

Because of what God has done and continues to do in the counsel of his will through the Son, the writer seeks to instruct his readers in a fuller understanding of what God is about to bring to pass (1.19). He calls upon them to remember the change which has occurred in them through his power. The contrast between the 'then' and the 'now' is as radical as between death and life (2.1ff.). Using the language drawn from Jewish proselytism, he reinterprets the bringing near of those who once were far off (Isa.57.19) to refer no longer simply to Israel's exiles, but to the inclusion of the Gentiles within the household of God. The Old Testament functions to confirm that this plan extended back into the very beginning of Israel's history. The church is the visible sign of the new reality which God has achieved in Christ by uniting all things under his rule.

Paul is vitally concerned that the new generation of Christians understand the nature of their access to the Father (2.18; 3.12). He makes clear that the Spirit is the guarantee of the inheritance not yet possessed (1.14) even though they have already tasted of all the blessings in the heavenly places (1.3). The church is the vehicle by which the witness to God's manifest wisdom is made known, but the church is carefully defined as the body of which the head is Christ. The church has no reality or role apart from its Lord. It provides the witness to God's purpose in offering a visible sign to the new reality which God has brought into being through his son. The church is the testimony to the present work of God in creating a unity between Jew and Gentile. By its own life it bears witness to the oneness of all creation, but it does not itself control the power. It remains a vehicle of Christ at work as the body under the dominion of the head. In sum, the claim that ecclesiology has replaced christology in the letter to the Ephesians badly misconstrues the message of the book.

In the light of the canonical function of this letter, the use of the term 'early Catholicism' (*Frühkatholicismus*) as a pejorative category allegedly to describe the theology of Ephesians is extremely ill-chosen and only breeds confusion. On the one hand, the canonical role of Ephesians provides an explicit warrant within the Pauline corpus for integrally relating christology to ecclesiology. On the other hand, the letter provides a major check against any ecclesiastical claims of autonomy – whether Catholic or Protestant – which would seek to ursurp the absolute, direct, and abiding authority of Christ over his church.

Up to this point in the analysis we have described the epistle to the Ephesians in terms of indirect Pauline authorship. In fact, the major exegetical problems do not turn on deciding the question of authorship in a strictly historical sense. Rather, the central problem lies in evaluating the role and the validity of this extended witness of the apostle Paul which the canonical process has received, nourished, and shaped. It is significant to observe that the church did not canonize the process as normative, but rather the interpreted text. The role of canon does not consist in stifling the church's continued search in understanding the truth of the gospel, but rather it stakes out the arena in which the church confesses the Word of God has been and will be heard by the community of faith.

17

PHILIPPIANS

Commentaries

C. J. Ellicott, ³1865
J. B Lightfoot, ⁶1881
M. R. Vincent, ICC, 1897
E. Haupt, MeyerK, ⁷1902
W. Lueken, SNT, ³1917
M. Jones, WC, 1918
P. Ewald, KNT, ⁴1923
K. Barth, 1928 (ET 1962)
W. Michaelis, THKNT, 1934
M. Dibelius, HNT, ³1937
H. Michael, MNTC, ⁴1946
P. Bonnard, CNT, 1950
E. F. Scott, IB, 1955

J. J. Müller, NICNT, 1955
G. Heinzelmann, NTD, ⁷1955
E. Lohmeyer, MeyerK, ¹¹1956
K. Staab, RNT, ³1959
K. Grayston, CNEB, 1967
F. W. Beare, B/HNTC, ³1972
J. Ernst, RNT, 1974
R. P. Martin, NCeB, 1976
J.-F. Collange, CNT, ET 1979
G. Barth, ZBK, 1979
J. Gnilka, HTKNT, ³1980
G. Friedrich, NTD, ¹⁵1981

Bibliography

G. **Baumbach**, 'Die Frage nach den Irrlehrern in Philippi', *Kairos* NF 13, 1971, 252–66; E. **Best**, 'Bishops and Deacons: Phil. 1.1', *StEv* IV, TU 103, 1968, 371–6; G. **Bornkamm**, 'Der Philipperbrief als paulinische Briefsammlung', *Neotestamentica et Patristica. FS O. Cullmann*, ed. W. C. van Unnik, NovTSupp 6, 1962, 192–202; reprinted *GA* IV, Munich 1971, 195–205; 'Zum Verständnis des Christus-Hymnus Phil 2,6–11', *GA* II, Munich 1963, 177–87; C. O. **Buchanan**, 'Epaphroditus' Sickness and the Letter to the Philippians', *EvQu* 36, 1964, 157–66; G. **Delling**, 'Philipperbrief', *RGG* ³V, 1961, 335; S. **Dockx**, 'Lieu et date de l'épître aux Philippiens', *RB* 80, 1973, 230–48; G. S. **Duncan**, *St Paul's Ephesian Ministry: A Reconstruction with Special Reference to the Ephesian Origin of the Imprisonment Epistles*, London 1929; New York 1930; 'Were Paul's Imprisonment Epistles Written from Ephesus?', *ExpT* 67, 1955/6, 163–6; G. **Eichholz**, 'Bewahren und Bewähren des Evangeliums. Der Leitfaden von Phil 1–2', *Hören und Handeln, FS E. Wolf*, ed. H. Gollwitzer and H. Traub, Munich 1962, 85–105; V. **Furnish**, 'The

Place and Purpose of Philippians: III', *NTS* 10, 1963/4, 80–88; H. **Gamble**, 'The Redaction of the Pauline Letters and the Formation of the Pauline Corpus', *JBL* 94, 1975, 403–18; D. **Georgi**, 'Der vorpaulinische Hymnus Phil 2,6–11', *Zeit und Geschichte, FS R. Bultmann*, ed. E. Dinkler, Tübingen 1964, 263–93; O. **Glombitza**, 'Der Dank des Apostels. Zum Verständnis von Philipper IV 10–20', *NovT* 7, 1964/5, 135–41; J. **Gnilka**, 'Die antipaulinische Mission in Philippi', *BZ* NF 9, 1965, 258–76.

P. N. **Harrison**, *Polycarp's Two Epistles to the Philippians*, Cambridge 1936; 'The Pastoral Epistles and Duncan's Ephesian Theory', *NTS* 2, 1955/6, 250–61; O. **Hofius**, *Der Christushymnus Philipper 2,6–11*, WUNT, 1976; M. D. **Hooker**, 'Philippians 1,6–11', *Jesus und Paulus, FS W. G. Kümmel*, ed. E. E. Ellis and E. Grässer, Göttingen 1975, 151–64; G. **Howard**, 'Phil 2,6–11 and the Human Christ', *CBQ* 40, 1978, 368–90; J. **Jeremias**, 'Zur Gedankenführung in den paulinischen Briefen, 4. Christushymnus Phil.2.6–11', *Studia Paulina in honorem J. de Zwaan*, ed. J. N. Sevenster and W. C. van Unnik, Haarlem 1953, 146–54; R. **Jewett**, 'The Epistolary Thanksgiving and the Integrity of Philippians', *NovT* 12, 1970, 40–53; 'Conflicting Movements in the Early Church as Reflected in Philippians', ibid., 363–90; E. **Käsemann**, 'Kritische Analyse von Phil 2,5–11', *Exegetische Versuche und Besinnungen* 1, Göttingen 1967, 51–95; A. F. J. **Klijn**, 'Paul's Opponents in Philippians III', *NovT* 7, 1964/5, 278–84; H. **Koester**, 'The Purpose of the Polemic of a Pauline Fragment (Phil.III)', *NTS* 8, 1961/2, 317–32; O. **Linton**, 'Zur Situation des Philipperbriefes', *Acta Seminarii Neotestamentici Upsaliensis* 4, 1936, 9–21; E. **Lohmeyer**, *Kyrios Jesus. Eine Untersuchung zu Phil 2, 5–11, Sitzungsberichte der Heidelberger Akademie der Wissenschaften*, Phil.-Hist. Klasse 1928; reprinted Darmstadt [2]1961; W. **Lütgert**, *Die Vollkommenen in Philippi und die Enthusiasten in Thessalonich*, BFChTh 13, 1909.

B. S. **Mackay**, 'Further Thoughts on Philippians', *NTS* 7, 1960/1, 161–70; T. W. **Manson**, 'St Paul in Ephesus: The Date of the Epistle to the Philippians', *BJRL* 23, 1939, 182–200; R. P. **Martin**, *Carmen Christi. Philippians 2,6–11 in Recent Interpretation and in the Setting of Early Christian Worship*, SNTSM 4, 1967; B. **Mengel**, *Studien zum Philipperbrief*, WUNT II.8, 1982; W. **Michaelis**, *Die Gefangenschaft des Paulus in Ephesus und das Itinerar des Timotheus*, NTF 1.3, 1925; *Die Datierung des Philipperbriefs*, NTF 1.8, 1933; 'Teilungshypothesen bei Paulusbriefen', *TZ* 14, 1958, 321–26; O. **Michel**, 'Zur Exegese von Phil 2,5–11', *Theologie als Glaubenswagnis, FS K. Heim*, Hamburg 1954, 79–95; J. **Müller-Bardorff**, 'Zur Frage der literarischen Einheit des Philipperbriefs', *Wissenschaftliche Zeitschrift der Friedrich-Schiller-Universität 7 1957/8*, Gesellschafts- und Sprachwissenschaftliche Reihe 4, 591–604; J. **Murphy-O'Connor**, 'Philippiens (Épître aux)', *DBS* VII, 1966, 1211–33; 'Christological Anthropology in Phil. II,6–11', *RB* 83, 1976, 25–50; T. E. **Pollard**, 'The Integrity of Philippians', *NTS* 13, 1966/7, 57–66; B. D. **Rahtjen**, 'The Three Letters of Paul to the Philippians', *NTS* 6, 1959/60, 167–73; W. **Schmithals**, 'The False Teachers of the Epistle to the

Philippians', ET *Paul and the Gnostics*, London and Nashville 1972, 65–122; O. **Schmitz**, *Aus der Welt eines Gefangenen. Eine Einführung in den Philipperbrief*, Berlin ⁵1934; G. **Strecker**, 'Redaktion und Tradition im Christushymnus Phil 2,6–11', *Eschaton und Historie*, Göttingen 1979, 142–79.

Because many of the larger issues involved in interpreting a Pauline letter from a canonical perspective have already been treated in some detail in earlier chapters (e.g. I and II Corinthians, Galatians), this analysis can be more narrowly limited to problems specifically germane to Philippians.

I. The Modern Critical Debate

A variety of critical issues have dominated the modern critical study of Philippians. Beginning with Lohmeyer's essay in 1928 on the christological hymn in 2.6–11, a lively discussion has continued up to the present on the structure of the hymn, its pre-canonical form, the nature of its tradents, and its theological significance prior to and following its inclusion in the Pauline letter. Many of the most important New Testament scholars of the last generation have been involved (Jeremias, Käsemann, Bornkamm, etc.). Because there have been numerous accounts of this history of interpretation (Martin, Hofius), there is no need for a repetition.

The debate over the geographical location of Paul's imprisonment as the setting of the letter to the Philippians belongs to the larger question which we have already briefly encountered. The designation of Rome, Caesarea, and Ephesus as the place of the writing have been the major options discussed. Although the traditional identification of Rome still has some important defenders (Jülicher, *Einl.*, Beare), and Caesarea has been virtually eliminated as a possibility (Lohmeyer), increasingly a broad consensus is emerging in support of Ephesus (Delling, Bornkamm, Friedrich, Gnilka). Especially for those scholars who envision a series of letters between Paul and the Philippian church, the proximity of Ephesus is highly attractive. However, this issue and its implications for the interpretation of the epistle have been adequately discussed in the standard Introductions and commentaries and do not need to be again rehearsed (cf. Kümmel, Schenke, *Einl.*, Beare, Gnilka).

There are, however, two critical issues which are closely related to the problem of describing the canonical shape of the book and these will need a more detailed treatment. Within the modern discussion the two issues are frequently intertwined. The first issue has to do with the nature of Paul's opponents, the second with the literary unity of the epistle.

As we have frequently observed, there is a widely accepted axiom of Pauline research that the sharper the profile becomes of Paul's historical opponents, the better the interpretation of his letter. As a result, much attention has focused on determining as well as possible the nature of the opposition against whom the apostle offers his polemic. The problem is unusually difficult because of the complexity in the description of the opponents. At first in 1.15 Paul speaks of opponents who 'preach Christ' but 'out of partisanship', as if the battle were an internal one within the church. Later in 1.28 the opponents appear to be persecutors of the church who deserved only destruction. Then in ch.3 the attack against the opposition mounts in intensity. They are characterized as 'dogs', 'evil workers who mutilate the flesh', and Paul opposes them as seeking righteousness through the law, much after the pattern in Galatians. In addition, shortly thereafter he appears to confront a form of perfectionism. Finally, he describes those who live as 'enemies of the cross' whose 'God is their belly' and who 'glory in their shame' (3.19).

Scholars differ on whether Paul is fighting on one or two fronts. Some speak of an internal and an external conflict. A wide variety of different solutions have been proposed in an effort to understand the complexity of the descriptions. In spite of A. F. J. Klijn's characterization of the opponents simply as Jews, the majority of scholars sees a far more complex phenomenon as some form of Jewish-Christian syncretism. Schmithal's important essay portrays the enemy as representatives of an anti-Pauline, Jewish-Christian Gnosticism by which he is able to join the features of legal observance and libertarian practices in the one group. Koester modifies Schmithal's proposal by denying that there were also libertarians at Philippi. Still others feel that the opposition in Philippi must be related to those enemies in II Corinthians, and that a proper description must be drawn from features of both epistles (Gnilka). The additional issue at stake is whether the description of the opposition varies in the canonical form of the letter because of the different historical periods which are reflected in the several original letters which comprise the present composition.

We shall return to this issue as we attempt to sketch the lines of a canonical interpretation. Our dispute in this regard does not lie in the historical enterprise of describing Paul's opponents as such, but in the manner in which the information is used to interpret the present canonical epistle.

The second major issue turns on the problem of the unity of the letter. This problem has called forth the most heated debate during the last three decades. Although the apparent disunity of the letter to the Philippians has long been recognized, most of the major Introductions (Jülicher-Fascher, Michaelis, Feine), and critical commentaries prior to 1950 (Haupt, Dibelius, Lohmeyer) defended the book's unity. The sharp shift in tone and content were explained in a number of ways. Either one argued for a psychological fluctuation of the apostle, or from his special technique of dictating his letters, or in terms of a change in circumstances which occurred after the writer had begun his letter. Often one spoke of digressions or even of interpolations, but still held to the basic unity of one letter.

Quite suddenly there has been a dramatic shift in approach, and a consensus is growing which holds that the present canonical letter is a composite of probably three independent letters. Several important essays appeared almost simultaneously and largely independently of each other, which defended this thesis (Müller-Bardorff, Schmithals, Rahtjen, Beare). More recently other strong voices have supported the hypothesis of separate letters in a composite (Bornkamm, Schenke, Vielhauer, Friedrich, Koester). To be sure, there remain significant voices of resistance (Kümmel, Delling, Mackay, Furnish), but the traditional position has been pushed on the defensive.

The major reasons used to support the compilation hypothesis are as follows:

(a) There is a sharp break after 3.1 with an unmediated polemic in 3.2–4.1 (cf. also the transition from 4.9 to 10).

(b) Numerous verses in ch.4 appear to have once served as conclusions to a letter (4.4–7,9,20,21–23).

(c) Different historical situations are reflected in the writing of the various parts of the letter.

(d) External confirmation is sought in Polycarp's reference to several Philippian letters (cf. Rahtjen).

In sum, three original letters are usually distinguished with some minor variations in the way in which the conclusions of chapter 4 are distributed. Schmithal proposes: Letter A=4.10–23; B=1.1–3.1; 4.4–7; C=3.2–4.3; 4.8. Beare suggests: A=3.2–4.1; B=4.10–20; C= 1.1–3.1; 4.2–9, 21–23. Bornkamm prefers: A=4.10–20; B=1.1–3.1; 4.21–23; C=3.2–4.9.

The important effect of this division, much like the analysis of the sources in the Pentateuch, is that a new historical dimension is recovered. Thus, it is usually argued that Letter A was Paul's immediate response to thanks upon receiving the gift from the church of Philippi and that he was already imprisoned. Letter B reflects a considerable passage of time for Ephaphroditus to have sickened and recovered. Possibly Paul had already made his defence and he was waiting for an imminent verdict (1.19ff.; 2.23). Letter C no longer speaks of imprisonment. Paul had meanwhile received fresh information regarding the opponents in Philippi to which he vigorously responded (cf. Bornkamm's reconstruction, 198ff.). In addition, it is thought that a more exact chronological relationship between the Philippian and the Corinthian correspondence can be established by means of source criticism of Philippians (cf. Schenke, 127ff.).

Of course, some important arguments have been advanced against the partition hypothesis. Kümmel contends that such a theory presupposes a liberty with Pauline letters, especially the elimination of original praescripts and postscripts, which does not accord with the recognized authority of Paul (333f.). More recently, a variety of rebuttals have appeared which stress elements of thematic unity in Philippians (cf. Jewett, 'Epistolary Thanksgiving', 19ff.; Furnish, Mackay, Pollard). It is pointed out that the continuity between Christ's humiliation and suffering and the faithful response of the community in its tribulation is obvious. Again, the theme of joy in suffering is consistent throughout the entire letter. Moreover, that there are parallels in several other Pauline epistles with breaks and digressions, can hardly be denied.

Nevertheless, I am inclined to believe that the case for the partition theory is the stronger, although the evidence remains somewhat inconclusive. Kümmel's argument that too much freedom has been assigned to the redactor of Paul's original letters to justify the partition hypothesis rests on an uncertain basis. We do not actually know how much redactional initiative was deemed commensurate with Pauline authority, but it would appear more than Kümmel wishes to acknowledge.

One of the strongest arguments against the partition theory was first raised by Michaelis ('Teilungshypothesen'), and more recently by H. Gamble. Both have argued that the question of the *Sitz im Leben* of the alleged redaction of originally individual letters into a larger corpus has not been adequately treated. The force of the objection is immediately evident, and as a result considerable effort has been expended by the recent defenders of the partition theory to describe a possible setting for the redaction. Schmithals ('On the Composition . . . ', 239ff.) and Müller-Bardorff ('Zur Frage . . . ', 66ff.) think that the redaction took place as part of the first collection of the Pauline corpus. There are strong objections to this position (cf. Gamble and Lindemann), and therefore Bornkamm has posited a redactional process independent of the Corinthian correspondence and the larger canonical collection (202f.). Also Gnilka (18ff.) and Marxsen (*Intr.*, 66ff.) have argued for the church's growing consciousness of Paul's enduring authority and its effort to preserve his literary legacy in a way which would retain the maximum quantity of correspondence. It is also proposed that the effect of Paul's martyrdom played an important role on the book's redaction. Finally, Marxsen (67) suggests that the original letters were arranged in such a way as to cast the most favourable light upon the church at Philippi. The framing of the last letter C which concerned the threat of heresy with the two earlier letters gives the impression that the church had indeed overcome the problem.

II. The Search for a Canonical Interpretation

At this point in the debate a canonical approach to the Pauline letters begins to diverge from the method of redactional criticism. Especially when interpreting the letter to the Philippians redaction critics focus their attention on determining the intention of those editors who gave the book its shape.In itself the enterprise is legitimate and can be affirmed, even though at times such reconstructions rest on scanty evidence. In contrast, a canonical approach shifts the interpreter's focus to the final form of the biblical text. That is to say, it seeks to determine how the results of the editing process affect the way in which the redacted letter now functions. The assumption lying at the heart of this approach is that the editorial activity does not reflect simply the idiosyncratic ideology of an individual, but is part of a larger canonical process of the community of faith who in the actual reception and use of Paul's letters struggles to do justice to their authority function. How then does the present text render the message of Paul?

A canonical approach to Philippians contends that the redactors have largely concealed their own footprints. Their particular intentions and motivations have not been afforded canonical significance. The edited letters do not serve to illuminate the identity of the tradents, but rather to render a different reality, namely, the apostolic testimony of Paul. For the canonical approach the historical process uncovered by redaction criticism is useful in so far as it aids in understanding the interpreted text, but it has no independent validity for interpreting the canonical text. The newly recovered depth dimension can often help in determining the exact profile of the text, but it cannot refocus the canonical text without distorting its theological function.

The differences in approach can be seen clearly in the application of the partition theory to the interpretation of Philippians. The redaction critics argue that the new historical reconstruction allows one to alter the present profile of the text and change the canonical balance between elements now assigned to the text's background or to its foreground. Thus, Paul is interpreted as being in prison only for letter B, possibly for A, but not in C. His enemies are recognized because new information reached him in letter C. In sum, a reconstructed profile is made the basis for interpretation which is often sharper and more detailed than that presented in the canonical letter, and one which is quite different from that presented to the community which works with the received tradition. Although the evidence is quite strong for a prehistory of the letter's growth in which once separate letters were subsequently combined, the hermeneutical debate turns on how this information is to be employed in the interpretation of Philippians as normative scripture for a community of faith and practice.

Interestingly enough, Marxsen, after reviewing the evidence for a redactional history, makes an interpretive move which comes close to the canonical. He writes:

In all this, however, the original circumstances in which the documents appeared are no longer of any significance, and the need to preserve the letters as items of correspondence addressed to a particular situation disappears. What is of interest is no longer the fact that Paul wanted to say something to earlier readers, nor what he wanted to say to them in particular, but his letters are now interpreted as an apostolic legacy to the whole church (*Intr.* 67).

What then are the main lines of the canonical shape of the Philippian epistle? Paul views his imprisonment and suffering in the light of a christological confession: Jesus Christ humbled himself in his incarnation and death, but God has exalted him through the resurrection and established his ultimate victory over all of creation (2.6ff.). Therefore, the apostle can rejoice because in his suffering the gospel is advanced, and he is confident that he will be vindicated on the day of Christ (2.16). He awaits his resurrection when he will assume a form commensurate with Christ's glorified presence (3.20ff.). Paul challenges the Christians of Philippi to live lives worthy of the gospel and to rejoice in their being called also to suffer for Christ's sake (1.29ff.). The eschatological peace of God – the Lord is at hand – has already become a present reality (4.4–7), and Paul admonishes the church to imitate him (3.17; 4.9) who has learned the secret of life with Christ (4.10ff.). Paul rejoices in their material support of him as a sign of their partnership in the ministry of the gospel (4.14ff.).

However, there is also the threat to the faith. There are those who seek to establish their own righteousness through the law (3.9) and boast in the strictness of their religious observance. Moreover, they consider themselves to have already arrived and to have attained a form of perfection in the eyes of God. Such heresy is equal to the crassest form of libertarianism and can only call forth destruction. These are the enemies of the gospel. They are false workers who lead astray and are to be avoided.

The Philippian letter serves canonically in a way akin to a last will and testament of the martyred apostle, who during the closing period of his struggle for the gospel offered a confident witness to a beloved church on how to respond faithfully and with joy to life with Christ even when the apostle is no longer present.

18

COLOSSIANS

Commentaries

C. J. Ellicott, [3]1865
J. B. Lightfoot, [3]1879
A. Klöpper, 1882
H. Oltramare, 1891–92
T. K. Abbott, ICC, 1897
E. Haupt, MeyerK, [7]1902
P. Ewald, KNT, [2]1910
W. Lueken, SNT, [3]1917
E. F. Scott, MNTC, 1930
W. Bieder, ZBK, 1943
C. Masson, CNT, 1950
M. Dibelius, H. Greeven, HNT, [3]1953
F. W. Beare, IB, 1955
F. F. Bruce, NICNT, 1957
C. F. D. Moule, CGTC, 1957

E. Lohmeyer, W. Schmauch, MeyerK, [13]1964
G. H. P. Thompson, CNEB, 1967
G. Johnston, NCeB, 1967
J. L. Houlden, Pel, 1970
E. Lohse, MeyerK, [15]1977, Herm, ET 1971
J. Ernst, RNT, 1974
R. P. Martin, NCeB, 1974
G. B. Caird, NCeB, 1976
E. Schweizer, EKK, [2]1980
J. Gnilka, HTKNT, 1980
H. Conzelmann, NTD, [15]1981
P. T. O'Brien, Word, 1982
A. Lindemann, ZBK, 1983

Bibliography

A. J. **Bandstra**, 'Did the Colossian Errorists need a Mediator?', *New Dimensions in New Testament Study*, ed. R. N. Longenecker and M. C. Tenney, Grand Rapids 1974, 329–43; P. **Benoit**, 'Corps, tête et plérôme dans les épîtres de la captivité', *RB* 63, 1956, 5–44; 'Paul, 1. Colossiens (Épître aux)', *DB*Suppl VII, 1966, 157–70; 'L'Hymne christologique de Col 1,15–20', *Christianity, Judaism and other Greco-Roman Cults, FS Morton Smith*, ed. J. Neusner, I, New Testament, Leiden 1975, 226–63; G. **Bornkamm**, 'Die Häresie des Kolosserbriefes', *TLZ* 73, 1948, 11–20; ET 'The Heresy of Colossians', *Conflict at Colossae*, ed. F. O. Francis and W. A. Meeks, 123–45; 'Die Hoffnung im Kolosserbrief. Zugleich ein Beitrag zur Frage der Echtheit des Briefes', *GA* IV, Munich 1971, 206–13; F. F. **Bruce**, 'St Paul in Rome, III. Epistle to the Colossians', *BJRL* 48, 1965/6, 268–85; W. **Bujard**,

Stilanalytische Untersuchungen zum Kolosserbrief, SUNT 11, 1973; C. **Burger**, *Schöpfung und Versöhnung. Studien zum liturgischen Gut im Kolosser- und Epheserbrief*, WMANT 46, 1975; J. **Burgess**, 'The Letter to the Colossians', (Proclamation Commentaries), *Ephesians, Colossians, 2 Thessalonians, the Pastoral Epistles*, Philadelphia 1978, 41–71; C. F. **Burney**, 'Christ as the 'APXH of Creation (Prov. VIII 22, Col. I 15–18, Rev. III 14)', *JTS* 27, 1926, 160–77; G. E. **Canon**, *The Use of Traditional Materials in Colossians*, Macon, Ga. 1983; J. **Coutts**, 'The Relationship of Ephesians and Colossians', *NTS* 4, 1957/8, 201–7; F. B. **Craddock**, ' "All Things in Him": A Critical Note on Col I.15–20', *NTS* 12, 1965/6, 78–80; J. E. **Crouch**, *The Origin and Intention of the Colossian Haustafel*, FRLANT 109, 1972.

R. **Deichgräber**, *Gotteshymnus und Christushymnus in der frühen Christenheit*, SUNT 5, 1967; G. **Delling**, 'πλήρωμα', *TDNT* VI, 288–311; M. **Dibelius**, 'Isisweihe bei Apulejus und verwandte Initiations-Riten' (1917), *Botschaft und Geschichte* II, Tübingen 1956, 30–79; K.-G. **Eckart**, 'Exegetische Beobachtungen zu Kol 1,9–20', *ThViat* 7, 1959/60, 87–106; 'Ursprüngliche Tauf- und Ordinationsliturgie', ibid., 8, 1961/2, 23–37; A. **Feuillet**, 'La Création de l'Univers "dans le Christ" d'après l'Épître aux Colossiens', *NTS* 12, 1965/6, 1–9; W. **Foerster**, 'Die Irrlehrer des Kolosserbriefes', *Studia Biblica et Semitica T. C. Vriezen dedicata*, ed. W. C. van Unnik and A. S. van der Woude, Wageningen 1966, 71–80; F. O. **Francis**, 'Humility and Angelic Worship in Col. 2:18', *StTh* 16, 1963, 109–34; *A Re-examination of the Colossian Controversy*, Diss. Yale 1965; 'The Christological Argument of Colossians', *God's Christ and His People, FS N. A. Dahl*, ed. W. A. Meeks and J. Jervell, Oslo 1977, 192–208; F. O. **Francis** and W. A. **Meeks**, eds., *Conflict at Colossae*, Missoula 1975; H. **Gabathuler**, *Jesus Christus, Haupt der Kirche Haupt der Welt. Der Christushymnus Colosser 1,15–20 in der theologischen Forschung der letzten 130 Jahre*, AbTANT 45, 1965; E. **Grässer**, 'Kol 3,1–4 als Beispiel einer Interpretation secundum homines recipientes', *ZTK* 64, 1967, 139–68.

H. **Hegermann**, *Die Vorstellung vom Schöpfungsmittler im hellenistischen Judentum und Urchristentum*, TU 82, 1961; E. G. **Hinson**, 'The Christian Household in Colossians 3:18–4:1' *RevExp* 70, 1973, 495–507; A. **Hockel**, *Christus der Erstgeborene. Zur Geschichte der Exegese von Kol 1,15*, Düsseldorf 1965; H. J. **Holtzmann** *Kritik der Epheser- und Kolosserbriefe*, Leipzig 1872; M. D. **Hooker**, 'Were there False Teachers in Colossae?', *Christ and Spirit in the New Testament, Essays in honour of C. F. D. Moule*, eds. B. Lindars and S. S. Smalley, Cambridge 1973; 315–31; E. **Käsemann**, 'Kolosserbrief', *RGG* ³III, 1959, 1727f.; 'A Primitive Christian Baptismal Liturgy', ET *Essays on New Testament Themes*, SBT 41, 1964, 149–168; N. **Kehl**, *Der Christushymnus im Kolosserbrief. Ein motivgeschichtliche Untersuchung zu Kol 1, 12–20*, SBM 1, 1967; J. **Knox**, *Philemon Among the Letters of Paul*, Chicago 1935, 13–24; 'Philemon and the Authenticity of Colossians', *JR* 18, 1938, 144–60; J. **Kremer**, *Was an dem Leiden Christi noch mangelt—Eine interpretationsgeschichtliche und exegetische Untersuchung zu Kol.1,24b*, BBB 12, 1956; J. **Lähnemann**, *Der Kolosserbrief. Komposition, Situation und Argumentationen*, StNT 3,

1971; J. B. **Lightfoot**, 'The Colossian Heresy', *St Paul's Epistles to the Colossians and to Philemon*, London [3]1879, 71–111; reprinted *Conflict at Colossae*, ed. F. O. Francis and W. A. Meeks, 13–59; E. **Lohse**, 'Christologie und Ethik im Kolosserbrief', *Apophoreta, FS E. Haenchen*, ed. W. Eltester, BZNW 30, 1964, 156–68; 'Pauline Theology in the Letter to the Colossians', *NTS* 15, 1968/9, 211–20; H. **Ludwig**, *Der Verfasser des Kolosserbriefes—Eine Schüler des Paulus*, Diss. Göttingen 1974; S. **Lyonnet**, 'Paul's Adversaries in Colossae', ET *Conflict at Colossae*, ed. F. O. Francis and W. A. Meeks, 147–61.

G. H. C. **MacGregor**, 'Principalities and Powers: the Cosmic Background of Paul's Thought', *NTS* 1, 1954/5, 17–28; R. P. **Martin**, 'An Early Christian Hymn (Col.1,15–20)', *EvQu* 36, 1964, 195–205; C. **Maurer**, 'Die Begründung der Herrschaft Christi über die Mächte nach Kol 1,15–20', *WuD* 3, 1955, 79–93; E. T. **Mayerhoff**, *Der Brief an die Colosser, mit vornehmlicher Berücksichtigung der drei Pastoralbriefe kritisch geprüft*, Berlin 1838; W. **Michaelis**, 'πρωτότοκος', *TDNT* VI, 865–82; G. **Münderlein**, 'Die Erwählung durch das Pleroma. Bemerkungen zu Kol.I.19', *NTS* 8, 1961/2, 264–76; E. **Norden**, *Agnostos Theos*, Leipzig 1913, reprinted Stuttgart 1956, 250ff.; W. **Ochel**, *Die Annahme einer Bearbeitung des Kolosserbriefes in Epheserbrief*, Diss. Marburg 1934; J. **O'Neill**, 'The Source of Christology in Colossians', *NTS* 26, 1979/80, 87–100; E. **Percy**, *Die Probleme der Kolosser- und Epheserbriefe*, Lund 1946; W. **Pöhlmann**, 'Die hymnischen All-Prädikationen in Kol 1, 15–20', *ZNW* 64, 1973, 53–74; J. B. **Polhill**, 'The Relationship between Ephesians and Colossians', *RevExp* 70, 1975, 439–50; W. G. **Rollins**, 'Christological *Tendenz* in Colossians 1:15–20', *Christological Perspectives. Essays in Honor of H. K. McArthur*, eds. R. F. Berkey and S. A. Edwards, New York 1982, 123–38.

E. P. **Sanders**, 'Literary Dependence in Colossians', *JBL* 84, 1966, 28–45; E. W. **Saunders**, 'The Colossian Heresy and Qumran Theology', *Studies in the History and Text of the New Testament in Honor of K. W. Clark*, ed. B. D. Daniels and M. J. Suggs, Salt Lake City 1967, 133ff.; H. -M. **Schenke**, 'Der Widerstreit gnostischer und kirchlicher Christologie im Spiegel des Kolosserbriefes', *ZTK* 61, 1964, 391–403; 'Das Weiterwirken des Paulus und die Pflege seines Erbes durch die Paulusschule', *Einleitung in die Schriften des Neuen Testaments*, I, Gütersloh 1978, 233–46; R. **Schnackenburg**, 'Die Aufnahme des Christushymnus durch den Verfasser des Kolosserbriefes', in *Evang.-kathol. Kommentar zum Neuen Testament, Vorarbeiten* 1, Zürich and Neukirchen-Vluyn 1969, 33–50; E. **Schweizer**, 'Die Kirche als Leib Christi in den paulinischen Homologumena', *TLZ* 86, 1961, 161–74; reprinted *Neotestamentica*, Zürich and Stuttgart 1963, 272–92; 'Die Kirche als Leib Christi in den paulinischen Antilegomena', *TLZ* 86, 1961, 241–56; *Neotestamentica*, 293–316; 'Zur Frage der Echtheit des Kolosser- und des Epheserbriefes', *Neotestamentica*, 429; 'σῶμα', *TDNT* VII, 1024–94; 'Die "Elemente der Welt"', *Beiträge zur Theologie des Neuen Testaments*, Zürich 1970, 147–63; 'Christ in the Letter to the Colossians', *RevExp* 70, 1973, 451–67; B. **Vawter**, 'The Colossians Hymn and the Principle of Redaction', *CBQ* 33, 1971,

62–81; F. **Zeilinger**, 'Die Träger der apostolischen Tradition im Kolosser-brief', in *Jesus in der Verkündigung der Kirche*, ed. A. Fuchs, Linz 1976, 175–90.

I. The Critical Debate

The modern discussion of Colossians has focused especially on three critical issues, the solution of which has been thought to provide a correct interpretive entrance into this complex material. The issues involve the problem of authorship, the nature of the deviant teaching being combated, and the literary redaction of the letter. On the basis of a study of these critical issues the hermeneutical key is sought by which to explain the peculiar theological profile of the letter which appears to reflect strong elements of both continuity and disconti-nuity with the undisputed letters of Paul.

A. The Authorship of Colossians

The history of the debate over the authorship of the letter has often been reviewed and need not be repeated here in detail. The authorship was first seriously questioned by Mayerhoff in 1838 whose theory was then developed by F. S. Baur and his school in the mid-nineteenth century. In the late nineteenth century various attempts were made to support some form of indirect Pauline authorship, either by a hypothesis of subsequent interpolations (Holtzmann), or by an appeal to Paul's use of an amanuensis. Although in the period before World War II, Bultmann and his school continued to characterize Colossians with Ephesians as part of the non-genuine 'deutero-Pauline' corpus, there was an impressive group of critical scholars who defended the book's authenticity, e.g. Dibelius, Lohmeyer. The comprehensive study of Percy in 1946 also added considerable support to the Pauline authorship.

However, within the most recent period it would seem that those who support the non-Pauline authorship form a new majority. Significantly the three latest critical commentaries from both Prot-estant and Catholic camps agree in characterizing Colossians as 'Deutero-Pauline' (Lohse, Schweizer, Gnilka). Naturally there remains an impressive minority voice (Kümmel, Moule, etc.). Meeks (114) voices a growing sentiment among some scholars that the question of authorship is actually less important than previously thought. He wonders whether the crucial task – regardless of what one decides about authorship – turns on interpreting the peculiar shape of Colossians which both has strong lines of continuity with Paul, and also diverges in significant ways from his other undisputed letters.

The reasons for questioning the authorship of Paul are several, but certainly the divergence in literary style, vocabulary, and syntax plays an important role. It has long been noticed that the number of *hapax legomena* is unusually large in Colossians, and that many of the familiar Pauline words are missing. However, this observation was always explained by appealing to the new content of the epistle and to Paul's adaptation of traditional material. Nevertheless a new stage in the debate was introduced by Bujard's closely analysed syntactical and stylistical investigation. He demonstrated the extent to which Colossians consistently differs from the genuine Pauline epistles in such matters as the use of genitives, the frequency of synonyms, and the unusual employment of prepositions. Admittedly the issue is complex and seldom is any one feature of Colossians totally absent from Paul's undisputed letters; however, the quality of the difference has a powerful cumulative weight. In addition, important conceptual distinctions are also stressed by those who support a non-Pauline authorship (cf. Schenke, Schweizer).

There remains considerable disagreement among this same group of critical scholars on how to explain the book's formation and role within the Pauline corpus. Those who defend a consistent pseudepigraphical position usually argue that an author from the school of Paul consciously imitated the letter to Philemon in his forming the praescript and concluding greetings of Colossians (Vielhauer, Schenke). Others stress that the author was trying to transfer the authority of Paul to other persons in the post-apostolic period and that the letter functioned therefore as a kind of pastoral letter (Marxsen, *Intr.*). Still others claim that the letter sought to describe a type of idealization of Paul (Gnilka), or to paint his portrait in heroic colours in the light of his martydom (Schenke). In my judgment, these suggestions are far from being persuasive. Rather, the hypothesis of Schweizer (*Kommentar*, 25) seems to come closest to explaining why the letter reflects an indirect authorship and yet does not stem from a later, post-Pauline period. We shall return to his theory in more detail when we discuss the present canonical role of the book.

B. The Nature of the Colossian Heresy

The second major critical issue involves the problem of describing precisely the nature of the heresy which appears to have evoked the letter to the Colossians in the first place. Meeks correctly characterizes the task of reconstructing the profile of the opponents as 'excruciatingly difficult'. His annotated edition of some of the classic essays on the subject (*Conflict at Colossae*, ed. with Francis) brings together succinctly the main positions of the century-old debate.

The problem turns on understanding a false teaching which is addressed only in fragments and in obscure catchwords in ch.2. The key verse in the debate is 2.18, a verse in which virtually every word is controversial. The false teachers demand observance of special feasts (2.16), and insist on dietary laws (2.16,21), claiming the need of some sort of ascetic practices to subdue the body (2.23). They appear to promote 'veneration of angels' (2.18) and submission to the 'elemental spirits of the world' (2.20). This 'philosophy' (2.8) appears to have a strong cultic cast, and is formulated in the cosmic speculative terminology of secret wisdom. Although there is a wide agreement that some form of Jewish syncretism is represented, there remains a continuing disagreement on the precise nature of the opposition. A large number of questions remain unsolved, and scholars differ on whether mystery practices outweigh speculative theology, whether it is an internal Christian development or largely an intrusion from without, and to what extent the teaching relates to a form of Gnosticism.

C. Literary and Redactional Features

The third major question relates to the literary shape of the epistle, particularly its redactional history. The interpolation theory of Holtzmann proved in the end to be unconvincing because of the consistently unified style of the entire letter. However, a new phase in the literary debate arose with the recognition that the author appeared to have used older, liturgical material. Above all, scholarly attention has focused on the passage 1.15–20 which has been widely accepted as poetic in nature. Käsemann's essay (1949) was decisive not only in correctly analysing the broad outlines of the poem which had been badly skewed by Lohmeyer, but also in sharply posing the redactional problems. His argument that the hymn stemmed originally from a non-Christian Gnostic source has not met with much positive response. However, his case for seeing a redactional supplement in the phrases 'the church' (1.18) and 'through the blood of the cross' (v. 20) has been widely accepted and has sparked much discussion. Although the debate continues on the details of the redactional process (cf. Gabathuler, Deichgräber, Kehl, Benoit, etc.), most critical scholars would agree with Schweizer's dictum (*Kom.*, 220f.) that the proper distinction between the genre of hymn and commentary is absolutely crucial for any further theological reflection on the letter. In my opinion, the modern redactional analysis of Col.1.15ff. offers a good example of the usefulness of this critical tool for exegesis; however, I would strenuously resist simply identifying a modern reconstruction – whether form-critical or redactional – with the canonical hearing of the biblical text.

Finally, on the basis of the history of critical research, the implications for the interpretation of the entire epistle have been drawn. The emphasis correctly focuses on both the continuity and discontinuity of thought with the undisputed Pauline corpus. The broad movement of the letter from indicative affirmation (1.9–2.23) to the imperatives for Christian living (3.1–4.6) follows generally the familiar Pauline practice. Likewise the linkage of apostolic office and tradition is thoroughly consistent. Conversely, the cosmological dimensions of Christ and his role as head of the body extends beyond anything in the homologoumena. Perhaps the crucial area of debate turns on the relation between eschatology and sacrament. Has the eschatological tension which is characteristic of Pauline thought been lost which understands the Christian hope in a spatial terminology (cf. Bornkamm, 'Hoffnung') as a reality already possessed (Käsemann)?

II. The Canonical Shape of the Letter

The first point is obvious, but needs to be stressed. The letter to the Colossians is firmly anchored to the apostle Paul, both to his person and to the gospel which he proclaimed. The mention of Timothy along with Paul in the praescript is so customary in the undisputed letters that it cannot be used as evidence for an indirect relationship to the addressee (cf. II Corinthians, Philippians, I Thessalonians, Philemon). In addition, any theory claiming that Epaphras was actually the author of the letter runs flatly in the face of the canonical role assigned him (1.7; 4.12f.). Then again, the conclusion follows the Pauline practice of conveying his personal greetings from his fellow workers to the congregation by means of a dispatched message (4.8). Finally, the letter is closed with Paul's personal signature (I Cor. 16.21; Philemon 19; II Thess. 3.17), and makes mention of his own situation of being prisoner.

Paul is also explicitly identified in the body of the letter (1.23ff.). The Colossians are admonished to stand in the tradition which they have received and of which Paul is a representative. In this passage and in 2.6f. Paul ties his apostleship to the same tradition of Jesus Christ on which their faith has been grounded. Although his apostolic authority is not being attacked, Paul links it explicitly to the selfsame faith which they have 'received' through the tradition.

The point has recently been made by Schweizer (*Kom.*, 21) and supported by Gnilka (*Kom.*, 23) that the use made of the expression 'I, Paul' in 1.23 differs from that of the genuine Pauline letters. In the latter occurrences (Philem. 19; II Cor. 10.1; Gal. 5.2; I Thess. 2.18) the phrase functions to establish a personal relationship between Paul and his addressees, whereas in the non-genuine letters, such as Colossians, the phrase functions to objectivize the apostle's office. In my judgment, this exegesis is tendentious and too greatly influenced by prior theories of authorship. Actually the phrase 'I, Paul' functions in a variety of ways within the Pauline corpus to render the *persona* of the writer. One of these functions is to establish a personal relationship with his readers (Eph. 3.1), but it is not an exclusive one, and often combines other elements as well. For example, the phrase in Col. 4.18 which is paralleled to II Thess. 3.17 establishes the Pauline authenticity of the letter. Again its function in I Thess. 2.18 is to distinguish Paul from Silvanus and Timothy. Finally, the exercise of apostolic authority is also present in Gal. 5.2 along with the personal appeal.

In sum, any discussion of the canonical function of the letter to the Colossians must take as its starting point the strong linkage of the letter to Paul. Regardless of how one subsequently handles the problem of the discontinuities with the usual Pauline style and thought patterns, the problem cannot be resolved by artificially weakening the explicit identification with the apostle himself.

Still the heart of the canonical issue of this letter has not been touched merely by insisting on the continuity with Paul. At this juncture a canonical approach parts company with traditional conservative exegesis whose major concern remains fixed on an apologetic defence of direct Pauline authorship (cf. Gloag, Zahn, Guthrie, *Intr.*, etc.). The crucial hermeneutical issue of the letter is how to understand the special canonical function which is realized by its peculiar literary shape.

Consistent with Paul's practice and fully obvious for this letter is the recognition that the apostle did not write a timeless theological tractate. Rather, the letter to the Colossians was evoked by a false teaching which had made inroads into the church and posed a serious threat. The letter was written to address this concrete issue, and much of its focus, both in terms of its form and content, was determined by the position which was being attacked. Because of the time-bound context of the letter which has influenced the shape of the biblical witness, it remains a continuing exegetical task to investigate the exact profile of the historical phenomenon which evoked the controversy. It seems increasingly clear that much of the basic theological language by which the false teaching was contested by the writer has its roots within the heresy itself (cf. especially the discussion of πλήρωμα, εἰκὼν τοῦ θεοῦ, πρωτότοκος). Yet as we have discovered elsewhere (I Corinthians, Galatians), the canonical context is not to be merely identified with the original historical situation of the writer. In Colossians a false teaching called forth a specific apostolic response which used the heresy as a transparency through which to unfold a new and positive witness to the truth of the gospel.

The basic theological issue confronted by the apostle's letter turns on the nature of Christ's presence in his church. That is to say, the problem of the link between God and his people lies at the heart of the controversy (cf. Lightfoot, 100f.). The false teachers had argued that between Christ and his church there now stood a hierarchy of cosmic powers which would only permit access to his salvation through various ascetic practices and self-humiliation. Through participation in the 'elemental spirits of the universe' or the 'mediators of angel worship' – the exact nuances are unclear – the worshipper entered into a religious experience which bridged the gap between the human and the divine. The fullness of God was thus distributed through a complex system of intermediaries.

The letter to the Colossians was written to address this threat to the church's access to Christ. Most important is to note how the response was made. Briefly stated, the author of the epistle translated Paul's temporal, eschatological language into a christological formulation by means of spatial terminology for the purpose of asserting the absolute, direct, and continuing supremacy of Christ over all creation.

The remarkable shift from the familiar idiom of Paul has long been observed. From his other epistles the apostle's dominant eschatological language emerges with clarity. Christ has redeemed the world from sin and death (Rom. 8); he has ushered in a new age (Gal. 1.4). The old has passed and in faith the believer has become part of the new. Yet the Christian lives in between the times. He is a new creation (II Cor. 5), buried with Christ in baptism (Rom. 6), set free from sin and bondage and walking by the Spirit. Yet he is still part of the old age with the old Adam (Rom. 6.6) and suffers the sentence of death (I Cor. 4.9; 7.25ff.). In faith he awaits his future resurrection (I Cor. 15), longing with the whole creation for the final victory of Christ (Rom.8).

However, Colossians speaks in a very different terminology. The reign of Christ has already begun and Christians have been delivered from the realm of darkness and transferred to Christ's kingdom (1.13). Sin is described as causing a hostile distance between Christ and his creation which has now been bridged (1.21). Ritual laws are only a shadow; Christ is the true reality (2.17). Christians who are buried wth Christ in baptism have already been raised with him (2.13; 3.1). The hope is of a salvation attained by Christ, and described in the spatial idiom of heaven above (3.2). The source of the change in emphasis clearly lies in the new christological formulation. Against a false teaching which would separate the world into different spheres of power, the letter to the Colossians bears witness to a cosmic Christ from whose creative power all existence derives, in heaven and on earth, visible and invisible (1.16). In the language of wisdom (Prov. 8), 'all things were created through him and for him' (1.16). He is before all things (1.17), not in terms of temporal precedence, but in the supremacy of his control. He fills up the void between the finite and the infinite and holds together all things (1.17). As the head of his body the church he is the sole mediator between God and the universe, and has reconciled the world through his atonement (1.20).

Nevertheless, it is a serious exaggeration of the function of the new language of Colossians to suggest that the theology differs completely from that of Paul. Lines of continuity are everywhere present. The redactional study of the hymn in 1.15ff. has only gone to emphasize to what extent the cosmic Christ of the original poem was reshaped to include the Pauline emphasis on Christ's atonement for the redemption of the church and the world. Similarly the commentary which follows in 1.21ff. brings the cosmic elements of wisdom teaching still further in line with Paul's insistence on the centrality of Christ's historical act of salvation. Moreover, in spite of the dominance of the spatial terminology, at crucial points the familiar eschatological tension has been retained. Christians still await their inheritance (3.24). Although they have been raised with Christ, there remains the future expectation of Christ's parousia when they will appear with him in his glory (3.4). Finally, the ethical implications of life of Christ (3.5ff.) largely run parallel to Paul's other letters.

Although many critical commentators have correctly seen both the elements of similarity and differences in respect to the undisputed Pauline letters, the canonical implications for understanding the function of Colossians within the Pauline corpus have seldom been addressed. Simply to focus on ideological differences (Käsemann) between the so-called 'genuine' and 'deutero-Pauline' letters is to overlook the effect of the New Testament canon. Rather, the shape of the letter to the Colossians provides a Pauline warrant for translating his theology into a different idiom which is faithful to the gospel. The letter establishes the parameters within which the continuing theological task is carried on. The fact that the corpus of Pauline letters contains material whose shape shows evidence of a process of expanding and adapting Paul's thought to a new and different situation indicates that Paul's letters were not regarded as a static deposit of unchanging doctrine, but as a living voice of apostolic instruction, supported by the authority of the exalted Christ, which was given to guide the church continually toward the obedient life. The final instruction of the epistle to have the letter read in other churches (4.16) already indicates the beginning of the canonical process at work. The letter functions as authority for Christians who do not share in the original historical situation of those at Colossae, but whose context within the community of faith is nevertheless addressed with a continuing word from God through his apostle.

Finally, there remains the task of explaining historically the peculiar shape of this letter which lays explicit claim on the authorship and authority of Paul. We have already expressed our dissatisfaction over those who would simply make use of a theory of pseudepigraphy to explain the Pauline claim. The parallel between the context of Colossians and that of Philemon does not reflect a contrived imitation. Nor are there any signs within the letter of a late doctrinal or ecclesiastical development such as one finds in the Pastorals. Nowhere does the letter turn its interest to building a tradition about Paul himself, which would make the apostle the object rather than the subject of the epistle. We, therefore, agree with Schweizer that the letter is not post-Pauline (*Kom.*, 25).

On the conservative side of the theological spectrum are those scholars who recognize the unusual features of the letter, but argue that it was Paul himself who 'translated' his message into a different idiom to meet the new situation. In my judgment, the philological and stylistic evidence speaks against the position. Moreover, it seems to me that the intensity of the conservatives' defence of a direct Pauline authorship stems from a traditional hermeneutic which ties the book's authority to the author's intentionality with little understanding of the function played by the canon. However, in respect to the letter to the Colossians, the issue of authorship can probably still be left moot without great exegetical effect. Nevertheless, the issue is part of the larger problem of an expanded Pauline corpus whose boundaries extend even further away from the undisputed Pauline core (cf. Ephesians, Pastorals, II Thessalonians).

Various theories have been proposed to explain the elements which point to an indirect authorship of the letter by Paul. Some argue that while he was in prison – whether in Ephesus or Rome – under those restricted conditions, he let a co-worker actually write the letter to which he penned his signature as a confirmation of his authority (Schweizer, *Kom.*, 25ff.). In spite of the attractiveness of such a hypothesis, the evidence is simply lacking by which to confirm it. However, even if it were true, the hard question remains as to how much exegetical ground has been won for interpreting the letter itself.

In my opinion, it is more important not to confuse the canonical shape and function of a letter with either radical or conservative theories of historical composition. In spite of our lack of knowledge in explaining the process by which the Pauline corpus was expanded to include features arising from an apparently indirect relationship to Paul, the letter's canonical function in applying the witness of the epistle to a different situation by means of a new theological formulation is not impaired. Obviously the Christian church had a different agenda from that of modern biblical scholarship when it received the letter as authoritative for its life.

19

I THESSALONIANS

Commentaries

C. J. Ellicott, [3]1865
C. A. Auberlen, ET 1868
G. Lünemann, MeyerK, ET 1880
G. G. Findlay, CB, 1891
J. Denney, ExpB 1892
W. Bornemann, MeyerK, [6]1894
W. Lueken, SNT, [2]1907
G. Milligan, 1908
G. Wohlenberg, KNT, [2]1909
E. von Dobschütz, MeyerK, [7]1909
J. E. Frame, ICC, 1912
A. Plummer, 1918
E. J. Bicknell, WC, 1932
M. Dibelius, HNT, [3]1937

W. Neil, MNTC, 1950
B. Rigaux, ÉB, 1956
C. Masson, CNT, 1957
L. Morris, NICNT, 1959
K. Staab, RNT, [3]1959
A. Oepke, NTD, [9]1963
K. Grayston, CNEB, 1967
A. L. Moore, NCeB, 1969
E. Best, B/HNTC, 1972
W. Marxsen, ZBK, 1979
G. Friedrich, NTD, [5]1981
F. F. Bruce, Word, 1982
I. H. Marshall, NCeB, 1983

Bibliography

E. H. **Askwith**, *An Introduction to the Thessalonian Epistles*, London and New York 1902; E. **Bammel**, 'Judenverfolgung und Naherwartung – Zur Eschatologie der I Thess', *ZTK* 56, 1959, 294–315; F. C. **Baur**, 'Die beiden Briefe an die Thessalonicher, ihre Echtheit und Bedeutung für die Lehre von der Parusie Christi', *ThJb* 14, Tübingen 1855, 141–68; C. J. **Bjerkelund**, *PARAKALŌ: Form, Funktion und Sinn der parakalō-Sätze in den paulinischen Briefen*, Oslo 1967; H. **Boers**, 'The Form Critical Study of Paul's Letters. I Thessalonians as a Case Study', *NTS* 22, 1975/6, 140–58; D. G. **Bradley**, 'The *Topos* as a Form in the Pauline Paraenesis', *JBL* 72, 1953, 238–46; R. F. **Collins**, *A Propos the Integrity of I Thessalonians*, Louvain 1979; C. **Demke**, 'Theologie und Literarkritik im I. Thessalonicherbrief', *FS E. Fuchs*, ed. G. Ebeling, Tübingen 1973, 103–124; A. M. **Denis**, 'L'Apôtre Paul, prophète "messianique" des Gentils. Étude thématique de I Thess II, 1–6', *ETL* 33, 1957, 245–318; K.-G. **Eckert**, 'Der zweite echte Brief des Apostels Paulus an die Thessalonicher', *ZTK* 58, 1961, 30–44; C. E. **Faw**, 'On the Writing of First Thessalonians', *JBL* 71, 1952, 217–25; G. **Friedrich**, '1.Thessalonicher 5,1–11, der apologetische Einschub eines Späteren', *ZTK* 70, 1973, 288–315; E.**Fuchs**, 'Die Zukunft des Glaubens nach I Thess 5,1–11', *Glaube und Erfahrung* (*GA* III), Tübingen 1965, 333–63; R. **Funk**, 'The Apostolic Parousia: Form and Significance', *Christian History and Interpretation. Studies Presented to John Knox*, ed. W. R. Farmer et al., Cambridge 1967, 249–68; R. **Gregson**, 'A Solution to the Problems of the Thessalonian Epistles', *EvQu* 38, 1966, 76–80.

W. **Hadorn**, *Die Abfassung der Thessalonicherbriefe in der Zeit der dritten Missionsreise des Paulus* BFChTh24.3/4, 1919; W. **Harnisch**, *Eschatologische Existenz. Ein exegetischer Beitrag zum Sachanliegen von I Thess. 4,13–15*, FRLANT 110, 1973; B. **Henneken**, *Verkündigung und Prophetie im Ersten Thessalonicherbrief*, SBS 29, 1969; J. C. **Hurd**, 'Thessalonians, First Letter to the', *IDB Suppl*, 900; R. **Jewett**, 'Enthusiastic Radicalism and the Thessalonian Correspondence', *Proceedings of the 108th Annual Meeting of the SBL 1972*, 182–232; B. N. **Kaye**, 'Eschatology and Ethics in I and 2 Thessalonians', *NovT* 17, 1975, 47–57; H. **Koester**, 'I Thessalonians—Experiment in Christian Writing', *Continuity and Discontinuity in Church History. Essays Presented to George Huntston Williams on the Occasion of His 65th Birthday*, eds. F. F. Church and T. George, Leiden 1979, 33–44; 'Apostel und Gemeinde in den Briefen an die Thessalonicher', *Kirche, FS G. Bornkamm zum 75. Geburtstag*, eds. D. Lührmann and G. Strecker, Tübingen 1980, 287–98; W. G. **Kümmel**, 'Das literarische und geschichtliche Problem des 1 Thessalonicherbrief', *Neotestamentica et Patristica. Freundesgabe O. Cullmann*, ed. W. C. van Unnik, NovTSupp 6, 1962, 213–27; F. **Laub**, *Eschatologische Verkündigung und Lebensgestaltung nach Paulus*, BU 10, 1973; J. B. **Lightfoot**, 'The Church of Thessalonica', *Biblical Essays*, London 1893, 253–69; *Notes on the Epistles of St Paul*, London 1895, 1–136; A. **Lindemann**, *Paulus im ältesten Christentum*, BHT 58, 1979, 28f.; W. **Lütgert**, *Die Vollkommenen in Philippi und die Enthusiasten in Thessalonich*, BFChTh 13.6, 1909; A. J. **Malherbe**, ' "Gentle as a Nurse". The Cynic Background of I Thess ii', *NovT* 12, 1970, 203–17; 'First Thessalonians as a Paraenetic Letter', Paper delivered at the SBL Seminar on 'The Form and Function of the Pauline Letters', 1972; 'Exhortation in First Thessalonians', *NovT* 25, 1983, 238–56; T. W. **Manson**, 'St Paul in Greece. The Letters to the Thessalonians', *BJRL* 35, 1952/3, 428–47; reprinted *Studies in the Gospels and Epistles*, ed. M. Black, Manchester and Philadelphia 1962, 259–78; W. **Marxsen**, 'Auslegung von I Thess. 4,13–18', *ZTK* 66, 1969, 22–37; C. **Maurer**, 'σκεῦος', *TDNT* VII, 358–67; J. **Munck**, 'I Thess. I 9–10 and the Missionary Preaching of Paul', *NTS* 9, 1962/3, 95–110.

E. A. **Nida**, *A Translator's Handbook on Paul's Letters to the Thessalonians*, Stuttgart 1975; E. **Pax**, 'Konvertitenprobleme im ersten Thessalonicherbrief', *BiLe* 13, 1972, 24–37; B. A. **Pearson**, 'I Thessalonians 2:13–16: A Deutero-Pauline Interpolation', *HTR* 64, 1971, 79–94; J. **Plevnick**, 'I Thess

5, 1–11: Its Authenticity, Intention and Message', *Bibl* 59, 1978, 71–90; B. **Reicke**, 'Thessalonich, Thessalonicherbriefe', *RGG*[3] VI, 1962, 850–53; J. T. **Sanders**, *'The Transition from Opening Epistolary Thanksgiving to Body in the Letters of the Pauline Corpus', JBL* 81, 1962, 348–62; R. **Scheppers**, 'The Pre-Synoptic Tradition in I Thessalonians II 13–16', *NovT* 8, 1966, 223–34; H. **Schlier**, *Der Apostel und seine Gemeinde*, Freiburg 1972; D. **Schmidt**, 'I Thess.2:13–16: Linguistic Evidence for an Interpolation', *JBL* 102, 1983, 269–79; W. **Schmithals**, 'Die Thessalonicherbriefe als Briefkompositionen', *Zeit und Geschichte, FS R. Bultmann*, ed. E. Dinkler, Tübingen 1964, 295–315; 'The Historical Situation of the Thessalonian Epistles', ET *Paul and the Gnostics*, Nashville 1972, 123–218; P. **Schubert**, *Form and Function of the Pauline Thanksgivings*, BZNW 20, 1939, 16–20; E. G. **Selwyn**, *The First Epistle of St Peter*, London [2]1947, 369–75; C. **Spicq**, 'Les Thessaloniciens "inquiets" étaient-ils des paresseux?', *StTh* 10, 1956, 1–13; K. **Thieme**, 'Die Struktur des ersten Thessalonicherbriefes', *Abraham Unser Vater, FS O. Michel*, ed. O. Betz et al., Leiden and Cologne 1963, 450–58; J. L. **White**, *The Form and Function of the Body of the Greek Letters*, SBLDS 5, Missoula 1972.

I. Modern Critical Issues

B. Rigaux's learned commentary of 1956 summarized well the full spectrum of critical questions which have been traditionally associated with the study of I Thessalonians. He carefully reviewed the historical background of the Thessalonian church, the circumstances evoking the letter, its literary character, authenticity, theological concepts, state of the text, and the history of its exegesis. Rigaux presented a virtual consensus which had been reached concerning some of these problems. The letter was written by Paul to the Thessalonian church shortly after his forced departure and is most probably the earliest of his extant letters. In more recent years scholars have tended to focus the discussion more narrowly which has led to an increased sophistication and refinement, both in posing and in answering the questions.

On the continent, following Eckart's initial article, Schmithals in 1964 proposed the theory that the canonical editor of the Pauline corpus had combined four original letters which were written to the Thessalonian church into the present two epistles. Among other things he argued that his theory resolved the old literary crux of interpreting the recurring thanksgiving sections (1.2; 2.13) as well as the premature benediction (3.11ff.). Of the four original letters, letter B comprised I Thess. 1.1–2.12; 4,2(3)–5.28, letter D I Thess.

2.13–4.1(2). Schmithals' general theory of the Thessalonian correspondence being made up of composite letters has received some support as well as modification from Schenke (*Einl.*I, 64ff.), among others. However, the theory has not been widely accepted by a majority of New Testament scholars, and particularly in Britain and North America, it has played no significant role in the ongoing debate (cf. Best,B/HNTC, 30ff.).

Rather, the major part of the current discussion over I Thessalonians has focused on determining the form and function of the letter when viewed from the perspective of its form-critical and rhetorical roles. Moreover, it is fair to say that recent critical analysis of I Thessalonians, in contrast to II Thessalonians, has been dominated by the American debate, which has had its centre in the seminars of the Society of Biblical Literature. The enterprise is misunderstood if viewed simply as literary analysis, but it is a broadly conceived, form-critical discussion in which author intentionality is viewed in relation to its extensive employment of Hellenistic epistolary conventions.

Although it is true that M. Dibelius' early form-critical and stylistic research formed the background of the modern discussion, the basic monograph which launched the newer phrase of the debate is clearly P. Schubert's *Form and Function of the Pauline Thanksgivings* (1939). Schubert argued in respect to I Thessalonians, that the introductory thanksgiving extended from 1.2–3.13. The so-called 'digressions' are in fact clearly announced '*topoi*' which form constitutive elements within the Pauline thanksgiving. The thanksgiving section actually constitutes the main body of the letter and is closely attached to the following paraenetic parts of the letter in chs. 4 and 5. Schubert's highly illuminating analysis evoked both support and disagreement. The respondents disagreed on whether to see Paul's purpose in writing the letter to lie in the autobiographical section (1–3), or in the concluding paraenetic portion (4–5). Appeals to *topoi* which were only loosely connected with a historical context were made by both sides.

Sanders, Funk and White argued for the centrality of the autobiographical section, albeit in somewhat different ways. Of great importance in the developing of this position was Funk's hypothesis of the apostolic parousia, which was thought to be a traditional literary form used to overcome the actual physical separation existing between the apostle and his hearers. By and large, these writers agreed in viewing 2.1–12 as the body of the letter which then resulted in viewing its main purpose to be apologetic. The exact nature of this apology is often debated, but the weight of the parallels suggest a defence of his gospel rather than a reference to personal attacks.

In a more recent article, H. Boers has sought to modify this conclusion by arguing that the purpose of the letter is 'disclosed by the inner connection of thanksgiving, apostolic apology and apostolic parousia' (153), and that the common feature which unites them all is *philophronesis* (the engendering of friendship). A key part of Boer's argument turns on his form-critical argument that if one eliminates 2.13–16 as an interpolation, following Pearson, what then emerges is a 'virtual metamorphosis of I Thessalonians' (152). By this he means that the apostolic apology and the parousia sections are joined. Pearson's argument is accepted by Koester ('I Thessalonians', 38), but rejected by Malherbe ('Paraenetic Letter', n.62).

On the other side of the debate are those scholars who basically support Schubert's analysis of the thanksgiving and lay the stress on the paraenetic function of the letter. Bjerkelund builds on Schubert initially, but then designates 4.1–5.11 as the body of the letter and sees the emphasis of the letter to lie in the summons to perfection in 4.1–2. However, the most consistent analysis of the epistle as a paraenetic letter has been done by A. Malherbe. In his 1972 essay Malherbe contends that the various features which have been described in ch.5.1–3 such as friendship, apology, and apostolic parousia all function as paraenesis. Moreover, the description of the readers as 'imitators' and the theme of remembrance all support a unified paraenetic purpose. He concludes that it is incorrect to contrast chs. 1–3 with 4–5 as being different in intention. In his 1983 essay Malherbe presses the argument even further, attempting to demonstrate how Paul constructed his letter by making a creative use of elements from the oratory tradition. By combining inherited traditional conventions such as the theme of freedom of speech (παρρησία) and friendship with his own pastoral method, Paul reshaped his material to stress the religious dimension of his ethical admonition.

In a similar direction, but even more aggressively argued, Koester seeks to describe how the message of the gospel, particularly with its eschatological setting, resulted in a drastic expansion of the traditional paraenetic genre. He emphasizes that simply to analyse the letter as a 'quarry of information for pieces of a genre or established tradition' (44) misses seeing the emergence of a highly creative experiment in a new form of Christian writing.

II. The Canonical Role of the Epistle

What implications can be drawn from reviewing the history of modern research on the form and function of I Thessalonians? Particularly the insights of Malherbe and Koester have made clear the role of the older, traditional elements which were reshaped to function as a particular kind of Christian paraenesis. It is also clear that the canonical process of collecting I Thessalonians to form part of the Pauline corpus did not seriously alter its original shape. At most the issue of whether or not 2.13–16 is a possible secondary expansion continues to be debated. What function can one attribute to its new canonical role in which it was joined to a larger collection and designated as normative scripture for a community of faith?

The effect of the canonical process did not alter its literary shape, but did influence how the letter was understood. This observation is not to suggest that an occasional letter was transformed into an authoritative treatise. Such a characterization badly misconstrues the canonical process. The original letter was written as a substitute for the apostle's presence and functioned as an authoritative vehicle by which to offer apostolic comfort and exhortation. Significantly, although it was addressed to one specific historical community, it was to be read from the start by the whole community of faith (5.27).

What occurred in the reading of the letter as a canonical writing was that its original paraenetic purpose was extended by the subsequent generations of readers to include themselves as the addressee. Moreover, the nature of the letter was such that with comparative ease the paraenesis was appropriated by others than the Thessalonians. The eschatological framework from which the admonition of holiness was made (3.13) applied equally to those latter-day saints who also awaited 'the coming of our Lord Jesus with all his saints'. Similarly the moral instructions which repudiated immorality and called for holiness as the will of God (4.1ff.) appeared to be equally applicable. Indeed, the delay of the parousia only increased the relevance and comfort of Paul's teaching regarding the simultaneous participation of the whole church in Christ's final victory (4.13–18).

It is also true that subsequent generations of Christians failed to grasp the full significance of many of the traditional Hellenistic features of the original letter. The effect was that almost immediately some features of the letter were blurred and misunderstood, even though its primary paraenetic function was clearly recognized. One of the positive features of the modern critical enterprise lies in its recovering the sharp profile of the original epistle as a paraenetic letter, thus confirming a significant continuity between various stages of the canonical process.

20

II THESSALONIANS

Commentaries

Cf. the list for I Thessalonians   W. Marxsen, ZBK II, 1982
W. Trilling, EKK, 1980

Bibliography

R. **Aus**, 'The Liturgical Background of the Necessity and Propriety of Giving Thanks according to 2 Thes 1:3', *JBL* 92, 1973, 432–38; J. A. **Bailey**, 'Who wrote II Thessalonians?', *NTS* 25, 1978/9, 131–45; F. C. **Baur**, 'Die beiden Briefe an die Thessalonicher; ihre Echtheit und Bedeutung für die Lehre von der Parusie Christi', *ThJb* 14, 1855, 141–68; O. **Betz**, 'Der Katechon', *NTS* 9, 1962/3, 276–91; W. **Bousset**, *Der Antichrist in der Überlieferung des Judentums, des Neuen Testaments und der Alten Kirche*, Göttingen 1895; H. **Braun**, 'Zur nachpaulinischen Herkunft des zweiten Thessalonicherbriefs', *ZNW* 44, 1952/3, 152–6; M. **Brunec**, 'De "homine peccati" in 2 Thess. 2,1–12', *VD* 35, 1957, 3–33; É. **Cothenet**, 'La IIe Épître aux Thessaloniciens et l'Apocalypse synoptique', *RSR* 42, 1954, 5–39; O. **Cullmann**, 'Der eschatologische Charakter des Missionsauftrages und des apostolischen Selbstbewusstseins bei Paulus. Untersuchung zum Begriff des κατέχον (κατέχων) in 2. Thess. 2,6–7' (1936), reprinted *Vorträge und Aufsätze 1925–1962*, Tübingen and Zürich 1966, 305–26; K.-G. **Eckart**, 'Der zweite echte Brief des Apostels Paulus an die Thessalonicher', *ZTK* 58, 1961, 30–44; J. **Ernst**, *Der eschatologische Gegenspieler in den Schriften des Neuen Testaments*, BU 3, 1967; R. M. **Evans**, *Eschatology and Ethics. A Study of Thessalonica and Paul's Letters to the Thessalonians*, Diss. Basel 1967; P. H. **Furfey**, 'The Mystery of Lawlessness', *CBQ* 8, 1946, 179–91.

C. H. **Giblin**, *The Threat to Faith. An Exegetical and Theological Re-examination of 2 Thessalonians 2*, AnBib 31, 1967; M. **Goguel**, 'L'énigme de la seconde épître aux Thessaloniciens', *RHPhR* 71, 1915, 248–72; J. **Graafen**, *Die Echtheit des zweiten Briefes an die Thessalonicher*, NT 14.5, Münster 1930; H. **Gunkel**, *Schöpfung und Chaos*, Göttingen 1894; A. **Harnack**, 'Das Problem des zweiten Thessalonicherbriefs', *SAB*, 1910, Berlin 560–78; A. **Hilgen-**

feld, 'Die beiden Briefe an die Thessalonicher', *ZWTh* 5, 1862, 225–64; G. **Hollmann**, 'Die Unechtheit des zweiten Thessalonicherbriefs', *ZNW* 5, 1904, 28–88; H. J. **Holtzmann**, 'Zum zweiten Thessalonicherbrief', *ZNW* 2, 1901, 97–108; J. C. **Hurd**, 'Thessalonians, Second Letter to the', *IDB Suppl*, 900f.; R. **Jewett**, 'Enthusiastic Radicalism and the Thessalonian Correspondence', *Proceedings of the 108th Annual Meeting of the SBL 1972*, I, 181–232; F. H. **Kern**, 'Über 2 Thess 2,1–12. Nebst Andeutungen über den Ursprung des 2. Briefes an die Thessalonicher', *Tübinger Zeitschrift für Theologie*, 2, 1839, 145–214; G. **Krodel**, 'The 2nd Letter to the Thessalonians' (Proclamation Commentaries), *Ephesians, Colossians, 2 Thessalonians*, Philadelphia 1978, 73–96.

F. **Laub**, *Eschatologische Verkündigung und Lebensgestaltung nach Paulus*, BU 10, 1973; J. B. **Lightfoot**, 'Thessalonians, Second Epistle to the', *Dictionary of the Bible*, ed. W. Smith, revised H. B. Hackett, Boston 1885, vol.IV, 3227–30; A. **Lindemann**, 'Zum Abfassungszweck des Zweiten Thessalonicherbriefes', *ZNW* 68, 1977, 35–47; W. **Lütgert**, *Die Vollkommenen in Philippi und die Enthusiasten in Thessalonich*, BFChTh 13.6, 1909; T. W. **Manson**, 'St Paul in Greece. The Letters to the Thessalonians', *BJRL* 35, 1952/3, 428–47; reprinted *Studies in the Gospels and Epistles*, ed. M. Black, Manchester 1962, 259–78; W. **Michaelis**, 'Der 2. Thessalonicherbrief kein Philipperbrief', *TZ* 1, 1945, 242–86; M. **Rist**, 'Pseudepigraphy and the Early Christians', *Studies in New Testament and Early Christian Literature*, ed. D. E. Aune, NovT Suppl 33, 1972, 75–91; D. W. B. **Robinson**, 'II Thess 2.6: "That which restrains" or "That which holds sway"?', *StEv* II, TU 87, 1964, 635–8; W. **Schmithals**, 'Die Thessalonicherbriefe als Briefkompositionen', *Zeit und Geschichte, FS R. Bultmann*, ed. E. Dinkler, Tübingen 1964, 295–315; E. **Schweizer**, 'Der zweite Thessalonicherbrief ein Philipperbrief?' *TZ* 1, 1945, 90–105; 'Zum Problem des zweiten Thessalonicherbriefes', *TZ* 2, 1946, 74f.; E. G. **Selwyn**, *The First Epistle of St Peter*, London ²1947, 369ff., 382ff.; J. A. **Sint**, 'Parousie-Erwartung und Parousie-Verzögerung im paulinischen Briefcorpus', *ZKT* 86, 1964, 47–79; L. **Sirard**, 'La Parousie de l'Antéchrist, 2 Th 2.3–9', *Studia Paulina* II, Rome 1963, 89–100; A. M. G. **Stephenson**, 'On the Meaning of ἐνέστηκεν ἡ ἡμέρα τοῦ κυρίου in 2 Thessalonians 2,2', *StEv* IV, 1968, 442–51; A. **Strobel**, *Untersuchungen zum eschatologischen Verzögerungsproblem*, NovTSuppl 2, 1961.

W. **Trilling**, *Untersuchungen zum 2. Thessalonicherbrief*, Erfurter Theol.Studien 27, Leipzig 1972; J. T. **Ubbink**, 'ὡς δι' ἡμῶν (2 Thess 2.2) – ein exegetisch-isagogische Puzzle?' '*Nederlands Theologisch Tijdschrift* 7, 1952/53, 269–295; J. C. **West**, 'The Order of 1 and 2 Thessalonians', *JTS* 15, 1914, 66–74; W. **Wrede**, *Die Echtheit des zweiten Thessalonicherbriefs untersucht*, TU 24.2, Leipzig 1903; J. **Wrzol**, *Die Echtheit des zweiten Thessalonicherbriefes*, Freiburg 1916.

I. Critical problems at Issue

Few books in the New Testament present such difficult problems of interpretation as does II Thessalonians. In spite of its brevity and seemingly minor role within the Pauline corpus, scholarly opinion is sharply divided on its dating, authorship, and function. The problems involve literary, historical, and theological issues and are as follows:

(*a*) The similarity in style, structure, and vocabulary between I and II Thessalonians is closer than any other two letters within the New Testament and seem to reflect some sort of literary dependency. The similarity extends beyond isolated vocabulary, but to unusual expressions and sequence of words which are peculiar to the Thessalonian correspondence. (Cf. the detailed comparisons in Wrede, 3–36; Rigaux, 76ff., 123ff.; Marxsen, *Der zweite Thessalonicherbrief*, 18–28.)

(*b*) In spite of these features of similarity there is no explicit reference made in II Thessalonians to the other epistle.

(*c*) The tone of II Thessalonians differs from I Thessalonians and has been evaluated by some scholars as impersonal and formal in character. In addition, there are a number of expressions which are thought to be uncharacteristic of Paul or even alien to his theology (Trilling, *Untersuchungen*, 64ff.; Braun, 152ff.).

(*d*) A shift in eschatology is discerned between I Thess. 4.13–5.11 and II Thess. 2.1–12. In the former the parousia is imminent, whereas in the latter it must be preceded by a number of events which include the appearance of the Antichrist. Scholars such as Krodel (75ff.) contend that the tension does not lie simply in conflicting concepts, but in the shift in the direction in which the eschatological argument points the reader.

(*e*) A use of Old Testament, apocalyptic tradition appears in II Thessalonians which is unexpected in the light of I Thessalonians (Bornemann, 460ff.).

(*f*) Finally, it is thought that there are indications of a later historical period which is characteristic of the post-Pauline era (Trilling, *Untersuchungen*, 109ff.).

II. Theories of Authorship

A variety of literary theories have been formulated in an effort to explain the difficulties. These can be conveniently grouped into three categories; (i) direct Pauline authorship; (ii) variations on direct Pauline authorship; (iii) pseudepigraphical authorship.

The traditional interpretation of II Thessalonians which attributes the letter to the direct authorship of Paul continues to have strong support from an impressive group of scholars. In fact, until very recently all the major critical commentaries continued to defend Pauline authorship (Bornemann, Milligan, Frame, von Dobschütz, Dibelius, Rigaux, and Best). With a remarkable openness to the critical issues von Dobschütz sketched out the exegetical alternative on the basis of two crucial passages by assuming pseudepigraphical authorship before rejecting the approach as less convincing than the traditional stance (258ff.; 303f.).

The traditional position takes as its starting point the explicit claim of Pauline authorship in the praescript, which is further strengthened by reference to Paul's own mark in 3.17. It argues that since Silvanus (Silas) and Timothy, according to Acts, were with Paul only during a limited period during the second missionary journey, the letter must have been written very shortly after the first. Often it is argued that the situation had worsened in the brief ensuing time both respecting the disturbance over the imminent parousia and the disorder resulting in idleness, and that Paul's second letter sought immediately to address these issues. The reference to the temple in 2.4 was once thought to be support for a dating before AD 70, but this argument has been generally abandoned as being a stereotypical feature. Several different explanations for the close literary similarity have been suggested. Zahn argued in his *Introduction* that Paul used a copy of his first letter, while Bornemann suggested that his memory of the earlier correspondence was still fresh and influenced his later writing. Then again, conservative scholars have made a rather strong case that the conflict between the two forms of eschatological hope is no grounds for questioning the authorship of II Thessalonians because such tension reflects a traditional apocalyptic feature which is still found, for example, in the Synoptic Gospels (cf. Marshall). Finally, the external evidence of its canonical attestation, probably by Polycarp but certainly by Justin and the

Muratorian fragment, sets a terminus within the first half of the second century (Rigaux, 112ff.).

In spite of these strengths, the traditional position has not been convincing to many when attempting to resolve several of the difficulties which surround II Thessalonians. The constant appeal to psychological bridges by which to link the two epistles is without textual warrant (cf. Bornemann's classic formulation, 484f., and Zahn's conjectures, *Intr.* ad loc.). Then again, the strange mixture of features of similarity with those of striking discontinuity has not been adequately faced (e.g. Marshall, 30ff.). It seems obvious that some critical scholars such as von Dobschütz and Best in the end fell back to the traditional position as the more plausible alternative although continuing to recognize some of the unresolved problems of this stance.

In the light of these persistent problems, a whole host of mediating solutions have been suggested. Because these theories have been reviewed by the various introductions and commentaries, it is unnecessary to rehearse the debate in detail (cf. Rigaux, 124ff.; Jewett; Schenke-Fischer I, 196f.). Briefly stated, the alternatives have been as follows: (i) II Thessalonians was written by Paul, but *before* I Thessalonians (Grotius, Manson). (ii) The letter was composed by Timothy in the name of Paul (Spitta). (iii) It was directed to a different audience from I Thessalonians, namely to a small circle of Jewish converts inside the Thessalonian congregation (Harnack, Dibelius). (iv) It was originally directed to another congregation, e.g. to Philippi (Schweizer). (v) II Thessalonians is a composite of several different, but genuine letters (Schmithals). Although it should not be denied that often some significant observations have emerged from these theories, it is also fair to say that none has so far evoked a wide affirmative response.

These mediating positions have been largely overshadowed by a consistent pseudepigraphical hypothesis. In the history of critical scholarship this alternative emerged by the end of the eighteenth century (J. E. C. Schmidt, 1798; selections are reprinted by Trilling, *Untersuchungen* 159ff.). After entering a period of disfavour, the pseudepigraphical theory was revived toward the end of the nineteenth century by Holtzmann, Hollmann, and especially Wrede. Although it continued to be supported by the so-called left wing (Schmiedel, Bultmann), the defence of the letter's authenticity by Dobschütz, Dibelius, and Rigaux, among others, did much to prevent the building of a consensus. However, within recent years the pendulum has begun to swing in favour of the hypothesis of pseudepigraphy. Among Protestants Friedrich (NTD) and Marxsen (ZBK) have defended the theory in their commentaries, and have received aggressive support from essays by Braun, Lindemann, Krodel and Schenke (*Intr.*). More striking has been the shift to the pseudepigraphical position among German Catholics. The work of Brox on the Pastorals had certainly prepared the ground, but starting with Trilling's monograph of 1972, followed by his commentary of 1980, a major attack on the letter's authenticity was launched which has received a growing support (Schelkee, Laub, Mussner, Giblin). Of course, this description does not imply that there were not significant variations within the hypothesis which are important to pursue.

Unquestionably, the most consistently brilliant formulation of the pseudepigraphical position was presented by Wrede. Basing his evidence primarily upon the literary dependence of II Thessalonians on I Thessalonians, Wrede argued that a post-Pauline author, claiming Pauline authority, composed a letter about AD 100 in order to legitimate a change in eschatological perspective. He used the church of Thessalonica as a fictitious setting for the treatise.

Recently, a more radical form of the pseudepigraphical thesis, first adumbrated in Hilgenfeld, has been developed by Lindemann, Marxsen, and Krodel. Accordingly, the function of II Thessalonians was to degrade I Thessalonians (cf. 2.2) and to replace it by a later pseudepigraphical letter. The effect was to challenge the authenticity of the genuine Pauline letter by an appeal to the legitimacy of the later pseudepigraphical letter. Krodel states it bluntly; 'In order to have his own writing accepted as apostolic writing our author used a trick in 3:17' (86).

A more conservative form of the pseudepigraphical theory has been developed by modern German Catholic scholars. Trilling (*Untersuchungen*, 133ff.) wrestles hard to give the literary phenomenon of pseudepigraphy a positive theological interpretation and to detach it from connotations of deceit and falsehood. He attempts to pursue the theory of Brox that the later writer saw himself standing in the line of Pauline tradition and sought to actualize the tradition for a later generation by interpreting (*auslegen*) the apostolic writings. He lays much stress upon the emergence of a 'portrait of the apostle' which provides an authentic prism through which to form a fresh formulation for a later era.

For anyone who has worked closely with both Thessalonian epistles, the attraction of the pseudepigraphical hypothesis is immediate and powerful. With a stroke one is able to develop a consistent theory by which to explain both the structural similarities of the letters, as well as the linguistic variations from the usual Pauline style. The theory also is consistent in positing a later situation by which to explain the growth in the status of Paul which is commensurate with the formation of a Pauline corpus.

Nevertheless, there remain some major problems, which derive from the pseudepigraphical model regardless of which form of the hypothesis is defended. The difficulties account for the continued resistance to the hypothesis by many critical scholars. It is far from obvious that the pseudepigraphical hypothesis has been successful in describing a suitable historical setting for the letter. The suggestions remain vague and hypothetical with little solid evidence on which to build. Some scholars posit a genuinely post-Pauline setting, others a fictive projection on the basis of I Thessalonians, while still others suggest a concrete, historical situation, but somewhere other than in Thessalonica.

There is general agreement among the proponents of the theory that the threat of a false eschatological hope did not stem from a form of gnosticism – Schmithals' voice is an exception – but from apocalyptic enthusiasts. However, the pseudepigraphical writer is thought to represent a later period in the development of the early church in which the hope of the imminent parousia had slackened and was being reinterpreted in order to accommodate the delay. However, the alleged parallels, e.g. II Peter 3.3, reflect a very different attitude in the congregation from that being combated in II Thessalonians, in fact, just the opposite. As a result, critics are forced to set the attitude of the pseudepigraphical author in contrast to his congregation, or to seek parallels for apocalyptic enthusiasm in the writings of Hippolytus (so Wrede). The point is that the alleged combination of enthusiasm, on the one hand, and the postponement of the parousia, on the other, does not have any clear parallels within the New Testament and requires a hypothetical construct.

Furthermore, it is largely assumed in the pseudepigraphical model that the overriding concern of II Thessalonians lay in correcting or replacing a false eschatological hope (2.1–12). This opinion holds good whether or not the situation described in the letter is interpreted as a genuine historical one, or as a literary construct, which functioned merely as a theological vehicle. It is, therefore, surprising that several features in the letter continue to have a largely independent function and have not been integrated into the one underlying purpose of the letter. It would have strengthened the case against the enthusiasts if the themes of disorder and idleness had been related to their false eschatological hope. However, this move did not occur within the letter. They remain independent themes which are never connected to the epistle's alleged purpose. Again, the theme of suffering is never discussed in such a way as to disassociate it from being understood as a sign of the messianic woes, which would also have strengthened the writer's main case. Conversely, if II Thessalonians were genuine, one could posit a situation similar to that of I Thessalonians in which Paul could address the issue of eschatology from one perspective (I 4.13), and then deal with the issue of the community's harmony from quite another, which is a practice common to his other letters. In sum, if II Thessalonians were pseudepigraphical, one would have expected the subordination of the various themes to the one theme of eschatology, but this literary move did not take place.

Finally, the two most recent attempts, by Trilling and Marxsen, to work out the pseudepigraphical hypothesis in the form of a commentary have demonstrated a new set of exegetical difficulties. Trilling's attempt to offer a positive interpretation of the phenomenon of pseudepigraphy must be commended, but it remains a question whether Brox's theory of an interpretive extension of the Pauline tradition in the Pastorals can apply also to II Thessalonians. The situation of the letter seems quite different. The effort to discover post-Pauline features, particularly to develop the idea of a portrait of Paul, seems often unconvincing and contrived. Many of the features of the post-Pauline era found in the Pastorals, such as the growth of ecclesiastical offices, are missing from II Thessalonians. Even the relation to tradition, while certainly present, differs strikingly from the Pastorals.

Marxsen's recent commentary is a highly conscious methodological attempt to exploit exegetically the pseudepigraphical hypothesis. He sets out at length his method (57ff.), especially his concern to discern the intention of the author who writes as if with the authority of Paul. The result is that a new form of psychologizing emerges in which Marxsen tries to reconstruct the thought process of the author which lies behind his formulation of Pauline doctrine. The critical concern to get as close as possible to the text apart from dogmatic biases seems to have come a full circle in Marxsen's case.

In sum, the attempt to do justice to the strange mixture of early and late features, and to the peculiar constellation of genuine Pauline and a mediated Pauline witness, has not yet been successfully accomplished either by the efforts on the right or the left of the theological spectrum.

III. Exploring a Canonical Alternative

The issue at stake is whether a different approach to the New Testament canon may provide some elements of insight which have not been exploited up to now. My intention is to begin with an analysis of how the letter functions canonically, and only then to pursue the relation of this canonical role to a putative Pauline authorship.

The letter clearly purports to be from Paul and his associates, and is directed to the church of the Thessalonians. The first real problem to adjudicate turns on how to understand the close parallelism between I and II Thessalonians respecting the praescript and the larger structure of the two letters. The peculiar problem in this relationship emerges because there is never an explicit reference made by II Thessalonians to I Thessalonians as a previous letter. It is neither cited, nor mentioned in any form. Therefore, the first implication to be drawn is that II Thessalonians cannot be seen as originally functioning as a commentary on I Thessalonians. The parallels lie in the content, but not explicitly related to the prior letter (cf. suffering II 1.5//I 3.3f.; parousia and assembly II 2.1//4.15; internal disorders II 3.11//I 5.14).

II Thessalonians, especially 2.1ff., seeks to supplement or correct a misunderstanding which is causing consternation in the congregation, specifically the belief that the 'arrival of the day of the Lord is at hand'. The sense of the expression in 2.2 is not fully clear and its interpretation depends on how one understands the larger situation. However, the effort to see the issue as arising from a gnostic reinterpretation of the mode of the parousia, as if the parousia had already come in secret, does not find any warrant in the text. Rather, the consternation arises from the fear of an imminent judgment which is associated with Christ's return (cf. Wrede). The exact source of this misunderstanding is not specified, but various possibilities are mentioned (word, spirit, Pauline letter). However, the emphasis falls on rejecting the teachings as false regardless of the origin.

There is no claim made in II Thessalonians that the writer is introducing a new eschatological teaching, but rather he is repeating what he had taught them when he was with them (2.5). Although the language is saturated with Old Testament imagery and allusion, there is no direct appeal made to the Old Testament by which to provide scriptural backing. Knowledge of Christ's parousia and the concomitant assembly is assumed. The sequence of eschatological events which precede the parousia is enumerated in terms of technical apocalyptic terminology (e.g. rebellion, man of lawlessness, the restrainer, Satan's activity, delusion, etc.). The text is not expounded in (say) a midrashic or *pesher*-type fashion, but actualized to the hearer by an appeal to his consciousness of what is occurring (e.g. 'remember', 'know', vv. 5f).

In ch. 3, specific commands are directed to the idle (3.1ff.) but without any reference to the situation having grown worse. The letter's role as the instrument of a specific ecclesiastical directive is made explicit (v. 14) and supported with a strong community sanction. In addition, the claim of Pauline authority is authenticated in 3.17 by means of a special mark by which to identify its true author. The sign serves to undergird the authority of Paul who in the letter offered his authentic teaching on the parousia as well as issuing a specific church order. Since there is no explicit reference to I Thessalonians in any form, the close parallelism in the style of the praescript and the letter's structure played no significant role in the canonical function of II Thessalonians. It emerged as an issue only when the larger collection of the two letters was joined within the Pauline corpus, and would have been read as a further extension of the apostle's claim: 'This is the way I write' (3.17).

To summarize, from a canonical perspective of II Thessalonians there is no indication of a hiatus between the letter and Paul's first-hand exercise of his authority over the Thessalonian church. Indeed the claim of authenticity is explicit and even apologetic.

However, there is another side to the canonical shape which must now be addressed. Is it possible that the present canonical function of II Thessalonians, which we have attempted to describe, is in fact a non-historical, theological construct? We have already sought to raise some of the difficulties associated with the radical pseudepigraphical hypothesis of Lindemann, Marxsen and Krodel in which the author fashioned his letter with the intention of deceiving his readers into rejecting the authority of I Thessalonians. However, is it possible within the canonical approach which is being suggested to recognize a distinction between a theological (canonical) construal and a prehistory of this canonical shape which reflected a different form in its early stage of development?

I think that the answer is clearly yes. The examples of other epistles which have been assigned a function within the Pauline corpus, such as the Pastorals, Ephesians, and Colossians, would support not identifying the final canonical role with the historical process of its composition. There is considerable evidence to buttress the argument that the canonical form of letters within the corpus often reveals an indirect relationship to Pauline authorship and that the apostolic witness has been extended beyond the historical Paul. The crucial issue turns on determining the effect of this form of extension of witness on the transmission of the tradition. As suggested earlier, the primary issue from a canonical perspective is not whether II Thessalonians accords with a reconstructed portrait of the historical Paul, but rather with the profile of the canonical Paul whose testimony has been preserved within the authoritative collection of the church's scripture. However, it should be immediately added that the relationship between the canonical and the historical Paul remains a significant issue for canonical interpretation, even if secondary to the primary one.

The effect of II Thessalonians was to extend Pauline eschatology in a new direction. Moreover, when the two Thessalonian letters were subsequently joined within the Pauline corpus, II Thessalonians performed the function of serving as a commentary on I Thessalonians. The eschatology of I Thessalonians was not replaced or suppressed, but its emphasis on the immediacy of the parousia was held in a tension with that of II Thessalonians which laid its emphasis on the signs preceding its inauguration.

Of crucial importance for the interpretation of II Thessalonians is to determine how the Pauline witness was extended by means of this letter. The second epistle did not repudiate the traditional Christian belief in Christ's imminent return, but it provided a new context for the doctrine which effected its understanding. A new historical situation which effected the eschatological hope in the parousia by producing a deep consternation in the church was addressed by an appeal to Old Testament imagery and to Christian tradition. The pattern of the coming of the Antichrist which had been formulated in Daniel and continued in apocalyptic tradition was now superimposed upon the earlier Christian eschatology of the Thessalonian church (cf. Luke 21.20ff.). The entrance of God's kingdom would surely come, and God would slay the lawless one through Christ. However, the end would be preceded by a variety of eschatological signs. The purpose of the message was to encourage the faithful in standing firm and holding to the faith (2.15). The letter claimed no new message, but appealed again to the tradition, both oral and written (2.15), and to the continuity with Paul's message (2.5).

We have argued up to this point that a canonical approach can take seriously the tension between its canonical role and its historical development. Specifically in terms of II Thessalonians it acknowledges the difficulties of assuming a direct Pauline authorship. Thus, although the stylistic similarity between the two letters functions canonically to undergird the selfsame authority of Paul, from a historical perspective it is difficult to attribute the imitation of the second letter to the apostle himself. Similarly the significant differences in theology and emphasis can hardly be denied. Finally, signs of a later period than that assumed by the tradition of direct Pauline authorship appear especially in the growth of Paul's authority through his letters.

The decisive question must, therefore, be faced in regard to II Thessalonians. Could the canonical construct have arisen through a process in which Pauline authorship was claimed for a pseudepigraphical work whose authoritative status was achieved by means of a literary ploy designed to deceive its readers regarding its actual origin? The issue, thus posed, stretches the tension between the letter's self-claim and its historical reconstruction to its fullest limits. The issue is far more extreme than that of the Pastorals or the so-called 'deutero-Pauline' epistles because of the nature of the book's self-claim. It also belongs to a different order from appeals to traditional authorship which appear in Old Testament books, such as Isaiah and Daniel.

The problem is difficult, if not impossible to decide in principle because direct historical evidence is lacking. One's decision depends to a great extent on the broader picture of the development of early Christianity into which the individual pieces of the puzzle are fitted.

It is also naive to suggest that dogmatic bias is present only on the side of those questioning the pseudepigraphical model. Perhaps it is wise to leave open the larger question and to address some of the specific details of the historian's reconstruction of II Thessalonians.

In my judgment, the form of pseudepigraphical authorship usually proposed for II Thessalonians faces serious historical difficulties. It underestimates the elements of genuine continuity with Pauline authorship. It has not demonstrated a consistently post-Pauline setting for the letter. Exegesis, when consistently pursued according to the new model, often loses credibility by being pushed to its logical conclusion. Above all, it is difficult to fit this portrayal of the process of canonization into the larger picture from the facts which are known. For example, the repudiation of the efforts of a pious Christian to enhance the reputation of Paul by means of a pseudepigraphical work (*Acta Pauli*) is indicative of the numerous types of ecclesiastical decisions, evoked in heated conflict, which characterized the canonical process. Admittedly the historical problem remains difficult and unresolved up to now. The dividing line was a narrow one between a process of extending Paul's apostolic witness which was considered legitimate and a process of pseudepigraphical composition which was rejected as deceptive by the church. (cf. the bibliography on the problem of pseudepigraphy in ch.21 below on the Pastorals).

The perplexity of the issue respecting II Thessalonians stems from the conclusion that the letter reflects neither the direct authorship of Paul, nor a later post-Pauline composition of a pseudonymous author. However, the general critical consensus appears to have concluded that there is no other alternative between direct Pauline or pseudonymous authorship. In my judgment, our historical knowledge is too fragmentary to preclude other possible options, one of which I will propose in the spirit of illustration rather than demonstration.

It is possible to conceive of II Thessalonians being written by someone under Paul's general direction, and signed by the apostle to legitimate the letter which was mediated in its actual composition by an associate. Such a theory would explain the strange mixture of genuine elements of continuity with the remarkable variations. The writer chose to imitate as closely as possible Paul's first letter in order to emphasize its Pauline origin and to minimize his own significance. Of course, I am aware that the objection is immediately raised that the praescript designates the authors as Paul, Silvanus, and Timothy, and that their ministry overlapped only during a brief period during the so-called second missionary journey.

However, the reference by Paul to his co-workers remains a traditional convention which can be easily abandoned when the apostle turns to address his readers in the first person singular. The inclusion of Paul's co-workers in the praescript of II Thessalonians would then belong to the writer's imitative style and would serve to assure his readers that II Thessalonians came with the same claim to authority as that of I Thessalonians. In my opinion, Hadorn's arguments for the conventional nature of the plural addressees (*Die Abfassung der Thess.*, 67ff.) have more force than usually recognized.

Then again, it would seem likely that II Thessalonians was composed at a period considerably later than suggested by the traditional position. This judgment is supported by the evidence of the growth of Paul's authority and the possibility of false claims being made in his name which were even supported by an appeal to his letters (2.2). Evidence by which to date the letter more precisely is lacking. The fact that II Thessalonians was included in the earliest stage of the canonical formation of the Pauline corpus, in striking contrast (say) to the Pastorals, would speak against choosing a date long after Paul's death. The attempt to correlate the dating of the epistle to a larger pattern of a growing disbelief in an imminent parousia seems to me highly subjective. Rather, the letter addressed a peculiar historical situation of one church, the exact details of which have been largely lost. The little which is known stands in striking discontinuity with the kind of threat later posed by Gnosticism, nor is it congruent with many features of Montanism.

To summarize, we have attempted to describe the canonical role of II Thessalonians which serves primarily to extend the Pauline eschatology in a new direction. Later when combined with I Thessalonians within the Pauline corpus, it marked one facet of his eschatological teaching which was held in a corrective balance with that of his earlier letter. Within this canonical construal the effect was to affirm the letter as an authoritative exercise of Paul's apostolic authority on which Christian tradition was grounded.

I do recognize that the letter reflects signs of a pre-canonical process which remains in considerable tension with the shape and function finally assigned the epistle within the canonical corpus. The hermeneutical issue turns on the extent to which exegesis of the letter is engaged from a reconstructed prehistory or from the context which the canonical process has assigned the book as scripture of the church. To put the question in another way, does the critical knowledge of the prehistory of the canonical process function to correct and even to repudiate the ecclesiastical decision, or does it serve rather as an aid in better understanding the nature of the canonical construal which is accepted as authoritative by the Christian church? A major concern of this introduction is that such issues be addressed from the broadest possible theological base in order to resist easy historical solutions whether made from the left or from the right.

21

THE PASTORAL EPISTLES

Commentaries

C. J. Ellicott, [4]1869
H. von Soden, HCNT, [2]1893
J. H. Bernard, CGT, 1899
B. Weiss, MeyerK, [7]1902
E. F. Brown, WC, 1917
R. S. J. Parry, 1920
G. Wohlenberg, KNT, [3]1923
W. Lock, ICC, 1924
A. Schlatter, 1936
E. F. Scott, MNTC, 1936
R. Falconer, 1937
B. S. Easton, 1947
D. Guthrie, Tyn, 1957
J. Freundorfer, RNT, [3]1959

W. Brandt, [2]1959
A. R. C. Leaney, TB, 1960
C. K. Barrett, NC1B, 1963
J. N. D. Kelly, B/HNTC, 1964
G. Holtz, THKNT, 1965
A. T. Hanson, CNEB, 1966
C. Spicq, ÉB, [4]1969
N. Brox, RNT, [4]1969
M. Dibelius, H. Conzelmann,
    Herm, ET 1972
J. Jeremias, NTD, [11]1975
J. L. Houlden, Pel, 1976
V. Hasler, ZBK, 1978
B. Van Elderen, NICNT, 1984

Bibliography of the Pastoral Epistles

J. A. **Allan**, 'The "In Christ" Formula in the Pastoral Epistles', *NTS* 10, 1963/4, 115–21; A. E. **Barnett**, *Paul Becomes a Literary Influence*, Chicago 1941; C. K. **Barrett**, 'Pauline Controversies in the Post-Pauline Period', *NTS* 20, 1973/4, 229–45; H.-W. **Bartsch**, *Die Anfänge urchristlicher Rechtsbildungen*, ThF 34, 1965; W. **Bauer**, *Orthodoxy and Heresy in Earliest Christianity*, ET London and Philadelphia 1971; M. **Baumgarten**, *Die Aechtheit der Pastoralbriefe, mit besonderer Rücksicht auf den neuesten Angriff von Herrn Dr Baur vertheidight*, Berlin 1837; F. C. **Baur**, *Die sogenannten Pastoralbriefe des Apostels Paulus aufs neue kritisch untersucht*, Tübingen 1835; H. **Binder**, 'Die historische Situation der Pastoralbriefe', *Geschichtswirklichkeit und Glaubensbewährung, FS Bischof F. Müller*. ed. F. C. Fry, Stuttgart 1967, 70–83; M. C. **de Boer**, 'Images of Paul in the Post-Apostolic Church', *CBQ* 42, 1980, 359–80; N. **Brox**, *Zeuge und Martyrer*, SANT 5, 1961; 'Amt, Kirche und Theologie in der nachapostolischen Epoche – Die Pastoralbriefe', *Gestalt und Anspruch* *des Neuen Testaments*, ed. J. Schreiner, Würzburg 1969, 120–33; 'Zu den persönlichen Notizen der Pastoralbriefe', *BZ* NF 13, 1969, 76–94; 'Historische und theologische Probleme der Pastoralbriefe des Neuen Testament', *Kairos* 11, 1969, 81–94; 'Altkirchliche Formen des Anspruchs auf apostolische Kirchenverfassung', *Kairos* 12, 1970, 113–140; 'Lukas als Verfasser der Pastoralbriefe?', *JAC* 13, 1970, 62–77; R. **Bultmann**, 'Pastoralbriefe', *RGG*², IV, 993–7; P. **Burke**, 'The Monarchial Episcopate at the End of the First Century', *Journal of Ecumenical Studies* 7, 1970, 499–518.

H. **von Campenhausen**, 'Polykarp von Smyrna und die Pastoralbriefe' (1951), in *Aus der Frühzeit des Christentums*, Tübingen 1963, 197–252; *Ecclesiastical Authority and Spiritual Power in the Church of the First Three Centuries*, ET London and Stanford 1969; P. **Carrington**, 'The Problem of the Pastoral Epistles, Dr Harrison's Theory Reviewed', *AnThR* 21, 1939, 32–9; R. F. **Collins**, 'The Image of Paul in the Pastorals', *Laval Théologique et Philosophique* 31, Quebec 1975, 147–73; E. **Dassmann**, 'Die Bedeutung des Alten Testaments für das Verständnis des kirchlichen Amtes in der frühpatristischen Theologie', *BiLe* 11, 1970, 198–214; M. **Dibelius**, 'ἐπίγνωσις ἀληθείας', *Neutestamentliche Studien für G. Heinrici*, Leipzig 1914, 176–89; G. S. **Duncan**, 'Paul's Ministry in Asia. The Last Phase', *NTS* 3, 1956/7, 211–8; E. E. **Ellis**, 'The Authorship of the Pastorals: A Resumé and Assessment of Current Trends', *EvQu* 32, 1960, 151–61; E. **Fascher**, 'Timotheus', 'Titus', *PW* II.12, 1932, 1342–54, 1579–86; B. **Fiore**, *The Function of Personal Example in the Socratic and Pastoral Epistles*, Diss. Yale 1982; J. M. **Ford**, 'Proto-Montanism in the Pastoral Epistles', *NTS* 17, 1970/1, 338–46; R. H. **Fuller**, 'The Pastoral Epistles', *Ephesians, Colossians, 2 Thessalonians, The Pastoral Epistles* (Proclamation Commentaries), Philadelphia 1978, 97–121; R. W. **Funk**, 'The Apostolic Parousia. Form and Significance', *Christian History and Interpretation. Studies Presented to John Knox*, ed. W. R. Farmer et al., Cambridge 1967, 249–68; K. **Grayston**, G. **Herdan**, 'The Authorship of the Pastorals in the Light of Statistical Linguistics', *NTS* 6, 1959/60, 1–15.

W. **Hadorn**, 'Die Gefährten und Mitarbeiter des Paulus', *Aus Schrift und Geschichte, FS A. Schlatter*, Stuttgart 1922, 65–82; E. **Haenchen**, 'Pastoralbriefe und Gnosis', *RGG*³, II, 1958, 1654f.;   A. T. **Hanson**, *Studies in the Pastoral Epistles*, London 1968; A. **von Harnack**, *The Constitution and Law of the Church in the First Two Centuries*, ET London and New York 1910; P. N. **Harrison**, *The Problem of the Pastoral Epistles*, Oxford 1921; 'Important Hypotheses Reconsidered: The Authorship of the Pastoral Epistles', *ExpT* 67, 1955/6, 77–81; *Paulines and Pastorals*, London 1964; H. **Hegermann**, 'Der geschichtliche Ort der Pastoralbriefe', *Theol. Versuche* II, 1970, 47–64; H. J. **Holtzmann**, *Die Pastoralbriefe, kritisch und exegetisch bearbeitet*, Leipzig 1880; J. **Jeremias**, 'Zur Datierung der Pastoralbriefe', *ZNW* 52, 1961, 101–4; L. T. **Johnson**, 'II Timothy and the Polemic against False Teachers: A Re-examination', *Ohio Journal of Religious Studies* 6–7, 1978/9, 1–26; E. **Käsemann**, 'Das Formular einer neutestamentlichen Ordinationsparänese', *Neutestamentliche Studien für R. Bultmann*, ed. W. Eltester, BZNW 21, [2]1957, 261–68; 'Ministry and Community in the New Testament', ET *Essays on New Testament Themes*, SBT 41, 1964, 63–94; E. **Kamlah**, *Die Form der katalogischen Paränese im Neuen Testament*, WUNT 7, 1964; R. J. **Karris**, *The Function and Sitz im Leben of the Paraenetic Elements in the Pastoral Epistles*, Diss. Harvard 1971; 'The Background and Significance of the Polemic of the Pastoral Letters', *JBL* 92, 1973, 549–64; K. **Kertelge**, ed., *Das kirchliche Amt im Neuen Testament*, WdF 439, 1977; G. W. **Knight**, *The Faithful Sayings in the Pastoral Letters*, Kampen 1968; O. **Knoch**, *Die 'Testamente' des Petrus und Paulus*, SBS 62, 1973.

S. **de Lestapis**, *L'Énigme des Pastorales de St Paul*, Paris 1976; J. B. **Lightfoot**, 'The Date of the Pastoral Epistles', *Biblical Essays*, London and New York 1893, 397–410,411–18; 'St Paul's History after the Close of the Acts', ibid., 421–37; A. **Lindemann**, *Paulus im ältesten Christentum*, BHT 58, 1979, 44–49; H. **von Lips**, *Glaube – Gemeinde – Amt: Zum Verständnis der Ordination in den Pastoralbriefen*, FRLANT 122, 1979; E. **Lohse**, *Die Ordination im Spätjudentum und im Neuen Testament*, Göttingen 1951; W. **Lütgert**, *Die Irrlehrer der Pastoralbriefe*, BFChTh 13, 1909; U. **Luz**, 'Erwägungen zur Entstehung des "Frühkatholizismus". Eine Skizze', *ZNW* 65, 1974, 88–111; D. R. **MacDonald**, *The Legend and the Apostle. The Battle for Paul in Story and Canon*, Philadelphia 1983; N. J. **McEleney**, 'Vice Lists of the Pastorals', *CBQ* 36, 1974, 203–19; J. **MacRay**, 'The Authorship of the Pastoral Epistles', *RestQ* 7, 1963, 2–18; H. **Maehlum**, *Die Vollmacht des Timotheus nach den Pastoralbriefen*, Theol. Diss. 1, Basel 1961; F. **Maier**, *Die Hauptprobleme der Pastoralbriefe Pauli*, Bibl. Zeitfragen III/12, Münster [3]1920; A. J. **Malherbe**, 'Medical Imagery in the Pastoral Epistles', *Texts and Testaments*, ed. W. E. March, San Antonio 1980, 19–35; C. **Maurer**, 'Eine Textvariante klärt die Entstehung der Pastoralbriefe auf', *TZ* 3, 1947, 321–37; H. H. **Mayer**, *Über die Pastoralbriefe*, FRLANT 20, 1913; B. M. **Metzger**, 'A Reconsideration of Certain Arguments against the Pauline Authorship of the Pastoral Epistles', *ExpT* 70, 1958/9, 91–94; 'Literary Forgeries and Canonical Pseudepigrapha', *JBL* 91, 1972, 3–24; W. **Michaelis**, 'Die Pastoralbriefe und Wortstatistik', *ZNW* 28, 1929, 69–76; *Die Pastoralbriefe und Gefangenschaftsbriefe. Zur Echtheitsfrage der Pastoralbriefe*, NTF I.6, 1930; O. **Michel**, 'Grundfragen der Pastoralbriefe', *Auf dem Grunde der Apostel und Propheten*, *FS T. Wurm*, ed. M. Loeser, Stuttgart, 1948, 83–99; C. F. D. **Moule**, 'The Problem of the Pastoral Epistles: A Reappraisal', *BJRL* 47, 1964/5, 430–52; F. **Mussner**, 'Die Ablösung des apostolischen durch das nachapostolische Zeitalter und ihre Konsequenzen', *Wort Gottes in der Zeit, FS K. H. Schelkle*, ed. H. Feld and J. Nolte, Düsseldorf 1973, 166–177.

W. **Nauck**, *Der Herkunft des Verfassers der Pastoralbriefe*, Diss. Göttingen 1960; W. E. **Oates**, 'The Conception of Ministry in the Pastoral Epistles', *RevExp* 56, 1959, 388–410; J. J. **O'Rourke**, 'Some Considerations about Attempts at Statistical Analysis of the Pauline Corpus', *CBQ* 35, 1973, 483–90; B. **Reicke**, 'Chronologie der Pastoralbriefe', *TLZ* 101, 1976, 81–94;

D. K. **Rensberger**, *As the Apostle Teaches: The Development of the Use of Paul's Letters in Second-Century Christianity*, Diss. Yale 1981; J. **Rohde**, 'Pastoralbriefe und Acta Pauli', *StEv* 5, TU 103, 1968, 303–310; O. **Roller**, *Das Formular der paulinischen Briefe*, BWANT 58, 1933; J. **Roloff**, *Apostolat – Verkündigung – Kirche. Ursprung, Inhalt und Funktion des kirchlichen Apostelamtes nach Paulus, Lukas und den Pastoralbriefen*, Gütersloh 1965, 236–71; 'Amt/Ämter/ Amtsverständnis IV. Im Neuen Testament', *TRE* 11, 509–33.

A. **Sand**, 'Anfänge einer Koordinierung verscheidener Gemeindeordnungen nach den Pastoralbriefen', *Kirche im Werden*, ed. J. Hainz, Munich 1976, 215–37; H.-M. **Schenke**, 'Das Weiterwirken des Paulus und die Pflege eines Erbes durch die Paulus-Schule', *NTS* 21, 1974/5, 505–18; F. **Schleiermacher**, Über den sogenannten ersten Brief des Paulus an den Timotheos, Berlin 1807; reprinted *Sämmtliche Werke*, 1. Abt.:Zur Theologie 2, Berlin 1936, 221–320; H. **Schlier**, 'Die Ordnung der Kirche nach dem Pastoralbriefen', *Die Zeit der Kirche*, Freiburg [2]1958, 128–47; E. **Schlink**, 'Apostolische Sukzession', *KuD* 7, 1961, 79–114; W. **Schmithals**, 'Pastoralbriefe', *RGG*[3], V, 144–8; W. **Schrage**, 'Zur Ethik der neutestamentlichen Haustafeln', *NTS* 21, 1974/5, 1–22; E. Schweizer, *Church Order in the New Testament*, ET, SBT 32, 1965; C. **Spicq**, 'Pastorales (Épîtres)', *DBSuppl* VII, 1961, 1–73; 'Pèlerine et vêtements (Á propos de II Tim.IV,13 et Act.XX,33)', *Mélanges E. Tisserant* I, Rome 1964, 389–417; F. **Spitta**, 'Über die persönlichen Notizen im zweiten Briefe an Timotheus', *ThStKr* 51, 1878, 582–607; A. **Stecker**, *Formen und Formeln in den paulinischen Hauptbriefen und den Pastoralbriefen*, Diss. Münster 1966; W. **Stenger**, 'Timotheus und Titus als literarische Gestalten. Beobachtungen zur Form und Funktion der Pastoralbriefe', *Kairos* 16, 1974, 252–67; G. **Strecker**, 'Paulus in nachpaulinischer Zeit', *Kairos* 12, 1970, 208–16; A. **Strobel**, 'Schreiben des Lukas? Zum sprachlichen Problem der Pastoralbriefe', *NTS* 15, 1968/9, 191–210.

J. **Thurén**, 'Die Struktur der Schlussparänese I Tim 6,3–21', *TZ* 26, 1970, 241–53; P. **Trummer**, '"Mantel und Schriften" (2 Tim 4,13). Zur Interpretation eines persönlichen Notiz in den Pastoralbriefen', *BZ* NF 18, 1974, 193–207; *Die Paulustradition des Pastoralbriefe*, BBET 8, 1978; D. C. **Verner**, *The Household of God. The Social World of the Pastoral Epistles*, SBLDS 71, Chico 1983; A. **Vögtle**, *Die Tugend- und Lasterkataloge im Neuen Testament*, NTAbh 16.4/5, 1936; K. **Wegenast**, *Das Verständnis der Tradition bei Paulus und in den Deuteropaulinen*, WMANT 8, 1962, 132–58; S. **Wibbing**, *Die Tugend- und Lasterkataloge im Neuen Testament*, BZNW 25, 1959; S. G. **Wilson**, *Luke and the Pastoral Epistles*, London 1979; H. **Windisch**, 'Zur Christologie der Pastoralbriefe', *ZNW* 34, 1935, 213–38.

Bibliography on Pseudepigraphy

Cf. bibliography in N. **Brox**, ed. *Pseudepigraphie in der heidnischen und jüdisch-christlichen Antike*, WdF 484, 1977, 335–42; K. **Aland**, 'Das Problem der Anonymität und Pseudonymität in der christlichen Literatur der ersten beiden Jahrhunderte', *Studien zur Überlieferung des Neuen Testaments und seines Textes*, ANTT II, 1967, 24–34; 'Falsche Verfasserangaben', *ThRev* 75, 1979, 1–10; H. R. **Balz**, 'Anonymität und Pseudepigraphie im Urchristentum: Überlegung zum literarischen und theologischen Problem des urchristlichen und gemeinantiken Pseudepigraphie', *ZTK* 66, 1969, 403–36; G. **Bardy**, 'Faux et fraudes littéraires dans l'antiquité chrétienne', *RHE* 32, 1936, 5–23, 275–302; A. E. **Barnett**, *Paul Becomes a Literary Influence*, Chicago 1941; L. H. **Brockington**, 'The problem of Pseudonymity', *JTS* NS 4, 1953, 15–22; N. **Brox**, 'Zum Problemstand in der Erforschung der altchristlichen Pseudepigraphie', *Kairos* NF 15, 1973, 10–23; *Falsche Verfasserangaben. Zur Erklärung der frühchristlichen Pseudepigraphie*, SBS 79, 1975.

J. S. **Candlish**, 'On the Moral Character of Pseudonymous Books', *Exp* IV. 4, 1891, 91–107, 262–79; J. A. **Farrer**, *Literary Forgeries*, London and New York 1907; J. C. **Fenton**, 'Pseudonymity in the New Testament', *Theology* 58, 1955, 51–6; K. M. **Fischer**, 'Anmerkungen zur Pseudepigraphie im Neuen Testament', *NTS* 23, 1977, 76–81; E. **Goodspeed**, 'Pseudonymity and Pseudepigraphy in Early Christian Literature', *New Chapters in New Testament Study*, New York and London 1937, 169–88; J. **Gribomont**, 'De la notion de "Faux" en littérature populaire', *Bibl* 54, 1973, 434–37; D. **Guthrie**, 'The Development of the Idea of Canonical Pseudepigraphy in New Testament Criticism', *Vox Evangelica* 1, 1962, 43–59; A. E. **Haefner**, 'A Unique Source for the Study of Ancient Pseudepigraphy', *AnThR* 16, 1934, 8–15; M. **Hengel**, 'Anonymität, Pseudepigraphie und "Literarische Fälschung" in der jüdisch-hellenistischen Literatur', in *Pseudepigraphia* I, Vandoevres-Genève 1972, 229–308; H. **Lietzmann**, 'Zur altchristlichen Verfassungsgeschichte', *ZWTh* 55, 1914, 97–153; reprinted *Kleine Schriften* I, Berlin 1958, 141–85; B. M. **Metzger**, 'Literary Forgery and Canonical Pseudepigrapha', *JBL* 91, 1972, 3–24; A. **Meyer**, 'Religiöse Pseudepigraphie als ethisch-psychologisches Problem', *ZNW* 35, 1936, 267–75; R. **Pesch**, 'Die Zuschreibung der Evangelien an apostolische Verfasser', *ZKT* 97, 1975, 56–71; M. **Rist**, 'Pseudepigraphy and the Early Christians', *Studies in New Testament and Early Christian Literature. Essays in Honor of A. P. Wikgren*, ed. D. E. Aune, Leiden 1972, 75–91; K. H. **Schelkle**, 'Biblische Pseudepigraphie', *Die Petrusbriefe. Der Judasbrief*, HTKNT, Freiburg 1961, 245–48; W. **Schneemelcher**, 'The Origin of the Pseudapostolic Literature', *NTApoc* II, 31–4; J. A. **Sint**, *Pseudonymität im Altertum. Ihre Formen und ihre Gründe*, Commentationes Aenipontanae XV, Innsbruck 1960; M. **Smith**, 'Pseudepigraphy in the Israelite Literary Tradition', *Pseudepigraphia* I, Vandoevres-Genève 1972, 189–215; W. **Speyer**, 'Religiöse Pseudepigraphie und literarische Fälschung im Altertum', *JAC* 8/9, 1965, 88–125; 'Literarische Fälschung', *RAC* 7, 1969, 236–77; *Die literarische Fälschung im heidnischen und christlichen Altertum – Ein Versuch ihrer Deutung*, HAW 1.2, 1971; E. **Stemplinger**, *Das Plagiat in der griechischen Literatur*, Leipzig and Berlin 1912.

F. **Torm**, *Die Pseudonymität im Hinblick auf die Literatur des Urchristentums*, Gütersloh 1932; W. **Trilling**, *Untersuchungen zum zweiten Thessalonicherbrief*,

Erfurter Theol. Studien 27, Leipzig 1972, 133–61; K. **Ziegler**, 'Plagiat', *PW*, 40, 1956–97; J. **Zmijewski**, 'Apostolische Paradosis und Pseudepigraphie im Neuen Testament, "Durch Erinnerung wachhalten"', (2 Petr 1,13; 3,1)', *BZ* 23, 1979, 161–71.

I. The Debate Over Genuineness

The modern discussion of the Pastoral epistles has been dominated by questions regarding the letters' genuineness. Are they the direct product of Pauline authorship, or do they stand in some indirect relationship to Paul, or are they actually pseudonymous? The majority of modern critics are unequivocal in asserting that this question must be decided at the outset because one's exegesis of the books depends to large extent on this judgment (cf. Dibelius, Wohlenberg, Brox, Trummer). Only occasionally are there dissenting voices which contest this starting point (Michel, Roloff).

The case mounted against the Pauline authorship of the Pastorals by historical critics began early in the nineteenth century, principally with Schleiermacher's powerful attack on I Timothy in 1807. This initial stage of criticism reached a climax in the analysis of Holtzmann (1880) which summarized with great thoroughness the literary, historical, and theological grounds for denying the traditional authorship. Finally, within the twentieth century P. N. Harrison's meticulous philological study of 1921 posed the literary argument against Pauline authorship with a new precision. In addition to these crucial volumes were numerous detailed articles and monographs which continued to expand the critical analysis.

The chief reasons raised against Pauline authorship are the following:

(*a*) An undisputed witness for the Pastorals by the Church Fathers cannot be established with certainty before the end of the second century (cf. Brox, *RNT*, 26ff. for the nature of the debate).

(*b*) The language, syntax, and literary style of the Pastorals vary greatly from the genuine Pauline epistles, both in respect to the vocabulary used and the familiar Pauline terminology omitted, to such an extent that the Pastorals appear closer to the Apostolic Fathers (e.g. Polycarp) than to the rest of the Pauline corpus (cf. Holtzmann, Harrison).

(*c*) The historical problem of fitting the ministry of Paul according to the Pastorals into the chronology of events known from the rest of the New Testament is exceedingly difficult. The most plausible construction is to posit Paul's release at his Roman trial, and another journey to the West, an assumption which raises other historical problems.

(d) The Pastorals appear to reflect a much later stage in the history of the early church with a more developed form of church structure, offices, and officers, and with forms of heresy which are more characteristic of the early second century.

(e) The theology expressed in the Pastorals differs markedly from that of the undisputed Pauline corpus and reveals a later, more developed theological reflection on the earlier Pauline tradition in the light of a changing historical situation.

Von Campenhausen summarizes the critical position in an important paragraph:

It is not the individual arguments against the genuineness (of the Pastorals), important as they are, which are decisive, but their complete and comprehensive convergence against which there are no significant counter-arguments. This convergence includes the late and tendentious external witness, the strangeness and improbability of the inner and outer depiction of the life of Paul, the non-Pauline concept of the community's structure, the completely different bland speech. Above all, there is the consistent alteration in the content which is indeed connected with Paul but in such a manner as both to continue and alter his thought according to the dogmatic needs of a later time . . . in the first half of the second century (*Aus der Frühzeit*, 200f.).

In response to the historical-critical position there has been called forth a strong and often learned defence of the direct Pauline authorship of the Pastorals which includes scholars of the stature of Lightfoot, Zahn, B. Weiss, Wohlenberg, Spicq among others. Their arguments proceed along the following lines:

(a) The attribution of the epistles to Paul does not rest upon a merely formal or peripheral relationship, nor is it analogous to the traditional ascriptions of authorship to the gospels. Rather, the Pauline authorship is an integral part of the letters' witness and is demonstrated in a series of personal, historical references which are not easily invented ('*unerfindlich*', Jeremias).

(b) The historical problems are resolved by positing a later missionary trip which is not recorded in either Acts or in the remaining letters. In addition, if the historical references were pseudepigraphical, would one not have expected agreement with the familiar history of Paul instead of disagreement? (Wohlenberg).

(c) The differences in vocabulary and style are to be explained either by a change in the historical situation addressed, or by the advanced age of the apostle.

(d) Finally, the elements of continuity with Pauline theology are sufficiently strong to support a unified authorship which has altered somewhat its theological emphasis in order to equip the church leaders in coping with new crises.

Within the conservative camp two important modifications of this traditional defence have been attempted which vary considerably in their degree of concessions. First, the thesis has been proposed that Paul was only the indirect author of the letters because the letters have been actually composed by a secretary under Paul's direction (Roller). The theory sought in this way to concede the difference in style while holding on to a Pauline source. Secondly, in order to account for the occasional personal references, such as II Tim.4.9ff., the hypothesis has been developed that epistles consisted of a group of genuine Pauline fragments which a later author formed into a new composition. However, these two attempts at modification have not generally been considered successful in mediating between the traditional and critical positions.

II. Recent Theories of Pseudepigraphy

A new phase in the debate over the question of authorship has opened up within the last two decades. It has been spearheaded by German-speaking Catholic scholars (Brox, Trilling, Kuss, Schelkle, Trummer, etc.), who have begun to exploit the new freedom of the period after Vatican II. These scholars have sought to develop in a positive way the exegetical potential within the genre of pseudepigraphy which they apply to the interpretation of the Pastorals. First, it is argued that the phenomenon of pseudepigraphy was widespread in the ancient world. It arose from a variety of different circumstances, and served very diverse functions. As a result, any generalization about its role is impossible, as if it were always uncritically accepted as a legitimate form of literature, or conversely, as if it were always regarded as fraudulent. These scholars contend that there were certain religious roles performed by pseudepigraphical writings which carried no odium, and that this recognition opens up new options for a positive historical and theological exegesis of the Pastorals.

While agreeing that the Pastorals are pseudepigraphical, this group of scholars has not yet formed a consensus regarding the exact function which the genre played in respect to these letters. Several suggestions have been proposed. Some argue that the Pastorals were written fifty years after Paul by a disciple of Paul who tried to address a new situation in the life of the church in a manner congruent with the apostle's teaching (Brox). Others have formulated the continuity in terms of a personalizing of the Pauline tradition (Trummer), or in terms of a commissioning office which continued to exercise the authority of Paul for a subsequent generation (Hegermann). Still others have sought to interpret the function of pseudepigraphical writing as a form of apostolic presence in the period following Paul's death (Stenger). Although the attractiveness of these hypotheses can be readily admitted, the difficulty remains that solid exegetical support has not yet been established. In fact, it is the virtual silence of the letters right at the crucial places where help is needed which continues to frustrate the interpretations.

One of the great advantages of the recent attempts to refine and apply the literary features of pseudepigraphy to the Pastorals in order to break out of the older impasse between the conservative and liberal positions has been its success in focusing the problem on the basic hermeneutical issues at stake in the debate. The heart of the controversy over authorship does not lie with the problem of historicity but with the nature of its referentiality.

The initial strength of the conservative position lies in its apparent ability to deal with the concrete biographical details which are found especially in II Timothy. Yet this one model of direct historical referentiality also proved in the end to be its undoing because large parts of the letters do not appear to lend themselves to the one hermeneutical model. The conservatives are forced to conjecture elaborate historical reconstructions, or to psychologize on Paul's declining health in order to bridge a growing historical gap between the Paul of the other letters and the Paul of the Pastorals.

The great strength of modern pseudepigraphical research lies in its recognition that such a literary model provides many other possibilities of theological referentiality whose truthfulness cannot be measured solely in terms of historical verisimilitude. For example, exploration into the function of this literary genre enables the interpreter to explain the typifying effect of its cliche-like language, or the reifying of ecclesiastical instruction. Moreover, some widely accepted warrants from modern Old Testament interpretation can now be exploited for the New Testament which finds an analogy in the theological extension of Mosaic authority to cover laws of a much later age. Finally, the new interpretive model appears to provide the flexibility to deal with the complex phenomena of 'double pseudepigraphy' (cf. Stenger) by which both the addressor as well as the addressee fail to reflect a simple historical referent.

However, in spite of the initial exegetical potential provided by the application of the genre pseudepigraphy to the Pastorals, some serious problems arise which have as yet not been adequately addressed by its proponents. In my judgment, the major problematical area does not lie with the description of the genre itself. That more research is needed beyond that begun by Sint, Speyer, Metzger, Brox among others would be readily admitted by all in an effort to bring its use more sharply into focus. However, the decisive hermeneutical issue turns on how one understands the problem of referentiality within the genre of pseudepigraphical literature. What is the hermeneutical effect on exegesis of applying this genre to the Pastorals?

First of all, among those scholars who have recently attempted to interpret the Pastorals as an example of pseudepigraphical literature the model of strictly historical referentiality of meaning continues to remain dominant. The literary genre is continually interpreted in reference to its allegedly 'real' historical situation, namely, one some fifty years after the death of Paul. The effect of this move is that the literary genre is actually viewed as something 'pseudo', whose true meaning only emerges when the genuine historical setting is reconstructed. A concomitant effect of this hermeneutical model is that the description of the Pastorals as pseudepigraphical usually functions to establish from the outset the referentiality of the letters to be derived largely from the creative imagination of the author. As a result, a rich variety of possible relationships, both simple and complex, between the literature and its referent is lost because the genre description simply decides the issue as if by reflex.

Then again, the purpose served by the Pastorals is strongly biased by its initial literary classification as pseudepigraphical. Its meaning cannot be obtained from the verbal sense of the text, but must be derived from a reconstruction of the author's 'real' intentions which have been purposely concealed. The pseudepigraphical text does not correctly render the biblical reality without its being critically reinterpreted. The model for determining true intentionality is bound to the original author's purpose which is established through a construct regarding the historical and sociological forces at work. The kerygmatic witness of the text is, thereby, rendered mute, and its interpretation is made dependent on other external forces which are set in a causal relationship.

In my judgment, the hermeneutical assumptions which derive from the application of the genre of pseudepigraphy to the Pastorals have resulted in several serious exegetical distortions. First, an exegesis which operates on the basis of the pseudepigraphical model effects a shift in the point of standing of the writer of the letters. The text is no longer interpreted according to its verbal sense with Paul writing in the first person, but rather the apostle's role has been altered to function in the third person. Paul is no longer the real subject of the letter, but its object. The letters are not from Paul, but about Paul (*ein Paulusbild!*). The crucial canonical shaping of the Pastorals has thus been seriously altered on the basis of an historical and literary critical judgment. In the canonical shape of the Pastorals the first-person role of Paul stands in striking discontinuity with the third-person role which Paul plays in the post-apostolic writings, especially in the letters of Polycarp. The effect of the modern pseudepigraphical interpretation is to lose this canonical distinction and to treat the Pastorals in the same way as the post-apostolic writings. Von Campenhausen's theory of Polycarp's authorship of the Pastorals is an especially dubious form of this move.

In addition, the pseudepigraphical model also effects a serious shift in the handling of the book's addressee. It is one thing to begin with the assumption of a simple addressee which stems from the normal conventions of letter-writing, but then to be forced to postulate a complex relationship between author and recipient in order to do justice to the peculiar features of the letter. It is quite another thing to begin with the historical assumption that the real addressee must be critically reconstructed in order correctly to understand the letter. Indeed, a close reading of the Pastorals confronts a variety of textual elements which have altered the normal portrait of a single historical recipient. The highly stylized representative role of the office extends the depiction of the historical Timothy almost to the breaking point. However, when the pseudepigraphical model first assumes that the true recipient must be recovered from an ecclesiastical situation obtaining some fifty years after the death of Paul, then the canonical depiction of Timothy and Titus by the Pastorals has been sacrificed to a hermeneutical theory of meaning as determined by historical referentiality.

Thirdly, the sharp profile of the Pastorals' characterization of the threat of heresy is significantly blurred by the use of the genre of pseudepigraphy. One of the striking features of the Pastorals is its fluctuation between viewing heresy as a present threat within the community (I Tim.1.3f.,19f.; 6.20f.; II Tim.2.16ff.; Tit.1.10f.), and in envisioning heresy within a prophetic oracle as a phenomenon of the future age (I Tim.4.1ff.; II Tim.3.1ff.,13; 4.3f.). When the interpreter shifts his point of standing to a period of fifty years after the putative writing of the book, this tension is collapsed. For example, Brox (RNT,42) is forced to argue that the motif of heresy is a purely literary one and on the basis of a better historical perspective can be flattened without significant loss. But is this really the case?

Trummer (*Paulustradition*, 73) has correctly characterized the chief exegetical problem of the Pastorals when he writes: 'The temporal and material distance of the Pastorals from Paul is indeed the basic assumption for its accurate interpretation.' However, the crucial hermeneutical issue is *how* one interprets this temporal and material distance from Paul. Is it the key for a critical reconstruction by which to establish the true historical perspective for interpretation, or is it considered an essential part of the canonical shape by which a new dimension of the Pauline witness is realized? In sum, one's decision on this hermeneutical option determines in large measure the manner in which scripture renders reality.

In spite of these criticisms of the pseudepigraphical model, it would be a mistake to underestimate the serious theological perception which often has supported its application. Especially in the use of this model by N. Brox one sees a responsible attempt at a theological reflection which would do full justice to the biblical text. Several significant exegetical points are emphasized by Brox. First, the Pastorals are late writings, but not inferior in quality (RNT, 55). He is thus careful not to carry over a negative judgment simply on the basis of its particular literary genre. Secondly, Brox has emphasized the genuine theological continuity between Paul and the subsequently developed Pauline tradition of the Pastorals. He formulates this position carefully:

> The letters interpret Paul (*auslegen*) in the situation which suits their time in the life of the church since only in this way can the word of the apostle be directive, instructive and supportive for the new situation (68).

Thirdly, Brox correctly stresses that the motivation for the growth of the Pauline tradition is related to the lively experience of the author with an authoritative tradition, rather than as a device for legitimating a particular ideology (69).

I would fully agree that Brox has offered some important historical and theological characterizations of the Pastorals in their role as pseudepigraphical literature which serve to correct some of the common impressions associated with the approach. However, I would contend that because of Brox's continued use of a basically historical referential model, he has been unable to exploit the potential in the directions outlined above, but he has been forced to compromise at decisive points in a way which runs in the face of the canonical shape of the biblical text.

It accrues to Brox's credit that he firmly resists all attempts to denigrate the Pastoral epistles theologically. He describes them as 'imitations', but of a high level of theological integrity. However, the reason why Brox has not depreciated this unknown pseudepigraphical author of the second century is that he comes to the New Testament in general with high regard for the direction in which the Christian church developed its tradition in this period. Brox carefully notes the differences between the Pastorals and the apostle Paul, but then evaluates the change of theology in a positive fashion in the light of an overriding assessment of the growth of church tradition. In my opinion, Brox is fortunately inconsistent in letting forces other than strictly historical ones effect his value judgments.

However, when Brox attempts to work out exegetically his interpretation of the Pastorals as a pseudepigraphical exegesis of Pauline tradition for a later period in the church's history, the effect of his hermeneutic of historical referentiality becomes evident. He does not view the new situation through the eyes of the extended Pauline witness, that is, through the canonically shaped text, but rather the reverse. He reconstructs the new historical situation which then becomes the measure for determining the meaning of the text. For example, the Paul of the Pastorals could not actually have needed his cloak left at Troas (II Tim.4.13); therefore, the verse must be a cliche-like phrase with a less than literal sense. Similarly, the nature of the experience of the developing church within the Pauline tradition is not interpreted primarily from the text of the Pastorals, but from the reconstructed historical setting from which the text is then read. Such a distinction in interpretive direction may seem at first incidental, but it actually proves to be crucial and decisively affects the exegesis of the letters.

Finally, there are certain implications from this discussion regarding the appropriateness of the term 'pseudepigraphical' to describe the Pastoral letters. My reservations do not arise from an attempt to defend the direct authorship by Paul. I am convinced that the relationship is an indirect one. There are many signs that the material stemmed from a period after Paul's death and that the addressee shared many features of a non-historical construct. The major problem is that the term pseudepigraphical arose within a context of historical referentiality and it does not as yet seem capable of functioning within another theological frame of reference. The material remains 'pseudo', and even when a fraudulent intention is removed, the interpretation is strongly affected by this initial judgment. The form-critical claim that the name merely designates a genre classification is not sustained by the actual exegesis according to the pseudepigraphical model.

In contrast, the point of a canonical interpretation is not to begin with either a judgment of historical authorship or with a denial of such, but to allow the peculiar features of the text's shaping to determine the meaning and role which historical and non-historical elements play within the text itself. In sum, it is the initial prejudicing of the content of the biblical witness, as well as the nature of the questions raised which call into question the exegetical usefulness of the term. Moreover, the debate focuses the question as to whether it is in fact wise to begin an exegesis of the Pastorals by first deciding on the issue of authorship. In the interpretation which follows an attempt will be made first to discern the letters' canonical shape in order to avoid the school pressures of both the right and the left within the scholarly guild.

III. The Search for the Canonical Shape of the Pastorals

Before turning to examine some of the detailed features of the canonical form of the Pastoral letters, a few general remarks are in order which will seek to clarify the approach being offered.

First, there will be no attempt made in this context to reconstruct a historical portrait of Paul. The historical enterprise, while fully legitimate within a certain context, is not identical with the theological enterprise of discerning the canonical shape of the material. Of course, historical elements will enter into the exegetical analysis, but it seems apparent that the canonical process of collecting, reordering, and interpreting the Pauline tradition has resulted in blurring the sharp historical lines. It is central to the canonical enterprise to seek to interpret the peculiar form into which the material has been rendered as the vehicle of the biblical witness.

Secondly, a major concern of a canonical exegesis will be to determine how the Pauline tradition was extended to address new situations and different addressees. At times critical literary and historical theories can aid in establishing the relationship of both continuity and discontinuity with the earlier stages of the tradition. However, a canonical interpretation of the new function of the literature is not directly dependent on the ability to establish an unbroken causal link.

Thirdly, the canonical witness of the Pastorals often was made with material which reflected a more advanced stage in the development of church tradition including ecclesiastical offices, legal structures, and church law. The mere presence of such elements within a time-conditioned sequence of the early second century does not in itself provide a canonical warrant for theological legitimation any more than does the presence of slavery in the society to which Paul ministered. Rather, the crucial factor is the canonical role which such new institutions were assigned in the extension of the tradition for successive generations of Christians. Thus, recognition of the hermeneutical function of canon is a major check against biblicism, whether arising from the left or the right of the theological spectrum.

It is now our concern to seek to sketch some of the broad lines of the canonical shaping of these letters. The major problem will be to interpret the strange mixture of genuine continuity with the undisputed Pauline letters and those elements of great dissimilarity. Our approach will be to interpret the effect of the peculiar shaping rather than to begin with a theory to explain how the Pauline tradition was extended. At the conclusion of our analysis some reflection on the historical process which lay behind the literary shaping of the letters will be attempted.

The three Pastoral epistles share the form of the genuine Pauline letters. Dibelius comments that the letters give the appearance of being truly occasional letters like the rest of the Pauline corpus, but they are really not (5f.). Certainly the letters reflect initially the formal features of Paul's style in the introduction. Paul identifies himself as the writer of the letter in his office as apostle. Next the addressee is identified (cf. Phil.1.1), which is then followed by a typical blessing formula. There is nothing in the prologue which would indicate any distancing from the historical Paul.

Moreover, portions within the body of the letters, especially in II Timothy, reflect a similar level of concrete historical specificity which is common to the other letters and which has resulted in their characterization as occasional letters. There are references to Paul's past missionary itineraries (I Tim.1.3; II Tim.4.20; Tit.1.5) and mention of future travel plans (I Tim.3.14). The author speaks of controversies and disputes (II Tim.3.11; 4.14), dispatches his co-workers on orders (I Tim.1.3; II Tim.4.11; Tit.3.12), and sends his customary greetings to friends (II Tim.4.19). References to such mundane features as the request to return his lost coat (II Tim.4.13) and dietary advice to improve Timothy's health (I Tim.5.23) reflect the highest level of historical particularity. The lack of typical legendary features such as abound in the *Acta Pauli* is indisputable.

Paul derives his apostleship from a divine command of God (I Tim.1.1; Tit.1.3) which has been entrusted him. At times he looks backward to reaffirm that his office to the Gentiles was grounded in the gospel (I Tim.2.7; II Tim.1.11). At times he looks forward in anticipating the approaching end of his task and his imminent death (II Tim.4.6ff.). Throughout the epistles the office of apostle is always viewed as a special commission which is unique to him. Never does Paul even hint that his apostleship will be passed on to his co-workers or extended into the next generation. When he speaks of his life functioning as an example for future believers, it is explicitly in his role as a forgiven sinner (I Tim.1.16). Those who follow Paul in his ministry are designated as 'children in the path', 'disciples', and 'good ministers of Christ Jesus'. They do not extend or inherit Paul's office, but rather are grounded upon his teaching of sound doctrine

(I Tim.4.6). Thus, in addressing the problem of how the Pauline tradition of the Pastorals was shaped in these letters any suggestion that his office of apostle was simply extended into the next generation is quite wrong. His role was *sui generis* and sharply distinguished from that of his disciples. Clearly the distancing from the historical Paul which is often felt in the Pastorals was not accomplished in this manner.

It has long been recognized that one of the major purposes for which the Pastorals were written was to oppose the threat of heresy. A recurring feature of the letters is their contrasting of the 'sound doctrine' of Jesus Christ with 'false teachings' (II Tim.4.3; I Tim.6.3). The latter is characterized as myths, speculation, and senseless controversies which produce dissention and error. The gospel is now referred to in the Pastorals as a deposit (παραθήκη) of truth which is to be guarded and protected. Right at this point the striking difference from the earlier Pauline letters, both respecting vocabulary and theology, can be clearly observed. Commentators have been quick to suggest that the genuine Pauline understanding of the gospel as the power of God for salvation has been replaced by a static, formalized concept of right doctrine (cf. Käsemann). Indeed, the contrast in the function of the gospel as testified to by Paul in Romans and Galatians cannot be denied. Nevertheless, the heart of the exegetical issue from a canonical perspective lies in interpreting the exact nature of the new function of the Pastorals respecting the gospel instead of immediately denouncing it as a distortion.

Perhaps the place to begin is with a careful distinction which has been observed by O. Michel in the Pastorals. He disputes the argument that the gospel has now been interpreted by a concept of 'sound doctrine', but argues rather for the reverse, that is, sound doctrine is defined by the gospel. Its content is measured by what 'accords with the glorious gospel' (I Tim.1.11). Likewise when the Pastorals speak of 'knowing the truth', the formula again receives its meaning in terms of a faithful testimony to Jesus Christ (I Tim.2.4ff.).

What has changed in the approach of the Pastorals is not the content of the gospel, but the manner by which the content is appropriated and treasured. Certainly a new formal element has entered the vocabulary, but this characterization is peripheral and has not touched the heart of the theological problem. In contrast to the rest of the Pauline letters, the Paul of the Pastorals does not apply his understanding of the gospel to a new historical situation. He does not develop the implications of his theology on a new fror˙. His relation to the churches in the Pastorals is strikingly different from (say) that with Corinth or Philippi. There is a shift from an active Paul to a passive one, not in a psychological sense, but rather that Paul does not himself break new ground in direct confrontation. Instead, his teachings have become the medium by means of which others are to confront falsehood and error.

Brox has suggested that the function of the Pastorals was to 'exegete' Paul for a new and later period in the life of the church. He has, thereby, seen the shift from the active to the passive role of the apostle. However, the crucial canonical issue lies in the nature of the 'exegesis'. The decisive point to make is that the Pastorals do not reinterpret Paul for a later age. His theology is not updated for a new generation. His theology is not extended in this way, nor did its actualization function according to this pattern within the canon. Instead, the canonical move, which in time sought to collect Paul's writings into a normative corpus of authoritative scripture, began to adumbrate the process of canonization with the Pastoral letters by encompassing Paul's theology within the category of 'sound doctrine'. His teachings were assigned the function of establishing the normative theological context from which position the later generations of Christians were to confront the threat of heresy. For that reason the Pastoral letters themselves do not engage in an active debate with false teachings (cf. I Tim. 6.3ff.), but rather instruct the next generation of the church's leaders on how the inevitable conflict is to be engaged. The continual imperative within the letter of preserving and guarding the tradition (I Tim. 6.20) re-emphasizes the canonical function of the Pauline teachings which for these congregations have become the normative guide of the faith.

A major concern in our earlier study of the Gospels was to describe the manner by which Jesus Christ was rendered accessible to later generations of believers through the various forms of written testimony. Again in the Pastorals, the issue of how the witness to the faith in Jesus Christ was made, played a significant role. First of all, it is clear throughout the three letters that the figure of Jesus Christ was confessed as the living Lord (I Tim. 1.12; 4.10) who had once entered the world to redeem sinners (I Tim. 1.15), but who is still alive and active in the present, 'desiring that all come to the knowledge of the truth' (I Tim. 2.4). The Christ of the Pastorals has been, in no sense, imprisoned within tradition. Rather, the Christian lives by the sense of his presence (I Tim. 5.21; 6.13) with hope set on the coming of Christ (I Tim. 6.14), awaiting the fulfilment of 'the blessed hope, the appearing of the glory of our great God and Saviour' (Tit. 2.13).

Yet it is seen in no way as a contradiction of the faith in the living Christ that he is appropriated through the tradition which has been entrusted to Paul. He has been appointed apostle, teacher, preacher (I Tim. 2.7; II Tim. 1.11) to bear testimony to Christ as the mediator between God and mankind. It is by holding fast to 'that which has been entrusted' (II Tim. 6.20) that Christ is honoured because the 'sound words' stem from Christ himself (I Tim. 6.3). He is the author of sound doctrine (Tit. 2.10). The 'sure word' is that which has been taught (Tit. 1.9) and entrusted to Timothy by the Holy Spirit (II Tim. 3.14). Paul explicitly reminds Timothy to keep in mind from whom he had learned the faith (II Tim. 3.14). The word of God preached by Paul is not fettered (II Tim. 2.9), but it issues in good deeds (Tit. 3.8). A sign of the truth of one's faith is that it equips the believer for good works (II Tim. 3.17). In sum, the Pastorals understand the doctrine testified to by Paul and received by the church as standing in no tension with the person of the living Lord whose truth constitutes the apostolic teaching.

Space is too limited to enter into a detailed debate with the recent interpretation of the Pastorals by Dennis MacDonald. He contends that the Pastorals arose in an effort to suppress the depiction of Paul reflected in the oral tradition of the *Acta Pauli* and transmitted in the stories told by women. As a result, the church's image of the apostle has been seriously distorted by the repressive, ecclesiastical (bishops!) ideology of the Pastoral letters. In my judgment, careful attention to the canonical process belies this description as a highly misleading caricature. It fails to reckon with all the signs – literary, historical, and theological – which support the critical evaluation of the church's transmission of the Pauline legacy as both faithful and truthful.

There is another important feature which shapes the canonical function of the Pastoral letters. Commentators have often noted the indirect quality of the addressee. Once again the exegetical issue turns on understanding the canonical role which this form of distancing plays. If we begin with II Timothy, one is struck by the effect of the concluding chapter on the understanding of the entire epistle. Paul offers his last will and testament (4.6–8) as he envisons

his imminent death. The effect on the whole letter is to explain why
the preceding instructions to Timothy appear largely to address
problems which lie in the future, that is, within a period later than
Paul's. When reference is made to the past (1.3–6; 3.14f.), it serves
to provide the theological warrant for Timothy's ministry in the
future. Knoch has rightly pointed out the parallel with Paul's farewell
speech to the elders at Miletus in Acts 20. The apostle's instructions
for his co-workers in the 'last days' also continue in I Timothy
(4.1ff.).

A similar theme is expressed in a different way throughout the
letters, but the effect is largely the same. Paul appears to be setting
forth his travel plans and reiterates his strong desire to visit (I Tim.
3.14; 4.13). Yet then he reckons with his delay and sets forth
instructions for his disciple and for the community as to how they
are to behave when he is not present (I Tim. 3.14f.). Similarly in I
Tim.4.13 within the same frame of expectation – 'till I come' – the
means of counselling the community of faith is outlined: 'attend to
the public reading of scripture, to preaching, to teaching'. Finally,
in II Tim. 3.15ff. the function of scripture for the church's nurture
is described in detail. It is a divinely ordained means for teaching,
for reproof, for correction, and for training in righteousness. Roles
which formerly Paul exercised by his physical presence among his
churches, have now been assumed by the collection of sacred writings.
Clearly the scriptures of the Old Testament are intended, but the
hermeneutical move has been initiated which would lead before long
to the church's assigning Paul's own letters to a similar function.

In the study of the Pastorals much attention has rightly been
focused on the peculiar features which characterize the roles of
Timothy and Titus as the addressees of the letters. In spite of the
historical problems connected with relating the concrete references
in the letters to any known missionary activity of Paul, there can be
no doubt that the dimension of historical specificity, when it appears,
is equal to any within the so-called genuine letters (I Tim. 1.3; 5.23;
II Tim. 4.9ff.,19ff.; Tit. 1.5,12). The various attempts of Brox (*BZ
NF 13*) and Trummer (*Paulustradition*, 78ff.) to undercut this feature
by means of a pseudepigraphical reading have not been successful.
Yet equally characteristic of these same letters are those features
which move the addressee away from the specific toward a more
representative role. The problem of interpreting this unusual

relationship forms the major problem respecting the letters' addressee.

It has long been recognized that the specific historical profile of Timothy, which emerges from Paul's other letters and from the book of Acts, plays little role in the Pastorals. The concrete features recede before a typifying profile of the office of pastor. Usually the movement from Timothy, the disciple of Paul, to the figure of pastor of the flock *par excellence* is quite frictionless and the historical exemplifies the typical. However, the critics have correctly observed some elements of friction which demonstrate that there are seams in the composition. For example, Timothy, who was historically a veteran missionary by this time, is still cautioned to flee youthful passions (II Tim. 2.22) and not to let anyone despise his youth (I Tim. 4.12). Similarly the reference to Timothy's training in the Christian faith from his childhood (II Tim. 3.15) stands in some tension with the account of Acts 16.1–3.

The major thrust of the three letters falls clearly on delineating the bearer of an office. Timothy is addressed as 'my child' (II Tim. 2.1), but also as 'man of God' (II Tim. 3.17), 'the Lord's servant' (II Tim. 2.24), 'good minister' (I Tim. 4.6), and 'workman' (II Tim. 2.15). He is to do the work of an 'evangelist', fulfilling his ministry (II Tim. 4.5) and is compared to a 'soldier of Jesus Christ' (II Tim. 2.3). His role as faithful tradent of the sacred tradition is constantly depicted. He is 'to guard the truth entrusted' (II Tim. 1.14), and 'follow the pattern of sound words' (II Tim. 1.13). Likewise, Titus is to 'hold firm to the sure word as taught' (Tit. 1.9), and 'teach what befits sound doctrine' (Tit. 2.1). The profile of the pastor also describes the qualities of his personal life. He is to shun evil, 'aim at righteousness' (I Tim. 6.11), 'train (himself) in godliness' (I Tim. 4.7), and 'set the believers an example in speech and conduct' (I Tim. 4.12). Much of the profile is concerned with outlining his duties including for whom he should pray, whom he should teach, and how he should exercise his office (I Tim. 4.15).

Of special importance is the detailed instruction on dealing with difficult officials within the church (I Tim.3.1ff.) and his instructions to various social classes: older men, older widows, younger women, and slaves. In contrast with Paul's other letters the instructions are not directed to actual situations within a local church, but constitute general rules which relate to the life of a typical congregation. Significantly the form of instruction is cast in terms of 'sure and worthy sayings' which includes general paraenesis (I Tim. 6.12), broad ethical paradigms (I Tim. 2.8), proverbs (I Tim. 6.6), and the application of both casuistic and apodeictic law (I Tim. 4.8; 3.5; 5.3). In spite of the variety of literary forms, they all function to establish the typical profile of the pastor, and do not arise as a response to any one historical incident.

We are now in a position to return to the question of the relationship between the specific and the typical features which characterize the addressee of the Pastorals. In spite of both elements being present in the letters, the effect of the reading of the letters as a whole is that the typical elements function in such a way as to establish the perspective which now dominates the whole. This is not to suggest that the specific elements are completely absorbed into the typical, but the literary effect tends to move them in that direction. For example, Paul's request for his 'cloak .. books, and especially the parchments' (II Tim. 4.13) gains immediately a typical significance and illustrates the single-hearted devotion of the apostle to his ministry who ended his life not even possessing a coat. Similarly Paul's advice to Timothy to 'use a little wine' (I Tim. 5.23) functions now as a warning to the pastor against forms of extreme asceticism. In this regard, the effort of the pseudepigraphical interpretation to interpret the personal notices in a less than literal sense has a certain literary warrant, even if it has not been correctly exploited by the proponents of this hermeneutical model.

This suggested literary reading of the letters is not to be confused with the historical question. It is one thing to suggest that the effect of the canonical reading is to typify the particular. It is quite another to argue that the specific elements stem from a pseudepigraphical construal of an idea in the form of the particular. The hermeneutical problem with the pseudepigraphical interpretation is that it fixes at the outset the semantic level of the text and proceeds to flatten those elements of the text which still retain a continuing movement from the particular to the typical. Thus, in the famous cloak passage (II Tim. 4.13), although this one element functions progressively as an illustration of the apostle's commitment, the concrete features of the surrounding passages continue to have independent life and cannot all be understood as an ideological construal. That is to say, historically it is more probable to see the primary level of the tradition consisting of elements of particularity, which in a new literary context moved in the direction of the specific to the typical, than to postulate with the pseudepigraphical model the reverse order, namely, the typical was primary in the tradition and was subsequently grounded in the particular.

To summarize, I have sought to interpret the Pastoral letters in terms of a canonical shaping which rendered the biblical material in a way unique to these letters. A distance was effected between the historical Paul and the apostle of the letters. His teaching was comprised in the form of authoritative doctrine which served as a guide to successive generations of Christians on how the entire Pauline corpus was to function. A tension was retained in the letters between the specific and typical elements which moved toward resolution into the latter.

In my judgment, it remains a largely unresolved historical problem to determine exactly how this interpretive process took place. The letters are themselves virtually silent on this side of the problem. As I have stated earlier, various theories have been constructed to explain the history in terms of an institutional or charismatic application of the Pauline tradition. Often elements of truth have been correctly recognized (cf. especially Brox, Hegermann, Trummer), and the need for such research is far from being over. However, the hermeneutical point must be stressed that the relationship between this set of historical questions and the canonical function of the biblical text is a dialectical one. Critical scholarship can indeed clarify a text's interpretation. Yet theologically the community of faith confesses that it has already been provided with a sufficient guide for understanding the Pastorals as sacred scripture.

22

PHILEMON

Commentaries

J. B. Lightfoot, [11]1892
H. Oltramare, 1892
M. R. Vincent, ICC, 1897
E. Haupt, MeyerK, [7]1902
P. Ewald, KNT, [2]1910
W. Lueken, SNT, [3]1917
E. F. Scott, MNTC, 1930
W. Bieder, ZBK, 1944
M. Dibelius, H. Greeven, HNT, [3]1953
J. Knox, IB, 1955
J. J. Müller, NICNT, 1955
C. F. D. Moule, CGTC, 1957

K. Staab, RNT, [3]1959
A. R. C. Leaney, TB, 1960
E. Lohmeyer, W. Schmauch, MeyerK, [13]1964
G. H. P. Thompson, CNEB, 1967
G. Johnston, NCeB, 1967
J. Ernst, RNT, 1974
R. P. Martin, NCeB, 1974
E. Lohse, MeyerK, [15]1977
G. Friedrich, NTD, [15]1981
P. Stuhlmacher, EKK, [2]1981
P. T. O'Brien, Word, 1982

Bibliography

S. S. **Bartchy**, μᾶλλον χρῆσαι. *First Century Slavery and the Interpretation of I Corinthians 7:21*, SBLDS 11, Missoula 1973; N. **Brockmeyer**, *Antike Sklaverei*, Erträge der Forschung 116, Darmstadt 1979; F. F. **Bruce**, 'St Paul in Rome, II. The Epistle to Philemon', *BJRL* 48, 1965/6, 81–97; G. **Eichholz**, *Die Theologie des Paulus im Umriss*, Neukirchen-Vluyn [2]1972, 278–83; F. V. **Filson**, 'The Significance of the Early House Churches', *JBL* 58, 1939, 105–12; E. R. **Goodenough**, 'Paul and Onesimus', *HTR* 22, 1929, 181–3; H. **Greeven**, 'Prüfung der Thesen von J. Knox zum Philemonbrief', *TLZ* 79, 1954, 373–8; P. N. **Harrison**, 'Onesimus and Philemon', *AnThR* 32, 1950, 268–94; H. J. **Holtzmann**, 'Der Brief an den Philemon, kritisch untersucht', *ZWTh* 16, 1873, 428–41; G. **Kernscherper**, *Die Stellung der Bibel und der alten christlichen Kirche zur Sklaverei*, Halle 1957; J. **Knox**, *Philemon among the Letters of Paul. A New View of its Place and Importance*, New York and Nashville [2]1959; R. **Lehmann**, *Épître à Philémon. Le christianisme primitive et l'esclavage*, Genève 1978; D. **Lührmann**, 'Wo man nicht mehr Sklave oder

Freier ist', *Wissenschaft und Dienst*, NF 13, 1975, 53–83; F. **Lyall**, 'Roman Law in the Witness of Paul. The Slave and the Freeman', *NTS* 17, 1970/71, 73–9; J. **Müller-Bardorff**, 'Philemonbrief', *RGG*[3], V, 331f.; W. -H. **Ollrog**, *Paulus und seine Mitarbeiter*, WMANT 50, 1979; T. **Preiss**, *Life in Christ*, ET, SBT 13, 1954; W. **Schrage**, *Die konkreten Einzelgebote in der paulinischen Paränese*, Gütersloh 1961; S. **Schulz**, 'Hat Christus die Sklaven befreit'?, *EvKomm* 5, 1972, 13–17; E. **Schweizer**, 'Zum Sklavenproblem im Neuen Testament', *EvTh* 32, 1972, 502–6; C. **Spicq**, 'Le vocabulaire de l'esclavage dans le Nouveau Testament', *RB* 85, 1978, 201–6; A. **Stuhl**, 'Der Philemon-brief als Beispiel paulinischer Paränese', *Kairos* 15, 1973, 267–97; W. L. **Westermann**, *The Slave Systems of Greek and Roman Antiquity*, Philadelphia [3]1964; J. L. **White**, 'The Structural Analysis of Philemon', *SBL Seminar Papers* I,1971, 1–47; U. **Wickert**, 'Der Philemonbrief – Privatbrief oder apostolisches Schreiben?', *ZNW* 52, 1961, 230–38; J. **Zmijewski**, 'Beobach-tungen zur Struktur des Philemonbriefes', *BiLe* 15, 1974, 273–96.

There are two major canonical issues respecting the letter of Philemon which are closely related. Why was this letter which gives the initial impression of being a private note of the apostle ever assigned a canonical status within the Pauline corpus? How does the letter function canonically within the New Testament? Of course, there are other critical issues regarding the letter which are not directly related to our present concern and the reader is referred to the standard Introductions and commentaries for a fuller treatment.

A variety of reasons have been suggested to explain the inclusion of the letter within the canonical collection. Lightfoot (*Philemon*, 314f.) makes reference to the strong bias against the letter in the fourth century because it was thought to be concerned with personal trivia without theological substance. Both the Latin and Greek Fathers sought to defend its place in the canon by pointing to its elements of wisdom and virtue. Later the Reformers praised the epistle as illustrating Christian love and demonstrating the compassion of the apostle.

In the modern period the most elaborate theory to explain its canonical status has been advanced by John Knox. He proposes a complex, and highly ingenious development. Knox argues that the actual owner of the slave Onesimus was Archippus who lived at Colossae, and that the church which gathered in his house (Philem. 2) was the Colossian church. Paul, who sought to intercede for Onesimus after his deserting his owner, sent him back to Archippus, but by way of Philemon at Laodicea in order to gain the support of the church leader. Onesimus was to proceed from Philemon at Laodicea to Archippus at Colossae with his special letter as well as with the general epistle to the Colossians. Moreover—and a key element in the reconstruction—it is his letter to Philemon which is mentioned in Col. 4.16 as 'from Laodicea', and the appeal to Archippus to fulfil his 'service' (διακονία) refers specifically to Paul's request for Onesimus.

On the basis of this reconstruction Knox then argues that Onesimus who is mentioned by Ignatius as the bishop of Ephesus is the former slave. Since Knox accepts Goodspeed's theory that the origin of the Pauline corpus took place in Ephesus and that the letter to the Ephesians was a covering letter to the entire corpus, he concludes that the letter to Philemon gained a place in the canon because of the special influence of Onesimus.

Knox's hypothesis has been gently criticized by Greeven, and much more severely by Moule (CGTC, 14ff.) and Schenke (Einl.I, 156). The theory is highly vulnerable at the outset because if any single element is removed, the entire construction collapses. Most critics are highly dubious that Archippus could be the real recipient of the letter and owner of Onesimus because of his position in the prologue. Again, it is unlikely that the letter to Philemon can be identified with the letter from Laodicea, particularly because Marcion knew of both letters as separate entities. Finally, the service to be fulfilled in Col. 4.17 appears to refer to a far broader obligation than Knox's interpretation allows.

Admittedly Knox's larger view of the canonization process of the Pauline corpus rests on Goodspeed's theories which have eroded badly in recent years (cf. Lindemann and Rensberger; see ch.24 below). But in any case, to derive the major force for the canonical inclusion of Philemon from the personal and political motivation of an individual stands in conflict with the early church's own understanding of the grounds for canonical decisions.

Finally, a new hypothesis has arisen in recent years regarding Philemon which stems from the conviction that the letter to the Colossians was pseudepigraphical and not from the apostle Paul. Accordingly, Schenke argues (154) that Philemon was published along with Colossians in an effort to provide the letter with the stamp of genuineness. But whether such a *tour de force* will gain wider support among other scholars can certainly be questioned.

A far more convincing line of argument regarding the grounds for the letter's canonicity has been suggested by Wickert, who addresses the issue from the perspective of our second major question, namely, the letter's form and function. At the outset Paul's use of all the same formal literary conventions which appear in his larger letters – the naming of the senders and addressees, greetings, and thanksgiving – cautions against categorizing it immediately as a private letter qualitatively different from his other epistles. However, the peculiar nature of the content would confirm that the relationship to his apostolic office is a subtle one. He makes use of the term 'obedience' (v. 21), but then relinquishes his right to demand it in order to give Philemon the freedom to surrender his just claims on Onesimus. Wickert mounts an interesting case that Paul's relation to Philemon is an illustration of the same apostolic freedom set forth in I Cor.9.19ff. Paul's human appeal to Philemon as a prisoner in Christ is ultimately grounded in the gospel and is not simply a private concern of the apostle based on friendship.

The inclusion of Philemon within the Pauline corpus would seem to indicate that the letter was so heard by the early church. However, once it was joined to the collection the force of its new intertextuality unleashed a fresh dynamic for its interpretation. Paul's teaching regarding slaves and masters (I Cor. 7.17ff.; Gal. 3.28) was now instanced by the apostle by means of a concrete example of the effect of Christ's transformation of human society in his image.

23

HEBREWS

Commentaries

F. Bleek, 1828–1840
F. A. G. Tholuck, ET ²1869
F. Delitzsch, ET 1868–70
J. C. K. von Hofmann, 1873
M. Stuart, ²1876
G. Lünemann, MeyerK, ⁴1878, ET 1882
A. B. Davidson, 1882
F. W. Farrar, CB, 1883
T. C. Edwards, ExpB, ²1888
C. J. Vaughan, 1980
B. Weiss, MeyerK, ⁶1897
A. B. Bruce, 1899
H. von Soden, HCNT, ³1899
B. F. Westcott, ³1903
A. Nairne, CB, 1921

E. Riggenbach, KNT, ²·³1922
J. Moffatt, ICC, 1924
H. Windisch, HNT, ²1931
A. Médebielle, SB, ³1951
C. Spicq, ÉB, ³1952–3
T. H. Robinson, MNTC, ⁷1953
J. Héring, CNT, 1954
W. Neil, TB 1955
H. Strathmann, NTD, ⁸1963
H. W. Montefiore, B/HNTC, 1964
F. F. Bruce, NICNT, 1964
O. Kuss, RNT, ²1966
G. W. Buchanan, AB, 1972
O. Michel, MeyerK, ¹³1975
P. E. Hughes, 1977
A. Strobel, NTD, ¹²1982

Bibliography

C. P. **Anderson**, 'The Epistle to the Hebrews and the Pauline Letter Collection', *HTR* 59, 1966, 429–38; C. K. **Barrett**, 'The Eschatology of the Epistle to the Hebrews', *The Background of the New Testament and its Eschatology*, *FS C. H. Dodd*, ed. D. Daube and W. D. Davies, Cambridge 1956, 363–93; M. **Barth**, 'The Old Testament in Hebrews', *Current Issues in New Testament Interpretation, FS O. Piper*, ed. W. Klassen and G. F. Snyder, New York and London 1962, 53–78; I. W. **Batdorf**, 'Hebrews and Qumran: Old Methods and New Directions', *Festschrift in honour of F. W. Gingrich*, ed. E. H. Barth and R. E. Cocroft, Leiden 1972, 16–35; K. **Bornhäuser**, *Empfänger und Verfasser des Briefes an die Hebräer*, BFChTh 35.2, 1932; G. **Bornkamm**, 'Sohnschaft und Leiden', *Judentum – Urchristentum – Kirche, FS J. Jeremias*, ed. W. Eltester, BZNW 26, 1960, 188–98; 'Das Bekenntnis im Hebräerbrief'

(1942), *Studien zu Antike und Urchristentum*, *GA* II, Munich 1963, 188–203; M. M. **Bourke**, 'The Priesthood of Christ', *To Be a Priest*, II, ed. R. E. Terwilliger and U. T. Holmes, New York 1975, 55–69; W. E. **Brooks**, 'The Perpetuity of Christ's Sacrifice in the Epistle to the Hebrews', *JBL* 89, 1970, 205–14; F. F. **Bruce**, '"To the Hebrews" or "To the Essenes"?', *NTS* 9, 1962/3, 217–32; 'The Kerygma of Hebrews', *Interp* 23, 1969, 3–19; 'Hebrews, Letter to the', *IDB Suppl*, 1976, 394f.; G. W. **Buchanan**, 'The Present State of Scholarship on Hebrews', *Christianity, Judaism and other Greco-Roman Cults*, *FS Morton Smith*, ed. J. Neusner, I, New Testament, Leiden 1975, 299–330; F. **Büchsel**, *Die Christologie des Hebräerbriefs*, Gütersloh 1922.

J. **Carmignac**, 'Le document de Qumran sur Melkisédeq', *RevQ* 7, 1970,348–78; K. W. **Clark**, 'Worship in the Jerusalem Temple after A.D.70', *NTS* 6, 1969/70, 269–80; A. **Cody**, *Heavenly Sanctuary and Liturgy in the Epistle to the Hebrews*, St Meinad, Indiana, 1960; N. A. **Dahl**, 'A New and Living Way. The Approach to God according to Hebrews 10:19–25', *Interp* 5, 1951, 401–12; G. **Dautzenberg**, 'Der Glaube im Hebräerbrief', *BZ* NF 17, 1973, 161–77; L. K. K. **Dey**, *The Intermediary World and Patterns of Perfection in Philo and Hebrews*, SBLDS 25, Missoula 1975; M. **Dibelius**, 'Der himmlische Kultus nach dem Hebräerbrief' (1942), *Botschaft und Geschichte*, II, Tübingen 1956, 160–76; E. **Dinkler**, 'Hebrews, Letter to the', *IDB*, II, 571–5; W. P. **Du Bose**, *High Priesthood and Sacrifice*, New York and London 1908; F. V. **Filson**, *'Yesterday': A Study of Hebrews in the Light of Chapter 13*, SBT II.4, 1967; J. A. **Fitzmyer**, '"Now this Melchizedek. . . . ." Heb.7:1; Ps.110:4; Isa.14:8ff.', *Essays on the Semitic Background of the New Testament*, New York and London 1971, 221–43; 'Further Light on Melchizedek from Qumran Cave II, ibid., 245–67; L. **Floor**, 'The General Priesthood of Believers in the Epistle to the Hebrews', *Neotestamentica* 5, 1971, 72–82; D. **Flusser**, 'The Dead Sea Sect and Pre-Pauline Christianity', *Scripta Hierosolymitana* IV, Jerusalem 1954, 215–66; R. H. **Fuller**, 'The Letter to the Hebrews', *Hebrews – James – 1 and 2 Peter – Jude – Revelation*, ed. G. Krodel (Proclamation Commentaries), Philadelphia 1977, 1–27.

E. **Grässer**, 'Der Hebräebrief 1938–1963', *ThR* 30, 1964, 138–236; 'Der historische Jesus im Hebräerbrief', *ZNW* 56, 1965, 63–91; *Der Glaube im Hebräerbrief*, Marburger Theol. Stud.2, Marburg 1965; 'Hebräer 1,1–4. Ein exegetischer Versuch', *Text und Situation, Ges. Aufsätze zum Neuen Testament*, Gütersloh 1973, 182–228; R. A. **Greer**, *The Captain of our Salvation. A Study in the Patristic Exegesis of Hebrews*, BGBE 15, 1973; R. **Gyllenberg**, 'Die Christologie des Hebräerbriefes', *ZSTh* 11, 1933–4,662–90; K. **Hagen**, *Hebrews Commenting from Erasmus to Bèze 1516–1598*, Tübingen 1981; A. T. **Hanson**, 'Christ in the Old Testament according to Hebrews', *StEv* II, TU 87, 1964, 393–407; A. **Harnack**, 'Probabilia über die Adresse und den Verfasser des Hebräerbriefs', *ZNW* 1, 1900, 16–41; W. H. P. **Hatch**, 'The Position of Hebrews in the Canon of the New Testament', *HTR* 29, 1936, 133–51; D. M. **Hay**, *Glory at the Right Hand: Psalm 110 in Early Christianity*, SBLMS 18, Missoula 1973; H. **Hegermann**, *Die Vorstellung vom Schöpfungs-*

mittler im hellenistischen Judentum und Christentum, TU 82, 1961; O. **Hofius**, *Katapausis. Die Vorstellung vom endzeitlichen Ruheort im Hebräerbrief*, WUNT 11, 1970; *Der Vorhang vor dem Thron Gottes*, WUNT 14, 1972; F. L. **Horton**, *The Melchizedek Tradition*, London and New York 1976; G. **Howard**, 'Hebrews and the Old Testament Quotations', *NovT* 10, 1968, 208–16; G. **Hughes**, *Hebrews and Hermeneutics*, Cambridge 1976.

W. G. **Johnsson**, 'The Cultus of Hebrews in Twentieth-Century Scholarship', *ExpT* 89, 1977/8, 104–8; C. P. M. **Jones**, 'The Epistle to the Hebrews and the Lucan Writings', *Studies in the Gospels. Essays in Memory of R. H. Lightfoot*, ed. D. E. Nineham, Oxford 1955, 113–43; E. D. **Jones**, 'The Authorship of Hebrews xiii', *ExpT* 46, 1934/5, 562–7; M. **de Jonge**, A. S. **van der Woude**, '11Q Melchizedek and the New Testament', *NTS* 12, 1965/6, 301–26; M. **Kähler**, *Der Inhalt des Hebräerbriefes in genauer Wiedergabe des Gedankenganges entwickelt*, Bonn 1865; E. **Käsemann**, *Das wandernde Gottesvolk. Eine Untersuchung zum Hebräerbrief*, FRLANT 55, 1938, ⁴1961; S. **Kistemaker**, *The Psalm Citations in the Epistle to the Hebrews*, Amsterdam 1961; B. **Klappert**, *Die Eschatologie des Hebräerbriefs*, TheolExH 156, 1969; J. **Kögel**, *Der Sohn und die Söhne: Eine exegetische Studie zu Hebräer 2,5–18*, BFChTh 8.5–6, 1904; H. **Koester**, 'Die Auslegung der Abraham Verheissung in Hebräer 6', *Studien zur Theologie der alttestamentlichen Überlieferung, FS G. von Rad*, ed. R. Rendtorff and K. Koch, Neukirchen 1961, 95–109; '"Outside the Camp": Heb.13:9–14', *HTR* 55, 1962, 299–315; H. **Kosmala**, *Hebräer—Essener—Christen. Studien zur Vorgeschichte der frühkirchlichen Verkündigung*, Studia Post-Biblica 1, Leiden 1959; O. **Kuss**, 'Der theologische Grundgedanke des Hebräerbriefes', *Münchner theologische Zeitschrift* 7, 1956, 233–71; reprinted in *Auslegung und Verkündigung* I, Regensburg 1963, 281–328; 'Der Verfasser des Hebräerbriefes als Seelsorger', *Trierer theologische Zeitschrift* 67, 1958, 65–80; reprinted *Auslegung und Verkündigung* I, 329–58; F. **Laub**, *Bekenntnis und Auslegung*, BU 15, 1980; U. **Luck**, 'Himmlisches und irdisches Geschehen im Hebräerbrief', *NovT* 6, 1963, 192–215; U. **Luz**, 'Der alte und neue Bund bei Paulus und im Hebräerbrief', *EvTh* 27, 1966/7, 318–36.

J. C. **McCullough**, 'Some Recent Developments in Research on the Epistle to the Hebrews', *Irish Bibl. Studies* 2, 1980, 141–65; G. W. **MacRae**, 'Heavenly Temple and Eschatology in the Letter to the Hebrews', *Semeia* 12, 1978, 179–99; T. W. **Manson**, 'The Problem of the Epistle to the Hebrews', *BJRL* 32, 1949/50, 1–17; reprinted *Studies in the Gospels and Epistles*, ed. M. Black, Manchester and Philadelphia 1962, 242–58; W. **Manson**, *The Epistle to the Hebrews*, London 1951; E. **Ménégoz**, *La Théologie de l'Épître aux Hébreux*, Paris 1894; O. **Michel**, 'Zur Auslegung des Hebräerbriefes', *NovT* 6, 1963, 189–91; G. **Milligan**, *The Theology of the Epistle to the Hebrews*, Edinburgh 1899; W. **Milligan**, *The Ascension and Heavenly Priesthood of our Lord*, London and New York 1892; A. **Nairne**, *The Epistle of Priesthood*, Edinburgh 1913; W. **Nauck**, 'Zum Aufbau des Hebräerbriefes', *Judentum—Urchristentum—Kirche, FS J. Jeremias*, ed. W. Eltester, BZNW 26, 1960, 199–206; A. **Oepke**, *Das neue Gottesvolk*, Gütersloh 1950; F. **Overbeck**,

Zur Geschichte des Kanons, Chemnitz 1880; reprinted Darmstadt n.d.; R. **Perdelwitz**, 'Das literarische Problem des Hebräerbriefs', *ZNW* 11, 1910, 59–78, 105–23; M. **Perry**, 'Method and Model in the Epistle to the Hebrews', *Theology* 77, 1974, 66–74; J. **van der Ploeg**, 'L'Exégèse de l'Ancient Testament dans l'Épître aux Hébreux', *RB* 54, 1947, 187–228; E. K. A. **Riehm**, *Der Lehrbegriff des Hebräerbriefes*, Basel and Ludwigsburg ²1867; J. A. T. **Robinson**, *Redating the New Testament*, London and Philadelphia 1976, 200–20.

J. R. **Schaeffer**, 'The Relation between Priestly and Servant Messianism in the Epistle to the Hebrews', *CBQ* 30, 1968, 359–85; H.-M. **Schenke**, 'Erwägungen zum Rätsel des Hebräerbriefes', *Neues Testament und Christliche Existenz, FS Herbert Braun*, ed. H. D. Betz and L. Schottroff, Tübingen 1973 421–37; F. J. **Schierse**, *Verheissung und Heilsvollendung. Zur theologischen Grundfrage des Hebräerbriefes*, MüThSt 9, 1955; G. **Schille**, 'Erwägungen zur Hohenpriesterlehre des Hebräerbriefes', ZNW 51, 1960, 112–31; 'Katechese und Tauflehre. Erwägungen zu Hebr 11', *ZNW* 51, 1960, 112–31; G. **Scholem**, *Major Trends in Jewish Mysticism*, New York ³1954, London 1955; F. **Schröger**, *Der Verfasser des Hebräerbriefes als Schriftausleger*, BU 4, 1968; E. F. **Scott**, *The Epistle to the Hebrews: Its Doctrine and Significance*, Edinburgh 1922; I. L. **Seeligmann**, 'Voraussetzungen der Midraschexegese', Supplements to *Vetus Testamentum* 1, 1953, 150–81; S. G. **Sowers**, *The Hermeneutics of Philo and Hebrews*, Zürich 1965; C. **Spicq**, 'L'autheticité du chapitre XIII de l'épître aux Hébreux', *ConNT* XI, 1947, 226–36; J. **Swetnam**, 'On the Literary Genre of the "Epistle" to the Hebrews', *NovT* 11, 1969, 261–69; 'Form and Content in Hebrews 1–6', *Bibl* 53, 1972, 368–85; 'Form and Content in Hebrews 7–13', ibid., 55, 1974, 333–48; F. C. **Synge**, *Hebrews and the Scripture*, London 1959; G. **Theissen**, *Untersuchungen zum Hebräerbrief*, SANT 2, 1969; K. J. **Thomas**, 'The Old Testament Citations in Hebrews', *NTS* 11, 1964/5, 303–25; J. W. **Thompson**, 'The Conceptual Background and Purpose of the Midrash in Hebrews VII', *NovT* 19, 1977, 209–23; 'Heb.9 and Hellenistic Concepts of Sacrifice', *JBL* 98, 1979, 567–78; W. **Thüsing**, '"Lasst uns hinzutreten.. . .." (Hebr 10,22). Zur Frage nach dem Sinn der Kulttheologie im Hebräerbrief', *BZ* NF 9, 1965, 1–17; H. **Thyen**, *Der Stil der jüdisch-hellenistischen Homilie*, FRLANT 47, 1955; C. C. **Torrey**, 'Authorship and Character of the so-called "Epistle to the Hebrews"', *JBL* 30, 1911, 137–56.

L. **Vaganay**, 'Le plan de l'épître aux Hébreux', *Mémorial Lagrange*, Paris 1940, 269–77; E. **Vanhoye**, *La Structure littéraire de l'épître aux Hébreux*, Stud. Neotest.1, Paris and Bruges 1963; 'La question littéraire de Hébreux XIII.1–6' *NTS* 23, 1977, 121–39; 'Situation et Signification de Hébreux 5,1–10', ibid., 445–56; G. **Vos**, 'Hebrews, the Epistle of the Diatheke', *PTR* 13, 1915, 587–632; 14, 1916, 1–61; H. **Wenschkewitz**, *Die Spiritualisierung der Kultusbegriffe Tempel, Priester und Opfer im Neuen Testament*, Angelos-Beihefte 4, Leipzig 1932; A. **Wikgren**, 'Patterns of Perfection in the Epistle to the Hebrews', *NTS* 6, 1959/60, 159–67; C. R. **Williams**, 'A Word-Study of Hebrews XIII', *JBL* 30, 1911, 129–36; R. **Williamson**, *Philo and the Epistle to the Hebrews*, Leiden 1970; A. S. **van der Woude**, 'Melchisedek als himmlische Erlösergestalt in den neugefundenen eschatologischen Midraschim aus Qumran Höhle XI', *OTS* 14, 1965, 354–73; W. **Wrede**, *Das literarische Rätsel des Hebräerbriefes*, FRLANT 8, 1906; G. **Wuttke**, *Melchisedeck der Priesterkönig von Salem. Eine Studie zur Geschichte der Exegese*, BZNW 5, 1927; Y. **Yadin**, 'The Dead Sea Scrolls and the Epistle to the Hebrews', *Scripta Heirosolymitana* 4, 1958, 36–55; T. **Zahn**, 'Hebräerbrief', *RE*[3], VII, 492–506; H. **Zimmermann**, *Die Hohepriesterchristologie des Hebräerbriefes*, Paderborn 1964; *Das Bekenntnis der Hoffnung. Tradition und Redaktion im Hebräerbrief*, BBB 47, Cologne 1977.

Few modern scholars would dissent from E. F. Scott's critical characterization of the letter of Hebrews as 'the riddle of the New Testament. . . . The more it is studied in detail the more it abounds in problems' (*The Epistle*, 1). Yet upon an initial reading the argument of the writer seems remarkably clear, even if strange and distant for the modern reader. The author is addressing Christians who are in danger of losing heart (3.12) and falling away from their earlier confession (3.14). He offers a 'word of encouragement' (13.22) which takes the form of a theological exposition of the nature of Christ's high priestly office and from which the writer develops his paraenesis (10.19ff.) in order to address the present crisis.

Wherein then does the difficulty of interpretation lie? It arises when one seeks to probe deeper into the surface meaning in order to establish a context into which to set the message and from which to understand it. Who is writing to whom and when? Why was the composition given this particular form? What are the concrete historical issues behind the letter? Above all, what is the nature of the conceptual medium through which the argument is presented? Because these issues have occupied much critical attention from the earliest times on, we shall have to pursue them in more detail.

I. Historical-critical Issues

At the outset, there has been much debate over the form of this composition. Is it really a letter after all? A good number of scholars (e.g. Scott, Moffatt) reject the idea that Hebrews is a letter, and emphasizing its oral features seek to describe it as a type of sermon.

The position that Hebrews has the form of a Jewish-Hellenistic homily has the recent support of both Thyen and Grässer (*ThR*, 153). Closely associated with this problem is the issue whether or not the author is addressing a specific audience. Particularly Wrede (5 ff.) mounted a case for seeing the composition as being composed of typical literary conventions without historical specificity. Conversely, other scholars, especially in England, agree with T. W. Manson (242) that there are enough concrete features within the letter to indicate a definite group rather than just the Christian church at large.

Two further features have emerged in the debate which relate to the beginning and conclusion of the composition. First, it has long been regarded as a problem that any composition claiming to be a letter would lack a praescript. Early theories that the introduction had fallen out, or that the letter was intended to be a round-letter proved unconvincing. Somewhat more plausible initially was the hypothesis (Zahn, Riggenbach) that the bringer of the letter supplied orally the missing introduction. However, the theory depended completely on another set of assumptions regarding the letter's recipients which was equally fragile. Increasingly a modern consensus has arisen that the composition never had a traditional introduction. Spicq (ÉB II,1ff.) has developed the theory that 1.1–4 function as a prologue to the epistle akin to John's Gospel, but support for the theory has been mixed.

The second issue turns on the letter's conclusion (13.19,22–25). A number of scholars have contended that the ending is a later, non-genuine addition (Wrede, C. R. Williams, Schenke). Especially Overbeck made out an elaborate case for seeing the ending as a part of the church's effort in the canonization process to legitimate the letter by means of an attribution of Pauline authorship. However, both Moffatt and Spicq are convinced that the ending is genuine. Moffatt finds it incomprehensible that such an alleged canonical motivation would have resulted in these enigmatic personal references, and Spicq discovers evidence of its genuineness in the continuity of themes from the body of the letter. Michel remains surprisingly cautious in his judgment. He allows for the strikingly different style of the conclusion and acknowledges the possibility of a redactional influence from Pauline circles. In the end, he leaves the problem unresolved.

We turn next to the issue of the letter's authorship which is related to the above issues. The early church's uncertainty over its authorship was revived in the Reformation and by the middle of the nineteenth century the denial of Paul's participation was virtually unanimous among critical scholars. There appeared to be a consensus that Hebrews differs from the Pauline style in structure, vocabulary, and theology. Moreover, it does not fit in with Paul's controversy with Judaism. Of course, various hypotheses were developed to replace the traditional authorship, and credit was given to Apollos, Barnabas and Luke, among others. Still the theories could never fully escape the charge of being purely speculative and of adding little to understanding the letter. Actually the main problem lies in the very vague profile of the author which emerges from the book. Apart from the conclusion, which in itself is far from precise, there are only a few hints to reveal the nature of the author such as his being a second-generation Christian (2.3). As a result, many would agree with Moffatt's characterization: 'to us he is a voice and no more' (xx).

Then again, the issue of the book's addressee has evoked much debate because this decision significantly affects how one interprets the letter. Although admittedly the title 'to the Hebrew' (Πρὸς Ἑβραίους) is not an original part of the letter, it has traditionally played an important role in determining the addressee. In the New Testament the term 'Hebrew' can refer to Aramaic-speaking Jews of Palestine in contrast to Greek-speaking Jews (Acts 6.1), but in the case of the letter to the Hebrews it is more likely a reference to Jews, whatever language they spoke, in contrast to Greeks or Gentiles (II Cor. 11.22; Phil. 3.5). From the title, therefore, it has been traditionally assumed that the letter was addressed to a group of Jewish Christians. However, if one dispenses with the title as providing insufficient evidence for an historical decision, the information about the original recipients of the letter to be gleaned from the letter itself is extremely vague. There are a few hints within the letter (e.g. 5.11ff.; 6.9ff.; 10.32ff.; 13.7) and some indication within the conclusion. However, unfortunately, even the reference to Italy (13.24) is ambiguous and can imply either that the author was in Rome and sends greetings from the Roman church, or that the writer was away from Rome and wished to be remembered to friends at Rome. One of the basic difficulties in reaching a decision is that much of the terminology of the letter is fluid (e.g. 1.1; 2.10), and can be interpreted either literally (descendants of Abraham=Jews), or figuratively (spiritual descendants = Gentiles).

Attempts to recover elements of a concrete historical situation have been often frustrated by the letter's portrayal of the crisis which evoked the response mainly in theological terms. The paraenesis is largely in the traditional terminology of exhortation (2.1ff.) or expressed in terms of analogies drawn from the Old Testament narrative, wisdom, or apocalyptic literature (4.2ff.; 10.19ff.). Only occasionally do apparently concrete elements emerge such as the neglect of meeting in assembly (10.25), or the loss of property, and abuse (10.32ff.). Earlier suggestions that the language of Jewish ritual reflects a period before the fall of Jerusalem have been largely abandoned. Likewise the traditional arguments for fixing the letter's destination at either Jerusalem, Rome, or Alexandria have become increasingly unconvincing to many scholars.

The final, and perhaps most difficult issue so far, has to do with the conceptual categories used by the biblical author, but never explicitly identified. Most critical scholars are fully agreed that the use of the Old Testament has been mediated through various Jewish-Hellenistic traditions of interpretation. The fact that the Old Testament is cited according to the Septuagint and not the Hebrew text indicates from the outset an important Hellenistic filtering of the tradition. In addition, there are numerous signs of midrash-like exegesis and the use of stereotyped homiletical techniques widely employed by both Jewish and non-Jewish Hellenistic authors. The use of technical philosophical terms and unusual cultic language adds to the puzzlement. However, the problem goes far beyond the employment of a few formal categories and touches on the question of whether the biblical material has been radically reshaped by means of very different ideological perspectives. This issue of the nature of the traditioning process and its effect on the shaping of the material remains the most difficult and controversial issue involved in understanding the letter to the Hebrews.

II. Some Proposed Solutions

Modern attempts to recover a concrete historical setting for Hebrews have divided into two major categories. One seeks to specify the addressee as Jewish Christians, the other as Gentiles. We shall treat each approach in turn.

The first proposal which has been the more traditional takes its

initial lead from the letter's title, and sees the major purpose of the
letter to be a defence of the superiority of Christianity over Judaism.
This theory then seeks to bring its description of the Jewish-Christian
recipients into much sharper focus. It is usually argued that the
original addressees were a specific group of Jewish Christians within
a larger congregation (Zahn), rather than being an entire Jewish
congregation or a general designation of Jews at large. Theories
which seek to characterize these Jews in more detail vary from those
arguing for a group with a rabbinic orientation or with a sectarian
perspective. Spicq even suggests a special circle of Jewish priests as
a possible addressee. The discovery of the Qumran material has
stimulated a variety of theories which have proposed parallels with
the Essenes (Yadin, Kosmala), or even a monastic sect of Zionists
(Buchanan), but the evidence for seeing a close analogy is far from
obvious.

Within these proposals much energy has been expended in seeking
to explain the nature of the historical crisis which evoked the letter.
The most frequent suggestion has been that the old forms of the
Jewish cult continued to provide a great attraction for Christian
Jews who were tempted to return to Judaism. Another suggested
motivation for apostasy was thought to be an appeal to Jewish
nationalism which erupted just before the destruction of the temple
and proved to be a great temptation. Still others contend that
disillusionment with Christian eschatology, specifically in the delay
of the parousia, or the lack of a more elaborate Christian cult, caused
the danger of relapse among Christian Jews.

In spite of the widespread use of some form of this reconstruction
(cf. Moule, *Birth of the NT*[3], 68), the difficulties of sustaining the theory
have increasingly undermined its cogency (cf. Scott, Käsemann,
Grässer). Above all, the basic polarity within the letter is not set in
terms of an opposition between Christianity and Judaism. Nowhere
are Jews and Gentiles played against each other. The contrast
between the new and the old covenant is not identified with Christianity's superiority over Judaism. The dialectic of the letter is of a very
different order as is shown by the writer's total lack of interest in
contemporary Judaism. He does not speak of the temple, but rather
of the ancient tent. He is opposing not Pharisaism, but a form of
Levitical worship portrayed in the Mosaic era. Moreover, the
argument is not polemical in the sense of Paul's debate with the
Galatians, but is a scriptural exposition of the Christian faith in

terms of its stages of revelation. The major threat described by the author appears to be abandonment of the Christian 'confession' (Bornkamm) rather than a relapse into Judaism. The various modern attempts to modify the thesis such as offered by Michel, Spicq and Hofius have not overcome the basic difficulty with this approach.

The second proposal which was developed in conscious opposition to the first, argues that the letter's title has misled traditional interpretation by obscuring the Gentile audience as the real addressee of the epistle. For example, both Scott and Moffatt pointed out that Gentile Christians also recognized the authority of the Old Testament, and that numerous phrases which appeared to apply only to Jews, were used metaphorically. In addition, certain idioms such as 'the living God' (3.12) were thought to suggest an antithesis between the true God and pagan idols. Similarly the moral exhortations of the letter were considered more suitable for Gentile Christians than for Jews. Finally, a major point derived from a cumulative argument regarding the development of the early church. The letter of Hebrews was thought to reflect a period somewhat after the fall of Jerusalem when new issues had replaced those of the Pauline era.

With the appearance of Käsemann's monograph *Das wandernde Gottesvolk* in 1939, the debate over the nature of the letter's Gentile recipients entered a new phase. He argued that the polarity of the letter turned on the contrast between the earthly and heavenly realities of Gnostic speculation, and that the Jewish cult functioned only as a specific representative of the earthly and imperfect sphere. Behind the basic motif of the wandering people of God to its heavenly rest lay the Gnostic concept of the heavenly journey of the soul. We shall return shortly to discuss Käsemann's theory in more detail.

The strength of this second position which envisions Gentile recipients lies in its negative criticism of the traditional hypothesis of a Jewish addressee. Its own positive alternative remains fragile and theoretical. Above all, the theory of a Gentile audience, particularly in its Gnostic formulation, results in a highly reductionist position. Eschatological motifs are dismissed as vestiges of inherited material with the paraenetic portions of the letter which have been replaced by the totally different spatial dialectic of a Gnostic ideology (Schenke, *Einl*.II, 252). Moreover, the second position has not been successful in getting close to the peculiar features of Hebrews. For example, it is far from evident that the theme of a heavenly journey of the soul, or Melchizedek as an *Urmensch*, illuminates the writer's train of thought.

Within the two larger historical proposals discussed above by which to arrive at a concrete setting for the letter various other attempts have been made as an indirect means of bringing precision to the discussion. Particularly if one could comprehend the ideological categories through which the material has been filtered, an avenue would be opened by which to interpret the assumptions, goals, and techniques of the author as well as those of his audience.

Ever since the initial suggestion of Grotius in the seventeenth century scholars have sought, above all, to find the key to unlocking the conceptual categories of Hebrews by means of a comparison with the writings of Philo of Alexandria. During much of the nineteenth and twentieth centuries an impressive list of major scholars has defended the fundamental influence of Philo on the author of Hebrews. A strong defence of this position was still made by Spicq in his learned commentary of 1952. He finds Hebrews to be impregnated with the same vocabulary, literary forms, and hermeneutical stance of Philo and he even argues that the author probably knew Philo personally (I, 89). Anyone who dismisses Spicq's case easily has not taken the time to study his evidence closely. Indeed, many of the strange features of Hebrews which set the author apart from the rest of the New Testament, and especially from Paul, find remarkable parallels in Philo. The concepts of the logos, of faith, angels, and perfection are often closely akin, but particularly a dualism between earthly and heavenly realities has elements in common with Hebrews.

Nevertheless, in recent years some strong voices have been raised in criticism of the close dependency of Hebrews on Philo. For example, S. Sowers still accepts Alexandrian allegory as the background of the epistle, but he wants to see a fundamentally different hermeneutic, that of *Heilsgeschichte*, consciously replacing the allegorical tradition. Detailed studies of certain features of the comparison, such as Barrett's on eschatology, have marked the striking dissimilarity between the two writers. Especially Williamson's very thorough comparison of shared vocabulary and themes has done much to undermine the theory of immediate dependency. His vocabulary statistics are decisive in dispelling loosely held impressions of similarity. In sum, the Hellenistic filtering which is reflected in Hebrews, especially by its use of the Septuagint, is far too complex to be explained simply by a comparison with Philo.

The long-standing interest in Philo as providing the closest parallel to Hebrews received an accidental blow which ironically cast a shadow on Spicq's work from the start. The discovery of the Qumran writings in 1947 unleashed a wave of new publications which sought to interpret Hebrews in the light of the new Hebrew sectarian material. Most noteworthy was the seminal article of Yadin. Kosmala's learned book which followed suffered from certain idiosyncratic tendences which lessened its impact. Yadin found important parallels in the sect's belief in two messiahs, in the figure of the prophet, in the role of angels, and in the wilderness calling. Subsequently, the even more exciting references to Melchizedek added a new dimension to the debate (cf. van der Woude, Fitzmyer). Now after several decades of scholarly discussion a consensus has emerged which would considerably modify Yadin's initial theory, but use the evidence from Qumran indirectly in sketching the syncretistic milieu of Palestine out of which Hebrews arose. Such a formulation of the contributions of Qumran as offered by Flusser seems especially judicious. However, the basic theological differences in perspective between a closed, ceremonially oriented community of Qumran, and the call for an open, christologically centred church of Hebrews continues to be obvious even to the casual reader.

Within the English-speaking world the proposal by Käsemann of a Gnostic background for Hebrews has received very limited suppport. However, within Germany a sharp debate has developed between Käsemann's supporters (Grässer, Theissen), and those who contend for some form of Jewish syncretistic influence, such as Jewish apocalypticism (Michel) or *merkabah* mysticism (Schenke, Hofius). Whereas Michel was at first willing in the second edition of his commentary to make a few concessions to Käsemann, Hofius' two monographs on Hebrews offer an unrelenting attack on the entire Gnostic proposal. Although in many details he has certainly undercut Käsemann's position (e.g. the concept of 'rest'), the larger issue of Gnostic influence has not yet been fully resolved. Bultmann's theory of a unified Gnostic *Urmensch* myth has, of course, been badly eroded in recent years, and Käsemann still assumes its validity quite uncritically. Nevertheless, there are some brilliant insights in Käsemann's monograph which will continue to attract adherents to his larger hypothesis. It is also clear that the defenders of the Jewish background of Hebrews have not made much contribution to the hermeneutical debate since many of them seem to assume that a positive exegetical yield derives automatically from a Jewish borrowing. This generalization needs some modification in the case of Schenke (*Einl.* II, 259ff.) who falls outside the 'Schlatter circle', and who explicitly explores the relation of the theology of Hebrews to a history-of-religions study of Jewish mysticism.

There is one final position to consider which has sought to reconstruct a plausible historical setting for Hebrews. The impact of William Manson's monograph of 1951 has been considerable in Britain. In these lectures he argues that within the Roman church there was a small enclave of conservative Jewish Christians who held to the principles of traditional Judaism. However, there was another wing who had accepted fully the implications of the Gentile world mission. The position of this group is best represented by the speech of Stephen in Acts 7. Manson finds a direct line from the teachings of Stephen to the epistle to the Hebrews. The author of the latter was also trying to convince Jewish conservatives of the church's world mission, and he develops the same eschatological and christological themes of Stephen. In fact, Manson describes eight different subjects which the two writing share (36ff.).

The initial similarity between Acts 7 and Hebrews is remarkable, and had been noticed before Manson's book. However, he deserves the credit for having mounted a highly consistent and imaginative theory which seems to interpret the similarities in a comprehensive manner. There remain some unresolved questions. It is speculative to posit a progressive and a conservative wing within Jewish Christianity along the lines which Manson sketches. Nor is it obvious that Stephen was the representative of an actual party. Then again, the major question posed by German scholarship which has been influenced by Conzelmann and Vielhauer turns on the issue of whether Acts 7 reflects an independent historical source or is primarily a Lucan composition. In spite of these reservations which have been voiced, Manson's theory continues to have an attraction for many and cannot be simply dismissed. In my judgment, his ability to bring the letter of Hebrews out of its position of isolation within the New Testament and to show important lines of theological connection with Acts is more significant than his detailed historical reconstruction which remains quite hypothetical.

To summarize, the various attempts to bring the book of Hebrews into sharper focus have been useful in part. The parallels, both Jewish and Greek, have demonstrated again that Hebrews was not written in a vacuum. Even such allegedly bizarre reflections as that on Melchizedek are now seen as being part of a larger tradition within the broad spectrum of Hellenistic religious speculation. The result of careful research has often been to bring words and concepts into clearer perspective. Larger patterns frequently akin to rabbinic and Qumran midrash have emerged and a general Hellenistic environment sharing complex hermeneutical tradition has received a clear profile. Yet no one key to interpret the letter has been produced, nor has it been possible to interpret the content of the letter successfully apart from its own unique theological message. Moreover, it is the contention of this introduction that the dimensions of the letter's reception by a community of faith which is the basis for its canonical form and function have not yet been adequately explored, and offer another approach to interpreting the letter's unusually vague setting.

III. A Canonical Approach to Hebrews

We began our study of the epistle by noting the problem of interpreting a writing whose concrete historical setting appeared so vague and imprecise. We have also reviewed different attempts of modern scholarship to recover an original context. The troubling question remains: how can a composition function with so little certainty regarding its original historical purpose? Are there any other exegetical avenues into the problem? When we studied the Pauline corpus, it became evident that the major canonical problem had to do with the later community's effort to broaden the high level of particularity in order to render the letters suitable for later generation of believers. The canonical problem of the letter of Hebrews is just the opposite. How can a letter function as normative religious literature which lacks a sharp, original profile? How is one to explain this vagueness? Above all, what are the signs left in the letter's final form which give an indication of how the epistle was heard and used?

A. The Function of the Title

There is general agreement that the letter's title 'to the Hebrews' is not an original part of the composition, but was added at an early stage in the second century, as is evident from the fact that the letter is only known under this title in all the manuscripts and versions. It also seems likely that the addition of the title was made under the influence of the Pauline titles as part of the canonical process of joining the letter to a larger corpus. There is no clear evidence to determine whether any historical memory was involved, but it appears more likely that the title was secondarily derived from a judgment regarding the letter's content. Frequently the opinion is expressed by commentators (Scott, Moffatt) that the title is not only misleading, but totally irrelevant for a correct understanding of the letter. Is this really the case?

It has long been noticed that the meaning of the term 'Hebrews' is ambiguous, and the problem is rehearsed by virtually every commentary (cf. especially Bleek, I, 33ff., and Zahn, *Intr.* II, 296). Within the New Testament the term can refer to Jewish Christians who retained their mother-tongue in distinction from Greek-speaking Jews (Acts 6.1). The term can also refer to all Christians who are Jewish by birth without reference to the question of language (II Cor.11.22; Phil.3.5). Since the letter was originally written in Greek and thus directed to a Greek-speaking audience, there is agreement that the term in the title is a reference to Jews by birth irrespective of language. We have already discussed the effort of Zahn to make this traditional title more historically concrete by posing various theories which assume a genuine historical memory.

Nevertheless, it is a different issue to raise the question as to how the title functioned canonically. The title construed the letter as being addressed 'to the Hebrews'. However, within the letter itself there is never a contrast made between Jews and Gentiles. Moreover, a remarkable feature of the letter is that it reflects no interest in the contemporary Judaism of the period. Again, by the end of the second century, when the title entered within the canonical process, the phenomeno of both Aramaic-speaking Jewish Christians, and Greek-speaking Jewish Christians had lost its major significance within the developing church.

The title does not therefore refer to any specific historical referent, whether Aramaic- or Greek-speaking Jews, but to those of the old covenant who form the major subject-matter of the epistle in contrast to those of the new covenant. In other words, the term is a theological construct in which an historical anachronism functions as a theological referent. The title correctly reflects the subject matter of the epistle which also involves a theological construct based on a scriptural reconstruction of Levitical worship rather than a polemic against contemporary Judaism. The reference to the Hebrews serves to generalize the addressee by including those who live under the old covenant, whether past or present, and whose situation is described by scripture. The generalizing role of the title is also compatible with further typological application, such as the linking of the old covenant with the earthly and the new with the heavenly. The one becomes identified with the ephemeral, the other with the eternal.

The title correctly construes the epistle as addressing the theological problem of the two dispensations. What is the relation of life under the old covenant with life under the new? (Obviously the issue is not between the Old Testament literature and the literature of the New which for Hebrews would be an anachronism). The scriptures of the old covenant continue to speak truthfully the voice of God concerning his eternal plan of salvation in his Son. The epistle to the Hebrews offers a programmatic statement of the theological relation of the two covenants, which receives its content from scripture and not from its historical setting in the 1st century. To suggest that Hebrews is lacking in concrete qualities is to misunderstand its theological purpose which is far from vague.

B. The Function of the Structure

Attempts to outline the epistle in detail continue to reveal great differences among the commentators. This observation should not come as a great surprise in the light of the different interpretations of the composition's genre as a whole, and whether it is primarily an oral or literary entity. It is clear that the various parts tend to flow into one another and present difficulties in establishing beginnings and endings of sections. A number of commentators have settled on a broad division of the letter into three main sections, 1.1–4.13; 4.14–10.18; 10.19–13.25 (Delitzsch, Westcott, Moffatt, Michel), but even these commentators differ on how much weight to attribute to the divisions. Moreover, ever since the critical essay of Vaganay in 1940 followed by the monograph of Vanhoye, various attempts have been proposed to discover a highly sophisticated literary work controlled by catchwords, symmetrical patterns, and calculated repetition.

In my judgment, the issue has not been fully resolved and more research is called for. Larger hermeneutical issues are also involved. It is not always easy to distinguish between structural elements which reflect an author's intentionality and a modern reader's imaginative construal of the material. Although I do not disparage either of these two aspects of interpretation, and believe that they should be related within the discipline of biblical exegesis, the two aspects are not to be identified. At this juncture, I remain unconvinced of Vanhoye's attempt to derive his detailed analysis of the epistle from the intention of the author.

Nevertheless, I believe that there is a feature of the book's structure which exhibits an original theological intention, and which continues to serve a canonical function in rendering the letter's message to future generations of readers. I am referring to the interchange between dogmatic and paraenetic sections of the letter.

Commentators differ in analysing the paraenetic sections (cf. Nairne, F. F. Bruce, Spicq). The situation arises because some exhortations are parenthetical, interruping an argument (2.1–4), whereas others form a climax to an entire section of the epistle or introduce the final hortatory chapters (10.19–25). The exhortation in 3.7–19 is developed on the basis of an extended exegesis of Ps.95, whereas 4.14–16 introduces a new section with an initial exhortative appeal. Although much discussion has taken place regarding the relation of the doctrinal and paraenetic sections, the major point to be stressed is that the two belong closely together. The doctrine leads to the exhortation and the exhortation derives from the doctrine.

The canonical significance of the interchange between doctrinal and paraenetic sections is in reminding the reader that the christological discussions of the letter have an immediate effect on the believer. The Christians who are addressed in Hebrews are in danger of falling away from their confession (3.1; 4.14; 10.23). The author of Hebrews sets out to remind them of the nature of the salvation which Christ, the subject of the confession, has procured. The issue is not a theoretical one, but focuses immediately on Christ's providing a way of access to God as high priest. He is a high priest who shared fully in human nature in order to overcome the threat of death which threatens every human being (2.14ff.). The author contrasts the old covenant and its earthly tent with the new covenant and its heavenly sanctuary in order to make clear the inability of the old dispensation to provide true communion with God. The eschatological emphasis of the writer is integrally joined to the liturgical because in the community's ongoing worship the presence of God is proleptically experienced (6.4). The author can move freely between doctrine and paraenesis because of the highly existential nature of the discourse. The subject matter is the 'living God' who speaks his word through his Son and who provides a way into his presence as an escape from his all-consuming judgment (12.18ff.). Any model for interpreting the epistle which characterizes the eschatological theme as a vestige from inherited material has missed the central dynamic of the letter which the canon has maintained in the structure of its final form.

C. The Function of the Conclusion

The critical debate over the conclusion of the letter (Wrede= 13.19,23f.; Michel=13.22–25; Spicq=13.20–25) has focused primarily on the genuineness or non-genuineness of these concluding verses of the epistle. We have already reviewed some of the literary problems involved. Nevertheless, without fully deciding whether the ending reflects a primary or secondary level of composition, there is an important need to discuss the canonical effect of the ending on the letter in its final form.

The concluding verses do not suddenly provide the reader with a volume of concrete historical information about the author or his community. The conclusion does not effect an alteration in kind from the vague historical context of the body of the letter. However, the ending does remove any doubts as to its being construed as a letter which was directed to a specific community with a real, if unexpressed, historical and geographical setting. The ending therefore strengthens the concrete qualities of the few particular references within the epistle (6.9ff.) and moves against the direction of interpreting the material as simply rhetorical and typical in quality.

A more important canonical effect of the ending turns on the issue of the letter's relation to the apostle Paul. Once again the critical debate has focused the issue largely on the historical question without ever posing the fundamental canonical question as to the relation of Hebrews to the Pauline corpus. The ending does not propose a direct link with Paul by attributing to him the authorship. Rather, it offers an indirect relationship through Timothy with whom the unknown writer shares a common ministry.

We have often observed in our study of the formation of the Pauline corpus that the New Testament has constructed a canonical Paul, who extends far beyond the boundaries which historical criticism has set for the reconstruction of the historical Paul. Indeed as an integral witness to the canonical Paul are the Pastoral letters and those of Ephesians and Colossians. However, it is significant that the letter to the Hebrews has not been brought within this circle. It has been assigned a position just outside this corpus.

Nevertheless, there is an important indirect link between Paul and Hebrews which the early church correctly sensed, but misinterpreted when it sought to solve the issue historically (e.g. Clement, Origen). The writer of Hebrews was a co-worker of Timothy, which means that from a canonical perspective, the letter is not to be interpreted within an historical context which assigns it to a late stage in the development of the post-apostolic church. Rather, Hebrews functions canonically as distinct and yet complementary to the Pauline corpus. Historically, W. Manson may be right in his theory of a link between Stephen and the writer of Hebrews, but canonically the letter's major function is in relation to the Pauline corpus.

The effect of the canonical ending, which has greatly influenced the usual positioning of the letter within the New Testament either before the Pastorals or after Philemon, is not to propose an easy harmonization with Paul, but to establish a context in which the different approaches to the great theological issues, shared by these authors, are viewed together as comprising the truth of the one gospel.

24

THE PAULINE CORPUS

I. Bibliography on the Literary Form of the Pauline Letters

C. **Andresen**, 'Zum Formular frühchristlicher Gemeindebriefe', *ZNW* 56, 1956, 223–59; G. J. **Bahr**, 'Paul and Letter Writing in the First Century', *CBQ* 28, 1966, 465–77; 'The Superscriptions in the Pauline Letters', *JBL* 87, 1968, 27–41; K. **Berger**, 'Apostelbrief und apostolische Rede. Zum Formular frühchristlicher Briefe', *ZNW* 65, 1974, 190–231; H. D. **Betz**, 'The Literary Composition and Function of Paul's Letter to the Galatians', *NTS* 21, 1974/5, 353–79; C. J. **Bjerkelund**, *PARAKALŌ. Form, Funktion und Sinn der parakalō-Sätze in den paulinischen Briefen*, Oslo 1967; N. A. **Dahl**, 'Letter', *IDB Suppl*, 538–40; E. **von Dobschütz**, 'Wir und Ich bei Paulus', *ZSTh* 10, 1932/33, 251–77; A. **Deissmann**, *Bible Studies*, ET Edinburgh 1901, 1–59; M. **Dibelius**, *Geschichte der urchristlichen Literatur* II, Berlin 1926, 5–9; W. G. **Doty**, 'The Classification of Epistolary Literature', *CBQ* 31, 1969, 183–99; *Letters in Primitive Christianity*, Philadelphia 1973; E. **Fascher**, 'Briefliteratur, urchristliche', *RGG*³, I, 1412–15; R. W. **Funk**, *Language, Hermeneutic and the Word of God*, New York 1966, London 1967, 252–74; 'The Apostolic Parousia: Form and Significance', *Christian History and Interpretation: Studies Presented to John Knox*, ed. W. R. Farmer et al., Cambridge 1967, 249–68.

R. **Jewett**, 'The Form and Function of the Homiletic Benediction', *AnThR* 15, 1969, 18–34; C. -H. **Kim**, *Form and Structure of the Familiar Greek Letter of Recommendation*, SBLDS 4, Missoula 1972; E. **Lohmeyer**, 'Probleme paulinischer Theologie I; Die brieflichen Grussüberschriften', *ZNW* 26, 1927, 158–73; R. N. **Longenecker**, 'Ancient Amanuenses and the Pauline Epistles', *New Dimensions in New Testament Study*, Grand Rapids 1974, 281–97; G. **Luck**, 'Brief und Epistel in der Antike', *Das Altertum* 7, 1961, 44–50; T. Y. **Mullins**, 'Disclosure: A Literary Form in the New Testament', *NovT* 7, 1964, 44–50; 'Greeting as a New Testament Form', *JBL* 87, 1968, 418–26; 'Formulas in the New Testament Epistles', *JBL* 91, 380–90; B. **Rigaux**, *The Letters of St Paul*, ET Chicago 1968; O. **Roller**, *Das Formular der paulinischen Briefe*, BWANT 58, 1933; J. T. **Sanders**, 'The Transition from Opening

Epistolary Thanksgivings to Body in the Letter of the Pauline Corpus', *JBL* 81, 1962, 348–62; P. **Schubert**, *Form and Function of the Pauline Thanksgivings*, BZNW 20, 1939; M. L. **Stirewalt**, 'Paul's Evaluation of Letter Writing', *Search the Scriptures, FS R. T. Stamm*, ed. J. M. Meyers et al., Leiden 1969, 179–96; J. **Sykutris**, 'Epistolographie', *PW* Suppl. vol.5, 1931, 199–200; P. **Wendland**, *Die urchristlichen Literaturformen*, HNT 1.3, [2,3]1912, 339–45; J. L. **White**, 'Introductory Formulae in the Body of the Pauline Letter', *JBL* 90, 1971, 91–97; *The Form and Function of the Body of the Greek Letter*, SBLDS 2, Missoula 1972; *The Form and Structure of the Official Petition: A Study in Greek Epistolography*, SBLDS 5, Missoula 1972.

II. Bibliography on the Formation of the Pauline Corpus

Cf. the comprehensive bibliography in **Lindemann**, *Paulus im ältesten Christentum* (below), 408–32.

B. **Aland**, 'Marcion: Versuch einter neuen Interpretation', *ZTK* 70, 1973, 420–47; E. **Aleith**, *Paulusverständnis in der alten Kirche*, BZNW 18, 1937; C. P. **Anderson**, 'The Epistle to the Hebrews and the Pauline Letter Collection', *HTR* 59, 1966, 429–38.

C. K. **Barrett**, 'Pauline Controversies in the Post-Pauline Period', *NTS* 20, 1973/4, 229–45; 'Acts and the Pauline Letter Corpus', *ExpT* 88, 1976/7, 2–5; A. E. **Barnett**, *Paul Becomes a Literary Influence*, Chicago 1941; W. **Bauer**, *Orthodoxy and Heresy in Earliest Christianity*, ET London and Philadelphia 1971; E. C. **Blackman**, *Marcion and His Influence*, London 1948; D. **de Bruyne**, 'Prologues bibliques d'origin marcionite', *RBén* 24, 1907, 1–14; C. H. **Buck**, 'The Early Order of the Pauline Corpus', *JBL* 68, 1949, 351–57; T. H. **Campbell**, 'Paul's "Missionary Journals" as Reflected in his Letters', *JBL* 74, 1955, 80–87; H. **von Campenhausen**, *The Formation of the Christian Bible*, ET London and Philadelphia 1972; K. L. **Carroll**, 'The Expansion of the Pauline Corpus', *JBL* 72, 1953, 230–37; O. **Cullmann**, 'Paradosis et Kyrios. Le problème de la tradition dans le Paulinisme', *RHPhR* 30, 1950, 12–30. N. A. **Dahl**, 'Adresse und Proömium des Epheserbriefes', *TZ* 7, 1951, 241–64; 'Welche Ordnung der Paulusbriefe wird vom muratorischen Kanon vorausgesetzt?' *ZNW* 52, 1961, 39–53; 'The Particularity of the Pauline Epistles as a Problem in the Ancient Church', *Neotestamentica et Patristica, FS O. Cullmann*, ed. W. C. van Unnik, NovT Supp 6, 1962, 261–71; 'The Origin of the Earliest Prologues to the Pauline Letters', *Semeia* 12, 1978, 233–77; A. **Deissmann**, *Bible Studies*, ET Edinburgh 1909, 3–59.

J.-A. **Eschlimann**, 'La rédaction des épitres Pauliniennes d'après une comparison avec des lettres profanes de son temps', *RB* 53, 1946, 185–96; W. R. **Farmer**, *Jesus and the Gospel*, Philadelphia 1982, 253–5; J. **Finegan**, 'The Original Form of the Pauline Corpus', *HTR* 49, 1956, 85–104; L. **Foster**, 'The Earliest Collection of Paul's Epistles', *JETS* 10, 1967, 44–55; H. J. **Friede**, 'Die Ordnung der Paulusbriefe und der Platz des Kolosserbriefs im Corpus Paulinum', *Vetus Latina: Die Reste der altlateinischen Bibel*, 24/2 Freiburg 1969, 290–303; G. **Friedrich**, 'Lohmeyers These über "das paulinische Briefpräskript" kritisch beleuchtet', *ZNW* 46, 1955, 272–4; H. **Gamble**, 'The Redaction of the Pauline Letters and the Formation of the Pauline Corpus', *JBL* 94, 1975, 403–18; *The Textual History of the Letter to the Romans*, Grand Rapids 1977; E. J. **Goodspeed**, *The Formation of the New Testament*, Chicago 1926; 'The Place of Ephesians in the First Pauline Collection', *AnThR* 12, 1930, 189–212; *Christianity Goes to Press*, New York 1940; 'Ephesians and the First Editor of Paul', *JBL* 70, 1951, 285–91; R. M. **Grant**, *The Formation of the New Testament*, New York 1965; P. L. **Hammer**, 'Canon and Theological Variety: A Study in the Pauline Tradition', *ZNW* 67, 1976, 83–9; A. **von Harnack**, Review of de Bruyne, *TLZ* 32, 1907, 138–40; *Marcion: Das Evangelium vom fremden Gott*, Leipzig ²1924; *Die Briefsammlung des Apostel Paulus und die anderen vorkonstantinischen christlichen Briefsammlungen*, Leipzig 1926; J. R. **Harris**, 'Marcion and the Canon', *ExpT* 18, 1907, 393; P. N. **Harrison**, *Polycarp's Two Epistles to the Philippians*, Cambridge 1936; W. H. P. **Hatch**, 'The Position of Hebrews in the Canon of the New Testament', *HTR* 29, 1936, 133–51.

E. **Kamlah**, *Traditionsgeschichtliche Untersuchungen zur Schlussdoxologie des Römerbriefes*, Diss. Tübingen 1955; L. E. **Keck**, *Paul and His Letters*, Philadelphia 1979; J. **Knox**, 'The Pauline Corpus', *Marcion and the New Testament*, Chicago 1942, 39–76; *Philemon among the Letters of Paul*, New York 1935, ²1959; 'A Note on the Formation of the Pauline Corpus', *HTR* 50, 1957, 311–14; 'Acts and the Pauline Letter Corpus', *Studies in Luke-Acts, FS P. Schubert*, ed. L. E. Keck and J. L. Martyn, Nashville 1966, 279–87; W. G. **Kümmel**, 'Paulusbriefe', *RGG³*, V. 195–8; H. **Lietzmann**, *Einführung in die Textgeschichte der Paulusbriefe*, HNT 8, ⁴1933, 1–18; J. B. **Lightfoot**, *Biblical Essays*, New York and London 1893, 287–374; A. **Lindemann**, *Paulus im ältesten Christentum*, BHT 58, 1979; G. **Lüdemann**, *Paulus, der Heidenapostel*, I–II FRLANT 130, 1980–83; T. W. **Manson**, 'St Paul's Letter to the Romans – and Others', *Studies in the Gospels and Epistles*, ed. M. Black, Manchester and Philadelphia 1962, 225–41; O. **Michel**, *Paulus und seine Bibel*, Gütersloh 1929; C. L. **Mitton**, *The Formation of the Pauline Corpus of Letters*, London 1955; A. Q. **Morton**, 'The Authorship of the Pauline Corpus', *The New Testament in Historical and Contemporary Perspective, Essays in Memory of G. H. C. Macgregor*, ed. H. Anderson and W. Barclay, Oxford 1965, 209–35; L. **Mowry**, 'The Early Circulation of Paul's Letters', *JBL* 63, 1944, 73–86; P. **Nautin**, 'Irénée et la canonicité des épîtres pauliniennes', *RHR* 182, 1972, 113–30.

F. **Overbeck**, *Zur Geschichte des Kanons*, Chemnitz 1880; reprinted Darmstadt n.d.; E. H. **Pagels**, *The Gnostic Paul*, Philadelphia 1975; S. **Pedersen**, 'Die Kanonfrage als historisches und theologisches Problem', *StTh* 31, 1977, 105ff.; J. D. **Quinn**, 'P⁴⁶ – The Pauline Canon?', *CBQ* 36, 1974, 379–85; D. K. **Rensberger**, *As the Apostle Teaches: The Development of the Use of Paul's Letters in Second-Century Christianity*, Diss. Yale 1891; J. A. T. **Robinson**, *Redating the New Testament*, London and Philadelphia 1976; J. A. **Sanders**, 'Torah and Paul', *God's Christ and His People, Essays honoring N. A. Dahl*, ed.

W. A. Meeks and J. Jervell, Oslo 1977, 132–40; W. **Schmithals**, 'On the Composition and Earliest Collection of the Major Epistles of Paul', ET *Paul and the Gnostics*, Nashville 1972, 239–74; W. **Schneemelcher**, 'General Introduction: 1. Canonical and Apocryphal', *NTApoc* I, 21–8; G. **Strecker**, 'Paulus in nachpaulinischer Zeit', *Kairos* ns 12, 1970, 208–16; A. C. **Sundberg**, 'Canon Muratori: A Fourth Century List', *HTR* 66, 1973, 1–41; J. **Wagermann**, *Die Stellung des Apostels Paulus neben den Zwölf in den ersten zwei Jahrhunderten*, BZNW 3, 1926; H. -F. **Weiss**, 'Paulus und die Häretiker. Zum Paulusverständnis in der Gnosis', *Christentum und Gnosis*, ed. W. Eltester, BZNW 37, 1969, 116–28; M. F. **Wiles**, *The Divine Apostle. The Interpretation of St Paul's Epistles in the Early Church*, Cambridge 1967; T. **Zahn**, *Geschichte des neutestamentlichen Kanons*, II/1, 344ff., 380ff.; II/2, 565ff.; G. **Zuntz**, *The Text of the Epistles*, London 1953.

It has long been recognized as a difficult and yet very significant New Testament problem to determine the history of the collection of the Pauline letters into a canonical corpus. During most of the history of the early church the letters of Paul were transmitted, not in isolation from each other, but within a collection. The earliest textual witnesses of his letters already reflect the form of a corpus (cf. Zuntz). Scholars have, therefore, struggled with a variety of problems which relate to this canonical formation. When, why, how, by whom and for whom did the Pauline corpus develop?

Not all of these questions can be clearly answered. The complexity of the task of assessing both the internal and external evidence should not be underestimated. Nor do all of the problems relate directly to the concerns of this introduction. However, it is equally clear that many of the literary, historical, and theological judgments regarding the formation of the Pauline corpus do affect one's interpretation of the letters both in their individual and corporate state. For example, it would be highly significant if Goodspeed's theory were right that Ephesians is a post-Pauline composition which was written by the collector to serve as an introduction to the whole corpus. Or again, important exegetical implications emerge for interpreting the individual letters if the historical process of collection ruled out the possibility for extensive reworking of the letters in their pre-canonical form.

The modern debate over the development of the Pauline corpus emerged in the long controversy between T. Zahn and A. Harnack. Zahn developed his position, which was supported with formidable scholarship, by an exhaustive study of the early canonical lists, Marcion, and the Apostolic Fathers, especially Clement, Polycarp, and Ignatius. He argued that the references to the Pauline letters in widely separated areas of the church (Rome, Corinth, Smyrna, Antioch) as well as the high level of uniformity among the epistles mentioned, could only be explained by assuming a process of conscious collection, the motivation for which Zahn attributed to the liturgical function of public worship. He assigned the process of the formation of the corpus of thirteen Pauline epistles, which he thought comprised the collection, to the period between AD 80 and 85, after the writing of the book of Acts. He located this canonical activity geographically in Corinth.

Harnack agreed with Zahn regarding the early age of the Pauline collection and set AD 100 as the *terminus ad quem* for the corpus, which had by then grown from ten to thirteen letters by the addition of the Pastorals. He also envisioned a growth which was motivated by the public reading of the Pauline letters in worship. However, Harnack differed at a decisive point from Zahn by sharply distinguishing between the public reading from a Pauline collection and the formal recognition of the corpus' canonicity. The latter decision constituted a restricting of the number of letters and attributing to them an authority equal to the Old Testament scriptures. For Harnack this latter process did not reach a conclusion until the end of the second century and was largely produced by Marcion who had first assigned to the Pauline collection a genuinely canonical function. Decisive in the shaping of the Pauline letters was the attempt to understand them as directed to seven congregations as a symbol for the universal church.

In spite of their differences Zahn and Harnack agreed in seeing the development of the collection of epistles as a gradual uninterrupted process which Moule designated 'the snowball theory'. It was this historical description which met with vigorous opposition beginning in the 1920s, and in the writings of Goodspeed, Knox, and Mitton unleashed a new phase in the debate over the development of the Pauline corpus. These scholars contended that the corpus did not gradually emerge, but must have been the product of a deliberate editorial activity which caused the collection to spring to life at once. They used as evidence the curious fact of the apparently complete ignorance of the Pauline letters as late as the composition of Acts, which period was immediately followed by full knowledge and recognition of a collection of ten epistles. Goodspeed further argued that the composition of Ephesians, as well as its position at the head of the corpus, played a major role in the process. However, Goodspeed's theory, even with the refinements of Knox and Mitton, has appeared increasingly idiosyncratic to most New Testament scholars. It is highly questionable that Ephesians ever held the first position in the sequence of letters. Even more damaging is the assumption that Paul had largely fallen into disfavour among orthodox Christians because of his popularity among the heretics, and was only rescued by the collecting and publication of his writings.

The contemporary discussion has continued to occupy itself with several of these older critical issues, but the form of the discussion has, by and large, moved in another direction. The theory that Paul was largely forgotten by the church has not been confirmed by recent research (cf. Lindemann, Rensberger). Then again, there is a growing consensus that Harnack and von Campenhausen have overestimated the crucial canonical role of Marcion. Even the theory of the Marcionite prologues to the Pauline epistles which de Bruyne first proposed in 1907 and which received Harnack's support, has been recently subjected to criticism and called into question (cf. Dahl, 'The Origin . . . ').

The reasons lying behind the canonization of the Pauline letters cannot be explained primarily as a reaction to some external threat, but derived from intrinisc theological concerns. In an illuminating essay Dahl has pinpointed the fundamental obstacle to the canonization of the Pauline epistles which lay not in their plurality, which was the problem of the Gospels, but in their particularity. How can occasional letters written to specific churches and concerned with particular situational conflicts function canonically as an authoritative norm? Wherein lies the universal and catholic authority of his letters? On the basis of both internal and external evidence Dahl was able to trace the church's struggle to universalize the function of the letters, but in such a way as to retain the basic particularity of the original epistolary setting. Dahl was able to show that the original corpus comprised a collection of letters to seven churches as a symbol of the universal church. Only later did another order arise which included thirteen (or fourteen) letters.

This history accounts for the complex diversity in the order of the letters, particularly in the Latin textual tradition. One of the implications to be drawn from this development is that a variety of different factors played a role in establishing the order of the letters, such as length, chronology, public or private letter, and age of inclusion (e.g. Pastorals). No great theological weight can be attached to the order which continued to fluctuate within different textual traditions. However, the conscious inclusion of Hebrews and the Pastorals within the collection, which was not an obvious canonical development, does carry significant theological implications which has been explored elsewhere.

Perhaps the most controversial issue which has emerged in the modern discussion turns on the relation between the alleged redaction of various Pauline letters and the formation of the Pauline corpus. Ever since the close critical study of the Pauline letters began, voices have been raised which would question the literary integrity of certain of the epistles within the corpus. Attention has focused especially on Romans, II Corinthians, II Thessalonians and Philippians (cf. the critical discussion in the prior chapters).

The argument for redactional activity has concentrated almost completely on internal evidence with the notable exception of Romans. However, as Schmithals has correctly pointed out, little attention has been expended on the larger canonical issues at stake in the assumption of such widespread redactional activity. How is one to explain such a process of reworking of letters which has few, if any, analogies in classical literature? Schmithals even speaks of a 'curious composition-psychosis' to characterize the idea of widely spread and independent editing of the letters (271).

In contrast to the theory of the independent redaction of the Pauline letters, Schmithals has presented a bold hypothesis which identifies the redactor of the letters with the first editor of the Pauline corpus. Moreover, he seeks to establish a specific *Sitz im Leben* for this activity which arose in the context of the Catholic church's attempt to combat the Gnostic threat with an interpreted edition of Paul's letters. An additional advantage of Schmithal's proposal is that it eliminates the puzzle of having a plethora of independent redactions of individual letters.

At this point it is unnecessary to pursue the specific weaknesses of Schmithal's reconstruction of the editorial process, which has received much criticism, but rather to concentrate on the larger principles at stake. The crucial problem respecting any theory which identifies the redactor and the editor of the corpus has been forcefully presented by Gamble (*JBL* 94). The theory assumes that the entire textual tradition of Paul's letters goes back to a single archetype, namely to the 'original edition' of the corpus. Gamble contends that the textual evidence of Romans makes this textual theory untenable. The text history of Romans shows that the letter underwent a lengthy transmission as an independent letter. Moreover, the case of Romans proves the rule that if textual revisions have taken place, they have left their marks within the textual evidence.

Gamble's contribution lies, not in his resolving the problem of the relation between the redaction and the editing of the corpus, but in clarifying the exact nature of the problem and in limiting the alternatives. Two major options seem left. Either the present corpus of the Pauline letters represents a collection of letters which underwent little change from the time of their original composition, or the redactional activity of the individual letters took place before the letters entered into the text-critical stream. With the first alternative the problem lies in adequately explaining the apparent internal evidence for a multi-layered text. With the second alternative the problem lies in explaining the rationale behind independent and diverse redactions of many of Paul's letters. In the light of the critical analysis of the Pauline letters which we have just undertaken, the second alternative seems clearly to be preferred in spite of the many unresolved problems respecting the process of redaction and canonization.

There is one final issue to discuss in this context. Dahl has correctly made the point that the canonical problem of the Pauline letters lay in their particularity. This insight is important and Dahl has traced historically the church's attempt to resolve it, both in terms of the textual evidence which reflected the struggle, and the explicit discussion of the issue in the literature of the early church. However, in my judgment, the issue of particularity is not the major theological issue at stake in the formation of the Pauline corpus. Rather, I would argue that the most important issue turns on the shape which the canonical collection has given the Pauline letters in greatly extending the profile of Paul far beyond that of his historical ministry. Regardless of how one decides on the relationship between the redactional and the canonical process of the collection, the present shape of the Pauline corpus has included letters which give the appearance of transmitting Paul's message within a variety of settings which cannot be easily identified with the known facts of his life. In sum, a profile of Paul has been shaped by the canon which transcends that of the historical apostle.

The detailed evidence for this assertion has already been offered in the analyses of the individual letters, but a few broad lines are in order by way of summary. The Pauline corpus now contains whole letters or at least portions of letters which do not stem directly from the historical Paul (e.g. II Thessalonians). In addition, Ephesians and perhaps Colossians appear to stem from a disciple or school of Paul which has actualized the teachings of Paul in such a way as to address the threat of Gnostic speculation and which has considerably influenced the shape of Paul's message within the New Testament. Again, the corpus contains a group of the so-called Pastoral epistles which in the name of Paul address a situation in the early church several decades after the death of Paul. Finally, one has the problem of understanding the relation of the corpus with the Paul of the book of Acts which, if nothing else, establishes a chronology of his life which interacts in some fashion with the figure behind the letters.

In the light of this literary evidence the usual approach employed by historical-critical research is to subject the Pauline corpus to a sifting process by which to isolate those elements which can be attributed to the historical Paul with reasonable certainty. Liberal and conservative New Testament scholars share this same approach and differ only in the amount which is confirmed to be historically reliable. The setting of a letter within the canonical corpus is usually dismissed as exegetically insignificant because it does not reflect author intentionality.

This introduction has attempted to move in a very different direction, cutting against both the left and the right of the theological spectrum in an effort to take seriously the effect of the canonical shaping on Paul's letters. It has sought to sketch the profile of the 'canonical Paul', while at the same time being aware of different degrees of tension between the historical figure and the apostle of the Christian faith. Although no one would suggest that all the difficulties associated with the position have been resolved, in my judgment, the canonical approach marks a fresh and promising new route for both critical and theological reflection on this important subject.

PART FIVE

THE CATHOLIC EPISTLES

25

JAMES

Commentaries

W. M. L. de Wette, ³1863
J. C. K. von Hofmann, 1871
E. H. Plumptre, CB, 1876
J. C. Huther, MeyerK, ET 1882
F. Spitta, 1896
W. Beyschlag, Meyerk, ⁶1897
H. von Soden, HCNT, ³1899
A. Plummer, ExpB, ³1901
R. J. Knowling, WC, 1904
F. J. A. Hort, 1909
J. B. Mayor, ³1910
J. H. Ropes, ICC, 1916
G. Hollmann, W. Bousset, *SNT*, ³1917
F. Hauck, KNT, 1926
J. Chaine, ÉB, ²1927
J. Moffatt, MNTC, 1928
J. Marty, 1935
H. Windisch, H. Preisker, HNT, ³1951

A. Schlatter, ²1956
E. C. Blackman, TB, 1957
B. S. Easton, IB, 1957
F. Hauck, NTD, ⁸1957
B. Reicke, AB, 1964
R. R. Williams, CNEB, 1965
C. L. Mitton, NICNT, 1966
J. Schneider, NTD, ¹⁰1967
E. M. Sidebottom, NCeB, 1967
J. Michl, RNT, 1968
J. Cantinat, SB, 1973
W. Schrage, NTD, ¹¹1973
J. B. Adamson, NICNT, 1976
M. Dibelius, H. Greeven, Herm, ET, 1976
S. Laws, B/HNTC, 1980
F. Mussner, HTKNT, ⁴1981
R. A. Martin, Augs, 1982
P. Davids, NICNT, 1982

Bibliography

K. **Aland**, 'Der Herrnbruder Jakobus und der Jakobusbrief', *TLZ* 69, 1944, 97–104; 'Jakobusbrief', *RGG³*, III, 526–8; P. **Althaus**, '"Bekenne einer dem andern seine Sünden". Zur Geschichte von Jak 5,16 seit Augustinus', *Festgabe für T. Zahn*, Leipzig 1928, 165–94; C. -B. **Amphoux**, 'Une relecture du chapitre I de l'épître de Jacques', *Bibl* 59, 1978, 554–61; E. **Baasland**, 'Der Jakobusbrief als neutestamentliche Weisheitschrift', *StTh* 36, 1982, 119–39; A. E. **Barnett**, 'James, letter of', *IDB*, II, 794–9; K. **Beyschlag**, 'Das Jakobusmartyrium und seine Verwandten in der frühchristlichen

Literatur', *ZNW* 56, 1965, 149–78; W. **Bieder**, 'Christliche Existenz nach dem Zeugnis des Jakobus', *TZ* 5, 1949, 93–113; J. **Bonsirven**, 'Jacques (épître de saint)', *DBSupp* IV, 1949, 783–95; J. A. **Brooks**, 'The Place of James in the New Testament Canon', *SWJT* 12, 1969, 41–55; G. **Braumann**, 'Der theologische Hintergrund des Jakobusbriefes', *TZ* 18, 1962, 401–10; C. **Burchard**, 'Zu Jakobus 2,14–26', *ZNW* 71, 1980, 27–45; 'Gemeinde in der strohernen Epistel. Mutmassungen über Jakobus', *Kirche. FS G. Bornkamm*, ed. D. Lührmann and G. Strecker, Tübingen 1980, 315–328; R. **Bultmann**, *Der Stil der paulinischen Predigt und die kynisch-stoische Diatribe*, FRLANT 13, 1910.

A. T. **Cadoux**, *The Thought of St James*, London 1944; K. L. **Carroll**, 'The Place of James in the Early Church', *BJRL* 44, 1961/2, 49–67; C. E. B. **Cranfield**, 'The Message of James', *SJT* 18, 1965, 182–93; K. -G. **Eckart**, 'Zur Terminologie des Jakobusbriefes', *TLZ* 89, 1964, 521–6; G. **Eichholz**, *Jakobus und Paulus. Ein Beitrag zum Problem des Kanons*, ThExH NF 39, Munich 1953; *Glaube und Werk bei Paulus und Jakobus*, ThExH NF 88, Munich 1961; P. **Feine**, *Der Jakobusbrief nach Lehranschauungen und Entstehungsverhältnissen*, Eisenach 1893; F. O. **Francis**, 'The Form and Function of the Opening and closing Paragraphs of James and I John', *ZNW* 61, 1970, 110–26; E. **Grafe**, *Die Stellung und Bedeutung des Jakobusbriefes in der Entwicklung des Urchristentums*, Tübingen and Leipzig 1904; H. **Greeven**, 'Jede Gabe ist gut, Jak 1,17', *TZ* 14, 1958, 1–13; R. **Hoppe**, *Der theologische Hintergrund der Jakobusbriefe*, FzB 28, Würzburg 1977; J. **Jeremias**, 'Paul and James', *ExpT* 66, 1954/5, 368–71; L. T. **Johnson**, 'The Use of Leviticus 19 in the Letter of James', *JBL* 101, 1982, 391–401; G. **Kawerau**, 'Die Schicksale des Jakobusbriefes im 16. Jahrhundert', *Zeitschrift für kirchliche Wissenschaft und kirchliches Leben* 10, 1889, 359–70; L. E. **Keck**, 'The Poor among the Saints in the New Testament', *ZNW* 56, 1965, 100–29; 'The Poor among the Saints in Jewish Christianity and Qumran', *ZNW* 57, 1966, 54–78; J. A. **Kirk**, 'The Meaning of Wisdom in James: examination of a hypothesis', *NTS* 16, 1969/70, 24–38; G. **Kittel**, 'Die Stellung des Jakobus zu Judentum und Heidenchristentum', *ZNW* 30, 1931, 145–56; 'Der geschichtliche Ort des Jakobusbriefes', *ZNW* 41, 1942, 71–105; 'Der Jakobusbrief und die Apostolischen Väter', *ZNW* 43, 1950/51, 54–112; W. L. **Knox**, 'The Epistle of St James', *JTS* 46, 1945, 10–17; H. **Köster**, *Synoptische Überlieferung bei den Apostolischen Vätern*, TU 65, 1957.

M. **Lackmann**, *Sole Fide. Eine exegetische Studie über Jakobus 2*, Gütersloh 1949; E. **Lohse**, 'Glaube und Werke— zur Theologie des Jakobusbriefes', *ZNW* 48, 1957, 1–22; reprinted *Die Einheit des Neuen Testament*, Göttingen 1973, 285–306; U. **Luck**, 'Weisheit und Leiden. Zum Problem Paulus und Jakobus', *TLZ* 92, 1967, 253–8; 'Der Jakobusbrief und die Theologie des Paulus', *Theologie und Glaube* 61, 1971, 161–79; M. **Meinertz**, *Der Jakobusbrief und sein Verfasser in Schrift und Überlieferung*, BSt X.1–3, Freiburg 1905; 'Luthers Kritik am Jakobusbrief nach dem Urteil seiner Anhänger', *BZ* 3, 1905, 273–86; A. **Meyer**, *Das Rätsel des Jacobusbriefes*, BZNW 10, 1930; R.

Obermüller, 'Hermeneutische Themen im Jakobusbrief', *Bibl* 53, 1972, 234–44; L. G. **Perdue**, 'Paraenesis and the Epistle of James', *ZNW* 72, 1981, 241–56; H. **Preisker**, 'Der Eigenwert des Jakobusbriefes in der Geschichte des Urchristentums', *ThBl* 13, 1934, 229–36; G. H. **Rendall**, *The Epistle of St James and Judaic Christianity*, Cambridge 1927.
H. **Schammberger**, *Die Einheitlichkeit des Jacobusbriefe im antignstischen Kampf*, Gotha 1936; G. **Schille**, 'Wider die Gespaltenheit des Glaubens—Beobachtungen am Jakobusbrief', *Theol. Versuche* 9, 1977, 71–89; A. **Schlatter**, *Die Theologie der Apostel*, Stuttgart ²1922, 87–119; W. **Schmithals**, *Paul and James*, ET, SBT 46, 1965; O. F. G. **Seitz**, 'James and the Law', *StEv* II, TU 87, 1964, 472–86; G. S. **Sloyan**, 'The Letter of James', *Hebrews—James—1 and 2 Peter—Jude—Revelation*, ed. G. Krodel (Proclamation Commentaries), Philadelphia 1977, 28–49; M. H. **Shepherd**, 'The Epistle of James and the Gospel of Matthew', *JBL* 75, 1956, 40–51; J. B. **Souček**, 'Zu den Problemen des Jakobusbriefes', *EvTh* 18, 1958, 460–68; P. **Stuhlmacher**, *Gerechtigkeit Gottes bei Paulus*, FRLANT 87, 1965, 191–4; D. O. **Via**, 'The Right Strawy Epistle Reconsidered: A Study in Biblical Ethics and Hermeneutic', *JR* 49, 1969, 253–67; R. **Walker**, 'Allein aus Werken. Zur Auslegung von Jakobus 2, 14–26', *ZTK* 61, 1964, 155–92; J. **Wanke**, 'Die urchristlichen Lehrer nach dem Zeugnis des Jakobusbriefes', *Die Kirche des Anfangs, FS H. Schürmann*, ed. R. Schnackenburg, Freiburg 1978, 489–511; R. B. **Ward**, 'The Works of Abraham: James 2, 14–26', *HTR* 61, 1968, 283–90; 'Partiality in the Assembly: James 2, 2–4', ibid. 62, 1969, 87–97; B. **Weiss**, 'Der Jakobusbrief und die neuere Kritik', *NKZ* 15, 1904, 391–439; K. **Weiss**, 'Motiv und Ziel der Frömmigkeit des Jakobusbriefes', *Theol. Versuche* 7, 1976, 107–14; W. H. **Wuellner**, 'Der Jakobusbrief im Licht der Rhetorik und Textpragmatik', *Linguistica Biblica* 43, 1978, 5–66; F. W. **Young**, 'The Relation of I Clement to the Epistle of James', *JBL* 67, 1948, 339–45.

The letter of James is one of the few books within the New Testament whose role within the canon has been long recognized to be of crucial importance. Luther's sharp formulation of the problem set the lines for the modern debate and his penetrating criticism of James from the perspective of Pauline theology continues to influence the discussion even today (cf. Kawerau, Meinerts, Eichholz, *Jakobus und Paulus*, 10ff.; Mussner, 42ff.). Nevertheless, the problem is older than Luther, and reflects a classic issue which stems from the phenomenon of the church's having a canon of authoritative writings.

Some thirty years ago Eichholz (*Jakobus*, 5ff.,27) raised many of the basic theological questions at stake. What are the limits of diversity within the New Testament canon? Is it legitimate for one canonical book completely to fall under the shadow of another? How does the integrity of a book's own witness relate to the canonical function which it acquires through the formation of the collection? In spite of the difficulty of these questions, most scholars would agree with A. Schlatter's observation: 'It does not make any sense to compare James with Paul before at least James has been understood' (*Glauben im NT*, ⁴1927, 419).

I. The Modern Critical Debate

In the modern critical analysis of the letter of James, two sharply conflicting scholarly assessments of the book have emerged. One group of scholars (Zahn, *Intr.*, Mayor, Kittel) dates the letter early, from AD 40–60, at times even claiming it to be the earliest writing of the New Testament. Another group of scholars, who perhaps now form the majority opinion (Dibelius, Eichholz, Kümmel, *Intr.*, Lohse), dates it much later, from the last quarter of the first century or the early second. Only a small third group has sought a compromise position (e.g. Davids).

A closer examination of the two positions indicates that far more than the problem of dating is involved, but rather two very different assessments of the letter emerge. Those holding the first position argue that the letter was written by James, the brother of Jesus who was leader of the Jerusalem church and representative of Jewish Christianity. The praescript is, therefore, to be taken literally in directing the letter to the dispersed Jewish Christians who were scattered after the death of Stephen (Acts 8.1). The early dating is further supported by the lack of reference to the Pauline letters, the strong eschatological notes, and the close continuity with the pre-literary synoptic tradition of the teaching of Jesus and the Jewish wisdom traditions.

Conversely, those defending the second position argue that the letter reflects a later Hellenistic period both in its use of polished Greek and of Hellenistic literary conventions, and its familiarity with the Old Testament in its Greek rather than Hebrew form. Its largely paraenetic style reflects a history of transmission of Christian teaching which finds its closest parallels in I Peter and in the Didache, rather than in direct, personal remembrances. Further evidence that the author was pseudonymous is found in the lack of harmony between the content of the letter and the portrait of James in the book of Acts and in Galatians. Finally, the long delay in the book's being accepted into the canon, particularly by the Western church, is thought hard to reconcile with its being written by a brother of Jesus.

Occasionally a compromise position has been attempted which could accommodate the strengths of each position. Recently, Peter Davids (22) has accepted in general the arguments of Kittel for an early date between AD 40 and the Jerusalem council, but then speaks of a final redaction between 55 and 65 or possibly between 75 and 80 which edited the book in an idiom more suitable to its new environment. Because of the lack of hard evidence, the compromise position has not yet evoked much support.

In sum, there has been no consensus reached regarding the historical problem which, as a result, has continued to call forth much disagreement on the book's function.

II. The Canonical Shape of James

Although we readily grant the difficulty of resolving the historical problems, nevertheless, there are some important observations which one can make regarding the canonical function of the letter which have not as yet been adequately explored, and which may also offer indirect access to some of the historical issues surrounding the book's composition.

The canonical shape of the letter of James appears to embrace features from both critical positions which offers an indication on how it envisioned the book to function. On the one hand, the letter is attributed to James. There can be little doubt that the canonical editors identified this James with the brother of Jesus and the leader of the Jerusalem church. James, more than any other person in the early church, was the representative figure of Jewish Christianity. The immediate designation of the addressee as 'the twelve tribes in the Dispersion' would further confirm their judgment that James' representative role respecting Jewish Christianity was intended. That this designation was shortly understood metaphorically by the church to include all believers does not gainsay the letter's primary canonical addressee. Indeed, the importance of the addressee may have been one reason for the editors' retention of the literary conventions of an epistle. The function of ascribing authorship to James was to assure a continuity between Jewish Christians and the teachings of Jesus which antedated the missionary activity of Paul. Moreover, there is a broad scholarly consensus that the letter of James does reflect a strong continuity with the teachings of Jesus in a pre-Pauline form closely akin to the paraenesis of the synoptic source Q (Mussner, 47–52; Davids, 47–51; Hoppe, 119–22).

On the other hand, the letter of James functions canonically in the context of the post-Pauline debate. In its present position within the canon of the New Testament it is quite impossible to read James without reference to the Pauline controversy. However, the relationship lies deeper than this, and did not simply arise from its later position within the larger corpus of sacred writings. Rather, the historical evidence is clear that the idea of a polarity between faith and works derives from Paul and was not a common inheritance from Judaism (*contra* Schlatter). Of course, the exact nature of the relationship between James and Paul requires a close examination of the letter. However, the point being made is that both from a canonical and a modern historical perspective James functions within a post-Pauline context. The letter cannot be adequately interpreted as an early witness which is totally unaffected by the Pauline idiom.

Of course it remains an important and difficult problem to understand the literary and historical processes lying behind this peculiar canonical construal of the material. However, our continuing concern is that the canonical function of the letter which emerges from its particular theological formation be not held captive to the modern critic's ability to trace all the steps which lie behind its present shape, or to resolve all the historical problems involved. Our immediate interest is to interpret in more detail the canonical function of the letter of James in a way commensurate with its peculiar shape. Once this has been accomplished, we shall return to a further consideration of the historical questions of authorship and dating.

III. The Teachings of Jesus

The epistle of James is, first of all, noteworthy because of the widespread use of the teachings of Jesus. Commentators have set out the extent and nature of the frequent parallels in a comprehensive fashion (cf. especially Kittel). There seems also to be much agreement that James is not dependent on the sayings of Jesus in any of the literary forms of the written Gospels, but rather reflects the pre-literary stage of the material. Moreover, the parallels are largely those of the Q material, clustered heavily in the Sermon on the Mount (cf. Mayor, lxxxv–lxxxviii; Mussner, 48–50; Davids 47f.). The form of the teachings of Jesus differs strikingly from that of the written Gospels since James does not set the sayings in the context of the life of Jesus.

Again, the sayings of Jesus are not presented within the epistle by means of citation formulae, but function as the prism through which the Old Testament is now understood. In a manner paralleled to Matthew's Gospel, James understands the entire Old Testament from a Christian perspective with Christ being its true interpreter. In 1.25 Old Testament law is the 'law of liberty', having nothing to do with ceremonial stipulations, and in its observance one responds obediently to the will of God. 2.8 speaks of the 'sovereign law' as interpreted by Jesus. His will from creation was the gift of salvation and God is its source. His implanted word (1.21) ushers in blessing to those who are doers of his will and not just hearers (1.25). The believer's confidence rests on God alone, not in the deception of the world, and he endures persecutions patiently awaiting the 'coming of the Lord' (5.7). Wisdom is a gift of God which is closely akin to the work of the spirit in producing works of righteousness.

The letter of James continues to present the Old Testament, when correctly understood, as the norm for Christian living. The author feels no need to defend the law, but simply assumes its validity. James develops no explicit christology, and yet it is a basic misunderstanding to suggest that the letter is a Jewish document with minor Christian interpolations (Spitta). A Christian orientation pervades the entire letter (1.18; 2.7,26), yet in such a way that Christ is not the object of faith. Rather, he continues faithfully to point the believer to God through the scriptures of the Old Testament. However, even this formulation is not completely correct. In 2.1 the writer uses the objective genitive to speak of a faith in Jesus Christ against which faithful human behaviour is measured. Partiality is an attribute which is incompatible with the glory of Christ.

The canonical significance of James' use of the teachings of Jesus can be seen in contrasting it with other New Testament writings. In one sense, James marks the opposite pole from Paul whose christology focuses almost entirely on the effect of Christ's death and resurrection in accomplishing salvation for the world. Moreover, even when compared to Matthew's interpretation of Jesus' teachings, the letter of James functions canonically in a unique way because of its post-Pauline context. The Gospel of Matthew offers a construal of Jesus' teachings as the true interpreter of the Old Testament law. Canonically Matthew functions as a witness to Jesus' earthly life leading up to his death and resurrection. However, James extends Matthew's understanding into the post-Pauline period. His letter is not just a check against a misunderstanding of Paul, but a positive witness for hearing the synoptic sayings in post-Pauline Christianity. The letter bears witness that, correctly interpreted, the Old Testament continues to function as a norm for Christian living even after the resurrection. Moreover, the witness is given in a consciously polemical manner and directed against those who would call it into question, allegedly from the perspective of Christian faith.

IV. Faith and Works

The epistle of James offers also an important canonical witness in relation to the problem of faith and works. Indeed, the alleged tension between the conflicting theologies of James and Paul on this subject has tended to dominate the entire discussion of the epistle since the Reformation. There are three different aspects to the problem which should be considered separately, even though finally they belong together. First, what is Paul's approach to the problem? Secondly, how does James address the issue? Finally, how are the two approaches related within the context of the New Testament canon? In respect to the final issue the problem does not turn merely on an original intentionality of each author who may or may not have been aware of the other witness, but on their function within a canonical collection for the Christian who accepts both writings as authoritative scripture.

Paul's treatment of the subject centres in Romans and Galatians, and is set within the context of his mission as an apostle of Jesus Christ to the Gentiles. For Paul, faith ($\pi i \sigma \tau i \varsigma$) is the basic term which expresses the only true human response to the message of the gospel, namely, that God has redeemed the world through the death and resurrection of his Son. Entirely on account of what Christ has done, man is declared justified through faith in him. He is made to share in the new creation which has already entered eschatologically into the world and which is embraced in faith. Life in Christ is lived 'through faith for faith' (Rom.1.17); it is characterized by the fruits of the Spirit which are the concrete signs of the new age. Paul can speak unhesitantly of the 'work of faith' (I Thess.1.3), but always in the context of an existence utterly dependent on the all-encompassing grace of God who calls forth the new life (Rom.14.7–8). The apostle does battle with the Judaizers who threatened the sufficiency of Christ's redemption by demanding obedience to the Jewish law as a condition for justification before God. Paul appeals to the Old Testament as evidence that righteousness has been manifest 'apart from works of the law' (χωρὶς ἔργων νόμου, Rom.3.28), and that Abraham's faith was reckoned to him as righteousness (4.22). It is thus constitutive of Paul's theology that his paraenesis is christologically grounded, a response called forth in the name of Jesus (I Cor.1.10; I Thess.4.1; Rom.15.30).

We next turn to the subject of faith and works in the letter of James and immediately enter a different theological world. The language is remarkably different, and even when some of the same expressions occur, the meaning is usually distinct. The style of the letter—paraenetic, ironic, disputational—sets a different context within an overarching wisdom framework which is reminiscent of the Old Testament. James stands in closest continuity with the faith of Israel, the true witness to which he finds in the teaching of Jesus. He does not carefully define his terms, but assumes that their content is already known.

In no sense does James derive salvation from a syncretism of human and divine co-operation. God is the source of every benefit. The believer's calling is to respond to the 'implanted word, which is able to save your souls' (1.21). Indeed, man's need of salvation is a major theme of the epistle (1.21; 2.14; 4.12). He must be justified before the coming day of the Lord. Wisdom is a heavenly gift, sent from above, and like the Spirit brings forth good fruit (3.13–18), instructing in the hidden, eschatological purpose of God.

For James the basic term which characterizes the obedient life is 'works' (ἔργα, cf. 2.14–16). The only true response to God is the doing of his word, not its hearing alone. A recurrent issue of the entire epistle is the guarding of the religious life against the trials and temptations of the world. True faith demonstrates itself in concrete deeds which support the poor against the rich (2.14–17), and the meek against the proud (2.1–7). It maintains itself in works of love and awaits God's justification in the coming judgment (2.14; 4.12).

James views faith completely from an Old Testament perspective. Faith (πίστις) is a commitment to God, a trust which seeks to fulfil the will of God through obedience to his commandments, a submission of one's whole life to God (5.13–18). The obedient response of Abraham combines completely his faith and his works. James testifies to the inseparability of faith and works, and opposes any theology which plays faith against works.

It is generally recognized that James' formulation of the relation of faith and works has been influenced by the Pauline debate, and is not simply a traditional idiom which he has inherited from Judaism. Yet the exact relation between the two writers remains enigmatic and is much debated. It remains a puzzlement to explain why James appears so distant from Paul? In spite of the polemical setting of his letter, the actual opponent seems to correspond only vaguely to Paul. The major theological dynamic of Paul's theology in which faith encompasses works of righteousness within the new eschatological existence which was accomplished in Christ, has been completely by-passed. Thus, an apparently minor shift in vocabulary from Paul's 'apart from works of the law' (χωρὶς ἔργων νόμου) to 'apart from works' in James (χωρὶς ἔργων) is actually of major significance, and reveals that an entirely different understanding of faith and works is operative. Paul is defending the sufficiency of faith in Christ's salvation against the claims of the law, whereas James is calling for a true faith which is demonstrated by concomitant deeds of charity. James' polemical adversary emerges as a caricature of Pauline theology (2.18).

From an historical perspective it is unclear how James' letter actually relates to Paul. That there is a relationship seems obvious, but to suggest that James is intentionally correcting a misunderstanding of Paul is to go beyond the evidence. Nor is there enough historical information from the early church to paint an exact picture of how Christian communities which were grounded in Paul's theology related to Jewish-Christian congregations who would have supported a form of the faith akin to that of James.

However, it is my strong contention that the issue of relating the two differing testimonies regarding faith and works cannot be left as an historical problem. The issue is above all a theological one, which the church correctly sensed, and its resolution involves the basic problem of the canon. Even if the historical relationship cannot be fully settled, the theological problem remains a lively one for the Christian church which uses both letters as an integral part of sacred scripture.

In his commentary on James, F. Mussner has been helpful in summarizing some of the classic attempts to harmonize Paul and James (148–50). For example, Augustine argued that Paul was speaking of the role of works which preceded faith, whereas James of works which followed faith. More recently, the tendency has been to harmonize by dissimilation, that is to say, to suggest the two letters reflect such different historical situations that they do not speak to the same theological problem.

One of the most serious theological attempts in the modern period to address the relation between James and Paul has been made in the several essays of G. Eichholz. After a careful exegetical study of both witnesses, he calls for a different understanding of the function of canon in order to confront the basic theological issues at stake (*Glaube und Werk*, 44f.). At the outset he argues vigorously that the two witnesses are neither to be harmonized nor historicized. Nor can one resolve the problem by falling back to the hermeneutics of 'a canon within the canon', which usually functions by using Pauline categories to correct James. A major point of Eichholz is that the relationship between the two witnesses is not that of two static sets of ideas. Rather, it is between two very different approaches to the subject, both of which entail a complete and discrete dynamic, which have arisen out of separate historical situations. The differences between James and Paul lie far deeper than different literary conventions or varying semantic ranges of words, rather between different theological streams of Christian tradition. Eichholz is eloquent in insisting that both bear witness to the one faith in Jesus Christ, and that the unity of scripture cannot be denied in spite of its diversity by an appeal to some theological principle, or to a reductionist kernel. His own positive solution is less clear. He emphasizes the need to retain a freedom to hear and to be flexible in reckoning with the changing fronts to which the biblical authors have sought to respond.

At this juncture, I would suggest that one must now move beyond Eichholz and draw out the full implications of biblical interpretation in the context of the whole New Testament canon. Eichholz is basically right in his negative polemics, but more must be said toward a positive approach which is commensurate with canon. Specifically, how is the reading of two different sets of writings, which reflect different original settings, affected by their role in a canon? First, both witnesses function normatively within sacred scripture and thus neither can be denied an individual integrity. Secondly, both are read as scripture, that is to say, in their canonically shaped form which is oriented towards its kerygmatic role within the community of faith. The scriptural norm of the church is the canonically shaped witness and not an original historical setting. The original context is important in so far as the canonical witness has often received aspects of its peculiar shape from its historical setting. However, invariably the canonical process has already re-ordered the original situation in such a way as to serve a kerygmatic function. Thirdly, the situation of the reader of the scriptures who seeks to discern their authority for a present community of faith shares neither the original historical context of Paul nor James.

Scripture addresses the theological realities of the faith in very different ways. On the one hand, Paul does battle with Judaizers who would derive human salvation from a co-operation between divine grace and human good works. Paul rejects this formulation as a threat to God's freedom and insists on seeing salvation totally as an act of divine intervention to which faith is a response to what God alone has achieved. On the other hand, James addresses a situation in which faith and good works have split apart. He defends the position that an obedient Christian response to God must entail both faith and a form of righteous behaviour commensurate with God's will.

It seems clear that Paul and James are addressing different questions from very different perspectives. Paul is asking about the relation between the divine and the human in acquiring salvation. James is asking about the relation between the profession of faith and action consonant with it. Together they are addressing different theological dimensions of the divine nature and the Christian life. The traditional attempt at harmony, say, by Augustine locates Paul's witness to the role of works in the period before conversion, and James' witness to the period after conversion. However, the chronological ordering of the two witnesses restricts the biblical witness too greatly by fitting them into a fixed temporal sequence. The theological issues at stake and the threats of misunderstanding for the modern Christian are greatly impaired by using only this one dogmatic framework.

Nevertheless, the traditional move is a serious attempt to understand the canonical function of these disparate testimonies for the continuing community of faith. It follows a correct theological instinct in interpreting both witnesses as constituting the one revelation of God, which Christian theology tries to comprehend. It thus rightly opposes the widespread modern hermeneutical option of seeking to discover analogous historical situations between the biblical authors and situations in the life of the modern church by which to actualize the historical particularity of the two separate witnesses. Such a move neglects completely the decisive role of the canon as offering an evaluative construal of the diversity within its collection.

It remains the continuing task of Christian theology, informed by the witness of the whole canon, to seek to discern God's will for the church and the world within changing historical contexts. At times in the life of the church the message of Paul will sound the primary note of the gospel, bearing witness to salvation by faith alone. At other times, the word of James will faithfully testify that faith and works are indissolubly joined in a faithful response to God. The role of the Christian canon is to assure that both witnesses are heard as part of the one divine revelation of truth, and that the Word of God is not restricted in its freedom to address the continuing needs of the church in the world.

V. Judaism and Christianity

There is one final subject which is greatly affected by the peculiar shape of the Christian tradition in the letter of James. The issue turns on the relation of Judaism to the Christian faith (cf. especially Schlatter, *Theologie der Apostel*, 101ff.). James offers an important canonical construal of the continuity and discontinuity which constitutes Judaism and Christianity. His understanding emerges in contrast to other formulations within the New Testament which describe the relationship in terms of an old and a new covenant, of promise and fulfilment, and of shadow to substance. James assumes an unbroken line of continuity between Israel and the obedient Christian life. His division does not fall between Judaism and Christianity, but rather between true and false religion. True faith is demonstrated by obedience to the one will of God, by a faith commensurate with Father Abraham, by following faithfully the law of liberty, and waiting patiently for the coming reign of God in righteousness.

One of the theological implications from the letter of James is that within the Christian canon there is a witness to a form of life which is formulated almost entirely in Old Testament terminology without an explicit christology. Yet its witness is no less Christian in substance. The original addressees of the letter of James appear to be Jewish Christians and the Old Testament is used to instruct them in an obedient Christian life. However, very shortly the letter of James was used to address Gentile Christians who saw themselves metaphorically as belonging to the Diaspora (1.1). In this context, which is our own, the letter of James plays a new and equally important role of providing a check against a misunderstanding both of Paul and of James respecting Judaism. Pope Pius XII had heard well this note from the epistle when he wrote: 'We Christians are also Jews' (cited by Mussner on the title page).

VI. Conclusion

Before concluding the study of James it is necessary to return again to the historical-critical questions which we raised at the beginning of the essay, and to explore the issue of authorship and dating in relation to the letter's canonical function.

It remains very difficult to attribute all the diverse elements within the letter simply to one author, whether to the historical James, or to a pseudonymous writer of the late first century. Rather, the relation between text and author appears to be a complex one. There are elements within the letter which reflect the strongest historical continuity with early Jewish Christianity. Yet it is equally true that the letter contains many other features which have extended the original witness into the post-Pauline era, apparently far beyond the original setting. In this regard, the complexity of the letter's authorship is fully in line with many of the other catholic epistles which also are only indirectly related to their traditional source. The historical stages through which the epistle of James developed are unknown, and the several reconstructions remain speculative. The danger of first deciding on a hypothesis regarding authorship and date of composition lies in twisting the subsequent reading of the canonical text in order to support the theory. Yet it is hard to deny that important exegetical insights have emerged both from the early model of Kittel and the late model of Dibelius.

For my part, it would seem wise to hold open the critical options because of their complexity and to strive to discern the canonical function of the letter which is only indirectly, in a dialectical fashion, related to the critical debates. In fact, it would appear that the canonical shaping process borrowed elements from both critical models by which to make its uniquely theological testimony to the gospel.

26

I PETER

Commentaries

J. C. Huther, MeyerK, ET 1881	J. Moffatt, MNTC, [8]1963
J. T. Beck, 1895	B. Reicke, AB, 1964
E. Kühl, MeyerK, [6]1897	C. Spicq, SB, 1966
J. F. A. Hort, 1898	A. R. C. Leaney, CNEB, 1967
H. von Soden, HCNT, [3]1899	J. Schneider, NTD, [10]1967
E. Bigg, ICC, [2]1902	J. Michl, RNT, [3]1968
E. Knopf, MeyerK, [7]1912	J. N. D. Kelly, B/HNTC, 1969
H. Gunkel, SNT, [3]1917	F. W. Beare, [3]1970
G. Wohlenberg, KNT, [3]1923	E. Best, NCeB, 1971
J. W. C. Wand, WC, 1934	E. Schweizer, ZBK, [3]1972
E. G. Selwyn, [2]1947	L. Goppelt, MeyerK, [8]1977
H. Windisch, H. Preisker, HNT, [3]1951	N. Brox, EKK, 1979
F. Hauck, NTD, [8]1957	K. H. Schelkle, HTKNT, [5]1980
C. E. B. Cranfield, TB, 1960	W. Schrage, NTD, [12]1980
A. F. Walls, A. M. Stibbs, Tyn, [2]1962	J. H. Elliott, Augs, 1982

Bibliography

D. **Balch**, *Let Wives Be Submissive: The Domestic Code in I Peter*, SBLMS 26, Missoula 1981; E. **Best**, 'I Peter and the Gospel Tradition', *NTS* 16, 1969/70, 95–113; 'I Peter II, 4–10 – a Reconsideration', *NovT* 11, 1969, 270–93; W. **Bieder**, *Die Vorstellung von der Höllenfahrt Jesu Christi*, AbTANT 19, 1949; *Grund und Kraft der Mission nach dem 1. Petrusbrief*, ThStud 29, 1950; M.-É. **Boismard**, 'La typologie baptismale dans la première épître de S. Pierre', *Vie Spirituelle* 94, 1956, 339–52; 'Une liturgie baptismale dans le Prima Petri', *RB* 63, 1956, 182–208; 64, 1957, 161–83; *Quatre hymnes baptismales dans la première épître de Pierre*, Paris 1961; 'Pierre (Première épître de)', *DBSuppl.* VII, 1966, 1415–55; W. **Bornemann**, 'Der 1. Petrusbrief, eine Taufrede an Silvanus', *ZNW* 19, 1919/20, 143–65; W. **Bousset**, 'Zur

Hadesfahrt Christi', *ZNW* 19, 1919/20, 50–66; W. **Brandt**, 'Wandel als Zeugnis nach dem 1. Petrusbrief', *Verbum Dei manet in aeternum, FS O. Schmitz,* ed. W. Foerster, Witten 1953, 10–25; H. **Braun**, *Das Leiden Christi,* Munich 1940; O. S. **Brooks**, 'I Peter 3,21 – The Clue to the Literary Structure of the Epistle', *NovT* 16, 1974, 290–305; J. P. **Brown**, 'Synoptic Parallels in the Epistles and Form-History', *NTS* 10, 1963/4, 27–48; R. E. **Brown**, K. P. **Donfried**, J. **Reumann**, ed., *Peter in the New Testament,* Minneapolis 1973; N. **Brox**, 'Zur pseudepigraphischen Rahmung des ersten Petrusbriefes', *BZ,* NF 19,1975, 78–96; 'Situation und Sprache der Minderheit im ersten Petrusbrief', *Kairos* NF 19, 1977, 1–13; 'Tendenz und Pseudepigraphie im Ersten Petrusbrief', *Kairos* NF 20, 1978, 110–20; 'Der erste Petrusbrief in der literarischen Tradition des Urchristentums', *Kairos* NF 20, 1978, 182–92; R. **Bultmann**, 'Bekenntnis- und Liedfragmente im ersten Petrusbrief', *Coniectanea Neotestamentica XI in honorem A. Fridrichsen,* ed. H. Riesenfeld, Lund 1947, 1–14; reprinted *Exegetica,* Tübingen 1967, 285–97.

P. **Carrington**, *The Primitive Christian Catechism,* Cambridge 1940; M. -A. **Chevallier**, 'I Pierre 1/1 à 2/10. Structure littéraire et conséquences exégétiques', *RHPhR* 51, 1971, 129–42; 'Condition et vocation des chrétiens en diaspora. Remarques exégétiques sur la 1ʳᵉ Épître de Pierre', *RSR* 48, 1974, 387–98; H. J. B. **Combrink**, 'The Structure of I Peter', *Neotestamentica* 9, 1975, Stellenbosch, 34–63; J. **Coutts**, 'Ephesians I.3–14 and I Peter I.3–12', *NTS* 3, 1956/7, 115–27; C. E. B. **Cranfield**, 'The Interpretation of I Peter III.19 and IV.6', *ExpT* 69, 1957/58, 369–72; F. L. **Cross**, *I Peter: A Paschal Liturgy,* London 1954; O. **Cullmann**, *Peter: Disciple–Apostle–Martyr,* ET London and Philadelphia 1953; W. J. **Dalton**, *Christ's Proclamation to the Spirits. A Study of 1 Peter 3:18–4:6',* AnBib 23, 1965; 'Interpretation and Tradition: An Example from I Peter', *Greg* 89, 1967, 17–37; F. W. **Danker**, 'I Peter 1, 24–2,17 – A Consolatory Pericope', *ZNW* 58, 1967, 93–102; D. **Daube**, 'Participle and Imperative in I Peter', in E. G. Selwyn, *The First Epistle of Peter,* London²1947, 467–88; G. **Delling**, 'Der Bezug der christlichen Existenz auf das Heilshandeln Gottes nach den ersten Petrusbrief', *Neues Testament und christliche Existenz, FS H. Braun,* ed. H. D. Betz et al., Tübingen 1973, 95–113; E. **Dinkler**, 'Die Petrus-Rom-Frage I', *ThR* NF 25, 1959, 189–230.

J. H. **Elliott**, *The Elect and the Holy,* NovTSuppl 12, Leiden 1966; 'The Rehabilitation of an Exegetical Step-child: 1 Peter in Recent Research', *JBL* 95, 1976, 243–54; *A Home for the Homeless. A Sociological Exegesis of 1 Peter, Its Situation and Strategy,* Philadelphia 1981; E. **Fascher**, 'Petrusbriefe', *RGG,³* V, 1961, 257–60; F. V. **Filson**, 'Partakers with Christ. Suffering in First Peter', *Interp* 9, 1955, 400–12; V. P. **Furnish**, 'Elect Sojourners in Christ: An Approach to the Theology of 1 Peter', *Perkins Journal* 28, 1975, 1–11; H. **Goldstein**, *Paulinische Gemeinde im Ersten Petrusbrief,* SBS 80, 1975; L. **Goppelt**, 'Prinzipien neutestamentlicher Sozialtethik nach dem 1. Petrusbrief', *Neues Testament und Geschichte, FS O. Cullmann,* ed. H. Baltensweiler and B. Reicke, Zürich and Tübingen 1972, 285–96; R. H. **Gundry**,

' "Verba Christi" in I Peter: Their Implications Concerning the Authorship of I Peter and the Authenticity of the Gospel Tradition', *NTS* 13, 1966/67, 336–50; 'Further Verba on Verba Christi in First Peter', *Bibl* 55, 1974, 211–32; A. **von Harnack**, *Die Chronologie der altchristlichen Literatur bis Eusebius*, I, Leipzig 1897, 451–65; D. **Hill**, 'On Suffering and Baptism in 1 Peter', *NovT* 18, 1976, 181–89; N. **Hillyer**, '"Rock-Stone" Imagery in 1 Peter', *TynB* 22, 1971, 58–81; C. -H. **Hunzinger**, 'Babylon als Deckname für Rom und die Datierung des 1. Petrusbriefes', *Gottes Wort und Gottes Land, FS H. -W. Hertzberg*, ed. H. Graf Reventlow, Göttingen 1965, 67–77.

S. E. **Johnson**, 'The Preaching to the Dead (1 Pet 3, 18–22)', *JBL* 79, 1960, 48–51; E. **Kamlah**, *Die Form der katalogischen Paränese im Neuen Testament*, WUNT 7, 1964; O. **Knoch**, *Die 'Testamente' des Petrus und Paulus*, SBS 62, 1973; J. **Knox**, 'Pliny and 1 Peter: A Note on 1 Pet 4,14–16 and 3,15' *JBL* 72, 1953, 187–9; E. **Kraft**, 'Christologie und Anthropologie im 1. Petrusbrief', *EvTh* 10, 1950/51, 120–26; G. **Krodel**, 'The First Letter of Peter', *Hebrews—James—1 and 2 Peter—Jude—Revelation* (Proclamation Commentaries), Philadelphia 1977, 50–80; A. R. C. **Leaney**, 'I Peter and the Passover: An Interpretation', *NTS* 10, 1963/4, 238–51; E. **Lohse**, 'Paränese und Kerygma im 1. Petrusbrief', *ZNW* 45, 1954, 68–89; D. **Lührmann**, 'Wo man nicht mehr Sklave oder Freier ist: Überlegungen zur Struktur frühchristlicher Gemeinden', *WuD* 13, 1975, 53–82; T. W. **Manson**, Review of E. G. Selwyn, *The First Epistle of St Peter*, in *JTS* 47, 1946, 218–27; R. P. **Martin**, 'The Composition of 1 Peter in Recent Study', *Vox Evangelica* 1, 1962, 29–42; J. D. **McCaughey**, 'Three "Persecution Documents" of the New Testament', *AustrBR* 17, 1969, 27–40; O. **Michel**, 'οἶκος', *TDNT* V, 119–59; C. L. **Mitton**, 'The Relationship between I Peter and Ephesians', *JTS*, NS 1, 1950, 27–40; J. **Moreau**, *Die Christenverfolgung im römischen Reich*, Berlin ²1971; C. F. D. **Moule**, 'Some Reflections on the "Stone Testimonia" in Relation to the Name Peter', *NTS* 2, 1955/6, 56–9; 'The Nature and Purpose of I Peter', NTS 3, 1956/7, 1–11; W. **Munro**, *Authority in Paul and Peter: The Identification of a Pastoral Stratum in the Pauline Corpus and I Peter*, SNTSM 45, 1983.

W. **Nauck**, 'Freude im Leiden. Zum Problem einer urchristlichen Verfolgungstradition', *ZNW* 46, 1955, 68–80; 'Probleme des frühchristlichen Amtsverständnisses (1 Petr 5,2f.)', *ZNW* 48, 1957, 200–20; F. **Neugebauer**, 'Zur Deutung und Bedeutung des 1. Petrusbriefes', *NTS* 26, 1979/80, 61–86; R. **Perdelwitz**, *Die Mysterionreligion und das Problem des 1. Petrusbriefes*, Giessen 1911; K. **Phillips**, *Kirche in der Gesellschaft nach dem ersten Petrusbrief*, Gütersloh 1971; L. **Rademacher**, 'Der erste Petrusbrief und Silvanus', *ZNW* 25, 1926, 287–99; B. **Reicke**, *The Disobedient Spirits and Christian Baptism. A Study of 1 Pet. III.19 and its Context*, Copenhagen 1946; K. H. **Rengstorf**, 'Die neutestamentlichen Mahnungen an die Frau, sich dem Manne unterzuordnen', *Verbum Dei manet in aeternum, FS O. Schmitz*, ed. W. Foerster, Witten 1953, 131–45; E. **Scharfe**, *Die petrinische Strömung der neutestamentlichen Literatur*, Berlin 1893; A. **Schlatter**, *Die Theologie der Apostel*,

Stuttgart ²1922, 44–64; *Petrus und Paulus nach dem ersten Petrusbrief*, Stuttgart 1937; K. L. **Schmidt**, M. A. **Schmidt**, 'πάροικος', *TDNT* V, 841–53; F. **Schröger**, *Gemeinde im 1. Petrusbrief*, Passau 1981; E. G. **Selwyn**, 'Unsolved New Testament Problems. The Problem of the Authorship of 1 Peter', *ExpT* 59, 1947/8, 256–9; 'Eschatology in 1 Peter', *The Background of the New Testament and its Eschatology*, *FS. C. H. Dodd*, ed. W. D. Davies and D. Daube, Cambridge 1956, 394–401; W. **Seufert**, 'Titus, Silvanus (Silas) und der Verfasser des ersten Petrusbriefes', *ZWTh* 28, 1885, 359–71; F. H. **Sleeper**, 'Political Responsibility according to 1 Peter', *NovT* 10, 1968, 270–86; K. R. **Snodgrass**, 'I Peter II.1–10: Its Formation and Literary Affinities', *NTS* 24, 1977/8, 97–106; C. **Spicq**, 'La 1ª Petri et le témoignage évangélique de saint Pierre', *StTh* 20, 1966, 37–61; T. **Spörri**, *Der Gemeindegedanke im ersten Petrusbrief*, Gütersloh 1925.

T. C. G. **Thornton**, 'I Peter, a Paschal Liturgy?', *JTS*, 12, 1961, 14–26; W. **Trilling**, 'Zum Petrusamt im Neuen Testament. Traditionsgeschichtliche Überlegungen anhand vom Matthäus, 1 Petrus und Johannes', *ThQ* 151, 1971, 110–33; W. C. **van Unnik**, 'The Teaching of Good Works in 1 Peter', *NTS* 1, 1954/5, 92–110; 'Christianity according to 1 Peter', *ExpT* 68, 1956/7, 79–83; 'Peter, First Letter of ', *IDB*, III, 758–66; D. **Völter**, *Der erste Petrusbrief. Seine Entstehung und Stellung in der Geschichte des Urchristentums*, Strassburg, 1906; J. W. C. **Wand**, 'The Lessons of First Peter. A Survey of Recent Interpretation', *Interp* 9, 1955, 387–99; B. **Weiss**, *Der Petrinische Lehrbegriff. Beiträge zur biblischen Theologie sowie zur Kritik und Exegese des ersten Briefes Petri und der petrinischen Reden*, Berlin 1855; *Der erste Petrusbrief und die neuere Kritik*, Berlin 1906; C. L. **Winbery**, 'Introduction to the First Letter of Peter', *SWJT* 25, 1982, 3–16; C. **Wolff**, 'Christ und Welt im 1. Petrusbrief', *TLZ* 100, 1975, 334–42; W. **Wrede**, 'Miscellen 3. Bemerkungen zu Harnacks Hypothese über die Adresse des 1. Petrusbriefes', *ZNW* 1, 1900, 75–85.

From the modern critical study of 1 Peter it would appear that two strikingly different assessments of the book have emerged. Conservative scholars such as Hort, Bigg, and Selwyn have defended the traditional authorship of Peter, the apostle. Liberal scholars such as Windisch, Knopf, and Marxsen (*Intr..*) have evaluated the letter to be pseudepigraphical. However, the true picture is far more complex than this polarity would suggest. First of all, the question of the book's authorship reflects a multiple gradation of opinion because of significant modifications and redefinitions of terminology which are involved. For example, the position of Selwyn, whose defence of Petrine authorship employs the mediation of Silvanus, does not differ greatly from Goppelt who in the end does not attribute the letter to the apostle. Secondly, the evaluation of the epistle as pseudepigraphical is no longer a judgment confined to so-called liberal scholars, but includes a wide variety of theological opinion. Especially the aggressive development of a fresh theological interpretation of pseudepigraphy by Roman Catholic scholars (Schelkle, Brox, Trilling) has radically altered the older picture.

This chapter will attempt to sketch the parameters of the modern discussion before setting forth a canonical approach which differs at crucial points from the various options being offered both on the left and the right.

I. The Modern Critical Debate

A. Literary Structure

There is much agreement that I Peter lacks a tightly constructed literary structure. Although central themes tie parts of the epistle together in a loose paraenetic fashion, it remains difficult for commentators to mount a case for any one particular outline. One of the first literary theories by which to explain the situation was proposed by Harnack who suggested that the letter comprised an originally anonymous Christian homily which was later made into a letter by the addition of epistolary conventions. A new phase of the discussion was introduced by Perdelwitz's theory of 1911 that the book originally constituted a baptismal homily. 1.3–4.11 formed the original liturgy and 1.1f. and 4.12–5.14 were later additions. In the subsequent years the liturgical hypothesis has been refined and expanded by Bornemann, Preisker, and Cross among others. Since the details of the hypothesis are discussed at length by the commentaries (Beare, Goppelt, Brox), it is unnecessary to rehearse them in detail. In more recent times the theory has been sharply criticized (Moule, Best), and in the original form of Preisker or Cross hardly commends any present support. Nor has Moule's theory that I Peter is a combination of two forms of one letter written to a number of communities, only some of which were suffering persecution, received a favourable reception. Rather, the overwhelming majority of modern scholars postulate the unity of the epistle which stems from one author.

B. The Question of Addressee

Another much debated issue turns on specifying the receipients of the letter. It is explicitly directed to the 'resident aliens of the Dispersion in Pontus, Galatia, Cappodocia, Asia, and Bithynia', which would appear to make it a circular letter. While scholars are generally agreed that the geographical designation is of Roman provinces and not territories, the more difficult question focuses on whether the addressees are Jews or Gentiles. The traditional interpreters (Greek Fathers, Erasmus, Calvin) assumed that the addressees were Jewish-Christians. The assumption rested in part upon the New Testament's characterization of Peter as the apostle to the Jews (Acts 15; Gal.1) in distinction from Paul, but additional support was found in the term 'Diaspora' (1.1) and in the frequent appeal to the Old Testament. The most persistent defender of this traditional theory, B. Weiss, even sought to date the epistle early and before Gentile Christianity had gained the ascendency in Asia Minor through the Pauline mission (*Intr.* II, 140f.), but this move has received no support whatever (cf. Jülicher-Fascher, *Einl.*, 194f.).

A large consensus has arisen that the addressees are Gentile Christians. The main evidence is supplied by those passages which mention the hopelessness of their former conduct inherited from their fathers and their life of immorality as heathen (1.14,18; 2.10;3.20; 4.3f.). However, in recent years some of the newer commentators (Brox, Goppelt, Elliott) have suggested a mixed congregation, although admitting the predominance of Gentiles. Van Unnik's theory of seeing the Gentile Christians as 'Godfearers' who had previously associated with the synagogue cannot be convincingly demonstrated. Finally, there has been considerable debate over the two terms in 1.1, 'resident alien' and 'dispersion' (cf. Elliott, *Home for Homeless*, 21ff.). The issue is important for the larger interpretation of the epistle (cf. below), but has not been decisive in itself in specifying the addressee.

C. Authorship of the Epistle

The most heated debate regarding I Peter has, of course, focused on the problems connected with the book's authorship, the dating of the composition, and the sources or traditions which underlie the material. In spite of the ancient identification of the author with the apostle Peter which was universal in Christian tradition, a very impressive group of modern scholars contest this traditional authorship in favour of some form of pseudepigraphical composition (Knopf, Beare, Kümmel, *Intr.*, Schelkle, Best, Trilling, etc.). Indeed, in the most recent period the advocates of pseudepigraphy have clearly moved into the majority opinion among critical scholars.

The study of this critical debate over the genuineness of the ascription to Peter is instructive in showing the changing profile of the discipline which abandoned some of its more radical theories in the course of the debate, but did not return to the traditional stance. The initial objection voiced against attributing the letter to Peter was the highly cultivated Greek style of the epistle which did not seem likely for a Galilean fisherman. Similarly, the consistent use of the Septuagint seemed strange for an Aramaic-speaking Palestinian Jew. In addition, it was argued that I Peter was dependent upon many of the other New Testament letters, particularly with Romans and Ephesians, and perhaps even James and Hebrews (Holtzmann, *Einl.*, 488f.; Jülicher-Fascher, *Einl.*, 194f.). Such evidence pointed to a late first-century or early second-century dating long after the death of the apostle. The attempt to pinpoint the dating more accurately turned on identifying which of the Roman persecutions was reflected in the letter (Nero, 64; Domitian, 95; Trajan, c.110). The choice fell between the latter two emperors. Finally, the case was made that the epistle stemmed from a Pauline disciple, but one who now stood at a considerable distance from him, which accounted for the diluted form of his message. The change from genuine Paulinism was also found reflected in the church polity of I Peter 5.

These are the arguments, following the critical tradition of Gunkel, Knopf and Windisch, which were still considered decisive by Beare in his commentary of 1946. However, he did include the debate over the epistle's unity initiated by Perdelwitz as an additional argument for its pseudepigraphical character, and found the lack of concern for the Spirit another sign of its post-apostolic age.

In response to these arguments there has emerged a strong conservative reaction which developed its defences in a way quite different from the earlier mid-nineteenth century defenders of the traditional position, such as B. Weiss. The most impressive formulation of the new conservative position was offered by E. G. Selwyn in his learned commentary of 1946. At the outset, Selwyn raised the question in what sense the epistle was authentic (7), which showed his change in perspective immediately. He then defended an elaborate theory for the indirect authorship of the apostle Peter who made use of Silvanus as an active participant in shaping the letter. Next he developed the hypothesis that the author made use of a common stock of teaching and hymnody which was current in the church. He divided the inherited material into four different categories: (i) liturgical, (ii) persecution fragment, (iii) catechetical, (iv) verba Christi. Selwyn went on to develop the last category in a way much akin to the earlier conservative position of Weiss and Scharfe in order to conclude that a common ground between the Gospels, Acts, and I Peter lay in the 'mind of St Peter' (36). In addition he argued that the persecution alluded to in the letter was of a persistent nature, extending over a lengthy period, and afforded no evidence for a specific dating.

Selwyn's commentary, coupled with some other important contributions (e.g. Bultmann, Preisker, Lohse) touched off the modern debate. On several of the older critical issues, Selwyn offered a major correction. His insistence that the letter reflected a common stock of liturgical and paraenetic language received strong support from Lohse among others, and did much to undercut the argument of a literary dependence on the Pauline corpus. Then again, the question of the Pauline influence on the letter has emerged in a different light in the newer debate. That I Peter had some unique features such as the great stress on the suffering of Christ like Isaiah's servant (2.21ff.) and the use of the stone imagery (2.6ff.) can hardly be denied. Nevertheless, it remains questionable whether one can really speak of a Petrine tradition (*contra* Elliott).

It has become increasingly clear that the relation of I Peter to the Pauline theology is a complex one. As has long been recognized there are some important similarities in christology, atonement, and eschatology, yet the differences are also striking, particularly the absence of a polemical setting and the debate over the role of the law. Brox makes an important point in warning against too sharp a contrast between Pauline and Petrine theology which would be anachronistic if projected back into the first century ('Tendenz', 118ff.). He concludes that I Peter is not literarily dependent upon either Paul or the deutero-Pauline school (EKK, 51). Finally, there is a growing consensus that the persecution reflected in the letter cannot be ascribed to a specific era, but was of a continuing nature (*Dauerzustand*). Elliott's sociological profile of the community of I

Peter and its relation to the state offers an interesting new approach to the older problem which has considerable potential for fresh insight.

On the negative side, several important positions which Selwyn defended have not been sustained in the continuing modern debate. The attempt to assign a decisive mediating role to Silvanus has not been successful in meeting the objections to direct Petrine authorship. The indirect relationship of Petrine authorship to the letter reveals a much more complex process than envisioned by assigning a major creative role to Silvanus as an amanuensis. Not only is the theory speculative, since we know very little about Silvanus' literary ability, but even more crucial, the letter reflects a religious idiom which has been formed and transmitted in the context of the Hellenistic synagogue.

Finally, the attempt of Selwyn both to recover a peculiar historical reminiscence by Peter of Jesus in the *verba Christi* of the Gospels, and to defend a unique form of Petrine doctrine which is shared by the epistle and Peter's speeches in Acts can only be deemed a failure. A major obstacle to the theory is that when certain words of Christ appear in I Peter, their form reveals a process of transmission which has undergone a lengthy traditional development in an ecclesiastical context. Gundry's articles, which elicited a response from Best, only served to confirm the serious inadequacies of this older approach. The positive gain which the critical method has produced is to undercut the widespread psychological interpretation of the gospel which marred Selwyn's otherwise impressive commentary.

D. *The Pseudepigraphical Hypothesis*

In the light of this history of scholarship through which the debate over authorship moved, it comes as no surprise that the issue of pseudepigraphy should have emerged in a new and vigorous form. Although the use of the term would imply a large degree of similarity between the composition of I Peter and the Pastorals, the significant fact is rather the recognition of how very different the two problems are. In terms of the Pastorals, the case for pseudepigraphy rested on the supposition that an anonymous second-century writer wished to evoke the authority of the apostle Paul in order to address a new ecclesiastical situation which arose some fifty years after his death. The writer accordingly constructed a portrait of Paul by which to actualize the apostle's authority. In sum, a clear profile of the intention and technique of the pseudepigraphical author was thought recoverable.

In marked contrast, those who characterize I Peter as pseudepigraphical find difficulty in establishing any relationship between the fictional authorship of Peter and the content, or historical circumstances of the epistle (cf. Brox). No attempt has been made by I Peter, in contrast to II Peter, to establish a portrait of Peter. Moreover, no obvious reason – historical, sociological, doctrinal – has been established for assigning the letter to the apostle. Nor is there any clear legitimating function provided by the appeal to Peter's authority.

Of course, various theories have been suggested by which to clarify the letter's alleged pseudepigraphical function. F. C. Baur, applying his *Tendenz* criticism to the epistle, saw it as a compromise document which sought to overcome the earlier friction between Pauline and Jewish Christianity. Trilling (120ff.), although making important modifications to Baur's hypothesis, continues to move in the same general direction when he describes the epistle's function as one of mediating between Pauline and Jerusalem tradition. Krodel also argues that the letter, which purports to enjoy the support of Paul's co-workers, witnesses to the true catholicity of the church (58f.). Also Elliott, taking a different tack, sees the pseudepigraphical function of the letter in preserving for a later period the peculiar tradition of a 'Petrine group', the broad lines of which he attempts to reconstruct ('Rehabilitation', 248ff.). Perhaps the least convincing explanation is that of Schenke who conjectures that the reference to Peter may well be a textual error (*Einl.* I, 203).

Finally, it is N. Brox who has worked the hardest on the problem in his many articles and commentary. The care and precision with which he approaches the problem is admirable. He admits that the only indication of a pseudepigraphical motivation from within the letter is the role of Rome as the locale from which the letter arose. In the end, Brox is only able to pursue some techniques common to pseudepigraphical writing which also could be reflected in I Peter. An adequate explanation of why the genre was employed for this letter continues to elude him.

In sum, although the difficulties of attributing authorship of this letter to the apostle Peter are enormous, it remains virtually impossible to penetrate behind the present literary function to a different, truly historical function which accounts for the form of the letter. From a hermeneutical perspective the effect of this impasse has been significant. Rather than following the method applied to the Pastorals in which the tension between the letter's literary function and its real pseudepigraphical intention is constantly exploited, most commentators on I Peter concentrate their attention on interpreting the ostensive purpose of the letter itself, which is ironically a stance akin to the canonical.

E. The Purpose of the Epistle

As one would expect, critical opinion varies considerably regarding the primary aim of the letter in its present form. It is generally recognized that the letter shares only a few formal features of a genuinely occasional letter. Some designate the letter as a theological tract which is directed to Christians at large. Others (Beare) stress the practical nature of the letter, and argue that the central doctrines are presupposed, but not expounded. Brox finds the theme of hope to be central, whereas Goppelt emphasizes its instructions in living the Christian life in a hostile world. Both Balch and Elliott approach the issue largely from a sociological perspective. Balch sees the main purpose of the letter as an effort to reduce the tension between society and the church. Elliott explores the issue in the framework of sectarian group formation and the letter's role as providing a communal identity and social cohesion (*Home*, 225). Although he is aware of the acute danger of reductionism in applying his sociological categories, in the end he falls back into the tedious American jargon of 'socio-religious solidarity', 'self-identity', and 'raising group consciousness'.

In sum, the historical critical decisions regarding the book's authorship and dating have not affected the book's interpretation as much as one might expect, say, in comparison with the Pastorals. Rather, exegetical decisions regarding the theology of the letter, its relation to Paul and early Christian tradition, and the sociological stance of the community have been more decisive in providing a shape for modern interpretation.

II. The Canonical Shape and Function of the Letter

A. The Form and Function of the Praescript

It is clear from the use of the conventions of a praescript and a conclusion that I Peter purports to be a letter and not a theological tractate or baptismal liturgy. Yet the effect of the canonical process at work within the early church is clearly evident. The epistle has retained the formal features of a genuine letter, but its function has been greatly altered. It does not address a particular community, nor does it concern itself with a specific historical situation. Its canonical shape which renders its message accessible to future generations of Christians is not the result of a secondary redactional process which modified its original, highly specific reference (*contra* Moule). Rather, like the letter to the Ephesians, its catholic quality lies firmly embedded in the original form of the epistle. Not only is it explicitly a circular letter, addressed to Christians at large, but its teachings are directed to faithful Christians living in the light of perennial threats to the faith. Brox speaks of 'every possible church in every possible epoch' (EKK, 15). The addressees are those who have not experienced Jesus in the flesh (1.8), and who have only recently been born anew into the faith (1.22; 2.2, etc.).

Although I Peter continues to employ a few conventions of the occasional letter, the actual dynamic of the epistle is provided by the homiletical, paraenetic mode of the sermon. As we have seen, this issue is usually treated from an exclusively diachronic perspective. In what sense did the letter stem from an original liturgical service? Yet from a canonical perspective it is far more significant to recognize—regardless of its prehistory—that the letter now functions to imitate the homily (cf. Gunkel, 248). The letter assumes the great doctrines of the faith, but seeks to actualize the faith by primarily addressing the will. The message does not progress by means of a tightly honed argument, but by a powerful use of repetition, by a constant appeal to Old Testament passages which evokes a virtual symphony of resonance, and by direct appeal of repeated exhortation.

The letter is addressed to the 'resident aliens of the Dispersion' (1.1). Much careful lexical work has been done on the exact meaning of this terminology (cf. K. L. Schmidt; Elliott, *Home*, 21ff.). Elliott in particular has mounted an extensive case against understanding the expression metaphorically. He argues that the contrast is not between an earthly and a heavenly home, but between being a homeless stranger and a fellow-citizen in the household of God. He has made a contribution in stressing the actual historical and sociological dimension of the biblical concepts, but it remains to me questionable whether he has correctly interpreted the function of the terminology within the present form of the letter. He has difficulty dealing adequately with the text's own explanation of the concept in 1.4: 'an inheritance which is imperishable, undefiled, and unfading, kept in heaven for you', which is a construal toward rendering the expression metaphorically. It does not actualize the term in the direction of his proposal. The relation is analogical, like the Hebrew exiles living in Babylon. I would, therefore, argue that the original sociological depiction of the 'resident alien', which Elliott sought to recover, has been subordinated canonically to the background of the text. Its new function provides a warrant for the correct hearing of the message of the epistle by later generations for whom the original sense of the expression in 1.1 has become blurred.

One of the implications of this reading of the praescript is that the old crux as to whether the addressees of the letter were Jews or Gentiles has lost its prime importance. The theological categories of 'newborn', 'elect', 'resident alien', function regardless of racial affiliation. Although the arguments which defend the original reference to a conversion from paganism are generally sound, the contrasts of the new with the old, of no people with God's people, of darkness and light, function as universal and enduring descriptions of Christian faith. To insist with the older, conservative commentators (Weiss, Zahn, *Intr.*) that Peter is the missionary to the Jews in I Peter just as in Acts is incorrectly to translate a canonical portrait into an historical statement.

Christians have been 'born anew to a living hope through the resurrection of Jesus Christ' (1.3). The author then interprets the function of Old Testament prophecy in defining Christian salvation by a forward-looking stance as an essential part of the Christian faith (1.10–12). The pattern which the prophetic witness to salvation established for the old covenant is the selfsame testimony of the Christian faith. Similarly the present divine support in the midst of intense suffering is a demonstration of the true grace of God in which the church is to stand (5.12). (Cf. K. Barth, *Church Dogmatics* III/2, 495–7.)

Much of the body of the letter is taken up with exhortation to follow in Christ's footsteps whose life was characterized by patient suffering (2.21ff.). As the elect people, called to holiness, the Christian is to live in the world in a way commensurate with his high calling. The writer describes the faithful Christian conduct of life in a highly practical fashion without the sophisticated dialectical categories of Paul. Particular emphasis is placed on maintaining a good report with the Gentile world (2.12ff.), and in sustaining the unity of the community of faith (2.18ff.).

Finally, we turn to the important issue of interpreting the function of Petrine authorship in its canonical context. We have already made the case that the letter itself does not establish a material connection between the content and the authorship of Peter. To make this observation is, of course, not to deny that some historical connection may have once existed, but only to reinforce the point that the canonical function of the present letter does not rest on establishing such a connection.

Peter is presented formally in the praescript as the author of the letter, and his role is defined as an apostle of Jesus Christ. The use of the name Peter, a graecized form of the Aramaic Cephas, instead of his personal name of Simon would tend to stress his ecclesiastical role in the church. Above all, he is an apostle of Christ. The term in Christian theology designates an authoritative office within the church which derives from his special witness to the resurrection of Jesus Christ and which is not extended to the next generation of believers. The praescript thus attributes the message of the letter to the apostolic authority of Peter. The grounds for connecting Peter's authority to this letter are not established historically, nor in terms of a chain of tradition, but simply asserted.

B. *The Conclusion of the Letter*

Several other pieces of information play a role in establishing a canonical context for interpreting the letter which are found in the concluding verses. The author sends greetings from the believers in Babylon who most likely are to be understood as the church at Rome. In addition, he commends Silvanus as 'a faithful brother' through whom the letter has been transmitted in some sense. Has he acted as an amenuensis or as the deliverer of the letter? Finally, he sends greetings from Mark, whom he designates his son (5.13). To the original addressees of Asia Minor both Silvanus and Mark would most likely have been known throughout these churches as co-workers of Paul, although the exact nature of the historical connection remains, in many respects, unclear. However, to later Christian readers to whom the letter of I Peter was transmitted as part of a larger Christian canon which included Acts and the Pauline corpus, the connection of Silvanus and Mark with Paul was certain.

To suggest that the letter functioned to establish a reconciliation between Pauline and Petrine parties within the early church is an erroneous conclusion for many reasons. It is certainly anachronistic, as Brox observes, to propose that the early church felt the need to harmonize two different theologies. At most one can infer that the references to Paul's co-workers in Rome, regardless of the original historical connection with Peter which has now been lost, functioned for later users of the whole canon to guarantee the catholicity of I Peter, which had the direct authority of Peter and the indirect support of Paul. However, there is no evidence that the original references ever functioned to legitimate a position under attack.

c. The Canonical Function of the Letter

What then is the canonical role of the letter besides legitimating its message with the apostolic authority of Peter? I would argue that the attribution of the letter to the apostle plays another important function of rendering the message within a canonical context. Selwyn and other conservative commentators have unsuccessfully tried to make the case for an historical continuity between the mind of Jesus and I Peter by means of an appeal to the *verba Christi* and the Petrine speeches of Acts. The basic error in this approach lies in confusing the canonical rendering with the claim of objective historical evidence. However, these scholars shared a correct observation in perceiving an important canonical link between the different parts of the New Testament.

I would suggest reversing the argument of Selwyn, and pursuing the effect of attributing the letter to the apostle Peter on the canonical rendering of the material. Even when the historical links lying behind the role of Peter are unclear, the effect of the ascription had a profound influence on the way in which the tradition was construed. A major characteristic of the letter was its general, non-specific paraenetic style which was addressed to Christian churches at large. By attributing the letter to Peter a vehicle was established by which to actualize the material through the person of the apostle. This move was greatly enhanced by the formation of the larger canonical corpus. The reader had access to Peter's own struggle for faith both in the Gospels and in Acts which, when read in conjunction with the letter, served to reify the material by evoking a resonance between the various parts of scripture.

For example, the admonition in I Peter 5.2: 'Tend the flock of God that is your charge', lends itself to be heard along with Christ's admonition to Peter: 'Tend my sheep' (John 21.16). Or again, the verse I Peter 1.8, 'Without having seen him you love him; though you do not see him, you believe in him and rejoice . . . . ', takes on a new sense when heard in concert with Jesus' words to Thomas, 'Have you believed because you have seen me? Blessed are those who have not seen and yet believe' (John 20.29). Numerous other examples from the Gospels and Acts can be presented which function in a like manner.

It is of crucial hermeneutical significance to understand exactly what is being suggested. This canonical function is not to be confused with recovering an author's original intention, nor proving historical continuity. Rather, it is a function of canon to establish an intertextuality between the parts as the context for its theological appropriation. It differs from a modern psychologizing of the biblical text in several important ways. First, it is a way of actualizing the material homiletically toward the end of making an exhortation concrete. Secondly, it works within the context provided by the parameters of the canon, and it interprets the material by refracting it through the larger context. Finally, it interprets the passage with a kerygmatic intention of engendering faith and is an enterprise somewhat analogous to the canonical harmonizing of the four Gospels (cf. ch. 20).

Finally, a word is in order regarding the implications of our canonical approach for the issue of the allegedly pseudepigraphical quality of I Peter. Admittedly, historical-critical research has opened up a new avenue of interpretation by presenting evidence which calls into question the direct literary activity of Peter. Still the point must be emphasized that in its canonical shape the letter of I Peter is attributed to the apostle, and its kerygmatic function is made a derivative of his authority. The effect of the historical-critical approach has been to force a distinction between the historical problem of authorship and the theological function of rendering the material according to a peculiar canonical fashion. At times it is possible to suggest ways of bridging the historical and theological perspectives (cf. the Pastoral epistles). In the case of I Peter, the evidence is simply inadequate to understand the relation between the historically indirect authorship of the letter and the direct apostolic attribution of the canonical construal. Of course, by using some general analogies from the rest of the Bible one can argue for a much looser concept of authorship than is often assumed by modern interpreters. Still the crucial hermeneutical issue is to allow for the integrity of the historical enterprise within its context, and also for the integrity of the canonical rendering of the material within its theological context, even when the connecting lines between the processes remain unclear.

A major objection to the use of the pseudepigraphical model for I Peter is that it often obscures the strikingly different functions which indirect authorship plays within the New Testament canon. We have attempted to illustrate the different role of authorship in I Peter from that of the Pastorals, or of Ephesians. The danger of the pseudepigraphical model is in lumping all books of indirect authorship under a category of 'non-genuine' writings, and thereby destroying any chance of discerning the nature of the canon's peculiar theological construal. The letter of I Peter offers a good illustration of allowing the complexity of the relationship between authority and authorship to strengthen a theological perception of the rich multi-dimensional quality of the apostolic witness.

27

II PETER

Commentaries

J. C. K. von Hofmann, 1875
E. H. Plumptre, CB, 1880
J. C. Huther, MeyerK, ET 1881
C. F. Keil, 1883
H. von Soden, HCNT, 1892
J. R. Lumby, ExpB, 1893
E. Kühl, MeyerK, 61897
C. Bigg, ICC, 21902
J. B. Mayor, 1907
R. Knopf, MeyerK, 71912
M. R. James, CGTSC, 1912
G. Hollmann, W. Bousset, *SNT*,
31917
G. Wohlenberg, KNT, 31921
J. W. C. Wand, WC, 1934
J. Chaine, ÉB, 21939
H. Windisch, H. Preisker, HNT,
31951

J. Moffatt, MNTC, 71953
F. Hauck, NTD, 71954
C. E. B. Cranfield, TB, 1960
J. Schneider, NTD, 91961
G. H. Boobyer, Peake, 1962
B. Reicke, AB, 1964
C. Spicq, SB, 1966
E. M. Sidebottom, NCeB, 1967
A. R. C. Leaney, CNEB, 1967
E. M. B. Green, Tyn, 1968
J. Michl, RNT, 21968
J. N. D. Kelly, B/HNTC, 1969
W. Schrage, NTD, 111973
W. Grundmann, THKNT, 21979
K. H. Schelkle, HTKNT, 51980
J. H. Elliott, Augs, 1982
R. J. Bauckham, Word, 1983

Bibliography

E. A. **Abbott**, 'The Second Epistle of St Peter', *Exp* II. 3, 1882, 49-63; 139-53; 204-19; D. **von Allmen**, 'L'apocalyptique juive et le retard de la parousie en II Pierre 3, 1-13', *Revue de théologie et de philosophie*, 16, 1966, 255-74; J. C. **Beker**, 'Second Letter of Peter', *IDB*, 3, 737-71; W. **Bieder**, *Die Vorstellungen von der Höllenfahrt Jesu Christi*, Zürich 1949; J. **Blinzler**, *Die neutestamentlichen Berichte über die Verklärung Jesu*, Münster 1937; G. H. **Boobyer**, 'The Indebtedness of 2 Peter to 1 Peter', *New Testament Essays. Studies in Memory of T. W. Manson*, ed. A. J. B. Higgins, Manchester 1959, 34–53;—'The Verbs in Jude II', *NTS* 5, 1958/9, 45–7; G. **Bornkamm**, 'Die Verzögerung der Parousie', *In Memoriam E. Lohmeyer*, ed. W. Schmauch,

Stuttgart 1951, 116–26; H. C. C. **Cavallin**, 'The False Teachers of 2 Peter as Pseudo–Prophets', *NovT* 21, 1979, 263–70; J. **Chaine**, 'Cosmogonie aquatique et conflagration finale d'après la Secunda Petri', *RB* 46, 1937, 207–16; F. H. **Chase**, 'Peter, Second Epistle of', *DBHastings*, III, Edinburgh 1900, 796–818; J. T. **Curran**, 'The Teachings of 2 Peter 1.20', *ThSt* 4, 1943, 347–68; N. A. **Dahl**, 'Anamnesis: Memory and Commemoration in Early Christianity', ET in *Jesus in the Memory of the Early Church*, Minneapolis 1976, 11–51; F. W. **Danker**, 'II Peter 3:10 and Psalm of Solomon 17:10', *ZNW* 53, 1962, 82–6; —'2 Peter 1: A Solemn Decree', *CBQ* 40, 1978, 64–82; 'The Second Letter of Peter', *Hebrews – James – 1 and 2 Peter – Jude – Revelation*, ed. G. Krodel (Proclamation Commentaries), Philadelphia 1977, 81–91; P. **Dexinger**, *Sturz der Göttersöhne oder Engel vor der Sintflut?*, Vienna 1966; K. P. **Donfried**, *The Setting of Second Clement in Early Christianity*, Leiden 1974.

C. **Ernst**, 'The Date of II Peter and the Deposit of Faith', *The Clergy Review* 47, 1962, 686–9; E. **Fascher**, 'Petrusbriefe', *RGG*[3], V, 1961, 259f; T. **Fornberg**, *An Early Church in a Pluralistic Society*, Lund 1977; R. M. **Grant**, *The Letter and the Spirit*, London and New York 1957; E. M. B. **Green**, *2 Peter Reconsidered*, London 1961; E. **Käsemann**, 'An Apologia for Primitive Christian Eschatology', ET *Essays on New Testament Themes*, SBT 41, 1964, 169–95; G. **Klein**, 'Der zweite Petrusbrief und der neutestamentliche Kanon, Ärgernisse', *Konfrontationen mit dem Neuen Testament*, Munich 1971, 109–14; J. **Klinger**, 'The Second Epistle of Peter: An Essay in Understanding', *St Vladimir Theological Quarterly* 17, 1973, 152–69; O. **Knoch**, *Die 'Testamente' des Petrus und Paulus*, SBS 62, 1973, 65–81; A **Kolenkow**, 'The Genre Testament and Forecasts of the Future in the Hellenistic Jewish Milieu', *Journal for the Study of Judaism* 6, 1975, 57–71; W. **Marxsen**, *Der 'Frühkatholizismus' im Neuen Testament*, Neukirchen 1958; W. **Michaelis**, *Der Herr verzieht nicht die Verheissungen*, Bern 1942; H. J. **Michel**, *Die Abschiedsrede des Paulus an die Kirche Apg 20, 17–38*, SANT 35, 1973; E. **Molland**, 'La thèse "La prophétie n'est jamais venue de la volonté de l'homme" (2 Pierre i.20) et les Pseudo-Clémentines', *StTh* 9, 1955, 67–85; C. F. D. **Moule**, 'The Influence of Circumstances on the Use of Eschatological Terms', *JTS* ns 15, 1964, 1–15; J. **Munck**, 'Discours d'adieu dans le Nouveau Testament et dans la littérature biblique', *Aux Sources de la Tradition Chrétienne*, *FS M. Goguel*, Neuchâtel 1950, 155–70; F. **Mussner**, *Petrus und Paulus – Pole der Einheit*, Freiburg 1976.

J. H. **Neyrey**, *The Form and Background of the Polemic in 2 Peter*, Diss. Yale University 1977; —'The Apologetic Use of the Transfiguration in 2 Peter 1:16–21', *CBQ* 42, 1980, 504–19; J. A. T. **Robinson**, *Redating the New Testament*, London and Philadelphia 1976, 140–99; E. I. **Robson**, *Studies in the Second Epistle of St Peter*, Cambridge 1915; G. **de Ru**, 'De authenticiteit van II Petrus', *Nederlands Theologisch Tijdschrift* 24, 1969, 1–12; K. H. **Schelkle**, 'Spätapostolische Briefe als frühkatholisches Zeugnis', *Neutestamentliche Aufsätze für J. Schmid*, ed. J. Blinzler et al., Regensburg 1963, 225–32;

J. **Schmitt**, 'Pierre (Deuxième épître de)', *DB Suppl* 7, 1966, 1455–63; J. **Sibinga**, 'Une citation du Cantique dans la Secunda Petri', *RB* 73, 1966, 107–18; F. **Spitta**, *Der Zweite Brief des Petrus und der Brief des Judas*, Halle 1885; 'Die Petrusapokalypse und der zweite Petrusbrief', *ZNW* 12, 1911, 237–42; E. **Stauffer**, 'Abschiedsreden', *RAC* 1, 29–35; A. **Strobel**, *Untersuchungen zum eschatologischen Verzögerungsproblem auf Grund der spätjüdisch-urchristlichen Gemeinde von Habakuk 2,2ff.*, NovTSuppl 2, 1961; J. **Snyder**, 'A 2 Peter Bibliography', *JETS* 22/3, 1979, 265–7; C. H. **Talbert**, 'II Peter and the Delay of the Parousia', *VigChr* 20, 1966, 137–45; A. **Vögtle**, 'Die Schriftwerdung der apostolischen Paradosis nach 2 Petr. 1,12–15', *Neues Testament und Geschichte, FS O. Cullmann*, ed H. Baltensweiler et al., Zürich and Tübingen 1972, 297–306.

B. B. **Warfield**, 'The Canonicity of Second Peter', *Southern Presbyterian Review* XXXIII, 1882, 45–75; 'Dr. Edwin A. Abbott on the Genuineness of Second Peter', *ibid.*, XXXIV, 1883, 390–445; H. **Werdermann**, *Die Irrlehrer des Judas– und 2. Petrusbriefes*, Gütersloh 1913; J. **Zmigewski**, 'Apostolische Paradosis und Pseudepigraphie im Neuen Testament. "Durch Erinnerung wachhalten" (2 Petr 1, 13; 3, 1)', *BZ* 23, 1979, 161–71.

I. II Peter and the Problem of Canon

It has long been recognized that the issue of the New Testament canon is of central importance for interpreting the letter of II Peter. Of course, how one assesses the significance of this process has sharply divided commentators. Käsemann agrees that the letter of II Peter documents the beginning of the canonical process, but at the same time he evaluates the letter as 'perhaps the most dubious writing' in the New Testament ('Apologia', 169). A far different judgment is offered by Vögtle who describes the letter as offering a significant key to the phenomenon by which the apostolic tradition was rendered into scripture ('Schriftwerdung', 297). These strikingly divergent assessments of the letter continue to present a challenge to any modern interpreter.

Throughout most of the nineteenth century the canonical problem of II Peter was not clearly in focus because it was generally thought that the issue was either identical with or closely akin to the problem of the book's authorship. As a result, the pattern emerged that the letter tended to be highly esteemed by those who defended the authorship of the apostle Peter (Weiss, *Intr.*, Zahn, *Intr.*, Warfield), and its value generally deprecated by those who denied its Petrine source (Abbott, Jülicher, *Einl.*, Knopf). In the English-speaking world the critical debate continued well into the first decades of the twentienth century. The ICC commentary of Bigg still sided with Zahn in 1901. However, the denial of the Petrine authorship by both F. H. Chase and J. B. Mayor did much to bring the nineteenth-century debate to a conclusion. Even though the book continued to be treated with reverence by these Anglican scholars (cf. Chase, 817), little theological contribution was made toward assessing the epistle's canonical function. Actually only in relatively recent times – note the hesitancy of Wikenhauser in 1958 – did an approach emerge among Roman Catholic scholars (Schelkle, Vögtle, Knoch) which sought to assess the book's theological role on the grounds of its pseudepigraphical authorship.

II. The Question of Authorship

The traditionally conservative defence of the Petrine authorship rested on the following points. The letter is explicitly attributed to the apostle and linked to I Peter in 3.1. There are clear references to Peter's eyewitness relationship to Christ (1.16ff.). Evidence for a post-Petrine dating is moot. Later church tradition, even if somewhat fragile, supports its genuineness (Warfield). In addition, conservatives tried to meet the critical attack on the letter's style by positing a different secretary from that of I Peter, or by suggesting that the 'first epistle' of 3.1 was not to be identified with the present canonical epistle (Zahn). Usually the priority of II Peter over Jude has been part of the defence (Spitta, Zahn), or an appeal was made to a common tradition in order to explain the relationship.

In spite of these arguments, the historical critics, making the following points against the Petrine authorship, won the day (cf. Schelkle, HTKNT; Chase, 796ff.).

1. The differences in style, vocabulary, and conception between I and II Peter are too great to be understood as the result of different secretaries, changing situations, or diverse audiences, but reflect different authors.

2. II Peter is literarily dependent on Jude, not *vice versa*, which indicates a relationship which one would hardly expect from an apostolic epistle.

3. A later stage in the life of the church seems apparent when

Paul's letters are described as functioning in a canonical collection along with the Old Testament, and already being interpreted authoritatively (cf. Chase, 810).

4. Signs of a post-apostolic age are evident in the death of the first generation of Christians (3.4), in the manner by which the apostles are addressed (3.2), and by the nature of the eschatological heresy being combatted (3.3ff.).

5. The portrait of Peter (1.13ff., 16ff.) reflects a traditional process at work, both in its form and function, rather than being derived from the personal reminiscences of Peter.

In sum, starting by the end of the nineteenth century and climaxing in the period following World War II, a very wide international and interconfessional consensus has emerged which agrees that the apostle Peter could not have been the author of the epistle of II Peter. The letter is thus described as pseudepigraphical, dated in the second century (125–140), and thought to be the latest addition to the New Testament canon. As will shortly become evident, my major disagreement with this critical consensus lies in the manner in which the non-Petrine authorship of the letter is interpreted. The danger of immediately applying the term pseudepigraphical to describe this indirect relationship of the putative author to the letter lies in focusing on certain features of this literary genre which do not touch at the heart of the real canonical function of II Peter (cf. below).

Conversely, the last major attempt by a conservative scholar to reverse the critical denial of Petrine authorship, that of Michael Green, simply updated the older traditional arguments for direct authorship, but without ever seeing the canonical problem (Tyn, 30). The result is that no real contribution was made in interpreting the canonical function of the letter. Like many of his nineteenth-century predecessors he identified the question of historical authorship with canonical function and turned exegesis into apologetics.

Finally, note should be taken of the recent position developed by R. J. Bauckham (131ff.), whose impressive commentary marks a new direction for conservative scholarship. He has abandoned the traditional defence of the authorship of the apostle Peter, and embraced virtually all the arguments of critical scholarship for pseudepigraphy. However, the uniqueness of his position lies in his argument that both the author and his original audience would have recognized immediately that the letter was 'intended to be an entirely transparent fiction' (134). It was never meant to be taken literally as a letter from Peter. Only at a later date, when a Gentile church no longer understood the convention of a Jewish genre, was Petrine authorship assumed. Significantly, Bauckham has moved away from the traditionally conservative position of identifying truth largely with historical accuracy in that he allows a non-historical genre to be the vehicle for the apostolic witness. In this respect his position is refreshing.

However, in my judgment, there remain several difficulties with his argument. First, there is no clear evidence that the letter was recognized either by its author, and especially by its recipients, as intentional fiction. The historical evidence for an early defence of the Petrine authorship points rather in the opposite direction. Secondly, his theory is too easy a solution for a complex problem, and obscures the genuine difficulty of the whole subject of New Testament pseudepigraphy. The critical position has established itself after a hundred years of hard debate and much resistance. To have its results now embraced as obvious to all its earliest readers, is hardly convincing. Certainly Zahn and his followers did not think it so evident!

III. The Debate over the Letter's Function

Generally speaking, the result of the modern critical debate has been that for several decades primary attention has turned away from the older issue of authorship to the real problem of understanding the function played by the letter within the canonical process of the Early Church. Yet even among scholars who recognize the non-Petrine authorship there remains the sharpest possible disagreement on a theological assessment.

The dominant critical view in Germany which Schenke (*Einl.* II, 321) characterizes as a consensus has reached the following conclusion: The epistle is conceived of as the testament of Peter in support of the emergence of early Catholicism. It is directed against the Gnostics, on the one hand, and to the growing doubt about the parousia, on the other hand. The author appeals to the authority of Peter to legitimate the apostolic tradition as the only avenue to the truth, and to transfer the teaching authority of the tradition to the established offices of the church, to which is assigned the sole right of interpretation.

A brilliant, if extreme, formulation of this same position is found in Käsemann's provocative essay, 'An Apologia for Primitive Christian Eschatology' (1952). He argues that this post-apostolic writer, in order to combat the attack by Gnostics on primitive Christian, that is Pauline, eschatology, launched a defence which proved fatal for Christian theology. The writer fell back on Hellenistic dualism in contrasting a corrupt world doomed to judgment with an incorruptible divine nature of the true Christian religion. Moreover, he changed the correlation of apostle and gospel to that of apostle and church doctrinal tradition, thus redefining faith as dogma and designating the church as sole possessor of correct interpretation. In II Peter *fides catholica* has already emerged.

During the period which followed Käsemann's essay, numerous writers have sought to contest various aspects of his reconstruction (Kelly, Talbert, Moule). For many scholars the heavy Lutheran bias in Käsemann's derogatory use of the term 'early Catholicism' appears not only tendentious, but destroys at the outset serious historical and theological reflection on the letter's role. Fortunately, a more positive evaluation of the book has begun which we shall exploit as we attempt to sketch the canonical shape of the book in a more systematic fashion.

IV. Canonical Function and the Formation of Scripture

The letter of II Peter is cast into the form of a farewell address and final testament. Recent form-critical studies (cf. Munck, Michel) have shown how widespread was the form in both the Old Testament and in post-biblical Jewish literature. However, the closest parallels to II Peter's usage of a farewell address are found in the New Testament itself, particularly in Paul's farewell at Miletus (Acts 20.17–38), and in the letter of II Timothy. In II Peter 1.14 the apostle is pictured as approaching his death of which he had been informed by Christ (1.14). Before the impending end he seizes the opportunity of both instructing and warning the Christian community. He seeks to remind Christians of the apostolic tradition and to guard them from the coming heretics (2.1–3) whose denial of the promise constitutes a sign of the last days (3.1ff.).

Peter's concern for the community of faith extends beyond his own life span. While he is still present with them, he seeks to arouse his readers by reminding them of the truth of the gospel (1.13). However, his main concern in the letter is to extend his apostolic function for future generations of believers after his departure. This expressed intention of the epistle makes it clear that II Peter was never an occasional letter, addressing specific problems within a given congregation, which was later edited to provide a wider canonical function. Rather, even more pronounced than the letter to the Ephesians, II Peter's primary function from the outset was to execute the canonical role of instructing future generations of believers in the faith.

In the epistle the figure of Peter functions as the representative *par excellence* of apostolic authority. He is the 'servant and apostle of Jesus Christ', but also the one who has already participated in the bestowing of 'honour and glory from God' (1.17) on Jesus at the transfiguration. Moreover, it was Christ himself who had revealed to the apostle word of his imminent death (1.14). Peter is not just a figure of the past, but he now functions as a vehicle for extending the apostolic tradition, of which he is the chief representative, into the future. The manner by which this is accomplished is of the greatest theological significance.

A sharp profile of the canonical function of the epistle emerges when it is both compared and contrasted with the Pastorals, especially with II Timothy. Both epistles share the literary genre of the farewell address and are directed to the coming generations of believers. Both letters warn of the danger of future heresy and seek to ground the faithful in the received tradition. Moreover, in both epistles a portrait of the apostolic author is sketched, namely a *Paulusbild* and a *Petrusbild*. Finally, neither epistle functions to 'update' the gospel in the name of an alleged apostle. Rather, the issue of both epistles turns on how the gospel is appropriated and faithfully extended to the next generation. However, it is in the manner by which this task was performed that the two epistles greatly differ.

In the Pastorals Paul's teachings are identified with 'sound doctrine' and are assigned the critical role by which the truth of the gospel is tested. The content of the gospel is not changed, but its faithful transmission to the next generation is guarded by encompassing it within the category of a summary of Pauline teaching. In II Peter the canonical question is addressed in a different manner. The issue does not turn on fixing the content of true doctrine. It is assumed throughout the letter that the true content of the tradition is fully known (1.12). The function of Peter as the primary representative of the apostolic tradition is to extend this apostolic authority to the next generation after the apostle's death. The apostle sets down in writing the authoritative tradition in order that his letter may continually 'at any time' remind the church of its message (1.15). The issue at stake is the creation of a written tradition in the form of an authoritative scripture in order to maintain the church in the truth of the gospel. Vögtle is certainly right in seeing in II Peter a primary witness of the rendering of the apostolic paradosis into a scriptural form (297).

From one perspective both the Pastorals and II Peter can be classified as pseudepigraphical. The writings are not the direct composition of an apostolic author. Yet my reluctance to use the term stems not only from the misconceptions inherent in the term – the flavour of 'pseudo' persists – but also from the unhelpful quality of the category. It offers little aid in pursuing the basic exegetical questions of how the apostolic tradition was shaped in the canonical process to render it accessible to later generations. The term pseudepigraphy continues to lead the discussion astray by wrongly concentrating on the alleged motivation of the pseudo-author in cloaking his own agenda in the guise of an authoritative figure of the past, rather than in focusing on a close reading of the text which has with great freedom assigned an astonishing variety of functions to the putative author of the apostolic tradition in performing its particular canonical role.

In my judgment, Bauckham's attempt (158ff.) to avoid the problem of pseudepigraphy in II Peter by his theory of an intended fictional genre has fallen into the same pitfall of much critical scholarship. In spite of some excellent observations on the role of the book's apostolic content, he also tries to determine the book's canonical role by probing the motives of the pseudo-author. However, in the canonical text this dimension has been obscured and is not the bearer of the text's witness. By tying his interpretation to the author's alleged intentionality he has not addressed the real canonical issue in which the church's reception of the message provides a crucial element in its form and function. Moreover, regardless of the extent of conventions used by the pseudepigraphical author, the letter was shortly received as genuine and functioned canonically as an historical construct. The genuine tension between the historical element of the text and its canonical function remains and cannot be so easily swept under the rug. Bauckham still ties the truth of the biblical witness to author intentionality which remains the crucial issue at the heart of the debate over pseudepigraphy.

For a genuinely canonical approach it is crucial to see how the apostolic tradition, represented by the figure of Peter, is extended to the next generation. Vögtle (300) emphasizes the remarkable fact that it is precisely not through the Petrine office that the extension is achieved. Unfortunately, this important point has been lost on those Protestant interpreters who continue to insist that II Peter is an egregious example of 'early Catholicism' in which the church lays sole claim to a teaching office through Peter's authority (Schenke, *Intr.*, 321; Käsemann, 176).

Nor is the gospel replaced by the church's doctrinal tradition (Käsemann, 176). The content of the witness has not changed, but the means by which the message is preserved and transmitted has been altered. Indeed, a new emphasis is placed on the content which constitutes the apostolic testimony (*fides quae creditur*), but then completely to deny this element of faith in the Pauline letters is to misunderstand the strong lines of continuity which are simply continued by the Pastorals and II Peter (Rom. 10.8; 12.6; Gal. 1.23; Eph. 4.5).

Dahl correctly emphasized the point that the function of the written word was primarily to evoke the church's memory ('Anamnesis', 17). Indeed the epistle is filled with constant references to 'remind' (1.12), 'to refresh your memory' (1.13), 'to recall' (1.15) and 'to arouse your mind by way of reminder . . that you remember the predictions of the prophets and the commandment of the Lord' (3.1f.). The widespread attempt, particularly of German Protestants, to contrast gospel and tradition has badly misunderstood the function of the tradition, whether written or oral, to actualize the gospel.

However, lest the emphasis on memory be misinterpreted as largely a psychological activity, it is important to follow the author's argument as he begins to develop a doctrine of scripture. The writings which function to guide the church in the Christian faith are not confined simply to Peter's epistle, but include the 'predictions of the holy prophets' and the 'commandment of the Lord' which were witnessed to by the apostles (3.2). Moreover, the reference to Paul's letters indicates that the effect of the canonical process was already at work. Paul's letters are received as having been addressed to them (3.15, 'our beloved brother Paul wrote to you'). The canonical function has shifted the weight from the original historical addressees to the present community of faith by whom they have been transmitted. They are now being interpreted along with the 'other scripture' (3.16) as a rule of Christian faith. The source lying behind Paul's letters is the 'divine wisdom which had been granted him' (3.15) and which assured their inspiration (cf. I Cor. 2.6f., 12f.).

In addition, there is a unity and continuity which pervade the sacred writings. The prophetic word has been confirmed by the apostolic experience which rendered the divine promise even more sure (1.19). Both I and II Peter have the same function of recalling the Old Testament prophecies and the evangelical commandments (3.2). Moreover, from the holistic perspective from which the Pauline epistles are now being read canonically, all of Paul's letters are speaking of the same eschatological promise as the prophets and the apostles (3.15f.).

However, with the development of a canon of sacred writings immediately comes the threat of misinterpretation and the writer of II Peter confronts this issue head-on. He begins by making the point strongly that 'no prophecy of scripture (γραφή) is a matter of one's own private interpretation' (1.20). No individual can claim to interpret the sacred writings according to personal whim. The reason for this prohibition then follows immediately, 'because no prophecy ever came from merely human impulse, but men impelled by the Holy Spirit spoke from God' (1.21). The prohibition derives from the source and effect of the prophetic word. As a result what is spoken bears God's message. A correct interpretation of scripture must therefore conform to the Spirit's intention.

Commentators have often argued that an alternative is being presented by II Peter which contrasts private interpretation with the official church rendering. The claim for an ecclesiastical custodianship of scripture is being made. Nor can it be denied that the early Catholic church did make such a claim in its battle with the Gnostics during the second century. However, caution is in order lest later ecclesiastical issues be read back into the epistle. The point being made in the letter is not to contrast unofficial with official interpretation, nor even private with communal. Rather, the writer is establishing the proper context in which scripture should function. He describes its role as the vehicle of divine communication by means of the Holy Spirit through the apostolic witness for the church. The biblical writer is making a theological statement which is not to be either politicized or institutionalized. The contrast is between interpreting scripture as every other product of human imagination which can be construed to sustain one's personal agenda, or in affording it a special status as the channel for the Word of God which must be received as authoritative. The link between scripture, apostolic witness, and church is being clearly made, but the dynamic of this theological claim differs sharply from its subsequent interpretation as a warrant for ecclesiastical custodianship. Heretics are condemned, not because they belong to a different party, but because they twist the truth for their own gain in lawlessness (3.16).

V. The Eschatological Hope

In ch. 3 the writer of II Peter focuses his attack against those who scoff at the hope of Christ's parousia. Käsemann's interpretation is typical of a widespread critical judgment that the delay in the return of Christ was a cause of great embarrassment within the church, and called forth an apology to check the growing disillusionment. However, Talbert has mounted a strong case for holding that it is the heretics (Gnostics) who were the ones disturbed by the church's traditional eschatology. They claim that things would continue as always. 'They are, then, people completely at home in this world, with no hope or expectation of life after death or a world to be renewed' (Neyrey, *Polemic*, 60). Because there would be no judgment, they could live in lawlessness in an alleged freedom. For the writer of II Peter this denial of the parousia struck at the heart of the Christian tradition. It rejected the truth of the divine promise, the reality of which had already been revealed in Christ's transfiguration. When Käsemann interprets II Peter as a relapse of Christianity into Hellenistic dualism, he shows a serious misunderstanding of the letter. The intensity of the response lies precisely in the christological implications of the heresy. Because God will fulfil his promise to bring forth a new heavens and earth, Christians are to respond with 'lives of holiness and godliness' (3.11ff.), growing in 'the grace and knowledge of Jesus Christ' (3.18). Unless God's promise is fulfilled, there is no hope of salvation.

VI. II Peter's Relation to I Peter and Jude

The canonical reading of II Peter approaches the material from a perspective which also throws new light on two classic problems in the epistle which have long exercised critical research.

The first issue turns on the relation of II Peter to I Peter. I have already rehearsed some of the interpretations regarding the explicit linkage of the two epistles in II Peter 3.1. From the conservative side, Zahn sought to maintain the Petrine authorship of the second epistle by positing the theory that the reference was to a lost first letter. He denied that there was an implied relation between the two canonical letters. From the liberal side, Knopf regarded the reference as a literary device of a pseudepigraphical author who sought to increase his own authority. In sum, both positions regard the alleged connection as having little significance.

In the light of this situation, it is refreshing to find a different approach being suggested in an incisive article by Boobyer which comes close to offering what I have described as a canonical reading. Boobyer is concerned to explore the manner by which the author of II Peter was reading I Peter. He raises the question as to how the writer could conclude that both of the letters serve the same function of reminding the reader of the 'predictions of the prophets' and of 'the command of Christ'. Boobyer argues that when viewed holistically, I Peter is addressing the issue of the second coming, the incorruptible heaven, and the coming judgment. Moreover, I Peter appeals to the Old Testament prophets, the spirit of Christ, and the apostles, which are the same authorities for II Peter, when speaking of the Christian salvation which Christ's parousia would inaugurate. From a canonical stance which allows the author of II Peter to identify the recipients of I Peter with his own readers, it becomes an easy step to identify the content of the two letters. Boobyer then proceeds to argue for an indebtedness of II Peter to I Peter which decisively shaped the structure of the second letter.

In my opinion, Boobyer's contribution lies in his posing the question of the relationship of the two Petrine epistles from a canonical perspective, rather than following the older lines which were unaware of the effect of the reinterpretation of their content in the light of a new canonical function within a collection of sacred writings.

The second classic critical issue involves the relation between II

Peter and Jude. Much of the debate focused on the question of the literary priority and a wide consensus has developed that II Peter is dependent on Jude. As a result of this literary decision, it is generally assumed as obvious, when there is parallel material between the epistles, (e.g. II Peter 2.1–18//Jude 4–16) that Jude supplies the original context against which II Peter is to be interpreted. In fact, the point is often made that II Peter 2.11 is incomprehensible without reference to Jude 9 because Peter chose to omit Jude's reference to the assumption of Moses.

From a canonical perspective it is significant to note that whereas an explicit connection is made between I and II Peter, no such linkage is made between Jude and II Peter. The relationship lies in the prehistory of the tradition and can be recovered to some extent through critical reconstruction (cf. Neyrey, *Polemic*, 119ff.). However, it is far from evident that this diachronic dimension plays a crucial role in interpreting the canonical function. Neyrey has made an important point in emphasizing that II Peter produced quite a different statement because he created a different context even though he incorporated Jude's text (143). While it can be granted that some verses in II Peter now appear in a blurred form when compared with Jude, the interpretive task remains to see how the material functions in its own integrity. The critical theory is certainly plausible that by the time of II Peter a more narrowly defined understanding of canonical writings had emerged which resulted in the elimination of references to 'apocryphal' writings still used by Jude. However, such historical explanations, whether right or wrong, are not a substitute for discerning exegetically the canonical role of II Peter in its own integrity within the context of scripture which includes the Old Testament and the Pauline corpus.

28

THE JOHANNINE EPISTLES

Commentaries

F. Lücke, 1826
J. C. K. von Hofmann, 1875/6
R. Rothe, 1878
E. Haupt, ET 1879
A. Plummer, CGTSC, 1886
B. Weiss, MeyerK, ⁶1899
B. F. Westcott, ⁵1908
H. J. Holtzmann, W. Bauer,
  HCNT, ³1908
G. G. Findlay, 1909
R. Law, 1909
A. E. Brooke, ICC, 1912
O. Baumgarten, SNT, ³1918
F. Büchsel, THKNT, 1933
J. Chaine, ÉB, ²1939
C. H. Dodd, MNTC, 1946
F. Hauck, NTD, ⁵1949
H. Windisch, H. Preisker, HNT,
  ³1951

A. Ross, NICNT, 1954
H. Asmussen, ³1957
J. Schneider, NTD, ⁹1961
N. Alexander, TB, 1962
E. Gaugler, ZBK, 1964
J. R. W. Stott, Tyn, 1964
R. R. Williams, CNEB, 1965
J. Michl, RNT, ²1968
F. F. Bruce, 1970
J. L. Houlden, B/HNTC, 1973
R. Bultmann, Herm, ET, 1973
M. de Jonge, PNT, ²1973
I. H. Marshall, NICNT, 1978
R. Schnackenburg, HTKNT, ⁶1978
K. Wengst, ÖTK, 1978
H. R. Balz, NTD, ¹²1980
R. E. Brown, AB, 1982
K. Grayston, NCeB, 1982
P. Bonnard, CNT, 1983

Bibliography

W. **Bauer**, 'Johannesevangelium und Johannesbriefe', *ThR* NF 1, 1929, 135–60; F. C. **Baur**, 'Die johanneischen Briefe. Ein Beitrag zur Geschichte des Kanons', *ThJb* 7, 1848, 293–337; 'Das Verhältnis des ersten johanneischen Briefes zum johanneischen Evangelium', ibid., 16, 1857, 315–31; R. **Bergmeier**, 'Zum Verfasserproblem des II. und III. Johannesbriefes', *ZNW* 57, 1966, 93–100; M.-É. **Boismard**, 'La connaissance dans l'Alliance nouvelle d'après la Première Lettre de Saint Jean', *RB* 56, 1949, 365–91; 'The First Epistle of John and the Writings of Qumran', in *John and Qumran*, ed. J. H. Charlesworth, London 1972, 156–65; J. **Bogart**, *Orthodox and*

Heretical Perfectionism in the Johannine Community as Evident in the First Epistle of John, SBLDS 33, Missoula 1977; G. **Bornkamm**, 'πρέσβυς', TDNT VI, 651–83; H. **Braun**, 'Literar-Analyse und theologische Schichtung im ersten Johannesbrief', *ZTK* 48, 1951, 262–92; reprinted *GS*, Tübingen ²1967, 210–42; R. E. **Brown**, 'The Qumran Scrolls and the Johannine Gospel and Epistles', *CBQ* 17, 1955, 403–19, 559–74; reprinted *New Testament Essays*, Garden City, N.Y. 1968, 138–73; ' "Other Sheep Not of this Fold": The Johannine Perspective on Christian Diversity in the Late First Century', *JBL* 97, 1978, 5–22; 'The Relationship to the Fourth Gospel Shared by the Author of I John and by his Opponents', *Text and Interpretation, FS M. Black*, ed. E. Best and R. McL. Wilson, Cambridge 1979, 57–68; *The Community of the Beloved Disciple*, New York 1979; F. **Büchsel**, 'Zu den Johannesbriefen', *ZNW* 28, 1929, 235–41; R. **Bultmann**, 'Analyse des ersten Johannesbriefes', *Festgabe für A. Jülicher*, ed. R. Bultmann and H. von Soden, Tübingen 1927, 138–58; 'Die kirchliche Redaktion des ersten Johannesbriefes', *In memoriam E. Lohmeyer*, ed. W. Schmauch, Stuttgart 1951, 189–201; reprinted *Exegetica*, Tübingen 1967, 381–93; 'Johannesbriefe', *RGG³*, III, 836–39.

H. **Conzelmann**, 'Was von Anfang war', *Neutestamentliche Studien für R. Bultmann*, ed. W. Eltester, BZNW 21, 1954, 194–201; M. **Dibelius**, 'Johannesbriefe', *RGG²*, III, 346–9; E. **von Dobschütz**, 'Johanneische Studien, I', *ZNW* 8, 1907, 1–8; C. H. **Dodd**, 'The First Epistle of John and the Fourth Gospel', *BJRL* 21, 1937, 129–56; K. P. **Donfried**, 'Ecclesiastical Authority in 2–3 John', *L'Evangile de Jean*, ed. M. de Jonge, *BETL* 4, 1977, 325–33; G. **Eichholz**, 'Glaube und Liebe im 1. Johannesbrief', *EvTh* 4, 1937, 411–37; 'Erwählung und Eschatologie im 1. Johannesbrief', ibid. 5, 1938, 1–28; 'Der 1. Johannesbrief als Trostbrief und die Einheit der Schrift', ibid. 5, 1938, 73–83; A. **Feuillet**, 'Étude structurale de la première épître de saint Jean', *Neues Testament und Geschichte, FS O. Cullmann*, ed. H. Baltensweiler and B. Reicke, Tübingen 1972, 307–27; F. V. **Filson**, 'The Significance of the Early House Churches', *JBL* 58, 1939, 105–12; 'First John: Purpose and Message', *Interp* 23, 1969, 259–76; F. O. **Francis**, 'The Form and Function of the Opening and Closing Paragraphs of James and I John', *ZNW* 61, 1970, 110–26; R. W. **Funk**, 'The Form and Structure of II and III John', *JBL* 86, 1967, 424–30.

E. R. **Goodenough**, 'John a Primitive Gospel', *JBL* 64, 1945, 145–82; J. J. **Gunther**, 'The Alexandrian Gospel and Letters of John', *CBQ* 41, 1979, 581–603; E. **Haenchen**, 'Neuere Literatur zu den Johannesbriefen', *ThR* NF 26, 1960, 1–43, 267–91; reprinted *Die Bibel und Wir*, Tübingen 1968, 235–311; A. **von Harnack**, *Über den dritten Johannesbrief*, TUXV, 3b, Leipzig 1897, 3–27; 'Das "Wir" in den Johanneischen Schriften', *SAB*, Phil.– Hist. Klasse, 1923, 96–113; W. F. **Howard**, 'The Common Authorship of the Johannine Gospel and Epistles', *JTS* 48, 1947, 12–25; P. R. **Jones**, 'A Structural Analysis of I John', *RevExp* 67, 1970, 433–44; M. **de Jonge**, 'The

Use of the word *Christos* in the Johannine Epistles', *Studies in John, FS J. N. Sevenster*, NovTSuppl 24, 1970, 66–74; 'An Analysis of I John 1.1–4', *Bible Translator* 29, 1978, 322–30; E. **Käsemann**, 'Ketzer und Zeuge. Zum johanneischen Verfasserproblem', *ZTK* 48, 1951, 292–311, reprinted *Exegetische Versuche und Besinnungen* I, Tübingen 1960, 168–87; P. **Katz**, 'The Johannine Epistles in the Muratorian Canon', *JTS* 8, 1957, 273f.; G. **Klein**, '"Das wahre Licht scheint schon", Beobachtungen zur Zeit– und Geschichtserfahrung einer urchristlichen Schule', *ZTK* 68, 1971, 261–326; W. **Landbrandter**, *Weltferner Gott oder Gott der Liebe: Die Ketzerstreit in der johanneischen Kirche*, BBET 6, 1977; R. **Leconte**, 'Jean, Épîtres de saint', *DBSuppl* IV, 1949, 797–815; E. **Lohmeyer**, 'Über Aufbau und Gliederung von ersten Johannesbriefes', *ZNW* 27, 1928, 225–63.

E. **Malestesta**, *The Epistles of St John: Greek Text and English Translation Schematically Arranged*, Rome 1973; *Interiority and Covenant*, AnBib 69, 1978; A. **Malherbe**, 'The Inhospitality of Diotrephes', *God's Christ and His People, FS N. A. Dahl*, eds. J. Jervell and W. A. Meeks, Oslo 1977, 222–32; T. W. **Manson**, 'Additional Notes: The Johannine Epistles and the Canon of the New Testament', *JTS* 48, 1947, 32f.; J. L. **Martyn**, *The Gospel of John in Christian History*, New York 1978; *History and Theology in the Fourth Gospel*, New York 1968; rev. ed. Nashville 1979; P. S. **Minear**, 'The Idea of Incarnation in First John', *Interp* 24, 1970, 291–302; F. **Mussner**, *ZŌĒ. Die Anschauung von 'Leben' im vierten Evangelium unter Berücksichtigung des Johannesbriefe*, Theol. Studien 1.5, Munich 1952; W. **Nauck**, *Die Tradition und der Charakter des ersten Johannesbriefes*, WUNT 3, 1957; J. C. **O'Neill**, *The Puzzle of I John*, London 1966; J. **Painter**, 'The Farewell Discourses and the History of Johannine Christianity', *NTS* 27, 1980/81, 525–43; O. A. **Piper**, 'I John and the Didache of the Primitive Church', *JBL* 66, 1947, 437–51; J. B. **Polhill**, 'An Analysis of II and III John', *RevExp* 67, 1970, 461–71; D. W. **Riddle**, 'The Later Books of the New Testament. A Point of View and a Prospect', *JR* 13, 1933, 50–71; E. **Riggenbach**, *Das Comma Iohanneum*, BFChTh 31.4, 1928; J. A. T. **Robinson**, 'The Destination and Purpose of the Johannine Epistles', *NTS* 7, 1960/1, 56–65; reprinted *Twelve New Testament Studies*, SBT 34, 1962, 126–38.

H.-M. **Schenke**, 'Determination und Ethik im ersten Johannesbrief', *ZTK* 60, 1963, 203–15; R. **Schnackenburg**, 'Der Streit zwischen dem Verfasser von 3 Joh und Diotrephes und seine verfassungsgeschichtliche Bedeutung', *MuThSt* 4, 1953, 18–26; 'Zum Begriff der Wahrheit in den beiden kleinen Johannesbriefen', *BZ* NF 11, 1967, 253–58; D. M. **Scholer**, 'Sins Within and Sins Without: An Interpretation of I John 5:16–17', *Current Issues in Biblical Interpretation, FS M. C. Tenney*, ed. G. F. Hawthorne, Grand Rapids 1975, 230–46; E. **Schweizer**, 'Der Kirchenbegriff im Evangelium und den Briefen des Johannes', *StEv* (I), TU 73, 1959, 363–81; reprinted *Neotestamentica*, Zürich and Stuttgart 1963, 253–71; F. **Segovia**, 'The Love and Hatred of Jesus and Johannine Sectarianism', *CBQ* 43, 1981, 258–72; J. **Smit Sibinga**, 'A Study in I John', *Studies in John, FS J. N. Sevenster*,

III, Paris 1959; B. H. **Streeter**, 'The Epistles of St John', *The Primitive Church*, London and New York 1929, 87–97; W. S. **Vorster**, 'Heterodoxy in I John', *Neotestamentica* 9, Stellenbosch 1975, 87–97; K. **Weiss**, 'Orthodoxie und Heterdoxie im I. Johannesbrief', *ZNW* 58, 1967, 247–55; 'Die "Gnosis" im Hintergrund und im Spiegel der Johannesbriefe', *Gnosis und Neues Testament*, ed. K.-W. Tröger, Berlin 1973, 341–56; H. H. **Wendt**, 'Die Beziehung unseres ersten Johannesbriefes auf den zweiten', *ZNW* 21, 1922, 140–6; K. **Wengst**, *Bedrängte Gemeinde und verherrlichter Christus. Der historische Ort des Johannesevangeliums als Schlüssel zu seiner Interpretation*, BTS 5, 1981; *Häresie und Orthodoxie im Spiegel des ersten Johannesbriefes*, Gütersloh 1976; A. **Westcott**, 'The Divisions of the First Epistle of St. John: A Correspondence between Drs. Westcott and Hort', *Exp* VII. 3, 1907, 481–93; W. G. **Wilson**, 'An Examination of the Linguistic Evidence adduced against the Unity of the First Epistle of John and the Fourth Gospel', *JTS* 49, 1948, 147–56; D. B. **Woll**, *Johannine Christianity in Conflict*, SBLDS 60, Chico 1981.

I. The Modern Critical Debate

The modern critical discussion of the Johannine epistles has been treated at great length by Haenchen (*ThR*), and most recently by R. E. Brown (AB). It is not my intention to repeat the discussion, but rather to offer the briefest summary possible.

The debate as to the relation of the writer of the Fourth Gospel and the writer(s) of the epistles has been vigorously pursued, but no longer in reference to John, the son of Zebedee, whose authorship of the Gospel has been dropped even by conservative scholars such as Schnackenburg and Brown. It is generally agreed that the question of authorship cannot be settled solely on the basis of linguistic or stylistic features. There are the strongest similarities and yet striking differences between the two. A majority of scholars would see an important temporal difference between them and assign the epistles to a later date. Dodd characterizes the author of the epistles as a disciple of the evangelist (MCNT, lvi). However, whether one attributes the authorship to one person over an extended period of time, or to a disciple of the evangelist, or to a Johannine 'circle' depends on a critic's larger construal of the evidence. The same judgment holds for the debate regarding the unity of authorship of the three epistles. Evidence is lacking by which to settle the issue decisively.

The issue of the form of the first epistle remains largely unresolved.

It is agreed that the major elements of an epistolary form are lacking, namely, a praescript and conclusion. Attempts to characterize the writings as a tractate or as a homily are unsatisfactory. Nor has Dodd's suggestion of regarding the epistle as a circular letter received much support(xxi). The historical specificity would also speak against describing the addressee as universal in character. The last two letters clearly reflect an epistolary form, but some scholars continue to contend for the fictional nature of the second epistle (Bultmann). Several notable attempts to postulate a *Sitz im Leben* for the first epistle have not met with any wide support (e.g. Nauck, O'Neill). Equally frustrating have been all efforts to determine the structure of I John in any detail. Many useful construals have been proposed, but the evidence by which to ground a particular scheme in the intentionality of the author has been missing up to now.

For several decades Bultmann's two articles have triggered a continuing debate regarding sources and redactions in the first epistle. Although some of his stylistic observations have been well received from his 1927 article, his application of these to a source theory has badly eroded (cf. Wengst, ÖTK, 21ff.). His second article of 1951 sought to apply his redactional theory regarding the Fourth Gospel to the first epistle. He attributed to a secondary ecclesiastical reworking passages which reflected a traditional eschatology (2.28; 3.2; 4.17), a concept of atonement (1.7b; 2.2; 4.10), and the conclusion (5.14–21). Generally speaking, only the issue which questions the integrity of the epistle's conclusion has drawn any wide support.

Finally, an important aspect of the modern debate has focused on questions respecting the background of the epistles. Two major options have emerged which are not mutually exclusive. Some scholars place the greatest emphasis on the impact from outside the community of Gnosticism. Others stress the force of the internal Christian controversy. Both Schnackenburg (14ff.) and R. E. Brown (55ff.) have wisely counselled against the danger of projecting later heretical movements within the early church back into the first century. In the issue of the nature of the conflict much attention has focused on III John in an effort to identify the contestants with larger movements and institutions. Käsemann's theory of identifying the Presbyter as a Gnostic served a function in stimulating the debate, but, as far as I can see, has been universally rejected (cf. Bultmann, Herm, 95).

II. New Directions of Interpretation and a Critique

The debate over the interpretation of the Johannine epistles has recently entered a new phase with the publication of a massive commentary by R. E. Brown. Certainly no future discussion of the issues can be deemed adequate which does not seriously deal with Brown's learned interpretation. Because the major interpretive issue turns ultimately on one's understanding of the purpose of the epistles, I intend to sharpen the issue of a canonical reading of these letters by comparing and contrasting it with Brown's proposal.

Brown (69ff.) depicts the background of I John as an internal struggle between two different groups within the Johannine community, both of which find a warrant for their positions in an interpretation of the tradition of John's gospel. Dissension had increased to the extent that a schism had occurred before the writing of I John. The author of I John writes his composition against the secessionists both to justify his interpretation of John's tradition and to strengthen his own group within the larger Johannine circle. The writer consciously fashions his composition to be a type of commentary on John's Gospel, even imitating the structural features of the Gospel. According to Brown, the heart of the controversy lay in a christological disagreement when the secessionists sought to relativize the salvific importance of Jesus' earthly life. Brown's exegetical method is first to reconstruct the theology of the secessionists which he then attempts to link directly to a particular interpretation of John's Gospel. Throughout his commentary Brown interprets the Johannine letters in a direct relation to this debate which he has reconstructed.

Brown concludes by suggesting that historically the secessionists were assimilated into later Gnostic movements which accounts for the Gnostics' enthusiasm for John's Gospel. Conversely, the path from the Johannine epistles led to Catholic Christianity. He summarizes the significance of the struggle: 'Thus the ultimate contribution of the author of I John to Johannine history may have been that of saving the Fourth Gospel for the church' (150).

In my judgment, Brown's approach to the Johannine letters, particularly to I John, reveals some major problems which touch upon the heart of the entire exegetical enterprise. First, Brown's exegesis of I John is made to rest completely upon his theoretical reconstruction of the opponents of the author. Much of the weight of the entire construct is built upon I John 2.19, which is assigned pivotal significance. Yet nowhere in the letter of I John is a clear profile of the opponents given. If there are other voices recorded within the epistle, they are not explicitly identified, but serve as foils for the author's positive christology. Nevertheless, Brown feels confident at every stage in identifying the opposition, their motives, and theology.

Secondly, a major element in Brown's thesis is that the writer of I John was consciously offering an interpretation of John's Gospel which was in opposition to its misconstrual by the secessionists. To support this hypothesis, Brown not only reconstructs the secessionists' position, but further attempts to trace the origin of each doctrinal stance in a reconstructed interpretation of some passage of John's Gospel. However, without solid evidence to support either end of the hypothesis, what purports to be an historical investigation is actually an exercise in creative imagination with very few historical controls. Repeatedly the reader is told what the secessionists 'probably' thought, or 'perhaps' intended. As a result, much of the exegesis rests on a highly speculative basis.

Thirdly, in order to support his theory regarding the purpose of the epistles, Brown is constantly forced to historicize the biblical text. This criticism is not to suggest that the text is devoid of concrete historical reference. Such an argument would be disproved by I John 2.19 alone. However, the different levels of historical referentiality within the letter are disregarded or flattened, and the text is interpreted in direct relation to Brown's reconstructed referent regardless of the level of clarity. The text receives the same referential interpretation whether the alleged historical element lies in the background or the foreground of the text. The text is translated in the same manner, always to make the same point. Although Brown takes note of stylistic differences, these differences in rendering reality play no significant role in determining the text's meaning.

The effect of this historicizing of the text is both a narrowing and a flattening of the epistle's message. Virtually every text functions as an anti-secessionist polemic. Thus, the 'sin unto death' (I, 5.16f.) is identified as the sin of the secessionists (636). The subtle balance between thesis and antithesis (2.4–11) is all rendered into a monotonous polemic against the same schismatics. Likewise, the prologue (1.1–4) becomes a deliberate refutation of the adversaries. The content of the entire first epistle turns out to be largely polemical, not because of the author's expressed purpose, but because an apologetic context has been established by Brown from the outset. Yet the real aim of the first epistle is not primarily polemical, as A. E. Brooke long ago recognized (ICC, xxvii).

Fourthly, Brown's thesis seriously threatens the independent integrity of the epistles, especially of I John (cf. Schnackenburg, HTKNK, 3). Although he avoids the terms, he interprets the epistles as a kind of midrash on the Gospel of John. That the epistles can be interpreted meaningfully in such a context cannot be denied. A particular dynamic has been set in motion by Brown which is certainly not unintelligible. Similarly one can interpret Genesis 1 as a direct refutation of the Babylonian myth of creation. Had not the Priestly writer direct contact with the traditions of Babylon and even used similar vocabulary? Nevertheless, it is generally recognized in Old Testament circles that to posit a context of intentional polemics is to misconstrue Genesis 1, and to set into motion an erroneous dynamic between two texts which are only indirectly related. The same analogy holds true for I John's relation to the Gospel. The extent to which Brown presses his theory of direct relationship appears in his strained effort even to find in the structure of I John an imitation of the Gospel (116ff.).

Lastly, there is a final point to make which is directly related to the question of canon. Brown has asserted that the ultimate contribution of the writer of I John was in saving the Fourth Gospel for the Christian church. In my judgment, the statement is an exaggeration. Nevertheless it does contain an important element of truth. Within the Christian church the epistle of I John became a significant guideline by which to read the Fourth Gospel from the late second century onwards. However, this statement is a description of a canonical function of the post-apostolic era. It describes a control which one part of the canon exercised on reading another. It assumes a community of faith which received as authoritative both writings and sought to interrelate the two.

In my judgment, Brown has misunderstood the nature of I John's canonical function. He has projected a later canonical role of the epistle back into the period of the epistle's composition, attributing it to the original author's intention. This move results in an anachronism. In the later stages of the New Testament canonical process, when the church possessed both writings within its collection of scripture, it used I John to assure a proper interpretation of the

Fourth Gospel against Gnostic distortions. However, Brown is forced to construct an elaborate and highly speculative hypothesis in order to defend the original function of I John as offering a guide to the Gospel. As a result, he has misconstrued the character of the epistle itself by making it into a largely polemical writing and confused the canonical process.

To summarize, in the case of the Johannine epistles the concern to understand the canonical function of a New Testament book illustrates an important exegetical control. It seeks to establish the various levels of meaning which the sacred text acquired, and to show their proper historical interdependence.

III. The Canonical Role of the Epistles

The concluding task is to offer a brief description of some of the important indices within the biblical text which serve the reader in discerning how the epistles are to function canonically.

The prologue of I John (1.1–14) offers the clearest indication of the writer's purpose. The similarities and differences between it and the prologue to John's Gospel have often been pointed out (Dodd, 1ff.; Schnackenburg, 49ff.; Wengst, 34). If the Gospel prologue is focused on the historical encounter of the Logos with the unbelieving world, the epistle has shifted the interest to the assurance of the experience of faith in the Eternal one, the proclamation of which has brought life to the believer. The exact meaning of the phrase 'from the beginning' has been much discussed, especially in the light of the parallels within the letter. At least two important features seem to be included in the phrase. 'That which is from the beginning' is certainly to be identified with 'the one who is from the beginning with the Father' (2.13), but in addition there is the function of the reception of the faith (2.24; 3.11), which involves a concept of tradition as well.

The writer of the prologue expressed himself in the most extreme fashion possible in emphasizing the experience of having 'heard, seen, looked upon and touched' the Word of life. However, it is not an individual voice which bears witness to the revelation from the beginning, but the community of believers, 'we', addressing a plural 'you'. The major concern of the witness is in first grounding its testimony in apostolic attestation by an eyewitness experience of the reality. Over against the various attempts to understand metaphorically the witness's claim to have been historically contemporary with the earthly Jesus, Schnackenburg has correctly insisted upon the author's intention to ground his witness in an event which was once-for-all manifested in an earthly appearance (53ff.). Moreover, to speak of 'an eschatological contemporaneity' with Jesus by the community (Conzelmann) does not do justice to the writer's thought in the prologue.

While the writer emphasizes that Christ was revealed in flesh and blood to a community of faith, the major concern of the prologue is to communicate the message of life to those – to 'you' – who have themselves not experienced Christ first-hand. 'That which we have seen and heard we proclaim also to you' (1.3). The witness of the 'we' is grounded in a physical experience of Jesus, but the present and future generations of 'you' experience the fellowship of eternal life through the proclamation of the message. The rest of the epistle then expounds the theological implications of fellowship with Christ for the Christian life, the emphasis falling on the need for love to manifest itself in deed and in truth (3.18).

The prologue offers an important canonical guide in attaching the witness of the 'we' firmly to the incarnation of Jesus Christ, but defining the 'you' as those who subsequently appropriate the gospel through its proclamation. When Brown restricts the addressees to contestants in a first-century controversy whose profile he details referentially by means of a reconstructed history, he sets up a dynamic which is not only foreign to the text, but which greatly impedes its continuing canonical function as scripture of the church. The referent of the letter is the theological reality of the gospel manifest in the human life of the believer. The function of the epistle is not in offering an apology for one party's correct reading of a tradition.

A second point of canonical significance is the lack of a praescript and a conclusion to the first epistle. Kümmel's suggestion (*Intr.*, 437) that I John is not to be understood as being in any way a writing intended for specific readers, 'but is a tractate intended for the whole of Christianity' falls into an error which is at the far side of the spectrum of Brown. The epistle is clearly addressed to a specific community which is known by the author. Moreover, the frequent reference to writing (13 times) confirms its epistolary nature and speaks against describing the composition as a homily. Although the epistle is saturated with the language and thought of the Fourth Gospel, there is no indication that the relationship between the two is on a midrashic level.

My own suggestion is to take seriously the later canonical inclusion of the Johannine epistles within the corpus of the 'catholic epistles' (*contra* Brown, 4). Even though the original addressee was a specific, historical community, the letter of I John was received as having a universal application. Already we have seen a clear pattern in the editing of the letters of Paul and Peter of attempts to generalize the particularity of the original function. It is possible that I John once had both a praescript and a conclusion. If it once had such, the loss must have occurred almost immediately in the transmission process since no textual evidence reflects the presence of either. Regardless of how one is to explain the omission, the effect of the present structure of I John is to move its interpretation in exactly the opposite direction from that proposed by Brown, and to universalize its message for the whole church. Again it is significant that Kümmel correctly recognized the letter's later canonical function, but was mistaken in failing to distinguish it from its original historical role.

Finally, I think it significant that all three of the Johannine epistles were included under the same canonical rubric as catholic epistles, even though the literary form of the latter two letters is very different from that of the first. Regardless of how one interprets the addressee of II John – is it to be taken literally or metaphorically? – the letter now functions in a generalized manner after the fashion of I John. The effect of the canonical rubric is the same for III John. The canonical ordering of the epistles is also a guide pointing toward the same end. One does not find the key to I John in the historical particularity of III John, but just the reverse. The last two letters illustrate the universal message of the gospel which is manifest in the daily life of the church.

29

JUDE

Commentaries

E. H. Plumptre, CB, 1880
J. C. Huther, MeyerK, ET 1881
H. von Soden, HCNT, 1892
E. Kühl, MeyerK, 61897
A. Plummer, ExpB, 31901
C. Bigg, ICC, 21902
J. B. Mayor, 1907
R. Knopf, MeyerK, 71912
G. Hollmann, W. Bousset, *SNT*
   31917
G. Wohlenberg, KNT, 31921
J. W. C. Wand, WC, 1934
J. Chaine, ÉB, 21939
H. Windisch, H. Preisker, HNT,
   31951
J. Moffatt, MNTC, 71953

F. Hauck, NTD, 71954
C. E. B. Cranfield, TB, 1960
J. Schneider, NTD, 91961
G. H. Boobyer, Peake, 1962
B. Reicke, AB, 1964
E. M. Sidebottom, NCeB, 1967
A. R. C. Leaney, CNEB, 1967
E. M. B. Green, Tyn, 1968
J. Michl, RNT, 21968
J. N. D. Kelly, B/HNTC, 1969
W. Schrage, NTD, 111973
W. Grundmann, THKNT, 21979
K. H. Schelkle, HTKNT, 51980
J. H. Elliott, Augs, 1982
R. J. Bauckham, Word, 1983

Bibliography

T. **Barns**, 'The Epistle of St Jude: A Study in the Marcosian Heresy', *JTS* 6, 1904/5, 391–411; J. C. **Beker**, 'Jude, Letter of', *IDB*, II, 1009–11; G. H. **Boobyer**, 'The Verbs in Jude II', *NTS* 5, 1958/9, 45–7; F. H. **Chase**, 'Jude, Epistle of', *DBHastings* II, 699–806; M. **Delcor**, 'Le mythe de la chute des anges et de l'origine des géants comme explication du mal dans le monde dans l'apocalyptique juive. Histoire des traditions', *RHR* 190, 1976, 3–53; E. E. **Ellis**, 'Prophecy and Hermeneutic in Jude', *Prophecy and Hermeneutic in Early Christianity*, Grand Rapids 1978, 221–36; I. H. **Eybers**, 'Aspects of the Background of the Letter of Jude', *Neotestamentica* 9, Stellenbosch 1975, 113–23; G. **Krodel**, 'The Letter of Jude', *Hebrews – James – I and 2 Peter – Jude – Revelation* (Proclamation Commentaries), Philadelphia 1977, 92–98; R. **Leconte**, 'Épître de Jude', *DBSuppl* 4, 1288–91; J. B. **Lightfoot**, 'The

Brethren of the Lord', *Epistle to the Galatians*, London 1869, 247–82; F. W. **Maier**, *Der Judasbrief. Seine Echtheit, Abfassungszeit und Leser*, Freiburg 1906; C. D. **Osburn**, 'The Christological Use of I Enoch 1.9 in Jude 14,15', *NTS* 23, 1976/7, 334–41; P. J. **du Plessis**, 'The Authorship of the Epistle of Jude', *Biblical Essays, Proceedings of the Second Meeting of Die Nieuwe-Testamentiese Werkgemeenskap van Suid-Afrika*, Potchefstroom 1966, 191–9; B. **Reicke**, *Diakonie, Festfreude und Zelos*, Uppsala 1951, 352–67; D. J. **Rowston**, 'The Most Neglected Book in the New Testament', *NTS* 21, 1974/5, 554–63.

K. H. **Schelkle**, 'Spätapostolische Briefe als frükatholisches Zeugnis', *Neutestamentliche Aufsätze für J. Schmid*, ed. J. Blinzler, Regensburg 1963, 225–32; A. **Schlatter**, *Die Theologie der Apostel*, Stuttgart ²1922, 119–26; F. **Spitta**, *Der zweite Brief des Petrus und der Brief des Judas*, Halle 1885; B. H. **Streeter**, *The Primitive Church*, London and New York 1929, 178–80; H. **Werdermann**, *Die Ihrlehrer des Judas- und 2. Petrusbriefes*, BFChTh 17.6, 1913; F. **Wisse**, 'The Epistle of Jude in the History of Heresiology', *Essays on the Nag Hammadi Texts in Honour of Alexander Böhlig*, ed. M. Krause, Leiden 1972, 133–43.

I. The Modern Critical Debate

The earlier critical discussion over the epistle of Jude which began in the mid-nineteenth century focused largely on two major problems. First, did the epistle reflect an apostolic or post-apostolic age, and secondly, what was the most probable identity of Jude? For those who argued for the apostolic age of the letter, Jude was thought to be the brother of James, the leader of the Jerusalem church (Mark 6.3), not an apostle, but one who did not mention his kinship with Jesus out of modesty. Support for this position was found in the rather strong attestation of its canonical status by the end of the second century. For those who argued for the post-apostolic age of the letter, Jude was a pseudonymous author who chose that particular name as the brother of James from some knowledge of his epistle, the exact nature of which is no longer fully understood (cf. Rowston, 560ff.). Part of this debate involved also the relation of Jude to II Peter and Jude's use of so-called apocryphal literature.

However, the evidence from the epistle itself was too sparse to resolve the issue decisively. Both sides were forced to construct the case from arguments drawn from a larger view of the development of early Christianity and from the history of New Testament canonization. Within the last several decades the pendulum has clearly swung in the direction of those who view the letter as post-apostolic and pseudepigraphical. Indeed, the large majority of Catholic scholars (Schelkle, Knoch, Vögtle) now support this latter position which was once defended only by radical Protestants. Still the interpretation of the letter is far from settled by the decision regarding its authorship and dating.

There has been a strong tendency among many critical scholars to polemicize against the letter along with II Peter. The author is thought to have little Christian message (Kümmel *Intr.*) and to reflect the worst side in the development of 'Early Catholicism'. The concept of faith has been described as having hardened into a fixed tradition of dogma (*fides quae creditur*). Those opponents who disagree with the author of Jude are scolded as heretics, but there is no positive content to the debate. The alleged false teachers are simply abused by the writer (Käsemann, Marxsen, *Intr.*, Krodel).

In recent years a somewhat different approach has emerged which has shifted the debate more in the direction of determining the role of the letter in the history of heresiology rather than in evaluating the contribution of its theological content by itself. Rowston, building on the earlier research of Werdemann, tries to describe the opponents of Jude without identifying them with any known system. He concludes by evaluating Jude's contribution historically. It serves as 'a reminder of the struggle against an ethically distorted and theologically diluted Christianity from c. AD 90, and through II Peter, until c. AD 190' (563). Jude tries to combat a growing antinomianism within the church by reviving a form of apocalypticism in order to check an erosion of the faith toward Gnosticism. J. C. Beker also evaluates the contribution largely historically. He sees Jude adding to our knowledge of the complex history of heresy within the church and documenting the early struggle between orthodoxy and heresy (*IDB* II, 1009).

Then again, in an important article F. Wisse attempts to determine the role of the epistle in the history of heresiology from a fresh perspective. He contends that the author had no concrete heresy in mind, which accounts for its lack of specific content, but the writer makes use of stereotyped stock phrases which he took from the description of eschatological false prophets in Jewish and early Christian literature. Moreover, the purpose of the letter was not to combat heretics within the early church, nor to rid the church of false teachers. Rather, his aim was to inform Christians that the enemies of the last days had arrived. The reference to the ancient evildoers was not simply to offer an illustration, but they are mentioned because these instances speak prophetically about the present. The ancient enemies are really portraits of the false teachers of the present.

Wisse has made several positive contributions. By addressing the issue of the letter's function, he has explained well the reason for the lack of specific content, and has undercut in large measure the polemic against the letter's theological originality. The use of the Old Testament figures as representative eschatological types also explains why the dimension of pastoral concern, so clear for example in Paul, is completely missing. Wisse's emphasis on the centrality of the expectation of the parousia is also highly significant. Yet ultimately Wisse has not adequately assessed the function of the letter, and certainly not its canonical role. Both Rowston, Beker, and Wisse remain content with viewing the letter simply as an historical document of the post-apostolic period without raising the basic theological question of how such an epistle functioned within the collection of authoritative writings for successive generations of Christians.

There is one final aspect to the modern debate which needs to be mentioned. In recent years it has become a widespread practice to refer to the New Testament's use of midrash, by which is meant a homiletical use of the Old Testament employing certain conventions of Jewish exegesis. For example, E. E. Ellis views the recognition of midrash as providing the key for interpreting the letter of Jude. Doubtlessly, many of the formal conventions of Jewish exegesis are reflected in the New Testament. Nevertheless, I have a growing conviction that the use of the term 'midrash' can be very misleading. Crucial to Jewish midrash is a particular hermeneutical under-standing of the biblical text which implies not only a closed corpus of canonical literature, but a dogmatic construal of the written text's relation to Jewish oral tradition. Jewish midrash is, therefore, text-oriented in a very different manner from that of early Christianity. If the term midrash is used for the New Testament interpretation, it should be carefully defined and probably limited to formal conven-tions of Hellenistic exegesis. The epistle of Jude is a good example of both elements of a continuity with Jewish, Hellenistic interpretation, and a striking dissimilarity in the function of the Old Testament within the New. To this canonical issue I now turn.

II. The Canonical Role of the Epistle

At the outset, it is important to recognize that in spite of similarity in content with portions of II Peter, the canonical function of the letter of Jude is not the same. II Peter's concern is to address the question of how the fixed apostolic traditions represented by the figure of Peter function as written scripture for later generations of Christians. Although Jude shares the witness to an established tradition – 'for the faith once-and-for-all delivered to the saints' – it is the converse side of this testimony which is now emphasized, namely, the heresy which threatens the true Christian faith.

The epistle of Jude addresses the phenomenon of heresy and not any one specific form of error. Indeed, what characterizes the approach is that heresy is now dealt with as a theological referent, and not simply as an historical danger confronting a particular congregation. Moreover, the writer makes clear that it is constitutive of the Christian faith to be always threatened by this terrifying dimension of falsehood. One cannot even talk of a common salvation without setting it in the context of a fundamental repudiation of this hope.

The identification of the threat of heresy by means of Old Testament figures serves to underline the major theological point that the alternative of unbelief was there from the beginning and is nothing new. Cain is the epitome of unrighteousness who murders his own brother. Balaam serves as the classic example of the corrupter who perverts for personal gain. Korah personifies blasphemy and rebellion against divine authority (cf. Wisse, 140). The selfsame threat continues at work in the false teachers who have secretly gained entrance into the community of faith.

The letter of Jude is a 'catholic epistle' *par excellence* in that it addresses from the outset a general audience of the faithful, and was never intended to be an occasional letter (*contra* Bauckham). In the light of the persisting threat of heresy of which the apostles had explicitly warned (vv. 17ff.), the Christian community is urged to maintain the faith which has been entrusted to it. However, Wisse is surely wrong in flatly historicizing the hope of the parousia. The eschatological tension of maintaining the foundation of the faith, of praying in the spirit, and awaiting the last day in expectation of Christ's return (vv. 17ff.) is constitutive of faithful Christian living for all times.

The function of the concluding doxology instead of the usual final greetings in the letter further emphasizes the catholic message of the epistle. The ultimate grounds for steadfastness in the faith lies with God, who rescues those who believe from destruction on the last day and whose authority extends from the past, to the present, and into the future. The eschatological hope is not a curious vestige of early Christianity, but an essential part of the promise of salvation, which is grounded in the 'glory, majesty, dominion and authority' of God (v. 25). When the canonical process collected the letters of the apostles along with their intense expectation of Christ's return to serve as authoritiative scripture, it extended the theological tension between promise and fulfilment into every successive generation of Christians. However, this move was not a peculiar concession on Jude's part, but an understanding which extends throughout the entire New Testament, and strives in a variety of ways to bear truthful witness to the full dimension of Christ's redemption.

The theological function, therefore, of Jude's letter cannot be understood in isolation from its role within the larger canonical corpus. The letter offers a theological description of the phenomenon of heresy rather than attacking a specific historical form of error. Nevertheless, a clear theological profile of heresy emerges. Error consists in 'denying our Master and Lord' (v. 4), in perverting God's grace by immorality and lawlessness (v. 7), and in rejecting divine authority for one's own advantage (v. 16).

The letter of Jude does not function canonically to provide the content of the apostolic tradition in an independent fashion. This subject-matter is assumed as known, received, and understood. Rather, the letter's function lies in guarding the tradition against corruption. A theological dynamic is set in motion by the canonical process. On the one hand, the epistle of Jude offers a larger theological appraisal of the phenomenon of heresy by which to interpret the specific historical examples in the rest of the New Testament, especially of the Pauline letters. On the other hand, the witness of the larger canon provides the actual content of the 'faith once-and-for-all delivered unto the saints' which the letter of Jude earnestly strives to preserve.

30

THE CORPUS OF CATHOLIC EPISTLES

Bibliography

H. **Balz**, *Die 'Katholischen' Briefe* (NTD[11]), Göttingen 1973, 1–4; E. **Fascher**, 'Katholische Briefe', *RGG*[3], III, 1198f.; A. **Jülicher**, E. **Fascher**, *Einleitung in das Neue Testament*, Tübingen [7]1931, 186–9; P. **Katz**, 'The Johannine Epistles in the Muratorian Canon', *JTS* 8, 1957, 273f.; J. B. **Mayor**, *The Epistle of St James*, London[3]1913, 290f.; W. **Michaelis**, *Einleitung in das Neue Testament*, Bern [3]1961, 147–9; J. **Michl**, *Die Katholischen Briefe*, Regensburg 1968, 5–13; A. **Plummer**, *St James and St Jude*, London and New York [3]1901, 1–10; A. **Strobel**, 'Die Kirchenbriefe in der neuen Auslegung', *Lutherische Monatshefte* 3, 1963, 1ff.; B. F. **Westcott**, *A General Survey of the History of the Canon of the New Testament*, London [7]1876, 548–90; T. **Zahn**, *Geschichte des Neutestamentlichen Kanons*, II, Erlangen and Leipzig 1890, 375–80.

In distinction from the collection of the four Gospels and the epistles of Paul, which first were accorded canonical authority, there was a third collection of New Testament writings which acquired the collective terminology of the 'catholic epistles'. Included were the seven letters of James, Peter, John and Jude.

The term 'catholic epistles' (*καθολικαὶ ἐπιστολαί*) first appeared in the Greek Church, but was originally used in the singular to designate a single letter as 'catholic'. In this usage it occurs frequently in Origen and Dionysius. Perhaps the earliest occurrence is found in Apollonius (c. 197) who designated the drafting of a catholic letter by the heretic Themison as a imitation of 'the apostle's' (John?) (Jülicher 187). The use of the plural term to describe a group of epistles in a closed collection appears first in Eusebius (*Hist. eccl.* II, 23.25; passage cited by Zahn, II, 376).

In spite of earlier controversy, there is now a general agreement that the term was initially a formal one designating a letter addressed to a general or wide circle of readers. It did not carry the value judgment of orthodox or canonical. Since Eusebius used the term for five epistles which belonged to the class of 'disputed' (*antilegomena*) and were not universally admitted to be canonical, the term could not refer to the book's reception as authoritative. There is no evidence that the term catholic originally marked the letter as authoritative in distinction from other letters. However, as the term was adopted by the West, it increasingly acquired the sense of authoritative or canonical (*epistolae canonicae*). Augustine occasionally referred to all the New Testament letters as canonical epistles which further blurred the original distinction. During the Middle Ages the terminology of the catholic epistles was again generally limited to the collection of the seven letters, but with the meaning of 'universal'. The term 'general epistles' is the English equivalent of the term, but derived from the Latin.

The sequence of the seven epistles varies greatly in the early catalogues (cf. Zahn II, 376ff.). The order: James, Peter, John, Jude is found in many of the Greek Fathers (Eusebius, Cyril, Athanasius). It was preferred by Jerome and thus became fixed in the Vulgate. However, several other ancient orders gave the lead position to Peter. Of perhaps more significance was the canonical ordering of the catholic epistles. The order which placed them immediately after the book of Acts was very ancient. Tischendorff and also Westcott and Hort attempted to restore this order in their editions of the Greek New Testament. However, the influence of Jerome through the Vulgate has been dominant; there the catholic epistles follow the Pauline.

In sum, the term remains a useful one to designate a collection of New Testament writings which is distinct from the Gospels and the Pauline corpus. It is neither a precise canonical nor a modern genre classification. Its usage has no great theological significance other than to reflect the church's growing concern that the New Testament letters be understood as universal, even when, in their original form, they often carry a specific addressee (cf. II and III John).

PART SIX

REVELATION

31

REVELATION

Commentaries

J. A. Bengel, 1740, [3]1758
J. G. Eichhorn, 1791
M. Stuart, 1845
E. W. Hengstenberg, [2]1861–62;
H. Alford, [3]1866
J. C. K. von Hofmann, 1874
W. Milligan, ExpB, 1886
F. Düsterdieck, MeyerK, [4]1887
W. Bousset, MeyerK, [6]1906
H. B. Swete, [2]1907
H. J. Holtzmann, W. Bauer,
    HCNT, [3]1908
F. J. A. Hort, chs. 1–3, 1908
I. T. Beckwith, 1919
R. H. Charles, ICC, 1920
A. Loisy, 1923
T. Zahn, KNT, 1924–26
W. Hadorn, THKNT, 1928
E.-B. Allo, ÉB, [3]1933
R. C. H. Lenski, 1935
W. Hendriksen, 1939

M. Kiddle, MNTC, 1941
J. Sickenberger, [2]1942
R. H. Preston, A. T. Hanson, TB,
    1949
K. Hartenstein, [3]1954
J. Behm, NTD, [7]1957
H. Lilje, ET [5]1958
M.-É. Boismard, SB, 1959
A. Wikenhauser, RNT, [3]1959
A. Farrer, 1964
T. F. Glasson, CNEB, 1965
G. B. Caird, B/HNTC 1966
L. Morris, Tyn, 1969
C. Brütsch, ZBK, [2]1970
G. E. Ladd, 1972
H. Kraft, HNT, 1974
G. R. Beasley-Murray, NCeB, 1974
J. M. Ford, AB, 1975
R. H. Mounce, NICNT, 1977
J. Sweet, Pel, 1979
E. Lohse, NTD, [12]1979

Bibliography

P. **Althaus**, *Die letzten Dingen*, Gütersloh [5]1949; C. A. **Auberlen**, *The Prophecies of Daniel and the Revelation of St John*, ET Edinburgh and Andover, Mass. 1856; D. L. **Barr**, 'The Apocalypse as a Symbolic Transformation of the World', *Interp* 38, 1984, 39–50; R. **Bauckham**, 'Synoptic Parousia Parables and the Apocalypse', *NTS* 23, 1976/7, 162–76; W. **Bauer**, 'Chiliasmus', *RAC* 2, 1954, 1073–8; W. A. **Beardslee**, 'New Testament Apocalyptic in Recent Interpretation', *Interp* 25, 1971, 419–35; J. **Becker**, 'Pseudonymität der Johannesapokalpse und Verfasserfrage', *BZ* NF 13, 1969, 101f.; A. A. **Bell**, Jr., 'The Date of John's Apocalypse. The Evidence of Some Roman Historians Reconsidered', *NTS* 25, 1978/9, 93–102; F. **Boll**, *Aus der Offenbarung Johannis*, Berlin 1914; G. **Bornkamm**, 'Die Komposition der apokalyptischen Visionen in der Offenbarung Johannis', *ZNW* 36, 1937, 132–49; reprinted *Studien zu Antike und Urchristentum, G* II, Munich ²1959, 204–222; W. **Bousset**, *Der Antichrist in der Überlieferung des Judentums, des Neuen Testaments und der alten Kirche*, Göttingen 1895; W. **Bousset**, H. **Gressmann**, *Die Religion des Judentums im späthellenistischen Zeitalter*, HNT 26, ³1926; J. W. **Bowman**, *The Drama of the Book of Revelation*, Philadelphia 1955; 'Revelation, Book of', *IDB* IV, 58–71; D. **Brady**, *The Contribution of British Writers between 1560 and 1830 to the Interpretation of Revel 13.16–18*, BGBE 27, 1983; F. C. **Burkitt**, *Jewish and Christian Apocalypses*, Schweich Lectures 1913, London 1914.

G. B. **Caird**, *Principalities and Powers*, Oxford 1956; 'On Deciphering the Book of Revelation', *ExpT* 74, 1962/3, 13–15, 51–3, 82–4, 103–5; L. **Cerfaux**, 'La Vision de la Femme et du Dragon', *ETL* 31, 1955, 21–33; R. H. **Charles**, *Studies in the Apocalypse*, Edinburgh 1913; C. **Clemen**, 'Die Stellung der Offenbarung Johannis im ältesten Christentum', *ZNW* 26, 1927, 173–86; A. Y. **Collins**, *The Combat Myth in the Book of Revelation*, Harvard Diss. in Religion 9, Missoula 1976; J. J. **Collins**, 'Pseudonymity, Historical Reviews and the Genre of the Revelation of John', *CBQ* 39, 1977, 329–43; G. **Delling**, 'Zum gottesdienstlichen Stil der Johannes-Apokalypse', *NovT* 3, 1959, 107–37; V. **Eller**, *The Most Revealing Book of the Bible: Making Sense Out of Revelation*, Grand Rapids, 1974; E. B. **Elliott**, *Horae Apocalypticae*, 4 vols. London ⁴1862; A. **Farrer**, *A Rebirth of Images: the Making of St John's Apocalypse*, London 1949; A. **Feuillet**, 'Essai d'interprétation du chapitre XI de l'Apocalypse', *NTS* 4, 1957/8, 183–200; *L'Apocalypse: l'état de la question*, Paris 1963; 'La premier cavalier de l'Apocalypse', *ZNW* 57, 1966, 229–60; E. S. **Fiorenza**, 'The Eschatology and Composition of the Apocalypse', *CBQ* 30, 1968, 537–69; 'Apocalyptic and Gnosis in the Book of Revelation and in Paul', *JBL* 92, 1973, 565–81; 'The Quest for the Johannine School: The Apocalypse and the Fourth Gospel', *NTS* 23, 1976/7, 402–27; 'The Revelation to John', *Hebrews – James – I and 2 Peter – Jude – Revelation*, ed. G. Krodel (Proclamation Commentaries), Philadelphia 1977, 99–120; 'Composition and Structure of the Revelation of John', *CBQ* 39, 1977, 344–66.

H. **Gebhardt**, *The Doctrine of the Apocalypse*, ET Edinburgh 1878; L. **Goppelt**, 'Heilsoffenbarung und Geschichte nach der Offenbarung des Johannes', *TLZ* 77, 1952, 513–22; H. W. **Günther**, *Der Nah- und Enderwartungshorizont in der Apokalypse des heiligen Johannes*, FzB 41, Würzburg 1980; H. **Gunkel**, *Schöpfung und Chaos in Urzeit und Endzeit*, Göttingen ²1921; A. T. **Hanson**, *The Wrath of the Lamb*, London and New York 1957; L. **Hartman**, *Prophecy Interpreted*, Uppsala 1966; D. **Hill**, 'Prophecy and Prophets in the Revelation of St John', *NTS* 18, 1971/2, 401–18; H.-U **Hofmann**, *Luther* *und die Johannes-Apokalypse*, BGBE 24, 1982; T. **Holtz**, *Die Christologie der Apokalypse des Johannes*, TU 85, ²1971; M. **Hopkins**, 'The Historical Perspective of Apocalypse 1–11', *CBQ* 27, 1965, 42–7; K. P. **Jörns**, *Das hymnische Evangelium – Untersuchungen zu Aufbau, Funktion, und Herkunft des hymnischen Stücke in der Johannesoffenbarung*, SNT 5, 1971; M. **Kaehler**, 'Die Bedeutung, welche den "letzten Dingen" für Theologie und Kirche zukommt', *Dogmatische Zeitfragen* II, Leipzig ²1908, 487–521; J. **Kallas**, 'The Apocalypse – An Apocalyptic Book?', *JBL* 86, 1967, 69–80; K. **Koch**, *The Rediscovery of Apocalyptic* ET, SBT II 22, 1972; H. **Kraft**, 'Zur Offenbarung des Johannes', *ThR* 38, 1974, 81–98.

S. **Läuchli**, 'Eine Gottesdienststruktur in der Johannesoffenbarung', *TZ* 16, 1960, 359–78; J. **Leipoldt**, *Geschichte des neutestamentlichen Kanons*, Leipzig 1907, 51–60; E. **Lohmeyer**, 'Die Offenbarung des Johannes 1920–1934', *ThR* NF 6, 1934, 269–314; 7, 1935, 28–62; E. **Lohse**, 'Die alttestamentliche Sprache des Sehers Johannes', *ZNW* 52, 1961, 122–6; F. **Lücke**, *Versuch einer vollständigen Einleitung in der Offenbarung des Johannes oder Allgemeine Untersuchungen über die apokalyptische Literatur überhaupt und die Apokalypse des Johannes insbesondere*, Bonn ²1852; G. **Maier**, *Die Johannesoffenbarung und die Kirche*, Tübingen 1981; P. S. **Minear**, 'Eschatology and History', *Interp* 5, 1951, 27–39; 'The Wounded Beast', *JBL* 72, 1953, 93–102; 'The Cosmology of the Apocalypse', *Current Issues in New Testament Interpretation, FS O. Piper*, ed. W. Klassen and G. Snyder, New York and London 1962, 23–37; 'Ontology and Ecclesiology in the Apocalypse', *NTS* 13, 1966/7, 89–105; *I Saw a New Earth*, Washington and Cleveland 1968; H. P. **Müller**, 'Die Plagen der Apokalypse', *ZNW* 51, 1960, 268–78; Isaac **Newton**, *Observations upon the Prophecies of Daniel and the Apocalypse of St John*, London 1733; A. T. **Nikolainen**, 'Der Kirchenbegriff in der Offenbarung des Johannes', *NTS* 9, 1962/3, 351–61; 'Über die theologische Eigenart der Offenbarung des Johannes', *TLZ* 93, 1968, 161–70; J. **Oman**, *The Book of Revelation*, Cambridge 1923; O. **Piper**, 'Johannesapokalypse', *RGG³*, III, 822–34; F. C. **Porter**, 'Revelation, Book of', *DBHastings*, IV, Edinburgh 1903, 239–266; P. **Prigent**, *Apocalypse 12: Histoire de l'éxegèse*, BGBE 2, 1959; 'L'Apocalypse: Exégèse Historique et Analyse Structurale', *NTS* 26, 1979/80, 127–137.

W. M. **Ramsay**, *The Letters to the Seven Churches in Asia*, London and New York 1904; M. **Rissi**, 'Das Judenproblem im Lichte der Johannesapokalypse', *TZ* 13, 1957, 241–59; 'Die Erscheinung Christi nach Off. 19, 11–16', *TZ* 21, 1965, 81–95; *Time and History: A Study on the Revelation* ET Richmond 1966; *The Future of the World*, SBT II 23, 1972; M. **Rist**, 'Apocalypticism', *IDB*, I, 157–61; J. A. T. **Robinson**, *Redating the New Testament*, London and Philadephia 1976, 221–253; A. **Sand**, 'Zur Frage nach dem "Sitz im Leben" der apokalyptischen Texte des Neuen Testaments', *NTS* 18, 1971/2, 167–77; A. **Satake**, *Die Gemeindeordnung in der Johannesapokalypse*, WMANT 21, 1966; A. **Schlatter**, *Das Alte Testament in der johanneischen Apokalypse*, BFChTh 16.6, 1912; H. **Schlier**, 'Jesus Christus und die Geschichte nach der Offenbarung des Johannes', *Besinnung auf das Neue Testament*, GA II, Freiburg 1964, 358–73; W. **Schmithals**, *Die Apokalyptik: Einführung und Deutung*, Göttingen 1973; R. **Schnackenburg**, 'Zur Vorgeschichte der "Antichrist"-Erwartung', *Die Johannesbriefe*, HTKNT, Freiburg ⁵1975, 145–49; R. **Schütz**, *Die Offenbarung des Johannes und Kaiser Domitian*, FRLANT 50, Göttingen 1933; E. F. **Scott**, *The Book of Revelation*, London 1939, New York 1940; F. **Spitta**, *Die Offenbarung des Johannes*, Halle 1889; E. **Stauffer**, *Christ and the Caesars*, ET London and Philadelphia 1955; K. **Stendahl**, 'The Apocalypse of John and the Epistles of Paul in the Muratorian Fragment', *Current Issues in New Testament Interpretation*, FS O. Piper, ed. W. Klassen et al., New York and London 1962, 239–45; M. E. **Stone**, 'Coherence and Inconsistency in the Apocalypses: The Case of "The End" in 4 Ezra', *JBL* 102, 1983, 229–43; N. B. **Stonehouse**, *The Apocalypse in the Ancient Church*, Goes 1929; H. **Strathmann**, *Was soll 'die Offenbarung' des Johannes im Neuen Testament*, Gütersloh ²1949; A. **Strobel**, 'Abfassung und Geschichtstheologie der Apokalypse nach Kap. 17, 9–12', *NTS* 10, 1963/4, 433–45; *Kerygma und Apokalyptik : ein religionsgeschichtlicher und theologischer Beitrag zur Christologie*, Göttingen 1967; L. **Thompson**, 'Cult and Eschatology in the Apocalypse of John', *JR* 47, 1967, 330–50; W. C. **van Unnik**, 'De la regle (μήτε προσθεῖναι μήτε ἀφελεῖν) dans l'histoire du canon', *VigChr* 3, 1949, 1–36; reprinted *Sparsa Collecta* II, Leiden 1980, 123–56; E. **Vanhoye**, 'L'utilization du livre d'Ezéchiel dans l'Apocalypse' *Bibl* 43, 1962, 436–76; P. **Vielhauer**, 'Apocalypse: Related Subjects, Introduction', 'Apocalyptic in Early Christianity, 1. Introduction', *NT Apoc* II, 581–607, 608–41; E. **Vischer**, *Die Offenbarung Johannes, eine jüdische Apokalypse in christlicher Bearbeitung*, Berlin ²1895; D. **Völter**, *Entstehung der Apokalypse*, Freiburg ²1885.

B. B. **Warfield**, 'The Millennium and the Apocalypse', *Biblical Doctrines*, New York 1929, 643–64; H. E. **Weber**, 'Zum Verständnis der Offenbarung Johannis', *Aus Schrift und Geschichte*, FS A. Schlatter, Stuttgart 1922, 47–64; J. **Weiss**, *Die Offenbarung des Johannes*, Göttingen 1904; C. **von Weizsäcker**, *The Apostolic Age of the Christian Church*, II, ET London and New York 1895, 173–205; J. **Wellhausen**, *Analyse der Offenbarung Johannis*, Berlin 1907; H. **Windisch**, 'Der Apokalyptiker Johannes als Begründer des neutestamentlichen Kanons', *ZNW* 10, 1909, 148–74.

The difficulty and attraction of the book of Revelation are evident throughout the history of the Christian church. No book within the New Testament exhibits such a wide range of disagreement on its interpretation. The controversy extends from the early church fathers to modern times, and has engaged many of the most brilliant minds (e.g. Isaac Newton, J. A. Bengel, Jonathan Edwards), often with disastrous results.

Commentaries and introductions frequently sketch the different hermeneutical approaches which have been used over the centuries (cf. Lücke; Bousset, 49ff.; Charles, *Studies*). Yet even before the rise of the modern critical method the extravagances and wild speculations associated with its interpretation caused many of the more sober exegetes of the church to view the whole enterprise with suspicion. Luther was largely negative in both editions of his Preface, and Calvin omitted writing a commentary on the book.

A lasting and positive contribution of the historical-critical method was in its rendering certain traditional interpretive options fully obsolete. There is a wide consensus that all interpretations which would see in the book a prefiguring of various epochs of world or church history are misconstrued. It is difficult now even to imagine that a volume like Elliott's *Horae Apocalypticae*, which offered a detailed correspondence between the structure of Revelation and the age of Constantine, the Reformation, and the rise of Islam, could have been widely viewed as the standard treatment in England during the mid-nineteenth century. Modern commentators, both conservative and liberal, are agreed that the book arose during a crisis of the first century and was addressed to the needs of its recipients of the same period within the thought patterns of that era. In sum, the book offers neither a blueprint of future history nor a timeless symbol system.

Of course, the crucial theological issue turns on whether the book offers anything beside being a tract for the times. How does it function as authoritative scripture in its first-century time-conditionality? Many modern commentators continue to be concerned with the theological issues, but are equally convinced that the interpreter's primary task lies in first resolving the critical philological, literary, and historical questions. For this reason the greatest energy of the modern period has focused on these latter issues. The shift of focus from Auberlen and Gebhardt to Bousset and Charles is unequivocal and characteristic of most modern critical research.

I. Historical-critical Issues

It was natural that the modern critical re-appraisal of the character of the book of Revelation would result in much attention being directed to the historical background of the period. The intense and highly developed scholarly discipline of classical studies, both in Europe and Britain, made the research into the Roman emperor cult and its effect on the early church an easy one. Fresh archaeological data respecting the cities of Asia Minor during the Hellenistic and Roman periods was also provided by W. R. Ramsay, among others. For a while it was thought that the interpretive task was largely one of correlating the biblical symbols with concrete historical events and personages of the period. Moreover, there seemed to be enough indications within the text to support this approach. The reference to the 'seven kings, five of whom have fallen' (17.10) seemed to cry out for correlation with the well-known sequence of Roman emperors. The difficulty lay in deciding where to begin one's calculation and whether all the emperors were to be included or only those involved in the notable persecutions of the church.

The historical approach seemed for many to have resolved once and for all two classic problems which were associated with the 'beast'. What was the meaning of the cryptic number 666 (13.18), and who was the 'wounded beast' (13.3)? By assuming a form of gematria in which the letters of the alphabet were used to denote numbers, and by translating the Greek form of Nero Caesar into Hebrew letters (cf. Beckwith, 403ff.), one obtained the required sum of 666. In spite of some nagging problems with this solution – why should one use Hebrew? – it appeared to many to offer a highly convincing warrant for the historical approach (Charles, I, 363ff.). In a similar way, the appeal to the legend of a reincarnated Nero who, after his suicide, was thought not to have died but to have escaped to Parthia in anticipation of his return (cf. Tacitus, Suetonius), was widely held to explain the imagery of the Antichrist in 13.3 as both wounded and healed (Charles, II, 80ff.).

Although few modern commentators would be prepared to reject these classic historical solutions out of hand – Minear is a bold exception (*New Earth*, 247ff.) – there is a growing dissatisfaction with the easy way in which biblical imagery and historical figures were correlated. The issues of symbolism, literary genre, and fluctuating tradition pose a complexity which does not allow for a simple method of 'decoding' the text. In the history of critical scholarship, a recognition during the last quarter of the nineteenth century of the complexity of the book's composition began to shift attention to a new set of problems away from simple interchange between text and history.

Traditionally, the issues associated with the book's composition have begun with a discussion of authorship and dating (cf. Beckwith, 343ff.). Many of the early church Fathers (Justin, Irenaeus, Tertullian, Origen) were convinced that the author of the Apocalypse was to be identified with the writer of the Fourth Gospel, namely, the apostle John, the son of Zebedee. Support for the unbroken continuity within the tradition was found in the wide ecclesiastical circulation of the Apolcalypse during the second half of the second century both in Asia Minor and in the West. However, the tradition was soon contested by Dionysius, bishop of Alexandria, who in the third century presented an elaborate argument, characterized by its critical sophistication, for defending a diversity of authorship. Especially forceful was his pointing out the differences in style, grammar and vocabulary between the Fourth Gospel and the Apocalypse. The problem of authorship became even more confusing in the modern period as the complexity of issues also surrounding the authorship of the Fourth Gospel multiplied. Although a few conservative scholars, such as Zahn, continued to defend the Johannine authorship of the entire canonical corpus, a majority ascribed the Apocalypse to a separate author, either to the cryptic John the Elder of Ephesus who was mentioned by Papias (Eusebius, *Hist. eccl.*, III, 39.4), or to an unknown apocalyptic writer. A few scholars followed Bousset's theory of a circle under the influence of the Elder from Asia Minor from which both writings emanated (179). However, the issue of authorship increasingly lost its significance as the unity of the book itself came under attack.

During the latter part of the nineteenth century there ensued a heated debate among those who felt that the duplications and inconsistencies within the book called into question the book's unity and required a more complex literary solution. Particularly disturbing were the apparent structural interpolations in chapters 7, 10–11, 12 and 17. Scholars such as Völter, Spitta, and Weizsäcker took the lead in offering a variety of different literary theories. Some envisioned the book as consisting of separate fragments much after the model of the Pentateuch which evolved through a lengthy process. Others, such as Vischer, posited a Jewish apocalyptic source which had been subsequently appropriated by a later Christian writer (cf. the most recent compilation theory of J. M. Ford). Still others contended for a complex redactional reworking of disparate parts into a relatively unified composition. Wellhausen thought that he

had discovered an independent oracle in 11.1f. which had been
written before AD 70 and which expressed confidence that the temple
in Jerusalem would be preserved. Among these critics it was generally
assumed that the incorporation of diverse material was part of a
rather wooden, even mechanical editing process.

Fortunately, by the end of the nineteenth century the predominantly literary approach to resolving the compositional problems of
the book of Revelation came under increasing attack from the history-
of-religions school of Gunkel and Bousset. Unfortunately for English
scholarship, the older literary approach to the book continued to
find its representative in R. H. Charles. His massive two-volume
commentary in the ICC series has remained the classic English
treatment, and is unexcelled in its thorough treatment of text,
grammar, and literary sources. Nevertheless, Charles' view that the
Apocalypse has been transmitted by a 'very unintelligent disciple'
who was 'profoundly ignorant of his master's thought' (II, xxii) is a
tendentious approach in the extreme and has done much to hinder
a more profound and empathetic handling of the biblical material
from emerging.

Much of the credit for a fresh approach to the book of Revelation
goes to Gunkel and his colleague, W. Bousset. In the concluding
portion of his brilliant monograph, *Schöpfung und Chaos*, Gunkel
turned his attention to the material in Revelation 12. In spite of
certain extravagances which Bousset later sought to modify, Gunkel
was able to demonstrate the elements of oral tradition of an extremely
early origin in the portrayal of the dragon's battle with the woman.
He argued not only that the material was originally mythological,
but that its roots reached back into the Babylonian era. Gunkel's
comparative method in the analysis of tradition was pursued vigorously by Bousset in a full-blown commentary. The effect of the
approach was to break out of the impasse between an uncritical
defence of the unity of the book and seeing it as an artificial
conglomerate of literary fragments.

Another contribution of the comparative method was in setting
the discussion in a much broader context and in pursuing the whole
question of the nature of the apocalyptic material, both in terms of
sociological phenomena and literary conventions. The comparative
material from Enoch, Baruch, and IV Ezra began to be fully
exploited. As a result, many of the features which in the nineteenth
century were thought illogical or simply bizzare began to be seen as

consistent with the general function of apocalyptic imagery in a particular situation of crisis.

In the contemporary debate over interpreting the book, there have been several attempts to apply the insights from the new literary tools toward resolving the complexities of the book's structure. For example, E. S. Fiorenza argues strongly for the unity of the book on the synchronic level. She has tried to describe literary techniques of intercalation as a key to understanding the structure, and concludes that the work is a 'carefully planned. . .artistic composition' (Proc. Com. 100). Others have sought to construe the book as a drama with its own inner laws of consistency (Bowman). In my judgment, the difficulty of many of these attempts lies in the claims of a demonstrable intentionality by the author for a particular reading. I would prefer a literary approach which would take advantage of the multi-layered quality of the biblical text by defining its unity more in functional terms in relation to its use by different circles of readers within varying contexts.

Finally, a word is in order concerning the theological understanding of the book. Although the major focus of critical research has not been on the theological dimension in a way comparable to the pre-critical era, the issue of how to deal adequately with this dimension of the text on the basis of a thoroughly critical exegesis of the book has not been completely overlooked. Was it possible to overcome the largely negative assessment of the book's theology which Bousset offered in characterizing it as a 'confusing conglomerate of different christological concepts' (140)?

Among English commentaries the older idealistic categories remain the dominant ones. Beckwith (291) still tries to distinguish between the 'permanent and the transitory elements' of the book. Caird applies Dodd's concept of 'realized eschatology' to the book, but with limited success. Perhaps the leading advocate of a theology of *Heilsgeschichte* is M. Rissi. His exposition is often profound as he seeks to develop a theology of history and eschatology. The problem remains, however, whether such a category which allegedly spans the entire New Testament can do justice to the peculiar features of the Apocalypse.

Then again, H. Lilje offers a powerful theological interpretation of the book as a witness to God's final history. He sees all the imagery focusing on the reality of the end of history and God's final victory. Undoubtedly, Lilje has recovered an important element of the book's theology, but others will question whether the full range of theological notes has been heard with this reading. Another powerful theological interpretation which grew out of the experiences of World War II is offered by K. Hartenstein. The book which is largely unknown in the English-speaking world, stands in the exegetical tradition of Auberlen and provides a modern actualization of the Apocalypse which is often profound and penetrating. Finally, serious attention must be given to P. Minear's sustained work in the theology of the book which has extended over a lifetime. In my judgment, Minear's most brilliant contribution is found in his article on 'The Cosmology of the Apocalypse', in which he broke new ground by exploring the peculiar theological stance which undergirds the biblical writer's view of reality. His later monograph was less successful in exploiting these earlier and exciting insights.

The concern of the rest of this chapter will be to see to what extent attention to the canonical process and its effect will aid in recovering a theological witness of the book which has suffered from yesterday's controversies.

II. The Canonical Shape of the Book

My study of the canonical shape of the book of Revelation will focus on two sets of issues. First, I shall seek to understand how the apocalyptic author structured his message in order to address a first-century Christian audience. Secondly, I shall seek to determine how this original function of the book was altered by its subsequent canonical role within the New Testament corpus. I feel justified in including the first question as part of the earlier stage of the canonical process because the writer sought to reinterpret inherited prophetic traditions in such a way as to witness faithfully to God's word for a new generation of Christians.

A. The Form and Function of the Book in the First Century

There is a general modern agreement that the writer of the Apocalypse sought to encourage first-century Christians who were facing grave persecutions under the Roman state by reference to God's great eschatological plan for the church and the world. The message is directed to the contemporary community of faith with a word for the future. The basic significance of chs. 1–3 lies in its firmly connecting the visions which dominate the rest of the book (chs. 4ff.) with an initial word of exhortation to seven local churches of Asia Minor. The visions do not rest on an historical prologue constructed by means of a *vaticinium ex eventu* which is typical of most apocalyptic writings, but are grounded in the perspective of the present (cf. J. J. Collins, 333ff.).

The crucial issue turns on the manner by which the writer achieved his purpose. As a Christian prophet he sought to bring to the churches a fresh revelation of God's plan which he experienced in a series of visions. He formulated his message in the imagery of the Old Testament, predominently from Daniel, and of the Synoptic Gospels, particularly the traditions of Matt. 24. Although the book of Revelation is completely saturated with the Old Testament – Westcott-Hort count 278 references in 404 verses – the writer did not employ a method of citations, but creatively adapted the ancient traditions to his own purpose. The use of the Old Testament is, therefore, prophetic in nature and not midrashic. His focus is not on the Old Testament text as such, but on an eschatological reality which he depicts by means of the Jewish scriptures. The writer can so easily combine the Old Testament with the apocalyptic traditions of Matthew 24 (and parallels) because the Synoptic Gospels had already given the prophecies of Daniel a canonical reading. Rome was the Fourth Kingdom spoken of by Daniel, and the coming of the expected Antichrist would be preceded by the 'desolating sacrilege' (Matt. 24.15) and the messianic woes. However, the central point to make, and indeed the heart of the canonical issue for the book of Revelation, is that the New Testament writer offered a profound reinterpretation of the whole Old Testament in the light of his understanding of Jesus Christ. But in order to develop this theme, some preliminary interpretation of the literary problems of the book is required.

The difficulty of analysing the structure of the book of Revelation has long been recognized. Because of the predominant role assigned to the symbol of the number seven – seven churches, seven seals, seven trumpets – the view has been defended by many that Revelation contains seven visions (Hadorn, 4). The major problem with this analysis is to explain the interpolations and expansions which seem to disregard this scheme. One option is to take the route suggested by Charles who assumed that the later redactor was incompetent, and as a result, the modern interpreter is required to recover some earlier and allegedly clearer stage of the literature. The high level of subjectivity in such a move is obvious. Another way to proceed is to take the final form of the present book seriously and seek to determine how the complex structure functions within the book as a whole.

The first observation to make is that there is a remarkable parallelism in content between the seven trumpets (chs. 8–11), and the seven vials (ch. 16). Bousset has charted the elements of parallelism (401f.). The intensification of judgment in the vial series does not obviate the common traits in both. The relationship between the first series of judgment in the seven seals (6.1–8.1) and the two latter septets remains contested. Hadorn (74ff.) and others argue that the seal septet is different in kind from the latter two and serves only a preparatory function. However, several other features enter the picture which would rather show that the three septets share a common function and are to be treated together.

First, each of the sections covers the same period within the divine economy, namely, from Christ's first coming to his second. Chapter 5 which introduces the opening of the seal septet speaks of the 'slain Lamb' (vv. 6, 9). There follows the depiction of the final judgment (6.12–17) in the terms of Isa. 34.4. Finally 7.9–14 portrays the deliverance of the saints who have already experienced the great tribulation (7.14.). Similarly, the sequence of the seven trumpets also depicts the final judgment and the reign of Christ (11.15–18) as a fulfilment of the prophet's word (10.7), at which time the saints are rewarded (11.18). Again, the description of the seven vials picks up the saying of Jesus about keeping awake for the coming of the bridegroom (Matt. 25.13), and moves to the fall of Babylon and the final judgment. Finally, chs. 12–14, which now separate the last two septets, follow the same pattern, and extend from the birth of the Messiah (12.2) to the coming of the Son of Man in final judgment (14.14ff.).

Secondly, the period of the great persecution preceding the end which Daniel depicted in the imagery of 'time, two times, and half a time' (Dan. 7.25) is adapted and continued in the book of Revelation. The prophetic number indicating the period of the tribulation appears within the expanded section of the seven trumpets (11.2) and also in the section describing Christ's battle with the dragon (12.6, 14). Therefore, it seems proper to draw the implication that the two sections are not set in a chronological scheme, but depict the same eschatological sequence from different perspectives.

Thirdly, there is the additional Old Testament warrant for seeing a pattern of reduplication in the structure of Revelation. The book of Daniel sets forth an initial prophetic vision of the future which moves through a sequence of four kingdoms until the last is destroyed by the coming of the kingdom of God. Chapter 7 then repeats the same sequence, but focuses attention on the period of the fourth monarchy in the coming of the divine rule. Again in chs. 8 and 10–11 the same pattern is followed and interpreted from yet another perspective. In spite of an intensification of the imagery the pattern of reduplication of the one prophetic sequence is evident.

To summarize the point, it should come as no surprise that the book of Revelation is constructed according to a traditional pattern of reduplication. The material is not chronologically ordered which probably accounts for the ease with which the original sequence was expanded by interpolations in order to enrich the basic eschatological pattern of the book.

The book of Revelation reflects a traditional apocalyptic scheme of the endtime which it shares with other apocalyptic sections of the New Testament (Matt. 24 and parallels; II Thess. 2; II Peter 3). The basic outline is provided by Daniel with the portrayal of the persecution of the saints, the coming of the messianic woes leading up to the great tribulation, and the appearance of the Antichrist. The New Testament prophet thus affirms the truth of the older prophecy respecting God's people. When the church has been taxed to its uttermost limit, the kingdom of God is ushered in with the coming of the Son of Man. However, this basic apocalyptic scheme of the New Testament has been enlarged and developed by imagery from other parts of the Old Testament. Psalm 2 provided the standard imagery for the rebellious nations (Rev. 2.26), Joel 2 for the cosmic disorders (Matt. 24.29f.; Rev. 6.12), and Isa. 66 for the hope of the new heavens and earth (Rev. 21.1).

The crucial theological point turns on the alteration of this traditional apocalyptic pattern which the writer of the book of Revelation effected. On the basis of a new understanding of christology a profound alteration of the apocalyptic tradition took place. The eschatological drama which consummated God's plan for his creation now takes place on two different dimensions of both time and space (cf. Minear, 'Cosmology').

There is the dimension of reality seen from the perspective of heaven. The book of Revelation begins with a description of God 'who is, and who was, and who is to come' (1.8; 4.8), the First and the Last (1.17). Obviously within this perspective human time is transcended. The same epitaph is repeated in 22.13, thus bracketting the entire book, but it has now been transferred to Christ as its referent. God is pictured enthroned above his creation, and being worshipped by everything living (4.8ff.). Indeed, the point is emphasized repeatedly in every cycle that God now rules his universe and his kingdom has come (7.10; 11.15; 19.6, etc.). Divine judgment has already taken place (14.7, 14ff.; 15.4; 16.4ff.). Satan has been defeated by the Lamb, and he has been cast out of heaven (cf. Luke 10.18). Moreover, the saints of God surround the throne, singing the new song in celebration of God's victory (5.11ff.; 14.1ff.). The Antichrist has been conquered once and for all by the Lion of Judah.

The effect of this christological understanding is that the whole apocalyptic scenario, inherited from Daniel, when viewed from the perspective of the heavenly reality has been reinterpreted as completed action. It does not lie in the future because Christ has encompassed the past, present and future into one redemptive purpose. In the light of this divine reality the entire Old Testament prophecy is interpreted as simply adumbrating God's purpose of judgment and salvation realized in Christ. Babylon has fallen (18.2), Michael has defeated the dragon (12.7), and the plagues of Egypt have been executed (chs. 8–11). The effect of this christological alteration is that the apocalyptic scenario has been turned into a peculiar kind of metaphor. It is no less true in this form, but it now serves to adumbrate the reality of God's judgment and salvation whose true profile is rendered only in Jesus Christ.

Yet there is another dimension of reality portrayed by the apocalyptic writer which is viewed from the perspective of the earth. The church still lives in time and space. There is a past, present, and future. There is Jerusalem and Rome. The church experiences the reality of suffering and death, and the face of the beast is mirrored in the emperor cult, which grows more threatening with the passing of each day (Günther, 67ff.).

The writer of the book of Revelation uses the apocalyptic visions of Daniel to identify both the Christ and the Antichrist. They bring into focus the nature of ultimate evil as well as the final triumph of good. They include cosmological evil, false prophets, and a city which personifies corruption. The author employs the apocalyptic material as a means by which to concretize that moment of time in the church's struggle with Rome within the framework of this eschatological scheme. Indeed, there are literary signs that the text was secondarily reworked in order to concretize even further the historical specificity within the apocalyptic events (17.1–14).

There are several implications to be drawn from this interpretation of the end. First, from the perspective of the earth, which the writer also shares with the suffering church, human time is taken seriously. The writer nowhere denies the reality of the church's persecution. Its suffering is not an illusion. The biblical writer allows the tension to continue between the two perspectives of reality, a heavenly and an earthly. Yet the major point being made is that in the cross, which is God's decisive moment within history, human history receives its meaning. Thus the cross bears witness to the church's earthly perspective of reality that the endtime lies in the past. Even the imagery of the future millennium serves to depict another aspect of Christ's ultimate victory over evil (20.7ff.) which unfolds gradually. Hartenstein articulates the concern succinctly: 'Eternity is not timeless, but unfolds in stages' (172).

Secondly, the christological reinterpretation of the apocalyptic tradition serves as a major source of encouragement to those living under severe threat. Frequently the writer of Revelation sounds the call for endurance (13.10; 14.12), even unto death (2.10). The grounds for the hope of the Christian derive from the present kingship of God, already being celebrated in heaven. The Christian, sharing a human perspective on time and space, lives in both confidence and acute tension. From this stance emerges the shrill cry: 'Come, Lord Jesus' (22.20).

Thirdly, the writer of the book of Revelation has encompassed all the cosmological evils which plague the church within the sphere of God's power. Judgment comes when God breaks the seals, signals the trumpets to be blown, and orders the pouring of the seven vials of his wrath. Because of the slain Lamb, the ancient enemies of the church have been robbed of their independent power and made to play out their subordinate roles within God's great plan.

B. The Canonical Interpretation of Revelation

The major theological issue in the church's continued use of this first-century book as scripture is clearly posed by Beckwith: '. . . what is its practical value for the faith and conduct of another age?. . . Rome was not destroyed, Nero did not return, Antichrist did not appear. . . and the End with its stupendous events has not come' (292). The canonical approach which we shall offer in response to this basic question stands in conscious opposition to the numerous theological options currently expoused: one can learn from the church's piety even if misinformed. There are some timeless ideas about God present in the book. Warrants for Liberation Theology are adumbrated. Endtime offers a current existential moment within human existence. These options have only in common their complete disinterest in the issue of canon as providing a hermeneutical guide in scripture.

We begin by observing the similarities and differences in the manner by which the apocalyptic material of Daniel and Revelation were shaped. Both books arose in periods of great crisis for the community of faith. Both writers presented a message of judgment and salvation in terms filled with concrete, historical specificity. Daniel envisioned the imminent end in association with the rise of the fourth monarchy from which the Antichrist emerged. When Antiochus IV Epiphanes did not prove to be the ultimate enemy, those receiving the book as a divine authority projected the entire vision of the fourth kingdom into the future and regarded Daniel's prophecies as still unfulfilled. The history of the interpretation of the book of Revelation indicated clearly that many Christians have sought to appropriate the New Testament apocalypse according to the same pattern which had been used for Daniel. Accordingly, the visions were loosened from their first-century moorings and pushed into the future. In our judgment, such a move has failed to reckon with the hermeneutical guides within the book of Revelation which the canonical process has provided in order to aid in its future appropriation by the community of faith.

As we have already argued, the writer of Revelation has radically reinterpreted the book of Daniel in the light of his christology. God's decisive event in defeating the cosmological power of evil lies in the past. In the event of the cross, God's reign was forever established and Satan defeated. Indeed the church continues to suffer in tension under persecution, but it lives in the confidence that victory has already been won. The apocalyptic imagery of Daniel now serves the function of identifying the defeated enemies of God and of the church who act from an earthbound perspective as if they were still in control.

From a canonical perspective the decisive move by which the book of Revelation could be appropriated by successive generations of believers has already been made by the original author. The continuing message of the book was indeed moored in history, namely, God's history in Christ. However, the traditional apocalyptic scenario which the first-century author has painted with a Roman backdrop now serves only as a vivid illustration of that recurring eschatological threat by which each successive generation of the faithful was challenged to endure. The witness of the book is equally true, whether concerning Nero, Genghis Khan, or Hitler. 'The kingdom of the world has become the kingdom of our Lord and of his Christ, and he shall reign for ever and ever' (11.15). To express the point homiletically: the supreme threat facing the world is not the possibility of a nuclear holocaust, but the absolute certainty of God's coming to judge his creation in righteousness.

As in the case with Daniel, the medium of apocalyptic symbolism greatly aided in providing a vehicle for the book's continued canonical function. Daniel never spoke of Antiochus, nor did Revelation ever identify the Antichrist with Nero. Even if the original author had intended to reveal the identity of the enemy with the cryptic number 666, the symbolism was such as to continue to function kerygmatically while allowing an original referentiality to become inoperative for later readers. If it were unclear for the first generation of Christians how literally to understand the exhortation, 'the time is near' (1.3; 22.12,20), for the later users of the book within the context of the whole New Testament, there are enough indicators given by which to interpret its true theological function. Günther speaks of the eschatological idiom as 'primarily a qualitative characterization of the endtime' (279). For the Christian living in the tension of a split vision of reality, an earthly and a heavenly, the appeal to the imminent coming of Christ serves as a constant reminder that God's reality is close at hand, evoking the proper response of faith: 'Then come quickly, Lord Jesus' (22.20f.).

In addition to these broad hermeneutical guidelines provided by the book, there are some specific literary features which serve an important canonical function. I begin with an analysis of the initial introductory section (1.1–3), called by some a superscription, and the epilogue (22.6–21). A comparison of their literary features brings out clearly the difference in function. In the epilogue many of the themes of the introduction are repeated. God affirms that the words concerning the future which has been given the prophet are true (v. 6), and a blessing is pronounced on those keeping the prophecy. Then the writer is instructed not to seal the book as Daniel had ordered because 'the time is near'. Then in v. 18 a warning is issued, usually ascribed to the heavenly messenger. No one is to add or subtract 'from the words of the book of this prophecy'. The verse is characterized by Bousset (459) as a 'canonization formula' stemming from Deut. 4.2, which became a widespread device in later Judaism (cf. Ps. Aristeas 311). Moffatt even brackets the verse as an editorial note directed to the copyist, but surely this is a misconstrual of its present function within the book.

The role of this verse is not canonical in the technical sense used by Josephus (cf. van Unnik), namely, a community's decision to define the scope of the authoritative literature. Rather, it is a warning addressed to the hearer in reference to the perversion of the truth of the book (cf. Beckwith). From the beginning the formula served to reinforce the authority which the book claimed. The book of Revelation was never simply a tract for the times or an occasional letter which later was assigned a religiously authoritative status, rather its author laid claim to its being divine revelation at the outset.

When one turns from the epilogue to the introduction of the book (1.1–3), its distinctive canonical function becomes immediately evident. The verses are presented by a voice different from the author (v. 4), and distinct from God and Christ who are also referred to in the third person. Someone else offers an introduction to the entire book in which its function for the reader is outlined. First, its content is defined: it is the revelation of Jesus Christ, who is its author. Next, its transmission is described: it was mediated by an angel to John by means of visions. Then its purpose is given: it testifies to Jesus Christ concerning what must soon take place. A blessing is then pronounced on its being heard and obeyed. Finally, the entire introduction is grounded in the urgency of the imminent end.

The introduction reflects a stage beyond that of the epilogue within the canonical process of the book. In the epilogue the author has reaffirmed the book's divine author. However, in the introduction, someone belonging to the community of faith who had received the book offers a canonical guideline by means of which the book was to function as authoritative scripture for generations long after the author. It defines the special quality of this writing which is not hindered by its time-conditionality from conveying the divine Word. That the Christian church understood almost immediately the seven churches in Asia in their representative, universal roles reflects a canonical reading fully commensurate with the introduction.

There remains one final canonical feature of the book to discuss. The book now bears the title 'The Revelation of John'. (The RSV has blurred the issue by its mistranslation.) Obviously the title is a secondary addition which stemmed from its canonical editor. Stendahl and Fiorenza have contended that the letter form of the Pauline corpus provided a major force within the canonization process of the Apocalypse. The evidence is insufficient to confirm the hypothesis, but at best the influence from Paul was minor. Rather, it is another apostle whose role must be considered. In the book's superscription we have a significant canonical construal regarding John. The issue is a theological one and must not be immediately translated into a historical debate.

The title provides an additional context from which the book is to be read. At first it is surprising that such a title should be used because it appears to disagree with the actual introduction which ascribes the Apocalypse to Jesus Christ. However, the editor's purpose is clear, and is not intended to contest the ultimate source of the visions. The book of Revelation is to be read in conjunction with the larger Johannine corpus. The point is not to harmonize the book of Revelation with the Gospel of John, but rather to affirm that there is a larger canonical unity to the church's scriptures which is an important guideline to its correct theological understanding. For the last book of the Bible such a canonical control is especially needful.

EXCURSUS I

THE HERMENEUTICAL PROBLEM OF
NEW TESTAMENT TEXT CRITICISM

Bibliography

K. **Aland**, 'The Present Position of New Testament Textual Criticism', *St Ev* [1], TU 73, 1959, 717–31; 'Glosse, Interpolation, Redaktion und Komposition in der Sicht der neutestamentlichen Textkritik', *Apophoreta, FS E. Haenchen*, ed. W. Eltester, BZNW 30, 1964, 7–31; 'The Significance of the Papyri for Progress in New Testament Research', *The Bible in Modern Scholarship*, ed. J. P. Hyatt, New York 1965, 325–46; 'Novi Testamenti Graeci editio maior critica. Der gegenwärtige Stand der Arbeit an einer grossen kritischen Ausgabe des Neuen Testamentes', *NTS* 16, 1969/70, 163–70; 'Der neue "Standard Text" in seinem Verhältnis zu den frühen Papyri und Majuskeln', *New Testament Textual Criticism*, ed. E. J. Epp and G. D. Fee, Oxford 1981, 257–75; K. **Aland** and B. **Aland**, *Der Text des Neuen Testamentes*, 1982; E. **Best**, R. McL. **Wilson**, eds., *Text and Interpretation. Studies in the New Testament Presented to Matthew Black*, Cambridge and New York, 1979; J. N. **Birdsall**, *The Bodmer Papyrus of the Gospel of John*, London 1960; 'The New Testament Text', *Cambridge History of the Bible*, I: *From the Beginnings to Jerome*, ed. P. R. Ackroyd and C. F. Evans, Cambridge 1970, 308–77; A. **Bludau**, *Die Schriftfälschungen der Häretiker: ein Beitrag zur Textkritik der Bibel*, Münster 1925; J. W. **Burgon**, *The Last Twelve Verses of the Gospel according to St Mark*, London 1871; *The Revision Revised*, London 1883; *The Traditional Text of the Holy Gospels Vindicated and Established*, ed. E. Miller, London 1896; *The Causes of the Corruption of the Traditional Text of the Holy Gospels*, ed. E. Miller, London 1896.

K. W. **Clark**, 'Textual Criticism and Doctrine', *Studia Paulina, FS J. de Zwaan*, ed. J. N. Sevenster et al., Haarlem 1953, 52–65; 'The Effect of Recent Textual Criticism upon New Testament Studies', *The Background of the New Testament and its Eschatology, FS C. H. Dodd*, ed. W. D. Davies and D. Daube, Cambridge 1956, 27–51; 'The Theological Relevance of Textual Criticism in Current Criticism of the Greek New Testament', *JBL* 85, 1966, 1–16; 'Today's Problems with the Critical Text of the New Testament', *Transitions in Biblical Scholarship*, ed. J. C. Rylaarsdam, Chicago 1968, 157–69; *The*

Gentile Bias and Other Essays, NovTSuppl 54, 1980; E. C. **Colwell**, *What is the best New Testament?*, Chicago 1932; 'The Complex Character of the Late Byzantine Text of the Gospel', *JBL* 54, 1935, 211–21; 'Genealogical Method: Its Achievements and its Limitations', *JBL* 66, 1947, 109–33; 'The Significance of Grouping of New Testament Manuscripts', *NTS* 4, 1957/8, 73–92; 'The Origin of Texttypes of New Testament Manuscripts', *Early Christian Origins, FS R. H. Willoughby*, ed. A. R. Wikgren, Chicago 1961, 128–38; *Studies in Methodology in Textual Criticism of the New Testament*, Leiden 1969; **Colwell** and E. W. **Tune**, 'The Quantitative Relationships between MS Text – Types', *Biblical and Patristic Studies in Memory of Robert Pierce Casey*, ed. J. N. Birdsall and R. W. Thomson, Freiburg 1963, 25–32; **Colwell** and D. W. **Riddle**, eds. *Studies in the Lectionary Text of the Greek New Testament:* vol. 1. *Prolegomena to the Study of the Lectionary Text of the Gospels*, Chicago 1933.

N. A. **Dahl**, 'The Passion Narrative in Matthew', *Jesus in the Memory of the Early Church*, Minneapolis 1976, 37–51; J. **Duplacy**, *Où en est la critique textuelle du Nouveau Testament*, Paris 1959; J. K. **Elliott**, 'Can we Recover the Original New Testament?', *Theology* 77, 1974, 338–53; 'Plaidoyer pour un éclectisme intégral appliqué à la critique textuelle du Nouveau Testament', *RB* 84, 1977, 5–25; 'Textual Criticism, Assimilation and the Synoptic Gospels', *NTS* 26, 1979/80, 231–42; E. J. **Epp**, *The Theological Tendency of Codex Bezae Cantabrigiensis in Acts*, SNTSM 3, 1966; 'The Claremont Profile Method for Grouping New Testament Minuscule Manuscripts', *Studies in the History and Text of the New Testament in Honor of K. W. Clark*, eds. B. D. Daniels and M. J. Suggs, Salt Lake City 1967, 27–38; 'The Twentieth Century Interlude in New Testament Textual Criticism', *JBL* 93, 1974, 386–414; 'The Eclectic Method in New Testament Textual Criticism: Solution or Symptom?', *HTR* 69, 1976, 211–257; 'New Testament Textual Criticism in America: Requiem for a Discipline', *JBL* 98, 1979, 94–8; **Epp** and G. D. **Fee**, eds., *New Testament Textual Criticism. Its Significance for Exegesis. Essays in Honour of B. M. Metzger*, Oxford 1981.

W. R. **Farmer**, *The Last Twelve Verses of Mark*, SNTSM 25, 1974; E. **Fascher**, *Textgeschichte als hermeneutisches Problem*, Halle/Salle 1953; G. D. **Fee**, 'Codex Sinaiticus in the Gospel of John: A Contribution to Methodology in Establishing Textual Relationships', *NTS* 15, 1968/9, 23–44; 'P[75], P[66], and Origen: The Myth of Early Textual Recension in Alexandria', *New Dimensions in New Testament Studies*, ed. R. N. Longenecker and M. C. Tenney, Grand Rapids 1974, 31–44; 'Rigorous or Reasoned Eclecticism – Which?', *Studies in New Testament Language and Text: Essays in Honour of George D. Kilpatrick on the Occasion of his Sixty – Fifth Birthday*, ed. J. K. Elliott, NovTSupp 44, 1976, 174–97; 'Modern Textual Criticism and the Revival of the Textus Receptus', *JETS* 21, 1978, 19–33; 'A Critique of W. N. Pickering's *The Identity of the New Testament*: A Review Article', *WTJ* 41, 1979, 397–423; D. O. **Fuller**, ed. *True or False? The Westcott – Hort Textual Theory Examined*, Grand Rapids 1973; Z. C. **Hodges**, A. L. **Farstad**, 'Introduction', *The Greek*

New Testament According to the Majority Text, Nashville 1982, ix–xliv; K. **Junack**, 'The Reliability of the New Testament Text from the Perspective of Textual Criticism', *The Bible Translator* 29, 1978, 128–40; M. **Karnetzki**, 'Textgeschichte als Überlieferungsgeschichte', *ZNW* 47, 1956, 170–80; G. D. **Kilpatrick**, 'Atticism and the Text of the Greek New Testament', *Neutestamentliche Aufsätze, FS Josef Schmid*, ed. J. Blinzler et al., Regensburg 1963, 125–37; 'The Greek New Testament of Today and the Textus Receptus', *The New Testament in Historical and Contemporary Perspective. Essays in Memory of G. H. C. Macgregor*, ed. H. Anderson and W. Barclay, Oxford 1965, 189–208; A. F. J. **Klijn**, *A Survey of the Researches into the Western Text of the Gospels and Acts*, Part Two 1949–1969, Leiden 1969.

M. J. **Lagrange**, Introduction a l'étude du Nouveau Testament: II. Critique textuelle, II, La critique rationnelle, Paris 1935; K. **Lake**, *The Influence of Textual Criticism on the Exegesis of the New Testament*, Oxford 1904; *The Text of the New Testament*, London 1959; J. B. **Lightfoot**, R. C. **Trench**, C. J. **Ellicott**, *The Revision of the English Version of the New Testament*, New York 1873; P. **Maas**, *Textkritik*, Leipzig [4]1960; B. M. **Metzger**, *Chapters in the History of New Testament Textual Criticism*, Leiden and Grand Rapids 1963; *The Text of the New Testament: Its Transmission, Corruption and Restoration*, New York and Oxford [2]1968; *A Textual Commentary on the Greek New Testament:*, London and New York 1971; *The Early Versions of the New Testament: Their Origin, Transmission, and Limitations*, Oxford 1977; D. C. **Parker**, 'The Development of Textual Criticism since B. H. Streeter', *NTS* 24, 1977/8, 149–62; M. M. **Parvis**, 'The Nature and Tasks of New Testament Textual Criticism; An Appraisal', *JR* 32, 1952, 165–74; W. N. **Pickering**, *The Identity of the New Testament Text*, Nashville and New York 1977; W. L. **Richards**, 'A Critique of a New Testament Text-Critical Methodology — the Claremont Profile Method', *JBL* 96, 1977, 555–66; D. W. **Riddle**, 'Textual Criticism as a Historical Discipline', *AnThRev* 18, 1936, 220–33; A. T. **Robertson**, *An Introduction to the Textual Criticism of the New Testament*, New York and London 1925.

F. H. A. **Scrivener**, *A Plain Introduction to the Criticism of the New Testament*, I–II, London and New York [4]1894; K. **Snodgrass**, 'Western Non-Interpolations', *JBL* 91, 1972, 369–79; A. **Souter**, *The Text and Canon of the New Testament*, rev. C. S. C. Williams, London [2]1954; B. H. **Streeter**, *The Four Gospels*, London and New York 1924; E. **Tov**, 'Criteria for Evaluating Textual Readings: The Limitations of Textual Rules', *HTR* 75, 1982, 429–48; H. J. **Vogels**, *Handbuch der Textkritik des Neuen Testaments*, Bonn [2]1955; B. B. **Warfield** *An Introduction to the Textual Criticism of the New Testament*, London and New York 1886; B. F. **Westcott**, F. J. A. **Hort**, *The New Testament in the Original Greek*, 2 vols., Cambridge and London 1881, New York 1882; F. **Wisse**, and P. R. **McReynolds**, 'Family E and the Profile Method', *Bibl* 57, 1970, 67–75; H. **Zimmermann**, *Neutestamentliche Methodenlehre*, Stuttgart 1978, 32–88; G. **Zuntz**, 'The Byzantine Text in New

Testament Criticism', *JTS* 43, 1942, 25–30; *The Text of the Epistles*, London 1953.

The non-specialist enters the field of New Testament textual criticism with considerable trepidation. And well he should. Not only is the field one of the earliest disciplines within biblical studies to have worked out a precise and subtle critical methodology, but it can also boast of a venerable stream of academic giants who have spent most of their lives wrestling with the problems of textual criticism. It would almost appear as if a special breed of scholar has been needed, equipped with unusual commitment, patience and technical competence to master the overwhelming mass of detail which is demanded by the task. It is also clear and not surprising that for several decades the field has been caught up in an intense debate in regard to its methodology. Our present concern is not to rehearse this debate which has been frequently reviewed (cf. the critical surveys of Aland, Clark, Colwell, Epp, Fee and Metzger), nor to seek to adjudicate between several competing models—rational eclecticism, text type trajectory, multiple reading techniques, etc.—which offer modern refinements to a large body of commonly assumed critical principles.

Rather, our concern is to focus on some of the basic hermeneutical issues at stake in the enterprise. In spite of the large amount of literature on different technical aspects of the critical enterprise, it is disappointing to discover how little sustained attention has been paid either to the hermeneutical issues involved or to the interpretive effects of the critical textual method. Occasionally there has been a promising beginning made in relating New Testament textual criticism to hermeneutics (cf. especially Fascher, 12ff., and several of K. W. Clark's articles), but it is obvious that the main interest and competence of the experts lie elsewhere.

We begin our reflection with the basic question as to the goal of New Testament text criticism. As is often the case, the apparently simple question turns out to be the most perplexing. F. J. A. Hort's answer, following Tregelles and Tischendorf, is completely straightforward: ' . . . an attempt to present exactly the original words of the New Testament, so far as they can now be determined from surviving documents'(1). Earlier Lachmann had been less ambitious and sought to restore only the text of the fourth century.

The majority of modern text critics (Streeter, Aland, etc.) would agree with Hort in principle, even though many are far more pessimistic about the possibility of ever recovering the original text (Epp, *Bezae* 36; Clark, *JBL* 85, 15). Interestingly enough, staunchly conservative scholars such as B. B. Warfield and A. T. Robertson fully supported Hort's goals and method. Warfield could even conclude: 'The autographic text of the New Testament is distinctly within the reach of criticism. . . .' (15).

At the other end of the spectrum from Hort is a minority opinion which rejects the idea that the goal of textual criticism should be the recovery of the original text. For example, Parvis (172) disputes that one form of the text should be given precedence over all others. He writes: 'There are no spurious readings; all are the product of the tradition of the church, whether they originated in the twelfth century or in the first' (*ibid*).

In between these two extremes are a number of mediating positions. K. Lake agrees with Hort that the object of text criticism is to recover the actual words of the writer, but he holds that an understanding of the history of the church's successive deviations from the original is also integral to the task (*Text of NT*, 1).

In my judgment, the chief problem with these various formulations of the goal of the discipline lies in their not adequately linking text with canon. This is to say, the issue of establishing a normative text cannot be separated from how the text was received, which involves the subject of canon. Hort seeks to recover the text as it was originally written by an author. His model is that of classical studies which had been long established since the Enlightenment, and which saw its task to restore the original composition from its later corruptions. However, the crucial hermeneutical issue at stake is whether Hort's approach does justice to the New Testament text which has been formed into a normative collection of received tradition. Can author intentionality be separated from community reception when dealing with a canonical text?

Conversely, Parvis has also separated text and canon, but in a different manner. Textual criticism has been turned into a branch of church history, and the authoritative text has been equated with ecclesiastical tradition. The qualitative difference between apostolic tradition and subsequent church tradition which the canon sought to establish has been completely blurred. The dialectical relationship of text and canon which seeks to relate what was written with what was heard has been sacrificed. Moreover, the subtlety of the hermeneutical problem is not recognized by simply joining the two positions, as Lake proposes, but requires far deeper methodological reflection.

Clearly there is an important parallel between tradition-historical developments of the canonical literature of the New Testament and the tradition-historical development of the canonical text. Indeed the line between them is quite fluid at times. Both processes involve the reception of normative tradition which includes an interpretation of the material along with the activity of its transmission. Even though the textual process normally reflects a more conservative, even passive stage in stabilization when compared with the enterprise of shaping and restricting the scope of the literature itself, nevertheless, a construal is also involved. The act of copying the sacred text, especially in the period from AD 50–125, included a significant element of interpretation. The major issue is not that of deliberate falsification, but, as Colwell has repeatedly emphasized (*Best NT* 52): 'The paradox is that the variations came into existence because these were religious books, sacred books, canonical books . . . . The devout scribe felt compelled to correct misstatements which he found in the manuscripts he was copying . . . .'. In other words, the process of canonization did not insure an uninterpreted 'neutral' text. Clearly Hort seriously underestimated the element of intentional change (Westcott and Hort, 282). Consequently, the polarity in the canonical process does not lie in a neutral or fabricated text, but rather in differing qualities of construal.

The point to be made is that textual criticism of the New Testament is part of the larger canonical process and must be seen in that light if the peculiar dynamic of its history is to be understood. Just as the growth of the literature of the New Testament as the normative writings of a religious community cannot be compared to inert sherds lying dormant for centuries, so also the peculiar features of the canonical textual process resist identification with the model of classical studies in the search simply for an original, uninterpreted text.

It is significant that the most vocal opposition to Westcott and Hort's critical Greek text first came from the Anglo-Catholic churchman, John William Burgon. In spite of the excessive rhetoric Burgon sensed that a theological dimension of the *textus receptus* was not being properly handled in the critical approach of Hort. He queried whether the Holy Catholic Church could have been misled from its inception by its use of a corrupt text. Could one discount the continuous witness from antiquity, the church fathers, the versions and lectionaries for a discarded text (Sinaiticus) which a German found in a waste basket!? (*Revision Revised*, 293ff.).

Unfortunately, in spite of a critical instinct, Burgon badly misunderstood the real theological issue at stake which had to do with the relation of text to canon, that is, the written word to the received word. He turned the debate into a misconstrued historical issue, arguing that the *textus receptus* represented the oldest text which was closest to the original apostolic autographs. He also sought to defend the lack of textual corruption with an appeal to divine Providence's special handling of the transmission process. Ironically, Burgon's defence of the Byzantine text was as historicist as Hort's, even if of an extremely poor quality, and shared the same lack of canonical understanding. Burgon's error has, unfortunately, continued among those scholars who have in recent times once again sought to defend the 'majority text' as the most historically accurate (Hodges, Pickering, Fuller).

During the last hundred years since the publication of the critical text of Westcott and Hort, the field has not stood still. Within the present state of the discipline a number of important criticisms of Hort's method have emerged which, in my judgment, lend support to a new attempt to relate text and canon. First of all, although it is theoretically reasonable to argue that the present multiplicity of copies derive from an original autograph, especially in the case of Paul's letters, the actual manuscript evidence presents a very different picture. The earliest levels of textual witness reveal a state of wide multiplicity, indeed, the model of a reservoir of tradition from which different streams flow is far more accurate than that of an ideal autograph at the source (Epp, 'Interlude', 396f.). K. W. Clark speaks of 'new evidence that textual bifurcation occurred in the earliest stage of transmission' ('Today's Problem', 162).

Secondly, the goal of textual criticism according to Westcott and Hort, which was the restoration of the original autographs, seems increasingly one-sided in the light of recent literary work on the New Testament. For example, N. A. Dahl, in his article on 'The Passion Narrative in Matthew' presents convincing evidence that there was an intermingling of written and oral tradition for a considerable period in the early church. At least in terms of the development of the Gospels, it can be seriously questioned whether there ever was just one original autograph, but rather a variety of traditions, written and oral, which competed for recognition in the ensuing period. Likewise for the Pauline epistles, Zuntz (*Text of Epistles*, 278f.) has argued that the extant manuscript evidence bears witness to the Pauline letters always in their collection form within the canonical corpus of about AD 100. Important things happened between the writing of the epistles and the formation of a canonical collection, a process which modern literary critical research has sought to clarify. Again the implications for text criticism move away from the model assumed by Hort to one which reckons with the best received text rather than that of an author's autograph.

Finally, recent criticism has become increasingly aware of the difficulty, if not impossibility, of reconstructing an adequate history of the New Testament's textual transmission in the period before AD 200. The recent papyri discoveries (Chester Beatty and Bodmer) have confirmed that the Egyptian text-type represented in the great fourth-century uncials reflect a textual tradition at least as early as AD 200. The papyri have also supported the textual value of the 'Western' text much beyond that recognized by Hort. Moreover, the late Byzantine text which Hort's genealogical method relegated to a consistently secondary role has been shown by the papyri to have preserved ancient readings from the second or third century for which there has been no other early witnesses (Metzger, *Chapters*, 38).

Several important methodological implications stem from this new evidence. First, there is no simply 'neutral' text from which one can recover a pure textual stream, but the early period reflects highly complex recensional activity from the outset. Secondly, in spite of the great value of Hort's genealogical method up to a certain point in the textual process, it is inadequate in adjudicating between the two or more ancient streams of tradition which extend back before AD 200 (cf. Epp, 'Interlude', 390ff.). A variety of different approaches are needed in a search for the best text, which is, of course, the reason for the present methodological debate among the experts.

It is significant to observe that the pattern of textual development for the New Testament text which has recently emerged has taken on a striking similarity to the development of the Hebrew text of the Old Testament (cf. Childs, *Introduction* [see p.xv above], 84ff.). Within the latter, the older picture of an original text which has suffered some corruption through transmission, but could largely be restored to its pristine purity through critical emendation has been replaced by a far more complex history of development. There is wide agreement that the earliest levels of textual transmission of the Hebrew text reflect a stage of much fluidity with a multiplicity of competing textual traditions, and that the direction of textual development moved from plurality to unity, and from fluidity to stabilization. Similarly, the New Testament text reflects a pattern of much fluidity with multiple competing traditions at its earliest stage which only slowly over several centuries reached a certain level of textual stability by means of a complex recensional history. The Hebrew text was stabilized in the Masoretic tradition, the Greek in the *koine*. Moreover, both processes were affected by both internal and external factors. For the Greek tradition this would include the dramatic decline of a knowledge of Greek in the West, the effect of Islam on the Christian hegemony in the East, and the ecclesiastical consolidation of the Greek Orthodox branch of Christendom.

Yet it would be a mistake to press the analogy too far. There are some important differences between the development of the Hebrew text within the Jewish synagogue and the Greek New Testament text within the Christian church. First, the Christian church did not develop an official, ecclesiastical position regarding one particular text which was analogous to the role of the Masoretic tradition within rabbinic Judaism. Secondly, the Christian church had a different attitude toward translations of the scriptures from that of the synagogue. The early and extensive use of Syriac, Coptic, and Latin translations of the New Testament resulted in a different dynamic of textual transmission from that of the Hebrew text. Thirdly, although both the Jewish synagogue and the Christian church transmitted their scriptures within a process of canonization, the understanding of the process was not identical. For the Christian church canonization was a derivative of christology. The New Testament scriptures gained their unique authority in their role as the apostolic and prophetic witness to Christ's death and resurrection which was also uniquely tied to the one specific period of his earthly life. The effect of the canonization of the Gospels was that the growth of church tradition always was tested as to its conformity with the normative apostolic witness. Because the post-apostolic church struggled to maintain this apostolic witness in a pure form, the concern for a true text of the pristine testimony was constitutive for the Christian understanding of canon.

It would, therefore, appear that within the development of the Greek New Testament two seemingly contradictory principles, both derivative of canon, were at work. On the one hand, there was the constant effort to preserve the 'best', 'purest', and 'oldest' text of the Gospels, a concern which was reflected in the various revisions and recensions of the Greek text. The Alexandrian school best represents this critical discipline, but the traditional view of a revision by Origen in Palestine, by Lucian in Antioch, and by Hesychius in Egypt, in spite of its historical problems, testifies to the extent of the concern within the church to restore a pure text. On the other hand, there was the textual activity, best represented by the Byzantine tradition, which expoused an inclusive principle. It sought to include the widest possible number of variant traditions actually in use by Christian communities through conflation and harmonization. However, the selection was critical to the extent that it also sought to establish fixed parameters for the Christian tradition outside of which only heretics ventured.

The crucial methodological question now arises whether or not one can redefine the task of New Testament textual criticism in such a way as to do justice to the text's peculiar canonical function within the Christian church. We have argued that a critical methodology, such as Hort's, which seeks to restore the original autographs of the author is inadequate for establishing the church's received and authoritative text. Conversely, a traditional method which identifies the canonical text uncritically with the *textus receptus* fails to reckon with the elements of corruption which have entered into the conflated textual tradition.

Theoretically, the goal of text criticism, which is commensurate with its canonical role, is to recover that New Testament text which best reflects the true apostolic witness found in the church's scripture. It is a goal which seeks to do justice to both the critical and inclusive principles at work in the history of its development, and tries correctly to balance the forces of promise and threat found in each. However, is such a goal feasible and can an actual textual method be outlined by which to achieve it? Is there any means of locating a text which is by definition different from the original author's autograph and at the same time is not to be identified with an uncritical text represented by the last stages of a stabilized *koine* tradition? No one should be deceived as to the difficulties involved in escaping the horns of this dilemma.

At the outset a crucial methodological decision turns on the context within which the enterprise is conducted. Because the text-critical goal has been defined as recovering the best received text, one begins by a self-positioning within the framework of actual ecclesiastical textual traditions, the outer parameter of which has usually been set by the Byzantine (*koine*) text. (For the Latin tradition the role of the Vulgate as a starting-point from within an inclusive ecclesiastical tradition would be roughly analogous). The use of the *textus receptus* as providing the initial context for textual analysis serves to describe a full range of textual possibilities which actually functioned in the church. It also offers an inclusive, if often distorted, textual tradition against which to test more and less pure textual readings. In addition such a context functions greatly to restrict the value of textual conjectures because these are by definition reconstructions without an actual historical tradent, but are dependent upon the rationale of an author's alleged intentionality.

The second step is equally decisive for the proposed method. Working within the initial context of the *textus receptus*, the text critic enters into a process of searching for the best received, that is, canonical text. One strives critically to discern from within the common tradition that text which best reflects the church's judgment as to its truth. The polarity is not between a neutral or an interpreted text, but between the qualities of received or interpreted texts. Moreover, the criteria by which these judgments are made are precisely those which critical scholarship has developed over the last two hundred years. One evaluates a variety of factors which includes the age of a text, the quality of its text type, the geographical breadth of its witness, the inner relationship of variants, and the inner consistency of style and content.

Although the enterprise of textual criticism is fully dependent upon the proper exercise of highly technical, scientific skills, the element of subjectivity should not be denied. As has become increasingly apparent within the discipline, there is a point at which the appeals to more or less objective criteria such as genealogical primacy or antiquity of witness offer inadequate means by which to adjudicate between competing traditions. Then an appeal to consistency of content is often made, but this decision involves a prior judgment which derives from a view of the whole. However, the recognition that the text critic is forced at some point to make his own construal should not be surprising in the light of the peculiar development of a canonical text. The modern critic's role becomes somewhat analogous to the earliest stages in the text's development in which transmission and construal were closely joined.

There is another significant element in the canonical model being proposed for New Testament textual criticism. The enterprise remains a continuing process. Although one cannot fault the preparation of critical editions of the Greek New Testament as a useful and necessary tool, the publication of such critical editions can result in seriously confusing the purpose of the enterprise by substituting a modern reconstructed text as a new form of the *textus receptus*. Rather, the canonical model of textual criticism proposes a continuing search in discerning the best received text which moves from the outer parameters of the common church tradition found in the *textus receptus* to the inner judgment respecting its purity.

The emphasis of this model on the activity of text criticism as a continuing process derives from several important reasons which are constitutive to the nature of the canonical enterprise. First, the search for the best canonical text within the circle established by the church's tradition takes place within the context of the multiple textual options which have been actually used in the church. These various traditions of interpretation provide the earliest commentary on the New Testament text and illustrate both the promise of understanding and also the threat of misunderstanding.

Secondly, the process of seeking to discern the truest witness to the gospel from within the church's multiple traditions functions to remind the interpreter of the canonical corpus that the element of theological interpretation is not only constitutive of the church's scriptures in general, but has also entered into the textual dimension of the tradition as well. This observation is not a defence of irrational subjectivity, but a further confirmation that the discipline of text criticism is not a strictly objective, or non-theological activity, but is an integral part of the same interpretive enterprise which comprises the church's life with its scriptures.

To conclude, it should now be obvious that the new proposal for New Testament textual criticism stands in closest relationship to the larger literary analysis of the canonical corpus which has been developed in the rest of this introduction. As the literary analysis starts with the outer scope of the canonical literature as received, so also the textual analysis begins within the parameters established by the *textus receptus*, to be more precise, by the *koine* text, as the best representative of the common tradition. Again, as the literary analysis seeks to discern within the corpus of scripture indices of how the tradents rendered the material in order for it to function kerygmatically for successive generations, so the text critic describes, analyses, and evaluates the competing textual traditions in an effort to discern the truest textual rendering. Finally, as the literary analysis requires not only an understanding of the church's construal of its scriptures, but also an important element of 'reader competence' in forming a modern construal, so also the textual task requires a similar element of construal in the final decision regarding a preferred reading. For these reasons the task of the church's understanding of its scriptures in all its various dimensions remains an ongoing responsibility for each new generation of believers.

INTERPRETATION OF THE PARABLES
WITHIN A CANONICAL CONTEXT

Bibliography

Full bibliographical resources are found in the following: J. D. **Crossan**, 'A Basic Bibliography for Parables Research', *Semeia* 1, 1974, 236–74; W. S. **Kissinger**, *The Parables of Jesus. A History of Interpretation and Bibliography*, Metuchen, N. J. and London 1979. M. **Black**, 'The Parables as Allegory', *B JRL* 42, 1959/60, 273–87; R. **Bultmann**, *The History of the Synoptic Tradition*, ET London and New York ²1968, 166–205; A. T. **Cadoux**, *The Parables of Jesus: Their Art and Use*, London 1930, New York 1931; J. D. **Crossan**, 'The Parable of the Wicked Husbandmen', *JBL* 90, 1971, 451–65; *In Parables. The Challenge of the Historical Jesus*, New York 1973; 'The Servant Parables of Jesus', *Semeia* 1, 1974, 17–62; 'Structuralist Analysis and the Parables of Jesus. A Reply to D. O. Via, Jr.', *Semeia* 1, 1974, 192–221; *Finding is the First Act: Trove Folk Tales and Jesus' Treasure Parables*, Philadelphia 1979; *Cliffs of Fall*, New York 1980; N. A. **Dahl**, 'The Parables of Growth', *StTh* 5, 1951, 132–66; reprinted *Jesus in the Memory of the Early Church*, Minneapolis 1976, 141–166; 'Gleichnis und Parabel', *RGG*³ II,, 1614–19; C. H. **Dodd**, *The Parables of the Kingdom*, London 1935, New York 1936.

G. **Eichholz**, *Gleichnisse der Evangelien. Form, Überlieferung, Auslegung*, Neukirchen-Vluyn 1971; P. **Fiebig**, *Altjüdische Gleichnisse und die Gleichnisse Jesu*, Tübingen 1904; D. **Flusser**, *Die rabbinischen Gleichnisse in der Gleichniserzählen Jesus*, Bern 1981; E. **Fuchs**, 'Bemerkungen zur Gleichnisauslegung', *Zur Frage nach dem historischen Jesus*, GA II, Tübingen 1960, 136–42; 'Das Fest der Verlorenen. Existentiale Interpretation des Gleichnisses vom verlorenen Sohn', *Glaube und Erfahrung. Zum christologischen Problem im Neuen Testament*, GA III, Tübingen 1965, 402–15; R. W. **Funk**, *Language, Hermeneutic, and Word of God*, New York 1966, London 1967; 'Beyond Criticism in Quest of Literacy: The Parable of the Leaven', *Interp* 25, 1971, 149–70; *Parables and Presence*, Philadelphia 1982; E. **Güttgemanns**, 'Die linguistische-didaktische Methodik der Gleichnisse Jesu', *Studia Linguistica Neotestamentica*, Munich 1971, 99–183; E. **Haenchen**, *Die Botschaft des Thomas-Evangeliums*, Berlin 1961; W. **Harnisch**, 'Die Sprachkraft der Analogie. Zur These vom argumentativen Charakter der Gleichnisse Jesu', *StTh* 28, 1974, 1–20; ed., *Gleichnisse Jesu. Positionen der Auslegung von Adolf Jülicher bis zur Formgeschichte*, WdF 366, 1982; ed., *Die neutestamentliche Gleichnisforschung im Horizont der Hermeneutik und Literaturwissenschaft*, WdF 575, 1982; J. **Jeremias**, *The Parables of Jesus*, ET of 6th ed., London and New York 1963; G. V. **Jones**, *The Art and Truth of the Parables*, London 1964; A. **Jülicher**, *Die Gleichnisreden Jesu*, Tübingen, vol.I ²1899, vol.II 1899; E. **Jüngel**, *Paulus und Jesus*, HUT 2, ³1967, 87–215.

M. **Kaehler**, *The So-called Historical Jesus and the Historic Biblical Christ* (1896), ET Philadelphia 1964; J. D. **Kingsbury**, 'Ernst Fuchs' Existential Interpretation of the Parables', *Lutheran Quarterly* 22, 1970, 380–95; H. J. **Klauck**, *Allegorie und Allegorese in synoptischen Gleichnistexten*, Münster 1978; H. G. **Klemm**, 'Die Gleichnisauslegung Adolf Jülichers im Bannkreise der Fabeltheorie Lessings', *ZNW* 59, 1969, 270–82; W. G. **Kümmel**, 'Noch einmal: Das Gleichnis von der selbstwachsenden Saat. Bemerkungen zur neuesten Diskussion um die Auslegung der Gleichnisse Jesu', *Orientierung an Jesus. Zur Theologie der Synoptiker, FS J. Schmid*, ed. P. Hoffman et al., Freiburg 1973, 220–37; E. **Linnemann**, *Parables of Jesus. Introduction and Exposition*, ET London 1966, New York 1967; H. **Montefiore**, 'A Comparison of the Parables of the Gospel according to Thomas and of the Synoptic Gospels', *NTS* 7, 1960/61, 220–48; D. **Patte**, *Semiology and Parables: Exploration of the Possibilities offered by Structuralism for Exegesis*, Pittsburg 1976; N. **Perrin**, *Jesus and the Language of the Kingdom. Symbol and Metaphor in New Testament Interpretation*, Philadelphia 1976; 'The Modern Interpretation of the Parables of Jesus and the Problem of Hermeneutics', *Interp* 25, 1971, 131–48; P. **Ricoeur**, 'Biblical Hermeneutics', *Semeia* 4, 1975, 29–148; J. M. **Robinson**, 'Jesus' Parables as God Happening', *Jesus and the Historian, Written in Honor of Ernest C. Colwell*, ed. T. T. Trotter, Philadelphia 1968, 134–50.

W. **Schrage**, *Das Verhältnis des Thomas-Evangeliums zur synoptischen Tradition und zu den koptischen Evangelienübersetzungen*, BZNW 29, 1964; B. T. D. **Smith**, *The Parables of the Synoptic Gospels*, Cambridge 1937; A. C. **Thiselton**, 'Parables as Language Event; Some Comments on Fuchs' Hermeneutics in the Light of Linguistic Philosophy', *SJT* 23, 1970, 437–68; R. C. **Trench**, *Notes on the Parables of our Lord*, London 1841, ¹⁴1882, New York 1884; H. **Weder**, *Die Gleichnisse Jesu als Metaphern. Traditions-und redaktionsgeschichtliche Analysen und Interpretationen*, FRLANT 120, 1978; A. N. **Wilder**, *Early Christian Rhetoric*, London and Philadelphia 1964, 79–96; *Jesus' Parables and the War of Myths: Essays on Imagination in the Scriptures*, Philadelphia 1982.

The purpose of this essay is to seek to relate a canonical approach to the New Testament with the specific problem of interpreting the parables of Jesus found in the Synoptic Gospels. Although this topic does not usually fall within the scope of New Testament introduction, there are several reasons for its inclusion. First, the interpretation of the parables plays a crucial role in determining how one understands the Gospels and the ministry of Jesus. Secondly, the intense modern debate on the parables provides an ideal arena for testing the canonical approach and for sharpening its profile in contrast to other hermeneutical options.

It is unnecessary to review in detail the modern history of the critical study of the parables which has been frequently rehearsed and is readily available (cf. Jones, Kissinger, Weder). Usually the beginning of the modern debate is attributed to A. Jülicher's epoch-making work which launched a massive attack against the church's traditional allegorical method of interpretation, best exemplified in the English-speaking world by the classic volume of Archbishop Trench. Jülicher argued that the original parables of Jesus had been misunderstood from the start by the church and buried under a layer of allegorical dust. The critical task lay in properly conceiving of the nature of Jesus' parables and then in recovering them according to their pristine form. He argued that the nature of the metaphor which is the root form of allegory is fundamentally different from the simile which is the form related to the parable. The simile consists of literal speech and needs no explanation, while the metaphor is non-literal by nature and requires explanation. The parable challenges the hearer to discover the point of comparison (*tertium comparationis*) which connects the picture-half with the reality-half. Jülicher assumed that Jesus was primarily a teacher of morals who sought to enlighten his hearers and elicit a response about the principles which govern the kingdom of God.

Jülicher's interpretation called forth widespread acceptance particularly regarding his devastating attack on allegory. To be sure, there were some criticisms voiced that he had overdone the antithesis between parable and allegory or that he had failed to reckon sufficiently with the Jewish background of the genre (Fiebig). However, no one doubted that a new era of interpretation had been initiated. The next clear stage in the history of the debate was inaugurated by C. H. Dodd and J. Jeremias, although their new approach had in part been adumbrated by Cadoux. Although there were some important differences between Dodd and Jeremias – Dodd was more closely patterned after Dibelius, Jeremias after Bultmann – they agreed in their basic criticism of Jülicher. His method of

interpretation ended with a moral generalization and failed to relate
the parable to the original historical situation which had called forth
the parable in the life of Jesus (Dodd, 24ff.; Jeremias, 18ff.). Both
Dodd and Jeremias in different ways construed the parable as a
weapon directed against historical opponents in a framework of
eschatological crisis.

Although Dodd's work was seminal, it was Jeremias who worked
out the historicist interpretation of the parables with great thoroughness and impressive learning. He made his hermeneutical position
clear: his goal was to recover the original voice of Jesus, which for
him alone remained authoritative (22). He agreed with Jülicher that
the levels of misunderstanding which reflected the erroneous manner
in which the parables had been received by the evangelists must be
stripped away. In a brilliant chapter entitled, 'The Return to Jesus
from the Primitive Church', Jeremias outlined the various factors
which had led to the distortion of the original parable. These included
such things as embellishment, allegorization, change of addressee, a
shift in the setting of the recipient, and various forms of redactional
editing. In his final section Jeremias offered an interpretation of the
message of the parables according to his reconstructed, original form.

In a real sense the contemporary debate which began in the 50s is
a direct response to both the strengths and weaknesses of Jeremias'
historicist position. With few exceptions Jeremias' approach was
commended as foundational in nature. His concern to recover the
original layer of Jesus' teaching was acknowledged as an indispensable component for correct interpretation. However, sharp criticism
arose regarding the adequacy of the historicist's interpretation which
fell into two different camps with considerable overlap. On the one
hand, there were those who disagreed with Jeremias from the side of
hermeneutics. On the other hand, there were those whose approach
focused on the literary aspects of parabolic interpretation.

The new debate concerning the hermeneutical issues involved
received a massive impetus from the writings of E. Fuchs, and the
so-called school of the New Hermeneutic. In Germany Fuch's
influence was reflected in Linnemann, Jüngel, and Weder, but it also
helped to stimulate an articulate new American school of interpreters
associated with the names of Funk, Perrin, and J. M. Robinson,
among others.

Although it is impossible to do justice to the various emphases of
each writer in a summary essay, there are certain common features

which ran through the new hermeneutical exegesis. First, a very different understanding of language was assumed as a necessity for understanding the role of a parable. The earlier distinction between the form and the content of the analogy was rejected as basically misleading, and the parable was conceived of as having a performative force. When Fuchs spoke of a 'language event' he interpreted the parable as opening up a new world and as having a power to impel the hearer to a decision. Secondly, and closely akin, most of these writers joined their view of language to an existential mode of interpretation. The decision which the parable called forth was not instruction in morals, but had to do with the hearer's existential understanding of reality. Thirdly, the role of the hearer of the parable played an integral part in the interpretive process. The hearer's function could not simply be historicized, nor could the parable be tied to a situation of the past. Rather, the hermeneutical problem was posed as the parable along with the hearer moved from the past to the present. Finally, there was a continued concern to interpret the multi-layered quality of the text which derived from its history of tradition in a positive manner rather than to conceive of the secondary layers as deposits of sediment which obscured its real meaning. Particularly in the exegesis of Eichholz and Weder one sees a sophisticated effort being made to overcome the legacy of Jülicher, Dodd and Jeremias and to do theological justice to the text's complex history of interpretation.

The new debate from the side of literary analysis followed many of the same lines of criticism which had emerged from the hermeneutical issues, but nevertheless the discussion moved in significant new directions. Moreover, in recent years, as the influence of the 'New Hermeneutic' sharply declined, the cutting edge of the modern debate shifted to the newer literary theories of the parable. The first great contribution of this school was in re-thinking the entire subject of the metaphor, and seriously calling into question Jülicher's literary analysis. Particularly the works of Jüngel and Weder in Germany/Switzerland, and Funk and Crossan in America have shown the function of metaphor to be constitutive to the parable. The issue of the polyvalent quality of the metaphor (Crossan) has largely undercut the search for one original meaning of a parable. Similarly the whole issue of allegory has been rethought and increasingly the complexity of the problem of sharply distinguishing between

different ways of actualizing the parable in the history of its growth
has become evident (cf. Jones, Weder).

Another important new emphasis of the new literary theory of
parables has been in focusing attention on the parable as having a
life and vitality of its own, simply by reason of its being a metaphor
(Perrin, *Interp*, 140). D. Via's characterization of the parable as an
'aesthetic object' (ix) stressed the autonomy of the parable as a
literary work of art which resisted all attempts to decode it for
historical or theological purposes. A. N. Wilder spoke of the parable
as an art form, full of creative flexibility, by means of which
Jesus' vision of reality was communicated through a compelling
imagination (79ff.). Finally, the issue of the role of the hearers of the
parable was raised and much attention was given to the ability of
the metaphor to transcend any one given historical situation and by
means of its open-ended quality be 'capable of transference into a
hundred other situations other than that of Jesus and his hearers'
(Perrin, 140).

In the light of these new and often stimulating proposals by the
modern interpreters of the parables, I feel a challenge to respond.
My concern is not an attempt to address the full range of interpretive
issues being raised, but rather to focus only on those areas which are
most closely related to the central concerns of canon. Although few
of the hermeneutical issues are totally new, some do appear with a
greater intensity because of the debate over the interpretation of the
parables.

From my perspective, the basic hermeneutical problem of the
debate arises from the discovery of the multi-layered quality of the
Gospel texts which contain the parables. There is every sign of a
lengthy and complex history of tradition which extended through
the oral, written, and redactional levels of development. One can at
times easily discern stages in the growth of certain of the parables.
There are frequent shifts in the addressee, later editorial frameworks,
and secondary applications to once independent stories. Sometimes
one can discern the original level of the parable and isolate it with
some certainty from subsequent commentary. The discovery of the
gnostic Gospel of Thomas offers a further aid in the recovery of the
earliest form of the tradition.

Nevertheless, my disagreement with the historicist position of
Jeremias is twofold. First, on the literary level the task of separating
the various layers seems to me far more complex than is often

realized. At times there are some objective indications by which to determine literary seams. However, when a method is committed in principle to recovering the original level, a large element of subjectivity is necessarily introduced. The decisive factor in determining the layers turns on each scholar's holistic construal of the original historical message of Jesus, apart from its later transmission. This point should be obvious ever since Martin Kaehler's book, but the search for the historical Jesus has taken on new life in relation to the parables. Thus, Jülicher's portrait of Jesus' original message reflects all the features of nineteenth-century Liberal Protestantism, Dodd's Jesus is fully encapsulated within a concept of 'realized eschatology', and Jeremias' Jesus seems never tired of repeating a very few ideas concerned with the coming kingdom (115ff.).

However, from a canonical perspective the major objection to the historicist position is hermeneutical. Jeremias is fully explicit when asserting his view that the authoritative form of the gospel for the Christian church is to be located in the reconstructed *ipsissima verba* of Jesus (22). Although a majority of critical scholars are dissatisfied with Jeremias's formulation, many, such as Dodd, agree in placing the highest value on the actual words of Jesus and deprecating the subsequent history of the church's transmission as full of misunderstanding and distortion. At this point the proponents of a canonical interpretation are insistent that the authoritive witness to the gospel is the apostolic testimony which the canon seeks to preserve. In sum, the Jesus of the Christian church – the Christ of faith – is only known by means of the authoritative witness of his disciples.

Again, the canonical approach welcomes many of the emphases of the new literary approach to the parables, particularly its concern for the text's own life and its continued vitality with new recipients. However, again basic hermeneutical issues are at stake which evoke serious disagreement. Much of the emphasis on the parables as artistic creations or as aesthetic objects assumes that the metaphor itself supplies its own context for interpretation, whether by means of laws of poetics or of deep structure. At times this school continues to work with the assumptions of the historicists that the parables 'involve something of the vision, the person, the *Selbstverständnis* of Jesus himself' (Perrin, *Interpr* 138), and the vitality of the metaphor is simply an extension of the historical. However, characteristic of this school is the assumption that the parable is to be interpreted independently of the ministry of Jesus in the theological terms of christology. As a consequence, the mode of interpretation is usually existentialist, and at most the earthly Jesus serves to raise universal questions addressed to common human existence. In my judgment, Jüngel has seen the fundamental theological issue at stake in this non-theological approach to the parables when writing: 'If the assertion then is true that in the parables of Jesus the new era of God's rule has already arrived, then those parables would be qualified in such a way as to distinguish them qualitatively from all other parables which ever were spoken on earth' (*Paulus und Jesus*, 101). The function of the canonical context is to assure that Jesus' words and actions are never separated, but heard together.

Finally, some of the most important hermeneutical issues of the modern debate have been raised by the traditio-historical critics. Of these, two stand out as being unusually penetrating in insight, G. Eichholz and H. Weder. Many of the concerns of these two interpreters are highly compatible with the canonical approach which is being suggested. Both authors are critical of Jeremias' attempt to restrict the interpretation of the parable to an original, reconstructed level. Both emphasize that the entire history of interpretation which is reflected in the multi-layered quality of the text is of equal theological importance, and dare not be dismissed as misleading accretion.

In addition, many highly significant observations of a positive nature have emerged from their research. They both stress that the presence of layers of interpretation surrounding each parable derives, not merely from general laws of narrative transmission in the Hellenistic world, but from a basic theological concern that the message of Jesus remain a living reality among its hearers rather than being consigned to the past. Moreover, Jülicher's attempt to dismiss all signs of allegory as secondary misunderstandings fails to interpret correctly the variety of ways in which the theological actualization of the parables operated, and that the category of allegorization needs major refinement as an interpretive tool of the parables (cf. especially Weder, 58ff.). Finally, the literary observations, both of Eichholz's chapter on the language and structure of the parables (17ff.) and Weder's research into the function of metaphor (58ff.), offer much insight and promise for future interpretation.

Nevertheless, there are some important points of disagreement which set the canonical approach apart from the traditio-historical and redactional. The basic issue of controversy turns on how one understands the relationship among the various levels of the biblical text. The issue is misconstrued if one describes it in terms of a polarity between a static concept of a fixed canonical text and a flexible concept of traditional process. Clearly a process is involved, but the nature of this history of tradition is determined by one's view of the function of the canonical text in relation to the process. The canonical form of the text offers a particular construal of the parables which it expresses by means of a complex history of development within the community of faith. The canonical text reflects the process by which several generations of tradents received and transmitted the text. The canonical text thus represents the final form in a process which follows a peculiar trajectory. Many options of construing the material are simply not represented within that particular process of transmission by the early church which in time was accorded an official ecclesiastical validation through canonization.

The hermeneutical issue at stake is whether one views the final form of the text from within the history of that particular construal, and uses the earlier levels to illuminate the final form of the text, or whether one seeks to stand outside of this history of tradition. On the basis of other criteria such as rival (Gnostic) construals, general laws of narrative transmission, or of a reconstructed history of the first century, one attempts to sketch other, so-called objective developments of the tradition. Even though within the canonical Gospels there is no level of tradition which viewed Jesus apart from faith, nevertheless, the issue is whether by the indirect means of critical method one can recover a Jesus of history from which to understand the Christ of faith.

In my judgment, the traditio-critical method falls into the danger of reconstructing a transmission process which does not reflect the actual growth of the tradition within the community of faith, but is a construct which seeks to penetrate behind the witness to the uninterpreted Jesus of history. For example, it appears to me that Weder's attempt always to recover a 'Jesus-level' of the tradition (108, 125, 139, etc.) does not reflect an early level of Christian witness within the canonical text, but a critical projection of what Jesus may have said apart from its reception in faith. The process is, therefore, different in kind from that history of witness whose faith construal was ultimately canonized as representing the authoritative, apostolic testimony. In sum, the so-called earliest level in the tradition often turns out to be qualitatively different from the earliest level of witness actually found in the Gospels. It is one thing to distinguish between the parable and its later applications. It is quite another to reconstruct the parable apart from its earliest kerygmatic shaping.

There are several other elements of controversy with the traditio-historical method which stem from this different hermeneutical stance. Weder is much concerned to distinguish in his analysis between the pre-Easter form of the parable and its post-Easter form. In itself, the concern is justified. However, there is a real danger in correlating a pre-Easter and a post-Easter form of the parables within a historical process. Rather, it is characteristic of the redactional shape of the Gospels that the relation between these different perspectives is a very subtle one, and for theological reasons certain Gospels retain elements of the pre-Easter perspective even as part of the post-Easter witness (cf. ch. 6 Mark). In this respect Eichholz's treatment is theologically more sophisticated and more sensitive to the multi-layered dimensions of the interpreted text.

Finally, it is highly important that the critical insights into the growth of the biblical text be correctly exploited. The suggested canonical approach is in no sense a return to Archbishop Trench. The various elements of growth, embellishment, and alteration which Jeremias has so carefully described should not be dismissed as distorting accretion, but rather considered as an aid in understanding the special nature of the church's construal of Jesus' message.

THE CANONICAL APPROACH AND THE 'NEW YALE THEOLOGY'

Bibliography

J. **Barr**, *Holy Scripture: Canon, Authority, Criticism*, Oxford 1983; H. **Frei**, *The Eclipse of Biblical Narrative*, New Haven 1974; *The Identity of Jesus Christ*, Philadelphia 1975; P. L. **Holmer**, 'Wittgenstein and Theology', *Reflection* 65, 1968, 1–4; D. H. **Kelsey**, *The Uses of Scripture in Recent Theology*, Philadelphia 1975; 'The Bible and Christian Theology', *JAAR* 48, 1980, 385–402; G. A. **Lindbeck**, *The Nature of Doctrine. Religion and Theology in a Postliberal Age*, Philadelphia 1984; J. A. **Sanders**, *Torah and Canon*, Philadelphia 1972; E. B. **Smick**, 'Old Testament Theology: the Historico-genetic Method', *JETS* 26, 1983, 146f.; C. M. **Wood**, *The Formation of Christian Understanding. An Essay in Theological Hermeneutics*, Philadelphia 1981.

The manuscript for this introduction had been completed and sent to the publisher when George A. Lindbeck's provocative book, *The Nature of Doctrine*, appeared. Although the main concern of his book is with a particular set of theological problems growing out of ecumenical discussions, the methodological proposals have important implications for the canonical approach which I have sought to describe. Upon reflection it seemed to me that the profile of my proposal could be sharpened by responding to Lindbeck's book, especially since there is a distinct family resemblance among several recent theological proposals stemming from Yale. Certainly any attempt to narrow the wide gap between dogmatic theology and biblical studies should be encouraged. I have translated his larger issues of religion and doctrine into a form more narrowly related to Bible and theology, but I hope without serious distortion.

Lindbeck's book is concerned to offer a new model for conceptualizing religion which he entitles a 'cultural-linguistic' approach. In order to delineate his position sharply, he first sets forth two other rival theories of religion and doctrine. The first type, which he calls the 'cognitive-propositional', stresses the ways in which church doctrine functions as informative propositions or truth claims about objective realities. Its best representatives are the traditional orthodoxies of Roman Catholic and Protestant theologies. Lindbeck argues that this traditional theory has been undermined by various aspects of the Enlightenment and post-Enlightenment eras which seriously called into question its metaphysical and epistemological foundation. The rise of historical criticism of the Bible would be an additional factor in its demise.

His second type, the 'experiental-expressive', is the liberal theological alternative represented by theologians from Schleiermacher to Tillich, and it interprets doctrines as non-informative and non-discursive symbols of inner feelings, attitudes or existential orientations. In spite of various formulations of the liberal approach, Lindbeck concludes that they all share the concern to find a single generic or universal experiential essence to religion. He criticizes the theory as basically reductionist and too narrowly representative of Western style modernity.

Lindbeck designates the third theory which is his own proposal as the 'cultural-linguistic' approach. It is a model akin to the function of language or culture which emphasizes the use of communally authoritative rules of discourse, attitudes, and action. Religion is viewed as a kind of cultural or linguistic framework which shapes the entirety of life and thought. It is a communal phenomenon which forms the subjectivities of individuals rather than being primarily a manifestation of such. Instead of deriving external features of a religion from inner experience, it reverses the relation of the inner and outer dimensions by viewing the former as derivative. The focus of the model is on the degree to which human experience is shaped, moulded, and constituted by cultural and linguistic forms as a means of construing reality. Lindbeck appeals for backing to the anthropologist, Clifford Geertz, and to the philosopher, Peter Winch. There are also frequent references to the works of Wittgenstein, Hans Frei, and David Kelsey, among others.

When I transfer this methodological debate to the current enterprise of interpreting the Bible, I am initially impressed with the insight which Lindbeck's categories bring to the problems discussed in this New Testament introduction. His classifications aid greatly in sharpening the profile of my canonical position by providing more precise tools by which to compare and contrast the canonical with other positions.

For example, when conservative and neo-Evangelical Protestants occasionally align themselves with portions of my canonical proposal, they accept the emphasis on the authority of the Bible, the role of the final form of the text, and the need for using the entire Christian canon. However, the caveat is quickly expressed that the historicity of the biblical accounts as the objectively verifiable foundation of the faith has been inadequately defended (e.g. by Smick). Lindbeck's first category is helpful in showing that the heart of my canonical proposal has been missed when this conservative theory seeks to ground biblical truth on objective propositions apart from the reception by a community of Christian faith and practice. Lindbeck is also illuminating in pointing out the degree of modernity present in the usual conservative formulation of the historical issue.

Again, Lindbeck's experiental-expressive category has been full of insight for me in distinguishing my position from the liberal theological model which continues to dominate modern biblical studies. For example, the majority of form- and redaction-critics appeal ultimately to a traditio-historical and literary process as the non-discursive bearer of religious values. Just as the ancient biblical writers sought to establish truth from an inherited legacy within a changing milieu, so the modern interpreter enters into an analogous process. Recently, James Barr has sought to base biblical theology on a return to the original historical experiences of the biblical people rather than on the later, ossified form of the biblical canon. Finally, one of James Sanders' major contributions, in my opinion, lies in his creative adaptation of the term canon to fit into the experiental-expressive mode of liberal theology. He interprets the role of the canon as a hermeneutical device for shaping Israel's identity by allowing an oscillation between the poles of stability and adaptability which process is tested by its conformity to an undergirding mono-theistic pluralism. From my perspective, much of the ongoing debate with these biblical scholars has been largely unsatisfactory because the basic theological issues have not emerged with the precision which Lindbeck's analysis demands.

I have also found Lindbeck's alternative proposal helpful in showing the significance of an intratextual context for a community of faith which seeks to render reality by its use of sacred texts. I largely agree with his understanding of the integral connection of faith and practice, and in his recognition of the dialectical relation between text and experience. Above all, I appreciate his stress on exploring the full range of the interpretive medium rather than in generalizing from disparate traditions—in my terminology, extra-biblical traditions.

Nevertheless, it is also true that the categorizing of theories can obscure as well as illuminate. For example, in a certain polemical, historical context the term 'neo-orthodoxy' had a legitimate meaning when it encompassed theologians as diverse as Barth, Brunner, Tillich, and Niebuhr within one group which was critical of Protestant liberalism. Yet when viewed in the context of constructive theological method, Tillich and Barth marked the furthest extremes within the modern theological spectrum and emerged as opponents rather than allies.

To draw the analogy, in a polemical debate with the theories of conservative propositionalists and liberal experientialists I find myself firmly within Lindbeck's third category. However, when I attempt to relate my own understanding of canon in a positive fashion to Lindbeck's cultural-linguistic model, I find innumerable problems arising. Of course, Lindbeck has recognized the difficulty when he allows for a continuing disagreement on the issue as to where proper grammar is to be found and who are the competent speakers of a religious language (113). I shall limit myself to three issues in order to illustrate the direction of my disagreement.

First, Lindbeck stresses that doctrine functions as an instantiation of rules rather than having a fixed propositional content (104). Similarly the Bible functions to provide the idiom by which the Christian community construes reality when it christianizes its inherited texts by various forms of typology. This hermeneutical approach derives from Lindbeck's theory of meaning as use rather than as proposition or experience. At this juncture, it is not my intention to argue the issue philosophically as to whether Lindbeck has correctly interpreted Wittgenstein's understanding of use when he turns it into a formal theory (cf. the article of P. L. Holmer). Rather, my concern is to point out that historically the New Testament canon functioned in a way which is not fully congruent with Lindbeck's theory.

The Christian canon established a context from which the gospel was to be understood. It was the arena in which the Word of God was heard through the medium of the Spirit. As a fixed body of literature it marked the range of legitimate diversity within the rule-of-faith, and had both a material and a formal role as the authoritative apostolic witness. Although the function of the canon in the early church was not propositional after the manner of Lindbeck's first category, the point to be stressed is that the church's *use* of its scripture involved a wide range of different models, one of which was propositional. There was a truthful apostolic witness to Jesus Christ, a faith once-and-for-all delivered to the saints, on which Christians grounded their existence. In spite of a variety of legitimate formulations of the one Christian faith, and in spite of the historical time-conditionality of the confessions, the Bible as the church's rule-of-faith laid claim to saving truth. In addition, it should be noted that experiential-expressive forms of appropriation were also included within the function of the canon. How can one understand the Psalms apart from the experience of God's forgiveness? In sum, to suggest that both doctrine and the Bible function simply as instantiations of rules does not do justice to either the cognitive or experiential dimensions of the canon.

Secondly, in agreement with the recent emphasis on 'narrative theology', Lindbeck stresses the 'intratextuality' of meaning. Indeed, the term has provided a much needed service in checking the abuses of a crude theory of historical referentiality which has dominated biblical studies since the Enlightenment (cf. Frei, *The Eclipse of Biblical Narrative*). Nevertheless, the concept is not without serious problems when used as a positive formulation of the Bible's relation to the external world. Above all, the New Testament bears witness to realities outside itself. The prophets and apostles spoke of things which they saw and events which they experienced as testimonies to what God was doing in the world. It is far too limiting to restrict the function of the Bible to that of rendering an agent or an identity. Rather, the nature of the biblical referent must be determined by the text itself which points referringly both to the Creator and the creation in a wide variety of different ways. To recognize that the Bible offers a faith-construal is not to deny that it bears witness to realities outside the text. Christians have always understood that we are saved, not by the biblical text, but by the life, death, and resurrection of Jesus Christ who entered into the world of time and space.

Thirdly, I am critical of any theological method which speaks of the Bible as a type of literary or symbolic construct (e.g. narrative, realistic novel, classic), but does not feel constrained to engage in continuous exegesis of the Bible itself as the indispensable ground for all Christian theological reflection. For a variety of theological reasons I find it basically unsatisfactory to assign the Bible a subordinate role within the creative imagination of the church where it functions merely as a source of imagery without a determinate meaning. If there is anything still left of the legacy of the Reformation for the church, it lies in the insistence that the enterprise of Christian theology must be carried on in an intensive wrestling with the scriptures, without which it can be neither true nor faithful.

In sum, the theological categories of Lindbeck are highly useful in describing with great precision the nature of some hermeneutical theories which stand in a negative relationship to the canonical approach of this New Testament introduction. However, when it comes to a positive formulation, the cultural-linguistic alternative appears to be of mixed value in describing the theological function of the canon as scripture of the church.

SELECTED COMMENTARIES FOR PASTOR AND TEACHER

Cf. the following bibliographies for further study:

J. C. **Hurd**, *A Bibliography of New Testament Bibliographies*, New York 1966; D. M. **Scholer**, *A Basic Bibliographic Guide for New Testament Exegesis*, Grand Rapids 1973; B. S. **Childs**, *Old Testament Books for Pastor and Teacher*, Philadelphia 1977; J. A. **Fitzmyer**, *An Introductory Bibliography for the Study of Scripture*, rev. ed., Rome 1981; R. P. **Martin**, *New Testament Books for Pastor and Teacher*, Philadelphia 1984.

The following list offers a small selection of New Testament commentaries which I would recommend for the person who is seeking to build a private theological library and needs aid in establishing priorities. The criteria for the selection are similar to those described in my earlier bibliography which is listed above. The opinions expressed are personal ones and do not attempt to reflect a consensus. Still I trust that the evaluations do not lead the reader astray and are fair. My purpose is to provide a practical and scholarly guide to the literature of the New Testament as a resource for the ministry of the Christian church. The overriding concern in these evaluations turns on a book's usefulness in the task of rendering the text as scripture of the church. However, the wide range of differing opinions within the church's tradition is recognized and respected.

1. Matthew

Of all the Gospels Matthew is least represented by good commentaries. The older, more technical English commentaries (Allen, McNeile) are badly dated. The most recent (Beare, Gundry) appear to me often idiosyncratic and unsatisfactory. Probably the best choice for the time being is the semi-popular volume of Schweizer, which is richer than Hill, but still often disappointing. My favourite commentary remains Schniewind which offers the most profound wrestling with the theological issues available. The monograph edited by Bornkamm (*Tradition and Interpretation*) is a good supplement to Schniewind and launched the new redactional study of Matthew. For technical analysis Klostermann's commentaries on the Synoptics are still indispensable, but devoid of theology. Chrysostom's sermons on Matthew remain a classic for Christian preaching.

2. Mark

The standard critical commentary on the Greek text is V. Taylor which is filled with useful and learned material. It combines a cautious form-critical analysis with an older form of liberal, free church theology which, in my judgment, often badly obscures the biblical text. Cranfield is very solid, and a good corrective to Taylor. Two inexpensive form-critical commentaries, those of Nineham and R. H. Lightfoot, are often full of insight and to be recommended. Again I prefer Schniewind to Schweizer. Haenchen's volume is of excellent quality, but represents a highly critical stance to the text out of the Bultmann school. Of the two most recent German commentaries, I would probably choose Gnilka. Pesch's great learning has tended to dissolve the text into redactional minutiae. Especially for the preacher a second-hand copy of Rawlinson may be found useful.

3. Luke

Fitzmyer's massive commentary will long be a standard reference work. However, the danger is acute of losing the biblical text in a mountain of endless historical and philological notes. Unfortunately, Marshall's learned volume is also strong on philology and weaker in exegetical insight. Schweizer's semi-popular volume may be useful in complementing these two more technical volumes. Unfortunately, the one commentary which is without a close rival, that of Schürmann, remains incomplete, but what is offered in the first nine chapters is priceless. Ernst's volume has profited from Schürmann's, and is of the entire Gospel, but his is not a substitute for Schürmann's masterful exegesis. The older ICC volume of Plummer is recommended, if purchased cheaply. It is less critical, but broader in scope than Creed.

4. John

Good commentaries are well represented and the difficulty lies in making a choice among many. R. E. Brown's two-volume set is extremely thorough and ecumenical in perspective, but not always satisfactory in terms of exegetical insight. Still it is recommended as a good purchase. Lindars is often more incisive, but less balanced. For a rich theological exposition my favourite commentary remains Hoskyns, but it is spotty in places. Probably the best all-round commentary is Schnackenburg's three-volume set, but it is expensive and can also be somewhat tedious. Bultmann's commentary is, of course, a brilliant classic. It is highly critical and profoundly theological, but for the uninitiated it is also esoteric. I do prefer it to Haenchen. On the second-hand market, Westcott's great classic offers a superb presentation of an older traditional Christian approach, richly informed by the fathers. Also Augustine's homilies on John should not be overlooked by the preacher. Godet has long been a favourite among homilists, but requires a critical discernment if used.

5. Gospel Harmonies

One needs a standard Greek Synopsis, and Aland is superior to Huck, but expensive. English editions of both volumes are available. It is difficult to find a commentary which addresses the problems of the Gospels' unity and diversity without falling into traditional rationalism or critical reductionism (cf. chs. 9–10 above). Calvin's *Harmony* can provide some help if used wisely. Chemnitz's massive tomes are rich and stimulating, but in Latin and generally inaccessible. Westcott's classic guide to the Gospels should not be disdained since, in spite of its many problems, it has never been adequately replaced. I have found the greatest homiletical aid from E. Mülhaupt's five-volume set of selections from Luther's exegesis of the four Gospels. Its exegetical value is equal to its practical, and not to be underestimated.

6. Acts

Haenchen's volume serves as the standard critical commentary, but for those who do not share his critical construal, the volume loses some of its value. The same judgment holds true also for Conzelmann. For technical work Foakes-Jackson and K. Lake's five-volume set has never been supplanted. The work is exhaustive in many respects, but is lacking in theological depth. The most recent German commentary by Schneider is very complete, but expensive and not always illuminating. My favourite commentary is clearly Bauernfeind, whose literary and theological penetration excels. For preaching aid I prefer the help of the old volume of Rackham over Bruce whose exposition tends to be solid, but unexciting.

7. Romans

Once again the problem lies in choosing from a wealth of rich offerings. My suggestion is to start with the old ICC commentary of Sanday and Headlam which has served many generations well, and then to add the newer edition of the ICC by Cranfield which is profoundly theological and sensitive to proclamation. Barrett's *Romans* is more lively than his *John* commentary. Dodd can be brilliant, but thin in many passages and even superficial. I have been disappointed with Käsemann's recent commentary. I find the format tedious and difficult to use. For those with patience, it can be rewarding, but I think it lacks the brilliance of his essays. Lagrange is a fine example of the best of traditional Catholic exegesis and extremely learned. Among German commentaries Schlatter is always stimulating and original. I prefer Kuss to Wilckens whose *Romans* tends to be unnecessarily verbose. Barth's famous commentary may be too difficult for many, but his shorter commentary in English is a priceless little volume. However, in the end, a library without Calvin's Romans and the magnificent English edition of Luther's commentary is sadly impoverished.

8. I Corinthians

There is much that is good in Conzelmann's commentary, which is fully up to date and theologically alert. However, the theology is one-sided and the exegesis is uneven in quality. It needs to be supplemented by other commentators. Barrett's semi-popular volume is filled with solid material and is probably the best choice in spite of a certain flatness in the exegesis. Orr's Anchor Bible has a long and informative introduction but the exegesis has been hampered by the book's format, and is thin. J. Weiss' commentary in the Meyer series is still the most thorough and brilliant exegesis available, but his radical literary theories undercut, in my opinion, much of the value for the teacher and preacher. The same holds true for Héring. Schlatter is not easy to use, but well worth the effort. The old ICC is still useful, but should be obtained second-hand. Karl Barth's *Resurrection of the Dead* is outstanding for theological penetration and is once again available in English.

9. II Corinthians

The choice is even more limited with II Corinthians. Barrett is solid and informative and to be preferred over Bruce's commentary. Bultmann is stimulating as always for the professional scholar, but not up to his *John* commentary in insight. Nor has it really replaced Windisch and Lietzmann in the scholarly debate. Plummer is old and somewhat wooden, but worth having if purchased cheaply. Héring is occasionally quite illuminating. The classic homiletical exposition of Denney is dated, but has retained some of its original force in a way which I do not find with Stanley's well-known commentary.

10. Galatians

The classic English commentary is Lightfoot. In spite of its age it remains impressive in scholarship and insight. His lucid English paraphrases of the Greek text offer an exegetical model. However, the theological exposition is inadequate. Burton's volume was one of the best in the ICC series and retains considerable value if supplemented. There is much to praise in Betz's learned commentary, although I think that his general construal of the epistle is badly skewed. Among German commentaries Oepke is a fine contribution. Also Mussner is outstanding and I prefer it over Schlier, which also offers serious exposition even when evoking controversy. Good homiletical aid is offered by Cousar, but once again, it is Luther's commentary on Galatians which has stimulated generations of readers to sense the power of Paul.

11. Ephesians

The old standard English commentary of Armitage Robinson has held up quite well, and is actually more useful than Westcott who is always impressive. M. Barth's commentary has much to offer the serious reader in a rich theological exposition; however, it is verbose and at times idiosyncratic. For the average reader Mitton's semi-popular commentary is probably the best choice, and makes an adequate attempt at interpretation. However, the Germans have dominated the field in recent years. Schlier is the most profound of modern commentators, but difficult to use and one-sided in approach. Mussner and Schnackenburg are both good commentaries, but the size and thoroughness of the latter allows for a richer exposition. For the homilist an excellent purchase is the reprint of Calvin's sermons on Ephesians which is a separate volume from his commentary.

12. Philippians

Lightfoot remains a classic, but Beare is probably more useful for the average reader. Martin would be a possible option. Lohmeyer's commentary has played a significant role in the modern critical discussion, but is increasingly out-of-date. I would judge that Dibelius has held up far better, and always has a literary flair. Gnilka has written the most recent, thorough commentary, but it is only average in exegetical insight. Again note should be taken of Barth's brief theological commentary available in English.

13. Colossians

Lightfoot's commentary still remains the basis for the modern study of the book and is of high quality as expected. However, it should be supplemented by Moule's careful study. Martin has a semi-popular contribution which is adequate. Both Lohse and Schweizer have provided solid critical contributions, but Lohse is to be preferred for the more thorough and detailed exposition. Schweizer probably has the edge over Gnilka. In general, on this book the Germans have more to say theologically than the English commentaries.

14. I and II Thessalonians

There are some fine commentaries from which to choose. The commentary of Milligan is still useful, and Frame was one of the better volumes in the ICC series. Best offers a good survey of the issues on a semi-popular level and for the average reader is a serious choice. However, the great classic in the field, which set a new standard, is Rigaux's massive French commentary which is both thorough and rich in exposition. Among German contributions Bornemann has never been fully replaced, especially for his history of exegesis. However, the more exciting volume is Dobschütz who often equivocates, but whose exposition is of high quality. In the most recent period Marxsen offers a brilliant exegesis from the far left, and Marshall a good rejoinder from the right. For some reason, Trilling's commentary on II Thessalonians is not as helpful as one might have expected.

15. Pastorals

One's choice on these books tends to be greatly influenced by the stance on the critical issues. Lock's ICC retains a value because he still equivocates on the authorship, but sets out well the problems and alternatives. However, Spicq's commentary is even more useful in covering the full range of exegetical issues and, although quite conservative, has been kept up to date with new editions. Kelly has a serious commentary for the average reader which I prefer to Barrett. Dibelius, now in English translation, offers the standard critical treatment of the book with brilliance, but without much theological insight. Credit goes to Brox for a serious new theological attempt to exploit the pseudepigraphical thesis, even if not fully successful. Calvin's reprinted sermons remain powerful.

16. Philemon

Commentaries on Philemon are usually included with the letter to Colossians. Consult Lightfoot, Lohmeyer, Moule, Lohse, and

Martin. The most exciting fresh attempt is the little commentary of Stuhlmacher who has included an essay on the history of exegesis.

17. Hebrews

Again there is a rich choice of scholarly commentaries. Westcott's volume remains impressive and is especially rich in patristic references. Delitzsch brings a wealth of Old Testament and Jewish material to bear on his interpretation and this old volume should not be overlooked. Moffatt is also a strong commentary, but more useful to teachers than preachers. In spite of his overdependence on Philo, Spicq's huge French commentary is indispensable for serious work. However, for theological penetration Riggenbach is more profound. The standard modern German commentary remains Michel, who is learned and thorough, but not always fully illuminating on this book. Kuss has possibly a more balanced exegesis. Unfortunately, most of the commentaries mentioned will be heavy going for the busy pastor. Good popularizations are rare. Bruce is certainly to be preferred over Montefiore who is thin. In general, the older volumes remain the best guides.

18. James

J. B. Mayor has long been considered the standard English commentary. It has impressive scholarship, but of a wooden sort, which is seldom useful. I think that Ropes has held up somewhat better. The translation of Dibelius has provided a sensitive literary study by a master, but theologically thin. The most thorough, recent German commentary by Mussner is of high quality and recommended as one of the best. I greatly prefer it to Windisch. Mitton has written a useful commentary which will fill the gap for many on a semi-popular level. However, there are some very new commentaries which take precedence. Laws is a useful, up-to-date study, but I would give my first choice to P. Davids' illuminating and thorough commentary on the Greek text.

19. I Peter

I would recommend having several commentaries which reflect the full range of the interpretation of this important book. Bigg is old, but useful for his technical material and a learned presentation of the traditional approach. Selwyn's commentary remains indispensable for any serious study, even though some of his brilliant theses have not held up. Beare is a good complement on the left and it is perhaps his best commentary. Among the German commentaries Schelkle is still the best guide, in my opinion. His commentary is rich and mature in theological reflection, and more profound than Brox's study. Goppelt is solid, but hardly outstanding. Of the popular commentaries Cranfield and Kelly are recommended. Best is also quite useful. For preaching the classic English homiletical work has long been Archbishop Robert Leighton's commentary (1693); however, I suspect that much skill and empathy are needed by any modern reader who seeks to benefit from its devotional insights.

20. II Peter, Jude

Among the older works I would again choose Bigg over Mayor for exegetical purposes. Among popular commentaries I would probably prefer Cranfield to Kelly, but both need supplementing by more detailed treatments. The recent English commentary of Bauckham is thorough, lucid, and of high quality. It would be my first choice. Among critical German commentaries Schelkle is greatly to be preferred, but still one can profit from Schrage.

21. Johannine Epistles

R. E. Brown's massive new commentary has overshadowed the earlier works of Brooke, Dodd, and Bruce. In spite of having some exegetical reservations concerning Brown's main thesis, I recommend it as a serious, and enormously learned piece of work which is reasonably priced. However, I do not think Westcott has been completely supplanted and evaluate it as a classic of lasting value. Bultmann is now available in English translation, but appears thin next to Brown. My first choice would be Schnackenburg whose commentary remains a model of careful exposition. Two older homiletical studies of high quality are those of Findlay and Law.

22. Revelation

It is extremely difficult to make a recommendation of commentaries on Revelation because of the enormous range of interpretations.

Charles is the standard English commentary, but wooden in the extreme, and theologically tone-deaf. Swete is also solid, but tedious. Beckwith offers a useful introduction, but his exegesis leaves much to be desired. Bousset is certainly the most brilliant German commentary and is a joy to read for its comparative insights, but it is theologically quite sterile. Probably I would select Hadorn as my first choice, but with some reservation. I confess to have found little help in Kiddle, Caird, Morris, and Ladd. Hendriksen's volume remains a classic in its way, and certainly is his best commentary. Whether one agrees or not, his construal is interesting. However, perhaps this last book of the Bible is best approached indirectly by other means than commentaries.

INDEX OF MODERN AUTHORS